ACTAR

IITAC PRESS

IITAC

to Kora, Miron, Eva, Filip and Maks

THE CITY AS A PROJECT

Portfolio of the "City as a Project" PhD Program at the Berlage Institute

2009 – 2010

VEDRAN

THE BERLA

BUILDING RELATIONS:
THE BERLAGE PLATFORM

Hrvatska akademija znanosti i umjetnosti Hrvatski muzej arhitekture u suradnji u Berlage institutom iz Roterdama poziva vas na otvorenje izložbe i seminar "Građenje odnosa : Berlage platforma" u petak 25. travnja 2008. u 14.00 sati u Hrvatskom muzeju arhitekture. Izložbe ostaje otvorena do 23. svibnja 2008. svaki dan od 11.00 do 18.00 sati. Projekt je realiziran uz potporu Veleposlanstva Kraljevine Nizozemske u Hrvatskoj.

The Croatian Academy of Sciences and Arts, Croatian Museum of Architecture in collaboration with the Berlage Institute based in Rotterdam in the Netherlands are inviting you for the opening of the exhibition and the seminar "Building Relations: The Berlage Platform," on Friday 25 April 2008 at 14.00 hours in the Croatian Museum of Architecture. Exhibition will be open till 23 May 2008 every day from 11.00 till 18.00 hours. This collaborative project between the Dutch Institute and the Croatian Museum of Architecture is financed through Dutch Cultural Funds.

MIMICA
GE AFFAIR

CONTENTS

ACKNOWLEDGEMENTS	08
PREFACE BY KENNETH FRAMPTON	11
INTRODUCTION	12
WHY THE BERLAGE AFFAIR?	14
WHO IS VEDRAN MIMICA?	17
INTRODUCTION	20
PERSONALITY NET	22
THE BERLAGE PLATFORM	24
THE BERLAGE EXPERIENCE	29
BUILDING CONSCIOUSNESS	46
ENGAGING REALITY	50
THE POWER OF ARCHITECTURAL THOUGHT	57
LEARNING WITHOUT TEACHING	63
THE ARCHITECTURE FOR CHILDREN	69
CREATION OF NEW WORLDS IN MINIATURE	80
UTOPIA AS TRADITION	88
STUDY LANDSCAPES OF HERMAN HERTZBERGER	96
THE BERLAGE INSTITUTE	104
THE NEW PUBLIC REALM	107
BERLAGE EXCHANGERS	116
PEOPLE DO STILL LIVE IN PLACES	120
2000 SHANGAY: THE SPIRIT OF MEGA	127
MID-SIZED CITY	131
NOT QUITE OBVIOUS DENSITIES	138
ZOKA, I LOVE YOU	140
THE MARSEILLE EXPERIMENT	143
A GOOD BUILDING MAKES YOU FEEL AT HOME	150
WEST BALKAN AFFAIR AND ARCHITECTURE OF TRANSITION	160
Croatia	
EAST-WEST: BLURRING TERRITORIES	164
ARCHITECTURE OF TRANSITION AND THE PRODUCTION OF MEANING	173
CROATIAN ARCHITECTURE, INVENTING REALITY	178
njirić+njirić: CHILDREN OF ST. PETER'S STREET	190
BALKAN TELETUBBIES AND DECONSTRUCTION OF MODERNISM	192
CHILDREN'S ROOM	197

NEXT EUROPE	201
MISSION IMPOSSIBLE? I DON'T THINK SO	204
EXERCISING EUROPE	210
BORDERS: THE OTHER SIDE OF GLOBALIZATION	215
NEW SCHOOL OF ARCHITECTURE IN THE CITY OF SPLIT	219
GYMNASIUM / QUANTUM LEAP IN MIROSLAV KRLEŽA STREET	224
EXITS ARE CLEARLY MARKED	227
WHERE IS (CROATIAN) ARCHITECTURE HEADED?	239
CITIES CAN CHANGE THEIR IDENTITY	243
Slovenia	
6IX PACK: CONTEMPORARY SLOVENIAN ARCHITECTURE	246
STRICTLY CONTROLLED SMOKING	253
Albania	
TIRANA METROPOLIS	258
SIX ANSWERS ON ALBANIA BY VEDRAN MIMICA	261
A VISION BEYOND PLANNING	262
Montenegro	
TOURISTS IN THEIR HOME TOWNS	271
BERLAGE TRANSFERS, ZAGREB SEMINARS AND NEW LIGHTHOUSES	274
FRAMES OF THE METROPOLIS	278
ZAGREB, TAKE A NAP	282
A CONVERSATION WITH KENNETH FRAMPTON	286
URBAN RULES	292
"NEW" NEW ZAGREB	294
SMALL CHANGES	298
DEMOCRATIZATION OF PUBLIC SPACE	301
MARE NOSTRUM	303
NEW LIGHTHOUSES	307
CROATIA – THE MEDITERRANEAN AS IT COULD BE	316
SPACE IS THE BASIC CROATIAN RESOURCE	319
INTERVIEW AT DAZ	322
CLOSING TIME	324
LIFE AFTER THE DEATH IN VENICE	328
CLOSING TIME!	337
UTOPIAN JOURNEYS	343
E LA NAVE VA	347
EPILOGUE BY WIEL ARETS	360
SELECTED BIBLIOGRAPHY	388
SELECTED CURATORIAL WORK	390
IMPRESSUM	392

ACKNOWLEDGEMENTS

Firstly, I would like to thank Anka Mimica, a Chilean born Croatian woman, for triggering my interest, with very little money and lots of love, in architectures of Paris and London, during my formative years. I will always be grateful to Jozara Mimica, a Titoist partisan and WWII hero, allowing me to proudly state that my family has always stood on the right side of world history. To my wife Sasha enormous thanks for the overall support.

Further I would like to thank and mention people who gave me the chance to enter into architectural discourses and writings, and who made my love affair with the Berlage Institute truly productive.

So, thanks to Neven Šegvić and Boško Rašica, my professors from Zagreb for opening to my generation the purpose and mysteries of architecture, art, ideologies and politics. To Josip Vaništa for telling us about his intimate conversations with Miroslav Krleža. To Veljko Oluić and Tonči Žarnić for being the best colleagues during my studies and at the beginning of our professional life. To Bere Radimir who believed I could teach and to Nikola Filipović who allowed me to link Zagreb school with the world.

Very special thanks to Herman Hertzberger for the entire pre-Berlage and Berlage affair. To Elia Zenghelis for teaching all of us how to teach others. To Kelly Shannon for editing my first book Notes on Children, Environment and Architecture, and providing a critical partnership for our research into school buildings. To Alejandro Zaera-Polo for support and belief in students' collective intelligence. To Yap Hong Seng, Joke Kemper and Rob Doctor for their belief in my service.

I would especially like to emphasize my gratitude to Kenneth Frampton: for having been teaching me all my life, lately through critically reading the manuscript of this book; for educating Berlage students with vigor and enthusiasm and being a strong pillar of architectural knowledge worldwide.

To Mick Morssink, Roemer van Toorn, Hans Tupker, Max Risselada, Winy Maas, Raoul Bunschoten, Bart Lootsma, Thomas A. P. van Leeuwen, Lieven De Cauter, Pier Vittorio Aureli, Peter Trummer, Joachim Declerck and Salomon Frausto and many other colleagues for total commitment to the Berlage and allowing my work to be truly pleasurable. To my first wife Visnja Pižeta who I collaborated with in my formative years.

Special thanks to Pero Puljiz, Branimir Medić, Tadej Glažar, Saša Randić, Reinier de Graaf, Don Murphy, Marina Lathouri, Kelly Shannon, Vasa J. Perović, Madir Shah, Lada Hršak, Norton Flores Troche, Penelope Dean, Pier

Vittorio Aureli, Martino Tattara, Peter Trummer, Bas Princen, Manuel de Rivero, Nanne de Ru, Martin Mutschlechner, Suitbert Schmitt, Im Sik Cho, Igor Kebel, Martin Sobota, Daliana Suryawinata, Marc Ryan, Ross Adams, Miguel Robles-Durán, Daniel Valle, Alessandro Martinelli, Pier Paolo Tamburelli, Petar Zaklanović, Dinka Pavelić, Maria S. Giudici, Felix Madrazo, Giorgio Ponzo, Agata M. Siemionow, Matrino Tatara, Joachim Declerck and other alumni which continued productive relation with the Institute by teaching studios, participating in masterclasses, addressing lectures, editing, writing, curating and in other means developing the legacy of the Berlage.
To Marina van den Bergen, Piet Vollaard, Jennifer Sigler, Roemer van Toorn, Salomon Frausto, Lucy Bullivant, Miodrag Mitrašinović, Petra Wollenberg, Nassrine Azimi, Liliane Schneiter, Zdravko Krasić, Hrvoje Bakran, Alan Kostrenčić, Maroje Mrduljaš, Ivo Babić, Damir Šarac, Igor Kebel, Mika Cimolini, Gudrun Hausegger, Gabriele Kaiser, Kristina Jerkov, Sabina Sabolović, Nives Rogoznica and Barbara Matejčić, who asked me the right questions.
To Vladimir Mattioni for more than twenty years of the most inspiring exchange and for support and engagement in keeping utopia alive.
To Maroje Mrduljaš who listened carefully what I had to say and for all what he taught me afterwards.
To Andrija Rusan for publishing my written work and allowing me to enter the stage at the Days of Oris.
To Hrvoje and Helena Njirić, Toma Plejić, Lea Pelivan, Sasa Randić, Bojan Radonić, Tatjana Medić, Idis Turato, Dado Katušić, Robert Plejić, Ante Kuzmanić, Gorki Žuvela, Eve Blau, Ivan Rupnik, Anna Grichting, Aron Betsky, George Brugmans, Hildegard Auf Franić, Bojan Baletić, Jasmina Siljanoska, Dietmar Steiner, Mathias Klotz, Flavio Janches, who thought I had something to say.
To Zoka Zola and Augie Mimica for their enormous generosity in my transition to Chicago and beyond.
Special thanks to the team who worked hard to make this project possible: Vladimir Mattioni for transforming my IIT tenure application document in a unique book format, Damir Gamulin Gamba for innovative design with ContextMapper, Ana Škegro for essential assistance in editing and design, Damir Žižić for essential photographic layer of the book, Bruno Babić for database visualization development of the book and Dado Čakalo for remarkable process of translation.
To Ramón Prat and Ricardo Devesa for their support and belief that this book shed light on one unique cultural and educational project. To Sonja Leboš for her supreme editing and to Wiel Arets for making this project possible.

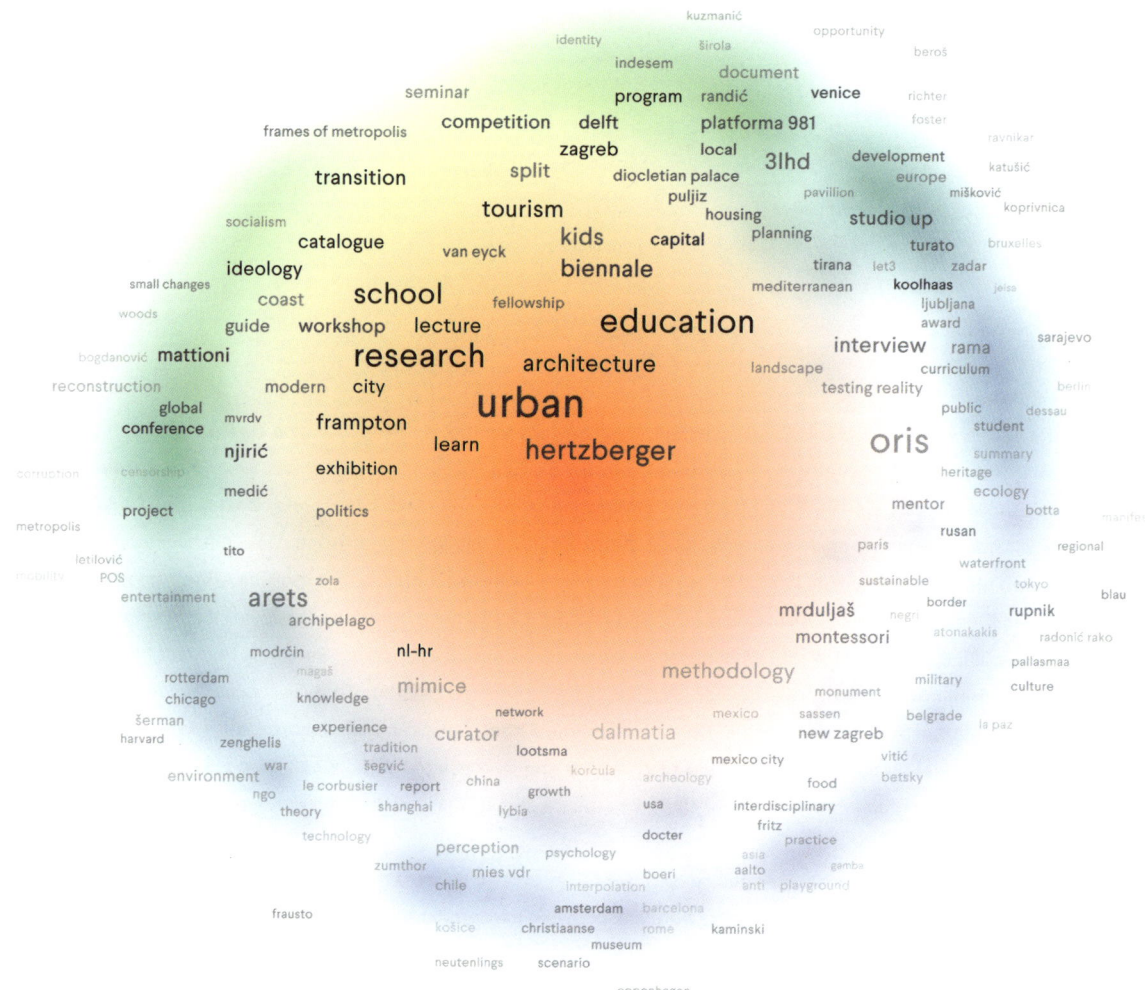

PREFACE

With this extraordinary book Vedran Mimica has, in effect, documented a large part of his life's work to date, which up to now has been inseparable from the evolution of the Berlage Institute. During the first twenty-two years of its existence as an independent institution (1990 to 2012), Mimica not only acted the school's main nexus of energy and inspiration, but also served as the essential organization man, as one director succeeded the next. He was the one other prime mover during the course of a changing nominal leadership, as it passed from Herman Hertzberger, who founded the school in the first place, to Wiel Arets, and finally to Alejandro Zaera-Polo. Throughout this trajectory, much of the day-to-day studio teaching, along with the initiation and organization of national and international workshops, were the responsibility of Mimica. And, in much the same manner as the charismatic role played by Alvin Boyarsky with his on-the-spot leadership of the Architectural Association School in London from 1971 to 1990, Mimica was the point man to whom faculty and students alike would necessarily turn to for guidance as to their specific momentary role in the affairs of the house.

This is a uniquely hybrid work, for it is, in the first instance, a wittily scrambled, diaristic record of the events through which the haptically fertile discourse of the Berlage would come sharply into focus. In addition, it is also an analytical account of the evolution of school design in Holland, this being an area of research with which Mimica was particularly involved at a thesis level, as we may judge from his book Notes on Children, Environments, and Architecture published in 1992, extracts of which are included herein. Otherwise, the book presents itself primarily as a series of essays, lectures, and taped interviews. Many of these perceptive texts have been already published elsewhere, whether in Hunch – the magazine of the Berlage itself – or in an NAi survey covering the span of its multifarious activities in pedagogy and practice, or, even more often, in the Croatian magazine Oris, edited out of Zagreb. Throughout this palimpsest, one is able to gather fragments here and there of Mimica's own development, from his basic education in Zagreb to his research work at TU Delft under Hertzberger's supervision in the late 1980s, to the large number of distinguished architects, theorists, and critics with whom he was in contact during the two decades of his teaching at the Berlage. In this respect, one is privileged to learn of Mimica's insider interaction with one "star" architect after another, including, apart from my own involvement with the school, such distinguished individuals as Jean Nouvel, Renzo Piano, Tadao Ando, Balkrishna Doshi, Saskia Sassen, Juhani Pallasmaa, Giancarlo De Carlo, Peter Smithson, Steven Holl, Henri Ciriani, Christian Gullichsen, Colin St. John Wilson, Oriol Bohigas, Thom Mayne, and Elia Zenghelis, not to mention the Dutch design elite to whom he was equally exposed, such as Rem Koolhaas, Wiel Arets, Max Risselada, Kees Christiaanse, Willem Jan Neutelings, Xaveer De Geyter, Jo Coenen, Mels Crouwel, Aldo Van Eyck, Adriaan Geuze, Ben van Berkel, and finally of course, Hertzberger himself.

Far from being a potted history, this is an exceptionally lively account of a unique institution, highlighting many of the ideological differences and debates of the time. What is truly surprising is the astonishing international scope of the Berlage workshops, from realistic feasibility studies in the Netherlands to projects as far flung as Albania, Turkey, Chile, and Croatia. One is enlightened and refreshed by the intensity of the exchanges and the creative formulations that emerged within the walls of the Berlage during Mimica's tenure there.

This account assembles the relatively random traces of that which, throughout the 1990s and beyond, was surely the most original European post-graduate design and research institution in the field. Under Mimica's stewardship, it was as much a forum for public debate as it was a place in which to concentrate on the design and substance of architecture.

All of this kinetic history, both as it transpired and as it is here recounted, would be totally overwhelming were it not for the wit and discretion with which Mimica has carried the discourse forward, both as a cultural entrepreneur at the time and now, in retrospect, as a writer.

Kenneth Frampton

INTROD

the BERLAGE
institute
AMSTERDAM
Postgraduate School of Architecture

Vedran Mimica
Van Kinschotstraat 174
Delft

IJsbaanpad 3
P.O. Box 7042
1007 JA Amsterdam
The Netherlands
tel. 020 - 675 53 93
fax 020 - 675 54 05

Amsterdam, 27 september 1994

Dear Vedran,

As we have discussed during the summer period I herewith would like to confirm your appointment to course director of the Berlage Institute.
Your tasks and responsibilities have been set in mutual agreement during the talks Herman Hertzberger, you and I had.

We also agreed that your salary will be Dfl. 6500,- bruto at 40 hours a week.
as per October 1st 1994.
I am convinced that our cooperation will stay as fruitful as ever.

With kind regards,

First year term project

Tuesday 27 June
Graduate Lectures part 1

Wednesday 28 June
Graduate Lectures part 2

All Public Events take place at the Berlage Institute, IJsbaanpad 1E (entrance via main entrance former Orphanage). Lectures start at 20.00 hrs and will be held in English. Admission is free. The programme is subject to change. For more information:
phone +31-20-6750-3, fax +31-20-67554
Berlagei@xs4all.nl

UCTION

The Berlage
Center for Advanced Studies in Architecture and Urban Design

Vedran Mimica
Head of Education

TU Delft Faculty of Architecture
Julianalaan 134 • BG.OOST.600
2628 BL Delft • The Netherlands
www.theberlage.nl • mimica@theberlage.nl
Tel. 015 - 278 23 84 • +31 6 14 32 53 42

WHY THE BERLAGE AFFAIR?

During the 1980s, with a great help of Herman Hertzberger, I found myself transiting from the enlightened authoritarianism of self-managed Titoist socialism to fully functioning democratic welfare state of the Netherlands. Herman guided me through the research at TU Delft and invited me to join him at the Berlage Institute in Amsterdam in 1990, where I kept working till its closure in 2012. Invited by Wiel Arets, in 2012 I first became a traveling visiting professor and Associate Dean at the Illinois Institute of Technology College of Architecture in Chicago while still trying to "save" what could be saved of the original Berlage Institute at The Berlage Center for Advanced Studies in Architecture and Urban Design at TU Delft.

Unfortunately, since it was not possible to continue the legacy of the original Berlage in Delft, I moved to Chicago by accepting to serve as a tenured professor at Illinois Institute of Technology. Since 2013 I have been fully committed to Wiel Arets' idea to present the Berlage's achievements in more detail to the American academia and wider public, in order to enrich student minds, spin off different forms of scholarship, and originate a new way of thinking about architectural education and culture.

Invitation by Wiel was a great honor for me and so was his request to compile my entire work in a digital document, in order to apply for tenure professorship at Illinois Institute of Technology. With great help from Mick Morssink, 'a genius at work' at the Berlage, whom I worked with closely for 22 unforgettable years, and with overall support of Sasha Žanko, a 1600 pages portfolio document was produced. Once produced, this portfolio represented more than 30 years of my life and work and provoked the thought to make it public.

Vladimir Mattioni took the task of biblical proportions to edit the material while Damir Gamulin developed a complex design strategy to make The Berlage Affair. Kenneth Frampton, Lluís Ortega and Hrvoje Njirić provided the essential critical readings of the manuscript while Wiel Arets provided the necessary structural support. Finally, Sonja Leboš copy-edited it all while engaging in truly inspiring critical debate about every argument presented.

The Berlage Affair is not a book about the Berlage Institute, it does not discuss the Institute affairs, but describes an autobiographical "love" affair with the Institute. During my appointment as the last Director of the Institute (2007-2012) we published The Berlage Survey[1] on the occasion of the Berlage Institute's 20th anniversary.

The Berlage Affair is a multi-layered book organized in seven chapters clustering diverse articles according to topics. Yet what all these essays, studies, reviews, and interviews share is their intellectual origin at the Berlage Institute.

Herman Hertzberger, Wiel Arets, Alejandro Zaera-Polo, Kenneth Frampton, Rem Koolhaas, and Elia Zenghelis, whom I have closely worked with for many years, as well as many leading architects and students from all over the word, developed a sort of institutional platform at the Berlage, that served for the construction and discussion of an array of contemporary architectural pursuits. In my professional engagement, as an educator, a writer, curator, and an initiator of some advanced architectural workshops, seminars, and events, I relied on this specific conceptual intelligence of the Berlage Institute.

---

1   The Berlage Survey of the Culture, Education, and Practice of Architecture and Urbanism, NAi010 publishers/Berlage Institute, Rotterdam 2011. Celebrating the twentieth anniversary of the Berlage Institute—the Netherlands' international training ground for architecture—this publication investigates how architectural models, insights and principles create a global architectural culture. With contributions by both prominent and up-and-coming architects, theorists, critics, historians and lecturers, The Berlage Survey examines the various fields that factor in the emergence of an architecture culture: education, practice, discourse and media. By means of critical reflection on the projects, theories, buildings and writings that have dominated the culture over the last two decades, the authors in this book preview the trends that will be decisive for architecture discourse in the coming years. Key texts address architecture policy in the Netherlands since the 1980s, the internationalization of Dutch architecture since the 1990s, the development and dissemination of Dutch expertise and the need for appropriate architectural visions for a globalized world.

The book opens with an introduction by Kenneth Frampton, who sees me within the Berlage as 'a spiritual leader of the school [...] with the everyday entire commitment to the Berlage'.

Chapters that follow present the theoretical principles of the Berlage Institute and explain its educational platform, organizational and methodological changes as they developed.
The Berlage initiatives constitute the acknowledgment that by the turn of the 21st century the exposure to global urbanization was an essential part of architectural education and research. This approach to research was recognized by an invitation to the Berlage to curate the 3rd International Architecture Biennale Rotterdam. Our curatorial position was that architecture must relate to reality through its own disciplinary tools, possibilities, and performances. Architectural disciplinary potentials are in juxtaposing ideas to existing urban conditions by re-imagining our urban world.

The Berlage Exchangers section underlines a growing sense of urgency around the questions of global urbanization. Much of The Berlage Affair is dedicated to the research of contemporary city. One would like to believe that architecture writings are well positioned to offer a synthetic overview in a debate about the contemporary city taking into account economy, ecology, sociology, art, civil engineering, history, anthropology, literature, politics, religion and ideology.

Following chapters focus on the countries of the Western Balkans that went through turbulent transitional processes, including the dramatic disintegration of the former Yugoslavia and the end of all forms of socialist government. In these circumstances the Berlage Institute launched several specific projects engaging the Berlage students in generating an entirely new dialogue about urban transformation in the transitional post-socialist democracies. The most influential was the project Croatian Archipelago New Lighthouses as part of the Matra program launched by the Dutch Ministry of Foreign Affairs to support the processes of social transformation in the countries of Central and Eastern Europe. The project was conceived and developed by the Berlage Institute while emerging Croatian architects and former Berlage students were invited to propose an alternative strategy to create favorable conditions for the development of the coastal areas without affecting their invaluable landscapes. This strategy was initially presented at the Rotterdam Biennale and further developed via seven projects that put forward a vision of new urban design and architectural standards for future coastal development.

The final chapter brings texts about the Venice Architecture Biennials, presenting Richard Burdett's Cities, Architecture and Society, an interview with Aaron Betsky on his Architecture Beyond Building, explaining the utopian aspect of the Croatian "floating pavilion" for the Kazuo Sejima's People Meet in Architecture and ending with a review of Rem Koolhaas' Fundamentals.

What sets The Berlage Affair apart from other literature on architecture is its very subject. Rarely do we learn about innovative or even alternative educational models that have produced and imparted applicable, real-world knowledge in our field. This knowledge was produced in an experimental environment as a result of exchange between the leading and emerging Dutch, North American, Japanese, and European architects and their students from all over the world, who were selected as the best graduates with some practical experience already behind them.

However, perhaps the most interesting keepsake from this book is the understanding how that global know-how was transferred to architectural schools with distinct local character, to local authorities dealing with city development, to cultural institutions, and to general public in more than 30 countries all over the world.

Vedran Mimica
photo by Bogdan Marov
Zagreb,1979

Yugoslav Passport
Zagreb,1985

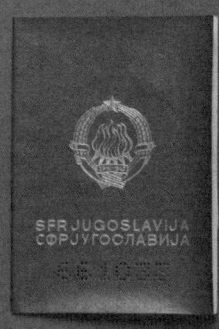

Croatian Passport
Bonn,1991

Dutch passport
Rijswijk,1995

WHO IS VEDRAN MIMICA?

Interview with Vedran Mimica by Marina van den Bergen and Piet Vollaard for ArchiNed, Dutch website for architecture, under the title Wie is Vedran Mimica?, Rotterdam, May 2007

From May 24 to June 10, 2007, Rotterdam will be the center of international world of architecture, says Vedran Mimica. Who is Vedran Mimica? And what is his relation with the International Architecture Biennale Rotterdam (IABR)? This is what we at ArchiNed tried to find out.

Q   How did the Berlage Institute get involved with the International Architecture Biennale Rotterdam?

VM That came about through articles on social and urban transition in the Balkan region I wrote a few years earlier. How can an advanced educational system be implemented in an area where it has not existed for the past fifty years? My work at the Berlage and the publications on transition introduced me to a circle of people, and it did not take long before I was asked to curate exhibitions. In the early 2006, the Berlage was asked by the IABR to make a "bid book". The theme the IABR board had come up with was Babylon. Board members inspiration was based on Saskia Sassen's books and lectures about global urbanization and that cities were important so that the Biennale should be about cities and their international and multicultural dimensions. But what the IABR did not really know was that the Venice Architecture Biennale in 2006 would be about more or less the same issues, namely cities, architecture, and society. Ricky Burdet's Venice exhibition was about data and statistics, but we want to do more than show data; we want to go a step further. We argue that the nature of the city is affected by invisible, either competing or collaborating, powers. In today's context, however, power is obscure. It is neither acknowledged nor discussed. Hence the theme "Power: Producing the Contemporary City".

Q   Can you tell us something about the general IABR program?

VM It turned out that we could not see through even as few as one tenth of the proposals we put in the "bid book". But we decided to go ahead as the Berlage Institute nevertheless. The Kunsthal offered accommodation. There is a lot going on in Rotterdam this summer: Wimby in Boijmans, a big Corbusier show at the NAi, Rotterdam City of Architecture 2007. You see, a Biennale can be "anything"; you do not come to the Biennale, you come to Rotterdam; and there is a lot happening. From May 24 to June 10, Rotterdam will be the international center of the world of architecture.

At the Kunsthal two exhibitions will be on show: Visionary Power and The New Dutch City. Visionary Power addresses issues like immigration, tourism, fear, commerce, and representation in fourteen world cities. The New Dutch City is a study of urban networks. What is very important is that we want an active Biennale, a research Biennale. Not a parade of starchitects, but presentations by architects genuinely dealing with the raw reality of everyday city life. That is why we are organizing a workshop that includes ten schools from around the world. Their assignment is to design community centers for various locations in Rotterdam South. We did not want a purely academic workshop. The locations and the programs were decided on with social workers, people who are directly involved and working for the local boroughs. The question to students is: what is urban renewal? Is it purely economic or is it a social issue? How can architecture contribute to the society? This brings us to the crucial issue: what is the power of representation? The workshop starts two days before the Biennale. Two to three teams will work on a proposal for a location. After the workshop, all proposals will be exhibited in South Rotterdam. There will also be a competitive element to the workshop. The idea for the workshop is to have a follow up in the Pact op Zuid (an agreement between the municipality, housing associations, and local boroughs to improve the social, economic, and urban environments in Rotterdam South.)

The fourth and entirely new aspect of the Biennale is the Power Lounge, which will last for two weeks. There will be a non-stop program in the lower gallery of the Kunsthal. Visitors will be able to relax on a sofa with a cup of cappuccino and enjoy the presentations and documentaries. The afternoons are planned for speakers. During these Power Conferences and Power Talks, economists, politicians, and academics will downstairs discuss issues highlighted in the exhibitions upstairs. We are kicking off the Power Lounge with a two-day conference entitled Producing the Contemporary City in which we will produce something of a mini-manifesto. The Power Lounge will finish with a discussion about the development of the cities in the Netherlands. The idea is to invite the new government ministers, but who will not be speaking but listening and taking notes.

Q   What will it take for you to consider the Biennale successful?

VM If we succeed in conveying a sense of urgency. Architecture and planning are important to the city, but architecture cannot confine itself to its own boundaries when you speak of the city. The new generation of architects is capable of achieving fundamentally important changes because they look beyond buildings. These architects will ideally, by giving a concrete form to a future of their own research and imagining, transport us to an elevated plane of existence.

Q   What is the story behind the Berlage Institute?

VM One day in 1989, Herman [Hertzberger], the founder of the Berlage Institute told me on the phone that he was starting a post-graduate school in Van Eyck's orphanage and asked if I wanted to join in. I said, "Come on Herman, you're kidding, a new international school in Van Eyck's orphanage?" But he meant it. Wiel Arets was there from the beginning, Van Eyck was there too, and Tadao Ando held a master class. It was a big success and huge step forward in creation of radically new model of education of architects. I supplied Herman with almost half the students for the Berlage Institute. For one reason or another it was fairly easy for students from Yugoslavia and Poland to get Dutch study grants at the time. I was able to convince my very best students from Zagreb to join me to the Netherlands. It was a perfect setting, even though there were a few hurdles to overcome in the beginning. All tutors worked part-time, all had their own offices. In hindsight, that was not very clever. Nobody was truly committed. In 1994, Herman, Kenneth Frampton, and Max Risselada asked if I wanted to become Course Director with a full time contract at the Berlage. My situation at the time was a bit schizophrenic. Yugoslavia was in the war. The very country my father had been fighting for as a Titoist partisan in World War 2. After the war, he helped build Yugoslavia, for a while acting as a government minister for agriculture. Returning to Croatia was therefore not an option. I found this thought bizarre, however, I kept permanent relation with Croatia and the region by engaging in various forms of postwar activities. My wife and children have already moved to the Netherlands. Since then I have lived in the Netherlands and worked at the Berlage. Currently I am the Director responsible for education and research.

Q   How are your past activities related to the current ones at the Berlage?

VM When we relocated from Amsterdam to Rotterdam we saw it as a great opportunity. Rotterdam was a laboratory to test our theories. With the Berlage Institute we want to propagate a way of thinking by developing a sort of collective intelligence about global urbanization. I have been able to do more in the Netherlands than I would have done if I had stayed in Croatia. For example, we staged more than 20 architectural and urban workshops in the former Yugoslavia. You might look at it as a form of development aid. We worked in Ljubljana, Zagreb, and Sarajevo just after the war, as well as in Skopje. We wanted to introduce the European way of thinking to the new countries in social, economic and political transition. Later the Berlage received great many students from South America. With their help, we had the opportunity to hold workshops in countries such as Bolivia, Chile, Dominican Republic, and Argentina. A number of years later we established

PUBLIC EVENTS SPRING '95

Berlage Institute, Amsterdam
1995

Public

Evening lectures
20.00 hrs.

Tuesday 9 May
John Körmeling The Netherlands
Recent work

Tuesday 23 May
Arie Graafland The Netherlands
Architecture of the uncanny

Tuesday 30 May
Vicente Guallart Spain
Contemporary architecture on CD-rom?

Tuesday 6 June
Kenneth Frampton United States
Museum culture

Wednesday 7 June
David Chipperfield Great Britain
Theorizing practice

Friday 9 June
Alvaro Siza Portugal
Recent work

Lunch lectures
13.00 hrs.

Friday 31 March
Peter Wilson Germany
The culture of schools

Tuesday 4 April
Vedran Mimica The Netherlands
Notes on children and architecture

Tuesday 25 April
Herman Hertzberger The Netherlands
The culture of schools

Friday 19 May
Abram de Swaan The Netherlands
The architect: politician without a party

Wednesday 3 May
Roemer van Toorn The Netherlands
Architecture and justice

Presentations
10.00-17.00 hrs.

LETTER

account of Vedran Mimica's study in Delft at TU Faculty of Architecture

Delft, 1988

closer ties with Japan and China, again in the form of workshops and research studios. And with the help from the European Union we held workshops in the European port cities such as Marseille, Barcelona, and Rotterdam. Supersudaca, Stealth, and Wonderland are the initiatives from former Berlage students. The Berlage network has spread all over the world.

Q   Born?

VM   In 1954, in Zagreb, then a city in Yugoslavia.

Q   Studies?

VM   I studied architecture at the University of Zagreb. Like so many young architects, after graduation I worked on many project proposals. One was a memorial primary school dedicated to a young partisan fighter killed by the fascists in World War 2. That was back in 1979. I worked on the project with two colleagues at the time of our graduation. After visiting London, a year before, I was fascinated by Cedric Price. We designed a glass memorial room on wheels and rails. With a push of a button the room would move out to the school front yard. Everybody thought it was a ridiculous idea. My professor Šegvić warned me: "Don't make jokes, Vedran; you could end up in prison". But surprisingly enough, we won the first prize. The design was never completed, but it did land us jobs at the university.

Teachers at the university taught courses, did research, and worked as architects. The university was affiliated to a semi-professional architecture firm. On paper this combination sounds interesting, but in reality it was not. The academic environment was far too removed from real architecture. It was not very inspiring. What is more, the teaching method was so very socialistic and polytechnic, almost exclusively focused on typology. At the time, I was doing research on school buildings, primary schools in particular, including Hertzberger's Montessori school. An advantage of working at the university was that I could apply for a grant to study abroad.

Q   And that is how you ended up in the Netherlands?

VM   Yes. On the form for Delft University you had to fill in three names of professors. Because of my interest in schools I wrote down Aldo van Eyck first, of course, and then Herman Hertzberger, and the third was Carel Weeber. All I had was a list of names, and there was no Google at the time. I had no idea who Weeber was but I still had to fill in three names. When Herman read the application, his first reaction was: "This boy is totally confused; he hasn't got a clue. Let's keep him away from Carel; that's poison. We have to help him." And so I ended up with Herman. All this happened in 1983, an interesting period in Delft. The group around Herman was working partly on what was a new research discipline at the time: environmental psychology. The underlying idea was that a good building has beneficial effects on its occupants. To design a good school, architects had to understand the behavior of students and teachers in the learning environment. The imminent retirement of Van Eyck was also a factor back then. A vacuum loomed, and everything seemed to be possible. To mark the Van Eyck's retirement, Herman organized the second INDESEM (International Design Seminar), the first having taken place 13 years earlier. This, together with the Stylos[2] activities, was of huge influence on education in Delft.

After six months I returned to the university in Zagreb, but I kept in touch with Herman. He arranged for me to get a scholarship in 1986 to do one-year research at the Delft University of Technology. The result was a book entitled Notes on Children, Environment and Architecture. In the years that followed I traveled back and forth between Delft and Zagreb, organized an INDESEM in Split in 1988, struggled for my daily bread, together with my wife and three children. The political situation in Yugoslavia was also deteriorating. Herman kept inviting me to come to the Netherlands. "Herman", I said, "how can you live in a country where it rains 260 days a year? I think you're very nice, I love Delft, the University has a fine library, but who could live in the Netherlands? It's not suitable for people."

2   Stylos is the independent student association of the Faculty of Architecture and the Built Environment at the TU Delft, founded in 1894.

Graduation project

Design Center in
Zagreb, Ilica 18

Zagreb, 1979

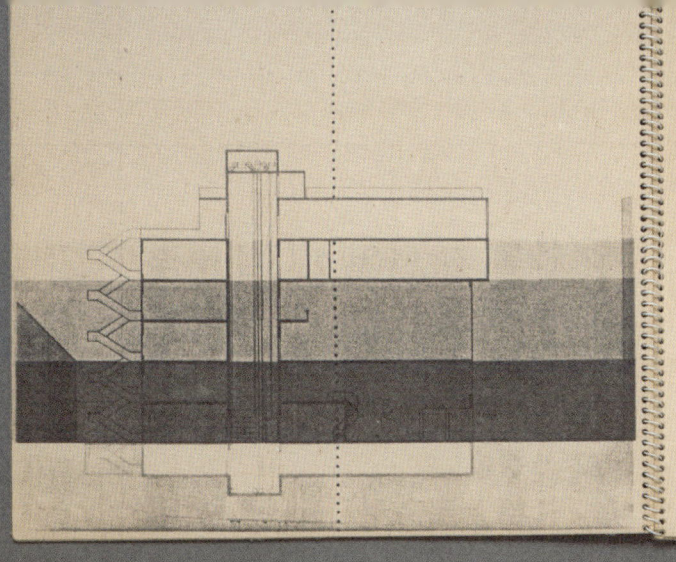

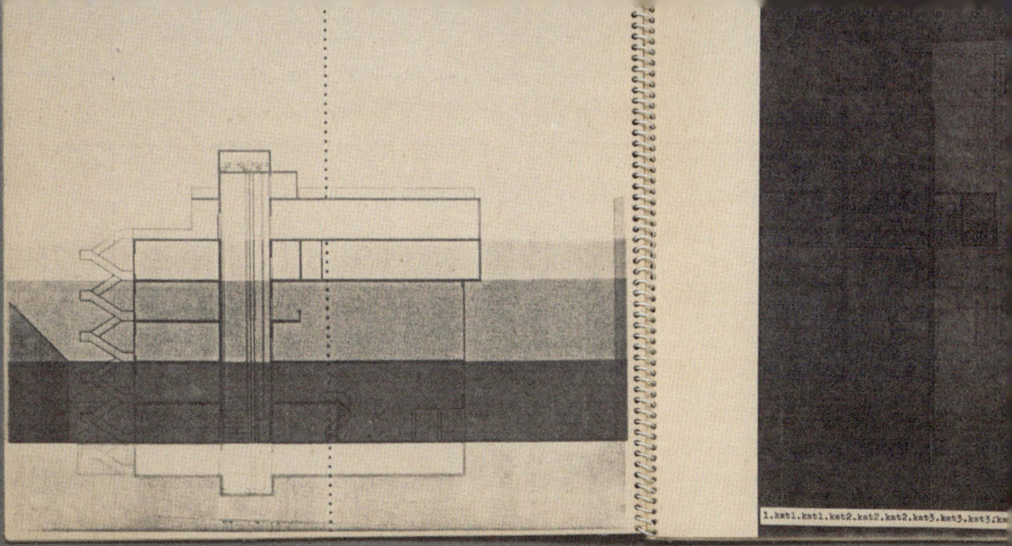

INDESEM '88

reports

Faculty of Architecture,
Delft University of
Technology

Delft, 1988

ZAREZ, I/6

Zagreb, 1999

Democratization of
public space, interview
with Vedran Mimica

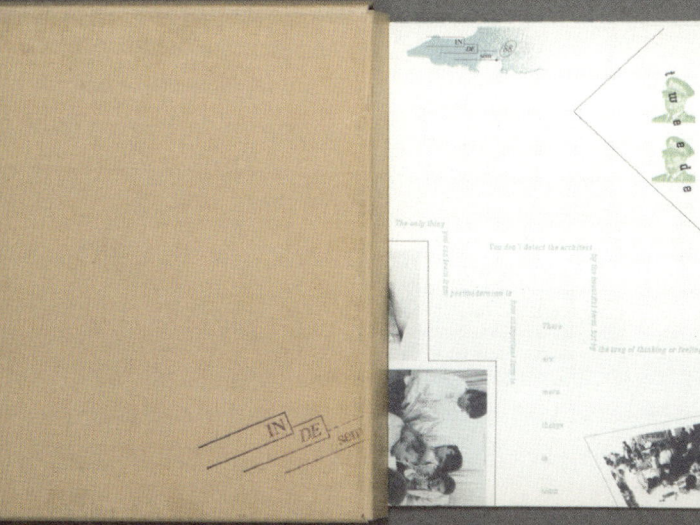

1990	1992	1994	1996	1997	1998	1999	2000	2001	2002	2003	20
Boro Doklestić			B. K. Boley			Rem Koolhaas			Andrea Branzi	Adriaan Geuze	
Children's room			Dimiti Waltritsch						Andrej Hrauski	Aldo van Eyck	
Ivan Čižmek			Robin Limmroth						Braco Dimitrijević	Alejandro Zaera-Polo	
Joschka Fisher			Tamara Roy						Daniel Libeskind	Andrea Branzi	
Niko Gamulin									Deyan Sudjic	Arne van Herk	Al
Ratko Miličević									Dietmar Steiner	Balhrishna Doshi	Al
Vladimir Mattioni									Hannes Svoboda	Bart Lootsma	Be
				Herman Hertzberger					Ignasi Sola Morales	Ben van Berkel	Bi
				Hilda Auf Franić					Igor Zidić	Caroline Bos	Be
				Kenneth Frampton					Jon Jerde	Christian Gullichsen	Be
				Marina Bertina					Joschka Fischer	Daniel Libeskind	Al
				Neno Kavurić					Joseph Beuys	Elia Zenghelis	Bo
				Patrick Schumacher					Lluís Hortet	Elizabeth Diller	Bo
				Tonči Žarnić					Manuel Castells	Giancarlo de Carlo	Bo
				Veljko Olujić					Michael Ignatieff	Greg Lynn	Bo
									Milan Kundera	Hani Rashid	Bo
									Njirić+Njirić	Henry Ciriani	Br
		Eleni Gigantes			Ante Kuzmanić				Oriol Bohigas	Herman Hertzberger	Da
		Elia Zenghelis			Eugen Širola				Slavoj Žižek	Ignasi Sola-Morales	Da
		Herman Hertzberger			Pamela Anderson				Tonko Maroević	Jacob van Rijs	Da
		Ignasi de Sola Morales							Vjeran Zuppa	Jennifer Sigler	Di
		Kenneth Frampton							Walter Maria Stojan	Jesse Reiser	Dr
		Rem Koolhaas							Wolfgang Petritsch	Jo Coenen	Ed
		Steven Holl								Joanna Regulska	Ell
		Thom Mayne								Joke Kemper	Ell
		Toyo Ito								Juhani Pallasmaa	En
		Wilfred Wang								Kees Christiaanse	Fra
										Kenneth Frampton	Fr
										Max Risselada	Fu
										Mels Crouwel	Ge
										Mick Morssink	Ge
		Aldo van Eyck				Elia Zenghelis				Oriol Bohigas	Ge
		Alvaro Siza				Kurt C. H. Ho				Peter Smithson	Ge
		Arne Van Herk				Northon Flores Troche				Raoul Bunschoten	Gr
		Bernard Tchumi				Rafael Gomez-Moriana				Rem Koolhaas	Ha
		Georges Descombes				Zhang Shao Hua				Renzo Piano	He
		Herman Hertzberger								Rob Docter	He
		Jean Nouvel.								Roemer van Toorn	He
		Kenneth Frampton								Saskia Sassen	He
		Kess Christiaanse								Stan Allen	Hr
		Rem Koolhaas								Stefano Boeri	Hr
		Renzo Piano								Steven Holl	Id
		Tadao Ando								Sylvia Lavin	Iva
		Toyo Ito								Terence Riley	Ja
		Willem Jan Neutelings								Thom Mayne	Je
										Wiel Arets	Jo
										Willem-Jan Neutelings	Ke
										Winy Maas	Ma
										Xaveer de Geyter	Ml
										Yap Hong Seng	Na
										Yorgos Simeoforidis	Nie
										Zaha Hadid	Ni
							3LHD				No
							Aldo van Eyck				No
							Aleksandar Laslo				Ol
							Bart Lootsma				Pa
							Bojan Radonić				Pe
							Charles Jencks				Pie
							Darko Fritz				Re
							Helena Paver Njirić				Re
							Hrvoje Njirić				Sa
							Jorgos Simeoforidis				Sa
							Jurgen Habermas				Sla
							Katrin Vandermerliere				Sla
							Kees Christiaansen				TB
							Kenneth Frampton				The
							Ivan Marušić Klif				To
							Manuel Gausa				To
							Njirić+Njirić				To
							Pero Puljiz				Ve
							Saša Randić				Vla
							Stephan Bell				Vla
							Steven Holl				Wi
							Theo Bosch				Wi
							Vladimir Šlapeta				Za
							Wiel Arets				Zd
							Yap Hong Seng				Zo
							Yorgos Simeoforidis				Zvj
							Irenée Scalbert				

2005	2006	2007	2008	2009	2010	2012	2014	2016
Aida Daidjić		Aldo van Eyck			Aldo van Eyck			
Aleksej Ivanko		Andrija Rusan			Bart Lootsma			
Bevk & Perović and Zorc		Ante Kuzmanić			Ben van Berkel			
Borislav Curcic		Ante Mardešić			Branimir Medić			
Braco Dimitrijević		Ante Nikša Bilić			Christian Keres			
Christoph Luchsinger		Boris Groys			Dado Katušić			
Dado Katušić		Boševski & Fiolić			David Van Severen			
Emir Kusturica		Branimir Medić			Elia Zenghelis			
Franjo Tudjman		Davor Lončarić			Hans Ibelings			
Hans-Dietrich Genscher		Dekleva and Gregorčič			Herman Hertzberger			
Herman Hertzberger		Edi Rama			Idis Turato			
Hrvoje Njirić		Feđa Vukić			Jean Nouvel			
Igor Kebel		Hans Ulrich Obrist			Kazuyo Sejima			
Ivo Banac		Helena Njirić			Kenneth Frampton			
Josip Broz Tito		Helena Paver Njirić			Kersten Geers			
Kenneth Frampton		Herman Hertzberger			Leo Modrčin			
Lebeus Woods		Herzog and de Meuron			Manuel Gausa			
Liliane Schneiter		Hrvoje Njirić			Marko Dabrović			
Maria Braut		Ivan Crnković			Njirić+Njirić			
Mika Cimolini		Ivo Opstelten			Pero Puljiz			
Nassrine Azlmi		Janez Koželj			Randić and Turato			
Nick Dodd		John Urry			Raoul Bunschoten			
Njirić+Njirić		Joschka Fisher			Rem Koolhaas			
Petra Marguc		Jurgen Habermas			Sanja Ipšić			
Radovan Karadzić		Kebel and Cimolini			Saskia Sassen			
Ratko Mladić		Kenneth Frampton			Saša Randić			
Rožić, Ostan and Zorko		Lea Pelivan			Tadej Glažar			
Slobodan Milošević		Leo Modrčin			Wiel Arets			
Slobodan Praljak		Lieven de Cauter			Winy Maas			
Stipe Mesic		Marijn Spoelstra						
Tadej Glažar		Marina de Vries						
Thom Mayne		Markus Schaefer						
Tina Gregorič	Alejandro Zaera-Polo	Max Risselada			Aaron Betsky	3LHD		
Vasa J. Perović	Ante Kuzmanić	Michiel Dehaene				Aldo van Eyck		
Vladimir Šlapeta	Bernard Cache	Mićo Gamulin				Anka Mrak Taritaš		
	Branimir Medić	Nenad Fabijanić				Andrija Rusan		
	Damir Martinović Mrle	Neno Kezić				Branimir Medić		
	Davor Katušić	Nikola Bašić				Bruketa & Žinić		
	Dubravka Šuica	Nikola Polak				Davor Katušić		
	Edi Rama	Nikola Popić				Francisco Mangado		
	Edwin Heathcote	Njirić+Njirić				Frank Gehry		
	Eugen Širola	Paolo Portoghesi				Helena Paver Njirić		
	Herman Hertzberger	Pero Puljiz				Hrvoje Njirić		
	Hugh Pearman	Petar Mišković				Maroje Mrduljaš		
	Ivana Franke	Pier Vittorio Aureli				Numen/For Use		
	Jennifer Sigler	Rem Koolhaas				Pero Puljiz		
	Lea Pelivan	Sadar and Vuga				Randić&Turato		
	Lionel Veehr	Saskia Sassen				Rem Koolhaas		
	Manfredo Tafuri	Stefano Boeri				Studio Up		
	Marijn Spoelstra	Tadao Ando				Thom Mayne		
	Markus Schaefer	Toma Plejić				Tonči Žarnić		
	Minas Bakalčev	Tonči Žarnić				Veljko Olujić		
	Mitko Hadži Pulja	Vladimir Mattioni		Aldo van Eyck		Zaha Hadid		
	Nicolai Ouroussoff	Zoka Zola		Boris Podrecca				
	Nives Kozulić	Ćurković and Zidarić		Branko Kincl			Wiel Arets	
	Pero Puljiz	Černigoj and Grmek		Brett Steele			Kenneth Frampton	
	Peter Trummer			Coop Himmelb			Vladimir Mattioni	
	Pier Vittorio Aureli			Daniel Libeskind			Andrija Rusan	
	Pope			Edi Rama			Maroje Mrduljaš	
	Radislav Jovanov Gonzo			Elia Zenghelis			Ante Kuzmanić	
	Randić & Turato			Elisabeth Riha			Sean Keller	
	Rem Koolhaas			Frank Gehry				
	Richard Sennett			Fuksas				
	Richard "Ricky" Burdett			Herman Hertzberger				
	Roemer van Toorn			Jean Nouvel				
	Rolling Stones			Kenneth Frampton				
	Saskia Sassen			Marc Auge				
	Saša Randić			Mladen Jošić				
	Stefano Boeri			Norman Foster				
	Terunobu Fujimori			Patrik Schumacher				
	Toma Plejić			Rem Koolhaas				
	Wiel Arets			Renzo Piano				
				Richard Florida				
				Ricky Burdett				
				Saskia Sassen				
				Thom Mayne				
				Velimir Neidhardt				
				Zaha Hadid				
				Ćurković and Zidarić				

THE BERLAG

Lunch lectures
13.00 hrs.

Friday 9 June
Alvaro Siza Portugal
Recent work

David Chipperfield Great Britain
Theorizing practice

Tuesday 4 April
Vedran Mimica The Netherlands
Notes on children and architecture

Friday 31 March
Peter Wilson Germany
The culture of schools

Tuesday 25 April
Herman Hertzberger The Netherlands
The culture of schools

Friday 19 May
Abram de Swaan The Netherlands
The architect: politician without a

Wednesday 3 May
Roemer van Toorn The Netherlands
Architecture and justice

Presentations
10.00–17.00 hrs.

Friday 23 June

THE BERLAGE EXPERIENCE
Rotterdam 2003
BUILDING CONSCIOUSNESS
Rotterdam 2011
ENGAGING REALITY
Rotterdam 2006
THE POWER OF ARCHITECTURAL THOUGHT
Zagreb 2007

PLATFORM

Public

Evening lectures
20.00 hrs.

Tuesday 9 May
John Körmeling The Netherlands
Recent work

Tuesday 23 May
Arie Graafland The Netherlands
Architecture of the uncanny

Tuesday 30 May
Vicente Guallart Spain
Contemporary architecture on CD

Tuesday 6 June
Kenneth Frampton United States

The texts in this section are a collection of thoughts on the changing and expanding role of architectural education in the face of rapid contemporary globalization and the attempt to position the Berlage Institute educational endeavors to train the emerging generations of architects able to steer unconventional and innovative processes in architectural and urban thinking.

The Berlage Institute represented a global architectural microcosm during the 1990s and 2000s.

From the beginning it was Hertzbergerian unorthodox cultural project, a sort of hybrid between the postgraduate school and cultural institution for exchange of Dutch and international architecture, initially ideally situated in Aldo van Eyck's former children orphanage in South Amsterdam. Wiel Arets redefined the Berlage as a 'postgraduate laboratory', rather than a school by emphasizing the individual students research activities and establishing Progressive Research PhD program. Alejando Zaera-Polo continued with strong research orientation of the Institute as a collective effort by introducing the new generation of tutors and associating the research to the reality of urban conditions. Finally, my role was to actualize the research portfolio of the Institute through internal publication of Studio Research Reports, engagement in international contract research projects as well as curatorial activities based on urban research.

The Berlage's research based curriculum encouraged dialogue and debates amongst different types of expertise and stances by inviting many prominent architects to work with postgraduate students.

It was very important that the Berlage was positioned in the real world that not only drew from but responded to contemporary social, economic, political and ecological issues. That kind of response, grounded in numerous analyzes of what at the Berlage we used to call 'real reality', resulted in alternative realities that were conceptualized as innovative urban strategies. The Berlage research based design was publicly presented at Ricky Burdet's Cities, Architecture and Society, Venice Architecture Biennial as an exhibition under the title Beyond Mapping, Projecting the City.

With no single dominant ideology, the Berlage was a platform for a discourse inciting many realities and forces in the contemporary city to occur, subsequently energizing and fostering the capabilities of architectural thought.

IMAGINATION

Rudi Supek

Zagreb, 1979

Zagreb, 1987

THE BERLAGE EXPERIENCE

Published in Hunch, the Berlage Institute report 6/7, Rotterdam, Summer 2003

It is perhaps premature to write the (hi)story of the Berlage Institute; it has existed for a mere 12 years. However, this is precisely what I was asked to do for this special issue of Hunch. I was not to ponder the fundamental questions posed to other contributors, but instead had to ask myself a host of other questions: how to write about the recent history, how to reveal the wider relevance of one institution within the late 20th and early 21st century architectural culture, and finally how to tell the story of the Berlage itself rather than of the individuals that comprise it?

These questions led to a chronology of themes, or better styles, of the three deans of the Berlage Institute. The sheer scope of events, issues, and ideologies that were constructed, debated, and quickly superseded, witness to the Berlage's commitment to establishing a critical attitude towards the present while simultaneously anticipating the future.

(Pre-)History of the Berlage

In 1985, Aldo van Eyck was forced to retire as a professor of architecture at the Delft University of Technology. But it was clear to everybody that it was virtually impossible to send Aldo into retirement; his spirit would be circulating through the Dutch architectural scene for many years to come. Herman Hertzberger decided to celebrate van Eyck's retirement by revitalizing INDESEM – International Design Seminar – which had originated in Delft in 1967, one year before the student revolution of 1968. INDESEM represented a new, self-organizing approach to teaching, with no formal ties to university bureaucracy; it was free from the institution.

The 1985 INDESEM was a huge success. Van Eyck worked with 40 students invited from schools all over the world, and with an international group of architects and teachers. Symbolically, it reestablished a critique of institutional bureaucracy and, perhaps more importantly, established new criteria for the conceptualization of education in architecture. One could almost argue that the students learned more in INDESEM's five-day workshops than during their entire studies, and that the experience of direct exchange with Rem Koolhaas, Renzo Piano, Aldo van Eyck, and others, had a crucial influence on their architectural development. Without a doubt, INDESEM was fundamental to Hertzberger's idea to organize a place for international postgraduate architecture studies in the Netherlands.

Simultaneously with Hertzberger's thoughts of establishing a new type of architectural education, two coincidences occurred. The first was the Memorandum on Architectural Policy (Architectuur-nota) presentation to the parliament, initiated by the Dutch Minister of Culture, Hedy D'Ancona. It established architecture as a fundamentally important discipline for the development of the country and resulted in the platform for the establishment of the Berlage Institute, the Netherlands Architecture Institute (NAi), and various funds for architectural research.

The second coincidence was the crisis surrounding Aldo van Eyck's orphanage in south Amsterdam, which led Hertzberger to start a campaign to save the structure. Built in 1960, the orphanage was considered the prototypical example of Dutch structuralism; its subdivided spaces overlapped with labyrinthine clarity, as van Eyck put it. The building initiated a completely new architectural language that was radically critical towards late-modernism and was based on his studies of the buildings of indigenous people all over the world. But by the mid-eighties, the system of care for orphans had evolved towards family-based arrangements and the orphanage became unnecessary. Van Eyck's canonical, yet poorly maintained building was threatened with demolition; with its surrounding land, the orphanage had been sold to developers of office space.

After an international campaign, in 1989 Hertzberger received enough support to convince the Dutch government to establish the building as a monument. The restored Van Eyck orphanage would become the Berlage Institute's first true home. During the reconstruction of the orphanage, Hertzberger gathered 15 students and – with enormous help from Mirjam Usseling and Yap Hong Seng – managed to start the Institute in September 1990 in a warehouse in Amsterdam's harbor. The place was to house the Institute only until completion of the renovation in the beginning of 1991. Appropriation of the "new orphanage" from day one was very important for the relation between the students and the space. No one would have believed, after Hertzberger's struggle to preserve the building, that only five years later the Berlage Institute would be forced out by the real-estate market, and the orphanage transformed into luxurious "Garden Courts" office space.

The orphanage as an architectural reference had no direct influence on the production of studio work during the Institute's first five years. Yet it took on an important presence as an existential frame for the life of the students and staff. The house – like all houses with a paradigmatic importance for the development of architecture – proved to be an ideal structure for a postgraduate school of architecture. In spite of Van Eyck's details, which were specifically designed for the different orphans' age groups, the architectural participants easily found and established their world in the building.

Aldo van Eyck used to visit us in the orphanage. He would come, uninvited, and wander around the building, surveying what was going on at the Berlage. In particular he would be annoyed with the messy state of the courtyards of the pavilions. We would explain that the courtyards were dirty because his project, a 10,000 m2 office building on the site next door is under construction, and that we were not responsible for the maintenance of outdoor spaces. This would not satisfy him. He wrote a big message on cardboard to be handed to Hertzberger: "pearls in front of pigs!"

Again and again, Van Eyck's feisty character would enliven the atmosphere. At the ceremony for the opening of his new building behind the orphanage, Van Eyck avoided all contact with the developers and guests. During the reception, he waited in the Berlage Institute's offices, explaining to students that the only reason he designed the office building was to save the orphanage. He stressed that he "was not an office-building architect". At the end of the talk, he provoked everybody by saying that today everyone is looking at OMA and not at OPA (in Dutch, Oma means grandmother, and Opa grandfather.) It is interesting to remember that Van Eyck was the member of the jury of the competition for the city hall in The Hague; it was he who promoted OMA's project in opposition to the winning scheme by Richard Meier, whom he characterized as a "white albino with postmodern misunderstanding."

Van Eyck did not have a particular influence on the creation of the curriculum at the Berlage, but he repeatedly urged us to put a shiny metal plate at the entrance, engraved with the names of the architects who should never be allowed to enter the building: Stanley Tigerman, Peter Eisenman, Michael Graves, and other "posts." Indeed, none of them came to the Berlage during Hertzberger's tenure. It is interesting to note that Van Eyck only came twice to see lectures, despite many invitations: he wanted to see the work of his friend Balkrishna V.Doshi and the work of Steven Holl.

When the time came, Van Eyck refused to accept or understand the departure of the Berlage Institute from the orphanage. He was furious and aggressive in his accusations of everybody from Hertzberger to government ministers. Aldo simply could not believe in the logic of the market or the ministry's refusal to pay the hugely increased rents for the space. He argued that beyond all bureaucracy and market logic, one must invest in culture and that by all means the Berlage must remain in the orphanage. Only in that situation would it be possible for the building to remain open for visitors from all over the world. Unfortunately, market logic won out and the building became privatized; visitors are not welcome.

Finally, there was also the dominant architectural ideology at Delft and elsewhere in the Netherlands during the seventies, with

(Pre-)History of the Berlage

In 1985, Aldo van Eyck was forced to retire as a professor of architecture at the Delft University of Technology. But it was clear to everybody that it was virtually impossible to send Aldo into retirement; his spirit would be circulating through the Dutch architectural scene for many years to come. Herman Hertzberger decided to celebrate van Eyck's retirement by revitalizing INDESEM – International Design Seminar – which had originated in Delft in 1967, one year before the student revolution of 1968. INDESEM represented a new, self-organising approach to teaching, with no formal ties to university bureaucracy; it was free from the institution.

Herman Hertzberger, during masterclass with Johan van der Keuken, 1994

Hunch 6/7

Berlage Institute Report
Rotterdam, 2003

FIELDS : THE BERLAGE CACHIERS 5 :
STUDIO '95 '96

010 Publishers
Rotterdam, 1997

One of the aims of the Berlage Institute is to stimulate cross-fertilisation between individual and group work, students and professors, practice and theory, in-depth research and contributions from critics and practitioners, including those from other disciplines.

Computer Laboratory The Berlage Institute tries to offer its students the most relevant and modern design facilities. Within this framework preparations are made for the installation of a well-equipped computer laboratory in December 1996. The computer laboratory will have a hybrid set-up and will include Power Macintoshes, Window NT machines, Silicon Graphics O2 machines, an A0 colour printer, an A3 black and white printer, an A4 colour laser printer, Internet, scanners and other accessories, as well as the software necessary for CAD, photo manipulation, animation and video productions.

Aldo van Eyck and Herman Hertzberger as its undisputed stars. Koolhaas viewed their popularity as a simple case of "polder blindness."
'In the polders, the absence of any comparative features can make a hare look as big as a cow… And in principle isn't it all Hertzberger ever talks about; that you need a special brick to put the milk bottles on at the front door? Even the average porno flick has subtler ideas about interactions between the housewife and the milkman… It's typical Montessori tyranny.'

Colenbrander, Bernard (1995) "The Inheritability of the Genius Complex". In: Reference OMA: The Sublime Start of an Architectural Generation, catalog for the exhibition at NAi, Rotterdam: NAi Publishers

Most architects today seem to have no higher aim than to produce something that becomes as close as possible to the mass-published "glamour realism" that appears to be demanded by society. The problem of the talented young architects of today is that they themselves are no longer capable of determining what they want, what their potential is, and who they are.

Hertzberger, Herman (1992) "Do architects have any idea of what they draw?"
Berlage Cahiers 1, Rotterdam: 010 Publishers

Hertzberger's Berlage: Montessori Paradise

In the early nineties, coinciding with the first years of the Berlage, Hertzberger published his Lessons for Students in Architecture, compiled from his lectures to undergraduate students at the Delft University of Technology. The book was immensely successful, and was later translated into eight different languages. But the post-professional program of the Berlage was not conceived as Herman Hertzberger's School. Hertzberger did not want Berlage students to pursue his architectural ideas. Rather, he wanted them to investigate and anticipate an architecture that would respond to present-day issues. Students came to Amsterdam believing in the mission of the Berlage Institute and with the utmost respect for Hertzberger at the helm. During studios, juries, and master-classes, students were simultaneously in contact with Hertzberger's generation of architects (Oriol Bohigas, Giancarlo de Carlo, Henry Ciriani, Peter Smithson, Juhani Pallasmaa, Balkrishna V.Doshi, Kristian Gullichsen, and especially Kenneth Frampton) as well as the new generation of the Dutch architects under the umbrella of OMA and Rem Koolhaas (Kees Christiaanse, Willem-Jan Neutelings, Xaveer De Geyter), and a group of Dutch architects outside of OMA (Adriaan Geuze, Ben van Berkel, Wiel Arets, Mels Crouwel, Jo Coenen, and Arne van Herk.)

The relation between the "old" and "young" architects provided the formative years of the Berlage Institute with a wide scope of ideas. The school's performance did not narrow in one direction, but conversely, opened the field of possible investigation and accumulation of knowledge from many different perspectives. The Berlage was a unique place where it was possible to compare the ideas of Doshi to those of Geuze, or Ciriani to Van Berkel. Precisely because of that strategy, Hertzberger was respected by Berlage students in spite of his critical attitude towards the work they produced; Hertzberger's critiques were always colored by the character of his own architectural practice.

The objective of architectural training must ultimately be to nurture the growth of the students' own sense of what constitutes quality, so that they may become aware of who they are, where they stand, what they have to say, and which formal means are the most appropriate in their specific cases. To design means to think... Our time, characterized by instability, rapid

Hunch 6/7

Berlage Institute Report
Rotterdam, 2003

Aldo van Eyck
Herman Hertzberger
Rem Koolhaas
Renzo Piano
Steven Holl
Oriol Bohigas
Giancarlo de Carlo
Henry Ciriani
Peter Smithson
Juhani Pallasmaa
Balhrishna Doshi
Christian Gullichsen
Kenneth Frampton
Willem-Jan Neutelings
Xaveer de Geyter
Adriaan Geuze
Ben van Berkel
Wiel Arets
Mels Crouwel
Jo Coenen
Arne van Herk
Elia Zenghelis
Max Risselada

Roemer van Toorn
Ignasi Sola-Morales
Yorgos Simeoforidis
Zaha Hadid
Daniel Libeskind
Stan Allen
Elizabeth Diller
Hani Rashid
Jesse Reiser
Greg Lynn
Terence Riley
Sylvia Lavin
Bart Lootsma
Winy Maas
Caroline Bos
Jacob van Rijs
Raoul Bunschoten
Alejandro Zaera-Polo
Joke Kemper
Rob Docter
Jennifer Sigler
Mick Morssink

42   The Berlage Experience   hunch

Aldo van Eyck's Orphanage, Amsterdam, inhabited by the Berlage Institute.

Aldo van Eyck, Victor Mani and Herman Hertzberger in front of a celebration cake of the Orphanage.

The 1985 INDESEM was a huge success. Van Eyck worked with 40 students invited from schools all over the world, and with an international group of architects and teachers. Symbolically, it re-established a critique of institutional bureaucracy and, perhaps more importantly, established new criteria for the conceptualization of education in architecture. One could almost argue that the students learned more in INDESEM's five-day workshops than during their entire studies, and that the experience of direct exchange with Rem Koolhaas, Renzo Piano, Aldo van Eyck, and others, had a crucial influence on their architectural development. Without a doubt, INDESEM was fundamental to Hertzberger's idea to organize a place of international postgraduate architecture studies in the Netherlands.

Simultaneous with Hertzberger's thoughts of establishing a new type of architectural education, two coincidences occurred. The first was the Memorandum on Architectural Policy (Architectuurnota) presentation to the parliament, initiated by the Dutch Minister of Culture, Hedy D'Ancona. It established architecture as a fundamentally important discipline for the development of the country and resulted in the platform for the establishment of the Berlage Institute, the Netherlands Architecture Institute (NAi), and various funds for architectural research.

The second coincidence was the crisis surrounding Aldo van Eyck's orphanage in south Amsterdam, which led Hertzberger to start a campaign to save the structure. Built in 1960, the orphanage was considered the prototypical example of Dutch structuralism; its

The Orphanage

building as a monument. The restored Van Eyck orphanage would become the Berlage Institute's first true home. During the reconstruction of the orphanage, Hertzberger gathered 15 students and – with enormous help from Mirjam IJsseling and Yap Hong Seng – managed to start the institute in September 1990 in a warehouse in Amsterdam's harbor. The place was to house the Institute only until completion of the renovation in the beginning of 1991. Appropriation of the "new orphanage" from day one was very important for the relation between the students and the space. No one would have believed, after Hertzberger's struggle to preserve the building, that only five years later the Berlage Institute would be forced out by the market, and the orphanage would be transformed into luxurious "Garden Courts" office space.

The orphanage as an architectural reference had no direct influence on the production of studio work during the Institute's first five years. Yet it took on an important presence as an existential frame for the life of the students and staff. The house – like all houses with a paradigmatic importance for the development of architecture – proved to be an ideal structure for a postgraduate school of architecture. In spite of Van Eyck's details, which were specifically designed for the different orphans' age groups, the architectural participants easily found and established their world in the building.

Aldo van Eyck used to visit us in the orphanage. He would come, uninvited, and wander around the building, surveying what was going on at the Berlage. In particular he would be amused with change, pressure and stress, asks for a continuous revision of our task, forces us to look for ever new formulations of that task in terms of spatial mechanisms and paradigms.

<u>Hertzberger, Herman (1992) "Do architects have any idea of what they draw?"</u>
<u>Berlage Cahiers 1</u>, Rotterdam: 010 Publishers

Yet, his educational message was that a student as an individual is the center of every pedagogical system. Obviously his educational thinking was influenced by his Montessori background; he believed in the basic Montessori principle of helping one to do it alone. In the beginning, the orphanage was like a big Montessori postgraduate course (as Aldo van Eyck once critically stated).

The Hertzberger spirit is still present at the Berlage and remains important for the quality of the educational environment. As much as "everything has changed," the Institute still has a "no-nonsense" attitude where communal intelligence supersedes the individual, despite the care targeted towards individual efforts. Still, bureaucracy is suppressed to the lowest possible level, students feel that they are the central interest, and teachers realize that they can introduce their programs without the fear of the "super-ideologies" from any side.

In regard to curriculum, Hertzberger believed that young architects should be able to work on many projects simultaneously. Therefore, students were involved in a series of design studios during their two years at the Institute. But after evaluating the first generation of students, it was obvious that the theory and history aspect of the curriculum needed strengthening. In addition, thesis work, which occupies most of the second year's time, needed to focus on one project. Both ideas were realized through contracts with Kenneth Frampton and Elia Zenghelis. Frampton developed, with Max Risselada and later with Roemer van Toorn, a history and theory course. From 1994 on Roemer included Cultural Studies and research on the Second Modernity.[3] In addition to regular lectures and theory-based projects, one masterclass per year would be dedicated to the critical comparative analysis of contemporary architectural production. Two people who were extremely influential in these discussions were the Catalan professor Ignasi de Solà-Morales and Greek architect and writer Yorgos Simeoforidis. Solà-Morales and Simeoforidis were unique individuals who were able to overlap the Mediterranean and Anglo-Saxon ways of thinking and analyzing architecture. Their observations and especially their work with the students in the studio were intimate, relaxed, and personal, but at the same time marked by a high degree of precision and discipline. Both Ignasi and Yorgos are simply irreplaceable.

I think that designing in itself, as far as it is a conscious and verifying process for others, should be acknowledged as research. And then the fuss about a project being realistic or not is irrelevant.

<u>Hertzberger, Herman (1994) "One-Day Conference on Education, Berlage Institute, 11 May 1993"</u> <u>The New Public realm, Berlage Cahiers 2</u>, Rotterdam: 010 Publishers

Elia Zenghelis came to the Berlage for a jury in the spring of 1993 and has remained ever since. Zenghelis' educational experience and his amazing ability to follow different projects simultaneously made him an ideal person for the second year thesis program. According to Hertzberger (and not only Hertzberger), Zenghelis is the world's best teacher of architecture. Rem Koolhaas, Zaha Hadid, and Greg Lynn were some of his students. For years, Zenghelis has managed to maintain love and a passion for teaching; a rare gift. He never tires or

3   Second modernity is meant here as a research agenda: theoretical and empirical explorations in the 'meta-change' of modern society, as according to the authors Ulrich Beck and Christoph Lau. See: Beck, U.& Lau, C. (2005) Second modernity as a research agenda: theoretical and empirical explorations in the 'meta-change' of modern society. In: The British Institute of Sociology, Volume 56, Issue 4, December 2005

TODAY AND WHERE THEIR PROFESSION MIGHT GO TOMORROW

Hunch 6/7

Berlage Institute Report
Rotterdam, 2003

BERLIN

excursion guide

Berlage Institute,
Amsterdam, 1992

FIELDS : THE BERLAGE CACHIERS 5 :
STUDIO '95 '96

010 Publishers
Rotterdam, 1997

PROSPECTUS '97 '98 (1999 - 2000)

Postgraduate Laboratory of Architecture
Berlage Institute Amsterdam

Amsterdam, 1997 and 1999

refuses to sit for hours with students and to help them to deliver quality work. Elia describes our students as "pregnant" with an idea or argument or concept, and himself as a "midwife" helping young architects to deliver. He has an amazing ability to recognize the particular obsession of each and every student and to "architecturalize" it, to develop it to its final stage.

The Berlage's pursuit of final, individual theses was always a controversial issue. Some critics argue that only the very best students are able to engage in individual research. Others support individual-based theses that do not develop personal preoccupations and obsessions but contribute to a larger body of collective research. Regardless of the argument, Elia was able to lift each particular student's production to its ultimate level.

Wiel Arets's Ambition

In the "constitution" of the Berlage Institute, Hertzberger established the principle of a five-year deanship. His argument was that progressive educational institutions on the postgraduate level must change their leading figures regularly. He simply did not believe in the dominance of one, however advanced, mind over others. He argued that new people should bring new ideas and new insights and research agendas into architecture. So after the first five years, the Berlage Institute was faced with the process of searching for a new dean. The dean had to be an internationally recognized architect with educational experience and with the ability to create a curriculum that would continually guarantee the Berlage Institute as one of the world's leading architecture schools. It was not difficult for the screening committee to see that Wiel Arets was an ideal candidate. Shortly after Arets took over in 1995, the Berlage moved from the orphanage to Marnixstraat, at the edge of Jordaan, the most local of all Amsterdam city center districts. From the old school building we occupied until late 1999, it was a pleasure to hop on a bike and arrive a few minutes later at Guus Kemme's Architectura & Natura bookshop, and then to have a cappuccino at Spanjaard, watching the Japanese tourists in the boats or waiting to get into the Anne Frank Museum. The city center of Amsterdam is not only a 17th-century theme park, but also a living city with particular qualities that Berlage students used in their particular ways. Studying in Amsterdam's center was not only about the complexities of Danny Libeskind's Hamlet studio, but also about coffee shops and Friday night techno-parties.

Schools are meant to educate people to do work in architecture and planning that is practical, ethical, and politically aware. In many schools around Europe there are factions which would like to impose ideals of homogeneity, typology of style; which follow an idea of eternity in architecture. But eternity begins in bed and ends in bed. This kind of frozen-ism is reactionary and obsolete. Students must be given the opportunity to question and respond in ways to the changes in society. A school must mirror the global transformations of technology and thinking; provide an international forum for creativity and thought. The Berlage Institute represents the most profound, innovative and critical approach to architectural education. It is a school that has made and will continue to make a seminal contribution to the world of both theory and practice.

Libeskind, Daniel. Speech for the opening of the new building in Marnixstraat, Amsterdam in 1995

The Marnixstraat time will obviously be remembered as Arets' time. Wiel's strong, almost obsessive belief that the architect must be a leading force in the development of society and not just a building master in that society led him to compose

Hunch 6/7

Berlage Institute Report
Rotterdam, 2003

ALLEN ANDO ARETS AURELI BEKAERT BELL
BENTHEM & CROUWEL VAN BERKEL & BOS BETSKY
BOERI & SIMEOFORIDIS BORDEN BOTTA BOUMAN
BRANZI BULLIVANT BUNSCHOTEN CACHE
CARBONERA DE CAUTER CHIPPERFIELD CHRISTIAANSE
CIMOLINI CLAUS & KAAN COENEN COHEN
COLENBRANDER VAN DIJK DIJKSTRA DUBBELDAM
EISENMAN & DAVIDSON FEIREISS FERNÁNDEZ-
GALIANO FLORES-TROCHE FRAMPTON FRETTON
GAUSA DE GEYTER GHIRARDO GÓMEZ-MORIANA
GRAAFLAND GRAFE HADID & SCHUMACHER HAYS
HERTZBERGER HERZOG VAN DEN HEUVEL HEYNEN
HOLL D'HOOGHE IBELINGS ITO JENCKS KLAASSE
KLOOS KRIER KWINTER LAVIN VAN LEEUWEN
LERUP LESAGE LOOTSMA MAAS DE MAESENEER
MERTINS MIMICA MOSS OBRIST ONE ARCHITECTURE
OOSTERHUIS OTTO PALLASMAA PARENT PIMLOTT
RASHID RAUTERBERG RIEWE SAFRAN SASSEN
SECCHI SEJIMA SHANNON SIJMONS SORKIN
SPEAKS STEELE STEINER TAYLOR TEYSSOT
TILMAN VAN TOORN TRUMMER UYTENHAAK
VENTURI & SCOTT BROWN VERSTEGEN VERWEIJ
VIDLER VIGANÒ WEEBER WHITING WILSON
WINGENDER ZAERA-POLO VAN ZEIJL ZENGHELIS

the Berlage Institute report No.6/7

109 PROVISIONAL ATTEMPTS TO ADDRESS SIX SIMPLE AND HARD QUESTIONS ABOUT WHAT ARCHITECTS DO TODAY AND WHERE THEIR PROFESSION MIGHT GO TOMORROW

hunch

Hunch 6/7

Berlage Institute Report
Rotterdam, 2003

The Berlage Experience

Wiel Arets's Ambition

In the "constitution" of the Berlage Institute, Hertzberger established the principle of a five-year dean. His argument was that progressive educational institutions on the postgraduate level must change their leading figures regularly. He simply didn't believe in the dominance of one, however advanced, mind over others. He argued that new people should bring new ideas and new insights and research agendas into architecture. So after the first five years, the Berlage Institute was faced with the process of searching for a new dean. The dean had to be an internationally recognized architect with educational experience and with the ability to create a curriculum that would continually guarantee the Berlage Institute as one of the world's leading architecture schools. It was not difficult for the screening committee to see that Wiel Arets was an ideal candidate.

Shortly after Arets took over in 1995, the Berlage moved from the orphanage to the Marnixstraat, at the edge of Jordaan, the most local of all Amsterdam city center districts. From the old school building we occupied until late 1999, it was a pleasure to hop on a bike and arrive a few minutes later at Guus Kemme's Architectura & Natura bookshop, and then to have a cappuccino at Spanjaard, watching the Japanese tourists in the boats or waiting to get in to the Anne Frank Museum. The city center of Amsterdam is not only a 17th-century theme park, but also a living city with particular qualities that Berlage students used in their particular ways. Studying in Amsterdam's center was not only about the complexities of Danny Libeskind's Hamlet studio, but also about coffee shops and Friday night technoparties.

The Marnixstraat time will obviously be remembered as Arets's time. Wiel's strong, almost obsessive belief that the architect must be a leading force in the development of society and not just a building master in that society led him to compose curricula that involved many tangential disciplines. Right away, he redefined the Berlage as a "postgraduate laboratory," rather than a "school," with the belief

Wiel Arets, 1997.

Schools are meant to educate people to do work in architecture and planning that is practical, ethical, and politically aware. There are in many schools around Europe, factions which would like to impose ideals of homogeneity, typology or style; factions which follow an idea eternity in architecture. But eternity begins in bed and ends in bed. This kind of frozen-ism is reactionary obsolete. Students must be given opportunity to question and respond in ways to the changes in society. A school must mirror the global transformations of technology and thinking, provide an international forum for creativity and thought. The Berlage Institute represents the most profound, innovative and critical approach to architectural education. It is a school that has made and will continue to make a seminal contribution to the world both theory and practice.

Daniel Libeskind, Speech for the opening of the new building on the Marnixstraat, Amsterdam, 1995.

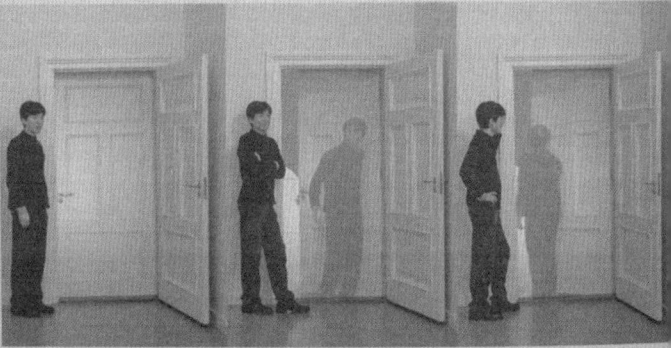

No way out, now way out, Project Jean-François Desmarais, Thomas Lettner, Hajime Narukawa, and Shohei Shigematsu

curricula that involved many tangential disciplines. Right away, he redefined the Berlage as a "postgraduate laboratory," rather than a "school," with the belief that postgraduate research should take a place in an experimental environment.

Arets came to the Berlage with teaching experience at the AA and Columbia University, and had taught at the Berlage during Hertzberger's tenure. From his own research on Luis Barragán in Mexico, which influenced his early work, Arets was convinced that individually conducted research as post-professional study is necessary for every young architect. He introduced to the Berlage and Dutch public his American colleagues: Stan Allen, Elizabeth Diller, Hani Rashid, Jesse Reiser, Greg Lynn, Terence Riley, and Sylvia Lavin. Through studios, masterclasses, and lectures, the "Americans" elevated the performance of the Berlage. Their knowledge, intelligence, and professionalism in terms of advanced research, running a studio, and giving public presentations, enriched the education of both students and staff.

The "American wave" at the Berlage overlapped with the "SuperDutch wave," to paraphrase Bart Lootsma's term for the "12 most innovative studios that are reframing international architecture's most central issues." It was clear that the opportunity to study in the Netherlands, in direct proximity to the practitioners and the work of these successful Dutch offices was a huge attractor. Willem-Jan Neutelings, Winy Maas, and Ben van Berkel and Caroline Bos used the Berlage to fuel their own research, resulting in mutual overlapping of interests between themselves and our students. Winy Maas and Jacob van Rijs started their Datascapes research at the Berlage in 1997. Datascapes were believed to present and represent a metropolitan reality and to work as a source of logic for manipulating that reality.

Datascapes are buildings that make visible some aspects and opportunities of the regulatory matrix that were never intended. They merge out of an apparently arbitrary extension of its logic, point to the arbitrages of the rules themselves and, at the same time, produce something unexpected. The result is both, rational and irrational, normal and monstrous, controlled and free, critical and affirmative.

Process, Berlage Cahiers 7, Rotterdam: 010 Publishers, 2000

Datascapes studios of 1997 and 1998 evolved toward the "3D-City" studio in 2000; "CapaCity," "MixMax," "Universal City," "Region Maker," "Berlage Mixer," and "Mini Machines" followed. Research into density was finally completed with the "Satellites Studio" with Wubbo Ockels[4] in 2002. The ideas, discussions, and results produced made an important contribution not only to the profile of the Berlage Institute, but equally to the development of the architectural discourse presented in numerous MVRDV publications.

As the number of Berlage students increased, Wiel Arets brought in two new tutors to work with Elia Zenghelis supervising thesis work – Bart Lootsma and Raoul Bunschoten.

Bart Lootsma, a leading critic, argued that "Research for Research," as he named his program, should be exclusively an analytical approach, dissecting the controversies and complexities of the contemporary world where the processes of individualization directly take place. Lootsma was able to drive his students to a remarkable product level; many of his thesis students have presented their work in world-renowned magazines, exhibitions, and seminars.

Raoul Bunschoten, a Dutch architect based in London with his office Chora, developed a research program and a methodology called "Urban Gallery." His charisma and his unique approach to teaching resulted in total devotion from his students, whose work constantly challenged the principles of urban

[4] Wubbo Johannes Ockels (28 March 1946 – 18 May 2014) was a Dutch physicist and an astronaut of the European Space Agency (ESA).

analysis and urban planning, and anticipated completely new urban realities.

Perhaps the most memorable – and tense – event of Arets's tenure was a public debate between Kenneth Frampton and Rem Koolhaas. Koolhaas did not want to lecture about his work, so he proposed a new format in which he would interview personalities who projected architectural "ideologies." He short-listed Frampton, Venturi, Rowe, and Smithson as possible interviewees. In the end he declared Frampton as today's one and only serious critic and a date was set. Koolhaas carefully prepared himself, diligently studying Frampton's books; finally, he composed a series of questions. The debate occurred and confirmed the obvious: a debate between the two most important architectural thinkers at the end of the 20th century is not really possible. It was clear that reconciliation between the Frampton's Frankfurt school ideological positions and Koolhasian poststructuralism is not easy and that common language is difficult to find.

For me, the issue of monumentality is related to an aphorism by Antoine Saint-Exupery that I like very much, where he says that we do not ask to be eternal beings, we only ask that things do not lose all their meaning. In her book The Human Condition, Hannah Arendt writes about the necessity of world creation for the maintenance of stability and continuity in a world where individual mortality is to be transcended. What I understand by monumentality is this continuity of the human world, the collective capacity that is to transcend death. The question then becomes of how can one still maintain this kind of activity today? The very fact that one can pose this question shows how precarious the issue is in a world that is constantly changing, in which the pressure of technological and economic change is so intense. It is obviously this intensity itself which makes the constitution of a human world extremely difficult; the maintenance of its stability, its identity, its physical presence even, becomes a difficult task before the escalation of technological and instrumental change. This is obvious not only in the field of architecture, but also for the whole question of national identity or for that matter other kinds of identity.

Kenneth Frampton BIA Interview with Inge Bobbink & Ellen Monchen, 1993.
The New Public Realm, Berlage Cahiers 2, Rotterdam: 010 Publishers, 1994

Finally, Frampton quoted Karl Kraus' famous sentence: 'He who has something to say, let him come forward and remain silent.' But, the studio at the Berlage in Marnixstraat was anything but silent. Continuous debate was influenced by different discourses that Frampton and Koolhaas promoted. In all the juries and studio debates, tutors and critics realized that they were of Wiel Arets generation (all roughly in their 40s), "Americans," and "SuperDutch." Zenghelis was the sole „in-house regular" representative of another generation and in situations of disagreement or misunderstanding of student project ideas, he was always the one who was able to introduce intelligence and wisdom into the debate. His views and argumentation would heal differences and refocus the debate on the real issues. Elia was obviously the only one who was able to reconcile the Ken-Rem divide by introducing a less determined argument, an argument that was not closed, but open to possibilities for a debate.

There is a game. It can be played anywhere – alone or in pairs. A ball is attached to an elastic cord, which is connected to a heavy weight. You hit the ball with a racket, in any direction, away from the weight. The

Komunikacija, magazine for architecture and urbanism

Beograd, 1992

interview with Vedran Mimica by Miodrag Mitrašinović

Hunch 6/7

Berlage Institute Report
Rotterdam, 2003

95

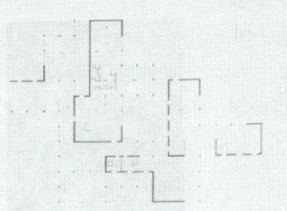

harder you hit, the further the ball is propelled from the weight, and the more erratic the return of the ball, pulled irrevocably back to the point of departure by the elastic. For Kenneth Frampton, the weight is and remains Constructivism. Once, I was a believer. I tried to hit the ball hard enough to break the cord. Frampton is happy each time it flies back to the center. I am confident that the most recent first review will be the last time.

Rem Koolhaas, Doubletake, The Berlage Papers

Wiel was never satisfied with the students' work; this made the students and the staff pushing harder to reach his standards. To his credit, he was always able to explain and argue these standards. Sometimes he used his own work to make an argument, but usually he would refer to Vers une Architecture, Delirious New York, L'architettura della città, or Eisenman's studies of Giuseppe Terragni as standards for theses. By successfully moving the Institute to Rotterdam and establishing a Berlage PhD program with Roemer van Toorn, in association with the Delft University of Technology, Arets laid the foundations for the new dean, Alejandro Zaera-Polo, to continue an exciting journey.

Zaera-Polo's Professionalism

Alejandro Zaera-Polo's educational approach is made clear in his interview with Roemer van Toorn. Zaera-Polo was no stranger to the Berlage before he became dean; quite the contrary. He was already "in" the Institute, having taught studios in previous years and followed several students in their thesis work. In 2002, Zaera-Polo and the Institute's advisory board very clearly re-endorsed the principles laid down by Hertzberger (who, incidentally, was the president of the selection committee for the dean). They agreed first to maintain the international aspect of the Berlage; second, to back a strong research orientation of the institute; third, to introduce a new generation of architects to the Berlage (when selected, Alejandro was not yet 40 years old); and finally to link the research of the institute to the "real world." After almost eight years from the first concept to the completion of the Yokohama port terminal building — one of the world's most exciting contemporary architectural achievements — Alejandro would face new challenges in the further development of an institution. He deserves the full support.

Students

If you are in the business of education, you have to love students; it is as simple as that. But your "love" cannot be unconditional and should develop differently in each case. Initially, the Berlage was a tiny school of 16 students; in recent years the enrollment has grown to 56. I have been in the fortunate position to follow every student's development from day one until graduation. Each of these students has undeniably left the Berlage with a completely different conceptual, intellectual, and professional level than when she or he entered. Two, or sometimes three years of working at the Berlage, followed by the work in top offices worldwide make many of our alumni leading professionals in the field. No doubt, these individuals would have been professionally successful without their Berlage Institute education, but the communal intelligence, skills, and capacity for critical thinking they developed at the Berlage has given them an edge. The Berlage has never been a school where a star architect helped a young architect to become another star architect. Rather, the Berlage has always been a place where the star architect was challenged by our students, therefore contributing to the development of the school's quality. From Hertzberger's attention to individuality, to Arets's ambition to become a leading force in the changing global culture, to Zaera-Polo's insistence on professionalism, the Berlage student body remains responsive and intellectually resistant. Student production at the Berlage had never followed a single style or ideology; instead it has

tecture, I construct a problematic that is, admittedly, both positioned and partial. Further, it is different from that of neotraditionalist architects who are also concerned about the current urban condition and address it with a return to reassuring built forms of the past. And it is different from a problematic focused on how current conditions are changing the profession and its opportunities, or, if critical, one which centers its critical stance in questions of the growing distance between the winners and the losers in the profession.

In emphasizing the importance of cities for architecture, I want to remember Ignasi Sola-Morales, who recently died tragically. He emphasized the growing importance of networks, interconnections, energy flows, subjective cartographies for architecture. He thereby opened up a field for transparent architecture in directions that diverge from the modernist engagement with *Glasarchitektur*. Sola-Morales constructs a theorization of liquid architectures centered not on the replacement of opaque with

Saskia Sassen is the Ralph Lewis professor of sociology at the University of Chicago, and Centennial visiting professor at the London School of Economics. Her most recent books are *Guests and Aliens* (1999), *Global Networks/Linked Cities* (2002), and *Denationalization: Territory, Authority and Rights in a Global Digital Age* (2005). Sassen is co-director of the Economy Section of the Global Chicago Project and is chair of the newly formed Information Technology, International Cooperation and Global Security Committee of the Social Science Research Council (USA).

This text is based on the author's introduction to a posthumous collection of essays by Ignasi Sola-Morales published by Editorial Gili (2003).

...she is someone who navigates multiple forms of knowledge and introduces the possibility of an architectural practice located in spaces ... where the naked eye or the engineer's imagination sees no shape, no possibility of a form.

Hunch 6/7

Berlage Institute Report
Rotterdam, 2003

studied, considered, and challenged everybody. In the very beginning, the heroic first generation of students told Hertzberger: "Dear Herman, we don't want to be taught, but we want to learn" and this remained a motto – a character of Berlage students. Work was incredibly diverse and individually framed. No recognizable idioms were followed or created. It is impossible to mention any student in particular. We take great pride in seeing them all over the world building, doing research, and teaching – sometimes back at the Berlage. In only 12 years of operation, there have been more than 100 leading young architects from Chile to Japan, all of whom, we can be sure, will refuse to merely conform to local commercial or bureaucratic logic, and will relentlessly pursue the installation of a piece of "Berlagian" spirit and intelligence into every project they undertake. I do not mean to measure their success in some sort of fundamentalist resistance to the market, but we know very precisely what we are talking about when we anticipate possible accommodation and resistance to contextual forces.

Building up Institutions in Culture

Although students have been our central preoccupation for the last 12 years, we have also been forced to engage in the political process of building up a particular institution of culture. Unfortunately, the institution cannot be totally free or liberated from politics or finances in order to remain concentrated on its prime function – education.

Since the Berlage has been a hybrid institution from the first day, it has been a difficult challenge to argue that ambiguity can be a virtue and that hybridity is congruent to contemporary life and society. The Berlage is neither a "school" in a strict sense nor it is a professional research institute. Rather, it is a cultural center for architectural debate and an international platform in the Netherlands for the discussion of very local issues. The Berlage is a vehicle for the export of Dutch culture as well as an import place for international architectural culture in the Netherlands. It is a private institute, but heavily subsidized by the Dutch government. The Berlage is run by a director and a dean. Since the beginning, we have seen these ambiguities as advantages, not as obstacles. Nonetheless, it has always been difficult to convince bureaucrats of the same.

One must admit that in Europe of the 1990s, the Utopian project of the Berlage Institute was only possible in the Netherlands. Today, while many cities in Europe are contemplating and actually establishing "copies" of the Berlage, one must emphasize the unique political and cultural environment in the Netherlands in the 1990s. In spite of ups and downs, support to the Berlage was never really in question from local political establishment, board members, or art council members. The Berlage's directors Yap Hong Seng, Joke Kemper, and Rob Docter have surfed the waves of Dutch politics to argue the purpose and performance of the Berlage, and finally to argue the very existence and importance of the place. This job was neither easy nor simple and was constantly under the pressure of arguing the Berlage's ambiguities between "culture" and "market".

Next

For the farewell ceremony of Arets and welcoming of Zaera-Polo, the Institute organized a moment to regroup – a brainstorm about how architectural education might evolve in light of the changing professional roles of an architect. That event, like this book, promoted—in the Berlage spirit—many voices. Roemer van Toorn asked six pregnant questions to a diverse international network of architects, including alumni of the Berlage Institute. With their responses, Jennifer Sigler, Mick Morssink, and Roemer van Toorn composed this publication. As always, hunch 6/7 demonstrates our belief in the cumulative effects of multiple readings. My attempt to retrace the crucial events in the (hi)story of the Berlage can perhaps help one to better understand how and why the Berlage Institute has become what it is today, as we begin our next chapter in postgraduate education.

Photograph of children playing in the courtyard of Herman Hertzberger's Montessori Primary School, 1981

Building Consciousness / Vedran Mimica / 2010

About

XX
The Berlage Survey of the Culture, Education, and Practice of Architecture and Urbanism
ed. Salomon Frausto
NAi Publishers / Berlage Institute, Rotterdam, 2010

Vedran Mimica: Building Consciousness

BUILDING CONSCIOUSNESS

Published in The Berlage Survey of the Culture, Education, and Practice of Architecture and Urbanism, Rotterdam, NAi Publishers/Berlage Institute, 2011

While the era of universal models and totalizing Utopian visions may be over, the need for new urban strategies is no less acute. The architect must, through his/her practice, intellect, and research, navigate those myriad currents that shape an urban reality in order to direct the shape of the built environment. To equip a new generation of architects to develop both themselves and new strategies, architectural education must produce new and in-depth knowledge of the forces that drive development.

Architects are increasingly aware of those complex factors beyond the traditional bounds of building construction that affect the built environment — from the flows of global capital to mass urban migrations. In this context, relevance in the practice of shaping cities and environments necessitates an engagement in permanent education. In order to keep up with the rapid transformations of society, architects must constantly engage in the practice of self-edification. To cite a famous mantra of Montessori education, the student of architecture must insist on "Help me to do it myself".

In the spirit of this undertaking and my perception of its necessity, I will introduce two characters, Maria Montessori – inventor of the eponymous educational philosophy, and Herman Hertzberger – a thinker and educator inspired by her ideas. Maria Montessori's system of education was inspired by the nineteenth-century Utopian ideal of liberating children from educational systems. According to Montessori, children do not benefit from an environment defined by patronizing ideological platforms but instead should grow in a space of free expression. Each child should be helped to learn and perform by himself.

While these pedagogical principles, meant traditionally for childhood education, cannot be entirely applied to the postgraduate level, in many ways Herman Hertzberger operated as a kind of Montessori teacher, allowing his students to freely express and direct themselves. Hertzberger, one of the founding fathers of the Berlage Institute, was an anarchist and a humanist. This vision of an early twentieth-century Utopia based on liberating children through education was among the anarchistic notions that Hertzberger adopted as a thinker, educator, and, to a certain extent, an architect.

For Herman Hertzberger, design and thought were intimately bound, designing was thinking, and architects were, or at least they should strive to be, – intellectuals. Architectural practice required a commitment to the lifelong education, to intellectual substantiation, and to a certain level of social consciousness.

Hertzberger's philosophies in many ways constitute the intellectual genealogy of today's Berlage Institute. Well-conducted postgraduate research opens new directions for a socially engaged design, fulfilling Hertzberger's mandate for action and expectation of an intellectually charged discipline. And when in the early 2000s the Berlage Institute changed its second-year program from individual thesis research to a collaboratively researched project, it enacted an ideal of collective intelligence on a structural level.[5] A laboratory is not formed of individuals researching but rather is structured around teams. In responding with sophistication to the realities of the contemporary world, collective action is required — we no longer can rely on single hands or minds.[6]

---

[5] The Berlage's second dean, Wiel Arets, described the Berlage Institute as a laboratory, rather than a school, in 1995. Alejandro Zaera-Polo, the dean from 2002 to 2006, tried to actualize this model.

[6] Elia Zenghelis, Bart Lootsma, Winy Maas, and Raol Bunschoten each led individual, research-based studios during the late 1990s and early 2000s. These four tutors and research methods were fertile for years at the Institute, producing discussion around how research based design can and should be operational. They advocated radically new approaches and manifestos that could be projective and progressive, conducting architectural research, producing thinking and theory oriented toward the future of metropolis.

It is this collaborative impulse which grounds the institute more generally, as the relations and exchanges that occur on the platform of the Berlage support its postgraduates, visiting tutors, and guests. It has been and continues to be important that there is no single dominant ideology in operation. The ideal environment accommodates different approaches, opinions, and ideas and allows them to influence production.

This cultural platform is meant not only for the education of architects on a postgraduate level, but also to bring foreign, young, and well-established architects into the Netherlands to discuss architecture. Since its beginnings, the Berlage has championed the importance of knowledge transfer on an international scale. It is thus not only an educational facility but also a cultural one. Participants return to their individual contexts and countries and alter the status quo, bringing an international perspective into their home countries. What emerged from this international initiative was a kind of family – a network, dispersed throughout the world.

This international student body came to the Netherlands with a certain anxiety about the places where and the ways in which they lived. While these individuals were not necessarily anarchistic or against any system, they were also not entirely at home in the particular structures they inhabited. They wanted to explore new techniques and a new teaching experience and perhaps, in this, to bring exposure to the background or cultures from which they came. From a position of distance in the Netherlands, the researchers observed the situation in their own cities and countries and considered how these places might be engaged and changed. When young architects come to the Berlage, they experience a freedom of thinking that allows them this self-realization.

Some argue that students without a deep understanding of their own roots, of their nationalities, histories, relationship to nature, politics, and local philosophies are not fit to enter the global world. Others maintain that a future, global world will promote and privilege those who speak many languages, are entirely mobile, and are not at all rooted in any particular culture, city, or family. In reality, both a stable background and a flexible mind are needed to navigate our society's fluid environments and identities. Such a preparation, centered on this notion of the flexible mind, allows one to enter other places. An education in a place away, at a distance from one's given background, can be extremely influential, encouraging critical and imaginative capacities.

And as an understanding of one's nationality might indeed require some geographical distance, an understanding of one's profession might insist upon a similarly removed perspective. The Institute's relative distance from the frustrations of an entirely professional environment engenders new modes of operations that would, in practice, encounter too many bureaucratic or political obstacles for implementation but nevertheless in their development contribute to a discourse. Working apart from the professional world but in an environment modeled on it, architects experience a formative freedom of expression and autonomy. Contributions, research, and design are less driven by the complications of client relations or by the political and economic agendas that necessarily exist in the professional sector. On the other hand, that the Institute takes practice as its model means that its approach to reality is not so distant from it to become ineffectual or irrelevant to actual conditions affecting the world.

Knowledge produced both within the Berlage and within our discipline should be relevant, applicable to reality, and not limited in scope to the ivory tower. This form of applicable knowledge is figured as somewhere between pragmatism and idealism and is not produced on the basis of the individual obsessions of students or tutors. Rather than to produce a sort of absolutely autonomous architecture or, in the other extreme, necessarily attach architecture to history, philosophy, economics, ecology, or sociology, this model looks to these disciplines with curiosity and consideration but develops, above all, our own discipline, our independence and professionalism. Architectural education does not need to be hermetically sealed from other realms. It would be impossible not to work in an interdisciplinary environment. The Berlage has aimed to develop research together with third-party collaborators in order to test strategies and scenarios for the use and development of the city. Our researchers are in close proximity to other disciplines, to external forces, and to the reality of the profession, so that they might understand the potential of architectural knowledge, applied.

The Berlage Institute encourages researchers to investigate and understand how the world is working, what is not working, and how it could work. The institute's prolonged engagement with such third-party collaborators and clients, like mayors Edi Rama of Tirana, Albania, and Osman Baydemir of Diyarbakir, Turkey, represent this Berlage commitment to a simultaneous rigor, idealism, and pragmatism, to a discipline applied beyond its boundaries. Working with these collaborators, the Institute designs scenarios and strategies that fundamentally challenge the performance of bureaucracies and organizations. The researchers deliver clear arguments and visions for different realities that reject uncritical, ideological constructions. The operations of the Institute, as much as they are meant to train architects, have also been paraeducational, beyond education.

Today, young architects aspire to engage with building, education, and research, and to articulate some degree of activism while doing so. Young architects would like to perform as public intellectuals, as people able to enter the public sphere and public debate. They aim at being not only fully educated, performing professionals, but also intellectuals determined to hold that position in society. The belief that the intellectual cannot exist outside of society is behind much of the thinking and the models within the Institute. Two years at the Institute allow researchers to not only understand and test different environments through fieldwork, develop-

ing projects that deal with a complex reality, but also to develop themselves intellectually. It would perhaps be a bit pretentious and naive to believe that study from within the studio, with just a week or two of cursory fieldwork, allows one to entirely enter local complexities. Instead, by truly investigating these areas, we try to analyze and discuss the impact of global forces that cause specific local issues or specific local understandings.

Those pedagogical priorities that found the research and direction of the Berlage implicate it, also, in an engagement with a world of inevitable and increasing complexity. Over the twenty years of its life, the Berlage has transitioned from analog to digital, from local to purely global. The decisions that drive change and development in particular cities are no longer exclusively linked to those particular locales. We actually live globalization; it is unavoidable and difficult to control, almost like the weather, or climate.

Observing those multinational organizations and global economical networks that drive development in so many cities internationally, the Institute has mostly focused its study on sites of increasing complexity and contradiction. It would be pretentious and naive to believe that study from within the studio, with just a week or two of cursory fieldwork, allows one to entirely enter local complexities. Instead, by truly investigating these areas, we try to analyze and discuss the impact that global forces have on specific local issues and understandings. This moment of understanding is the key moment in a studio. In a research based design studio "When Economies Becomes Form: Micro-economic Models as spatial Prescriptions in Northeast Brazil"[7], researchers worked on the impact of a five-star

7   "When Economies Becomes Form: Micro-economic Models as spatial Prescriptions in Northeast Brazil" was a research based studio led by Tina DiCarlo and Markus Miessen that investigated a strategy for local intervention within the emerging sub-urban economy of Northeast Brazil. It took place at the Berlage in 2009. More at: www.theberlage.nl/galleries/projects/details/when_economies_ become_form, accessed August 22, 2016

resort on the development of surrounding villages, studying the local fallout manifested by a global phenomena, in such cases, they tried to take a position not as observers, but as an active force that could, through the use of planning and design tools, actively participate in future development while enacting a sort of reverse globalization.

This responsibility must be evident in the way a studio is set up and then, of course, in its execution. The ultimate responsibility for development is beyond the studio, however, and comes from a higher degree of consciousness about the processes at works—an awareness that demands research. Equipped with an understanding of the influences and operative agendas of urban development, planning and architecture can operate in a way alternately critical or supportive.

Researchers should be more than observers, also an active force that can, through the use of planning and design tools, actively participate in future development. At the Berlage exists an almost unwritten and unspoken consensus that another world is possible – a world that is more just and fair, which can benefit us all.

The results of this approach are what Saskia Sassen calls "counterprojects" or counter-specialties.[8] Within the global flow of goods, money, and people, there exists the possibility for alternative projects that might, and do, redirect our focus. If we continue our dominant models of development, our society will remain limited to a pendulum of mediocrity – a little bit better here, a little bit worse there – the seemingly inevitable performance of capitalism in the last 250 years.

We must investigate models, technologies, and ways of organizing the different programs of a city not based purely on consumption. We should strive to produce more than we consume. We must design urban environments in which people, rather than the automobile or mobility, are central. We must establish a set of tools that visualize and idealize new cities. Architects can navigate between pragmatism and idealism, power and powerlessness, critically discussing visions for an urban future. Compartmentalized realms of knowledge dissolve in the service of some new intellectual synthesis and this situation offers architecture an incredible possibility. Architects are beginning to curate, moderate, and manage, while continuing to design. In these new involvements, architects must strive to perform as public intellectuals, negotiating between different forces to project a direction for development in the future. The Utopias of the future will be radically different from the Utopias of the past. Grand narratives have disappeared and neoliberal optimism fails to promote projects with real social orientation. Architects will need to cultivate their abilities—the skills gained from their training and education—to engage with complex and controversial processes. Architects must somehow transgress the unquestioned global experience by gaining knowledge and experience of global forces and reapplying these skills as equipment for action in local settings. The translation between the global and the local will be a key intellectual challenge for this young generation of architects. Society, as a whole, is increasingly aware of the strong relationship between the quality of the urban environment and the quality of life. And as our lives continue to be influenced by urban networks and systems, the need to design new cities will remain. The challenges awaiting young architects will continue to grow in complexity, and their role as public intellectuals, as critical voices that provide direction to society, must be confronted more deliberately today than ever.

---

8   Saskia Sassen quoted in Mimica, Vedran (2007) "The Power of Architectural Thought." In: Visionary Power: Producing the Contemporary City. Rotterdam: NAi Publishers

ENGAGING REALITY

Interview with Vedran Mimica by Jennifer Sigler and Roemer van Toorn in Projecting the City, Beyond Mapping, a special issue of Hunch to accompany the Berlage Institute's installation at 2006 Architecture Biennale in Venice. 10th edition of the Biennale, directed by Richard Burdett, was centered around Cities. Architecture and Society and focused on the global cities themes.

Question   What makes the Berlage Institute unique?

Vedran Mimica   In the last five years, the Berlage Institute has taken a very particular position in terms of merging academia with the real world, addressing urgent issues engaging reality. To engage reality does not mean to submit to it; it does not imply just to perform mapping, sampling or deciphering reality but, primarily, it means to take a pro-active position toward reality. At the Berlage Institute, real conditions which are influencing the development of the cities are embraced through the relations with third party collaborators. These are like external "clients", people whom we work with, cities' representatives, urban planning offices, cultural institutions, biennials, triennials, different agents with different themes of urgency and different needs for cultural performances. By engaging with reality we develop concepts, strategies, scenarios and projections which could fundamentally influence urban environments. In order to change urban environments where the Berlage Institute is operational, one definitely needs dedicated students, students who are passionate about their profession and students who are actually wondering why they are at the Berlage and what they can do after the Berlage; how they can influence a change. In that sense, I think the Berlage is fortunate to have these extremely engaged young architectural intellectuals who try to understand through research the core issues of architectural discourse. They try to link these issues with the social, economical and ecological issues which are both fundamental and political in order to project alternative realities. In that sense, one may argue uniqueness through production, through the method of working, through the results of the production. At the Berlage we dislike the star system, instead of focusing upon the individual, we invest and promote teamwork. The studio professor operates as a coach of a team instead of as a master who teaches students.

Q   Why is this approach important?

VM   One of the critical aspects of production is definitely the group work in the second year program. This is something which has changed in the last five years with Alejandro Zaera-Polo, where we moved the research from individually based research to more a group based research. By that I mean that the urban issues which we researched in each project, with certain strategies and scenarios, were incredibly complex, and at a certain moment we did not believe any more that it would be possible for a single student to accomplish an important research task or a project within one single year of studying. Therefore, the collective attitude, I think, is fundamentally important where a group researches a certain phenomena, or a certain city, or a certain process, and then eight to twelve students really can add to the research in a way in which they bring individual contributions to the overall theme. It is an interesting position to take because of trends in recent production and in the debate about the position of a contemporary architect. Is an architect someone who belongs to the star system producing the buildings of iconic value which would then support the branding of the city, or is an architect someone who is an agent of change? Perhaps a public intellectual who would be able to guide and steer the social processes toward the different performances? This is precisely where the Berlage stands. When we engage in research in China, we do not believe it is enough to understand the processes and then learn the basis of the process, but we want to manipulate the process or to present the strategies in which the government, the villagers and the developers will act differently.

In Brussels, the capital of Europe, we researched urban form and architecture as constitutional parts of the city of Brussels, looking in an office quarter of the European commission which hosts 29,000

IN-BETWEEN :
A book on the Croatian coast, global
processes, and how to live with them

Saša Randić, Idis Turato

Rijeka, 2006

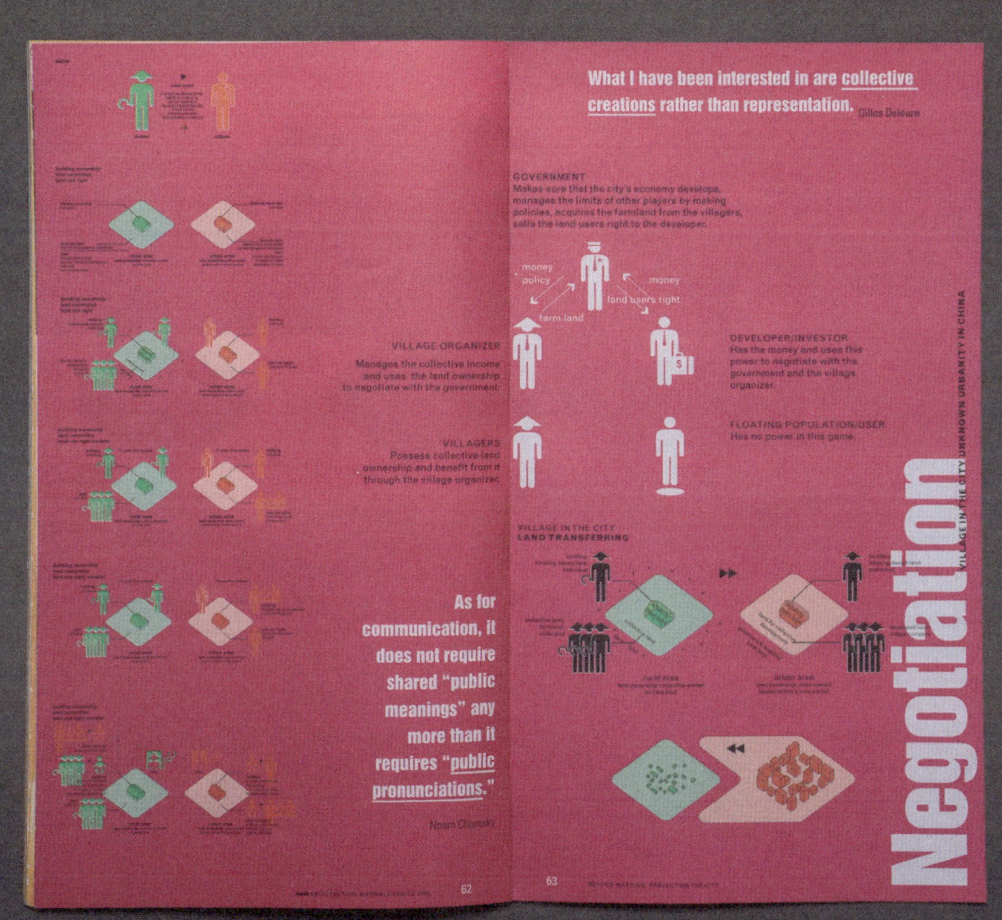

Jennifer Sigler
Roemer van Toorn
Edi Rama
Herman Hertzberger
Wiel Arets
Alejandro Zaera-Polo
Bernard Cache
Peter Trummer
Pier Vittorio Aureli
Markus Schaefer
Marijn Spoelstra
Yushi Uehara

HUNCH, BEYOND MAPPING : PROJECTING THE CITY

Berlage Institute Rotterdam
2006

Engaging Reality, interview with Vedran Mimica by Jennifer Sigler and Roemer van Toorn

XX

The Berlage Survey of the Culture,
Education, and Practice of
Architecture and Urbanism

ed. Salomon Frausto
NAi Publishers / Berlage Institute
Rotterdam, 2010

THE SNIPER'S LOG : ARCHITECTURAL
CHRONICLES OF GENERATION X

Alejandro Zaera-Polo

Actar, Barcelona, 2012

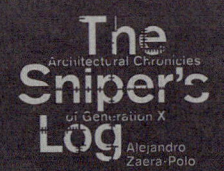

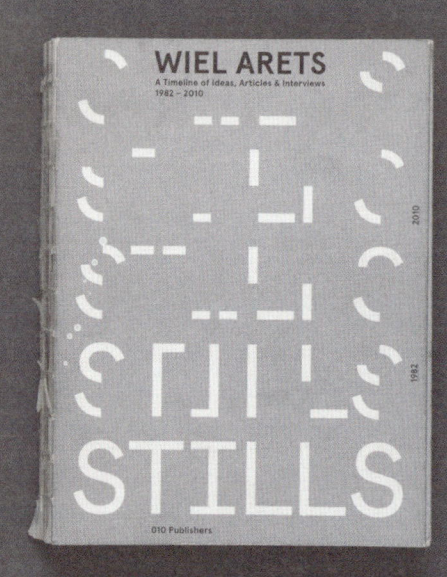

WIEL ARETS : STILLS

A TIMELINE OF IDEAS, ARTICLES
AND INTERVIEWS, 1982 - 2010

010 Publishers, Rotterdam, 2010

bureaucrats. We are discussing, again, a highly complex political relationship between the European Union and the city of Brussels, between the Brussels region and the city and the European Union. In order to decipher those policies, the research needs very provoking ideas projected in terms of the architectural resolution of the issues which could frame and present the new capital of Europe.

In some situations, the Berlage Institute has been incredibly fortunate to have a specific client, or an external agent – epitomized by Edi Rama, the Mayor of Tirana. Tirana Metropolis, the publication presenting the Berlage Institute research and the summer school results, became an official document for the development of a regulatory plan for the city. Again, I would say it is a fortunate relation and the level of understanding which we developed with the city mayor and the city administration. Here, we can talk about the development of communal intelligence which was not based within the space, or within the walls of the Berlage, but projected toward a new European capital, the city of Tirana. In that sense, the urban strategy for Tirana, project by our students, will be fundamental for the development of the city. In so doing, the Berlage would break standard academic performance, which too often ends within the walls of academe. Hopefully, the Berlage's pro-active approach to Tirana will shape the future of the city. What has been, additionally, very interesting is that many of our students continued working in Tirana as professional architects. Edi Rama invited the students to work as urban planners and designers of the major extensions of the city center. In this case, the Berlage provides the bridge between academe and the real world because a project started here continues working in the real world.

Q   Are you not afraid that we could get the critique from traditional academia that we surrendered to the client with our applied research? How do you view the working for a client or commission?

VM First, I think that academia cannot establish itself as a copy of the outside world, the professional world. That is simply impossible. Academe or the Berlage particularly, embraced the external parties or the people whom we call the clients in a way in which we could develop the projects with them. So in every sense, we want them to participate and work with our students and professors. That is one thing. The second thing is that the projects we are doing are always investigatory stories, they are always projects based on a particular investigation which perhaps in a real commercially oriented commission would not simply happen. Thirdly, the Berlage Institute engages, always understanding the conditions in which many offices or institutions, especially in the newly developing countries or the countries which are seeking development, are not able to perform by themselves. We test those investigations through the exhibitions, public debates and publications which we project into the city where we do research. Those public moments of debate are educational as well as professional indicators for the value of the research which we produce. If we do not have a sense of the real world within the Institute, we would not be able to argue the usefulness or the imaginative power of certain strategies we produced. So here again, it is a step from traditional academia toward a more dynamic institute which does engage with reality, but is not submitting itself to certain powers in those realities. Instead of believing in one unit system at a school, we believe in a dialogue and debate among different types of expertise and architectural stances.

Q   Could you explain why?

VM From the very beginning of the establishment of the Berlage Institute, from Herman Hertzberger to Wiel Arets and Alejandro Zaera-Polo's strategies, the Berlage was never conceived as centered around one personality, one ideology, one idea or one dominant logic. It has always been a platform, a place which invited people with opposite views, people with different, but interesting ideas,

ideas which can anticipate the future development of the discourse. We have been extremely careful in selecting and inviting different guest professors and promoting some internal PhD candidates in collaboration with the University of Delft, elevating them to a level of tutors in order to stage a debate. I have incredibly appreciated the link between the PhD research and studio research as a structure at the Berlage where some of our PhD researchers, most of them being our Berlage alumni, tested the concepts and ideas which they partly developed. So in that sense, it was an internally generated debate. Obviously, the debates have been influenced by clients, by external parties, by invitations to manifestos, to the biennials of Venice, Rotterdam and Beijing, where you have particular statements from the curators and particular ideas to research. All this creates a multi-layered curriculum where the students have a possibility of choice and a great ability to shape their professional careers toward a particular subject, conceptual construct or research oriented systems. This is precisely how a curriculum is created in order to give a choice to the students, no matter how small the school is – with only five to six studios, to create a tailor-made curriculum structure for each student according to his/her own interests. The condition of the city today demands education to develop new architectural knowledge, what we at the Berlage call "expertise".

Q Can you elaborate this?

VM Historically, we bridged the situation in which more than half of the world's population lives in cities and that is not that interesting until you recall world's population doubled in the last 40 years. In 1966, we had 3 billion people and now we have 6 billion people. In China, in the next 15 years, if the GDP continues at the same rate, there will be a need to house 400 million people in urbanized areas. This is a massive task confronting our profession. The question presents itself as to what models, strategies and planning we should perform. The Berlage is deeply committed to unconventional and innovative structures, scenarios and procedures to construct new urbanity, to construct the new urban environment in which one would feel, perhaps, a different status of citizenship as well; so something which accepts a political, social, economical status of the modern women and men. This is, obviously, a tall order. It is a huge task and we try to perform it with particularly focused agendas. How to bring the innovation is a critical question. No one seriously believes in great new narratives anymore, everybody is more convinced that in a postmodern, post historical time, we need moderation and mediation of our practice in order to engage with the political and social realm. This, instead, is precisely where architects need to gain new knowledge, a new sort of expertise appropriate for the new times. There is no possible way to deliver this new knowledge top-down. We deeply believe it has to come from research of the environment in which one operates. This is not entirely enough. The new research has to be supported with the development of new technologies, new computational techniques, and the techniques in social research. It is what constitutes the multilayered, curricular structure at the Berlage. The question is then, would our students be able, in the foreseeable future, to exercise those techniques and perform the knowledge that they begin gaining at the Berlage? We deeply believe they would, not only relying on the network of Berlage alumni who operate all over the world in academia, offices and businesses, but also via engaging with different realities all over the world, and again by permanently educating themselves – and this is what we hope to teach at the Berlage. Permanent education is absolutely necessary to be in touch with the radical changes of our globalized world. When we declare that our research should go beyond mapping, it assumes mapping and maps are presenting a frozen reality captured at the certain moment which is then diagrammed and presented. The fundamental question is how we should use those diagrams or maps in order to project new realities.

Q Can you give me an example of a project that created alternative realities? What has gone beyond mapping?

VM There is another aspect of the Berlage Institute, explained under the umbrella of contract research, where we engage with outside parties. One particular project was developed with the Croatian Association of Architects, called Croatian Archipelago: New Lighthouses, a project for the development of seven sites on the Croatian coast where we develop an operational method. Such an approach to a new and advanced model of planning, using alumni and expertise from the Berlage Institute, is projecting a transitional environment for countries like Croatia. So in that sense, we could argue the project and a book present an operational manual, influencing the urban realities in Croatia. If we talk about a studio project developed in the last years then, obviously, in Tirana it went pretty far because it almost became an official document related to the regulatory plan. We not only develop new urban concepts, new urban forms, but we are also into parametric manufacturing of urban furniture.

Q Could you say something about manufacturing, clients etc?

VM One very particular aspect of the Berlage was developed by Bernard Cache and Peter Trummer in the first Associative Design Studio (in this hunch, you find the result of Associative Design 2). It was research into a new combination of techniques, specifically into Top Solid software modeling which produces a manufacturing file while you design the product. That was very important for the Berlage because it links urban research and planning, architectural design and manufacturing of urban furniture.

Q And future endeavors...

VM I would like to see more operational performance of our research into a reality. What we develop here at the Institute can steer unconventional, innovative and different processes in terms of urban thinking. If one looked at the territories where such thinking is possible, or needed, or it somehow could prove operational, then one should definitely look toward the extension of the European Union, to countries in transition looking to develop and meet the European standards. The second territory is definitely phenomena of development in China, India and Asia where new megalopolises are in creation and where we believe new models need to replace top-down traditional planning, which would introduce the creation of new terms of urban environment, life and lifestyles. Further, we would continue exploring new technologies leading toward more new typologies and then this typological research, or the research on the prototype or prototypical urban entities which perform as hybrids in a programmatic sense, would definitely influence the life of cities and their future performance. The Berlage should look very precisely into the creation of new lifestyles, the multitude of social performances and their relation to architecture and in general, relation to the visual. Examine how the new visual culture can be supported by architecture which creates a more vibrant dynamic urban environment. I think in the next years, we will perform in order to answer the question: What is the city in which you and I would like to live in the future?

Q What do you mean by embracing reality?

VM In order to engage with reality, you have to get your hands dirty. Hence, you have to go deep into the fundamental processes which shape the social realities. And in order to understand that, you have to understand what powers are at stake in the development of the contemporary city and how, in one way or another, you might be able to steer, manipulate and control those powers, which are your possibilities as an urban planner or architect. Going deep into the processes which are shaping the contemporary city, one would be able to shape a new process where architecture and planning would play, not a leading role, but would contribute to the development of different environments not based on purely economical logic or political strategies.

IN-BETWEEN:
A book on the Croatian coast, global processes, and how to live with them

Saša Randić, Idis Turato

Rijeka, 2006

HUNCH,
BEYOND MAPPING,
PROJECTING THE CITY
Berlage Institute, Rotterdam, 2006

Engaging Reality,
interview with Vedran Mimica by
Jennifer Sigler and Roemer van Toorn

Q   Do you think a lot of other schools fall short of this?

VM I think a lot of schools really embrace mapping analysis along with sampling and architectural journalism, and my answer to this is good, very interesting, but it is not enough. It is simply not enough for the student, the researcher, to just understand what is out there. He/she must act upon that understanding.

Q   Is the Berlage about new visions?

VM It is partly about visions; it is also about shaping the processes. What Pier Vittorio Aureli is doing is to use architectural representation in order to shape a particular process. Peter Trummer uses new software and computational techniques in order to shape the creation of new neighborhoods. Yushi Uehara understands the incredible intricacies of the Chinese political system and the influence of that system on the development of the city and uses this knowledge in order to find unique strategies for the development of Chinese cities. And finally, Markus Schaefer and Marijn Spoelstra use economical and architectural analyses in order to project a development model for the new European capital city in Ljubljana. So in that sense, there is always a vision based on the research of social, economic and cultural realities of cities. What is perhaps important here is that visionary attitudes are representing a critique of these realities while shaping the processes for urban change.

Q   Anything that you want to be critical of?

VM I want the Berlage not to become a supermarket, not to become a place for consumption, but a place for production. This metaphor, obviously, says many schools are tending toward pure consumption of certain knowledge and not the creation and production of knowledge. So if you ask me what I would like to see, I would like to see more passionate students in the production of the work at the Berlage. The students who bring a passionate way of understanding the reality and the desire to change it, but also with some strategies or intelligence we can all embrace; not based on individual obsessions or individual dreams and nightmares.

THE POWER OF ARCHITECTURAL THOUGHT

Published on a basis of the curatorial statement for the 3rd IABR, International Architecture Biennale Rotterdam, "Power – Producing the Contemporary City" in Oris 46, Zagreb 2007

Visionary Power in particular is a treasure room of ideas that should be a must-visit for the whole... preferably under inspired guidance, because of the...maps, photos, and plans.

de Vries, Marina (2007) Inspiring Belief in the Power of the City. Volkskrant, May 26, 2007

The Board of the International Architecture Biennale Rotterdam (IABR) invited the Berlage Institute to curate the 3rd IABR of 2007[9]. After a little over a year of intensive research, workshops with exhibitors, fund raising and public relations exercises, the Biennale entitled Power – Producing the Contemporary City opened in Rotterdam Kunsthal on 24 May and will close on 2 September. The opening speech was delivered by Rotterdam Mayor Ivo Opstelten, followed by Edi Rama, Mayor of Tirana, Herman Hertzberger, the founder of Berlage Institute and Vedran Mimica, the Institute's director and the Biennale's head curator. By inviting an institute instead of an individual curator (such as Francine Houben in 2003 and Adriaan Geuze in 2005), the Biennale's Board seems to have counted on the wide range of urban studies carried out by the Berlage Institute, on its operative research network, dominated by the Institute's former students, and its organizational and production potential. This article focuses on a single aspect of the Biennale, that is, on the exhibition entitled Visionary Power. This exhibition seems to best reflect the current state of development of the Berlage Institute and hopefully promotes the specific values of the new generation of architects, with a little help from its curators.

Powers producing the contemporary city

In this era of globalization – more than ever before – the city is the space where cultural, economic and

[9] It was the first time that an institution was invited instead of an individual curator.

Marina de Vries
Ivo Opstelten
Edi Rama
Herman Hertzberger
Pier Vittorio Aureli
Lieven de Cauter
Michiel Dehaene

John Urry
Saskia Sassen
Rem Koolhaas
Kenneth Frampton
Keller Easterling
Alfredo Brillembourg
Hubert Klumpner

ORIS 46
Zagreb, 2007
Vedran Mimica
The Power of Architectural Thought

MUSEUM 21+ VELA SPILA,
ARCHIVE OF SIMULTANEOUS TIMES

project study
report on the workshops, reader 1

2006

BUILDING RELATIONS:
THE BERLAGE PLATFORM

exhibition and seminar
Croatian Museum of Architecture,
Zagreb, 2008

political forces interact, where various powers and phenomena compete or collaborate in continuous evolution. This reality confronts us with the questions of who is producing the city and envisioning its future and what visible and invisible powers are shaping its production. This exhibition is the result of the quest by an international selection of leading scholars and emerging architects and researchers to position themselves vis-à-vis these issues. By exploring the global political and economic conditions and powers defining the development and livability of today's cities, this younger generation of architects focuses on how tactical urban strategies and architectural interventions can concretely contribute to the contemporary discourse on the city. The twenty-first century is an age of urban migration and movement, a time when people – rich and poor alike – flock from South to North, from East to West, from country to city, in search of prosperity and security as part of our inevitable existence. As the stage upon which cultures meet and civilizations clash, cities are now the hubs of networks through which the fast flows of global capital surge and the focal points for an unrelenting media blitz. They bear the brunt of new world wars and are the targets of international terrorism. With the experience and entertainment economies in fast mode, these same cities accommodate huge streams of consumers, shoppers and tourists on a daily basis. The city is the platform where all of these forces come into play, where different and indiscernible powers confront and interact with each other. The impact of the force of commercial capital or the power of government on the fabric of the city is perhaps easily identified. But the powers of fear, desire, religion or law are just as strong in shaping the city. Consider the way the European Union facilities in Brussels currently shape the need for security; the way zoning laws affect the development of Manhattan as much as that of Shenzhen; how a cartoon of Mohammed may reshape the architecture of future embassies; how the fact that immigrants will soon account for as much as 40% or more of the population of cities such as Amsterdam and Rotterdam emphasizes the need for rethinking of its urban planning; or how "powerless" individuals themselves create huge squatter cities, favelas, barriadas, katchi abadis and bidonvilles of this world.

Investigating five forces

As curators, we asked five international teams of theorists and architects to reduce their knowledge of the forces that affect cities – like migration, fear, commerce, tourism and representation – to a well-defined problem: an urgent question about the possible future of the city. The Biennale subsequently asked young and talented architects from all over the world to comment on the propositions that were put forward. They were given a threefold assignment: "Select an urban force that matches your own projects and research; indicate a city in which this force is strikingly manifest; and create an architectural strategy to deal with this phenomenon." Out of close to 100 responses, the curators chose 14 cities and teams of architects that are now part of the Visionary Power project.

The "Capital Cities" section of the exhibition explicates that the need for cultural and geopolitical centers has not been eliminated by the demise of nation states. The new global geography is defined by the cities that are emblematic for their economic significance as well as for their cultural and political importance. In view of this development, Pier Vittorio Aureli argues the necessity for rethinking the contemporary city as a representative and symbolic entity – or as a social, political and political center – rather than the result of flux and flows. The "Corporate Cities" section maintains that particular urban areas located within cities are transforming themselves into exclusive business or shopping districts. Understanding that this phenomenon undermines, and even colonizes, the central and public functions of the city, Keller Easterling demonstrates that these enclaves are subject to global political and economic forces that form new free economic zones, thereby creating a new urban paradigm. While commercial parties aim to create introverted worlds that are seemingly neutral, these areas become more powerful than the cities themselves and subsequently often lead to local cultural conflicts. The respective cities try to counter the homogenization of these districts by stimulating functional variety, or by activating them as structuring elements for urban growth.

"Informal Cities" references the informal social, economic, political, architectural and urban practices in relation to the more formal physical and spatial aspects undertaken to engage in urban life. The result of massive urban migrations, these spontaneous phenomena have rapidly exploded around formal urban cores in South-East Asia, Africa and Central and South America. Alfredo Brillembourg and Hubert Klumpner maintain that the organizational, ecological and economic potential of these developments should be embraced and enlisted as an urbanization model to be further developed in close collaboration with the inhabitants/builders. This blending of formal and informal urban elements could potentially lead to a new and inclusive city geography.

The growing fear caused by globalization's by-products, such as illegal immigrants, is explored in "Hidden Cities". According to Lieven de Cauter and Michiel Dehaene, the two urban paradigms appearing in the contemporary city are heterotopias and camp. The former is understood as offering protection by serving as a vehicle for urban development; while the latter defines a spatial condition that deprives people of their fundamental human rights. Both of these spatial organizations operate according to their own regulations which cause them to be isolated from normality. In today's "new world order", "Spectacle Cities" postulates that cities may only be taken seriously as cultural and political entities by creating museums, festivals, sporting events, universities and especially iconic buildings to sustain themselves. In an age where former sites of labor are being transformed into sites of visual consumption, John Urry points out that this is necessary in order for cities to compete in the global race for recognition. At the same time, cities copy each other's formulas and specific characteristics at the expense of the identity of these cities. By this thematic zoning, the essential role of cities as centers for revolution, individual development, new ideas and socio-cultural representation of different groups is eliminated. The urgent question is how to reconcile the spectacle city with the real city.

Beyond mapping, projecting the city

Within the complexities of these global phenomena, the city becomes central to the contemporary architectural debate. As Saskia Sassen stated in a 2004 public lecture at the Berlage Institute, "City space is the key zone where a lot of the power projects of global corporate capital play out, and where the new political interventions of even the poorest organizations can also be enacted." And then more recently at the London School of Economics Urban Age conference in Berlin from November 2006: "Architecture needs to confront the massiveness of urban experience, the overwhelming presence of massive architectures and massive infrastructures in today's cities, and the overwhelming logic of utility that organizes much of the investments in cities." Yet, as Rem Koolhaas pointed out in another public lecture held by the Berlage Institute in February 2006, architecture has reached an impasse: the concept of the city is disintegrating.

Presented throughout the clusters of the Visionary Power exhibition are series of projects by a younger generation of architects and urbanists that bridge theory and practice to investigate today's urban conditions. These ambitions — merely mappings of contemporary trends — depict how architecture and architects can initiate a transformative impact on the production of the contemporary city. As Kenneth Frampton instructs us, I am paraphrasing here: one is tempted to suggest that the great nemesis of our time is maximization irrespective of whether it is a maximization of profit or firepower. You may well ask where does this leave the architects of our time? This is a question that here, as elsewhere, is painfully difficult, if not impossible, to answer in a satisfactory way. One can only say that the responsibilities of being an architect are as much to be constantly engaged in political discourse and advocacy as to be involved in the design and realization of a built form.[10]

By not searching for statistical truth, these proposals allow us to see the world lucidly as it currently exists: as a means to empower us — as architects — to take action. From arguing that cities like Beirut should create new networked city-state paradigms by exploiting their inherent social and cultural differences to unmasking the urban interiors of Johannesburg, these projects unfold and unpack reality as it is by direct engagement with the real world.

Projects — like the one for Rome investigating the ability of architecture to achieve coexistence between tourism and heritage, or the use of Havana as a tourist attraction to develop a new global identity — call for a renewed commitment of architectural imagination. The research into Mexico City's unrelenting urban expansion, or the presentation of the seemingly neutral transitory spatial conditions along the border of Ceuta, reject the prevailing tendency to view the growing complexity of our urban environment as a pretext for an end to the relationship between architecture and the city. The time for universal urban models may be over, but the need for new strategies for the city — like using energy management methods to urbanize Busan — is no less acute. In order to equip a new generation of architects to develop these strategies, a new and in-depth knowledge of the powers and forces that drive development is required. Each presented project takes a stance, to reveal the similarities and differences between cities and cultures to suggest how architects and urbanists can influence and improve our future. By clearly understanding how these forces operate, these proposals — such as the scenario for blurring political power with market hegemony in Luoyang, or the reshifting of corporate activity from the metropolitan centers to the suburban peripheries as in the case of Jersey City — show how to intelligently subvert by working with, and around, these conditions.

These projects go beyond the current obsession with mapping and pose direct questions to the discipline of architecture by directly engaging in the quest for changing reality or elevating society to a different level of existence.

Architecture as power, or return to the discipline

It is clear that this current impasse in architecture is related to the inability of the architectural profession to form a clear idea about the contemporary city. Urban projects, as Lyotard's concepts of grand narratives, are long gone — along with the times when architects would make rigorous attempts to understand and project the city. As Koolhaas also pointed out in his recent lecture, the writing of architectural manifestos ceased in the late 1960s — precisely at the moment when urbanization exponentially increased on a global scale. This loss of engagement with the city, as a conceivable collective entity, produces a breaking point between architecture's theory and practice. In today's world, we believe that architecture should no longer attach itself to other disciplines, such as sociology and philosophy, or work through sophisticated computational techniques or other state-of-the-art processes, in order to reactive itself. The position throughout this exhibition is that architecture must be connected to reality through its own disciplinary tools, possibilities and performances. In order to truly take action to change our world, we must make architecture a discipline that other disciplines relate to, instead of architecture always looking to other disciplines to revitalize itself. The architect is a figure who — through his or her professional performance, intellectual capabilities, and research investigations — is able to fundamentally understand the forces shaping contemporary urban reality. Throughout this exhibition we show how architecture must be connected to reality through its own tools and possibilities. By delivering a juxtaposition of ideas and positions, these projects precisely implement an architectural reaction to found urban conditions by re-imagining our world. This is the power of architectural thought.

---

10   Paraphrasing from the text Between Monumentality and Immaterial (Kenneth Frampton in Contemporary Croatian Architecture: Testing Reality by Maroje Mrduljaš, Vedran Mimica and Andrija Rusan. Zagreb, Arhitekst, 2007).

THE ARCHITECTURE FOR CHILDREN
Delft 1992
CREATION OF NEW WORLDS IN MINIATURE
Zagreb 2003
UTOPIA AS TRADITION
Milan 1997

STUDY LANDSCAPES OF HERMAN HERTZBERGER
Zagreb 2011
THE BERLAGE INSTITUTE
Belgrade 1992
THE NEW PUBLIC REALM
Rotterdam 1994

MUZEJ ZA UMJETNOST I OBRT, ZAGREB
MUSEUM FOR ARTS AND CRAFTS, ZAGREB, YUGOSLAVIA

LEARNING WITH

RMAN HERTZBERG

ARHITEKTURA

projects multiplied and they created many emblematic buildings, for example in Los Angeles in 1925 (Richard Neutra), in Amsterdam in 1930 (Jan Duiker) or in Suresnes in 1935 (Eugène Beaudouin and Marcel Lods). By the end of the thirties, Open-Air Schools would number in the thousands. A large number of them were called into question after 1945 because of the effectiveness of a new treatment of tuberculosis by streptomycin. However, the movement did not run out of steam. New establishments were constructed, benefiting from the pre-war experiences. Other international congresses took place, in 1949 in Italy, then in 1956 in Switzerland.

This colloquium strives to understand the emergence and the evolution of Open-Air Schools due to national and international approaches (which will be emphasized) and some monographic studies. The

OUT TEACHING

Vedran Mimica

41000 ZAGREB
Radnički dol 52

SINOPSIS disertacije na temu PRILOG
OSNOVNE SKOLE KOD NAS NA OSNOVU ANALI
MONTESSORI

Sadržaj disertacije

Oblast : tehničke znanosti
Područje: arhitektura i urbanizam
Matična disciplina : arhitektonsko pro

Tema: PRILOG RAZMATRANJU PROSTORNOG MO
NA OSNOVU ANALIZE ARHITEKTURE SK

1.0.0. Uvod

Definiranje konteksta arhitekt
moderne arhitekture kod nas i

2.0.0. Školski okoliš

Osnove teorije ekološke psiholo
fizičke strukture školskog pros
ponašanja.
Ispitivanje međuodnosa korisnik
školskog okoliša.

The texts that follow where written primarily as reflections on my academic practice and research, developed across my successive engagements at the University of Zagreb, Technical University Delft and early Berlage Institute. My postgraduate research in Delft was greatly influenced by Herman Hertzberger where I learned that structuralism could support the effort to understand the world. That means that content is significantly more important than form, and that the structuralist notion of spatial possibilities can be interpreted in terms of architecture being a spatial frame in which users can influence a constructed space. Focus in the research was on extensive study on the school typology from a multifaceted perspective. The relationship between educational spaces and the teaching methodology from various cultural and historical backgrounds are contrasted in a study to demonstrate the importance of educational environment as a caring nursery of new ideas for upsetting the status quo, and ideally creating new school worlds.

Architecture must take advantage of its capacity to transcend through moments in time, catalyzing an enlargement of programmatic scope of school's spaces that increase habitability and flexibility in such buildings. The school is a survivor of architectural typologies that is continually morphing while it is still seen as an institution or object in the city, whereas many other spaces have succumbed to the forces of the information technology age.

A set of texts explored the implementation of various theories of making educational spaces in different contexts, with a notable review of Hertzberger's pursuit of anarchistic humanist spaces that inspire independence in learning, especially within a Montessori educational ideology. Montessori education calls for spaces that allow for dynamic movement, encouraging learning through the interactive child's play.

Similarly, the later installments of this collection of essays draw on the idea that the dissemination of knowledge should be done in a way that invokes inquisitiveness about urban issues.

The Hertzbergerian discourse was transgressed into the early Berlage by introducing a comprehensive framework of very real contemporary contexts that have a sense of ambiguity, capable of provoking discourse and allow students to test various possibilities.

NOTES ON CHILDREN, ENVIRONMENT AND ARCHITECTURE

Vedran Mimica

book mock-up

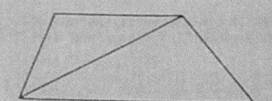

Fig. 15. Most people see this primarily as a trapezoid with a diagonal, rather than as two superimposed triangles, though the other interpretation remains possible too.

Fig. 16. The law of proximity. The top row is perceived as consisting of points in pairs. If the points are unequal in size, grouping takes place, not according to the law of proximity, but to the law of equality, in pairs of equal points.

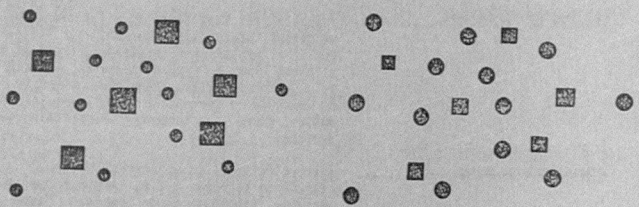

Fig. 17. Whether the equality of elements in a configuration will be recognized depends – as always – on the prevailing conditions. The squares on the left are easily recognized as being equal, because they also differ in size. On the right, the squares and circles are equal in size, and therefore harder to distinguish. On the left, a difference in form is enhanced by a difference in size. The recognition of similarities or equalities becomes still more difficult if variations in form and size do not coincide, e.g. with large and small squares and large and small circles.

Fig. 18. Continuity and closure. Perception has a tendency to continue lines as they started: a straight line as a straight line, a zigzag as a zigzag, a wavy line as a wavy line, for such continuation does not add information. Closure is shown on the right: the four angles are sufficient to perceive a rectangle, though only a minor portion of its total outer edge is drawn. Information is concentrated at the corners, where the edge changes its direction. The intermediate parts of the edges are filled out by the law of continuity. Center: closure works, even if the edges are not straight, as in this 'triangle' with its quasi-bent edges

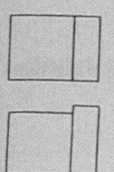

Fig. 19. Simplicity of discontinuity of the edg ceived. Even if the divid two hexagons.

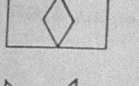

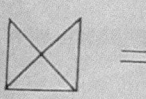

Fig. 20. More examples gular line going up and d interpretation is simpler t first resolves itself into fig than the last two figures of

Kora, Miron, Eva

Zagreb, 1987

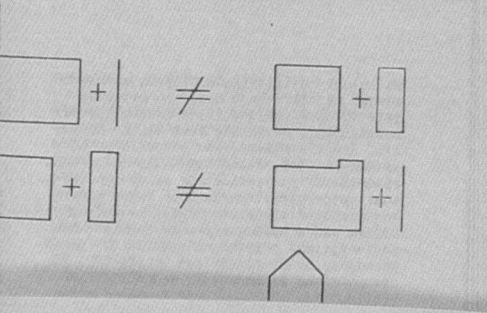

NOTES ON CHILDREN, ENVIRONMENT AND ARCHITECTURE

Vedran Mimica

Publikatieburo Bookwunde, Delft, 1992

user-form relation

as a platform to sit on, as a place to put things down, as a stage from which to make announcements, or just to become taller. They play games around and on it. To them it is an island-the floor the sea.

In every circumstance, this fixed point acts as a magnet towards which one is unintentionally drawn; it becomes a "touchstone", the articulation of the space, enlarging the scope of the hall's habitability. That such a block can be interpreted in so many different ways means not only that it can fulfil several roles, but also that the children are stimulated by it to greater diversity in the roles they play.

Not only do we interpret the form, the form at the same time interprets us, shows us something of who we are.

entrance

porch

In its limited sense the school entrance is a door which is used only for a few short moments at the beginning and end of the school day. A sort of entrance porch has been made, so that the building can already house the children before school, and provide a place to wait for each other or just hang around after school. This is as much an outward extension of the hall as an inward extension of the playground; it is the in-between area where one feels not yet within but yet not entirely outside the school.

playground

The playground outside is public area, part of the street. Even when classes are not in session, when the school is not to open at all, neighbourhood children are attracted by this place where they apparently feel at ease, somewhere to meet each other and to hang around. It has become a meeting place quite out of its context as a doorstep of the school. At these times it appears

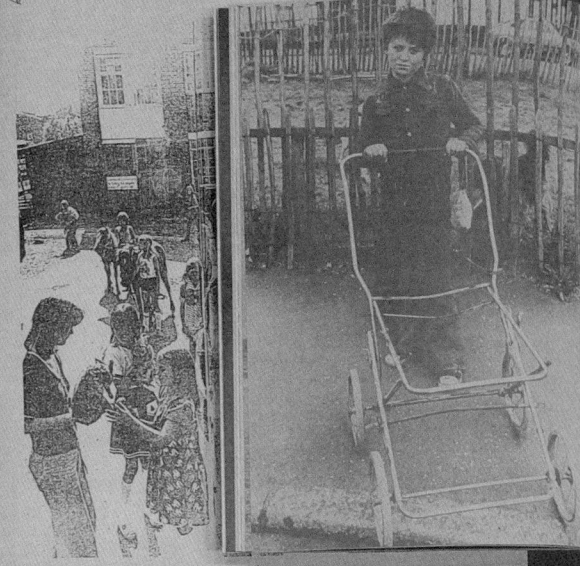

NOTES ON CHILDREN, ENVIRONMENT AND ARCHITECTURE

Vedran Mimica

book mock-up

NOTES ON CHILDREN, ENVIRONMENT AND ARCHITECTURE

Vedran Mimica

Publikatieburo Bookwunde, Delft, 1992

Éugene Beaudouin
Marcel Lods
Jan Duiker
Richard Neutra
Giuseppe Terragni
Arne Jacobsen
Paul Rudolph
Aldo van Eyck
Aldo Rossi
Herman Hertzberger
Thom Mayne
Manuel Castells
Andrea Branzi

ORIS 20

Zagreb, 2003

Article based on a paper Creation of New Worlds in Miniature
(co-authored with Kelly Shannon) December, 2001

THE ARCHITECTURE FOR CHILDREN

Excerpts from Vedran Mimica's book Notes on Children, Environment and Architecture, published by Publikatieburo Bouwkunde, Delft 1992

Architecture is the discipline which has the potential to 'carry out that part of sensory reality which is abstract in the art of painting, as well as to create harmony between people and their environment in the future.'[11]

Piet Mondrian in the 1920's

Children's World and the World of Art

The relationship between the world of children and the world of art is important element in the architectural structure of places built for children. Plato (428-348 B.C.) considers this element as complementary on many different levels. He says: 'Teach the child to experience joy and pain from the things that surround him... The right things are those which, irrespective of which branch of art they belong to, transmit a direct aesthetic pleasure for they alone are objectively true.' He includes here works of painting and sculpture, architecture and crafts, and in fact everything that has beautiful form, nobility of content, and a perfectly realized goal. All grace and harmony in life, which form the human soul, are determined by aesthetic feelings, by the perception of rhythm and harmony.

Pedagogues of the 18th and 19th century stress the importance of the environment in the process of education. Their views often coincide with those of Plato. In his novel Emile, J.J. Rousseau (1712-1778) tells teachers to base the education on a child's contact with things.

Heinrich Pestalozzi (1746-1827), the great preacher of the unity of life and education, names the house, the living-room, the garden and the things in them as being necessary for an active education. His ideas are fundamental to modern pedagogy: 'Life forms and molds... Everyday life is not a matter of words, but of deeds.'[12]

Maria Montessori (1869-1956) stresses the importance of an artistic environment for a child's life. She explains new relationships in classrooms, and stresses the importance of the environment in the process of education. Beside the traditional relationship between children and teachers, she points to the relationships between children and the environment and teachers and the environment. She says that every school-environment should offer possibilities for self education. Talking about the furniture in the classroom, she says: 'The furniture must represent an artistic reality.'[13] In this case, beauty is not the result of affluence and luxury, but modesty and harmony of forms and colors combined with the absolute simplicity of furniture. Concerning the way how children actually learn, Montessori says: 'Children accept knowledge with all their physical abilities. Impressions do not only enter into their world, they also form it and become innate.'[14]

Herbert Read, in his works Education through Art[15] and Education for Peace,[16] explains the importance of art in the process of education. He says: 'Child and artist stand in a close spiritual relationship to one another, and by the adoption of the right educational methods the artist must be developed and brought out in the child. Art is representation and science is explanation of one and the same reality. Artistic education is of more fundamental importance than intellectual scientific training.'[17]

---

11 Quoted from: Holtzman, Harry & James, Martin.S. (1987) The New Art, the New Life: The Collected Writings of Piet Mondrian (Documents of Twentieth-Century Art). London: Thames & Hudson Ltd

12 Quoted from: Roth, Alfred (1957) The New School. Zürich: Ginsberger

13 Ibid.

14 Montessori, Maria (1965) Spontaneous Activity in Education. NY: Schocken Books

15 Read, Herbert (1974) Education through Art

16 Read, Herbert (1949) Education for Peace

17 Quoted from: Roth, Alfred (1957) The New School. Zürich: Ginsberger

The transcendental and metaphysical relationship between children and architectural space form the children's visual, cultural and human level of development. Only the architecture of the highest aesthetic value can meet the demands of the fantastic child's world. It means neither the classical nor the modern, up to date aesthetic, but the aesthetic determined by the child's world.

According to Heidegger, the essence of art can be experienced by entering the un-hidden essence, by entering and belonging to the truth, which is expressed in a work of art. We are convinced that "the mindlessness of childhood"[18] actually unveils the truth, and sets us in some way into the un-hidden essence, and shows us the truth, which is being realized in a work of art – in the world.

I want to stress the simple fact that architecture of a school building or any other physical structure built for children will be of greater aesthetic value if it tries to be as near as possible to the aesthetics of the child's world. Realizing this fact, the architecture will express the spirit of the built object (Loos)[19]. An object has to be what it wants to be (Kahn) and a house has to be, as the architect wants it to be (Venturi)[20]. Understanding these complexities we shall come nearer to the idea of architecture that we imagine. The architecture of the child's world must reach the complexity of the world of art, whereas the aesthetics of the child's realm is that of an artist's.

Complexity of Architecture

Many authors are actually concerned about the complexity of physical environment and regard this as a key to understanding the relationship between people and their environment. Amos Rapoport and Robert E. Kantor (referring to psychologists who research the complexity of the human environment) conclude that people prefer a more complex environment.[21] Many psychologists say that the human organism has to be stimulated in many other ways besides food and drink. Richard Held and Alan Hein proved that the combining of visual impulses and manual activities resulted in the development of adequate and acceptable behavior. Healthy behavior is in its nature exploring, venturous and various (Rapoport and Kantor)[22]; it therefore demands an adequate environment. The exploring kind of behavior actually stimulates mutual influences between an individual and his surroundings. These mutual relationships are important for the functioning of every organism. The non-static environment, one which encourages movement, naturally increases learning.

The limit of complexity is not clear, but instead depends upon every individual, his visual interest and experience. This limit is much higher for children than for adults. It is clear that a non-static and complex environment does not only consist of complex forms, but also of complex functions which take place in that same environment. Form cannot be separated from meaning. Schools should therefore carry certain meanings. But we can also ask: what effects do these schools have on children, and how do the forms of schools affect children's behavior? One must return to the open, dynamic and purposeful process of visual perception which is very much influenced by the strong meaning of forms. Besides other mechanisms of perception, we know very little about the significance of forms in perception. There are two aspects of form significance:

1 / The denotative aspect – an aspect which refers to understanding; to those things we know and recognize through archetypes (e.g. we recognize a building as a church, school, hospital or factory). This aspect answers to simple questions like "What is this?" or "What does it represent?".

---

18 Quoted from: Grlić, Danko (1983) Estetika IV. Zagreb: Naprijed (Translation by the author)

19 Loos, Alfred (1957) Ornament i zločin. Zagreb (Translation by the author)

20 Venturi, Robert (1966) Complexity and Contradiction in Architecture. NY: MoMA

21 Rapoport, A.&Kantor, R. (1967) "Complexity and Ambiguity in Environmental Design". In: Journal of the American Institute of Planners, 33(4)

22 Ibid.

2 / The connotative aspect refers to emotions; to the way we experience forms (meanings). This aspect answers to the question: How do you like something?

The denotative and connotative aspects are omnipresent and mutually dependent.

The denotative aspect is based on archetypes, and the forms of these archetypes depend on our experience, social status, cultural context, and the era we live in. Subculture also influences the formation of stereotypes. This denotative aspect and the basis of archetypes are formed during childhood. It is therefore a very important period in the development of a child's visual and cultural level. The pre-school and school environments influence that formation. The connotative aspect of the meaning of forms can dually be connected with the question of liking and the question of identity. Many authors stress that man searches for a sense of security and self-identity.

Home is certainly the space which offers the strongest feelings of belonging and identity. But some research like for example Kevin Lynch's UNESCO research[23] shows that school is actually the dearest place in the world for children of Ecatereca, the slums of Mexico City. School occupies the first and most important place in their perception of environment.

In his book Complexity and Contradiction of Architecture Robert Venturi talks about the richness and duality of our modern experiences and of an architecture that is complex and contradictory in itself. Venturi prefers richness of meaning rather than clarity of meaning. A valid architecture evokes many levels of meaning and combinations of approaches. Its space and elements become legible and productive, working in several ways at once.
He stresses the great contrast between the means and goals of every architectural program. The means involved in building a school represent no special problem, but the relationship of goals and means is very often complex and Venturi speaks in favor of such architecture which consists of many levels of meaning between the elements within a hierarchical system.
Such architecture contains elements which are at the same time good and bad, great and small, open and closed, continuous and broken, round and square, constructive and spatial. Simultaneous perception of these elements involves struggles and hesitation for the observer, and makes perception more vivid.

Venturi explains the importance of double functioning elements. Contradiction between levels of function and meaning, appear in these elements – a double meaning. This double meaning is the result of a more or less ambiguous combination of the old meaning, called upon by association (archetypes), with a new meaning created by the modified or new functions (constructive or programmatic), as well as the new context.
Venturi's research of form does not refer directly to the relationship between the user and space. He describes the consequences of visual perception of certain forms. In 1962, when Complexity and Contradiction in Architecture was written, the book was accepted as a strong and critical view of the situation in architecture. It also anticipated new ways of thinking and new approaches to architecture.

Hertzberger's Architecture of School Buildings

The architecture of the children's world can be conceptualized as the mutual influences between children and the elements of physical structure. Some of the most significant contributions on the practical and theoretical level of schools can be found in the Netherlands. This long tradition is being enriched in the 20th century by the works of

23 Lynch, Kevin (1978) Growing up in the Cities. Cambridge, MA, MIT Press

M. Dudok, J. Duiker, J.P. Kloos, A. van Eyck, J. Verhoeven, H. Hertzberger and many other architects. Many schools built by these architects are well known.

A significant contribution to the architecture of the children's world has been made by Herman Hertzberger. His schools have achieved purely architectural qualities that are timeless and have set new standards for the relationship between children and the elements of physical structures.

Hertzberger formed his attitudes to designing space for education during the design process. However, he also directs a critical eye towards his own work and earnestly uses post occupancy evaluations.

In the articles published in the Harvard Educational Review: Architecture and Education, "Montessori primary school in Delft, Holland", Delft in 1969, and in the De Architectuur van de Montessori-School, Stichting Montessori Uitgeverij, Montessori and Space, in 1985, Hertzberger discusses the approach and results of designing schools.

Hertzberger's structuralism approach is based on the works of Ferdinand de Saussure, Claude Lévi-Strauss, Noam Chomsky, Michel Foucault and Jean-Paul Sartre. His structuralist approach to architecture was also influenced by his teacher and mentor Aldo van Eyck.

Before analyzing Hertzberger's texts on designing school environments I shall quote the text written by Roland Barthes in 1964, talking about the character of structuralism: 'The goal of all structuralist activity, whether reflexive or poetic, is to reconstruct an "object" in such a way as to manifest thereby the rules of functioning (the "functions") of this object.'[24]

The structure is then simply a semblance of the object, but an orientated and interested semblance, because the imitated object makes visible something that was not so before, or that was unintelligible in the natural object. The structural man takes reality, disassembles it and reassembles it. Between these two phases of the structuralism activity something new is produced, and this something is nothing less than the general intelligibility: the semblance is then the intellect added to the object, and this addition has an anthropological value, because it represents the whole human being, its history, its situation, its freedom and nature's resistance to its mind. In this manner one may speak of structuralism activity. Creation and reflection are not, in this case, original "impressions" of the world, but a true fabrication of a world similar to the original, not in order to copy it but to make it intelligible. These ideas of Barthes explain and correspond with the conceptual framework of Hertzberger's work.

Hertzberger's schools represent above all the true product of the world, the fantastic world of Maria Montessori's educational methods.

In the texts mentioned, Hertzberger elaborates the basic ideas about his approach to designing and to the relationship between the Montessori method and space. In discussing the essence of his architecture of schools, that is the relationship between the object and the inhabitant (physical structure and an individual), Hertzberger argues:

'Everything we make must be the catalyst to stimulate the individual to play the roles through which his identity will be enriched. The aim of the architecture is then to reach the situation where everyone's identity is optimal, and because user and thing affirm each other, make each other more themselves, the problem is to find the right conditioning for each thing. It is a question of the right articulation that things and people offer each other. Form makes itself, and that is less a question of invention than of listening well to what person and thing want to be. A thing, exclusively made for one purpose, suppresses the individual because it tells him exactly how it is to be used. If the object provokes a person to determine in what way he wants to use it, it will strengthen his self-identity. Merely the act of discovery elicits greater self-awareness. Therefore

---

24 Barthes, Roland (1964)1972 "L'activité Structuraliste." In Id., Essais critiques, 221–28. Paris: Seuil. Translated by Richard Howard as "Structuralist Activity," in Id., Critical Essays, 213–20. Evanston: Northwestern University Press

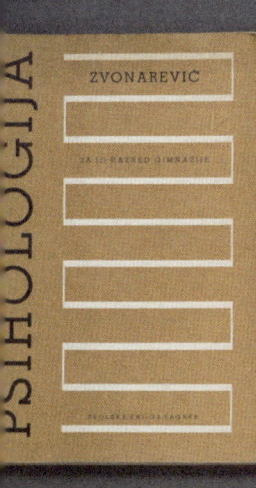

PSYCHOLOGY
for the 3rd grade
of high school

Mladen Zvonarević

Zagreb, 1971

ART OF
DESIGNING

press clipping

Zagreb, 1987

SEVEN
OPENINGS

press clipping

Zagreb, 1987

ARCHIS : HERMAN
HERTZBERGER -
RECENT WORKS

magazine, catalogue
of the exhibition

Amsterdam, 1986

a form must be interpretable – in the sense that it must be conditioned to play a changing role. It must be made in such a way that the implications are posed beforehand as hidden possibilities, evocative but not openly stated.
Everything must be formed so that one can make it relevant to himself according to his own nature, with adequate implications for everyone. In this sense the building acts as a framework to be filled in by everyone according to his own predilection.' [25]

Anarchistic humanity of Herman Hertzberger creates a theoretical tension, which enables one to come nearer and understand the importance of the manifold and complex relationship between Montessori method and space. After his experience with the new school in Amsterdam on Apollolaan, he was convinced by the interrelation of movement and space with the educational method, which Montessori had envisioned herself. A movement (voyage) through space is omni-present in a Montessori school. Children identify themselves with certain spatial situations which offer them a sense of security, take care of the things around them and build their own space and surroundings. There is a continual movement through space, which offers free, intellectual and creative learning.

Talking about the relationships in a school environment, Hertzberger describes his school in Delft, and says: 'This school has been made to answer the specific demands of a non-traditional teaching system, as far as was possible within the framework of the rather strict building regulations for primary schools in this country.'[26]

Each classroom is considered and equipped as a complete unit, a house in itself. The houses open into a central space, the street; here all activities take place between students of many ages, interrupting the unity of the classroom-groups, which are merely children of similar age.
The working method in a Montessori school is not dominated, as it is the case in traditional teaching methods, by fixed and static relationship between teachers and children, but exploits the infinite variety of relationships of child to child, child to work and child to teacher. Everybody makes his own choice of what kind of work he is going to do. As a result, the system is characterized by many different activities occurring simultaneously.
In the traditional rectangular classroom the variety of activities generally tends to create a rather chaotic situation in which the children become a disturbance to their neighbors. Children, who have difficulty in concentrating, or those doing demanding work, are consequently at a considerable disadvantage.

In Montessori primary school in Delft, the classroom has been modified to an L shape form and given a floor level variation of two steps, so that a child is no longer forced to take in the activities of all the other children at once. By suiting the parts of the classroom to the various categories of activity-like rooms of the house, one achieves a situation where children disturb each other as little as possible.
Those who have the most difficulty in concentrating can be given their permanent place in the quietest corner; those doing arithmetic, where concentration is difficult, will not be as easily distracted by the painters, modelers, and sketchers who at that moment do less demanding work.
There are small tables for individual work, and a child can work either alone or in co-operation with others at the big table by the window, or in the "corner for self-expression," each one either alone amidst others or in social contact with them.
While the teacher is occupied with a single child, or with groups of varying size, the others work on their own projects. By making a great variety of space qualities, it will obtain the potential to contain several activities simultaneously; its adhesive potential increases.

---

25   Hertzberger, Herman (1969) "Montessori primary school in Delft, Holland", in Harvard Educational Review: Architecture and Education, Vol 31, No 4.

26   Ibid.

**OPEN-AIR SCHOOLS
OF THE 20th CENTURY**

description of the seminar

Sorbonne, 2001

**HERMAN HERTZBERGER
ARCHITECTURE**

poster
Museum of Arts and Crafts
Zagreb, 1987

The hall space is the street onto which all classrooms and general facilities are grouped. Here perhaps the most important part of school life is centered. This hall is the big communal classroom, the complementary form and the extension of the classroom element taken as a whole. The stepped arrangement of the classroom creates a great many corners where children can work individually or in groups near their particular classroom.

The most active and complex point of the building is where the classrooms and hall open onto each other. These are the points where the children will work in the hall as though outside in front of the house on one's own ground, outside the security of one's classroom, yet not shut out, still under the eye of the teacher – still belonging.

In these places which are part of the social, as it were, sort of public area, classroom and hall give each other mutual definition. It is at these points that the roof domes let in daylight, and at night let out artificial light. With its strongly articulated form, this hall can suitably contain the most diverse activities: a podium and many dark corners cater to specialized lessons, such as handy work, traffic instruction, and music; at the same time all the classes can continue to function normally. The central point of the hall is the brick podium that is used for formal gatherings as well as spontaneous expression. One might tend to think that the hall space would have a greater potential if one could move the block aside once in a while. On the contrary, its being immovable is crucial. Flexibility leaves every theoretical possibility open, in the sense that nothing is a priori excluded but, on the other hand, it does not initiate anything either.

Due to its presence as the focal point of the building, the block evokes a response for any occasion; it reacts to every action, and can be interpreted in a variety of ways, playing different roles, each one accommodating a different circumstance.

Besides, the podium can be extended in all directions with a kit of wooden elements that are revealed out of its interior to make a real stage for bigger theatrical, dance and music performances. Curtains are rigged to an overhead track around it, so that the stage can look in different directions. The children take the block for granted. They use its porch as a platform to sit on, as a place to put things down, as a stage from which to make announcements, or just to become taller. They play games around and on it. To them it is an island in the sea. In every circumstance, this fixed point acts as a magnet towards which one is unintentionally drawn; it becomes a touchstone, the articulation of the space, enlarging the scope of the hall's habitability. That such a block can be interpreted in so many different ways means not only that it can fulfill several roles, but also that the children are stimulated by it to greater diversity in the roles they play. Hertzberger will argue: 'Not only do we interpret the form, the form at the same time interprets us, shows us something of who we are.'[27]

In its limited sense the school entrance is a door, which is used only for a few short moments at the beginning and end of the school day. A soft of entrance porch has been made, so that the building can already house the children before school, and provide a place to wait for each other or just hang around after school. This is as much an outward extension of the hall as an inward extension of the playground; it is the in-between area where one feels not within but yet not entirely outside the school. The playground outside is public area, part of the street. Even when classes are not in session, when the school is not open at all, neighborhood children are attracted by this place where they apparently feel at ease, somewhere to meet each other and to hang around. It has become a meeting place quite out of its context as a doorstep of the school. At these times it apparently has a meaning of place unrelated to being a doorway, formed by the walls. The opportunity has been taken wherever possible to increase the number of available uses of each object. Window ledges, for instance, and other

27   Ibid.

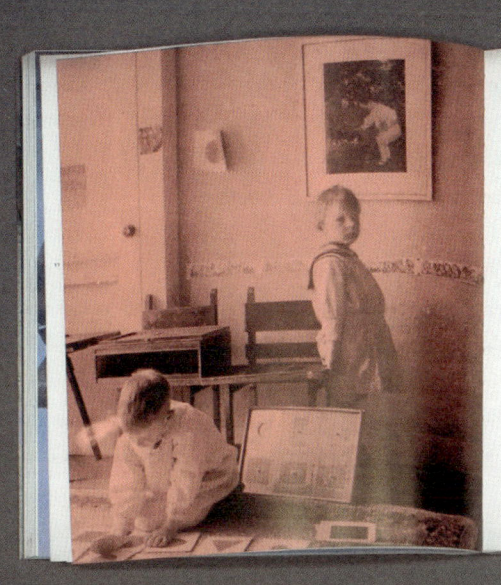

KID SIZE :
THE MATERIAL WORLD
OF CHILDHOOD

Vitra Design Museum,
SKIRA Editore, 1997

Vedran Mimica and
Kelly Shannon:
Utopia As Tradition

HERMAN
HERTZBERGER
ARCHITECTURE

poster
Museum of Arts
and Crafts
Zagreb, 1987

Ph.D.
Dissertation synopsis

Zagreb, 1991

Vedran Mimica and Herman Hertzberger
Zagreb, 1995

places which lend themselves similarly, have been dimensioned so that the children can display on them many unbelievably beautiful things they make. Each class will interpret these elements differently. Thus the differences between the classes will be emphasized and their specific identity strengthened. The yield can be increased without doing injustice to the primary function.

Originally, only a four-classroom school was to be built, with the understanding that the addition of one or two classrooms would be possible.

There is continuing uncertainty over what is going to happen to the form of the school. In fact – there can be no talk of a definitive form at all. Since we cannot continually be in an environment that is incomplete in itself, a building must constantly fulfill its function in every respect.

This is achieved by making such elements that each one is complete in itself, and at the same time its addition makes a new whole. In this case the classroom is the building block, a small school in itself. The roof domes play a significant role in the defining of the building block. While being internally the most important articulation of the hall, they simultaneously perform a similar function externally for the building. The protruding transparent cubes identify each classroom, visually determining the location of each within the whole.

In the article "Montessori and Space" Hertzberger describes the experiences of the new school in Amsterdam: 'A classroom in a Montessori school must be organized in such a way, that a teacher cannot see all the activities at once. The surface of the classroom is designed according to Dutch norms, regardless of the Montessori demands for a classroom which should offer possibilities for many different and simultaneous activities. The basic concept is the idea of a shell of a snail, which represents a kind of movement outwards.'[28]

The "kitchen" element is placed in the part of the classroom suggested by the teacher. It occupies the largest spare part of the classroom and therefore presents classic organization of the work.

The space develops diagonally and therefore stimulates dynamic and creative organization of classroom activities. Related to the central hall, the opposite classrooms are built on a split-level. This very organization creates an amphitheatrically central space for a very convenient visual communication between opposite classrooms.

Special attention is paid to the classroom entrance. This space is formed as an access to the classroom and the central hall. Approaching the classroom a pupil is already there in his thoughts (the formation of space causes that feeling). The space in front of the classroom offers possibilities for individual work, although a pupil is physically outside, in the central hall.

The connection between the classroom and the central hall is achieved by a door divided horizontally (either part can be open or closed). There is a shelf by the door, where every class has its small exhibition. Spatial qualities of the central hall offer possibilities for individual work. The hall can therefore have a function of a large classroom. Steps function as desks and each child can use these desks in his own way. The form does therefore not define the use. In this sense, the steps are actually analogous to the central block in Delft. They stimulate all kind of use but they also present the central space at school.

The essence of prepared environment of the Montessori method is the congruence of the essence and form. Children become „stone investigators", and we should add stone to a certain space in order to expand its possibilities.

The notion that every child should contribute to the image of a building is not a utopian idea. The window ledges are made of tiles, which are the pupils' handy work. A good organization of space does not mean that space has to be defined. Space has to be made, and to be made free at the same time. Every space must offer possibilities for change, association and freedom to choose.

28 Hertzberger, Herman (1985) "Montessori en ruimte". In: De Architectuur van de Montessori School. Amsterdam: Stichting Montessori Uitgeverij

ORIS 20

Zagreb, 2003

Éugene Beaudouin
Marcel Lods
Jan Duiker
Richard Neutra
Giuseppe Terragni
Arne Jacobsen
Paul Rudolph
Aldo van Eyck
Aldo Rossi
Herman Hertzberger
Thom Mayne
Manuel Castells
Andrea Branzi

ECOLOGICAL
CHILD
PSYCHOLOGY

Beograd, 1985

PSYCHOLOGY
for the 3rd grade
of high school

Mladen Zvonarević

Zagreb, 1971

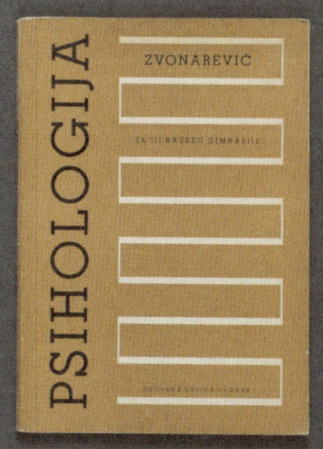

ALDO VAN EYCK

Herman Hertzberger,
Addie van Roijen-
Wortmann, Francis
Strauven

Amsterdam, 1982

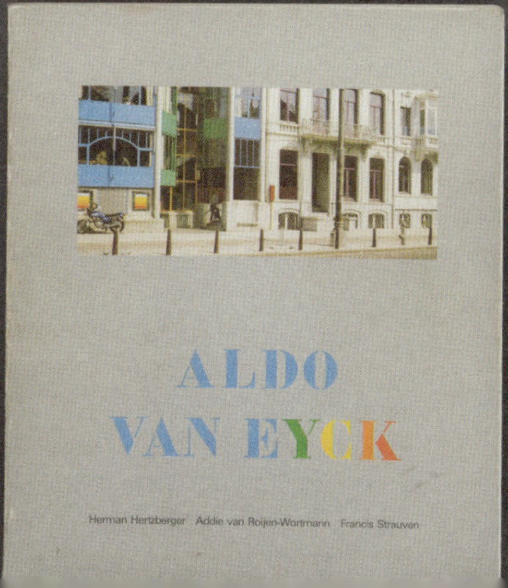

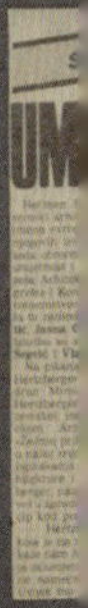

CREATION OF NEW WORLDS IN MINIATURE

Published in Oris 20, Zagreb 2003

Article is based on a paper Creation of New Worlds in Miniature (co-authored with Kelly Shannon) from the seminar Les Écoles de Plein Air au XXe Siècle, Histoire d´une expérience éducative et de son architecture, Sorbonne, Paris (December 2001)

An Innate Utopian Drive?

Every civilization has the necessity to create ideal islands, enclaves and missions. The modernist "utopian spirit" was grounded in the understanding that the future could fundamentally transcend the present.

Utopias – literally "no-man's lands" – often appeared as radical visions, ideal worlds opposite to the status quo. It was often argued that, in fact, utopias were necessary in order to "correct" modernization and the progress of civilization. The fate of the utopian thinker hinged upon the paradox: to be a realist means to demand the impossible.

In the Occidental world, within the Modernist tradition, the wheels of progress have been kept in-line by "utopian ideals" that sustained dissent and the movements of social change.

However, by nearly all contemporary accounts, the avant-garde is dead and utopias are obsolete. Instead the modern world is overrun with information technology, lifestyles and mediA

identity, brands and commodities are what society demands. The market has consumed its so-called utopias – there is no critical discourse within the late-capitalistic mode of production.

What, then, is the value of dreaming the world of tomorrow? If the unfinished modern project has finally been abandoned, what is there to fill the void?

Built Utopias

Along with the other arts, architecture is a discourse that has created images of utopia. Unique to architecture is the fact that it affords the possibility of physically representing the ideal world.

Although literally grounded in reality and the present, architecture has the capacity to transcend particular contexts and moments in time.

The fundamental power of architecture in the creation of culture, through materialization of universal values, is manifested in the design of the built environment.

In the twentieth century, school buildings represented a particular typology that encapsulated aspects of the utopian, ideal world.

The meaning of a school – within society as an institution and within a city as an object – inheres in its being a place of formal mediation between the world of adults and the world of children.

School buildings encode the values of culture through design, construction and use; it is the spatial encounters of early childhood that provide a framework for visual, cultural and societal development.

The most radical paradigmatic shifts in the history of school buildings paralleled new ideas in pedagogical standards, themselves a reflection of radical changes in the economic, environmental and socio-political arenas.

The open-air school was an important canonical break in (re)creating school typology.

Radically different from their surroundings, usually the dense urban fabric of the 19th century, these educational machines created built utopias for the material world of childhood.

Post-war experiments in education led to another fundamental break in the development of school typology.

Today, the premise for education has again taken a drastically new perspective and the architectural world has yet to respond.

Brave New Worlds

The most direct translation of the particular ideology associated with the open-air school movement is commonly attributed to the 1932-36 construction in Suresnes by Eugène Beaudouin and Marcel Lods. This school banishes the commonly held notions of style. Kenneth Frampton refers to the Perretesque nature of the building but indeed it is a crossbreed between Auguste Perret's transformation of beaux-arts symmetry with respect to the needs of reinforced concrete and a decisively modern architecture, fitting the Corbusiean spirit of the times. Beaudouin and Lods adopted the engineering logic and brilliance of their mentor Jean Prouvé, which resulted in a logical and common sense school typology as city-in-miniature. The school redefined the relation of the exterior and interior, whereby the border of the two are literally blurred by sliding walls and the outside is treated as a functional territory. The composition of the archetypal elements is developed in parallel with the new functional and symbolic development of open spaces. Suresnes was also an important element of the equipment urbain. The city, understood as an organism, was serviced by various interventions – equipment urbain – which were able to guide and regulate public behavior. The vulnerability of children to the evils of contemporary society is paradoxically safeguarded by the most modern techniques – prefabricated elements, special heating systems and the most advanced use of new materials are employed in the creation of a healthy new world.

Duiker's School (1929-30) on Cliostraat, within Berlage's South Extension plan in Amsterdam, reveals apparent simplicity but is actually the result of extremely complex architectural strategies, not only in terms of the violation of symmetry, but also in the composition of details, employment of colors and use and design of the structure. Jan Duiker's faith in the new society, the new institution, is embodied in a completely new type of school building. As an engineer, Duiker created the Constructivist character of the school by exploiting the nature of new materials – reinforced concrete, glass and steel:

It may be the working of chance, but the programs of Duiker dealt with appear in retrospect to be central to a new sort of society – a new view of society... One imagines that the Constructivist dream was to create architecture capable of dealing with just such problems in the most ordinary of materials – steel, concrete, glass, and it was Duiker's luck and genius to make a slightly mad but quite real machine poetry from this ordinary stuff, not in Holy Russia but in Bourgeoisie Holland. And perhaps there is no paradox in that.

Smithson, Peter (1961) Statement on Duiker. Forum, November 1961

Duiker's engineering logic was able to consume and then recompose all the contemporary influences in order to build architecture of "economy of means." The fact that the school for the emerging new society required ample light and air only supported Duiker's preoccupations. The rationalism of Duiker must be counterbalanced by his deeply rooted humanistic concerns. He spoke often of a concept of "spiritual economy."

The Open Air School represents Duiker's ideological position and his strong belief in the direct usefulness of new architecture:

Now it has become necessary to give these children back their health, now the things that have been withheld from them in the past suddenly become necessities, sunlight, ultra-violet rays, rest after exercise, ample fresh air for poisoned lungs, toughening-up, in short ... hygienic conditions. Injurious school conditions gave rise to a movement for open air schools both in our country and abroad...
It is a strong hygienic power that is influencing our life; one that will develop into a style, a hygienic style!

J. Duiker, 1932

Some years before Beaudoin, Lods and Duiker, Richard Neutra was experimenting with similar ideas in America. The ultimate draw for the Viennese émigré was the most liberating and young part of America – southern California. Here, fuelled by an ideal climate and the invigorating atmosphere of the "California Modern", Neutra continued work on a project (begun in Berlin) that would occupy him over his entire career in the United States. Rush City Reformed was a utopian world, with far-fetched dreams of an entirely new city sitting alongside realistic visions for housing and radically new forms of education. Neutra believed building programs could be interpreted as making a direct contribution to the psycho-physiological well-being of its occupants. Relating to education, Neutra's conviction that tensions begin to accumulate in childhood when one is taken from the home and living room and put into a school and classroom led to his conception of classrooms resembling living rooms filled with group action.

His first school, the 1926 Ringplan school, was part of the Rush City Reformed oeuvre. Its parti was rooted in that of the monastery and California's indigenous Spanish Colonial houses, which made wide use of arcade passages. However, instead of merely focusing upon a communal space inwards (to the cortile), Neutra developed a system whereby its circle of connected classrooms expanded to outside patios. Although the Ringplan school was not realized until 1961 in Lemore, California (constructed of stucco, as opposed to the originally designated metal), it stirred much comment following its inclusion in the 1932 Museum of Modern Art show.[29] In 1935, the addition to the Corona Avenue School in southeast LA was completed. Essentially, it was the Ringplan school without the ring. The L-shaped wing, one classroom deep, devoted practically all of the floor space to areas of instruction.

The Corona School banished the "listening classroom", while moveable chairs and desks, easily portable between indoors and out, replaced traditional furniture.

The radicalism of the school was evident in the derogatory names by which it was referred to – "a drive-in market", "an airplane hangar" and "a penthouse on Mars." Yet most of Neutra's innovations in the school type were incorporated throughout California schools.

Further interpretations of the open-air classroom can be seen in the series of rural schools Neutra designed in 1944 for Puerto Rico, the Kester Avenue Elementary School (1951), the Alamitos Intermediate School of Garden Grove (1957) and the Elementary Training School at UCLA (1958).

The Puerto Rico schools are a testament to Neutra's desire that good design should be available to people of modest means. Over 150 sites on the tropical island had minimalist versions of the Ringplan and Corona Avenue Schools. The buildings were sited as to take advantage of the prevailing breezes and were constructed of hurricane-resistant reinforced concrete in standardized, replicable, expandable sections allowing different arrangement for different sites, all possible by using unskilled labor. Each unit had two solid walls, a third with strip ventilating louvers near the ceiling, and the fourth with three wide glass panels that could be lifted like overhead garage doors to a horizontal position. During the school hours the doors were always open.

Beyond the Open Air School

Similar to the ambiguity of Beaudouin and Lods' school in Suresnes, Giuseppe Terragni's Asilo Sant'Elia nursery school in Como, Italy (1934-37) represents the continuum of historical, classical principles transformed within the syntax of the modern. Terragni, working within the tenets of Italian Rationalism, re-interpreted the cortile. The school embraced the spirit of space as envisioned

---

29   Modern Architecture: International Exhibition is the title of an exhibition that took place in 1932 at the Museum of Modern Art in New York City. Curated by Philip Johnson and Henry-Russell Hitchcock, the exhibition introduced an emerging architectural style characterized by simplified geometry and a lack of ornamentation; known as the International Style, it was described by Johnson as "probably the first fundamentally original and widely distributed style since the Gothic." The exhibition, along with an accompanying catalog, laid the principles for the canon of Modern architecture.

in the new educational program of Mussolini and Terragni's faith in the new society (institution) is embodied in a transformed typology. The central zone for recreation (indoor and outdoor) separates the classroom wing from the dining and supportive facilities, materializing in a structure that is simultaneously intimate and monumental. The poetic functionalism of Terragni is expressed through asymmetrical distortions in a predominately rational ordering system. Dynamism to the entire complex is achieved through technologically sophisticated detailing, culminating in an elegance of expression. The manipulation of daylight and the series of layered spaces of increasing openness create a school environment rooted in mediation and dialogue with the elements of nature. Each classroom has an outdoor terrace defined and shaded by canvas awnings (inflated by the wind) supported on a concrete frame.

Arne Jacobsen's Munkegård School (1954-56) in Gentofte, a suburb of Copenhagen, represents a city-in-miniature adapted to Nordic functionalism.[30] Sophisticated detailing of the interior world softened a highly organized and rational plan, with pairs of soundproof classrooms linked to individual gardens. A balanced combination of scale, light and a decidedly intimate atmosphere resulted in the Danish version of the total work of art. The Munkegård School is canonical in terms of its interior world, where well-designed objects not only serve functional purposes, but also produce a subconscious change in the pupils' perception of the built environment.

Costly public investment in elementary schools confirms that architecture for the world of childhood can define high national standards for the relationships of users and living environments in general. The corollary to the welfare state's investment in the 1950s is the fact that in the 1990s the European Union's richest societies build the cheapest schools.

Aldo Van Eyck's Nagele schools (1956) as well as the Orphanage (1960) in the Netherlands portray perhaps the last possibilities of "heroic modernity". The proto-structuralist buildings poetically articulate large/small and inside/outside vis-à-vis interlocking contingent units, materializing Van Eyck's reciprocal house-city image:

```
"tree is leaf and leaf is tree – house
is city and city is house – a tree
is a tree but it is also a huge leaf
– a leaf is a leaf but it is also
a tiny tree – a city is not a city
unless it is also a huge house – a
house is a house only if it is also
a tiny city".
```

A. Van Eyck, 1963

Paul Rudolph's John W. Chorley School (1964-69) in Middletown, New York represents a radical break-through in the typology possible by way of a major shift in terms of pedagogy.

The school-without-walls, a prelude to the larger social movements of 1968, although premised upon different principles of the open-air school, nonetheless remains interesting as a comparison in terms of the relation of pedagogy to school typology. Rudolph created a physical form to correspond to the pedagogy's emphasis upon non-hierarchical relationships and the de-institutionalization of the institution. The school and its immediate exterior environment were conceived as a landform. Interior spaces were designed as landscapes, with manipulated ground plans and maximum transparency. The short life of the acceptance of the diminished image of schools resulted in the abandonment of the school-without-walls by the mid-1970s.

In an extreme reaction to the populism of the 1970s, Aldo Rossi's Falagno Olona School (1972) heralded a return to the typologies and constructional forms of the second half of the 19th century. The school's archetypical organization of highly rationalized,

New style of functionalism was first mentioned in Finland in 1926.

ordered, symmetrical forms and spaces of the old "type" must be viewed within the voice of the "Tendenza", the Italian Neo-Rationalist movement. Retro-garde expression sought to regain the loss of timeless, eternal and metaphysical values.

Since the 1960s, Herman Hertzberger has firmly been propagating the cultural importance of architecture, with a particular emphasis on the school building within the Montessori pedagogical system. The invention of Hertzberger's 1980-83 Apollo Schools – split-level organization and amphitheatrical central hall – has been successfully multiplied in the Montessori College Amsterdam (1998-99), resulting in an array of suspended wooden amphitheaters (resembling elevated urban squares) and multiple choices of circulation routes.

The classroom block simultaneously creates opportunities for seeing and being seen and precariously balances spatial freedom with panoptical control.

All thresholds are exploited as opportunities for the creation of spaces for social encounters and individual/small group study to occur.

In the recent Diamond Ranch High School, Pomona, California (2000) of Thom Mayne and Morphosis, clusters of classrooms are ingeniously arranged on a sloping territory, which encompasses outdoor teaching areas as well as collective spaces.

The school for 1200 students reflects the reality of suburban America – 700 parking places were required. Increased mobility requires areas around schools, at least in the United States, to be not unlike the vast areas surrounding shopping malls; seas of asphalt for car parking.

Schools of Flows

The non-linear dynamics of the information technology revolution ushered in a truly interactive world in which decentralization and diffusion of the power of information has the potential for fundamental architectural and town planning consequences.

Manuel Castells, in his massive trilogy of what he terms The Information Age focuses upon the space of flows, a term he developed to represent the dominant spatial manifestation of power and function in contemporary societies.

He opposes the historically rooted spatial organization, the space of place (in which horizontal relationships are more prominent and meaningful), to that of the space of flows (involving the rapid movement of capital, technology, labor and information). Nonetheless, he admits that

… people do still live in places. But because function and power in our societies are organized in the space of flows, the structural domination of its logic essentially alters the meaning and dynamic of places. Experience, by being related to places, becomes abstracted from power, and meaning is increasingly separated from knowledge. It follows a structural schizophrenia between two spatial logics that threaten to break down communication channels in society. The dominant tendency is toward a horizon of networked, ahistorical space of flows, aiming at imposing its logic over scattered, segmented places, increasingly unrelated to each other, less and less able to share cultural codes. Unless cultural and physical bridges are deliberately built between these two forms of space, we may be heading toward life in parallel universes whose times cannot meet because they are warped into different dimensions of a social hyperspace.

Castells, Manuel (1996) The Rise of the Network Society (The Information Age: Economy, Society and Culture, Volume 1). Malden, MA: Blackwell Publishers.

Paradoxically, he concedes that schools and universities are the institutions least affected by the virtual logic embedded in information technology, in spite of the foreseeable quasi-universal use of computers in the classrooms of advanced countries.

But they will hardly vanish into the virtual space. In the case of elementary and secondary schools, this is because they are as much childcare centers and/or children's warehouses as they are learning institutions. In the case of universities, this is because the quality of education is still and will be for a long time, associated with face-to-face interaction.

Castells, Manuel (1996) The Rise of the Network Society (The Information Age: Economy, Society and Culture, Volume 1). Malden, MA: Blackwell Publishers.

The school can be viewed as a transitory hardening in the flows of the 21st century.
The symbolism of the institution is mutating and oscillating between the new world of virtual education via information technology (the Internet) and the old world of schools as physical places of developmental social encounter.

In schools, software – the floating, invisible and ephemeral flows of the contemporary global information society – demands state-of-the-art hardware that not only fulfils technical requirements but also provides stability, security and anchorage within local communities.

(Re)Schooling Society

The end of the old world coincides with its continuity. Not, though, an immobile, not a petrified continuity, but continuity powered by a slow earth-movement of transformation; by mild tectonic tremors that do not conspicuously alter the landscape (urban and domestic) but subject it to a subtle evolutionary transformation. And this deep though secret change is a mental, not a formal one.

Branzi, Andrea (1998) 2028: the escape from entropy. In: Domus 800, January '98

Ideally, education and the schools in which childhood matures progressively mediate the changes between one generation and the next. From this perspective, schools may be viewed as the leading interactive environments from which to introduce change in a society. In the early- and mid-twentieth century, the possibility to create radical architectural expressions in school buildings was due not only to the genius of their creators, but also to the impassioned search by educators for new teaching methods. The success of the open-air schools and the failure of the 'school without walls' is reflected in the acceptance and space-time constraints of new methods and 'new worlds'. The legacy and spirit of these creations represent a disappearing world. At the beginning of the new millennium, radicalism has become commodified and utopias are retreating into the flows of media. Nonetheless, school buildings remain as a typology, which can be radically transformed vis-à-vis the enormous potentials of the information technology and communication revolution.

Architects and educators need to become initiators of evolutionary transformations; and, as Branzi commented, these transformations demand their beginnings in the realm of conceptual and strategic thinking. The changes in the relations between individuals, knowledge and the access to / dissemination of information need to be paralleled in radically new interactive environments. Architects must continue to question the nature of institutions and the typology of the school. The world of childhood, reflecting the larger image of society in the digital age, simultaneously embraces a higher degree of individualization and diversity. Schools should provide a degree of cultural cohesion while still accommodating cultural difference. Schools do not necessarily have to become educational islands of resistance in the commodified world, but instead can once again engagingly become (re)created civic realms. The global world of flows has to be appropriated into the local community in a process of (re)schooling society.

2
Terragni's final plan of the
Asilo Sant'Elia nursery
school, Como.

3
Front (Via Andrea Alciato)
and side (Via dei Mille)
elevations and east-west
section through the Asilo
Sant'Elia.

MUZEJ ZA UMJETNOST I OBRT, ZAGREB
MUSEUM FOR ARTS AND CRAFTS, ZAGREB, YUGOSL

KID SIZE :
THE MATERIAL WORLD
OF CHILDHOOD

Vitra Design Museum,
SKIRA Editore
1997

Vedran Mimica and
Kelly Shannon:
Utopia as Tradition

Giuseppe Terragni
Benito Mussolini
Herman Hertzberger
Mies van der Rohe
Maria Montessori
Bruno Zevi
Siegfried Giedion
Thomas Schumacher
Peter Buchanan
Kenneth Frampton
Reyner Banham

HERMAN HERTZBERGER :
EXHIBITION OF ARCHITECTURE

Museum of Arts and Crafts, Zagreb

May 1987

UTOPIA AS TRADITION

Published in Kid Size – The Material World of Childhood,
Vitra Design Museum, Skira Editore, Milan, 1997 (co-authored with Kelly Shannon)

There exists an enormous challenge in designing the fantastic world of childhood: that of enriching the sense of wonder and imagination as the innocence of childhood evolves to understanding. The built environment poses a series of complex relations, scales and forms, many of which are daunting from the perspective of a child. Nonetheless, the spatial encounters of early childhood frame visual, cultural and societal development. Therefore, the material world of childhood demands the utmost attention by architects and designers. The fundamental power of architecture in the creation of culture, through materialization of universal values, should be manifested in the design of the built environment for children. Architecture of a children's world needs to ground a sense of identity. A school signifies a place of formal mediation between the world of adults and the world of children. The school building as a "type" has been transformed by various cultures and individual architects throughout history. The meaning of a school – within society as an institution and within a city as an object – is expressed not only through the formal characteristics of the buildings but also through the social and pedagogical structures of education. Historically, schools have encoded the values of culture through design, construction and use. Two elementary schools will be discussed here, providing an awareness of different strategies that have been employed in achieving architectural value, symbolic meaning and environmental nurturing. A more direct relation to the design environment will also be addressed, since their respective architects also designed the furniture of these schools. The immediate sensorial and psychological encounters with the material world are embodied in the design of desks, chairs, tables and play apparatus.

Giuseppe Terragni's Asilo Sant'Elia nursery school in Como, Italy (1934-37) and Herman Hertzberger's Apollo Schools (the Montessori school and the Willemspark school) in Amsterdam, the Netherlands (1980-83) represent two canonical typologies of material worlds for children. These schools express paradigmatic breaks within the revolutionary changes of the twentieth century in the development of the "school type", and establish a clear relation between the inseparable notions of tradition and innovation.

Terragni, working within the tenets of Italian Rationalism, re-interpreted the cortile (monastery cloister) as a "glass house for learning."[31] His Asilo Sant'Elia represents the continuum of Classical principles transformed within the syntax of the Modern. Half a century later, French linguistic structuralism strongly influenced Hertzberger. His introspective, Apollo schools, exploit the compactness of a historic type, the urban villa and infuse a spatial richness created by the split level.

Asilo Sant'Elia School by Giuseppe Terragni

Now Terragni reaches his poetic stage – the Sant'Elia School is his masterpiece. It erases all dogmatism, forgets the exhausted quarrel with the Regime and comes from a human understanding, full of well-educated and popular inventiveness. It is the kind of architecture which . . . [is] controlled by contents and functions, simple and bright, molded by lived-in spaces more than volumes, holding a kind of dialogue between the inside and the outside because it has some panoramic connections. The school is not easy to analyze by European criteria; its inspiration comes from everyday experience.

Zevi, Bruno (1968) Omaggio a Terragni, Milano: Etas Kompass

The fifth and most humane of his significant buildings in Como is an infant school, the Asilo Sant'Elia,

[31] Schumacher, Thomas (1991) Giuseppe Terragni. Milano: Electa

the most fairy-godfatherly compliment ever paid to the young by a modern architect. Here, Terragni's passion for open frames and courtyard plans produces a delicate environment of airy, lightly-shaded spaces and framed views of greenery beyond, unaffected (though not without its formalism) and still, to my mind, the best school built in Italy in this century.

Banham, Reyner (1975) Age of the Masters: A Personal View of Modern Architecture, Harper & Row Icon Editions; first American Edition edition

Giuseppe Terragni (1904-43) was an enigma, an architect who carried through only 26 works in his brief career spanning 15 years. His revolutionary designs, in nearly every category of building type, have only recently been revisited in respect of their importance in the history of the twentieth-century modern architecture. Terragni was a passionate, visionary architect who lived and died with a fervent belief in Italian Catholicism and in Fascism.

The Modern Movement was imported to Italy four years after Mussolini seized power; avant-garde architects, therefore, had to respond to a changing and progressively conservative social order which masqueraded itself as revolution. Before 1935, Mussolini was considered not only a savior of Italy, but also an international statesman. Two competing architectural forces strove to win his favor – the nationalistic, Roman revival expressed through the work of Marcello Piacentini, and the abstract modern idiom of Italian Rationalism. Unlike Hitler and Stalin, Mussolini never formally endorsed any particular architectural vocabulary to represent the ideology of Fascism; he patronized both, as long as they expressed the grandeur of the regime.

The Italian Rationalists sought a rational synthesis between the nationalistic values of Italian Classicism and the structural logic of the machine age. Terragni was influenced by architectural and artistic movements, as well as personalities: Russian Constructivism, the Bauhaus, de Stijl and Le Corbusier.

In addition, his background as a painter, where he focused upon the dialogue between abstraction and figuration, was also highly instrumental in his development of architectural form. For Terragni, 'architecture, a measure of civilization, elementary, rising clear, perfect when it becomes the expression of a people who select, observe and appreciate the result, which, laboriously reworked, reveals the spiritual values of all'.[32] The progressive and traditional aspects of Fascist mythology emerged as a poetical expression of Rationalism as the new institution for Italian society of the 1930s. Italian architecture of the 1920s and 1930s was an architecture of the state, and the work of Terragni was no exception.

The design of the Asilo Sant'Elia, actually done with the assistance of Terragni's brother Attilio, was meant to be a prototype for nursery/elementary schools of the Fascist regime. However, due to Terragni's departure for the Russian Front during the war, his submission of wider-ranging plans to government headquarters was compromised, although this school certainly embraced the spirit of space as envisioned in Mussolini's new educational program. Terragni's faith in this new society is embodied in a transformed "school type." The school stands south of the city walls of Como, in the new Sant'Elia working-class quarter of the city, which had been developing since the early 1900s. The site is a corner lot, and the building is at a diagonal to the street plan with which the surrounding buildings conform. The ground plan consists of volumetric massing on three sides, opening towards a courtyard on the north-eastern side. The south-east wing houses four generous classrooms and a cloakroom. The north-west wing contains the refectory which connects to the section at an oblique angle on the north-west side to the kitchen.

The central zone for recreation (indoor and outdoor) separates the classroom wing from the dining and supportive facilities, materializing in a structure that is simultaneously intimate and monumental. The poetic functionalism of Terragni is expressed by asymmet-

32   Zevi, Bruno (1968) Omaggio a Terragni. Milano: Etas Kompass (quoting from a manuscript by Terragni)

rical distortions in a predominately rational ordering system. Dynamism to the entire complex is achieved through technologically sophisticated detailing, culminating in an elegance of expression. The manipulation of daylight and the series of layered spaces, of increasing openness, create a school environment rooted in mediation and dialogue with the elements of nature. Here, as in most of Terragni's buildings, exists the golden section of 8:13, carefully hidden in the plan. In the Asilo, Terragni showed his understanding of the essence of the Open Air School in Amsterdam by Johannes Duiker (1929-30). Duiker's vertical organization of semi-outdoor protective spaces for small children has been transformed horizontally. Each classroom has an outdoor terrace defined and shaded by the canvas awnings (inflated by the wind), supported on a concrete frame. The entirety of the Asilo conquers outdoor space by dissolving boundaries into transparency, projecting volumes into the outside – refectory, corridor running alongside classrooms, and balcony complex and canopy roof over the main entrance. The tight interplay between interior and exterior is revealed through the dynamic treatment of openings, including hopper upper lights that tip on a central horizontal axis, operated by rods, and the light rhythmic verticals of the entry porch. Terragni designed all the furniture and fittings for the Asilo. In spite of a high ceiling, emphasized by the vertical glazing, the stairs, furniture, door handles, radiators, counters and bathrooms were all designed to accentuate the scale of a child. Innovative solutions in detailing transposed the classical Roman conception of stability towards the modern inclination to flexibility and dynamism. In the classrooms, teaching areas have a layered series of moving vertical surfaces; partitions between the classrooms consist of sliding wooden panels collected in a bellows stack, allowing them to be combined for assemblies.

There exists an obvious relation between the poetic functionalism of the furniture and Terragni's abstract conception of flexibility. Chairs and desks, made of tubular steel and plywood, were extremely light, and therefore easy to move. Their elementary nature worked from the precedents established in the Weimar Bauhaus. Marcel Breuer, Mart Stam and Mies van der Rohe had all been experimenting with contemporary machine methods and an array of new materials. 'The tubular steel chair is as truly a part of the heroic period of the new architecture as are the transparent shells of glass that replace bearing walls,' according to Siegfried Giedion.[33] Terragni re-interpreted their basic geometrical forms, built up from an analysis of details and function, to educational furniture, scaled to the child. Like the Bauhaus chairs, the weight-supporting framework was of tubular steel while the plywood non-structural parts, in more direct contact with the child, were less abstract and softer in character.

Apollo Schools by Herman Hertzberger

To visit the Apollo Schools at the end of the school day, as classes slowly wind down and parents come to collect children, is a joy. Children, teachers, parents all use the building so fully and variously that there is a tangible atmosphere of enjoyment and belonging. Rarely does an architect's description of how a building should work seem to accord so well with practice as here.

Buchanan, Peter (1987) New Amsterdam School/Herman Hertzberger/Apollo Schools. In: The Architectural Review, no 1055, 1987

This is a school as a city-in-miniature, the school as compensation, one might say, for the loss of a public forum in the community as a whole. It is difficult to imagine a more specifically political gesture than this and it would be hard to find any school built during the last twenty years that is of comparable critical subtlety and depth.

Frampton, Kenneth (1986) The Structural regionalism of Herman Hertzberger. "The cause of architecture in a Taylorized age". In: Herman Hertzberger, Recent Works, catalog of the exhibition derived from Archis no. 12/86

[33] Giedion, Siegfried (1947) Mechanization Takes Command. New York: Oxford University Press,

THE ARCHITECTURAL REVIEW

London, 1985

THE ARCHITECTURAL REVIEW

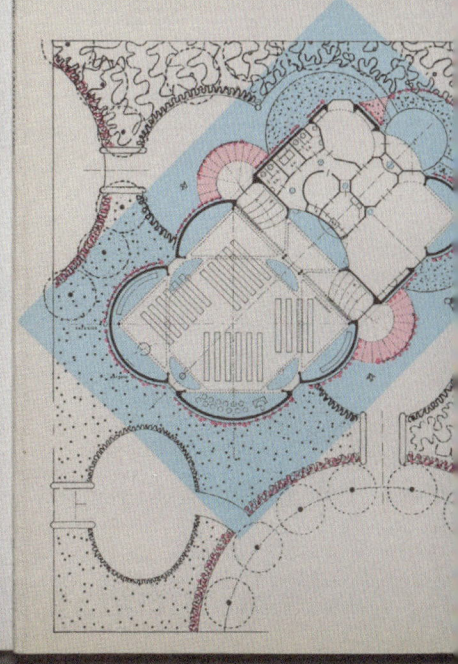

London, 1990

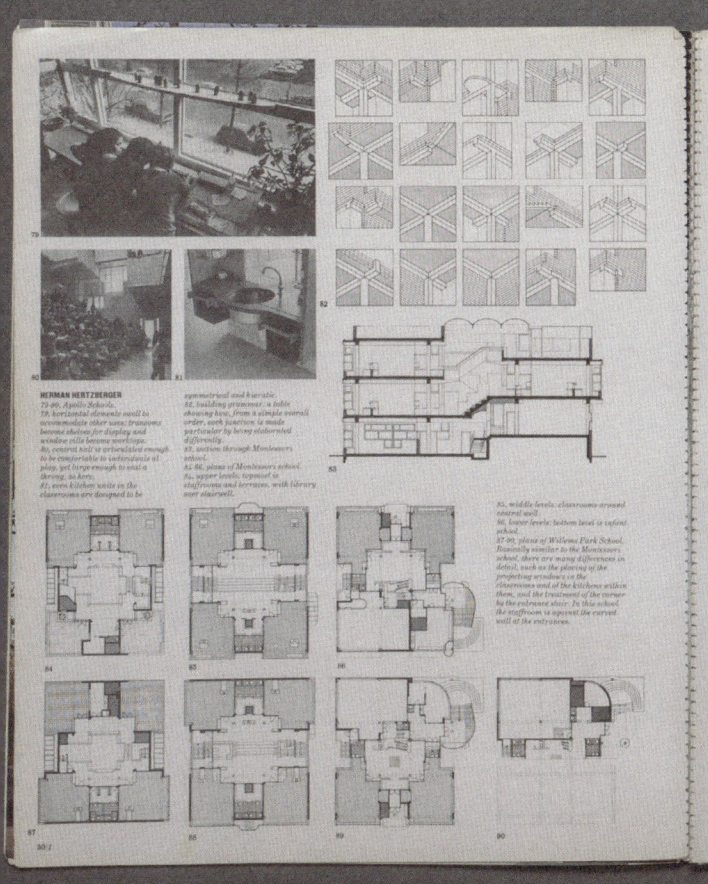

THE ARCHITECTURAL REVIEW

London, 1990

THE ARCHITECTURAL REVIEW

London, 1985

Herman Hertzberger (born 1932), Dutch architect, critical intellectual and humanistic anarchist, firmly believes in propagating the cultural importance of architecture. To date, he continues his struggle against the positivism of contemporary culture through impassioned writing, practice and the education of a younger generation of architects. The school type holds a special fascination for Hertzberger, and through his numerous designs he has made a significant contribution to the architecture of the children's world. The timeless qualities of his schools have set new standards for the relationships of users and the built environment. Holland, one of the most stalwart proponents of the welfare state, has a societal structure that reflects Dutch mercantile and land reclamation traditions. The national character is rational, pragmatic, culturally open, religiously tolerant and socially progressive. Moralistic soberness, economic shrewdness and political respect for democratic institutions create a homogenous, collective body that does not promote extreme ideologies. Hertzberger practices concurrently in accommodation of, and in opposition to, Dutch culture. However, through the prism of the Montessori subculture, he is selective towards the more liberal aspects of Dutch society. The Montessori pedagogical methods were established as a vision for a way of life, as opposed to merely being an alternative educational system. The Italian educator Maria Montessori (1870-1952) stressed the importance of an architectural environment in the development of childhood. According to her, 'children accept knowledge with all their physical abilities. Impressions do not only enter into their world, they also form it and become innate.'[34] Education is not something the teacher does, but a natural process that develops spontaneously in human beings: it is not acquired through word, but by virtue of experiences in which the child acts on its environment. The "prepared" environment is one that encourages the self-creating process of the child. In 1980, the authorities of Amsterdam South planned two primary schools with an identical program, albeit with different pedagogical systems, on Apollolaan, a wide green boulevard which is a major axis of the urban extension of the city planned by H. P. Berlage in 1915 (South Plan). In conceiving the plan, Hertzberger questioned the rigidity of structuralist design principles by a sensitive contextual approach towards the site. Responding to the requirements of division (the dissimilar educational methodologies) and unity (the massing of the site), Hertzberger developed two villa-like buildings. They continue the character of the urban residential fabric of Apollolaan, but architecturally they emphasize a striking transformation of the 1920s urban villa. The three-store compact volume of each split-level "villa" contains eight classrooms, a small gym hall, central hall and teachers' support space. The central, amphitheatrically shaped, atrium, with two free standing staircases, creates the schools' dynamic performance setting. This place-form, void as space of public appearance, is the spatial focus of all programmed areas of the school. The complex overlapping of the public and private realms and the spiral circulation movement are congruent with the progressive pedagogical methods of the Montessori movement. Hertzberger himself describes importance of the void as 'a movement (voyage) through space [which] is omnipresent... Children identify themselves with certain spatial situations which offer them a sense of security. Children take care of the things around them and build their own space and surroundings. There is a continual movement through the space, which offers free, intellectual and creative learning... Spatial qualities of the central half offer possibilities for individual work. The hall can therefore have a function of a large classroom. Steps can function as desks and each child can use these desks in his own way. The use is therefore not defined by the form.'[35] While designing his first school (Montessori Primary in Delft, 1968), Hertzberger developed a unique theoretical concept concerning the relation of an object to an individual: 'everything we make must be the catalyst to stimulate the individual to play the roles through which

---

34 Montessori, Maria (1965) Dr. Montessori's Own Handbook, New York, Schocken Books, 1965

35 Hertzberger, Herman (1986) Apolloscholen Amsterdam, Archis no.12

his identify will be enriched. A thing, exclusively made for one purpose, suppresses the individual because it tells him exactly how it is to be used. If the object provokes a person to determine in what way he wants to use it, it will strengthen his self-id entity. Merely the act of discovery elicits greater self-awareness. Therefore, a form must be interpretable – in the sense that it must be conditioned to play a changing role. It must be made in such a way that the implications are posed beforehand as hidden possibilities, evocative but not openly stated.'[36] This concept has been employed in the design of the interior elements of the "prepared" Montessori environment. Transitional zones and thresholds are enabling spaces for activities to happen. Montessori pedagogy demands environments that offer possibilities for different and simultaneous activities. Strict Dutch building regulations concerning the allowed square meterage of classrooms led Hertzberger to place a freestanding kitchen element in the classroom, and then extend the classroom space towards the central atrium. In the transition zone between the classroom and the central hall are small, individual workplaces for students. Direct contact between the classroom and the central hall is achieved by a horizontally divided door of which either part can be open or closed. A shelf by the door is provided for individual classroom exhibitions. Tiles painted by children animate the classroom window ledges. Similarly, a projection of the children's work is presented to the outside world: window mullions are crafted to accommodate the creative efforts of the pupils. In the nurseries, Hertzberger innovatively re-interpreted the transitional floor surface as a gridded series of wooden box-chairs. The exact uses of these elements are left to the imagination of children and teachers. Hertzberger's unique effort in the complete fusion of architecture and furniture defines a design strategy which proves successful in daily use. The colors in the exterior and interior of the school are extremely neutral (white, light grey and light green), providing a frame for the colorful world of childhood to flourish.

Conclusion

Terragni and Hertzberger, drawing on their respective cultural heritage as well as contemporary European theories on teaching methods, successfully realized approaches to the world of children through design. Both architects creatively transformed references from the rich heritage of modern architecture in the detailing of their schools, adding to the multi-valent readings of spatial relationships.

Terragni's design demonstrates that it is possible to satisfy the needs of children and contribute to their education by starting directly from the environment – from volumes, from light and from air. The considerable size of the glazed areas and meeting zones (the play areas and refectory) enables the children to enter into a dialogue with the world.[37] Through the play of light, poetic detailing, furniture design and spatial concepts; Terragni expressed an optimism and enthusiasm for the belief in children's abstract thinking. The Asilo presents a new school type, a sharp contrast to the heavy, static and stable representation of the Roman era. The codes and messages embedded in Terragni's abstract functionalism frame an environment conducive to the imagination and wonder of a children's world. The Montessori school of the Apollo Schools is the most intense and elaborates expression of Hertzberger's vision of the children's world. By following the basic principles of Montessori pedagogy, Hertzberger has created a space that is at the same time physically determined and programmatically undetermined – a space for children that offers possibilities for change, association and freedom. His "inviting form" strategy and the richly detailed physical structures allow for individual reading and interpretation, with the use of metaphors. The lessons to be learned from both architects stem from their drive for an ethical consistency and an absolute freedom of spatial experimentation. Ultimately, their visionary achievements reflect their utopian passion to confront the challenges in building the fantastic world of childhood.

---

36 Hertzberger, Herman, Montessori Primary school in Delft, Harvard Educational Review, Vol. 39, no.4.1969

37 Marcianò, Ada Francesca (1987) Giuseppe Terragni: opera completa 1925-1943 Rome: Officina edizioni

ORIS 68

Zagreb, 2010

Vedran Mimica:
Study Landscapes of
Herman Hertzberge

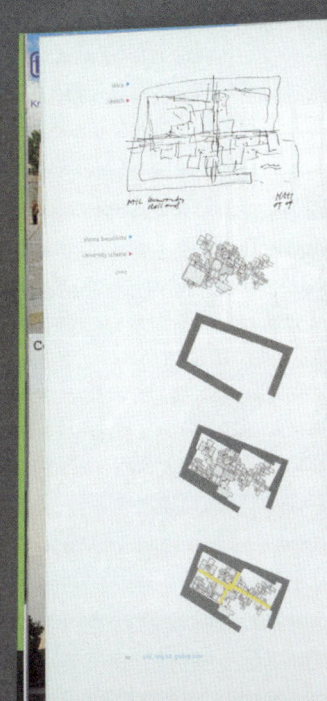

STUDIO '92 - '93 :
THE NEW PUBLIC REALM,
the Berlage cahiers 2

010 publishers, Rotterdam, 1994

Herman Hertzberger
Aldo van Eyck
Abe Bonnema
Max van Rooy
Royal Highness
Princess Maxima
Pierre Chareau
Bernard Bijvoet
Le Courbusier
Jean Nouvel

Herman Hertzberger
Elia Zenghelis
Eleni Gigantes
Toyo Ito
Thom Mayne
Steven Holl
Rem Koolhaas
Wilfred Wang
Ignasi de Solà-Morales
Kenneth Frampton

STUDY LANDSCAPES OF HERMAN HERTZBERGER

Published in Oris 68, Zagreb, 2011

To write about one's teacher's architecture is always sensitive, and probably also ungrateful. Nevertheless, to write about the phenomenon of Hertzberger is today certainly necessary, perhaps even more than in the time of the teacher's "golden structuralist" time, from the late 1960s to the mid 1980s.

I met Hertzberger for the first time in Delft in 1983 as a postgraduate student with a scholarship from the Croatian Ministry of Science. Stipe Šuvar was the minister at the time.[38] I remember, as if it were yesterday, that I waited impatiently for my first meeting with my mentor on the fourth floor of the former building of the Faculty of Architecture in Delft which burned down in fire a few years ago. After I presented my portfolio and the work of my professors Neven Šegvić[39] and Božidar Rašica[40] (Hertzberger was extremely impressed by their scope of interest), his first question was related to the basics of the Western European culture. I attempted then, in my broken English, to make connections between Aristotle and Leonardo da Vinci, and the French Revolution and the Encyclopaedists. Professor Hertzberger observed all this with a slight frown and interrupted me with the sentence, "The basis of Western European, and especially Dutch culture, lies in the organized quality of society." And this was how twenty-eight years of my "companionship" with Hertzberger began. You could learn from Hertzberger that anarchy and humanism are in no way separated discourses. That structuralism helps in the effort to truly understand the world. That "content" is significantly more important than "form", and that the structuralist notion of "spatial possibilities" can be interpreted in terms of architecture as a spatial frame in which users will influence a constructed space. That the educational environment can be a true nursery of new ideas for changing the status quo, and that we never should give up the possibility of creating new worlds in which we will all be able to recognize one another, instead of only some of us. And finally, that you should never stop listening attentively to new generations: their ideas, and reasons for radical change of the existing.

And so, Hertzberger as a humanist, anarchist, architect and teacher has tirelessly been building the foundations of a unique cultural phenomenon for more than half a century; to be more precise since 1959, when Aldo van Eyck invited him to the editorial board of Forum, the Dutch part of Team 10. Related to this professional involvement, the Berlage Institute, which he established in 1990, represents perhaps the most important aspect of his mission in education.

Hertzberger was introduced to the Croatian architectural scene through a series of seminars, lectures and exhibitions. The 1986 exhibition in Zagreb's Museum of Arts and Crafts, the 1988 INDESEM (International Design Seminar) in Split's Diocletian's Palace, The Frames of the Metropolis in Zagreb from 1995, as well as his "return" to the Palace in the form of the 1996 seminar "Split 1700+" should be singled out. My humble person was tremendously lucky and given the true privilege of spending almost 12 years in an intense exchange with Hertzberger as the mentor and teacher, in every aspect of architectural and human activity.

---

38 Stipe Šuvar held a title equal to the minister of culture and education of the Socialist Republic of Croatia (then a part of the Socialist Federal Republic of Yugoslavia) from 1974 to 1982. From 1988 to 1990 he was a member of the Presidency of the Socialist Federal Republic of Yugoslavia.

39 Neven Šegvić (1917-1992) graduated from the prestigious Academy of Visual Arts in Zagreb, where Drago Ibler conducted a Masterclass in Architecture. PhD in Architecture in 1975. The UHA (Association of Croatian Architects) annual award for criticism, scientific and theoretical work, established in 1996, was named after Neven Šegvić. Source: Uchytil, A., Barišić Marenić, Z., Kahrović, E., eds. (2009) Leksikon arhitekata atlasa hrvatske arhitekture 20. stoljeća. Zagreb: Arhitektonski fakultet Sveučilišta u Zagrebu

40 Božidar Rašica (1912-1992) was born in Ljubljana and studied in Rome, Belgrade, Warsaw and Zagreb. Worked as an independent architect, but also as a professor at the Faculty of Architecture of the University of Zagreb. Awarded for his architectural achievements, he was also a member of the famous EXAT 51 Group of architects and visual artists. Source: Uchytil, A., Barišić Marenić, Z., Kahrović, E., eds. (2009) Leksikon arhitekata atlasa hrvatske arhitekture 20. stoljeća. Zagreb: Arhitektonski fakultet Sveučilišta u Zagrebu

Today, Herman Hertzberger is a vital seventy-eight-year-old who goes to work in his Amsterdam office every day. The office has always been the second, or often also the "first" family for Hertzberger; it is the place where his numerous associates spent their entire active lives starting in 1958. Hertzberger truly believed that neither he nor his office would "survive" the 1990s, and that they would simply be left without new commissions. Exactly the opposite happened: the need for new public programs, schools, museums, community centers, but also office buildings for the galloping Dutch and German economies in the mid 1990s and at the beginning of the millennium did not allow Hertzberger to retire. It is interesting that the office was also given tasks to redesign and make extensions to some of their canonical realizations which created the image of the Dutch structuralism, like the offices of Centraal Beheer Insurance Company in Apeldoorn (1968-1972) and Vredenburg Music Palace in Utrecht (1973-1978). These are exactly the tasks on which the office of Herman Hertzberger built a platform for their activities from the 1990s to the present time.

Space for this contribution does not allow analysis of "poststructuralist" activities by the office during last 20 years; therefore we will focus on the NHL (Noordelijke Hogeschool Leeuwarden) building as perhaps the most representative instance of recent production by the office.

NHL University is located in Leeuwarden, which is the capital of the Frisland province in the north of the Netherlands. Leeuwarden is a town with 95,000 inhabitants and, along with Grooningen, represents the most important urban centre in the relatively poorly inhabited north of the country. Leeuwarden was established in the 10th century, and it gained autonomy in 1435. In 1901, the town had 32,000 inhabitants. Historically, the most renowned inhabitants of Leeuwarden were Stadtholder William IV, Prince of Orange-Nassau, who was the sovereign of all Dutch provinces in the mid 18th century; M.C. Escher, the phantasmagoric painter from the beginning of the last century; and Mata Hari, the dancer and spy from the same period.

The first NHL building was designed by Abe Bonnema at the beginning of the 1980s. The building was opened in 1984 for the needs of the technical college. Abe Bonnema was born in Frisland and was one of the most significant architects of his generation (1928-2001). As a student in Delft during the fifties, he manifested an inclination for functionalist language under the influence of van den Broek, and post-war Netherlands was at that time constructed in this style. Bonnema was a neo-Miesian architect, meaning that "less means more", and he designed "well-oiled machines" for living and working. Max van Rooy described Bonnema in one phrase as: Friese no-nonsense bouwer (a no-nonsense builder from Frisia). Bonnema's most significant works are his own house in Frisia, in Hardengarijp, from 1963 and the Delftse Port office tower for Nationalle Nederlander, an insurance company in Rotterdam, from 1992 which is still, along with the Erasmus bridge by Ben van Berkel, the main icon of Rotterdam's urban landscape.

It is interesting that Bonnema's design for NHL is under the influence of Dutch structuralism, in other words, of van Eyck and Hertzberger's architecture of school buildings from the 1960s and 1970s, which is surprising in relation to his entire opus. In his lecture at the Berlage Institute in 2009 when he was describing the history of his involvement in the NHL University project from 2004 to 2010, Hertzberger mentioned that students often used to approach him with the magazine in which this building had been published and ask him for his autograph, being totally convinced that he was the author of that building.

On that occasion, he also mentioned that the management of the new university in Leeuwarden also thought that his office should be commissioned for the extension of the building on the basis of the European tender since he would execute the task "most naturally."

The project task required preservation of the existing building of 20,500 m² and an additional construction of 21,500 m². This enlargement to almost 42,000 m² was the result of a fundamental change in the structure of the University of Leeuwarden which became the centre of a new international European university institution, thus creating the Kenniscampus (Campus of Knowledge) in collaboration between NHL and the Catholic University of the Netherlands (CHN), Van Hall Institute (VHI), the town of Leeuwarden and the province of Frisland. Namely, many Dutch universities accepted the Bologna Declaration as an extraordinary opportunity to create new university programs at undergraduate level and a total internationalization of teaching. In practice, this means that NHL University can accommodate up to 10,000 students at the present time, that lectures are held in English, that students attend courses in the Dutch province from virtually the entire world, and that courses are organized on the principle of preparing students for clearly defined professions. NHL possesses a "menu" of studies that consists of 50 different programs within four institutes. These are the Institute of Healthcare and Welfare, the Institute of Technology, the Institute of Education and Communication, and the Institute for Business and Management Studies. The curriculum is based on "problem-based learning", instead of "subject-based learning" in which students acquire knowledge via a direct link to tasks which are real and related to practice. A significant part of study is spent on real tasks in companies, government and other institutions which all have cooperation contracts with NHL. In this manner, students acquire knowledge about professional qualities in the earliest phase of their graduate education which is necessary in the contemporary European labor market. Students are also allowed to choose a selection of 'subjects' from different programs, but within the same institute and in this way they 'design' their individual curriculum which enables a higher level of job competitiveness in the end, after completion of their undergraduate studies.

Since this model has shown remarkable results in many university environments in the Netherlands, the management of NHL commenced construction of a new integrated and united campus in 2004, with all the institutes on the same location. The project task therefore insisted on concentration on one location and creation of a new, modern and dynamic learning environment for students and employees. It required anticipation of state-of-the-art technology, like wireless Internet (Wi-Fi) in all spaces, modern multifunctional study areas, a café, a large canteen, a theatre hall, an Internet lounge, a big car park for vehicles and bicycles, as well as attractive exterior spaces. The entire investment was supposed to be realized within the sum of approximately 55 million Euros.

The building was ceremoniously opened by Her Royal Highness Princess Máxima on May 27, 2010 as part of a number of ceremonies under the motto "Education for Everyone."

It is interesting that Her Royal Highness did not bother the guests with her speech on the occasion of the opening, but merely "clicked" on the laptop and a huge screen displayed the following message: "I wish you success in your new beautiful building. Máxima."

Hertzberger's office spent almost six years in researching, programming, designing, and finally constructing the NHL University building. This process could not have been a continuation of the research which led to the structuralist language of the 70s, but is a clear continuation of the practice from the 90s which manifested itself as extremely successful on the occasion of the reconstruction and extension of Centraal Beheer in Apeldoorn and Music Palace in Utrecht. If this phase of the HH office's work ought to be given any "style" features, which is at present in itself rather awkward for any practice, then one could say that where Hertzberger is concerned, interest for "French Tech" prevailed during the 1990s and 2010s.

That is Hertzberger's indeed long-ago developed interest for one, almost uninterrupted, trend in

HERMAN HERTZBERGER :
EXHIBITION OF ARCHITECTURE

Museum of Arts and Crafts,

Zagreb, 1987

NEGATIVE GRADE

Marijan Vogrinec

press clipping
Zagreb, 1997

ORIS 68

Zagreb, 2010

French architecture which started with Henri Labrouste, via Auguste Perret, to Pierre Chareau and Bernard Bijvoet (Dutch collaborator of Chareau), Le Corbusier's realizations in steel, like Maison Clarte in Geneva, and ending with early Jean Nouvel.

Hertzberger would probably not agree, but the extension to the NHL University building in Leeuwarden seems to me a little bit like an homage to Abe Bonnema; here, he frames Bonnema's structuralist construction with a "well-oiled functionalist" frame.

Hertzberger himself will say, with a typical dose of somewhat false modesty, "We respected the existing building and wanted to make a modern, simple building around it."

It is almost as if Hertzberger is here having a "self-critical" conversation with his own influence on Bonnema and other epigones, who were perhaps not supposed to be impressed very much by the structuralist code from the 1970s. In opposition to this, perhaps rather stretched, thesis, Hertzberger's lecture Tracing Dutch Structuralism at the Berlage in 2009 should be mentioned. In it he explained that the basic concept of the extension of NHL was framing structuralist "cancerogenic" growth by functional reasons, in other words, by the possibility of extending individual institutes in the direction of spaces within "the frame", in their immediate vicinity.

Hertzberger's critique of Bonnema's building is primarily related to unclear communications within the structure of the building, to the "labyrinth-like fuss", as well as urban unrecognizability or appearance. The project strategy of framing the existing building presented the possibility of preserving the existing edifice almost intact, except for the space of the sports hall, and to be connected with surgical precision to the extension frame.

Exactly these places of connecting the new and old are the most important points of the new complex's organizational structure. The spatial operation is extremely interesting: namely, Hertzberger is here reminded of one of his favorite lessons, that of Diocletian's Palace. To be more precise, the points of connecting the new and old structures of the NHL building create a cardo and decumanus, and in this manner order and meaning are introduced to the organization of the new complex.

The office has, namely, accumulated a really true design experience which is no longer determined by the structuralist canons, but more according to the historical experience of architecture.

Hertzberger will emphasize that the process of "drilling streets through the labyrinth" represented a huge structural and financial problem; therefore, the 'streets' were finally given dotted skylights instead of long linear ones, which nevertheless provide sufficient quantities of natural light, while the floor surface is painted a bright yellow color.

Such a strategic design perhaps best speaks of the HH office in last 20 years.

The office has, namely, accumulated true design experience which is no longer determined by structuralist canons, but more according to the historical experience of architecture.

The next fundamental design intervention was the tectonic defining of the multi-storey frame structure. In terms of structural design it is a steel space truss which enables a free span of 12 meters without any supporting walls or pillars. Hertzberger will stress that this structure is an expression of his understanding of the notion of generic in architecture, where this notion enables an almost absolute flexibility of organization of a modern university program, but also a possible future change of program of the same building.

The space truss enabled extreme flexibility and transparency of the frame in a vertical sense as well. This is exploited through a radical elevation, in other words, separation of the frame structure from the ground floor on over more than half the area, thus creating exterior semi-public spaces of the university campus which open up towards the town's space and enable visual connection with the original NHL building.

The tectonics of the building also enables interior vertical linking of the first and second floors with the ground floor, thus creating spectacular three-storey terraced study landscapes, as well as three-storey streets, illuminated by zenith light. Here, the HH office again uses their incredibly rich experience in the construction of more than twenty school buildings in which they have used – starting with the 1983 canonical project of the Apollo, Montessori and Willemspark Schools in Amsterdam – the "split-level" organization of the school's vertical space, as well as multi-level spaces of school auditoriums, forums or, as Hertzberger calls them, "educational landscapes". However, mere creation of such spaces is not sufficient for their programmatic and educational use. Hertzberger will point out that the careful articulation of "space units" within the large multi-level central spaces is needed. The articulation here includes creation of "spatial units" as structural elements for free use on the part of users. The office pays special attention in realization of the "spatial units" to the design of furniture, partition walls, staircases, and use of materials and colors. The "spatial units" should on one hand enable focusing on studying which mostly means "interface", computer screen, but also a view of the real world. In this manner, a space for studying close to the concept which Maria Montessori within her pedagogy called a "prepared environment" was created. Hertzberger developed this concept of use of didactic aids in classroom spaces towards a total educational environment and projected it especially towards semi-public educational landscapes (semi-public spaces in front of the very classrooms). From the very beginning of his practice in constructing school buildings, from the Montessori elementary school in Delft (1960-1966), Hertzberger has insisted that the most important spaces for studying lie precisely on the boundaries, the thresholds between the space of classrooms and corridors, and between classrooms and exterior spaces.

In the NHL building, the space of the three-level terraced educational landscape in the southern section of the edifice clearly possesses qualities of a 'prepared environment', but it also possesses an almost theatrical quality. Kenneth Frampton, in his text on the Apollo Schools in Amsterdam, notices that Hertzberger's architecture, through the creation of semi-public central forums, amphitheatres, and spaces of 'public appearance', is a criticism of and response to the disappearance of such spaces in our contemporary urban environments.

After the presentation of NHL in the already mentioned lecture, Hertzberger also presented the building of the Dalton Secondary School in Dordrecht, where he used similar design methods in the design of the edifice's central interior street. As a reference and inspiration, he showed Dubrovnik's Stradun, or 'Placa', as the clearest example of a street which structurally determines a town or which, according to Hertzberger, is in fact "the structure of the town".

Hertzberger will tirelessly emphasize the importance of the notion "content" in relation to "form", where the "content" of a space is in fact a social situation or relational situation of human activity and architectural space. I dare claim that it is possible to critically observe Hertzberger's work during the last 50 years solely within a discourse which is defined in this manner.

To all who are truly interested in the construction of educational landscapes, I can give only one piece of advice: visit NHL and/or other educational edifices by the architectural office HH and you will enjoy, without much theoretical effort, in a unique architecture which creates spaces of true cultural value and educational imagination. Google will not help you here; you yourself have to be in the space, in the actual space. And best of all, as a "student."

FIELDS : THE BERLAGE CACHIERS 5 :
STUDIO '95 '96

010 Publishers
Rotterdam, 1997

PROSPECTUS '97 '98 (1999 - 2000)

Postgraduate Laboratory of Architecture
Berlage Institute Amsterdam

Amsterdam, 1997 and 1999

Peter Smithson, 24-10-1995 Alejandro Zaera-Polo, 23-4-1996 Kazuo Shinohara, 23-10-1995

Felix Claus, 12-3-1996 Kees Kaan, 12-3-1996 Silvia Kolbowski, 11-10-1995

John Körmeling, 19-3-1996 Hani Rashid and Lise Anne Couture, 14-11-1995

Mels Crouwel, 11-1-1994 Ignasi de Solà-Morales, 3-5-1992 Raoul Bunschoten, 31-10-1995

Prospectus '97 '98
the BERLAGE institute AMSTERDAM
postgraduate Laboratory of Architecture

Prospectus 1999 2000
the BERLAGE institute AMSTERDAM
postgraduate Laboratory of Architecture

THE BERLAGE INSTITUTE

Interview with Vedran Mimica by Miodrag Mitrašinović, published in the magazine Communication, Belgrade, January 1992

The Berlage Institute is a postgraduate school of architecture without a real faculty, tenures, hours, typical hierarchy, and exams. When you graduate, you do not get a scientific degree. It is a school in which you can have your coffee and a chat with Kenneth Frampton, Herman Hertzberger, Rem Koolhaas, Alvaro Siza, Tadao Ando, Georges Descombes, and Renzo Piano. And these architects are only a fragment in the line of visiting teachers from all over the world.

Miodrag Mitrašinović Judging by my brief stay at the Institute and everything I read about it and heard from you, it looks as though these visiting teachers provide essential help to students in solving the tasks at hand. In other words, it is the selection of guests that influences the participating students' education and the way of thinking.

Vedran Mimica Yes, exactly, this is one of the most important aspects of the Institute.

Q Considering their short stays at the Institute, how much knowledge and experience can they actually pass on to the students? And what are the selection criteria for the visiting teacher?

A A few months ago, Aldo Van Eyck witnessed our discussion about who should and could be invited to teach. He joined in saying that it does not really matter who you invite but who you do not, so he proposed that the Institute should put up a plaque at the entrance with the names of architects who should not be entering. He named a few: Eisenman, Tigerman, Graves, Rossi, and Bofill. Of course, this was an allusion to his famous article: "What Is and What Isn't Architecture; à propos of Rats, Posts and Other Pests (R.P.P.)", published in Lotus International in 1981. What he probably meant is that people who were championing the "modern project" had probably no reason to be at the Berlage, unlike those who questioned it and sought to transform it into something new, using modern means. Bottom line, it is all about two generations of architects. One generation is represented by the architects such as Giancarlo de Carlo, Henri Ciriani, Alvaro Siza, Renzo Piano, Otto Steidle, Kristian Gullichsen, and Oriol Bohigas and the other generation by mostly Dutch architects such as Rem Koolhaas, Wiel Arets, Kess Christiaanse, Arne Van Herk, and Willem Jan Neutelings. The profile of our visiting teachers and their visiting schedules reflect, in fact, their importance for architectural culture today. As a bonus, students get to speak with the architects such as Alvaro Siza, Renzo Piano, Tadao Ando, or Jean Nouvel.

Q Is there a kind of meta-structure that steers the progress through the education process at the Institute and is there a progress at all, in the sense of departure from one point and arrival to another?

A This is the fundamental question that concerns many interpretations of the world today, not only in terms of whether education is possible, but also in terms of whether the "modern project" is still possible. Does the idea of departure from one and arrival to another point, the dialectic of it, the positivism of the "modern project" correspond to the contemporary context at all? This fundamental question not only concerns the present moment, but the future even more so. In as far as it is built today, perhaps, but is it modern in the way "Modernism" was modern in the 1920s, 30s, 40s up to the 1980s? I think that after 1984, the Netherlands and the world saw a paradigmatic breakthrough that has fundamentally shifted the perspective of architecture, especially in the light of Jean Nouvel's, Bernard Tchumi's, Toyo Ito's, and the latest OMA projects (I particularly refer to the Paris National library competition). We can hardly speak about progress from one point to another any longer. But let us stick to education. The Berlage is multifaceted: one facet is that it is a school with students and teachers, the other that this is an institute with architects who collaborate.

Q The next Master Class is more theoretical, and will be run by Kenneth Frampton. I would like to know how much attention the Institute pays to the theory of architecture. You mostly hear of projects, designs, and drawings as the starting points for discussions about architecture, but do you draw an imaginary line between theory and practice?

A Theory and work on it have been closely associated with design. We spend a lot of time investigating how a certain idea that leads to a building is put into a concept. How that concept is derived, what is its cultural and social background, what context does it spring from, to what extent it is global or local, how it relates to a project – all this has to do with theory. To make it perfectly clear, the school does not distinguish between theory and practice. But when Frampton first came to the Institute, he conducted an interview with the students to see how familiar they were with the theoretical fundamentals of the 19th and 20th century architecture. He asked them about the relations between Vilmos Huszár and Gerrit Rietveld, between László Moholy-Nagy and Bruno Taut, and between Peter Behrens and Le Corbusier. The students had little to say, so he decided to start with a series of lectures that relied on his book Modern Architecture: A Critical History with a few updates on views and conclusions. This Frampton's first visit to the Institute left a strong impression on the faculty and the students, and he was asked to dedicate as much time as he could to teach at the Institute. This is when we started to talk about projects of a more theoretical nature and this is when The Other Moderns project started. It is the brainchild of Max Risselada and Kenneth Frampton and it looks into local interpretations of the modern project in Europe and the world. For example, Croatian Modernism between the two world wars or Nikola Dobrović[41] and Milan Zloković[42] in Belgrade were completely unknown to Europe. Our Master Class and The Other Moderns are complementing each other in an attempt to identify the criteria that would define architectural quality: what was the quality of architecture in the past and what is it now.

Q You told me earlier that you have no fixed working hours and no hierarchy, yet you still have a very precise and flexible motivating structure that never stops changing and upgrading itself. In this context, can you compare the Berlage with other leading postgraduate schools of architecture and say what distinguishes it from them?

A This is what we always ask ourselves at the Berlage. The students who have enrolled here could have just as easily enrolled at the Architectural Association or Cooper Union or the Frankfurt School, while Peter Cook was still there, or maybe to Düsseldorf, where James Stirling is now. The Berlage could not and would not fall in the steps of the AA or Cooper Union for the simple reason that we see no sense in recycling a successful model by other means. It would have been a poor head start. In addition, this model is not close to Hertzberger's view of architecture. A lot of people wanted the Berlage to be the last line of defense of ARCHITECTURE before it fell victim to deconstruction, to be the last obstacle to the downfall of Modernism. But this is not what the Berlage is; just take a look at the students' works. It is perhaps too soon to compare the Berlage with other postgraduate schools, because our first generation is still with us and we still have not published a single book presenting the Berlage projects. What is important at this point and what distinguishes this school is that it questions the existing architectural values and theories and seeks to arrive at its own view/conclusion of architecture in general.

---

41   Nikola Dobrović (1897-1967) was an architect, teacher and urban planner. He designed the building of Yugoslav Ministry of Defence, later destroyed during the 1999 NATO bombing of Belgrade. Dobrović left en extensive mark on Dubrovnik as well, which has been thoroughly tackled in the book Dobrović in Dubrovnik – A Venture in Modern Architecture (by Krunoslav Ivanišin, Wolfgang Thaler and Ljiljana Blagojević, published by Jovis, 2016).

42   Milan Zloković (1898-1965) was a Serbian architect, professor at the University of Belgrade, Faculty of Architecture. He was one of the founders of the Group of Architects of Modern Expressions (Grupa Arhitekata Modernog Pravca, GAMP), which existed from 1928-1934.

FIELDS : THE BERLAGE CACHIERS 5 :
STUDIO '95 '96

010 Publishers
Rotterdam, 1997

lectures

Distributions, Combinations, Fields

Stan Allen

Geometry lesson The diverse elements of classical architecture are organised into coherent wholes by means of geometric systems of proportion. Although ratios can be expressed numerically, the relationships intended are fundamentally geometric. Alberti's well know axiom that "Beauty is the consonance of the parts such that nothing can be added or taken away" expresses an ideal of organic geometric unity. The conventions of classical architecture dictate not only the proportions of individual elements but also the relationship between individual elements. Parts form ensembles which in turn form larger wholes. Precise rules of axiality, symmetry or formal sequence govern the organisation of the whole. Classical architecture displays a wide variation on these rules, but the principle of hierarchical distribution of parts to whole is constant. Individual elements are maintained in hierarchical order by extensive geometric relationships in order to preserve overall unity.

The Mosque at Córdoba, under construction over a span of nearly eight centuries offers an instructive counter-example.[1] In the first stage of construction, [c. 785-800] the established typological precedent was respected, resulting in a simple structure of 10 parallel walls perpendicular to the quibala, supported on columns and pierced by arches, defining a covered space of equal dimension to the open court. The directionality of the arched walls (toward the quibala) operates in counterpoint to the framed vistas across the grain of the space. The columns are located at the intersection of these two vectors, forming an undifferentiated but highly charged field. Complex parallax effects are generated as the viewer moves throughout the field. The entire west wall is open to the courtyard, so that once within the precinct of the mosque, there is no single entrance. The axial, processional space of the Christian church gives way to a non-directional space, a serial order of "one thing after another".[2]

By comparison with western classical architecture, it is possible to identify contrasting principles of combination: one algebraic, working with numerical units combined one after another, and the other geometric, working with figures (lines,

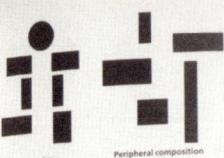

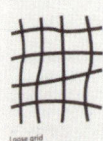

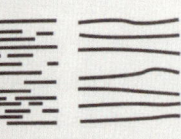

Axial symmetry   Peripheral composition
Patchwork 1   Field vectors
Loose grid   Felt
Patchwork 2
Striated

PROSPECTUS '97 '98 (1999 - 2000)

Postgraduate Laboratory of Architecture
Berlage Institute Amsterdam

Amsterdam, 1997 and 1999

Thanks to the Dutch architectural background, the Berlage has a fantastic privilege to have access to an incredible amount of the latest information about architecture. Our students keep abreast with projects and publications that have just been completed and released. Our communication with other schools and publishers is also fantastic, so everything that goes on at the school makes part of the latest architectural discourse. Our work suffers from no delays, no missed references to whatever has just been published. Of course, this is a bulk of material that physically cannot be processed entirely by using standard architectural methods based on the earlier education of these students...

Q You seem to be very pleased with what you do at the Institute, with your, not small, part in all this?

A One likes to find a place that corresponds to one's intellectual mindset and his views of life and work. When you recognize something that suits your way of thinking and hope that your way of thinking will contribute, then you can only feel lucky to be in the motivating environment such as this. This happened to me when I worked with Hertzberger in 1984 and 1986, and it is happening now. I have been part of the Institute since its establishment, and now I am deeply involved. How pleased will I be will greatly depend on what we manage to do during the first trimester. In other words, a project is measured exclusively by the resulting product, nothing else. If the product is good and the criteria that say it is good are high, the pleasure is greater. My position at this school is less important, and it is in fact an advantage when you are not important and you can still enjoy. The need to be important in order to enjoy is more specific to our situation back at home. Not to be important, that is, to be as important as anybody else, and to be able to participate means that you learn democracy on one hand and progress on another. These are the lessons that everyone could benefit from. This school is where you see Hertzberger's anarchistic humanism in its full splendor.

NEW PUBLIC REALM

Excerpts from The New Public Realm: Berlage Cahiers 2
010 Publishers, Rotterdam, 1994 (co-authored with Nicholas Dodd, Miodrag Mitrašinović, Vasa Perović and Kelly Shannon)

Introduction

The New Public Realm is an anthology of the Berlage Institute's work during the academic year 1992-1993. This document is a presentation of the studio work together with a partial record of other events, lectures, discussions and interviews that have made up the Institute's educational environment. As an international postgraduate educational institution, the Berlage Institute seeks to combine design practice with theoretical discourse. To this end, it intersperses the trimester long design projects with the short, intense Master Classes led by visiting international architects and teachers of stature and devoted to design and critical analysis. The overall didactic experience is complemented by a number of excursions. The first section of this publication, entitled Education of an Architect has been assembled here as a record of an on-going debate that was consciously initiated the last year. It took the form of a series of interviews with various protagonists, both within and outside the Institute, with colleagues and, above all, with visiting architects and lecturers.

The second section of The New Public Realm is a record of the various short and long term design themes addressed throughout the year. The design work for the academic year 1992/1993 reflects a multitude of fragmented architectural influences and ideologies. These seem to be succeeding each other with increasing speed and decreasing duration. The dissemination of information produces a situation in which no single theory or method of interpretation can possibly encompass the plurality of discourses. There is no longer a commonly accepted foundation for the production and representation of civic meaning.

The publication attempts to acknowledge the new civitas that results from the ever-increasing privatization of consumer society along with consequent instability of its programs. The projects presented here attempt to redefine the notion of the public realm and its architectural representation.

The projects are presented through six conceptual subsets which, in retrospect, constitute our collective reading of the "New Public Realm." These subsets are:

New Living Conditions – created by the above mentioned changes in the contemporary society with regard to their impact on the housing field.

Peripheral Territories – resulting from the notion of "dispersive" centers and the subsequent reclamation of vacant territories for development.

Urban Landscapes – created for metropolitan centers as a response to a recognized loss of the „natural," landscaped environment.

Media Culture – responding to information/media communication which is one of the most influential surrogates for the "public" realm.

Cultural Plurality – balancing of intercultural influences in order to maintain both the positivist aspects of globalization and site specific / local identities.

Utopia versus Reality – reacting to the conditions of the "global" culture by attempting to create a critical architectural interpretation of The New Public Realm.

The grouping of the design work within these headings is by no means absolute; it is merely a method applied for the purpose of identifying the subjects addressed by the participants as a set of generic responses to specific situations. Needless to say, the final form of these works has arisen as a result of observation and criticism from the visiting and permanent faculty. The third section of the publication is "Methods of Evaluation of Architecture," a selection of critical reflections on the 1993 Theory Master Class, "Tectonics and Representation in Public Buildings." This class was focused on the theme of the "poetics of construction" as this has manifested itself in public building works. Renowned public buildings from the last 30 years were comparatively analyzed. The criteria upon which to base such an analysis became controversial and difficult to determine in light of recent cultural change. This section also includes the Theory Master Class Lecture, "Polarities," by Colin St. John Wilson.

The results published here constitute a non-linear, non-chronological record showing the way in which we felt the need to respond to the overriding conditions and themes of The New Public Realm at the end of the twentieth century.

Education of an Architect

Things are not so difficult to do, what is difficult is to get ourselves in the right state of mind to do them.

Constantin Brancusi, quoted by Herman Hertzberger in his Berlage Institute introductory statement, September 1990

Over the past year, the Berlage Institute formally initiated a process of questioning the nature and methods of the international postgraduate architectural education. We have had to ask ourselves – what are the pedagogical and research procedures that would appear to be conducive to authentic architectural "invention?" This question has gained increasing urgency as we have come to realize the inherent limitations of maintaining the status quo, with its perennial emphasis upon product rather than upon process. We have also had to ask ourselves how to most effectively internalize our knowledge of the discipline. Thus, throughout the academic year 1992-1993 a series of in-house, public discussions and interviews were conducted between the participants and visiting professors. An anthology of the interviews has been assembled here in order to indicate the precarious state of contemporary education, particularly in relation to the ever-changing social and urban context.

FIELDS : THE BERLAGE CACHIERS 5 :
STUDIO '95 '96

010 Publishers
Rotterdam, 1997

edge field I core design-project Andrew MacNair & Hugo Schut 25

dynamics, models and diagrams

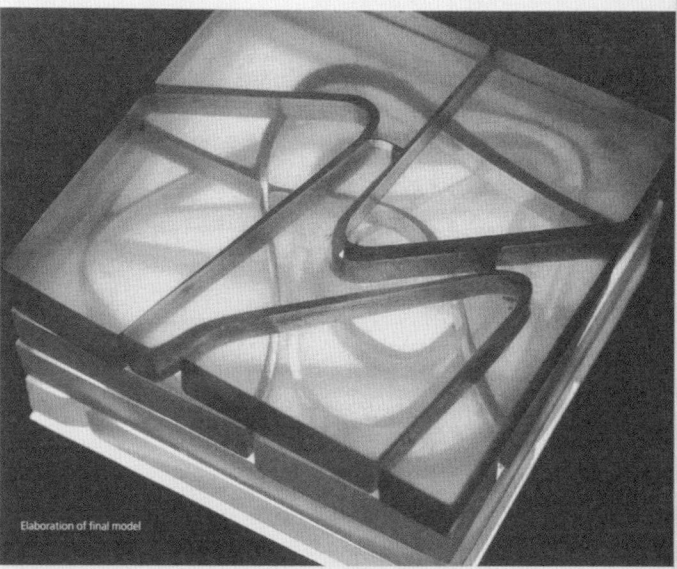

Elaboration of final model

New Living Conditions

The standards upon which we base housing today are the outcome of certain decisions made in Frankfurt in 1929 by the architects of GAM according to their concept of "existence minimum." This "existence minimum" has in fact become the norm, the standard applied to all housing. Housing is thus based on the strict economic priorities. This is the poverty of our contemporary situation.

Elia Zenghelis and Eleni Gigantes, BiA Lecture, May 25, 1993

Contemporary urban phenomena have been supported by technological changes. One of these changes is the telephone. Telephones have nothing directly to do with architecture, however, they change the way society works. This media destroys our traditional, concentric and hierarchical space. Twenty-four hours a day the telephone can invade space, whether the person likes it or not. This phenomenon should affect the plans of our houses. When a family is living in a house, the area or room which faces the community is commonly the living or dining room. However, because of the telephone, or the other media, each individual can now participate in society through his or her own private networks.

Toyo Ito, BiA Lecture, November 27, 1992

Are we at the "end of housing?" Is it time we begin to think of other ways of accommodating ourselves in order to adapt to these new conditions?

Herman Hertzberger, BiA Mid-term Review, November 1992

Housing typologies, as well as their corresponding urban morphologies, have remained basically unchanged since the Industrial Revolution. Lifestyles have changed drastically as a result of the rapid evolution of our post-industrial society, in terms of globalization of programs and cultures. The way in which Western cultures continue to build their housing stock, however, has not kept up with the scale and speed of these events. The contemporary condition is recognized as a complex structure of networks. The response to this reality, particularly in the design of contemporary housing, has taken distinct attitudes in terms of the relationship to this context. Several projects established systems of networks as extensions to megalopolitan "imploded infrastructure" situations, while others created sets of personal, closed-off environments, individual oases, within the distorted mental maps of contemporary cities.

Peripheral Territories

City space consists of two things, immovable buildings and roads; a mix of social and natural phenomena as well as invisible phenomena. This is the city that we actually feel and experience, not visually but aurally and tactilely.

Toyo Ito, BiA Lecture, November 27, 1992

The contemporary urban condition brings with it a series of consequences which are, I think, highly architectural. The first has to do with an absolute breakdown of the most basic notions of coherency. An understanding of the organism is no longer present. A part of that is the complete breaking down of any notion of boundary, of threshold, of inside and outside.

Thom Mayne, BiA Lecture, March 2, 1993

The conditions of contemporary civilization have radically changed and the traditional notion of "centering" has been lost. Political, socio-cultural and economic realities have instead shifted the emphasis towards a decentralized society. The mono-centric "organic" city has imploded, its traditional center being replaced by a multiplicity of (sub)urbs at its edge. The phenomenon of "ring-culture," a string of fragmented, individualized "centers" fed by the highway and by global electronic communication has virtually eliminated the requirement for physical, material centers.

In some instances, the "ring culture" was highlighted by interventions which qualitatively added to the context. Other designers devised new "tissue typologies," new spatial organizations on, along and under the "edge" condition.

Urban Landscapes

The urban condition represents the manifestation of the modern paradigm, the "metropolis"; one that we can define as a collection of infinite numbers of events, movements, objects, one which is based on information and an interactive society. It is this condition, which we have to come to grips with: its unknowability, its incomprehensibility. We understand this „metropolis" as an enigma and as something that is unstable and is understood by culture as a more-or-less accepted condition.

Thom Mayne, BiA Lecture, March 2, 1993

All seemingly natural places are subject to the same disciplines and rules as the metropolis, only in subtler and more organic ways... there is now really no difference between city and nature. There is only one universal, global framework with its subtle differences of degree rather than differences of kind.

Elia Zenghelis and Eleni Gigantes, BiA Lecture, May 25,1993

An architectural project is an operation within an existing context, a structure traditionally read as a physical, delimited and identifiable entity and as either "urban" or "natural." With metropolitanization and suburbanization, land reclamation and redevelopment, the ability to distinguish such absolute conditions within the contemporary situation is diminished. This situation suggests that the presence of an "outside" necessary is no longer necessary to delimit and differentiate a physical context as an "inside." This together with the proliferation of published information means that the external influences upon the context of a project are potentially limitless. With such an incomplete or ambiguous contexts and with the possibility of adding to such new contexts by fragments rather than by making tabula rasa beginnings, the projects express the current range of possibilities, between being "readings" or "outside impositions" laid over the situation or of being suspended between places of "human appearance" and the organization of autonomous systems. The recognition of this equalization and loss of "limits" prompts the investigation of new structures capable of accommodating the indeterminate variables of human life, nature, density, void, infrastructure, technology, economy, programmed and non-programmed space.

Media Culture

Architecture might become more about showing memories of the media-explosion phenomenon; it might become something that simply transmits information. Buildings might transmit phenomena, images of movement, of "running" through the city. How to make a physical building from such images and experiences is the question that architecture is facing today. My belief is that it is now best to describe ourselves as a community of nomads in the world of media.

Toyo Ito, BiA Lecture, November 27, 1992

As the study of essences, phenomenology seeks to ground experience in perception. This is potentially a very fruitful territory for architecture, because in a certain way it has the power to put essences back into existence. For my Palazzo del Cinema competition in Venice the concept stemmed from the belief that time could be the connection between architecture and cinema. Architecture can never win against cinema, film being a media so much more powerful.

Steven Holl, BiA Lecture, May 28, 1993

The impact media is having on contemporary society and culture has been investigated through various projects. The fascination with images inevitably influences the very nature of our culture, and of our architectural raison d'être. From large cinematic cultural centers to small fair pavilions and exhibition installations, a non-phenomenological approach has been taken in order to recognize and analyze the essence of the immaterial, the media, the message and the image, as design pedagogy. Today, the relationship between a human being and its environment has become defined more by the "visual" (id est image, sound and color), rather than by the "tactile."

One of the values of this work is its "contemporaneity," its parti pris in terms of trying to create an architectural narration which parallels the narration of the media and cinema itself.

Claudia Dias and Sven Grooten, *Lost Dimension*

FIELDS : THE BERLAGE CACHIERS 5 :
STUDIO '95 '96

010 Publishers
Rotterdam, 1997

seminar Silvia Kolbowski 45

Takeo Ozawa and Rajan V. Ritoe,
The Complex Meaning of the White Wall

rchitect as a literal facilitator of social interaction and alleviator of alienation. The rogramme's demand for "an architecture 'vocabulary', informed by aesthetic / terary strategies, rather than the other way around" was formulated so as to dicate the necessity of recognising that each profession works within given social nd disciplinary limits at any moment in history. While these limits can and should be tretched at any given time in order to attempt social critique, it was recognised that isregarding these limits in a more comprehensive way can make the interventions hemselves invisible to established social modes of perception and interpretation.

Lost dimension. The lack of comparable scale The projects lustrated here show two very different ways of interpreting the terms of the rogramme. Claudia Dias and Sven Grooten, identified a "neutral" urban site as an d-hoc one lacking scale (the unprogrammed, yet heavily utilised space between a rain station and a major office high-rise), and chose to superimpose an indexical sign f recognisable scale (crosswalk graphics). This intervention into an urban site was hen documented from above rather than at eye-level, and projected against the loped underside of the stair in the underground, and little-used, bicycle storage pace of the Institute, creating distortions of scale in the images, and physically ontorted viewing positions. By bringing together an unprogrammed yet heavily ccupied site with programmed, yet scarcely used space, this project highlighted, in a ubtle yet distinct way, the social 'neutrality' of the various spaces involved, as well as he representational dimensions of the sites, and of the modes of documentation nd presentation.

The meaning of the white wall The project by Rajan V. Ritoe and Takeo Ozawa utilised a very different methodology, insisting on a very literal interpretation of "white wall" and a very broad identification of urban site / object as the city itself. But they inverted the terms of the programme. By bringing the wall to the city, and utilising the inherent framing capacity of the video camera, echoed by the way in which the "white wall" created a hole, or an absence, in each frame, they were able to highlight aspects of urban space and inhabitation which are normally overlooked. They were able to use the video camera to collapse the space of the city into sequential frames which de-emphasised the more typical gestalt experience of such spaces and programmed activities. Their choice of specific sites – such as the edited contiguity of museum and highway – served to re-present the city within the content of the programme's call for the inscription of the institutionality of "white" spaces.

First & Second Year Studio / Seminar / Winter 1996
Guest professor: **Silvia Kolbowski** *Studio Tutors:* **Roemer van Toorn, Vedran Mimica**
Participants: **Eddy Arinto, Seong-lok Bae, Martina Cafaro, Niall Cain, Penelope Dean, Claudia Dias, Northon Flores Troche, Marie-Paule Greisen, Sven Grooten, Jan Richard Kikkert, Volker Mencke, Takeo Ozawa, Wim Poppinga, Chris Rankin, Rajan V. Ritoe, Madir Shah, Igor Stipac, Dan Stuver, Keisuke Tamaru, Peter Trummer, Sofia Vyzoviti, Dimitri Waltritsch, Anna Webjörn, Christine Yadlowsky, Carlo Zavan** *Critics:* **Silvia Kolbowski, Vedran Mimica, Roemer van Toorn**

Cultural Plurality

The different interpretations of reality that we make, reflect qualitative differences between Northern and Southern Europe, in Northern Europe there exists a tendency to see reality as a regrettable accident; as something that used to be better and that is now going badly. Therefore, in the north there is the worry about impending disasters - we are heading towards self extinction. In the south, it is believed that the north has a very enviable reality. However, reality there is quite often squalid but nonetheless seen as possessing quality — as going forward.

Elia Zengelis, BiA Interview with N. Dodd and N. Joustra, May 22, 1993

I regard the hyper-activity of the hybrid culture as the 21st century phenomenon which is positive... I am not so excited about mono-cultured societies; instead I find the intellectual and poetic potentials of many cultures co-existing more exciting.

Steven Holl, BiA Interview with N. Dodd and N. Joustra, May 5, 1993

> The international character of the BiA adds to the depth and variation of cultural, ideological and architectural influences. When different cultures meet, the confrontation may generate various reactions. The globalization of contemporary society coupled with the quickly expanding communication network, makes mediation between contemporary socio-cultural conditions and the identity of individual cultures a crucial issue for architectural design. The way in which architecture may mediate between the conflicting forces of global and "regional" identity, has been strongly emphasized.

Utopia versus Reality

"Architecture is about moving intelligent articulation into the work and ultimately the work has to have that articulation, otherwise one is merely a programmer or a critic."

Thom Mayne, BiA interview with T. Corsellis, March 3, 1993

Architecture is monstrous in the way in which each choice leads to the reduction of possibilities. It implies a regime of either/or decisions, often claustrophobic, even for the architect... Many of our recent and not so recent projects have been investigating how to deal with the fatalities of architecture to exclude possibilities and reduce possibilities. We have been struggling with how to create a situation of programmatic instability in a situation where programs are not very clear and how, under these circumstances, it might be possible to still generate an architecture that is different from a stable architecture; in other words, how we can find a way of developing an architecture which deals with programmatic instability without becoming a victim of it.

Rem Koolhaas, BiA Lecture, May 28, 1993

We cannot escape from our culture – that is a Utopia. The only thing we can do is to make it work, rather than destroying it. With our culture, we can let it destroy us or we can address it in creative ways. These alternatives always exist. It is not inevitable that our culture will ruin us.

Elia Zenghelis, BiA interview with N. Dodd and N. Joustra, May 22, 1993

The distance between "Utopias" and "realities" is rapidly diminishing, due to the media/image impact on contemporary perception of "reality;" everything is possible and accessible via the excesses of communication. The search for new "Utopias" becomes a critical means, with the primary drive of broadening the gap between perception and reality. The radical character of these projects occasionally escapes the particularities of its locality and addresses more global issues, often within a critical framework. The projects presented invariably led to heated discussion during their reviews and were powerful in their inspiration. The conditions of society were questioned and alternative forms and expressions were made with the aim of creating a critical discourse. The projects which follow explored the notion of design as a research with two basic approaches. The first set of projects is on the "border" of the architectural domain; they manipulate with the means of communication (the text, the word and the simulation) in the critical questioning of the nature of architecture. The second approach directly exercised "Utopia" as a formal expression of contemporary programs. The new modes of organization and composition of these forms and programs work with the belief in creating new social networks.

Evaluation of Architecture

Architecture is a practical activity; the theoretical moment comes after a building is finished, not to light up the future, but the past. That process starts with art and finishes with ethics, which has to do with judgment. Architecture does not make any sense without public judgment.

Wilfried Wang, the Master Class final discussion, BiA, March 1992

Architecture is a network. Empiricism of fact is the only way to find out what architecture is. The final aim of criticism is to understand the present time.

Ignasi de Solà-Morales, the Master Class final discussion, BiA, March 1992

Comparison is problematic because all of the buildings analyzed contained, to some degree, anomalies and contradictions, or what one may call "faults." In our "success obsessed" state such failures are not to be tolerated, and therefore they are simply regarded as not being of value.

Kenneth Frampton, the Master Class final discussion, BiA, March 1993

Our ability to be critical in a constructive sense is rather weak, not only because of the lack of common consensus and value before the diversity of buildings studied but also because of our inability to judge them all equally. In March 1992, the first theory Master class led by Kenneth Frampton raised the issue as to what are the qualities which throughout history have been the basis for a high level architectural production. An answer was attempted by asking a number of established critics to select ten canonical buildings from the period 1945 to 1992 (five from 1945 to 1968 and five from 1968 to 1992), and to give their criteria on which they based their selection. The participants also had to prepare an analytical commentary about the same ten buildings together with a number of substitutions of their own choosing. In the second Theory Master Class held in March 1993, the analytical focus shifted to the theme of the manner in which the public building has been articulated in this century by comparing the expression of its structure and the mode of its construction. It was suggested that the comparative criteria to be used for this Master Class should be derived from Gottfried Semper's essay The Four Elements of Architecture: the earthwork, the frame and roof, the infill walls, and the hearth. While the comparative criteria were deliberately limited, other aspects of the works that concerned the current crisis of the public realm cannot be adequately discussed solely through a consideration of their tectonic attributes. Many groups expanded the discussion so as to include questions of site, typology and spatial organization, in order to pose the question as to "what is the contemporary public realm, and how are its intrinsic values to be expressed?"

BERLAGE E

PEOPLE DO STILL LIVE IN SPACES
Zagreb 2002
2000 SHANGHAI: THE SPIRIT OF MEGA
Zagreb 2000
MID-SIZED CITY
Zürich 2008
NOT QUITE OBVIOUS DENSITIES
Zagreb 2004
ZOKA, I LOVE YOU
Zagreb 2004
THE MARSEILLE EXPERIMENT
Marseille 2003
A GOOD BUILDING MAKES YOU FEEL AT HOME
Zagreb 2013

CHANGERS

Edited by Nicola Schüller, Petra Wollenberg and Kees Christiaanse

Urban Reports

– Urban strategies and visions in mid-sized cities in a local and global context

In recent years, it has been increasingly evident that architectural discourse has become related to the inability of the architectural profession to form a clear idea about the contemporary city. This section features a set of texts documenting the journey of an educator, exploring the constant shifts in the quest to create knowledge through sensitive research and incorporate it into new forms of urban existence. Utopias of the future will be radically different from the Utopias of the past.

The Berlage Exchangers addressed the phenomenon of global urbanization focusing on public urban domains. The definition of public sphere has been continually recalibrated through advanced probes into both historical and emerging domains of urban life, and the multiple facets of contemporary urbanization including politics, culture and the collective memories of places. The discussion is extended into various scales of this global phenomenon, once again trying to understand the role the architectural discipline can play in the areas of complexities in contemporary transformations of the built environment. This chapter is especially thorough in addressing the challenges of a contemporary architect in engaging with the actual transformative forces of urbanization. Ambitions of contemporary architects to investigate new urban configurations come along with the ambition

to think with the larger environment, a reality which is now, at this particular stage of capitalism, organized more to follow the market. So, this chapter ultimately discusses the degree to which architecture can contribute to the face of urbanity and the emblematic appearance of the city while engaging effectively with different regimes of power.
The translation between the global and the local will be a key intellectual challenge for next generations of architects.

The society as a whole is increasingly aware of the strong relationship between the quality of the urban environment and the quality of life. As our lives continue to be influenced by urban networks and systems, the need to design new and different cities will remain, as well as the need to redesign the existing ones.

The chapter ends with an "exchanger" between Wiel Arets and myself in relation to almost twenty years of collaboration, first during the golden years at the Berlage and currently at Illinois Institute of Technology Chicago. In an interview form, both Arets' autobiographical and autodidactic approach to the practice of architecture and progressive social views about architectural education are revealed.

PEOPLE DO STILL LIVE IN PLACES

Published in Oris 14, Zagreb, 2002

People do still live in places. But because function and power in our societies are organized in the space of flows, the structural domination of its logic essentially alters the meaning and dynamic of places. Experience, by being related to places, becomes abstracted from power, and meaning is increasingly separated from knowledge. It follows a structural schizophrenia between two spatial logics that threaten to break down communication channels in society. The dominant tendency is toward a horizon of networked, ahistorical space of flows, aiming at imposing its logic over scattered, segmented places, increasingly unrelated to each other, less and less able to share cultural codes. Unless cultural and physical bridges are deliberately built between these two forms of space, we may be heading toward life in parallel universes whose times cannot meet because they are warped into different dimensions of a social hyperspace.

Castells, Manuel (1996) The Rise of the Network Society (The Information Age: Economy, Society and Culture, Volume 1). Malden, MA Blackwell Publishers.

After carefully reading Manuel Castells' words, we can stop deluding ourselves about the victory of the virtual over the actual, of the digital over the physical, and of networked spaces of flows over places. In the near future, and quite likely in the distant future as well, we will be finding ourselves in both worlds, the digital and the real, but we will have to be sure to build bridges between them. This text will focus on the actual, physical world of public urban spaces. It will address the changes and the influences on the civitas and on different manifestations of the public domain or the civitas in our times and in different cultures. Siena and Dubrovnik, Boulevard Haussmann and Tiananmen will belong to the past soon enough in terms of the requirements of the public urban life for which they were built. Although we are no longer attached to the public domain and space, we have not entirely forsaken our sense of belonging, of community, even if it means shopping malls, stadiums, airports, or the Internet. Bombarded with incredible technological breakthroughs, human nature, which has not changed much from Homer over Hamlet to Milan Kundera, needs and/or seeks the collective as a counterweight to the individual. In terms of urban life people will need public as well as private spaces.

Andrea Branzi accurately observes that, when it comes to the urban and domestic landscape, the ongoing changes are more of a mental than a formal nature. This does not mean that architectural and urban discourse should not respond to these changes, but that they need to be understood on a conceptual level before they can be responded to. This introductory article is my modest attempt to illustrate, through a number of examples, certain worldwide tendencies in the production of the urban landscape, and to find a concept for understanding the public urban spaces of Croatia.

Learning from Croatia

Historically, public urban spaces display, or in the case of Croatia, – "carved in stone," the foundations of the culture of an area. Perhaps it is going too far, but I dare assert that the basic Croatian cultures are dominantly urban, and that this urban historical infrastructure places us in the European cultural context, much more than, say, Vratoslav Lisinski,[43] or Marija Jurić Zagorka.[44]

43 Vatroslav Lisinski (1819-1854), Croatian composer, one of the champions of the Croatian nationalist movement. Note by the translator.

44 Marija Jurić Zagorka (1873-1957), Croatian writer and journalist. Women's rights activist. Best known for her pulp fiction. Note by the translator.

To make my point without observing the strict scholarly hierarchy and systematization, I will single out a few Croatian urban "wonders" which place our urban culture alongside that of the rest of the world.

The first "wonder" is the geometric prodigy of the historical city of Ston and salt works. Its "urban" and functional grid is superimposed on the town's own grid and represents a textbook example of the relationship between intact nature and public urban spaces through the abstract grid of the salt works. Urban settings such as this reveal layers of set values anticipating concepts of approach to a new construction which observe the spirit of the place. In that case, the spirit of the place or genius loci is not understood as a frozen historical category, but as a dynamic code (gene) anticipating considerations about new urban entities which reinterpret the historical layer. Thinking about the public urban spaces in this region today, the lesson of Ston, which is the lesson on the relationship between the landscape and the urban grid, as well as on the hierarchy of public urban spaces, simply must be learned.

The second "wonder" is Croatia's brand name – Dubrovnik, as communicated by CNN's New Year's world celebration broadcast. Stradun, or Placa, is the "ultimate" public urban space; it is an eminent, cosmopolitan and multicultural space of the economically and culturally sound Republic of Dubrovnik. In its urban essence, Dubrovnik is a very dense structural grid which has "produced" poets as well as civitas. The maths required to calculate urban density is simple: one should add up the square meters of the residential, business, church, and public spaces and divide it by the total area.

When in November 1991 Montenegrin paramilitary forces and Yugoslav Army Navy ships started to shell Dubrovnik, some European cultural and political circles realized that Croatia had been under attack all along. The irony is twofold, as both Europe and the war criminals have somehow realized that Croatian identity equaled urban, and that which was urban was Croatian. The third "wonder" is Split and Diocletian's Palace as the paradigm of transformation from the absolutely private (an imperial palace) to the absolutely powerful urban mix of public and residential spaces (a Croatian town).

The Croatian barbaric genius transforms one man's house into a town for five thousand people, and this is the premise for any discussion about public and private spaces in this corner of the world. The shift is creative, functional, and establishes a very sophisticated and dynamic relationship with the past. The best illustration of the earliest anticipation of Croatian modernity is perhaps St. Martin's church above the Golden Gate of Diocletian's Palace from the 6th century A.D.

The final "wonder" is Zagreb and its horseshoe-shaped green area. It is Milan Lenuci's[45] reading of Semper's Ring Strasse, a supermodern project freely placing public institutions within city gardens, as an ideal of the bourgeois understanding of the urban.

The Croatian historical urban palimpsest is an open textbook inviting discussion about the concepts of public urban spaces in the times of social transition. For as long as the Croatian economy evades absolute domination by global economic systems, it will be possible, and desirable, for new architecture to draw on concepts taken from our rich historical textbook. Once Croatia integrates with the global economy network, however, the ties with tradition will weaken and currently inconceivable concepts, strategies and urban projects will become conceivable under the logic of neoliberal flow of capital.

---

45 According to S. Knežević, an acclaimed architectural historian, Lenuci was the first urban planer of Zagreb, Croatian capital. He is most famous for his interpretation of the idea of the continuous park belt framing the city's center from 1883 (the year when a new regulation plan for Zagreb was issued, urged by the earthquake that had occurred in 1880) which today still shapes the popular green horseshoe form in the center of Zagreb.

URBAN REPORTS

Urban strategies and visions in mid-sized cities in a local and global context

eds. Nicola Schüller, Petra Wollenberg, Kees Christiaanse

Zürich, 2008

Mid-sized City, interview with Vedran Mimica by Petra Wollenberg

Manuel Castells
Andrea Branzi
Milan Lenuci
Ignasi de Solá-Morales
Burle Marx
Jon Jerde

Frank Gehry
Zaha Hadid
Coop Himmelb(l)au
Rem Koolhaas
Saskia Sassen
Richard Florida
John Urry
Mike Davis
Richard Sennett
Alejandro Zaera-Polo
David Harvey

ORIS 14

Zagreb, 2002

Vedran Mimica: People do still live in places

Barcelona, a breath of democracy

Barcelona set new criteria in the treatment of public urban space through democratic changes after Franco and through the Olympic Games project. As the main town planner, Joan Busquets successfully integrated the requirements of the Games in the master plan for the new Barcelona. He was followed by the chief Barcelona architect Oriol Bohigas who wittily integrated the Olympic program with the new infrastructure of the city. Barcelona's success story starts from the understanding of infrastructure as the motor of this emerging Mediterranean metropolis. While Ignasi de Solà-Morales was meticulously reconstructing Mies van der Rohe's Pavilion on its original site at the foot of Montjuïc, a group of young and super-talented Catalan architects were designing and building new city railway stations, bridges, garages, transferiums, cemeteries, and parks, and were redeveloping the existing public urban spaces. The spirit of van der Rohe's Pavilion floated over the drawing boards and computers of Enric Miralles Moya, Carme Pinós, Santiago Calatrava, Ignasi de Solà-Morales, Albert Viaplana, and Helio Piñón. The most representative public urban spaces in Barcelona have been designed almost as an extended living room in a flat of a an architect. Details, expensive materials and the design of the urban furniture have been given to the extraordinary attention. Stainless steel, granite, teak, and steel were used to make pergolas, lighting fixtures, benches, walls, and billboard supports. This gave both the new and the old spaces a new ultramodern abstract layer, putting a strong accent on the new democratic spirit of post-Franco Spain. This Barcelona phenomenon has been studied by Ignasi de Solà-Morales who writes about the character of public urban space and anticipates the new phenomenon of collective urban space. This space is neither public nor private, yet it is both at the same time. In other words, the traditional border between the two clearly delineated spaces, public and private, has become transparent. Solà-Morales speaks about traditional public spaces used for private purposes as well as of private spaces used for public purposes. This "uncertainty" in defining the public vs private is the result of the increasing commercialization of the public urban space. The basic feature of these "new" public urban spaces is their "mobility" and "interactivity". "Mobility" is a spatial feature enabling the use of public urban space by more than one user over the cycle of the day, whereas "interactivity" refers to the shaping of public space which invites people to use it in an active and dynamic way. Commercialization has contributed to the greater "mobility" and "interactivity" of spaces, and what is perhaps more important, to an increased city budget.

Rio, the green magic of Roberto Burle Marx

Roberto Burle Marx was born to a German immigrant family in Rio de Janeiro in 1909. His father took him to Germany to study music and letters in Berlin, where he first beheld the beauty of tropical vegetation in the greenhouse of Dahlem Campus at the Freie Universität Berlin.[46]

Only after his return to Brazil he embraced the irresistible beauty of his country's flora. Music and letters became his hobbies, while landscape architecture and painting became his true calling. Roberto Burle Marx collaborated with radical modernists of the Brazilian circle such as Lúcio Costa, Oscar Niemeyer, and Affonso Eduardo Reidy, who exerted considerable influence on his work. The Roberto Burle Marx Association designed over 2,500 parks, gardens, squares, and other public urban spaces. His perhaps most interesting project

[46] Habelschwerdter Allee 45 (the "Rost- and Silberlaube") and Fabeck Street 23-25 ("Holzlaube") together are the location of the largest university building complex in Dahlem. The complex houses several humanities and social science subjects, as well as 14 smaller departments from the Department of History and Cultural Studies. Various institutes and departments are spread over the Dahlem campus. The School of Business and Economics, the Department of Law, and the Otto Suhr Institute for Political Sciences are all situated near the Henry Ford Building and the University Library. North of Habelschwerdter Allee 45 are the Department of Mathematics and Computer Science, the Department of Biology, Chemistry and Pharmacy, and the Department of Physics as well as the John F. Kennedy Institute for North American Studies. Also included on the Dahlem campus is the 106-acre one-of-a-kind Botanic Garden containing more than 20,000 wild plants.

URBAN REPORTS

eds. Nicola Schüller, Petra
Wollenberg, Kees Christiaanse

Zürich, 2008

ORIS 14

Zagreb, 2002

Vedran Mimica:
People do still live in places

was the landscaping of a nearly ten-kilometer long waterfront in Rio de Janeiro. From Flamenco Park to Copacabana and Ipanema, there runs a border area of immense and pure beauty between the ocean and the city. Burle Marx succeeded in reconciling nature and the city in an unprecedented, and as yet unequaled, manner. His pedestrian areas dance with the samba, and his parks and gardens represent the Brazilian jungle. Combined with the character of Cariocas, the inhabitants of Rio, and their sense for public space, for living outdoors, on the beach, this concept reveals Marx's genius in its full splendor. The spaces of Marx's parks and public areas seem as if they have always been there and they are an integral part of one of the most attractive modern cityscapes ever created.

The Jerde Partnership and the theme city

Jon Jerde is the charismatic figure behind the Jerde Partnership International from Santa Monica, Los Angeles. He and his team of 150 people are the heroes of the new public spaces-linked exclusively with the consumerist culture. Try as I may to explain that any number of their mega shopping malls have been built in troublesome downtown areas, which in turn improved the security level of the neighborhood, that is, the crime rate dropped, the only reason for the ultimate success of their buildings is their fabulous consumerist reasoning. The thing is that the Jerde Partnership "patented" the "armature" as the basic operation method in the construction of the new generation of shopping malls. The "armature" is a total concept, transforming the classic suburban shopping mall into a multi-story crossbreed acting as a mall, car park, catering and refreshment area, theme park, multiplex, hotel, and above all an exciting and entirely themed public space. It would be too farfetched to describe this public space as completely urban, because it is run by the rules of the corporation, which built it. In the American case, public political speech is forbidden in such places, there is a special kind of policing and the rules of behavior differing from those in the city. The rationale is that these public spaces are secure, well lit, clean, pleasant to stroll in, have direct access to a multi-story garage, and above all, are completely open to commercial content.

Jon Jerde started his career by designing the visual identity of public urban spaces in Los Angeles for the Olympic games in 1984. He owes his success to thematizing the public urban space as a sports event, thus demonstrating that it can be successfully themed and that this operation is economically viable, as well as that everyone – politicians, developers, and the citizens – is more or less happy with it. As for the concept, the density and the complexity of the city are dealt with through a series of reductions pointing toward the meanings, which are in the exclusive domain of the marketing. Jerde continued his success story in Las Vegas, where he designed the Treasure Island casino as one of the first themed casinos with a reenacted sea battle between pirates and the English navy taking place on the lake in front of the casino four times a day. During our visit to Las Vegas, we had the misfortune to miss the show due to strong winds, which increased the risks involved with maneuvering full-scale sailing ships in the limited space of the lake. The most impressive works of the Jerde Partnership are the Canal City Hakata in Fukuoka, Japan and the Universal City Walk in Universal City, Los Angeles. Both projects date from the mid-nineties and both were incredibly successful, or as Jon Jerde would succinctly put it, "Fukuoka, big success, Universal Studio, big success", where "success" is exclusively measured by the profit earned per square meter of a business area (US$ per m^2). The key to this "success" is the public or semi-public space, which takes the visitor to the place of consumption. The "armature" method channels the visitors and the merchandise routes with perfect precision to reach every single corner of the center. One of the basic ideas of Jerde's "armature" is that prominent public content such as a multiplex is located on a higher floor to make visitors pass through spaces with stores, restaurants and other consumer "machines". The Jerde Partnership employs about 150 architects and designs shopping malls all over the world, including Europe, with its first completed buildings in Rotterdam and Hamburg.

Las Vegas – the triumph of the artificial

Three decades have passed since Venturi's and Scott Brown's charismatic book Learning from Las Vegas, and while their students were mapping signifiers on the Vegas Strip, juxtaposing the phenomenon of the sign with the phenomenon of the object, and clearly showing the sparkling Vegas-wise shift from modernist to postmodernist. The US developers, aided by figures such as Jon Jerde, created a metropolis with the fastest population growth rate in North America. The ultimate triumph of the city that is always on the move is the import of high culture, that is, the opening of no less than two Guggenheim & Hermitage museums which have been "carved into" the tissue of the new mega hotel-casino The Venetian. Both museums have been designed by Rotterdam OMA and through them Koolhaas established his controversial dialogue with the "devil" of radical American corporate mentality. With its Egyptian and Roman themes in the Luxor and Caesar Palace casinos, and city themes in Rio, New York and Venice casinos – the last with another reenacted form – Canal Grande and gondolas and Piazza San Marco and Duke's Palace; Las Vegas affirms the theming of urban content as the potential/future urban identity of developed capitalism.

However appalling this absolutely artificial and ahistorical method may seem to the European critical circle, the undisputed success of Vegas, Disney, and Hollywood indicate that themes will be more and more present in public spaces, even in the European urban context. How far are we from the horrid idea of accommodating a super shining casino Imperator in the cellars of Diocletian's Palace?

New Croatia: renaming of public urban spaces – lessons learned

Even though this issue of Oris deals with a series of successful interventions in the urban spaces of Southeast Europe, we must conclude that the past decade saw little besides the renaming of nearly all the major public urban spaces and their blunt commercialization in the entire region. New street signs were accompanied by huge amounts of green carpeting which "enhanced" the gray socialist asphalt and marked radical changes in the social and economic order. Renovations of public urban spaces, particularly of those in Zagreb, provoked surprisingly bitter arguments and protests from architects and art critics, less from the general public. However angry with the quality of interventions in the heart of the city we architects and art critics may be, it is as clear as a sunny day that the city center stages a lively parade of nouveaux riches displaying the latest sunglasses on sunny Saturday mornings while everyone else enjoys their coffee on terraces. It may be a little embarrassing to conclude that we architects did next to nothing to contribute to it, and that we are still waiting for quality urban landscaping to come this way and bring us closer to some European standards. To make such a project viable, Zagreb should rise to a new international dynamic level and be able to offer a high quality of life to the convincing majority of its citizens. To achieve that, it has to define and develop its strong points. We should be thinking about Zagreb in terms of the development – stimulating, attractive, hospitable, open and smooth-running place. To achieve that, it takes political engagement, the participation of citizens, and metropolitan architecture. If we embrace the idea that Croatian culture is based on the urban fundamental, and that urban life is the key descriptor of life in this region, then everyone will clearly see the importance of public urban space. What we need is the consensus of politicians, architects, developers, and the public on creating a new urban landscape in which the majority of our citizens would be able to recognize themselves.

2000 SHANGHAI: THE SPIRIT OF MEGA

Published in the magazine Čovjek i prostor, 1-2, Zagreb 2000

To get rich is glorious

In the early 1980s, as China barely entered the fourth decade of communism – a wink of an eye of 7000 years of its written history – Deng Xiaoping started to revise Maoism under a new slogan: To get rich is glorious. Soon this new political, social, and economic tide gave a fantastic boost to the development of Chinese cities. In April 2000, the Berlage Institute, an Amsterdam-based postgraduate laboratory, visited Shanghai for an urban research project, and this essay is about our first impressions.

To get rich is glorious was launched seven years after China's Great Shame ended its 150-year-long history that started with the Hong Kong occupation by the British Empire. Having won the First Opium War in 1842, Great Britain forced China to open five major ports to free trade. Hong Kong became a British colony, and Shanghai a free port under concession first to the British and then the French, Americans, and Japanese. Parts of the city came under the jurisdiction of concessionaires instead of local Chinese administration. Dual administration with two distinct systems – colonial and feudal – persisted from the end of the 19th century until the Maoist revolution in 1949. When Hong Kong changed hands in 1998, after 150 years of British rule, this dual system became part of one country. China clearly vouched not to mess with Hong Kong's turbo-capitalism and granted to it, instead, to act as a virus of changes in other Chinese cities. The concept was introduced in the so-called free trade zones with varying success, but in Pudong, Shanghai success was the most spectacular by far.

Chinese social laboratory

What is it all about? China wanted to avoid the pitfalls (in their own words) of the East-European transition, and decided to focus on a thorough economic shift instead of political. The post-Berlin Wall experiment that introduced free trade and parliamentary democracy failed miserably and was certainly not the road for China to follow. With its global ambitions, China in the early 1990s adopted the heavy-handed Hong Kong and Singapore-style capitalism as a model that could thrive in the highly regulated communist political environment, abandoning the old Leninist tenet that only social revolution could bring change to the relations of production. Instead, the slogan to get rich is glorious welcomed the widening social gap, but also the rise in standard for all, however unequal it may have been. To introduce capital or capitalism to a highly controlled economy, China needed partners and came up with another fantastic solution – diaspora from Hong Kong (which after the handover was diaspora no longer), Singapore, the US, Taiwan, and other Asian countries that were willing to invest. It was a momentary thing; foreign (yet Chinese) capital poured in the southern cities, which were ready to receive it, Shanghai in particular. In Shanghai, a point is always made by telling a visitor that Shanghai is not China but a Chinese social laboratory: the most liberal, the most democratic (whatever that may mean), and the most welcoming city in the country. How has this city managed to have a complete makeover in less than ten years (1991-2000)? What has drawn so much fresh capital to build millions of square meters for businesses and residences (over 10 million square meters a year for residences alone!), 300 kilometers of elevated highways running above the broader downtown area, two metro lines, a new airport, a stadium for 80 thousand people, renewed city center, a new opera house, new museums, new parks?

Oversimplified answers would be: China recovering from the madness of the cultural revolution and opening to the West; the mere fact that this is the most populated country in the world and therefore the most attractive market; highly organized and wealthy diaspora willing to invest into a safe and attractive new economy... Whatever the reasons, several players had a key role in it: consultants, developers, politicians, city planners, and architects.

Deng Xiaoping
Kurt C. H. Ho
Zhang Shao Hua
Jiang Zemin
Rem Koolhaas
Lou Oswald

Čovjek i prostor, 1-2

Zagreb, 2000

Vedran Mimica
2000 Shangay: The Spirit of Mega

40x40 METARA VELIKE MAKETE GRADA SA IZLOŽBE URBANOG PLANIRANJA U SHANGHAI-U. MAKETA PRIKAZUJE RAZVOJ SHANGHAIA DO GODINE 2020. U CENTRU SLIKE JE PU DONG POSLOVNO STAMBENA ZONA.

vedran mimica |→ ARHITEKT, DIREKTOR INSTITUTA BERLAGE U AMSTERDAMU, GOVORI O ISTRAŽIVANJU URBANOG RAZVITKA KINESKIH GRADOVA

shanghai - the spirit of mega

To be rich is glorious. Nakon samo 40-tak godina komunizma u Kini, što je sasvim zanemariv period u bogatoj, 7000 godina dugoj povijesti pisanih dokumenata, Deng Xiao Ping je kao reformator maoizma početkom 90-tih "pustio u eter" novi slogan: To be rich is glorious. Ova političko-socijalno-ekonomska promjena je vrlo brzo utjecala na fenomenalan urbani razvoj kineskih

Kurt C. H. Ho – developer

From what we have understood from a conversation with Mr. Humbert Pang (who works for FPD Savills, International Property Consultants as an associate director), consultants or investment and development experts provide services for investors and developers. They scan the market, identify developing potentials, analyze building programs, sound the political waters, analyze city planning requirements and programs for particular locations, and propose their own programs and terms of lease and sale. Big investors and/or developers can have their own teams of consultants instead of outsourcing, but the job description is pretty much the same. The process starts with a developer with a specific short and long-term profit in mind. Shanghai developers count on long-term profit as a rule; if they cannot buy land, they will take it in lease for 50 to 70 years, and run it as agreed with the city. Long-term is the kind of arrangement that determines their business strategy; there is no room for the take-the-money-and-run way of thinking. The idea is to keep the developer present (as a lessor) in a city with its buildings and programs for 50 to 70 years and to tie the profit to stable economic development. Developers have been the key players as they collect and bring money for Shanghai's modern development.

In the interview for the Berlage, the CEO of Sun Hung Kai Properties Mr. Kurt C. H. Ho (Kurt not being an unusual name for a Hong Kongese) said that he had been in Shanghai for three years and proudly presented his achievements that included several business and shopping centers. The buildings are typically Hong Kong-style and consist of several parking levels, a shopping mall and two to three-story galleries with luxury stores and a 40-story business tower with offices for sale or rent. Kurt explained his reasons for coming to Shanghai. Five years ago, Shanghai had only one such business center, the Portman Ritz Hotel and Business Center, which attracted the pioneers of the new Chinese business world like flies, being the single complex providing the electronic infrastructure (such as internet and e-mail) for online finances. The rent per square meter was about 4 US dollars a day, which translates to 12,000 US dollars a month for a 100 square meter office back in 1993, when China was still considered a backward country at the end of the world. This was a clear sign for developers who spoke Chinese and had good consultants that something big was going on in Shanghai and that it would definitely be their next stop.

Two billion people won't be wrong

If we remember that this is the country where the central TV news report on ribbon-cutting ceremonies on a daily basis, with local politicians witnessing to the achievements of our Party that leads us along the road to success, where President Putin is our dear and sympathetic friend, and where we are always right (the remark that even Rem Koolhaas picked up to conclude his lectures on China, probably impressed by Deng's slogans: two billion people won't be wrong), then there is no wonder that the Shanghai-type reformed politicians play an exciting part in the development of the city, juxtaposing their Communist rhetoric to the thundering advancement of global capitalism.

Even if there is something to the Eurocentric criticism, this type of homo duplex has definitely nothing to do with the newfangled Confucian theory and practice. The second hottest seat to the head of the country is that of the Shanghai mayor, who as a rule becomes the President of China. The case in point is Jiang Zemin, who enjoyed outstanding popularity as Shanghai's mayor. In the interviews we had with Hong Kong developers and consultants, they had only words of high praise for the top city politicians and planners and nothing but criticism for the communist red tape that requires obtaining over 80 licenses to build a single building.

City services

In this boiling economic pot, politicians hold the key to decision-making about those million-dollar investments that pour into the city budget. As the land is leased instead of sold, and annual income is measured in billions (exact figures are not available for the public), Shanghai too has taken the role of infrastructure and public building developer (such as hospitals, schools, museums, and apartments).

Residential standards have significantly improved over the last decade, from 4 to 8 square meters per capita. While still far below the European standards, this is an unprecedented leap in Chinese history. Political decisions about city development are therefore focused on the financial success, as only 40% of foreign investment in China brings profit.

Not that anyone is concerned about it; BDP is soaring – 10% every year – and every foreign investor thinks that this is the right time to invest in China, because profit will turn up eventually. Everyone counts on the corruption-free and open political environment. Who would ever have imagined that the high-stake, global capital would so depend on a communist government! And finally, this high-speed development cannot do without local planners and architects.

The Berlage paid a visit to the Shanghai Institute of Architectural Design & Research (Co., Ltd.) or, as the business card of its employees adds Formerly Shanghai Municipal Institute of Civil Architectural Design. In other words, the former monopoly holder has become a free-market research institute. The Institute's director Zhang Shao Hua explained to us that his institute employed 1200 people, including 500 architects, who competed for planning and design contracts for all types of buildings on the free market. One of their collaborative projects is the business Jin Mao ("golden prosperity") Tower, the tallest building in Shanghai and the third tallest building in the world. It has been designed by SOM Architects (Skidmore, Owings & Merrill), a team of renowned tower specialists, who won the 1992 competition launched by a state-owned company China Shanghai Foreign Trade Center (CFTC).

Jin Mao Tower is located in the Pudong/Lujiazui area, the financial center of Shanghai. With its 88 stories resting on a six-story platform it reaches 450 m in height. The first 50-odd floors are offices, whereas the floors above belong to the super luxurious Grand Hyatt Shanghai Hotel topped by a belvedere. Total floor area exceeds 270 thousand square meters.

Lou Oswald from SOM Architects described the collaboration between SOM and the Shanghai Institute of Architectural Design & Research as a joint effort that resulted in a fascinating experience in spite of communication and cultural differences. SOM won the 1992 competition because it offered a good project due to great experience in business tower design and very solid business reputation. The Shanghai Institute of Architectural Design & Research contributed with its knowledge of the local setup and all shop drawings and documentation for the contractors. Jin Mao Tower gave a boost to the Chinese steel industry, as all earlier towers were done in reinforced concrete. It took 2000 people to complete the tower, working three shifts, 24/7, from May 1994 to mid 1999.

Meanwhile, the designs and licenses for the new tallest building in the world are ready; the 94-story, 460 m tall Shanghai World Financial Center is the collaborative project of KPF (Kohn, Pedersen & Fox) and the "inevitable" Shanghai Institute of Architectural Design & Research. The impressive, recently launched permanent Shanghai urban planning exhibition, set in a new building at the main square just by the new opera house and the city council, showcases a 40x40 m scale model of the entire city. There, in the Pudong area, side by side with the Jin Mao Tower and the Shanghai World Financial Center, a new 500-meter tower is planned to crown Shangai's ambitions for at least 20 years to come. As the accompanying text puts it, the vision of Shanghai is that of an information technology city of the future. By 2020 it will catch up with the technological development of the developed countries. By that time, the city might fall out of the Berlage's focus of interest in terms of postgraduate urban research, but we are almost certain that globalism will find some new development formulas and conquer new territories. It only remains for us to see to what extent it will involve architects as a profession, for to be an architect does not seem glorious at all.

MID-SIZED CITY

Vedran Mimica talks to Petra Wollenberg about the mid-sized city.

Published in Urban Reports – Urban strategies and visions in mid-sized cities in a local and global context; eds. Nicola Schüller, Petra Wollenberg and Kees Christiaanse, gta Verlag, ETH Zürich, Zürich 2008

Petra Wollenberg During the symposium, we heard about the urban development strategies adopted by six midsized European cities. They have each found individual ways of dealing with similar problems and challenges resulting from global forces and special local circumstances. What do you think the advantages and disadvantages of midsized cities are in comparison with megacities?

Vedran Mimica When we are thinking about the category of mid-sized cities, it may be necessary to create categories according to the continents or regions involved. Mid-sized cities in China and India are obviously different from those in the European situation or definition. The advantage of such cities is that they can remind us of cities the way they 'used to be' – cities with a clearly defined center and a periphery, cities in which certain programmatic layers are still recognizable in the city-scapes. Mid-sized cities in Europe may still have a certain degree of social and cultural consistency, due to the way in which their institutions function. The disadvantages of mid-sized cities are that they are not really able to generate the critical mass of exchanges of information, goods and people on a global level.

PW Does this mean they are not really influencing the global discourse?

VM Mid-sized cities have hardly any influence on genuinely global discourses. However, it is useful to consider them, because they are very interesting case studies for the development of a critical approach towards megacity environments.

PW Are they capable of acquiring a special role in a globalized context?

VM Yes, they can acquire a special role in a globalized context, but only with socialized functions in terms of culture, commerce, or politics that would relate to the global context.

PW The impacts of the global phenomena such as migration, security demands, demographic developments, consumerism, tourism, etc., affect the urban development of cities on different scales. Which ones would you regard as being influential and significant for the future? What possible strategies are there for dealing with these challenges?

VM We studied the global phenomena in our curatorial work at the Third International Architecture Biennale in Rotterdam in 2007. We gave the Biennale the theme "Power: Producing the Contemporary City". In this era of globalization, the city is, more than ever before, a space in which cultural, economic and political forces interact, where various power structures and phenomena compete or collaborate in continuous evolution. This reality confronts us with the questions of who is producing the city and envisioning its future, and what forces are shaping its production. The twenty-first century is the age of urban migration and movement, a time when people – rich and poor alike – are flocking from south to north, from east to west, from country to city, in search of prosperity and security, as an inescapable part of existence.

The city is the platform where all of these forces come into play, where different and obscure powers confront and interact with each other. The impact of the force of commercial capital or the power of government on the fabric of the city is perhaps easily identified. But the powers of fear, desire, religion or law act just as strongly in shaping the city.

PW In the case of Bilbao and the development company Bilbao Ría 2000, we have seen a quite unusual (administrative) and successful model for urban development. Why do you think this model has been so successful? Which aspects of it are decisive? And in this context, how do you see the role of leadership?

VM The company Bilbao Ría 2000 represents an incredibly successful model for urban redevelopment. The city of Bilbao, which was completely run down economically, with incredible social and political tensions, has been redeveloped using the model of giving political decision-making power to the company. The company created a cluster of stakeholders from the economic, social and political sectors to redevelop the city, mainly through private-public partnerships. The key aspects for the success of the model were the importation of the managerial expertise from Britain and the establishment of a culture of consensus in decision-making processes. A very sophisticated relationship between political influences on the development of the city was combined with the private interests of developers and investors. Generating trust in the company's performance created a series of win-win situations. Many traditional values, norms and regulations were questioned in order to develop a common-sense approach towards the city's development. Top-down approaches were merged with bottom-up trends in order to improve social and economic aspects of the city's fabric. In the way in which Bilbao Ría 2000 performed, the traditional role of leadership from either the political or economic sector was redefined through a culture of consensus, which was then further developed by constant re-evaluation of the decision-making process. So it is neither strange nor extraordinary that the Guggenheim Foundation became involved in developing a new museum in Bilbao.

PW The Guggenheim Museum has become an icon for Bilbao and is regarded as a guarantee that successful urban development can be promoted in the same way elsewhere as well. Do you agree, and are architectural projects (and the image they are able to communicate) important for urban development and the identity of a city in the global as well as in the local context?

VM The Guggenheim Museum in Bilbao is indeed regarded as being an icon for the successful redevelopment of an entire city. I do not completely agree with this view, since it was precisely the way in which the Bilbao Ría 2000 company worked that laid the foundations for the Museum. Gehry's building is merely the outcome of very ingenious work on the part of the company in developing this project. Many other Guggenheim Museum projects have not been successfully implemented, as the conditions in other cities have not been able to match the ambitious quality of this type of project. The Bilbao museum created the so-called „Bilbao effect", which is probably a negative aspect of its global influence. The Bilbao effect created a belief among many politicians that it is sufficient to build an iconic building designed by an architectural superstar in order to fundamentally change a city's image and context. So the inflationary increase in objects by figures such as Frank Gehry, Zaha Hadid, and Coop Himmelblau are now creating a sort of confusion of the local identities of particular cities in interaction with global ambitions. In this sense, new localities are almost being imported and fabricated in response to global market demands. This development raises a cluster of difficult questions that we need to find answers for, in the search for a definition of authentic local development within the globalized world.

PW Still, most of the current development strategies are based on the idea of the master plan. Is the master plan still an adequate planning and design tool for a time of rapid change like the twenty-first century? Or do we need to develop other tools, and can you imagine the kind of tool that would be able to replace, or rather complement, the master plan?

VM The master plan in the traditional sense is not an adequate tool for developing contemporary cities. However, political bodies in many countries, and especially in transitional countries (as in Eastern Europe, for example) still need and use a master plan to regulate the development of the city. As a

The European megalopolis

In terms of absolute numbers, the growth of mo
phenomenon that is playing out primarily in the
2015, there will be twenty-three cities with over
Only two of these twenty-three megalopolises w
known as the Western world – New York and Los
of them will be in Europe.

Megalopolises are characterized by their rapid
tion density. In contrast, the development of cit
appears to be characterized by ever-decreasing d
any growth does take place here, it is in the still-
cities. In 1960, for example, the city of The Hag
ants. In 2000, The Hague, Delft and the new city
also had 600,000 inhabitants. The intervening 40
to constant building activities that resulted in a
doubling of the number of motorways, and a co
scape. Forty years of development focused solely o
number of inhabitants at ever-decreasing density.

The increased use of cars is both the cause and e
ment. Nowadays, less than half of the inhabitant
live in the same location as where they work. U
outwards to escape the city, but despite this – in a
manage to live without it. The drawing-power of
strong that remote parts of the French countrys
out. Not having any choice, new 'immigrants' are
velles that surround Paris.

In the 'centre' of Europe, the situation is quite d
ized agglomeration of the Dutch Randstad connec
agglomeration and the German Ruhr area. In this
countryside is not emptying out, but instead fill

URBAN REPORTS

eds. Nicola Schüller, Petra
Wollenberg, Kees Christiaanse

Zürich, 2008

Mid-sized City, interview with
Vedran Mimica by Petra Wollenberg

political document, a master plan basically creates additional obstacles to development, rather than opening up opportunities. Even in the 1990s, many cities – such as Barcelona – abolished comprehensive master planning for the city and replaced it with the development of specific city projects. The development of such projects is intended to be consistent with an overall vision or strategy on the part of the city's government, but the projects are not subject to the standardization involved in a master plan that is implemented from the top down. The new tools that should be developed would need to seriously address the increasing instability of economic and social developments in cities. They would need to negotiate between regulation and deregulation, establishing a proper balance between determined and non-determined aspects of the city's growth. New strategies and plans will be needed in order to establish a meaningful balance between the public interest and the private sector.

PW Kees Christiaanse once mentioned that his office is testing its urban projects with regard to how much "bad architecture" an urban plan can tolerate. What kinds of qualities need to be defined or set in the urban plan? How much should be left open?

VM Christiaanse is right in arguing that urban plans, or rather urban designs, should have internal qualities and that the built urban environment should not necessarily depend on the architectural quality of particular buildings. The urban design should focus primarily on the relation between the public realm and the private sphere. The utmost care should be taken in designing public spaces and the ways in which people meet and share their interests in a common space. The urban plans should anticipate the creation of new neighborhoods with different lifestyles and should create opportunities for different groups and individuals to express themselves in the public sphere.

PW An issue that is widely discussed is the concern that global culture is replacing local culture, resulting in the homogenization of the life—world. How important is it to preserve, reinforce and strengthen local identities in contrast to global impacts?

VM It can be argued that genuinely authentic local values and identities are basically subject to constant negotiation relative to global pressures. Authentic local values and interpretations are therefore constantly being redefined, and the degree of homogenization of urban environments worldwide is a consequence of such processes. There is a tendency to create secure, clean, regulated, and usually highly commercialized city areas. These areas usually replace city fabrics that have been abandoned or are in decay, by implementing strict market logic in creating new opportunities for real-estate development.

One would wish that local identities could somehow be miraculously preserved. But the only way to achieve this is for them to become global values or trends, and this is a paradoxical situation in the world we live in today. Not all of the local values and identities will have disappeared within a short time, but the newly emerging generations of city dwellers, from Lisbon to Vladivostok, do have an increasingly similar consumer-oriented value system.

PW Cities have to deal with tensions and apparently blatant contradictions arising from local interests and global powers. How important is it to have a clear, overall vision in setting up urban policies for a city in times in which the conditions for urban development change every five to ten years? How would you assess the ability to implement a vision under the growing influence of economic forces?

VM It is clear that contemporary architectural discourse is related to the inability of the architectural profession to form a clear idea about the contemporary city. Social and urban concepts which Jean-François Lyotard would name as "grand narratives" are long gone, along with the period when architects were still making serious attempts to understand and project the city by drafting different manifestos.

As Koolhaas also pointed out in his lecture at the Berlage Institute, architects and urban planners "stopped thinking at precisely the same time that the city is now being constructed all over the world. This enormous gap is a sad territory, because in the meantime, as architects are reluctant to step into this void, others are stepping into it with a degree of eagerness that is about to change the whole nature of the city."

This loss of engagement with the city as a conceivable collective entity is producing a fracture line between the theory and practice of architecture. Koolhaas points to business players and real-estate corporations that collaborate very closely with local government in developing new cities and reconstructing old ones, with only marginal influence from architectural offices. We really have to ask ourselves who it is that is developing the new cities and what the prevailing logic is in these processes. Who is it that is establishing a vision of new Dubai's and other free economic zones, who is it that is conducting experiments, and how can any of the critical qualities that were previously intrinsic to the architect's work be accommodated in these processes? Keller Easterling, a leading scholar writing about the issues involved in relationships between the global market and city development, would argue that the architect is only able to introduce a "germ" or a "virus" into systemic planning in order to resist the expected results from global market players.

PW In recent years, the role of the historic city center has been changing. It has been seen merely as a shopping center and as a place to entertain tourists, but not necessarily as a place to live in. Now people are moving back into the centers to live there. How do you see the future development of historic city centers?

VM At the Berlage Institute Masterclass lecture from 2002, Saskia Sassen would argue for the importance of the cities by saying that „City space is the key zone where a lot of the power projects of global corporate capital play out, and where the new political interventions of even the poorest organizations can also be enacted". However, the renaissance of the city center that took place during the 1990s as a result of the „return to the centers", with what Richard Florida, calls a „creative class", was still somewhat surprising. In today's "new world order", cities can only be taken seriously as cultural and political entities through the creation of museums, festivals, sporting events, universities and in particular iconic buildings, in order to sustain themselves. In an age in which what were previously industrial and working sites are being transformed into locations for visible consumption, John Urry has pointed out that this is necessary in order for cities to compete in the global race for recognition. At the same time, cities are copying each other's formulas and specific characteristics at the expense of their own identities. As a result of this thematic zoning, the essential role of cities as centers for revolution, individual development, new ideas and sociocultural representation of different groups is being eliminated. The urgent question is how to reconcile the city of the spectacle with the real city.

PW As you have already mentioned, cities are presenting themselves as competitors in the global marketplace – to attract inhabitants, tourists and investment. City marketing is therefore becoming more and more important. How do you judge the need for city marketing and how important is it to develop and communicate a "city brand?"

VM Branding has developed recently as an important strategic marketing activity for cities. In a postmodern society, values are communicated through images, and cities can be successfully branded. However, brands often do not correspond to the genuine reality of a city and are used more to trigger people's imagination about the city.

PW There is an increasing desire for protection against uncontrolled and criminal influences. Surveillance technology and gated areas are constantly and increasingly present in our cities. These issues have also negative effects, such as complete or partial inaccessibility of large parts of the cities, which have been severely criticized by Mike Davis, for example. How could or should cities deal with this topic, and is it still possible nowadays to have a "real" and "authentic" public space (in the classic sense)?

VM Even in the mid-1990s, our students at the Berlage Institute were studying the sophistication of the surveillance-camera system in the shopping zones in Amsterdam's historic center. This was all before 9/11, but the conclusion was that entire zones of public and semi-public spaces in Amsterdam are being constantly monitored. The events of 9/11 radically changed the situation, and today we simply live in controlled environments. One can question some hypotheses that have been proposed in Mike Davis's books, and we are not yet entering an Orwellian darkness – but the effects of division, separation, and the disappearance of links in society are more than visible. Richard Sennett argues in favor of the concept of the „open city", featuring porosity, transparency and well-maintained, genuinely authentic public domains – but when contrasted with Kabul, Baghdad, Beirut, and the Gaza Strip, this beautiful academic voice does not resonate well.

PW Planning is often criticized for its lack of three-dimensional thinking, for the absence of a relationship to reality, and much more. Against the background of your teaching experience at the Berlage Institute, could you describe your ideas in this area and what kinds of skills the urban planner needs to learn and apply today?

VM At the Berlage, during last five years, I have worked in close relation with Alejandro Zaera-Polo and my answer is based on the research and educational program developed at that time. What needs to be taught and ultimately learned is subject to a permanent process of research and discovery. Architectural research at the Berlage Institute addresses fields of knowledge that are supra-disciplinary (economics, sociology, philosophy) and sub-disciplinary (engineering, construction, management, advanced technology). We are seeking to create knowledge and carry out research into new forms of urban existence through advanced definitions of sustainability and by defining the public sphere for contemporary urbanization processes. At the Berlage Institute, we regard architectural research as being a form of applied research, which should be immediately applicable by producing design solutions that have a concrete and transformative impact on the built environment. We want to address the transformations through which contemporary urban environments are shaping traditionally strong cultures by confronting the shift from state-driven to market-driven economies. We investigate the impact of massive immigration into the cities, the completely new relationships that have arisen between work and leisure, heritage and tourism routes and mobility, and local and global influences in specific urban settings. In addressing contemporary transformations of the built environment and understanding its complexities and the areas of ambiguity in which the discipline tends to break down into compartmentalized areas of expertise, we are faced with the challenge of directly engaging with the real forces that are transforming the built environment, while simultaneously having to develop a new genre of architectural understanding that combines speculation with realistic implementation.

PW City administrations often lack the financial means to develop important projects involving the cultural or technical infrastructure. Do you think that models involving public-private partnership can be successful?

VM From a south-eastern European perspective of development in transitional environments, the public-private partnership model has proved to be a highly desirable one. It is precisely the process of negotiation between public and private participants that is needed for the development of the new members of the European community. The public-private partnership model is forcing the various interest groups involved to negotiate in order to clearly define public and private interests, and this is miraculously reducing corruption and creating a more democratic process in urban development. The public-private partnership idea requires conceptual and technical development of the local administration to enable it to articulate public values and interests. Conversely, private partners gain greater security for their investments when they participate in projects in collaboration with the public authorities.

PW There is continuing debate regarding participation by citizens in urban planning. Is it possible for there to be effective communication between city authorities and the citizens without a loss of strong ideas and focus?

VM As Saskia Sassen has argued, the cityscape is a theater for political action on the part of every sector of society. Particularly vocal are non-governmental organizations assembled under the slogan 'the right to the city.'[47] These groups involve various political ideologies, but their main argument is that a city belongs to everybody and not just to the consumer society.

David Harvey would argue that a radical democratization of urban space is necessary in order to prevent the prevailing consumer-society landscapes from penetrating every domain of city life. For this purpose, it would be necessary to carry out educational work and engage in exchanges and involvements in local affairs, and public communication of radically different policies would be needed. This type of activity could be achieved by organizing biennial exhibitions and other cultural events, but such events would primarily have to enter the political sphere. Only articulate positions with clearly defined arguments would be capable of establishing the critical dialogue needed for the development of contemporary cities.

PW More and more people want to live in cities, or are being forced to. How do you see the development of mid-sized cities in 20-50 years from now? Will today's mid-sized cities become tomorrow's megacities and today's villages tomorrow's mid-sized cities? And what do you think the main challenges will be for mid-sized cities in the future?

VM We are living in an urban age in which more and more people will be living in cities and in which completely new cities will emerge, and historically unprecedented growth of the existing cities will take place. Many mid-sized cities in countries like China or India will become megacities, with their polycentric structures. The European mid-sized cities will probably experience slower growth, but they will be investing heavily in a redefinition of their position in the global networks. They will need to create city programs that can communicate on a local and global level with the larger cities and with the global economy. They will need to compete with and contest the quality of life that is possible in larger cities. They will need to reform their administrations, which are often slow and tradition-bound, and they will need to attract various participants to become involved in their development.

Harvey, D. (2008) The Right to the City, New Left Review, 53

NOT QUITE OBVIOUS DENSITIES

Published in Oris 28, Zagreb 2004

In 1991, Winy Maas, Jacob van Rijs and Nathalie de Vries founded MVRDV, an architecture and town planning office in Rotterdam. According to Rem Koolhaas' foreword to a monumental monograph S, M, L, XL, Winy Maas 'has left a deep imprint on individual buildings made by the Rotterdam OMA, and has significantly contributed to an intelligent office as a whole.' MVRDV operates through research, design, construction and teaching, which are the basic activities of the leading team members. None of these activities starts from concepts based on some developed theoretical or French post-structuralist discourses, but from a highly accurate and pragmatic study of distinct facts which define contemporary architectural practice. MVRDV works with economic indicators, building regulations, consumerist behavior, corporate structures, program hybrids and computer programs. In a number of aspects, MVRDV's space and time arrangements are influenced by the reality of the New Europe in which the flow of money, ideas and people follows ever more complex patterns. Amsterdam harbor of the mid nineties is one such paradigm of extremely complex patterns of socioeconomic flow of a variety of interests focused on a specific area. Amsterdam harbor gradually withdrew from the city center zone toward the North Sea, and was abandoned by the last of the squatters by the end of the nineties. A huge grain silo, the last of the squatters' bastions, fell without a fight and is being transformed into subsidized housing. MVRDV won a competition for a new Amsterdam super-hybrid that was to be erected in the immediate vicinity, on a pier which was no longer in use. This residential Silo(dam) is the result of the joint effort of housing corporations, developers (housing and business) and the city of Amsterdam. With the highly democratic environment such as the Dutch, and business environment relying on consensus and pragmatism as the basic means of operation, designing a hybrid in a top location was by no means a mission impossible. In this setup, an architect acts as an overarching process director, and MVRDV is very successful in that role. It starts with a painstaking study of all design aspects and uses diagrams, statistics and data mapping to come up with the most logical "spatial" solutions. In this process, creative force never assumes spectacular shapes, but redefines current requirements. By finding new

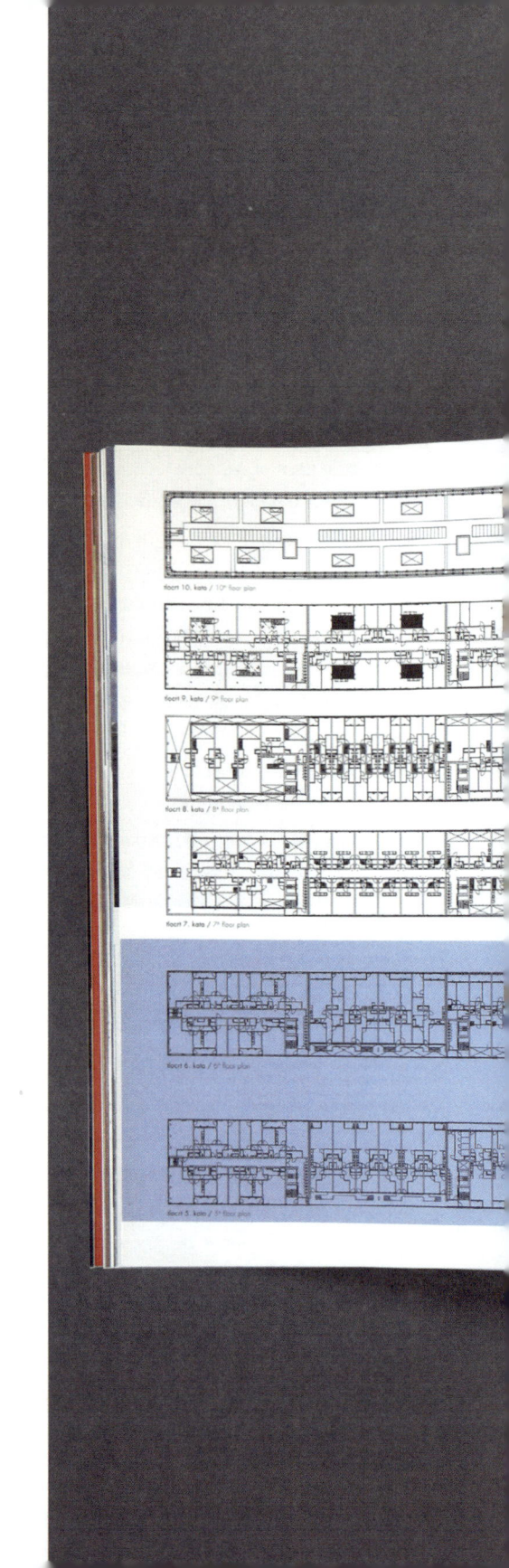

ORIS 28

Zagreb, 2004

Vedran Mimica: **Not Quite Obvious Densities**

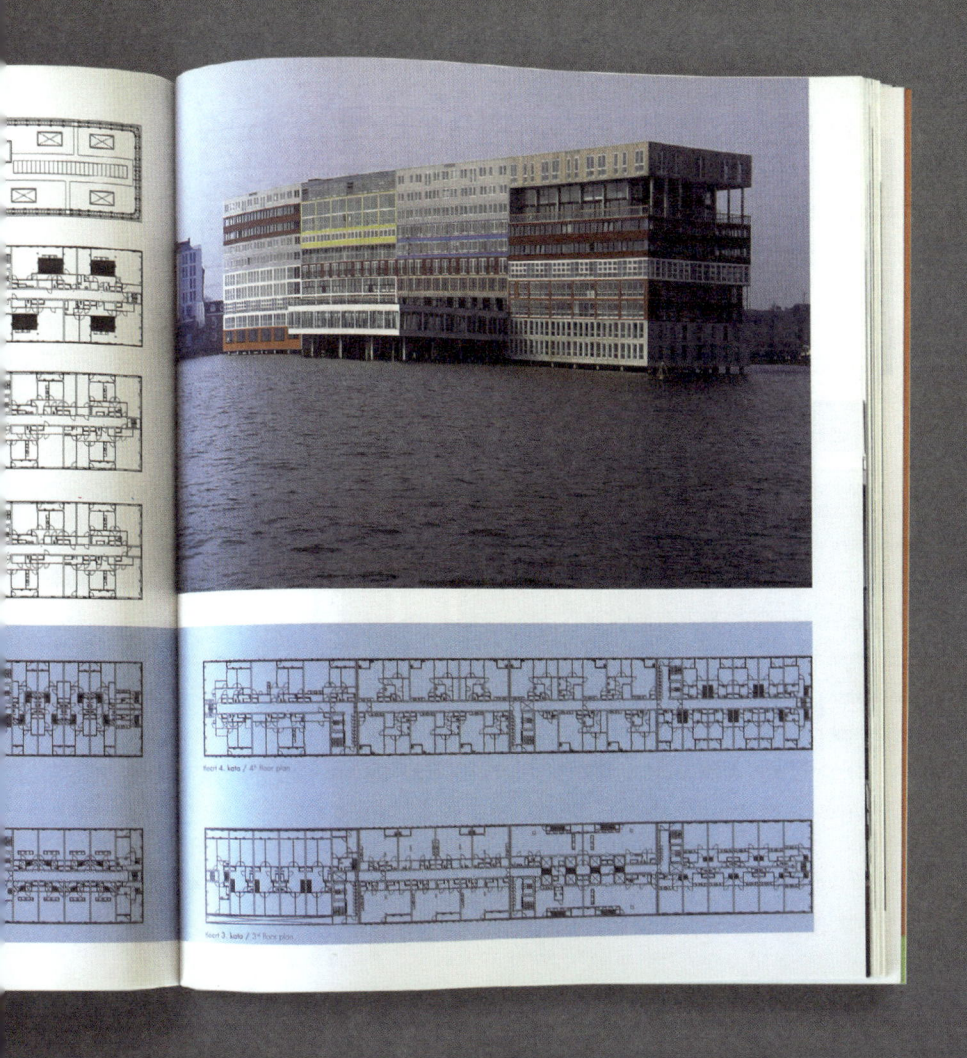

ways to describe or investigate hybrid configurations, MVRDV demonstrates its virtually unfaltering ability to come up with some unexpected solutions. This method can be described as a series of "switches", each opening a new organizational level. The result is an optimal spatial organization of a variety of contents. Nothing is made up and everything seems accounted for and rooted in reality. MVRDV first demonstrated its self-assuring ability in composing housing hybrids as early as Europan 2 in Berlin. The Amsterdam Silo(dam) is therefore a continuation of this research. The Silo(dam) project provides for 160 dwelling units, offices, businesses and public areas. Silo(dam) is an almost literal interpretation of MVRDV's organizational quest. Even its basic programmatic models manifest the principle of the vertical clustering of different typologies into mini residential neighborhoods. The building thus becomes a process "built", a reflection or manifestation of a negotiating process between several systems. Even the façade treatment reflects this rationale by underlining the variable contents behind it, as required by the client and end-users. Unfortunately, the completion of the pier as a public space, or more exactly, as the main communication with the city was not realized after the awarded design due to an extremely low budget. Regardless of the budget, however, the Silo(dam) is one of the most radical solutions in recent Dutch hybrid collective housing building practice. Enclaves or clusters create images of Giddens' abstract systems, at the same time detaching themselves ironically from these systems. This dichotomy is perhaps the most interesting stage in the process of translating datascapes (a term used by MVRDV to encompass all input related to a task) into a project and finally into a completed building. These buildings have a particular way of transforming ordinary biographies of an industrial society into chosen or, according to Giddens,[48] reflexive biographies of new members of a post-industrial society.

[48] Giddens, Anthony (2013) The Consequences of Modernity. Cambridge, UK: Polity Press. Namely, in the first chapter of the book Giddens begins discussion about reflexivity with the point that what is inherent to the idea of modernity is a contrast with tradition. There is a fundamental sense in which reflexivity is a defining characteristic of all human action: this is because we all keep in touch with what we are doing as an element of doing it. Giddens calls this the 'reflexive monitoring of action.'

ZOKA, I LOVE YOU!

Published in Oris 27, Zagreb 2004

The human will pass through another decisive step, in which the subject, despite its satisfaction, fails to be sufficient unto itself. Desire metamorphosed into an attitude of openness to exteriority. Openness that is appeal and response to the other. The proximity of the other, origin of all putting into question of self.

Levinas, Emmanuel (1999) Alterity and Transcendence. Columbia University Press

I do not respect Mies,
I love Mies.

Koolhaas, Rem (2004) Miestakes. In: Content, Taschen

Pfanner House is the embodiment of Zoka Zola's understanding of the concept of open space. It is a unique architectural concept of freedom. In establishing the relationship between architectural expression and the concept of freedom, Zoka relies on recent research in philosophy, art and social sciences. These disciplines address the issue of individual or group opening toward other entities, as opposed to making them same or similar. Zoka believes that architecture is the ideal medium for exploring the opening of "one" toward the "other", because it involves constant "opening" of one space to another space. As quite expected, in Zoka's interpretation there are few genuinely open spaces in the history of western architecture: Wittgenstein's house, Melnikov's spaces, Asplund's houses and some of Alberti's and Bernini's spaces.

Zoka's ethics about constituting a relationship between self and other is perhaps best explained in her Beijing lecture: "Much was said in the recent years about the Self and the Other.

Zoka Zola
Emmanuel Levinas
Rem Koolhaas

ORIS 27

Zagreb, 2004

Vedran Mimica
Zoka, I Love You!

ORIS 65

Zagreb, 2010

Oblique Strategies, interview with Dado Katušić by Alan Kostrenčić, Vedran Mimica

That would mean that in order to accept another person we do not need to expect them to be like us, not even essentially different than us, but just accept them as being Other. Other means just that – OTHER – without judgment, comparison, pretenses towards the other, without categorizing the other, (without saying "he or she is like this or like that"), but instead acknowledging the Other. There is a certain "COOLNESS" that is involved, in a way that we need to be glad of the distance and in the same time very aware of the Other."[49]

The philosophical base of the Zoka's concept of open space, of openness or open situation draws from her research on French philosopher Emmanuel Levinas. Levinas' main concern was the ideas of the relationships between people, which he claimed to be the main subject of ETHICS, the first and the most important origin of philosophy. Levinas is investigating the concept of TRANSCENDENCE. He claims that in Western philosophy since antiquities, the transcendence, which could be interpreted as going beyond oneself, has been wrongly searched in the higher selves. Levinas further says that the reason the transcendence is never properly understood in Western philosophy is because of its continuous interest in ONE. Levinas insists that the only true transcendence is in our RELATIONSHIP WITH THE OTHER.

This study of Levinas' philosophy and her architectural research provided the grounds for conceptualizing the Pfanner House. It is an independent and authentic piece of architecture whose interpretation of concepts is not literal but tangential or transcendental. Without Zoka's investigative drive, however, the Pfanner House would not have the power and the beauty of a fundamental architectural piece it is. There lies the essential distinction and the value of a single piece of architecture.

Let us see some of the concepts, which influenced the appearance of this house. The first was perhaps the most challenging for Zoka. How to design a house for oneself and one's family, a house that will accommodate an architect's studio too? How to avoid the self-referential domestication? How to strike a balance between freedom and safety? Then there is also the concept of exposure. The house opens to the exterior in many elements; (the lot is not separated from the street by a fence and one can easily cross it at the corner.). Zoka makes it clear that the interior opens up to "other people," "so that [they] can inhabit it as part of their own mental space." The third concept is proximity. The view that is framed through the façade openings does not follow the principle of "a good view," but it is a reminder of where the house is. The fourth concept is pleasure. Zoka says that the Pfanner House is a house of pleasure for being "there" and "then." There is more than one aspect of pleasure: bodily pleasure, social pleasure, and pleasure with a passage of time, pleasure with the sun, air and trees. Finally, there is the concept of unowned house. Zoka underlines that the house has been designed not to feel owned. When a building feels owned, it has an impoverished relationship with the rest of the world. This is why the host and the guest are treated equally in this house.

It is interesting to note that US critics recognized the value of the Pfanner House and gave it a number of awards. I have an intimate wish to spend some time with Zoka, her family and colleagues in this house, so that I can understand and experience the possibilities of this architecture as safeguard of our critical conscience.

Beijing International Forum, (China) May 18th 2004

THE MARSEILLE EXPERIMENT

Interview with Elia Zenghelis published in "Making the City by the Sea Forum & Workshop Marseille," Berlage Institute – Fundació Mies van der Rohe / IFA – Institut Français d'Architecture 2003

After the 2000 Venice workshop organized by the IFA, the Fundació Mies van der Rohe and the Berlage Institute concentrated on the city of Marseille in 2001. In the preparatory documents of the workshop, Marseille was presented as a new Euro-Mediterranean metropolis. The city is representative of the cleavage between the new Europe and the Mediterranean center.

Elia Zenghelis, how would you reflect upon this new European Mediterranean metropolis? Or, how do you define this new sort of political or programmatic entity?

Elia Zenghelis For the Marseille workshop, the focus of the program was to exploit the opportunity of a city, which was also a port. In other words, the city represents juxtaposition of the extreme conditions of a metropolis that finishes by the sea, the face-to-face between the extreme conditions of nature with the extreme condition of a city. That was one consideration. The other consideration was the fact that the ambition of architects is now to control what happens in the larger environment, how to think with reality – a reality which is now organized more to follow the market at this particular stage of capitalism or so called modernity. One must adopt a stance because the issue at stake is in making a city. In preparing for the workshop, I decided to explicitly challenge the status quo of education and of the profession – wherein architects are losing the ability to take positions. The ability to take positions has been forgotten, I remember that during the time of my education it was a very important thing. This workshop provided an opportunity to reintroduce the notion that participants should declare a very strong view and develop concepts that they could defend in projecting a future for the city. This links to the Euroméditerranée project[50] in that it deals with the front; the frontline of the city, the fins that face the sea with a new facade. Marseille had an emblematic facade in the nineteenth century, which gradually became eroded by additional highways, infrastructure, transformations of the port, etc. After the city's economic decline, it is now involved in the process of acquiring a new facade, a new sea front, which in turn gives rise to the opportunity to discuss architecture and the iconography of architecture as a kind of theoretical, symbolic aspect. This is the degree to which architecture contributes to the face of the city, to the emblematic appearance of the city. And this also leads to the idea, also very strongly illustrated, perhaps by default, of architecture not being contextual, but always generating context.

VM Let's now go to the task and discuss the introductory or a little exercise those participants were expected to complete before the formal beginning of the workshop in Marseille. Quite provokingly, you asked them to develop an ideal city on a border between the sea and the land. During the workshop, this ideal (or prototypical) city was to be transformed to the site specificity of Marseille.

EZ In order not to waste time at the beginning of the workshop, this introductory exercise was the jumpstart. When one has a workshop of only one week or five days, the first three days can easily be completely wasted on arguing and debating "what shall we do?" and then the work is produced in solely one day. The assignment ensured that we already had a body of work from day one, as a kind of foundation on which we could build. The exercise also forced participants to deal with the power of abstraction. Participants were forced to adopt a position vis-à-vis nature and the city in projecting an ideal city between water and land. Abstraction to an ideal condition required participants to rely on their memories and previous experiences of cities by

50 http://www.euromediterranee.fr/ , accessed August 14, 2016

the sea – whether these cities were visited, lived in, imagined, or dreamed of.

VM Once in Marseille, Dominique Cervetti and other organizers took us all to the project sites. Following site visits, we reviewed a series of global referral images of port renewal projects – from cities such as Baltimore, Buenos Aires, Athens, Piraeus and Genoa – that repealed new radical relations between the evolving functions of both harbors and cities. It became evident that the core challenge of the Euroméditerranée was how to create a kind of metropolitan dynamism in which the pressures of urban politics can marry functional requirements. In many examples of port rehabilitation, the tendency towards „disneyfication" or stigmatization of the port comes to the fore, especially in the examples from South and North America. In Europe, there appears to be a belief that port functions and city functions could coexist. What do you think in general about the approach one should take when the city starts actually appropriating a part of the port? This is very obviously the case in Marseille, as it was also in Baltimore, Capetown and Puerto Madero in Buenos Aires. Areas that were formally highly protected, functional, industrial harbors are transforming into civic urban areas – complete with public places, places of entertainment and commerce.

EZ Yes, this is moving beyond the scope of the particular exercise, it became clear during the exercise that there is an incredibly delicate balance, and an incredible danger of loss of authenticity of ports, which are in danger of stigmatization and a sort of romantic „disneyfication" as the ports begin to lose their connection to the real life of cities. Indeed the Euroméditerranée restoration of the old docks, planned in a linear way, accepted the division between city and sea. As René Borruey commented, they could have been used more as a porous element that links the city to the port. In the exercise, we did try to remain more radical and tried to avoid a sentimental re-use of port facilities. We also discovered (specially coming from Rotterdam) that territorially; a port and the city are two distinct entities in France. The municipality of Marseille

LOS ANGELES STRANGER THAN FICTION

The Berlage Institute research report No.33

Rotterdam, 2010

MAKING THE CITY BY THE SEA

Actar, Barcelona, 2003

The Marseille Experiment, interview with Elia Zenghelis by Vedran Mimica

ROME:
THE CENTRE(S) ELSEWHERE

A Berlage Institute Project study

SKIRA, Milano, 2010

has a kind of frontier between itself and the port – the port is like another country. The problem arises along the facade of Marseille. The area which has the port in front of it is not an issue. However, the territory that was released by the port (next to the Fort Saint-Jean) to the municipality proved difficult for the students. The area is ambiguous in that there is no clear boundary between where the port ended and the city began. Another side to the same issue is the fact that the city has realized that its well-wishing sponsors are calling for a renewed public domain, public ground. Sponsors have imagined a civic entity that, in fact, does not exist anymore. The notion of urban space as the Roman public forum has been replaced by a commercial (shopping) alternative to the contemporary public realm. In the end, these expectations lead to the "disneyfication" of an authentic object.

VM Nonetheless, in creating a new public realm for Marseille, students and city planners alike rely on manipulating the infrastructure. The city's elevated highways were seen by many as protecting the city from merging with the port. The question involves the degree to which manipulation with infrastructure provides new programmatic possibilities beyond simply occupying extra public space.

EZ Without a doubt, the studio was very concerned with this whole issue of infrastructure – especially since the highway infrastructure was very much present and has formed the newest front of the city. Marseille's first front was the nineteenth-century Haussmanian blocks that were built in the triangle between Place de la Joliette, Vieux-Port, Fort Saint-Jean and Rue de la République and finally the docks. Then there were the raised highways, and then beyond these came the warehouses of the harbor. Between the harbor and the city, there has been this kind of infrastructure, or barrier, which was extremely present. Many projects made an attempt to turn infrastructure into architecture. In other cases, infrastructure was suppressed in order to open up the space. However in both cases – conquering the territory or opening up the space

– there was always the problem of that barrier, visible or invisible, between Marseille as a city and the port as a national territory. In recent times, customs have moved to the North and a large area has been released more for passenger use and ferry boat traffic, in this sense, this area of the port belongs to the city. The barrier becomes a pity in this instance – because the change of program resulted in the life of the port having a dialogue with the life of the city. The dialogue was rooted in a life of movement – a life of flows, with boats coming and going, cars arriving and leaving, and passengers circulating.

VM Turning to the work of the participants, it became clear that all the groups developed a clear attitude to conquering new ground – either by manipulation of infrastructure or by actually creating a new ground in a vertical sense above the harbor ground.

EZ In fact Dominique Cervetti encouraged us by saying that there have been negotiations – negotiations between the city and the port. However, for participants, these negotiations were problematic in that they were read as a horizontal duality of levels, by layering the city over the port. There was often a kind of loss of definition that one wanted to achieve by reproducing a new front or a new context for the city, as seen from the sea.

VM In the middle of our workshop, the September 11 attack occurred on the Twin Towers in New York. After that shock, I think many of our beliefs or concepts fundamentally changed. Could you now, after almost one year, summarize the effect of September 11 on the architectural debate?

EZ This is something I do not even need to talk about very much. It definitely gave us a shock. There were at least one or two days in which the whole project remained in suspended animation. It was the shock of the suspension of the entire project. But of course it was also the blow to the face of globalization and of the global free market that the assaults on the World Trade Center conveyed. The very realization of what this sort of economic imperialism was doing to make this kind of operation possible. In other words, suddenly one saw in front of one's own eyes the impossible becoming possible. But strangely, it was also something that many of us, without ever having had the imagination to articulate, were expecting. In other words, there was also something that was not a surprise, something familiar, some kind of nightmare that we have all had was coming true. And that had an effect on the project, or at least on the way the project was conducted. Whether it had any effect on what the results were, I do not know.

VM What was equally interesting perhaps in a kind of post-workshop political development was the fact that something like a multi-cultural metropolis was promoted, conceived, and not debatable – all as we concluded in the Marseille workshop. However, the recent French presidential and Dutch parliamentary elections proved that the immigration issue and the multi-cultural basis of modern European democracies seem to be in question. Of course, it is always very difficult – and one could even say on slippery ground – to question how urbanism can engage with these issues.

EZ It is a very hard thing to be able to summarize in any kind of intellectual or objective way. When you are dealing with the issues of a collective or unconscious psychology, you might call it retrenchment. At its most basic, collective psychology automatically becomes the most reactive – becomes conservative and reactionary. This is the psychology of the masses, if one had the time to sit back and examine the situation more philosophically; one becomes more critical if you like. But one's sense of critical faculties goes somehow, and that is what you get. Everybody is looking after their own skin.

VM The final question relates to the unbelievable degree of French hospitality in Marseille we experienced throughout the workshop. In our understanding of the potentials of such a city, not only the physical properties were clear, but also cultural aspects and the very spirit of the city. So the question might be if the radical changes are taking place under the pressure of globalization, or the market, how could we look into the future of the metropolis vis-à-vis the national culture and spirit which has been developed on that site for the last 2400 years since the very first Greek colonization of the city?

EZ There are a number of issues here. One is of course – which I have to mention separately – the question of hospitality. Being amongst the locals, amongst the French people, was a kind of redeeming factor of the otherwise horrible shock of September 11. The counterpart was the pleasure of having such incredible hospitality, and dealing with such a really magnificent city. But then on the other hand, one has to admit that the scope of the exercise in terms of reshaping the metropolis was limited. It was limited to its formal and emblematic levels. On the one hand, it was also my intention to limit it to that; because in the time we had available it was impossible to embrace the enormous complexities of a metropolis. It was an abstraction that was necessary to make in order to focus on an issue of urbanism and architecture that did not seem to be in focus anymore. It does not seem to be a part of their agenda. It was an attempt to look at an emblematic or paradigmatic vision for the city. On the other hand, we have to admit that the Euroméditerranée is really focusing on – if you like – the fashionable part of Marseille, the golden triangle of Marseille. It is not paying any attention to the Quartiers Nord, where the problems of Marseille are of a completely different category – and they are the problems of a metropolis that one cannot deny. If we were asked to deal with them, I would have backed out; it would not have been within my ability to handle such an enormity. But we should not fool ourselves into thinking that we have dealt with the problems of Marseille or with the problems of a metropolis. But, in an abstract way, again returning to the formal aspect of the emblematic appearance of a city by the sea, of which the docks of Marseille were a very useful example.

MAKING THE CITY BY THE SEA

Actar, Barcelona, 2003

CROATIAN ARCHIPELAGO : NEW LIGHTHOUSES

Progress Report
Interim Substantial and Content Report nr. 2
01/11/2005 - 30/04/2006

Interlude 2
Workshop Ambience

A GOOD BUILDING MAKES YOU FEEL AT HOME

Published in Oris 83, Zagreb 2013
Wiel Arets in conversation with Vedran Mimica
In Chicago, August 23, 2013

My conversation with Wiel Arets started in 1991, when we met in the orphanage of Aldo van Eyck, at the Berlage Institute in south Amsterdam, and have carried on until today, at Mies's Crown Hall, where we work together, at the Illinois Institute of Technology College of Architecture.

The conversation we had recently in Chicago is just a small "pixel" from our continuing intense exchange of ideas regarding our professional and private lives, which will, I hope, help the readers to learn more about the underlying motivation of an exceptional architectural scope of work.

For the purpose of this leading article I will quote the critical observation of Robert McCarter from the book Wiel Arets: Autobiographical References (Robert McCarter, ed, published by Birkhäuser, Basel in 2012)

'Wiel Arets is an architect with an exceptional sense of self-awareness; a profound ethical approach to architecture, based on his deeply-held beliefs; a humble desire to learn from certain works by others – works for which he has sympathy because they relate to his beliefs; a clear-eyed recognition of his own obsessions and intense interests, and a willingness to engage them in his projects, making his method truly autobiographical.

Arets' works are too anchored in their places and circumstances, too directly the result of his autobiographical and auto-didactic method, too clearly an outcome of his progressive social views and too much a product of his dialogical practice of architecture, to be appropriately characterized as a part of any style, school of thought, or a general mode of making architecture.

The critical importance of Arets' dialogical approach to design lies in his ability to respond to a client, site, program, place, and circumstance, engaging each with the greatest respect and without preconceptions, while simultaneously exercising the most remarkable capacity for transforming reality in an entirely unforeseen way.'

Vedran Mimica Wiel, I would like to begin by asking about your formative years; your studies in Eindhoven; growing up in the south of the Netherlands; and your student travels to Russia and Japan, which allowed you to see the world during this very important time in your life. Would you conclude that this multi-cultural environment you grew up within, in the Netherlands, alongside the Belgian, German, Dutch, and French cultures and languages, is a situation that you will carry with you for the rest of your life? How has this unique upbringing affected your teaching and practice of architecture?

Wiel Arets My family and I always travelled when I was young. We often traveled to nearby Belgium, Germany, Luxembourg, and Switzerland. I remember that my parents were always very interested in other cultures, yet strangely enough; we hardly ever traveled within the Netherlands. I do not even remember the first time I went to Amsterdam with my father. What I do remember is going to Cologne, Antwerp, Liege, Frankfurt, and Munich – we always went south. Though, I would say that we mostly traveled in Germany and France. Being born in an area with many people, from all over the world – amongst teachers, engineers, and miners – allowed my childhood to be very open and modern, in the sense of its context. My parents' house was quite normal, yet its furnishings were what some would call 'Mid-century Modern'; our furniture had stainless steel frames and ovdje u Chicagu? ¶ WIEL ARETS — Nastava ili vođenje u akademskim ustanovama kao što su AA, Columbia, Cooper Union, Institut Berlage, UdK, a sada i IIT CoA, sve su bile promišljene odluke, kako bih si omogućio potragu za trenutkom. Osjećao sam da mogu pridonijeti tim fakultetima. Paralelno sa svojom karijerom arhitekta, uvijek sam smatrao da su ta imenovanja bila ispravne odluke. Da budem na fakultetu, gdje mi radovi koje proizvodim kao arhitekt, bilo da se radi o pisanju ili zgradama, omogućuju da premostim profesionalnu praksu arhitekture njezinim više akademskim interesima. Ponekad čovjek ne zna zašto reagira na određeni način na neko pitanje ili situaciju. Ali kad sam u jesen 2012. prvi put došao predavati u Chicago, mogao sam osjetiti da grad ima nevjerojatno pozitivan stav i da je njegova javna domena iznenađujuća, a to vrijedi i za njegovu kulinarsku scenu, što također smatram važnim. Grad je vrlo gust u određenim područjima, a ipak 200 metara dalje prema, na primjer, istoku, nalazi se jezero Michigan, a na zapadu je Avenija Michigan, sa svojim glasovitim trgovcima. Život koji vodim u Chicagu i način na koji međunarodni zamah fakulteta dobiva na brzini, uz pozitivnu političku klimu grada, omogućio mi je da mislim da stvarno mogu pridonijeti ovom fakultetu. ¶ Nakon moje dvije najnovije teme istraživanja, na UdK u Berlinu, *Unconscious City* i *Tokyo Utopia*, znao sam da je istraživanje nešto u što sam se ponovno spreman udubiti. Ovdje u Americi ljudi svakodnevno stvaraju nove ideje i nove izume; primjer koji možda najviše obećava električni je automobil Tesla. Mi, kao ljudska bića, planiramo za život na Zemlji. No, kao što sam napisao u *Wiel Arets: Autobiographical references* (Birkhäuser, 2012.), svijet je postao jedan veliki grad pa bismo trebali shvatiti da će nas se uskoro ticati i područje izvan orbite ovog planeta. ¶ Arhitektura i njeno zanimanje za tehnologiju na IIT-u smatraju se jako važnim. Moj prethodnik, Mies van der Rohe, radio je na mnogim zanimljivim zgradama ovdje u Illinoisu, uključujući stanove na Lake Shore Driveu, Kuću Farnsworth, i naravno, zgrada Tehnološkog sveučilišta u Illinoisu (IIT CoA), S. R. Crown Hall. Od stanovnika Chicaga možemo učiti o tome kako bismo trebali pristupiti ovim novim područjima. Uvjerenje da živimo u prirodnom toku tehnologije, naročito ovdje u SAD-u, gdje nova tehnologija stalno prodire u svakodnevne živote, jedan je od razloga zašto ja doista vjerujem da će moja nastojanja ovu školu učiniti značajnijom adresom arhitektonskog obrazovanja diljem svijeta. Čikaški je gradonačelnik odličan, čelnici IIT-a ugledni, osoblje i uprava fakulteta spremni su za početak školske godine 2013./14. ,a uvjeren sam i da će trenutačna politička klima u gradu osigurati kontinuirani uspjeh ovog fakulteta još dugo nakon moga mandata.

WIEL ARETS, Intervju

Oris 83

Zagreb, 2013

A Good Building Makes you Feel at Home,
interview with Wiel Arets by Vedran Mimica

fantastic colored fabrics. I grew up in a very modern and very-multicultural environment. I studied at the Technical University of Eindhoven (TU/e), where I was very curious about, and very interested in, physics. During my childhood, a scientific journal would arrive in the mail every week, showcasing the world's latest innovations and discoveries. These feature articles always captured my imagination. When this journal came each week, I always read it. But just a few years later, the media landscape changed, and suddenly TV took precedent, in terms of communicating new ideas to the world. At the TU/e, I began my studies as a physics student, and during that time the school was very much hands on, and focused very much on engineering. It was there that I first worked with a computer, but we also used our hands. My idea was that at the university I would be, each day, in the library for three hours. And that is what I did. It was an incredible environment to be in, reading about philosophers and architects that perhaps others at that time were not interested in. During this period I also become interested in what was happening in the USA and Japan, but also within Europe. I also went to Paris quite often. And there were always lectures within a few hours drive of Eindhoven, and I was very much involved in the events happening within that radius. And then of course, I went to Russia.

VM After your graduation, and after you established your office in Heerlen, you were invited by Alvin Boyarsky to teach in London at the AA School of Architecture. At that time the school was, perhaps, in its golden years of architectural education, with Rem Koolhaas and Zaha Hadid and Elia Zenghelis, and many others present. How did this experience, of being in London during the early 1980's, immersed within this very intense environment, affect you and your outlook towards architecture?

WA First, one has to understand that I studied in Eindhoven and not in Delft. This may not seem like a big difference to someone unfamiliar with the Netherlands' architectural educations, but the Technical University of Delft (TU Delft) is a design school, and the TU/e is a polytechnic. At the TU/e, Geert Bekaert was a very important Belgian professor for me, and probably the person who first introduced Koolhaas to the Netherlands. Bekaert's writings are very important, both to many others and myself. Because of him, a lot of philosophy was imparted within the school. At that time, the university was interested in highly technical ideas and problems, and Bekaert gave the university a completely different outlook on what that meant, via his interest in philosophy. At that time, Hans Tupker was also a young professor at the TU/e, and perhaps he did not have the biggest architectural firm, but what he was doing was travelling around the world, and he introduced to that school, and to me as well, the work of Judith Turner and Zaha Hadid, who at that time had just graduated at the AA. These people were incredibly interesting to me then, and they continue to be interesting to me today. The years I spent alongside Alvin Boyarsky, who was at that time the AA's director, were highly influential. And I was very much aware of the debates concerning Postmodernism and Deconstructivism, and all of these movements happening in architecture. But I was not interested in all that, and neither was the TU/e. Instead, that school looked in other directions, such as the debates happening in Italy and the USA, for instance. When I arrived in London, Zaha, alongside Rem and Peter Cook and Peter Wilson, confronted me as professors, at the time when Bernard Tschumi had just left. Everything happening at the AA at that time was not only an internal debate. The AA was not a part of the ism's being practiced outside the school, except for Charles Jencks, who very often initiated debates on Postmodernism. Boyarsky always wanted to include everyone. He was clever enough to understand that he needed to invite different contemporary voices to the school. When Ben van Berkel finished his studies, he also taught at the AA. It was not a school where students worked all day on their projects, but instead a place where dialogue and discourse happened. There was just no space to work there, in the sense of producing physical things. But there was space for lectures and debates and discussion. The AA was an integral part of London. I flew back and forth between England and the Netherlands every week for many years, during the time that Boyarsky had also invited Peter Eisenmann, Tony Vidler, and John Hejduk to teach, and suddenly, the American architecture scene flew back and forth to London, too.

VM Wiel, it is clear that your time spent studying, and the periods directly thereafter, were of great importance to your own architectural development. Continuing in time, I would like to ask about your first major building, the Academy of Art & Architecture in Maastricht. I remember, during our time together at the Berlage Institute, that students were always approaching me, asking me to arrange a study trip to visit the building. And we did end up visiting the project with the students. A couple of months after, I went there again, this time with Kenneth Frampton. In one of his texts on the building, Frampton noted how he had never seen such a level of maturity in a work by such a young architect. Indeed it was, for everyone at that time, being there and seeing this building, in this medieval setting of Maastricht's inner city, completely unique. And as Frampton noted, it is a very mature work. Wiel, could you explain the importance of this building to your practice, your office, and your own architectural definitions?

WA When I was shortlisted for Academy of Art & Architecture in Maastricht, I had just finished a small shop around the corner, the Beltgens Fashion Shop. While working on that shop, I was interested in the idea of the entrance door being higher than the front façade's window. The back window of the shop, which overlooked the courtyard, and the front door aligned, so that the whole building block became the façade. It was an attempt to compress the space's features into a flat image, when seen from the street, in which the viewer could simultaneously see through the entire space. The client had a small budget, and so I chose to use only one oversized piece of Corten steel, and cut the window and door from this one steel sheet. If you were to ask me why I used steel, the decision was of course conscious, as that part of the city has a burnt-maroon cast to it, due to the surrounding brick facades. So I had to consider what the shop would look like as it began to age. Shortly after it was completed the city was awarding an architecture prize, for the very first time. The jury shortlisted about 10 different buildings, excluding this shop. There were three jury members, two from Belgium, one from the Netherlands, and they decided who would win the prize. One of those members was Geert Bekaert. After their selection of the award's winner, the jury walked by the shop on their way to dinner, and during that dinner they discussed this shop, and asked themselves, and the city officials, why it was not shortlisted for the prize. There was a heated debate, and to make a long story short, this shop was eventually awarded the prize. It was a great honor. There is even a drawing of the shop published in the book Wiel Arets: Inspiration & Process in Architecture (Moleskin, 2012), showing its compression in axonometric projection, and rendered in fantastic colored pencil.

Regarding the Academy of Art & Architecture, nine architects were shortlisted, including myself. Every one of them presented a conventional design that shuffled the given program. I approached the jury, explaining that the site had three trees, that it was disjointed, and further explained that the building would certainly need to be divided into two separate building, with a bridge connecting them. I ended up telling the building's design competition jury the same narrative Alvin Boyarsky had once told me about the AA; I explained to the jury that there needed to be lecture rooms, installations, a gallery, a café, a library, and a large staircase. The narrative was a mental construct of the building, explaining how its bridge would work, if the routing of the building were to be weaved through it. Then the question was: What should we do with the façade? The school did not want to the building to impose on the surroundings — a medieval city — and they certainly did not want students to be constantly moving behind windows, with rubbish visible from the exterior, adding a sort of visual pollution to the neighborhood. I proposed that we would make the building's glass frosted, so that the people inside would be able to concentrate, and the people outside would only see the glow of the building at night, and the figures moving behind its façade. I also presented an image of a jellyfish, with its tentacles, to the jury. When I was awarded the building's design, we had to translate that idea into a physical material, and so we ended up constructing the building in concrete, using glass brick to cover the floors, ceilings, and windows. It is obvious when one looks at this building that the glass block is perhaps too industrial, or too reminiscent of Maison de Verre. But I never considered that work to be a precedent in any way. With this building, as well as with the Beltgens Fashion Shop, my architectural language began to shape; it stemmed directly from these projects. In that respect, I could also mention the Allianz Headquarters, currently finishing construction in Zürich; it has four bridges and each bridge has been covered with glass, both below and above. For me, architecture is never an image. But of course, what one sees, visits, experiences, and digests influences one's perception. The people in my office know that I always try to reset, from the beginning of every project. I always begin with a blank piece of paper, and really attempt to create something new. But I never do this for the sake of new. The moment one begins to copy-paste, in my opinion, they will never arrive at the essence of what the work really is, or perhaps should be.

VM Another building from your oeuvre that I would like to discuss, as it is quite canonical, is your library on the Uithof campus of the Utrecht University in the Netherlands. My daughter Kora studied at the Faculty of Medicine, and saw the library open on the campus. She experienced the library as a student, as a user, and she found herself incredibly focused when studying inside. It is not a library where one simply comes to read books. Today this type of building would more than likely be restricted due to diminished budgets, but this building really is an incredibly important contribution to the entire Uithof campus in Utrecht, and it was built during a very ambitious time in the university's history.

WA I am happy you mentioned your daughter in relation to this project, because she is a layperson. What I like about the Politea is that the architect and the layman are in discussion. And that is another reason why I started to write the publication I am currently working on, called the Unconscious City. Most people that deal with buildings are not architects, or specialists — they are laymen. When the client of the shop in Maastricht asked me to do that building, I had to have many debates about the window being low, and how people would be able to look inside, among many other points of discussion. At this time I was also doing research on cinema at the TU/e, and I knew that cinema was either for layman-layman, who only want to be entertained — something we could compare to pop-architecture — and that there is also cinema, where people allow themselves more time to observe. And even if one is not a director or expert on film, one can gain much from it.

Back to the library in Utrecht; it was a competition. And Aryan Sikkema was the director of the head of building at the university, and a very interesting and powerful person. The director of the library was however, a very clever guy whose knowledge about architecture at that time could have been considered to be that of an interested layman. Yet he knew everything about how a library should operate, and was very clever and open to developing the entire programmatic strategy of the building over many meetings and dinners. At that time, I was also presenting my design for the MoMA extension in Manhattan, and there were four board members on the jury. I presented the project in Manhattan, and the jury had asked us for two options. But of course when one has to present two options it will always be more difficult. 10 architects had to present two options each, totaling 20, and I knew that that could potentially be very confusing. After presenting my design for the MoMA, someone from my office met me at Schiphol Airport in Amsterdam, and gave me a carousel with 84 slides in it, to present to the jury in Utrecht. I arrived in Utrecht a few hours later, fresh off the plane, knowing that I had only one hour to present

Filip, Sasha, Maks

Los Angeles, 2016

Oris 83

Zagreb, 2013

my design for the university's library. I decided to take a postcard out of my pocket, which one of the jury members of the MoMA competition had given me during my presentation. It was a postcard of Mondrian's 'Broadway Boogie-Woogie'. I knew that I had just made a big mistake during my presentation in Manhattan, where we were only allowed to present 20 slides; the jury was totally confused. Instead, I decided to explain the design to the library's jury, and so I sketched my presentation, and eventually sketched the whole building. The sketch showed that there were some clouds; these clouds would be the building. I explained to the jury of the library that if their university were to put 42 million books in that space, and if we together were to condition this space, in a very specific way, that it would be able to become their library. In the end, the jury wanted to see these 84 slides, and I briefly flipped through them. But I explained that they would not be happier after that, because this is the building, and this is what we will do. I also explained – and this is very important – that I could not tell them more, because I had to know my client. That is crucial for me: I want to know my client and I need to have a concept. In my work, one will always see that it is the program, flexibility, routing, and the materials that construct or bring light through a façade. Acoustics are also incredibly important to me. Like a good restaurant, a good building should make you feel at home. And that is what we tried to do, and achieved with the Utrecht University Library.

VM I would like to continue with two smaller houses from your oeuvre, the Hedge House and the Jellyfish House. With the Hedge House, which you built in a protected garden of a 17th century castle, the project was labeled as an art gallery, yet was built under the guise of a garden shed. And the Jellyfish House, in the Mediterranean context, has been an incredibly interesting contribution to the rather standard private villas in Marbella. I have read about your relation to the tradition of the total work of art (Gesamtkunstwerk), and the belief that we can still have expressions of total works of art, where the client and architect work towards a private or semi-public typology. This often leads to your clients living in extremely cultural environments, within their private domains. Could you elaborate on these two works?

WA I was very impressed when I visited Cape Canaveral for the first time, seeing the spaceship that was on the moon. There, one can see how this vehicle was made. And I was impressed not only because of its design, but also by the fact that it worked for its purpose without striving to aestheticism. The reason why I am against formalism, and the reason why I am against beauty for the sake of beautification, is that it is fashionable and short minded, and therefore will not last. Aging is not a bad thing. Humans are part of a momentum in history, and we should change with that path and enforce its limits. Just because we can walk on our hands, why should we? So the engineering of these space vehicles is important to me, as are their stories. How can one combine stories, engineering, making, and programming, and what is the purpose of all that? I always try to go one step further in every project I do, in order to understand the question of the client. And that is a question the architect cannot answer. The Hedge House began at the same time as the Jellyfish House. The clients of the Hedge House were art collectors, and they had been following my career. When I received the Maaskant Award in 1989 they approached me to say that they were interested in working with me, though they were not yet sure for what. In the end they asked me to design a small house for their chickens, and whether that was a joke or not, I still do not know. The husband later invited me for a glass of wine, which he hosted in the stables on his castle's grounds. He showed me a small area of the garden, and asked if we could perhaps build something small, perhaps a chicken house or an orchid room. He knew what he was doing, knowing that he was not allowed to build on these grounds due to the fact that his house is listed as a state monument in the Netherlands, meaning it and its grounds are protected. We decided to put a structure there, and when we first presented it to the city hall, they said it was impossible to build. So instead, we made a stable for chickens, an orchid room for his wife, with a kitchen and dining room, and an art gallery as well. In section one sees these four programs, sunken into the garden's grounds. We combined these programs into one entity, with the museum spaces below. In the end, the project became a hedge house, for chickens, garden tools, and orchids. And it is also a museum.

Key to that project was the engineer. And in all of my work, including this one, the collaboration with engineers has been vital. Van Rossum and Rob Nijsse are engineers I have collaborated with on almost all the buildings my office has done. Later I began to work with others, but these two were initially very important to me because we always worked towards building a structure that was not covered with cladding. The structure is instead the end product, and that is very difficult. Most of my work with engineers has not been to make a building's shape work, but to make its climate work instead. For how small the Hedge House is, it was extremely difficult to create its construction, given installation needs and other practicalities that come with building in the Netherlands. A lot of concrete in this building is actually hanging in tension and is not under pressure; the same is true of the AZL Pension Fund Headquarters in Heerlen. With the Hedge House, the routing from the exterior to interior is incredibly important, and so it needed to be able to be programmed differently, during various periods of the day. Buildings simply need flexibility.

The Jellyfish House, on the other hand, took us about ten years to build, and that time was spent pushing the work as far as we possibly could. We ask a lot from our clients, engineers, and consultants; yet we never spend more money doing this – it is always done within the budget. For this particular house, the client asked us to build a house in Los Monteros, Spain. It is a very interesting location on the coast of the country, between Marbella and Málaga. Within the development from the 1960's, there was one plot that had not yet been built. It was a rectangular plot close to the water, and the client – who is Belgian – after just completing a new house for his family in Belgium, told me that he wanted this house in Spain, to encourage and invite his family to relax there. I am not sure if this was another joke or not, but when I asked what he would like to have in his house, he said an aquarium. Because of this rectangular plot, we were given the opportunity to flip the house upside down, since the site's sun was mostly blocked; and so I proposed to build the pool on the roof. It made sense. The roof became the structure, with one column, with a glass floor and veranda to the kitchen, so that when one's cooking, people can be seen swimming. We challenged the contractors with this project. And at one point they even called the client, asking to no longer be responsible for the building, once the pool was filled, which of course did not happen. Though when the pool was first filled, to test it, the building deflected only 3mm, after 24 hours. It is a house that is built in such a way that the owners' children can go to the beach, enter the site, and head directly to the pool on the roof without ever going inside the house. The exterior routing, from the sea to the roof, is completely independent of the house interior; it is both slow and quick. The experience of swimming in this pool is simply amazing. The client recently told me, that no matter what happens, his house would always be there.

VM Indeed, that house will be there for a very long time. Wiel, I would like to continue with a situation you have found yourself in during the last five years. In terms of architectural offices, you have actually experienced the enlargement of your office and the scope of your professional activities, by working in Chicago and opening offices in Switzerland and Germany. What are your reasons for these recent changes, and how have these changes affected the development of your projects Schwäbisch Media in Ravensburg, and the Allianz Headquarters in Zürich, two projects that best exemplify the state of your work, as it is right now?

WA Schwäbisch Media came about due to our winning a design competition for the new office of this publishing company. It is situated in the center of the medieval city of Ravensburg, Germany. We developed a strategy for an office with 350 people, which is also freestanding. We explored the idea — drawing inspiration from the surrounding traditional German fachwerk villas — of setting up five separate 'villas' for these employees to work in. And all the other competitors had designed great buildings, but none of them searched for a new typology. The company is composed of several smaller companies, and we wanted to give them a smaller scaled environment, where all branches could work in one building. Because of this, we wanted to impart a domestic atmosphere on these working spaces, by connecting them to the more communal spaces, such as a lobby and café. There are gardens between these 'villas', and a glass fence surrounds the project's site, becoming its façade at certain points within this perimeter. The volumes on the first, second, third, fourth, and fifth floors all look toward one another, with gardens separating them. And by going downstairs, employees can access these other villas. Our idea was to give to this rather large property, a building with 350 people, the sense that its employees would be living and working in this environment; they have the possibility to be outside, to meet one another, and to communicate in a very informal way, while still being 'at work'. By allowing and encouraging this, the building is always alive, both during the day and night, both inside and out. These employees now feel at home. That notion helped me to understand that it is not only me, and other architects, who are living in this 24-hour condition. And in that way, it is a very crucial work for my office.

Regarding the Allianz Headquarters, Switzerland is a very different country, in terms of its building practices. About 15 years ago I was asked to be on a sort of jury to advise the city of Zürich on its ideas for its redeveloping areas, such as Escher Wyss, which I think is one of the most interesting areas right now in Europe. It is defined by its roughness, as it is a former industrial area, yet that 24-hour life has already begun to appear. My office developed a strategy for the city called 'rough premium', which was for the western side of the city. And my office has also done proposals for the ETH in Zürich, and the city continues to become even more interesting for us. When we were awarded the Allianz Headquarters we decided to open an office there, too, and it is the first building that we will complete in Switzerland.

The Allianz Headquarters is very near the Zürich airport, in an area called Wallisellen. It is an emerging district with offices, shops, and housing, and it will be very important to the city's public realm. We were able to have a debate about the urban proposal, and within this constellation we were awarded the area's tower, and a smaller five-story building, which at the beginning were not connected. The client is Allreal, as a developer, and the user is Allianz, who has a long-term lease. And so we had to consider what would happen to the building in the future, and who would be renting which portions of it. Maybe in 15 years it is a very diverse hybrid building; we just do not know. While working on the tower, and the adjacent five-story building, we started to develop the idea of a larger company working in this massive tower and the smaller building. People can freely move throughout these connected buildings without using an elevator, as the floors are connected with voids and staircases, so that people can move through the building as a landscape. At a certain point, it was clear that to activate the adjacent Richti Square, and to create an urban context near this building, its ground floor would need to contain shops and retail spaces, accessible from the square. These two building are connected by a series of four bridges, which are for circulation, but can also be used as conversation places, as each is 8 meters wide. We started this project as an urban proposal, and after much debate, while working with the client we developed the strategies for the structure, the façade, and the ceiling. This project was actually the first time that we really spent endless effort on a building's ceiling, which became a sort of fifth façade. The heating, acoustic, and ventilation needs of the building are all met by components of this ceiling. The Allianz Headquarters' façade is composed of a closed cavity system, with a metal curtain hanging in this space that moves to shade the building in accordance with its changing daylight needs. If one were to look up at this building from below, there is the question of what exactly the building is; is it an office, a school, housing? We did not want the façade to show the program. The lower stories are hybridized, used for conferences, restaurants, and even espresso bars. The building animates the public realm, and the public realm activates the building. Working 'in progress' on the building allowed me to realize that it already had a life before it even began its first occupied life, knowing it will have many more lives in the years ahead. And I am sure that this building will be recognized as a new typology. I hope that it has been seen as a positive virus, changing its surroundings when they are confronted with it, while giving the people who use it some new opportunities concerning their daily flexibility. Buildings should be state of the art, but not in a way that they are high-tech machines. A building is still a one of a kind product, developed by an architect, for a client, on a particular site, during a particular moment in time. We should understand, in regards to 'Rethinking Metropolis', that buildings play an important role in the constraints of a city.

VM I would like to conclude with a question concerning why we are here, in Chicago, conducting this interview on the South Side of the city, at the one of the historically most famous architecture school in the world, the Illinois Institute of Technology College of Architecture (IIT CoA), where you are currently the Dean. Where would you like to take the school in the years ahead, and in what ways will Nowness, the school's first publication under your direction, and the conceptual umbrella of 'Rethinking Metropolis' influence the research and education here in Chicago?

WA Teaching or leading within academic institutions, such as the AA, Columbia, Cooper Union, Berlage Institute, UdK, and now the IIT CoA, have all been conscious decisions, to allow me to look for a moment. I felt I could contribute to these schools. And alongside my career as an architect, I always considered these appointments to be the right decisions. Being at a school, where the work I produce as an architect, whether it be writings or buildings, allows me to bridge the professional practice of architecture with its more academic concerns. Sometimes one does not know why they react to a question or situation the way they do. But when I first came to Chicago, to lecture in autumn 2012, I could feel that the city had an incredibly positive attitude, and that its public realm is amazing, and that the same is true of its culinary scene, which I also find important. The city is very dense in certain areas, and yet 200 meters further to, for instance, the east, is Lake Michigan, and to the west is Michigan Avenue, with its famed retailers. The life that I experience in Chicago, and the way the school's international momentum is gaining speed, alongside the positive political climate of the city, has allowed me to think that I could really contribute to this school. After my two latest research topics, at the UdK in Berlin – Unconscious City and Tokyo Utopia – I knew that research was something I was once again ready to delve into. And here in America, people are creating new ideas and new inventions everyday; perhaps the most promising example is the Tesla electric car. We, as humans, plan for living on Earth. Yet as I wrote about in Wiel Arets: Autobiographical References (Birkhäuser, 2012), the world is becoming one big city, and so we should understand that the area outside this planet's orbit will one day soon concern us, too. Architecture and its concern for technology are seen as very important at IIT. My predecessor, Mies van der Rohe, worked on many interesting buildings here in Illinois, including the Lake Shore Drive Apartments, the Farnsworth House, and of course the home of the IIT College of Architecture, S.R. Crown Hall. We can learn from Chicago locals about how we should approach these new realms. The belief that we live in a natural flow of technology, especially here in the USA, where new technology continually infiltrates daily lives, is one reason why I truly believe that my endeavors at this school will make it the address within architectural education, worldwide. Chicago's mayor is excellent, IIT's leaders are distinguished, the CoA's faculty and administration are poised to begin the 2013-2014 school year, and I am certain that the city's current political climate will ensure the sustained success of this school, well beyond my tenure.

Croatia

EAST-WEST: BLURRING TERRITORIES
Geneva 2005

ARCHITECTURE OF TRANSITION AND THE
PRODUCTION OF MEANING
Zagreb 2000

CROATIAN ARCHITECTURE, INVENTING REALITY
Zagreb 2007

NJIRIC&NJIRIC: CHILDREN OF ST.PETER'S ST.

BALKAN TELETUBBIES AND DECONSTRUCTION OF
MODERNISM
Zagreb 2001

CHILDREN'S ROOM
Zagreb 2003

NEXT EUROPE
Zagreb 2002

MISSION IMPOSSIBLE? I DO NOT THINK SO
Zagreb 2001

EXERCISING EUROPE
Zagreb 2005

BORDERS: THE OTHER SIDE OF GLOBALIZATION
Zagreb 2003

NEW SCHOOL OF ARCHITECTURE IN THE CITY OF
SPLIT
Zagreb 2006

WEST BALKAN ARCHITECTURE

GYMNASIUM/QUANTUM LEAP IN
MIROSLAV KRLEŽA STREET
Zagreb 2007

EXITS ARE CLEARLY MARKED
Zagreb 2008

WHERE IS (CROATIAN) ARCHITECTURE HEADED?
Zagreb 2010

CITIES CAN CHANGE THEIR IDENTITY
Split 2013

Slovenia

6IX PACK: CONTEMPORARY SLOVENIAN
ARCHITECTURE
Ljubljana 2006

STRICTLY CONTROLLED SMOKING
Zagreb 2007

Albania

TIRANA METROPOLIS
Rotterdam 2004

SIX ANSWERS ON ALBANIA BY VEDRAN MIMICA
Vienna 2010

A VISION BEYOND PLANNING
Rotterdam 2004

Montenegro

TOURISTS IN THEIR HOME TOWNS
Kotor 2014

AFFAIR AND OF TRANSITION

With the fall of the Berlin Wall, the raison d'être of the buffer zone between geopolitical east and west, known as Yugoslavia, disappeared. A Pandora's box of political nightmares was opened. Incredibly tragic wars in former Yugoslavia, based on Slobodan Milošević and Radovan Karadžić's proto fascist ethnic cleansing policies, resulted in the loss of more than 130 000 lives, 3,5 millions of displaced people[51] and radical destruction of cities. Just to remember Vukovar[52] in Croatia and Sarajevo in Bosnia which suffered unimaginable destruction and human loss.

The Western Balkans as a neologism was coined to describe the countries of ex-Yugoslavia (Croatia, Bosnia-Herzegovina, Serbia, Montenegro and the Former Yugoslav Republic of Macedonia minus Slovenia) and Albania.

The texts included within this section discuss the political engagement of architecture in a post-socialist transitional society. Transition from one party political system and state regulated economy to parliamentary democracy and free markets was characterized by disappearance of unquestionable authorities, universal dogmas and basic ethics. Social transition introduced the falling to pieces, instability, uncertainty and lack of definition. Under such circumstances, defining language, speech, expression, creativity and discipline represents a titanic effort for architects in Western Balkans countries.

My answer to those questions, albeit perhaps oversimplified, mostly

---

51 Source: The UN High Commissioner for Refugees. www.grida.no/graphicslib/detail/refugees-and-displaced-people-from-the-former-yugoslavia-since-1991_0c5a#, accessed September 10, 2016

52 Vukovar is a beautiful town in eastern Croatia and its largest river port, located at the confluence of the Vuka and Danube rivers. Once a strong commercial and industrial center, Vukovar was completely destroyed in 1991 by the radicalized members of Yugoslav Peoples' Army. It has been slowly rebuilt since 1995.

had a political tone, by emphasizing the importance of the European integrations processes. Perhaps we who represent a large minority, with double identities, citizenship, as well as working and professional experiences, from both Western Balkans and Western Europe, could be able to generate an entirely new dialogue about urban transformation in the transitional post-socialist democracies. These processes will most certainly include critical negotiations between the global discourse and a local one, and probably a radical reduction of differences between them.

The most successful and productive relation in external engagement of the Berlage studio work happened, surprisingly for all of us, in Tirana, Albania. From 2000, when elected the Mayor, Edi Rama[53] engaged in a utopian project to modernize Tirana, the most undeveloped of all European capitals. Berlage studio production greatly influenced the development of the regulatory plan for Tirana, while many students continued working in Tirana on new metropolitan projects as practicing architects after their graduation at the Berlage. I served as mayor Rama's adviser for urban development, chairing many invited international architectural competitions for development of major projects for Tirana's economic, infrastructural, cultural and residential projects. Those architectural competitions were won by Henning Larsen architects, 51N4E, MVRDV, Xaveer de Geyter, BIG and Boles&Wilson and in toto marked Tirana's future development.

---

53   Edi Rama has been the Prime Minister of Albania since 2013.

EAST-WEST: BLURRING TERRITORIES

Published as a transcript of the lecture in Actes du Colloque Urbicide~Urgence~Durabilité: Reconstruction et Mémoire (Acts of the Colloquium: Urbicide, Urgency, Durability: Reconstruction and Memory) eds. Rémi Baudouï and Anna Grichting. Geneva: Institut d'Architecture de l'Université de Genève 2005

Upon receiving the invitation to speak on the subject of "Urbicide, Reconstruction and Memory," I was very enthusiastic, as it was a lecture that I have wanted to do for a long time. However, I was also a little apprehensive, as it is very difficult, or nearly impossible, to talk about this subject. It is quite rare that architecture schools get involved in the more humanitarian side of the art of construction.

Geneva offers the potential for a contextual debate, with many globally active institutions active in operational work, prevention and research: the United Nations, the Red Cross, and the United Nations High Commission for Refugees, UNESCO, and many other non-governmental institutions.

I am probably a kind of nomad, basically with roots from Dalmatia, Split, but living and working in the Netherlands, which explains why, with the help of Photoshop, I have superimposed a painting by Mondrian with the plan of Diocletian's Palace in Split. I think that the image describes my hybrid "DNA."

The concept of "balkanization" is an attempt to theorize the last conflicts in the Balkans. However, without any academic background or method, one has considerable difficulties fitting this period of conflict into a particular historical, cultural, sociological or geographical theory. Of course, as an academic, one can, should and is expected to "theorize." Nonetheless, my personal experiences and views as an insider/outsider tread upon incredibly slippery ground. History is an extremely dynamic concept, and in the particular case of the Balkans it is constantly evolving. For example, during WWII my father believed that Joseph Stalin was a charismatic leader; Borislav Ćurčić and my generation believed that Tito was a great leader, and the younger generation in Croatia has been told that Franjo Tuđman was an excellent statesman. All this happened in less than one century. It should be obvious as to why the ground is so slippery.

At the time of Tito's funeral in 1980 Yugoslavia was a buffer zone between East and West, invented as a result of the Treaty of Yalta from 1943, conceived by Churchill, Roosevelt, Stalin and others. In 1943, there was a 50/50 influence within Yugoslavia between Stalin and Western powers. There was a fear that the "haven," known as Yugoslavia, would disappear and dissolve after Tito's death, but this did not happen immediately. Tito was a political genius. One can look at Yugoslavia within the terms of Tito's political success. Between 1945 and 1980, Yugoslavia received foreign aid of 109 billion dollars from both East and West. A couple of billion of these dollars were spent on defense (precisely how well the military used their weapons was shown to us by Borislav Ćurčić in his lecture on Sarajevo) but the rest was mostly implemented in the industrialization and modernization of the country. The reason Yugoslavia ceased to exist in the late 1980s was the fall of the Berlin Wall (1989). Nobody believed this would happen, and the geostrategic reason for Yugoslavia's existence, as some sort of buffer zone between the "good" guys in the West and the "evil" guys in the East, or vice versa, became obsolete. In the time-space travel map of Europe with Berlin in the center, France appears as a small country because the high-speed railway lines of the TGV compress time-space relations, inversely, Albania, Bosnia, and Croatia figure as very big countries because one travels endless hours through them. In 1994, a number of us (Croatian architects living in western Europe) went to Zagreb to explain to fellow Croatians that Croatia could not develop independently after the war – and after the fall of Yugoslavia – but must find a way to integrate into Europe. In place of the seemingly difficult inclusion into Europe's political structure like The European Economic Community (EEC), Croatia should at least strive to strategically place itself within the continent's infrastructure networks.

The Berlage Institute organized seminars in Zagreb together with local emerging architects and the municipality, and we developed a series of diagrams and maps to demonstrate how to strengthen the potential of Croatian cities. We believed that the ideas produced during these encounters could

ACTES DU COLLOQUE:
URBICIDE - URGENCES - DURABILITE:
RECONSTRUCTION ET MÉMOIRE

Geneva: Institut d'Architecture
de l'Universite de Geneve, 2005

Vedran Mimica
East-West: Blurring Territories

PROJECT OF THE MONUMENT
ON PETROVA GORA

ed. Andre Mohorovičić
Acta architectonica, Zagreb, 1981

ORIS 9

2001

Vedran Mimica
Mission Impossible?
I Don't Think So

BALKANOLOGY
Architekturzentrum Wien
22/10/09 - 18/01/10

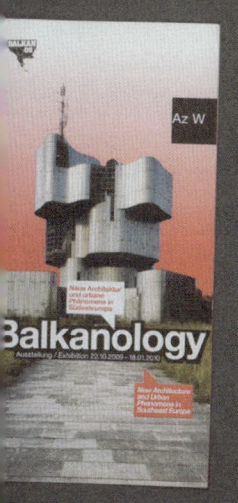

Tito: The Story from Inside

Milovan Djilas
Harcourt publishers, New York, 1980

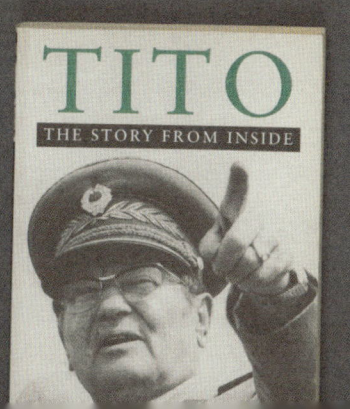

contribute to the development of possible strategies for the future sustainable development.

Going back in history, the Austrian-Hungarian Empire was a very interesting, multi-ethnic, cosmopolitan state with (more or less) equal rights to all citizens.

Zagreb was situated in the Hungarian part of the Empire and in the mid 19th century it sought greater autonomy and the way to break away from Hungarian dependency through Pan-Slavism. With the end of WWI in 1918, Zagreb became a city in the Kingdom of Yugoslavia.

However, the things did not go smoothly. A radical Serb and a Member of Parliament shot Stjepan Radić, a Croatian politician, who died in the Yugoslav parliament in Belgrade in 1928. This was a clear message from the Serbian nationalists, that those Croatian dreams of independence or at least equal rights should not and would not become realities. This incident took place in parliament and took the form of a parliamentary "debate" with guns.

In the beginning of the 20th century, Zagreb was a prosperous city, where numerous Croatians participated in a sort of Austro-Hungarian multiculturalism. But then, quite different ideologies came to this part of the world – Stalinism and Titoism, as a result of WWII. In 1948, President Tito resisted Joseph Stalin when the Soviets attempted to interfere with political development in Yugoslavia, as they later did in Hungary in 1956 and Czechoslovakia in 1968. This made Tito a very powerful man in the view of many, inside and outside the country. However, his grip on power became shaky in the beginning of the 1970s, when a group of young Croatian and Serbian politicians proposed a revised version of Titoism.

One of the youngest and particularly strong voices of this revision was Savka Dapčević Kučar, one of Tito's young partisans during WWII. Her revision proposed a decentralized Yugoslavia, which gave more power to the economy and less to ideology, a federalist state with more control over public matters and finances. Tito made a huge historical mistake in not heeding or promoting these young politicians, who were ideologically "healthy" and economically advanced. Instead, he promoted a bunch of old apparatchiks – and they succeeded him as a kind of collective body to rule Yugoslavia, after his death in 1980. Tito's successors provoked a nightmare situation, and much of what happened in Yugoslavia in the 1980s was due to Tito's inability to transform the country in the 1970s.

Maria Braut, a photographer from Zagreb, represents the soft atmospheres of Zagreb in the 70's – life in the city was pleasant, new housing was being built and the quality of architectural production was quite high.

Quite important and powerful was the "new art" from 1964 to the late 1970s. Braco Dimitrijević was one of the most well known artists of this period, and these contemporary artists were in close contact with Joseph Beuys. The argument put forward by many artists was to oppose the destruction of Yugoslavia in the 1980s and 1990s, which was a wide-scale catastrophe, and to promote the substantial social and cultural life that the country had produced in the 1960s and 1970s.

In the early 1990s, when it was obvious that things were not going well, the first person was killed in Zagreb. He was not killed because the war started in Zagreb, but because he was protesting against the intervention by the Yugoslav Peoples Army in Slovenia, which basically represented the beginning of the war in Yugoslavia. Slovenia sent a message to Belgrade proposing to Milošević and other members of the government that the Slovenian, Serbian, Croatian, Macedonian, and Bosnia-Herzegovinian governments form a confederation, in which confederate states would govern their own matters, and whereby only the military and foreign affairs would remain central. This was a clear attempt to avoid any form of armed conflict. The radical Serbs, especially Milošević refused, saying that there were no way these republics could control their borders, and Yugoslav Peoples Army was sent to Slovenia to "protect" the borders. This was the beginning of the large-scale catastrophe. The war in Croatia begun in August 1991 with Yugoslavian troops and tanks on the streets of Osijek and the subsequent shelling of other cities and the displacement of enormous numbers of refugees. Numerous atrocities were committed towards the civilian population. The argument put forward to justify this intervention was that the Serbian minority in Croatia was in danger. The city of Vukovar, situated on the Danube river, at the border between north-east Croatia and Serbia, was nearly totally demolished. The International Red Cross ran a hospital in Vukovar, which nursed 2000 victims or injured soldiers from both sides of the conflict. When the Yugoslav Peoples Army (at that time predominantly Serbian) captured the city, the Red Cross was asked to leave. However, they protested, claiming that according to the Geneva Convention, they should not and could not leave Vukovar and all its casualties. The Serbian general insisted and they were finally forced to leave. Subsequently, 1,400 bodies were excavated from common graveyards and Vukovar was declared a Croatian holy place.

Srebrenica on the Eastern Bosnian border with Serbia, was declared a safe-haven by the United Nations and abandoned by the Dutch military under the Serbian attack. These remarks are not intended as a criticism or accusation of the Dutch military, but to explain that in the Balkans, the strategies for preventing the conflict were not effective at all, especially when one witness more than 7000 Muslim men killed and buried in Srebrenica.

These events did not seem to disturb the international community. However, what did shock world public opinion was the shelling of Dubrovnik, a tourist destination on the Adriatic, which was badly damaged. To return to the concept of "urbicide" – how can one make a military target of such a beautiful city? Hans-Dietrich Genscher, the German Minister of Foreign Affairs, and ally of the Croatians, believed in the beginning of the 1990s that the conflict in Yugoslavia could have been stopped if the international community had recognized the new states. But the British and French were opposed to this idea and Europe was totally divided on the issue. The war in Croatia ended with the recognition of Slovenia and Croatia, but this left the Bosnian territory open for discussion. Towards the end of war in Croatia, Stipe Mesić[54], went to the European parliament in Strasbourg and alerted the European Community that they had to do their utmost to stop the war in Bosnia, whereas it was quite clear that Milošević intended its ruination. Milošević, together with seriously demented people like Radovan Karadžić and General Mladić, had lost war in Croatia, but still occupied a great part of the country with his powerful war machine. They appeared unstoppable. Unfortunately, Mesić's appeal was lost in a vacuum – there was no response, nobody listened to this important message and some European politicians just hoped the Bosnian war would not happen.

Mostar was one of the most beautiful cities in Bosnia and Herzegovina, where Serbs, Muslims and Croats lived in some sort of harmony. Eastern Mostar is predominantly Muslim while western Mostar is predominantly Croatian, although a small Muslim enclave exists also in the western part of the city. This proved to be a big problem for Croatian politicians and paramilitaries from Herzegovina. They decided it would be a good idea to shell the Muslims and push them to the other side of the river, without any important strategic or military reasons to justify their actions. The iconic Mostar bridge[55] was demolished separating the Muslims from the Croats. This became one of the visual and conceptual symbols of the war. Prior to the war, the bridge was renowned as an exceptional example of the Ottoman art of building bridges.

In the megalopolis of Bombay 250,000 people live in the Dharavi, the largest slums of Asia. One can make an analogy to Yugoslavia, with its previous Austro-Hungarian heritage of order and efficiency, which today, in some areas, resembles the slums of Bombay. A certain chaos and confusion reigns – a lot of questions remain unanswered – where to go, whom to help? Our architectural moral and conceptual backgrounds are questioned. During the golden years, Yugoslavia naively believed that its privileged situation would continue eternally. The damaged and destroyed buildings, in certain cases being of archi-

54   The president of Croatia from 2000 to 2010.

55   Old Bridge, as it used to be, was a 16th-century Ottoman bridge. It was destroyed in 1993 and reconstructed in 2004.

tectural interest, are witness to this radical change.

Having visited Sarajevo three times, I can say that during the Olympics in 1984 it was one of the most beautiful cities on the entire planet. The second visit, after the war, proved, as Ćurčić also said, that one can kill a city – destroy the National and University library and burn manuscripts, witnesses of the city's multi-ethnic history – but the spirit of the city cannot be killed. A special spirit kept the people of Sarajevo alive and during their hardships they developed a sense of humor and even a new slang. The municipal soccer training field in Sarajevo was transformed into a graveyard, and it became a black joke to describe where people were buried – "Oh, she is in the 16 meter line (box), in front of the goal." An image of the main railway track a hundred meters from Sarajevo main railway station shows a process of "ruralization" of the city's infrastructures. A shepherd is looking for his animals beside the railway track, something that was truly unimaginable in the city before the war. Nevertheless, it will probably take more than a hundred years to restore the city to its former physiognomy. It is important to be aware that it is not a question of "reconstruction" but a question of large-scale catastrophe recovery.

Should we do something for Sarajevo? What are people doing for Sarajevo? Aida Daidžić fled Sarajevo for Darmstadt and created a body of architects at the Technical University of Darmstadt, who then went to Sarajevo immediately after the war. It is important to mention that two well-known architects visited Sarajevo during the war for a workshop, Thom Mayne and Lebeus Woods. Thom Mayne understood that in a context of war, it was not about architecture, but about cigarettes and whiskey – he arrived well equipped. Together, he and Lebbeus Woods created a new institution, a student organization (body), in the middle of the war while doing the workshop.

I went with Petra Marguc and a group of the Berlage students to Sarajevo to conceive a project for the Open University. The project investigated how the former military barracks built by Marshal Tito could be converted into the Open University. Before starting to elaborate the project for this competition, I asked the Berlage students to investigate if there was any money for this project. The organizers announced that there were 200 million DM available for the project. The students investigated the UN offices in New York, Geneva, and Brussels, to find out if there were really some funds allotted to build the Open University in Sarajevo, but they discovered that there was no funding.

If a convincing proposal was put forward, there could be some funding for basic infrastructure. The students wanted to know what was the involvement of the Press, what was going on? So they interviewed journalists. As the Berlage students are very pushy we came really to the top. The most interesting interview was with Aleksej Ivanko, a Russian who was the official United Nations spokesman during the war in Sarajevo. He told us a lot of very interesting stories. Ivanko discovered that no politician in Sarajevo was truly interested in what happened to the city, that no international relief organizations were really concerned, and that big business was thriving there. The New York Times reported that from 1995 to 1999, the Bosnian government had "stolen" one billion US dollars from the foreign aid deposit. One can question the New York Times sources but it was a common thing to steal foreign aid in Balkans during the war.

So, how should we act? Is there any ideology left, is there any radicalism? How can we understand these two concepts of "culture" and "market" which are getting blurred more and more? Is this some sort of new, natural e-commerce, economy promise for the Balkans? So, we have the scenario of the Balkans as a stage for the end of the 20th century. A couple of Serbian architects, theorizing a big change in Belgrade, were using a leaflet with Richard Burton on the cover, who actually embodied Marshall Tito in a movie[56] from 1973.

While the UNHCR was busy making the high technology GIS/GPS maps that Mr. Bouchardy presented to us, some Albanians in Kosovo were

---

56 The Battle of Sutjeska, the film directed by Stipe Delić, featuring Richard Burton as Marshal Tito.

ACTES DU COLLOQUE:
URBICIDE - URGENCES - DURABILITE:
RECONSTRUCTION ET MEMOIRE

Geneva: Institut d'Architecture
de l'Universite de Geneve, 2005

Vedran Mimica
East-West: Blurring Territories

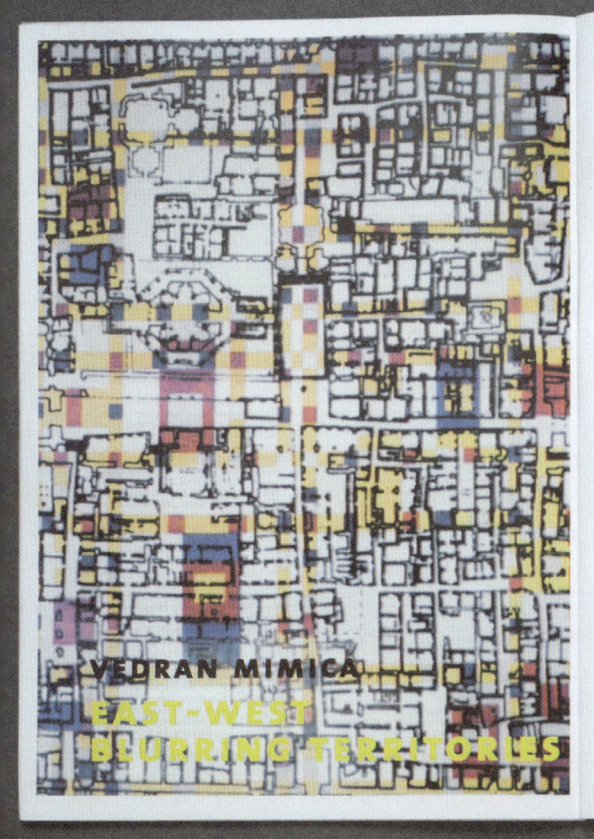

Josip Broz Tito
Borislav Ćurčić
Maria Braut
Braco Dimitrijević
Slobodan Milošević
Hans-Dietrich Genscher
Radovan Karadzić
Ratko Mladić
Slobodan Praljak
Aida Daidjić
Thom Mayne
Lebeus Woods
Petra Marguč
Aleksej Ivanko
Franjo Tudjman
Nassrine Azlmi
Ivo Banac
Liliane Schneiter
Emir Kusturica
Herman Hertzberger
Kenneth Frampton

BALKANOLOGY

Architekturzentrum Wien
22/10/09 - 18/01/10

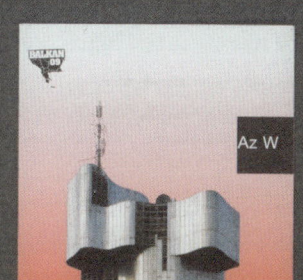

PROJECT OF THE
MONUMENT ON
PETROVA GORA

ed. Andre Mohorovičić
Acta architectonica,
Zagreb, 1981

searching for windows for their shelters. A lot of Serbs were still fleeing and some abandoning their cars. One Albanian man took a door from one of these cars, and made a window for his shelter.

So you see, tomorrow never dies in Balkans.

Questions

Nassrine Azimi The way you presented Yugoslavia, it appears that until Tito died, things were going rather well. In the mid-eighties, I had the opportunity to work with a group of brilliant scientists from ex-Yugoslavia on some environmental GIS applications, and we had a workshop in Split. I recall very well that, one day, during a discussion with six of them – all Croatians, young, well educated, and really extraordinary people – the conversation came down to the difference between Serbs and Croatians. I was astonished by the violence of their words and their feelings, and the level of hatred and rage was shocking, in people that we imagined had overcome them. We are referring to events that happened about five hundred years ago. Are you saying that today, as then, things have not really changed? Or do you see differences in your town of Split that, even though they are painful to acknowledge, have the advantage of reflecting clearly a given situation.

Vedran Mimica I think that is a very essential question. A lot of my friends in Zagreb, architects and non-architects, were Serbs, but I did not know they were Serbs before the war started in 1991. A lot of them ended up as soldiers in the Croatian army, despite the fact that they were Serbs. But what is even more amazing is that a lot of Serbs were "imported" by the Austro-Hungarian Empire from the 15th century on, as soldiers to defend the Empire. When WWI started, Serbs attacked the Austrians and asked them to surrender, then the Austrians, being "imported" Serbs, said "Serbs never surrender". You are immediately in difficulties when you try to analyze the situation. Croats have been perceived as fascists because of the pro-nazi government during WWII. If you look into the facts, Tito was a Croat himself – my father, who was a Croat, killed perhaps more German soldiers during the WWII than the entire Dutch resistance movement, which is my argument towards the Dutch when they say the Croatians are fascists. Most of Tito's partisans were Dalmatian Croats. Serbian radicals are complaining that in WWII concentration camps the Croats killed 700,000 Serbs, which is a crazy number. Yes, indeed, they killed, according to the recent scientific research, 70,000 people, mostly Serbs, also Croatian communists and Gypsies but the numbers are not the most important here; what matters is that we do not operate with the correct data, clear conceptions, and correct histories. The very interesting book I read about Croatian/Serb relations is by Ivo Banac, a Croatian professor at Yale University, and a linguist – "Controversy of the Croatian Language". In this book, he explains that all the Croatian politicians who argue clear Croatian causes, always put Serb-isms in the Croatian language, and all the Serbian nationalists who would like a pure Serbian language put Croatian words, not really knowing what they are arguing for. So it is, as I said before, pretty, pretty slippery. This is what I am trying to say: when you are trying to establish the facts, it is always difficult. Tito, being a communist, inherited a rural country full of peasants. The Yugoslavia of 1945 was basically a rural country. The Avant-Garde of communism are the working class – so what he did was to build factories, cities, and infrastructures. He was not a "banana-republic" ruler; he used these 109 billion dollars to build the country, even if he lived a lavish life-style. Politically, he was obviously a genius, playing the game between East and West. Tito's Yugoslavia can be described, as an example of "enlightened autocracy", (he was named President for life) which functioned economically. It was fake and real – it was fake in the terms that it was not entirely the product of the Yugoslavian economy, but it was real as the result of unbelievably successful global politics. Then Tito came in between Khrushchev and Nixon, between the Soviet Union and the USA, as a sort of non-aligned, non-bloc politician, and he gained unbelievable support from Nehru in India, from Nasser in Egypt and from other countries, creating some sort of relevant non-aligned political movement. So, internally, he was introducing something unbelievably advanced, a workers' self-management economic strategy, but this was perhaps too advanced, especially the social and economic issues. I remember that, at the University, we discussed the curricula with the cleaning ladies, which was the ultimate expression of the self-management of the university. Secondly, there is no unbiased history, because there was a big ideological pressure on historians at the time. There has been a lot of good movies, but some movies like those of Emir Kusturica, "Underground", are a little shaky. Kusturica pictures Milošević in the beginning of the nineties as the young, advanced, positive politician who was able to succeed Tito. It is a little bit tricky, because at the same time, Aljoša Mimica, my cousin, who is professor of sociology in Belgrade, was linking Milošević to the Tchetniks, Serbian nationalist paramilitaries supporting Nazis in WWII. Milošević was pictured as a sort of communist leader and a positive politician by intellectuals like Kusturica, but there were warnings in the early nineties that Milošević was already in ties with the extreme right wing of Serbian politics, which was extremely worrying for that period and proved to be totally true. No-one could believe that Milošević would act as he did, but if one wants to study Yugoslavia in the nineties, one has to study media. One would never believe that the destruction of Vukovar by the Serbian army had never been shown on Serbian television until after Milošević died. Namely, Koštunica, a Serbian president at the time, was showing to the Serbian population what happened during all these years. Serbian people were totally shocked during the NATO bombings – I still have a lot of Serbian friends and I tried to explain to them but they did not understand – they were not getting the message. They were totally manipulated by the media. You can say it is impossible; people nowadays have e-mail, satellites, and connections. No. The role of the media in ex-Yugoslavia was terribly dirty, terribly, terribly dirty. One cannot accuse the media or journalists for war atrocities – it is impossible, one should not do that. But if one sees the latest pictures from Belgrade, one can see the Director of Television being beaten by the people.

Liliane Schneiter Could you say a few words about the Berlage Institute.

Vedran Mimica The Berlage Institute is a postgraduate laboratory for architecture. It is funded by the Dutch government, as they believe that architecture is important for the state, so there is a political "note" which says that the Dutch government will invest in architecture. It is quite a unique political act in Europe. Based on this political decision, the Berlage Institute, the Netherlands Architectural Institute, and a series of organizations funding competitions, publications and scholarships for young Dutch architects were established. We have been operational for 10 years. Herman Hertzberger, professor in Delft, was the founder of the Institute and the Institute operates with a curricula structure of two years for a Masters Diploma. It has produced 75 graduates (Alumni) these are our "warriors" who come from all over the world. It is interesting to work in Berlage as you work with people from Chile, Argentina, Peru, South Korea, Japan, Europe and it is a very international body. Our strategy is to educate these people and then to send them back to their countries to be some sort of "urban guerrillas" – provocative agents, terribly active people. Are we succeeding or not? I think they are succeeding and we are providing two years of education that is very dense, highly expensive, and for them, very enriching.

Liliane Schneiter Basically, you want to make the students into "provocative agents"?

Vedran Mimica Basically, yes, this is taken from a statement by Kenneth Frampton. You have to take into account the nature of Herman Hertzberger, who established the Institute, and the Dutch culture, as it is "normal" in the Dutch culture to say that an Institute will function along some sort of "anarchistic" lines.

FRAMES OF THE METROPOLIS:
ZAGREB URBAN PLANNING
SEMINARS 1995 & 1996

Horetzky, Zagreb, 1996

MODERN ARCHITECTURE :
A CRITICAL HISTORY

Kenneth Frampton

Globus, Zagreb, 1992

RANDIĆ & TURATO : THE ARCHITECTURE OF TRANSITION

Kenneth Frampton, Darko Glavan, Vedran Mimica
Arhitekst, Zagreb, 2010

Vedran Mimica : Architecture of Transition and the Production of Meaning

ARCHITECTURE OF TRANSITION
AND THE PRODUCTION OF MEANING

Published in Randic & Turato, The Architecture of Transition, Arhitekst, Zagreb 2000

Transition:
Architects as Managers of Change

Transition in a social sense is a change from one system to another. Globally, the modernist paradigm changed to the post-modern with the disappearance of central authorities, universal dogmas and foundational ethics. The post-modern world introduced fragmentation, instability, indeterminacy and insecurity. Architectural responses to these conditions occurred as a 'semantic nightmare' of the post-modern discourse and/or the attempted completion of 'the modern project.'

Locally, in Croatia, transition occurred as a quantum leap from the socialist, one-party, state-controlled market system, into a capitalist, parliamentary democratic, free-market system. In 1989, with the fall of the Berlin Wall, disappeared the raison d'être of the 'buffer zone', known as Yugoslavia.

Yugoslavia disintegrated into 5 new independent nation-states: Slovenia, Croatia, Bosnia-Herzegovina, Yugoslavia (Serbia and Montenegro) and the Former Yugoslav Republic of Macedonia. The surprising national optimism and excitement upon which these states were formed quickly back-fired. The war, in the beginning of the 1990s, completely destroyed the Croatian economy, especially the tourist industry. The war in Bosnia-Herzegovina, in the mid 1990s, transformed Croatia into an enormous refugee camp. The compounded effects of the war and transition of the political and economic system, in fact, placed Croatia amongst the levels of Third World countries. A corresponding cultural transition returned Croatia to the romantic nationalist sentiments of the mid 19th century.

The transitional field within the Croatian architectural profession of the 1990s was widened to surrealistic dimensions while a simultaneous narrowing of actual realizations occurred. In order to survive, architects had to fundamentally change their status and role within society. The architect was no longer a "gentleman", with a bow-tie and cigar, waiting for a patron to develop canonical national institutions of historical importance. The architect becomes an "extra", a free-lance actor without a previously assigned role, without a script. Randić and Turato are able to anticipate and transform this transitional atmosphere. Randić and Turato are transitional architects who have fully understood and accepted these realities without ontological disturbances and professional nostalgia. Architecture of Transition is a way of intervening in the new market conditions where the "role assignments" are no longer grounded in the established state-regulated economy. In the free, non-regulated market, they use even the slightest opportunity for activity. Their work is widening the traditional field of the architectural profession, whereby Randić and Turato have become dynamic managers of change.

City of Rijeka: Border Conditions

The city of Rijeka represents the historical and conceptual background of Randić and Turato. Historically, geographically and conceptually, the city of Rijeka represents a borderland between sea and land, east and west, order and chaos, the province and the center and the horizontality of its sea and the verticality of its mountains. Rijeka is a harbor city, where the port and its industry represent the urban more significantly than the morphological organization of the city center. Rijeka's skyline is dominated by the silhouette of numerous harbor cranes and social housing skyscrapers – function and pragmatism dictates the city form.
Saša Randić (1964) and Idis Turato (1965) were both born in Sušak, the eastern quarter of Rijeka. Both come from the families of architects; Randić's father is an urban planner and Turato's father is an architect while the grandfather was a builder. Randić and Turato completed primary and secondary school in Rijeka and studied architecture in Zagreb from the mid 1980s to early 1990s. Their education at the Faculty of Architecture at the University of Zagreb further attests to the particular context upon which their foundation rests. The University of Zagreb never accepted post-modernism as a dominant direction; quite to the contrary, it sought the completion, so to say, of the modern movement. During the 1980s, for example, students and professors would carefully study the work of Cedric Price rather than that of nearby Aldo Rossi, while Paolo Portoghesi's 1979 Venice Biennale, which showcased the early work of OMA, was congruent with the sensibilities of the Zagreb students.

New modus operandi

Saša Randić, similar to many other excellent students of his generation, not only received the solid grounding at the faculty, but also educated himself with an insatiable curiosity about the contemporary international architecture scene. In his exchange with the world, he was awarded a prize in a competition organized by the RIBA, the Oasis competition in 1989 for the redesign of Le Corbusier's Ville Radieuse housing tower as a new typology for future housing. Idis Turato, as a secondary technical school student in Rijeka, often spent time in his father's library, which was full of books of Oscar Niemeyer and Richard Neutra. It quickly became apparent that Turato was destined to continue the family business. He completed his studies in Zagreb as one of the best students of his generation and was awarded a prize in the Rotring and Ove Arup student competition for a 'house for a media lover.' His diploma work (1991) was for a villa in Crikvenica nearby Rijeka as a micro-version of OMA's La Villette strategy, where the different programs are organized as linear strips and the event is created as a perpendicular movement through different programmatic fields.
During their studies, Randić and Turato, together with Damir Rako, Toni Poković and Saša Bradić formed the student group Ax5. The work of the group was nationally recognized within the Youth Salon of Architecture in 1988 in Zagreb. The group dissolved after the members graduated in early

1990s. From the fall of 1990, Randić studied at the Berlage Institute in Amsterdam, a post graduate school of architecture, as one of the students of the first "heroic" generation in a conceptual environment created by Herman Hertzberger (founder and creator of the Institute) and Kenneth Frampton (history and theory chair). Randić spent two dynamic years together with a generation of outstanding European young architects, including Reinier de Graaf, Marina Lathouri, Pero Puljiz, Branimir Medić and Tadej Glažar. The phenomenon of the contribution and performance of the Croatian student at the Berlage is probably deserving a separate monograph, however, Randić and his comrades created (within Aldo van Eyck's orphanage) strategies and scenarios for the reconstruction of the troubled ex-Yugoslav region following the war.

A very important element within the education environment of the Berlage was the existence of the international competitions. Europan was a logical choice as a competition for the new housing typologies for young European architects. Randić and his partner Sanja Ipšić (a painter) were awarded the prize for the site in Sète, France. Following his diploma work, Turato carried out the "Simona" cafe interior in Rijeka and thereafter worked as a free-lance architect in Veneto, Italy. Upon the 1992 return of Randić from Amsterdam and Turato from Veneto, the Randić-Turato architectural office was established in Rijeka as an operational platform for architectural activities in a transitional environment. It was a strategic decision to establish an office in Rijeka; leaving the west and returning to the homeland was based upon the possibilities to act within the completely changed conditions of the Croatian architectural market. The establishment of their office in Rijeka was logical in terms of filling a gap in the transitional market – where large state offices did not manage to transform themselves. Nonetheless, the waves upon which Randić and Turato began to sail were rough, disorientating and pulled by a strong under-current. To a certain extent, the seas they began to re-navigate were, in many aspects, surreal.

Croatia, in the beginning of the 1990s, was a "laboratory of transition" where the central authorities, universal dogmas and foundational ethics of socialism were replaced by a series of (unsuccessful) economic and cultural experiments embedded in new romantic nationalist values. Following the privatization of state-owned companies, the so-called Croatian free market became, in fact, an oligarchic system of control where the entire market was in the hands of a number of ruling elite families. Croatia acquired a social and economic system which was very similar to so-called banana republics of the Third World. Perhaps the only possible way to act in such an environment was to pragmatically accept the chaos of transition (fragmentation, instability, indeterminacy and insecurity) while super-intelligently accommodating the context.

Randić and Turato had to create a new system of values and a new modus operandi for their architectural practice. The principles of their transitional 'manifesto': Don't Bother with the Future, Keep an Open Mind, Define the Circumstances, Work in a Group, Condense the Solution, Use Existing Elements and Dispose after Use, reveal an extra-intelligence that is necessary in order to practice architecture – when it is still considered a conceptual discipline – in the contemporary Croatian context. All difficulties aside, one should also recognize that such a context also offers advantages: to a certain degree everything is possible; creation of the new is compulsory; the dynamism makes for never boring commissions.

Production of Meaning

Randić and Turato's architecture of transition has uniquely positioned itself. In their uninterrupted struggle for the production of meaning, Randić and Turato are simultaneously "flying" as a cloud above the context and in the daily contact with the context. The production of meaning is then reflected through the conceptualization of strategies in order to answer assignments and finally to carry out their work. This so-called extra-intelligence from which Randić and

Turato are creating their operational strategies is based upon sophisticated analytical research. This research in itself translates to the deconstruction of the process by which the project is evolving. Their analyzes concentrate on the causes of changes in the context, which are defining the specificity of the place, rather than the superficial appearance of these changes. Merely understanding the physical context and the program is not sufficient anymore. Now the architect has to act convincingly as a problem-solver, instead of a mere form-provider.

Randić and Turato's most intensive work occurs in the conceptual phase of their projects, when the investors and developers do not really know what they want to build and from where they are going to finance the planned project. Within this environment of instability, Randić and Turato operate with a high degree of openness towards the ceaseless changes of the project's development. This tactic is possible only if one approaches the project without a stable model and hypothesis but much more with an anticipatory instinct for the development of the project.

Randić and Turato, very correctly, emphasize that contemporary architectural practice has to develop special strategies for performing within three very different fields: virtual, legislative and constructional. Communication in each of these fields must be moderated according to the actors within the phasing of the project. The method Randić and Turato have developed to achieve this involves the simplification of the project to the level of its basic concept, which then can be successfully communicated within each of these fields. The operational engine for the success of the project is a successful communication of the concepts of the project.

Randić-Turato: Production 1992-2000

During the last 8 years the Randić and Turato office has produced previously unfathomable quantities of work: 31 projects, 25 urban design studies/master plans and 19 competitions. All of these works have been produced within the environment of a think-tank workshop. In the atmosphere of the workshop the quality of the idea was much more important than the authorship of the idea. The group, workshop atmosphere is an aspect Randić no doubt carried with him from his days at the Berlage Institute. The critical adoption of the laboratory-like Berlage atmosphere to the Croatian environment required a shift from a conceptually-based and "instant" project formulation to a pragmatically-based operational code – which sought to maintain the unbearable beauty of initial ideas and concepts.

The essay by Darko Glavan[57] about the 20th century cultural environment of Rijeka emphasizes the city's multi-layered and cosmopolitan character. His contribution affirms that there is no innovation without tradition and that it is virtually impossible to erase a historical and cultural production in the time of transition. However, the fundamentally changed cultural context of Rijeka in the early 1990s is the space in which Randić and Turato operate. Almost all of their completed works indicate, to different degrees, the "impossibilities of architecture" in Croatia in the 1990s. What is positive is the experience which the office gained through the building process, through the exchange with clients, investors and politicians, all of which is a necessary accumulation of knowledge for future activities.

Within a transition Randić and Turato are generating endless strategies and scenarios for their activity. Their work is a link with Rijeka's cultural and architectural production of the last century as well as anticipating and embracing the nature of a transitional context. The production of meaning, as the premise of existence and operation of the office, has to transform in the future into the production of urban and architectural culture on the regional level. In spite of everything, Randić and Turato possess the energy for that task.

---

[57] Darko Glavan (1951-2009), Rijeka born Croatian rock critic, curator and art historian, especially dedicated to pop culture.

Joschka Fischer
Paolo Portoghesi
Feđa Vukić
Vladimir Mattioni
Boris Groys
Hans Ulrich Obrist
Aldo van Eyck
Herman Hertzberger
Kenneth Frampton
Stefano Boeri
Jurgen Habermas
Nikola Polak
Davor Lončarić
Ivan Crnković
Nenad Fabijanić
Ćurković and Zidarić
Boševski & Fiolić
Ante Nikša Bilić
Ante Kuzmanić
Neno Kezić
Nikola Popić
Ante Mardešić
Nikola Bašić
Njirić+Njirić
Branimir Medić
Pero Puljiz
Zoka Zola
Leo Modrčin
Miće Gamulin
Andrija Rusan

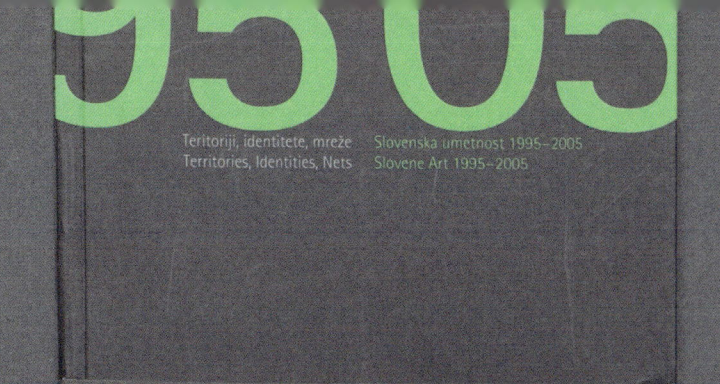

TERRITORIES, IDENTITIES, NETS:
SLOVENE ART 1995 - 2005

eds. Igor Španjol, Igor Zabel
Moderna galerija, Ljubljana, 2005

CONTEMPORARY CROATIAN
ARCHITECTURE - TESTING REALITY

Maroje Mrduljaš, Vedran Mimica, Andrija Rusan
Ahitekst, Zagreb, 2007

Vedran Mimica: Croatian Architecture, Inventing Reality

CROATIAN ARCHITECTURE, INVENTING REALITY

Published in Domus 873, Milan, 2004 and an extended version in Contemporary Croatian Architecture: Testing Reality. Zagreb, Arhitekst 2007

In September 2004 Domus no. 873 published an essay entitled Don't cry Croatia, let's invent reality. Oris editors then asked me for permission to publish the integral and amended version of this text. This took a little shuffling through the 38 issues of Oris to find articles on Croatian architects and their projects, but it has refreshed my knowledge about what has been going on in Croatia since I have not lived there for over fifteen years. What follows is the result of my subjective interpretation and an attempt to speak critically of what I found. I use the adverb "critically" not in the sense of "objectively" or "scientifically," but in the good old Šegvić's sense of intuitively and subjectively.

We who look on all this from the "other" side enjoy a specific position in the academic community as our layered experience goes in both directions. We spent our formative years in the east, under communism, and developed professionally mainly in western environments without losing our connections with the former surroundings. Is our knowledge reality-grounded and operational? Perhaps it is; but how can we reconcile the differences and play with our multiple layers of identity? This essay is an attempt to answer that question.

Fall of the Wall

When Rem Koolhaas presented the time line 1989-2003 under the regime of "YES" in his last book-magazine Content, a collage captured my attention: the Spice Girls holding the European flag on the bridge in Mostar with buildings in flame beneath. Even without AMO's expert photoshopping viciousness, the last 14 years have indeed been a "great decade for fans of turmoil." Although it is hard to take the image "Spice on the Bridge", it holds a great deal of significance. One could have used the image of dead bodies in plastic UNHCR bags from the "safe haven" in Srebrenica or the image of the Koševo football stadium in Sarajevo turned into the public graveyard but the Spice Girls on the Bridge simultaneously captured the drama of and hope for the Balkans at the dawn of the new millennium. If one is about to continue with the AMO time-line one should be able to picture George Bush and Jacques Chirac opening a "new" bridge in late July 2004.

Meanwhile, Bush never appeared at the opening, and the new Old Bridge connected the two banks of the Neretva. Eventually, it entered the UNESCO list of the World Heritage at its conference in Durban in July 2005, the newest structure ever to enter the list. Now Emir Balić[58] and his chaps are willing to dive from the bridge in front of the hordes of foreign tourists on a daily basis at the asking price of 30 euro a dive.

But let us start from the "beginning" – the fall of the wall.

Croatia as a country was "born" in the middle of the turmoil in the Balkans, one of six ex-Yugoslav republics seeking independence. The biggest war on European soil after WWII was a catastrophe. The fact that the main proto-fascist "freak" Slobodan Milošević died in a Scheveningen jail before his trial was over by no way compensates for the large scale catastrophe caused by his policies.

Transition

From WWII, Croatia developed within the Yugoslav federation under the influence of Tito's concepts of state-regulated workers' self management in economy and an independent foreign policy. Titoist concepts created a social landscape incredibly different to those found in other eastern European countries under the influence of the Soviet Bloc.

[58] Emir Balić is a legendary diver from Bosnia and Hercegovina who used to dive from the Old Bridge in Mostar. Balić jumped off the Old Bridge for the last time in 1996, at the age of 61.

Tito's enlightened authoritarianism accepted artistic freedom, small private enterprises, and freedom of movement, private bank accounts in foreign currencies and many other social and cultural activities totally unknown at the time in the world behind the Iron Curtain. Nonetheless, the specifics of the Croatian socio-cultural landscape in the second half of the 20th century when compared with western European social environments are characterized by two phenomena.

First is the fact that it was almost entirely spared the influences of the 1968 student revolution.

The revolution in universities had a tremendous influence upon the development of western democracies, especially towards the end of the 1970s, when revolutionaries joined the establishment and took up leading roles in the universities, business and politics. The latest in this sequence is Joschka Fischer, former German Foreign Secretary. 1968 put an end to the incoherent totalitarian hierarchy of various institutions. University offices' doors opened or were removed, and the discourse of the society shifted towards horizontal methods of decision-making and production.

Secondly, the young liberal-communist revolt colored by national aspirations of 1971 sadly failed. Even if it had succeeded, the democratization of society would have probably remained without the revolutionary influence of 1968.

Tito's death in 1980 somehow coincided with Paolo Portoghesi's Strada Novissima at the first Venice Biennale. Titoist Yugoslavia did not immediately disintegrate; however in Kosovo, Milošević introduced a "post-modern" political discourse as a return to the historical symbols of "the sacred" Serbian nation. As we know, the future was extremely bloody. Milošević's schizophrenic arguments that the Serbs in Croatia and Bosnia were threatened by the new democratically elected governments in these republics sparked the wars of the 1990's.

Croatia entered, in a dramatic way, the process typically referred to as transition. The political and economic changes were paralleled with a war for independence. The market economy and parliamentary democracy that developed countries of the West "sprayed" upon Croatia radically changed its political and economic landscape.

The transitional field within the Croatian architectural profession of the 1990s was affected with almost surrealistic tremors including a change in the political and economic system paralleled by a war, while a simultaneous narrowing of actual architectural accomplishments occurred. In order to survive, architects had to fundamentally change their status and role within society. The architecture of transition was created by way of intervening in the new market conditions, where role assignments were no longer grounded in the established state-regulated economy. The architect became an "extra," a free-lance actor without a previously assigned role, without a script.

In an essay City Plan, published in the book Zagreb – Modernity and the City edited by Feđa Vukić, Vladimir Mattioni gave a precise description of difficulties Croatian architecture and city planning encountered in the transitional 1990s.

… In the condition of a reduced public domain, architectural discourse suddenly found itself in a "no-man's land." By its very nature architectural practice has always been oriented towards the public aspect, but it represented that aspect from a certain professional distance enabled by the yet unspent aura of a special social status. Then, it suddenly found itself caught unaware by an abrupt change within the entire professional environment. The aura had vanished, and the architect's role in the public domain had also suddenly altered. Somewhere between the zone of self-isolation and media aggression, architectural discourse had lost its authenticity. …

….Regional and urban plans are being produced in conditions characterized by an environment rendered unstable as a result of constant social, political and economic changes. The key aspects of such unstable conditions are manifested in: the absence of a long-term role for the central government and for towns within a wider geo-political environment; the dearth of long-term development strategies for individual sectors of the economy, which made a profound impact on urban changes (industry, tourism, transport, agriculture ...); the poorly defined public sector role in the policy of urban development (public standards and public services); the unreliability of the legal system and political responsibility; lack of knowledge with regard to the way the instruments of planning function in conditions of a market economy, combined with weak political will; inferior training in professional institutions acting in conditions of instability, uncertainty and rapidly changing situations (inability to comprehend a situation, a lack of readiness to adjust, and the uncritical adoption of models).

... There is barely anything left of the notion of public. Led by a weak will, public interest has been deleted from all the operations that include private capital. Regardless of the size of the investment, private capital is paradoxically serviced by public institutions, as if public services existed only to underpin private interests. Mixed public/private undertakings are inconceivable.

... In that way, the logic of low investment in land development and of high profits reaped from the positions that act as parasites on the existing, a developed city infrastructure, both technical and social, has been actualized. Without investing a single kuna (Croatian currency) into that infrastructure, these centers are expanding their potentials without restrictions, the only limitations being the vision of their protagonists. They are guaranteed a high level of attraction through the novelty of their supply and by offering completely new environment conditions compared to those which we were familiar with. To be there, to shop there, means enjoying a certain social prestige...[59]

59 From Vladimir Mattioni's City Plan, an essay published in a book Zagreb – Modernity and the City edited by Feđa Vukić in 2003. Published by AGM in Zagreb.

Boris Groys in Zagreb

Discussion with Groys about relations between East and West and about transition is always very interesting. He was born in East Berlin and educated in the Soviet Union. He defected in 1981 and in 1994 became the head of Philosophy and Media Theory at the Academy for Design in Karlsruhe, Germany. Groys is an outstanding intellectual with experience of both sides of the Berlin Wall, before it fell.

Boris Groys' concept of "double erasure" is perhaps a key one to understand the specificity of Croatian cultural development. Strikingly different from other east European countries, Croatia did not witness the first erasure since Tito won the political battle against Stalin in 1948. Therefore, the modernist avant-garde discourse was a feature on the scene. In Croatia, the Stalinist erasure was delayed by half a century. It occurred due to the totalitarian nationalist culture of the 90s. This period of erasure purged most socialist achievements, relegating them as disturbances in the stream of the national culture. EUROKAZ (International theater festival), Festival of Contemporary Dance, the exhibition of kinetic and constructivist art were a few of remaining cultural programs from the previous period. The dynamic NGO scene as well as the creation of the NGO network Zagreb- Cultural Capital 3000 worked on transformation of the dominant governmental tendencies in the development of national, traditional and rigid culture.

Groys would explain at Zagreb Domus workshop: 'Speaking with people from Russia and Eastern Europe, I am confronted with the attitude that communism was an interruption in the development of society during the 19th and 20th centuries. It was a kind of delay or "blank space." It was the erasure of national tradition and society. And now what we are doing is the erasure of erasure, the destruction of destruction. We should erase or destroy communism because communism is destructive itself. It is an interesting discourse because in a certain sense it is generally Stalinist. Following the discussions of the 20s and 30s in the Soviet Union, at the time of change from classical avant-garde to Stalinism, theorists of Stalinist culture said they were against the avant-garde because it was the erasure of traditional culture; it was only negation, destruction and reduction. They were against reduction for saving the national heritage and re-using it in terms of the new socialist society. So in a strange way, the post-perestroika or post-communist rhetoric of re-using national heritage under contemporary cultural conditions (understood as erasure of erasure, as destruction of destruction of the forces that did not allow such re-use) is a repetition and recycling of the Stalinist ideology. And this makes me very suspicious because we should not see communism as a time of delay or non-existence. We must not commit the same mistake as Stalinist culture did in relation to the avant-garde. We should rethink communism itself as a practice of creation of public spaces, and think about the positive re-formulation of these. We should analyze what kind of potential was created in the communist time: not only as a factor that delayed western-style neo-liberal economic development, but also as a kind of specific organizational form of social spaces.'[60]

Another theme of Groys may be applied to Croatia's recent history – his concept of utopia, whereby a truly utopian experience is one of visiting and then leaving:
'I think it is very interesting because if you look at Utopian literature in general, from Plato to now, it was always based on the same movement of visiting Utopia and then leaving it. It is like a drug experience: there are two problems, how to get in and how to get out of it. I think it is something that has been forgotten because Utopian literature is not only about going to Utopia; it is also about getting out of it. So what we actually have now is completed Utopia. We only have a completed Utopia now because we have got out of it. So we now know how to get into it and how to get out of it. And that is precisely what makes this experience operational. If you only know how to get in, it is inoperative, but if you know how to get in and out it is operational; it is technical, you can make it. You can do it as an individual project or you can do it as a collective project and so on. You can understand what happens if you organize some collective aesthetic experience and how you can manage it. It is about collective emotional ecstasy, it is an aesthetic experience. You experience something from it and you experience something when you get out of it. And that is precisely what creating contemporary public space with artistic or architectural or political means actually is. If we look at these carnivalesque, non-government, anti-global things, it is like Bakhtin and his series of carnivals. You go in, and there is a certain state of affairs coming out of it. This going in and coming out is a post-communist experience that should actually be understood as a completing of the communist experience. It is not something that brings us out of it but something that completes Utopia, because now Utopia is there as a technical device and to forget it just means to forget technical knowledge, to forget to know how to deal with a Utopian experience. [...] What we really need is a technical side to the whole experience. We should reflect on this.'[61]

In the case of Croatia it can be argued that the Titoist utopian experience and technical knowledge could have theoretically inspired Croats to imagine some kind of a "third way" that would not blindly follow the Euro-Atlantic integration. It is an unbelievably interesting prospect but there is a painful lack of the minimal critical mass among the cultural and political elite of Croatian society for even starting a debate about it.

European integration and how to get there is a dominant subject in the discourse of the Croatian establishment. Assuming that this process works out, Croatia would approach European standards

---

60 From a transcript of Groys's lecture at the Domus workshop in Zagreb, 2004.   61 Ibid.

within the following 30-50 years. At the moment, Croatia is a country without an immediate future that has only started mastering true democracy on its way to transformation.

Learning from Croatia II

In 1956, a CIAM conference was held in Dubrovnik. The young rebels Alison and Peter Smithson, Aldo van Eyck, Jaap Bakema were plotting against the "masters" while simultaneously being engaged in an intense debate amongst themselves. The modernist project was on review and inspirations to bury it partly came from the Adriatic coast. Dubrovnik and Split immensely inspired the rebels. Jaap Bakema published a brilliant essay about the transformation of Diocletian's Palace into the city center of Split in the Dutch magazine Forum (2-1962).

For Van Eyck and Hertzberger, the transformation of the Roman emperor's villa into the medieval and then contemporary city represented a paradigmatic case for the revision of radical modernism.

In Croatia, the historical urban spaces, carved in stone, literally and symbolically provide the cultural foundations. As I already mentioned, it might seem a bit farfetched, but it could be declared that the basic Croatian culture is predominantly urban. Indeed, the country's urban historical infrastructure provides its identity within the European cultural context, much more than music, literature or other forms of art. To make this point, without strict scholarly hierarchy and systematization, a number of Croatian urban "wonders" can be singled out.

The first "wonder" refers to the geometric prodigy of the Ston salt works. Urban settings such as this reveal a layered set of values and potentially anticipate concepts for new projects that observe the spirit of the place. In this case, the spirit of the place or genius loci is not understood as a frozen historical category, but as a dynamic code (gene) that is capable of anticipating considerations about new urban entities. Regarding the present-day programmatic densification of the Adriatic coast, the lesson of Ston lies in its relationship between the landscape and the urban grid, as well as in the hierarchy of public urban spaces.

The second "wonder" is Dubrovnik as Croatia's brand name. Stradun or Placa mark the ultimate public urban space; it is an eminently cosmopolitan and multicultural space. In its urban and cultural essence, Dubrovnik is a very dense structural grid which has generated poets as well as civitas during 800 years of the glorious Republic of Dubrovnik.

The third "wonder" is Split and Diocletian's Palace, paradigm of a transformation from the ultimately private (an imperial palace) to the private-public (a Croatian town). The Slavic barbaric genius transformed a single-occupant house into a town for five thousand people, and it is this action that serves as the premise for any discussion about public and private spaces in this corner of the world. The shift from private to public was creative and functional. It established contemporary urbanity in a very sophisticated and dynamic relationship with the past.

The final "wonder" is Zagreb and its horseshoe-shaped green belt. It is Lenuci's reading of the Vienna Ring Strasse, a super modern project which placed public institutions freely within city gardens – an ideal of the bourgeois understanding of urbanity.

Croatia's historical urban layer is an open textbook inviting discussion about concepts of new urban spaces in the times of social transition. If the CIAM group could get inspiration for a theoretical revision of radical modernism fifty years ago, there could be hope for contemporary Croatian and foreign architects to draw on this historical layer as inspiration and reference.

Croatian Architectural Discourse, Terra Incognita

Internationally, Croatian urban miracles are at least known as iconic tourist destinations, while Croatian architectural history of the last century is a huge terra incognita. Croatian pre-WWII as well as post-WWII modernism deserves comprehensive research, publications, promotion and debate.

Viktor Kovačić, Otto Wagner's student and a proto-modern architect of European importance, is the Croatian variation of Plečnik[62] or Berlage; Drago Ibler, Josip Seissel, Josip Pičman, Ivan Zemljak, Ernest Weissmann, Slavko Löwy, Stjepan Planić are representatives of the great generation of first Croatian modernists while the work of Ivan Vitić, Božidar Rašica, Lovro Perković, Neven Šegvić, Drago Galić and Vladimir Turina represent a continuation of the modern project in post-WWII era.

In more recent history, as mentioned, the Architectural Faculty of the University of Zagreb never accepted post-modernism as a dominant direction but it sought some sort of completion of the modern project. Education was based upon the concepts of the modernist tradition of the 1930s, when the so-called "Zagreb School" was an active part of the European Modernist scheme. The legacy of these architects as practitioners and teachers is still present in recent production and education. It is in a way ironic that most of Croatia's architectural efforts are still geared towards "trying to finish the great modern project" in a time of radical changes in almost everything. It could be claimed that such a "delay" is not really fertile, but somehow eclectic, neo-modern and out of time.

"Fertile delay"

Stefano Boeri's beautifully promising "fertile delay" concept is painfully struggling with the obvious impossibilities of originating an authentic "third way" policy. Boeri is perhaps right in saying that Croatia cannot learn a lot from the European experience, but it will be more than a miracle if the "extravagant breakthrough of generosity" of the new generation of Croatian architects succeeds to be indeed operational in the larger social framework.

In his text for the 38th Zagreb Salon catalogue, Boeri pinpoints the major controversies troubling the future of the Croatian city and makes it clear that Croatia has no directly applicable model to follow.

'Croatia today is being offered, more than any other eastern country, a considerable chance to use its delay in a fruitful way, closely studying the foundations of European urban planning. In particular, a number of pertinent questions have come to the fore:

How can one avoid having large shopping centers generating a "void" in their surroundings, like some gigantic spaceships, and instead create the opportunity for new forms of public and communal space?

How can one redirect the energies that pulsate in the diffusion of family homes and force them to also produce public spaces and infrastructures?

How can one protect the coast, the land's true great resource, and direct, curb, and occasionally redefine – but not lose – large projects along the coast which are being generated by foreign capital.

How can we prevent the islands from becoming tourist theme parks and have them retain the complex diversity of their functioning and way of life?

These are all inevitable and difficult questions because there are no previous experiences – far or near – to which we can look.'[63]

Boeri's questions hit the point and are relevant for the future of the Croatian landscape as a whole and not only of the towns; but the sordid reality of Croatian transition leaves little hope that this "fertile delay" will be of any good in answering to them. In the absence of a critical mass that would start any relevant discussion about these burning development issues, looking back seems far more "comforting" and almost "promising".

---

[62] Jože Plečnik (1872–1957), the most famous Slovenian architect who shaped the identity of modern Ljubljana (Slovenian capital). Plečnik also accomplished the modification of Prague Castle, the work that was entrusted to him by the first Czechoslovakian president Tomáš Garrigue Masaryk.

[63] Quote from Stefano Boeri's essay Fertile Delay, published in the catalog of the 38th Zagreb Salon in 2003.

Three "realities:" post-modern, neo-modern and transitional

A closer look at Oris, ČiP[64] and the Zagreb Salon catalog shows that there are three streams, three directions, three groups of concept- and/or generation-related modern Croatian architects.

The first includes architects whose theoretical and practical ideas were formed in the postmodernist 1980s, that is, after Portoghesi's Strada Novissima of the first Venice Biennale of Architecture. This group gathered around the Gallery of Contemporary Art in Zagreb and the journal ČiP, whose postmodernist discourse was mainly influenced by Nikola Polak and Davor Lončarić.

In charge of the 1991 exhibition Distinctive Features of Croatian Architecture of the Eighties, Nikola Polak in his accompanying text questions the true merits of this group in reference to modernist tradition: 'Will this architecture preserve any of the original value, freshness, topicality and verve of its time and will its ethics and aesthetics, following the basic tenets of Modernism, be able to convey the message about its destiny for this day and beyond? Or will the illusions and the pressures of current nationalist realism outlive the illusions and the pressures of the former socialist realism. To keep this cultural disaster in check, the current revision of our immediate heritage is not enough, but we also have to revise our goals by thinking beyond the xenophobic apathy of a nation in transition.'

As a curiosity, in 1984 the architects Ivan Crnković, Nenad Fabijanić and Nikola Polak established a group which they called Nebo (Heaven) and which was "as different from the group Zemlja[65] (Earth) as heaven and earth." The group supported Eisenman's postmodernist approach to architecture as an independent discipline, whose social aspect was more or less secondary. This is partly why the influence of Nebo on Croatian architecture was as different from Zemlja's influence as heaven and earth.

The second group, or should I say tendency, is characterized by the belief that Modernism is not just over yet and that the Modernist code has still something to say within the contemporary cultural context. Koolhaas would call this architecture confusing, for you cannot tell whether it was built in the 1930s or 1990s. Frampton instead, would probably go for Habermas's belief[66] that the Modernist project may still be unfinished.

The activity of this group is related to the functionalist teaching at the Zagreb Faculty of Architecture and to the faith of that institution in the continuity of Zagreb school of architecture. Hereby I refer to a particular kind of neo-modernism that is quite authentic in the context of the previously mentioned fertile delay in which Croatian architecture and culture got caught.

The list of people belonging to this stream is long, but I would single out the "modernist perfectionism" of Tomislav Ćurković and Zoran Zidarić, the soundness of Studio Boševski & Fiolić with Mira Tadej and Tom Pavelić, the verve of Ante Nikša Bilić, the Adriatic interpretations of Ante Kuzmanić, Neno Kezić, Nikola Popić, Ante Mardešić, and the specific neo-corbu interpretation of the given context by Nikola Bašić.

What is certain is that in the transitional darkness and devastation of the landscape, this group distinguishes itself by making professionally sound architecture.

---

64 ČiP, pronounced as [chip], which is an acronym for Čovjek i prostor (Man and Space), one of the Croatian long-lasting journals for architecture, spatial and artistic practices, has been published in Zagreb since 1954 by the Croatian Architects' Association.

65 Zemlja group (the Earth Group) was a Croatian arts collective which brought together artists, architects and intellectuals. The group was active in Zagreb from 1929 to 1935. It had strong socialist affinities.

66 Habermas, J. (1987) The Philosophical Discourse of Modernity: Twelve Lectures. Cambridge, MA: MIT Press. See also: Passerin d'Entrèves, M. and Benhabib, S. ed. (1997) Habermas and the Unfinished Project of Modernity: Critical Essays on The Philosophical Discourse of Modernity. Cambridge, MA: MIT Press; and the original version of the speech given by Habermas in September 1980, when he was awarded the Adorno Prize by the City of Frankfurt (the German text was published in Habermas' Kleine Politische Schriften I-IV, Frankfurt: Suhrkamp, 1981).

The third group includes the most interesting contemporary architects in Croatia, most of whom presented themselves at the 38th Zagreb Salon, and one can hardly disagree with Stefano Boeri's interpretation of 450 buildings included in the recent Croatian output. It only needs to be amended by the output of "Croats" abroad.

This group is conceptually the most diverse of the three, but it can generally be described by two documents. The first is Njirić's mini-manifesto of the Kalvariengürtl[67] catalog accompanying an exhibition set up in deSingel, Flanders' international arts center in Antwerp in 2001 with an unpretentious title njiric+njiric arhitekti hints and the second is the paradigmatic graduation project Parasite by Petar Mišković, mentored by Professor Tonči Žarnić.

Both the hints and the Parasite, the latter displayed in the Muzej narodne revolucije (Museum of the Peoples' Revolution) in Rijeka, send a clear message: if we want to address the real issues of today's world, Modernism will prove more or less inoperable as a discourse and discipline. To paraphrase Njirić, Modernism will be replaced by new architecture, the collective will extinguish the heroic, complexity will give way to simplicity, and definite solutions to open possibilities. Intelligence will outdo god-given talent, and practicality and usability will replace the metaphysical and artistic instant.

Diaspora

Many Croatian architects, after graduation in Zagreb, entered the international architectural scene. Among many hard working architects there are three practices, or four architects, who could be singled-out. They all reveal a particularly interesting way of parlaying their background into an international context. Branimir Medić and Pero Puljiz are partners in de Architekten Cie. in Amsterdam, while Zoka Zola runs her own studio in Chicago, as also does Leo Modrčin in New York. Being further educated at the Berlage Institute Amsterdam in the case of Puljiz and Medić, AA London in the case of Zoka Zola (where she was an intermediate unit teacher) and the Pratt Institute in Brooklyn, New York for Leo Modrčin (where he also taught design studios), they internalize the lessons from their respective post-structural discourse and are all producing work of a particular intensity.

Perhaps Kenneth Frampton's usual ability to name or characterize different works can be called upon. He would explain the work of Medić and Puljiz as 'Slavic, laconic, dynamic minimalism'[68]. In a text where he was reflecting upon the responsibility of the present generation for 'the critical and ethical necessity of accepting the limits of the Habermas unfinished modern project in all its aspects,' he recognized that Medić and Puljiz's work does this 'only this time with different repetition. The creation of unexpected relations in their projects is obviously in a domain of creativity.'[69] Their new configurations are reconstructed and again, according to Frampton, 'rational orthogonal planning folded about itself to make yin-yang composition of surprising dynamism.'[70]

Medić is very precise when arguing that they belong to a generation that inherited modernity and its developed feelings for the social and public realm; a sort of modernist honest ideology in debate with economic reality. The best example of such an attitude is revealed in their recently completed Acanthus building in South Amsterdam. They almost surprised the unprepared free market, performing as some nostalgic protectors of fundamental values. Ingrained commercial principles were seen from an unexpected and distorted angle. Medić and Puljiz were able to create a paradoxical opportunity to transform ordinary

---

67 A country road nearby Graz. It was chosen as the title of Njirićs' exhibition because they lived there during the time they spent in Graz.

68 Frampton, Kenneth (1995) "Different Repetitions". In: Architectural Agency MPG 1992/95, Amsterdam/ Ljubljana/Zagreb.

69 Ibid.

70 Ibid.

commercial mass-products into unique objects. Inherited discipline replaced "context-specific modernist" responsibility for generic material. Anonymous, commercial square meters for unknown users have been configured as a unique, tailor-made product.

In the Pfanner House in Chicago from 2001 Zoka Zola explored the architectural issues of boundaries, space and freedom, and specifically how to open one space into another. This research she almost obsessively continued from her Zagreb studies, through the AA course and teaching, to, finally, her first built work. Zola will argue that modernist spaces are rarely truly open because they mostly just extend themselves through their openings. Her work is truly questioning modern principles while establishing completely new relations in order to discuss the relations between open space and freedom.

Leo Modrčin is a New York-based architect of Croatian origins. After working as independent architect in New York from 1990, Modrčin started uRED Architecture in 2001. The firm designed and in 2004 completed 59E59 Theaters, a three-theatre off-Broadway complex in Midtown Manhattan, for the Elysabeth Kleinhans Theatrical Foundation. This Midtown wonder is clearly presenting the ethical and cultural background of Modrčin's heritage, a sort of inherited modernism that communicates with contemporary New York as a live container for theatrical performances.

Tendencies

Post-historical times discourage any kind of classification, but still may serve a purpose in reviewing or interpreting recent Croatian architecture. Instead of classification, perhaps it would be wiser to talk about the tendencies and directions defining transitional Croatian architecture at the turn of the millennium. It has democratized itself, just as the society has. But what does this mean? It means that architectural culture no longer depends on the exclusive support of government institutions and that the number of active creators has increased. Needless to say, these new creators of architectural culture, liberated from government bonds and working according to free market principles, are far more dynamic and interesting than the slowly awakening government institutions.

The paradigms of these new forces in Croatian architecture are the independent publisher Arhitekst and the non-governmental organization Platforma 9,81. Even though far apart, they have both embraced the transitional architectural reality as their field of action and when it comes to publishing and education through a variety of public lectures, workshops and research, they have practically replaced the old and rusty government institutions.

In this context the magazine Oris has lit a Promethean torch in the transitional darkness of the new cultures of the Western Balkans. Thanks to the efforts of Oris editors to present us multicultural and multidisciplinary texts, we can gain an insight into the state of architectural and cultural affairs in this part of the world at the beginning of the third millennium.

Vladimir Mattioni is a Croatian transitional phenomenon in his own right. He was one of the leading figures of the Nova umjetnička praksa (New Artistic Practice) in Yugoslavia of the 1970s and 1980s, a conceptual artist, a town planner and now the editor and graphic designer of a number of books fundamental for understanding the tectonic shifts in transitional Croatia.

Croatian transition is probably best illustrated by remarkably impressive photographies published in Oris. The transitional reality exposed in front of the cameras of Ivan Posavec, Boris Cvjetanović, Mladen Tudor or Aleksandra Vajd is sometimes even more fascinating than the contributions by their architect colleagues on other pages in Oris. The first Internet influences on architectural discourse started with the web pages www.urbanizam.net and www.arhitektura.info, meticulously edited by Vladimir Mattioni and Miće Gamulin. However, blog discussions on architecture, a trend of more recent date, show that younger generations are still not ready to use the achievements of information society for critical discussion about architecture. The greatest surprise is that these generations seem to care for issues of regulations far more than for conceptual ones.

There are a few positive trends that should be attributed to the efforts made by "reformed" municipal and government institutions. Since 1995 Gradski zavod za planiranje razvoja grada Zagreba (City Bureau for Zagreb Development Planning) has been organizing a series of seminars in cooperation with the Dutch Berlage Institute and other European institutions, addressing issues related to the development of Zagreb as the capital of a new nation. A series of seminars entitled Frames of Metropolis looked into the development of Zagreb along the railway lines, addressed new regulations for the development of several Zagreb estates, investigated the possibilities of development using "small steps" that allow local communities and urban subcultures to participate, and opened a discussion about the construction of office towers in Zagreb.

It is a great pity that virtually none of the ideas presented at the seminar ever got into city development plans or lived to be considered for implementation. There were about forty outstanding projects proposed for public spaces at the seminar Small Changes that would radically have changed the public spaces of Zagreb for the better.

Far more successful and radical has been the State-Subsidized Housing Program (POS), launched by the Ministry of Public Works, Reconstruction and Construction. After ten years of disregarding the need for social housing in transition, this program has enabled young families to move out of their parents' homes and have something of their own. Over a series of public competitions it made the way for a new generation of very young architects who knew how to meet high and sometimes contradicting building requirements set before them. Helena Paver Njirić's building "log" of her POS building experience in Rovinj is one of the most indicative texts presenting the difficulties an architect had to overcome in this new transitional reality. Despite them, POS housing is the best that could happen to current Croatian architecture. In addition to the housing project in Rovinj, worth mentioning are the neo-modernist housing experiments in Đakovo by Loher, Mišković and Rajčić, phenomenological interpretations of locality by Iva Letilović and Morana Vlahović in Krapinske toplice, critical interpretations of locality and modernity in Delnice by Vladimir Kasun and Ivica Plavec, a Mediterranean deconstruction of mega-structures in Cres by Ivana Ergić, Vanja Ilić and Vesna Milutin, and finally an outstanding context-aware building in Krapinske toplice designed by Vesna Mravinac and Dubravka Vranić.

Another tendency in recent Croatian architecture is going small-scale, that is, focusing on the interior. Worth mentioning are residential and office building interiors designed by Vedrana Ergić and Marko Murtić. Lovorka Prpić and Miljenko Bernfest with their hairdressing salon and gallery La Coulisse and Andrija Rusan with his design for the Lisinski Small Concert Hall set sky-high standards that are still limited to the interior. In fact, these and similar projects fully meet the international standards of design and use of materials, but they also provide an ironic comment on the poverty of the setting and show an absolute discrepancy with the new Croatian elite for which they were made, with a few exceptions. For the cultural level of the Croatian nouveaux riches are poles apart from the efforts of "interior designers" built in these projects.

What transition brought along as its basic urban activity is individual consumption, with a number of shopping malls parasitizing on the existing infrastructure. The sad truth is that none of these "boxes" has brought a new quality to the semi-public urban space, regardless of their popularity among the new middle class. Yet another, cultural, type of consumerism has dominated architectural competitions for a number of new museums. The competition for the Zagreb Museum of Contemporary Art is a paradigm of the utter ignorance of the new temples of cultural consumption in the world. Only Hrvoje Njirić with his hybrid between a museum and a shopping center seems to have opened a critical discussion about the function of this new program in the transitional environment.

All things considered, it is possible to discern a number of activities that constitute a basic architectural discourse in Croatia, measured by European standards that is. These include the foundation of the Chamber of Architects, the activities of the Croatian Architects' Association (UHA) and Zagreb Architects' Association (DAZ), the First Congress of Croatian Architects in Zadar, independent publishing, reform of the Faculty of Architecture in Zagreb according to the Bologna Declaration, new non-governmental organizations addressing city planning issues, architecture web portals, and public debate on architecture issues in the media.

One can only hope that all these efforts will redirect and manipulate the strong currents of global capital flows into the creation of an authentic and specific architectural culture, contributing to European cultural exchange in the years to come when Croatian architectural production should not invent its own realities but be part of a social reality.

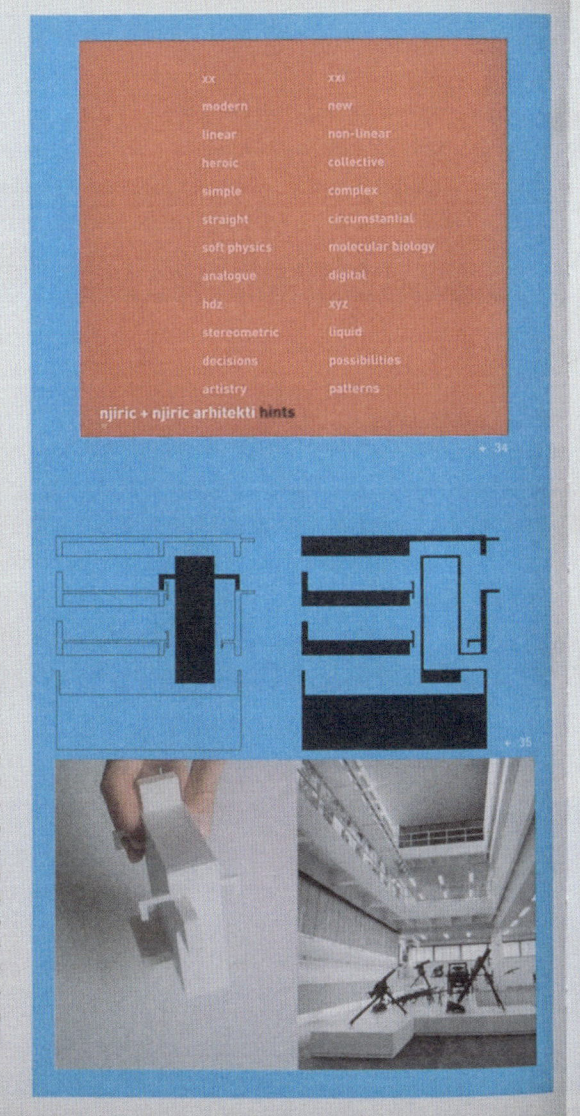

CONTEMPORARY CROATIAN ARCHITECTURE - TESTING REALITY

Maroje Mrduljaš, Vedran Mimica, Andrija Rusan
Ahitekst, Zagreb, 2007

Vedran Mimica: Croatian Architecture, Inventing Reality

xx	xxi
modern	new
linear	non-linear
heroic	collective
simple	complex
straight	circumstantial
soft physics	molecular biology
analogue	digital
hdz	xyz
stereometric	liquid
decisions	possibilities
artistry	patterns

njiric + njiric arhitekti hints

\+ 34
"njiric+njiric arhitekti hints"
u katalogu "Kalvariengürt-
Vandermaliere u antwerpe
vjerovatno najreprezentat
europskom kontekstu do c
Klif i Lala Rašić prikazali s
strategija "balkanskih man
"njiric+njiric arhitekti hints
ed in the Kalvariengürtel e
held in Antwerpen deSing
perhaps the most represe
European context in whic
Klif and Lala Rašić showed
operational strategies dev

\+ 35
Diplomski rad iz 2000. gor
Žarnića nije samo uzbudu
Boerija (jedna od 3 jednak
salona arhitekture) već je
najmlađih hrvatskih arhite
Žarnićeve "kabanice".
Not only did Petar Mišković
by Assistant Professor Žar
(receiving one of the three
of Architecture), but it also
Croatian architects bred ur

NJIRIĆ+NJIRIĆ
CHILDREN OF ST. PETER'S STREET

Essay in a monograph "Aftermath", to be published by Actar

Helena and Hrvoje Njirić are true children of Zagreb, Maksimir[71], or to be even more local, of St. Peter's Street. Every milieu has architects which are somehow different, whose work is visibly detached from their own surroundings. However, those who are familiar with the Njirićs' cultural milieu can see that they have captured the best it had to offer. Back in the eighties, Helena and Hrvoje Njirić were enrolled in the Faculty of Architecture at the University of Zagreb, which still chewed on an eclectic variation of the „unfinished modernist project." The information they were receiving as students of architecture was revealing enough to show them what was built in the big wide world, but not enough to make them understand what was really going on out there. Life at the margins, on the periphery, or limes, if you will, has its advantages; one can more readily change the big wide world in his or her mind if one does not really know it.

The Njirićs belong to Zagreb, conceptually speaking, inasmuch as they draw from certain cultural wells there are in the city, and far less because of their university education or local architecture. Zagreb greatly influenced them through its Zagreb School of Animation of the 1960s (particularly Dušan Vukotić, who won the Oscar for animated film Surogat/Substitute in 1961), through the New Art Practice of the 1970s and 1980s, and through its own generation of digital artists of the nineties.

The Njirićs know, all to well, how enormous is the distance between the two worlds, they know that their home has little to do with Europe and the West. Yet these "little green people from the Balkans" have proved that they can give to that old Europe a good shake, and they owe it to their background. Their world has been determined by their Zagreb background, but rather as an antithesis to that background, as a reaction to the milieu and to its modernist culture with clear-cut rules of behavior, socialist hierarchy, xenophobia, and narrow mindedness. Their reaction is remarkably committed, intelligent, and radical. They dug their way out from the debris of a dying system, and created an entirely new world and a new system which opens a myriad of possibilities. The Njirićs have created a platform for action that is specific enough – yet retains its generic potential – to distinguish their practice as one of the most interesting European practices at the beginning of the century.

How did it occur? They chose to ignore the lessons taught at the Faculty of Architecture in Zagreb, according to which function still followed form while communists led the people toward a brighter future where architecture was a heroic discipline, and replaced them with a radically different code. While it is true that the code was changing with the fall of the Berlin Wall, European integration, and the war in the former Yugoslavia, this change took a somewhat different direction from the optimistic vision of "post-Dayton" arcadia proposed by the Njirićs.

A World of Its Own

How is that? First, for the Njirić's, architecture is no longer a heroic discipline founded on simple, linear modernist solutions, but an operating discourse embracing complexity and different patterns. This discourse renounces formalism once and for all, it is the "end" of estheticism, and a step toward the abrogation of "authorship" and city planning. Accordingly, architecture should emerge "just there," or rather "just be there." Its primary concern is its client, not ideology; it relies upon "ready-made" strategies and practices, it makes its own infrastructure visible, it makes use of corporate logos and forms a new and dynamic consumerist culture.

The war-ridden Croatia of the early nineties was not appropriate for testing the Njirić's strategies. Europan, instead, was an ideal testing laboratory.

71 Maksimir is a city district in Zagreb.

In two Europans, the Njirićs won three prizes for projects on three locations. Unfortunately, the Dutch, the German and the Scottish locations were not ready for their architecture. Within the frame of European housing, the Njirićs presented their idea of the "new urban landscape" in which the privacy of home belonged to a vast territory of a new megalopolis, that is, to a public domain which combined all scales at the same time. The Njirićs' faith in a New Europe and noble intentions of Europan bumped into the wall of local red tape. Notwithstanding, Europan started to create a new world which unambiguously dealt with issues of the "everyday life." A vernacular emerged, which was new and still very familiar. This new world, which was created according to a Kees Christiaansen, communicates with the public through highly sophisticated means, often using rich animation and underlining the new technologies with human character. This human aspect which may be attributed to the great tradition of the Zagreb School of Animation, is the feature that distinguishes the Njirićs from the highly sophisticated "blob" generation of the "big wide world", not only in presentation, but also in the concept. Bart Lootsma remarked that the Njirićs' world and their presentations were brimming with humor and playfulness, which was rare in their generation.

Vladimir Mattioni shrewdly observed that, in no more than a decade, the Njirić's designed so many diverse projects which, if put together, could catalog an entire city. And we are not talking about town planning here, but architectural design proper. An entire imaginary city has been designed (not planned!) in a fashion which sets a solid framework for its real existence regardless of "where" and "when". Should some "after-modern njirić city" emerge from this extraordinary phenomenon, it could be itemized by using the following words: housing + commercial + life & leisure + office + cultural + educational + religious + memorial = the city!

Post-Dayton Arcadia

The "post-Dayton" era has been all but arcadian, and our irony expresses the hope of better future. Even though arcadia has a prominent utopian ring to it, nearly all Njirić' projects and strategies are meticulous about the possibilities of arcadia in the Croatian context.

The conceptual implementation of these strategies borders with schizophrenia, if one bears in mind Croatian reality. On the other hand, this is the only "way out" — to get to Europe — which seems to be without alternative. While the "third way" between the Balkans and Europe, between free market and social welfare, and between democracy and autocracy, is a purely an academic issue, through their projects and writing the Njirić's offer a new "arcadian" reality which brings market pragmatism closer to the new consumerist culture. When it comes to the presentation of global issues to local community, this exercise in conceptual thinking betrays faith in double intelligence.

This double intelligence is best seen in situations in which the Njirićs, instead of asking what the Museum of Contemporary Art should look like, ask how to get there, how to bring it to life. For instance, when they describe the church in Aljmaš[72], they speak about rusty barges, which would take thousands of pilgrims to pay their respect to the blue cloak of St. Mary of Aljmaš. They conclude that "it is not then unreasonable to wrap the church in rusty panels of corrugated Corten steel and paint the entire pilgrim area in blue, with the exterior spiraling like Le Corbusier's interior and stopping high above the altar, opening a vista toward the Danube." This betrays an almost schizophrenic conceptual exercise which employs "double intelligence."

Yet, it is precisely this area between real and unreal, or even surreal, which is so exciting in the Njirićs' world. If we put aside our real world for a moment, if we embrace their world as a possibility,

---

72 Aljmaš is a village in the Erdut municipality in eastern Croatia. It lies on the right bank of the Danube.

not as a cartoon, but as an operating structure, what would this new Croatian arcadia be like? The new churches in Trnje[73] would have a "video campanile," "digital stained-glass windows," our "red" Trešnjevka would be an ideal spot for new types of buildings such as "drive-in villas" or "baby skyscrapers." The Museum of Contemporary Art would be a hybrid of four supermarkets and a museum, and the new monuments would be abstract laser structures resting on an "intelligent hill" or an "electronic mound."

Why not, and why not now? The Njirićs have practically been bombarding the Croatian community with these brazen questions. They make it seem as if our only option is to rush toward the post-Dayton arcadia. On our way there, we should implement Njirićs' world and strategies, not as the only available, but definitely as indispensable for a new culture of a region laden with history, yet with a perfect landscape. Should Njirićs' worlds come to life, both Croatia and Europe would become the meccas of some new pilgrims and the wells of some new lives. Just like that.

---

[73] Trnje and Trešnjevka are two city districts in Zagreb, both mostly inhabited by workers' population.

BALKAN TELETUBBIES AND THE DECONSTRUCTION OF MODERNISM

Published in Čovjek i prostor, 1-3, Zagreb, 2001

Kees Christiaanse: [...] this show is very clever. The Njirićs are really able to put an answer to everyday life into very conceptual and very strong architecture without taking the risk of not being accepted [...]

[...] their work brings a new vernacular, but even though it is very new, it is also very familiar. It corresponds to a very conceptual way of everyday life. I like the animation very much and how architecture is communicated. This is all highly modern. That is very important. They give an iconographic quality to the animations, but at the same time they are very strong, very sophisticated, and very human in using new technologies.

Bart Lootsma: It is a very playful exhibition, and what I find very impressive is that all the presentations are using new media; it is an architectural exhibition with lots of humor, which is very rare.

[...] it is always very difficult to represent architecture when you are not there with a building, because either you have the drawings, which means you do not get to see the detail or you have a model but you do not get to see the inside, you lack the scale. You always have to construct the experience of a building from many different media. You have to learn about it. I like this exhibition very much in all its playfulness, in the way it really wants to be modern, in the way it links up to its media culture. On the other hand, I have seen the buildings in Maribor, and they are very well detailed, very sharp, very tough, very good buildings, and all that is now transformed into a media experience. That aspect of the work is a bit blurred. This is the difference between the real world and the exhibition. On the other hand, you can consider this exhibition a piece of architecture.

(Excerpts from a video interview with Kees Christiaanse and Bart Lootsma by Darko Fritz at the opening of Kalvariengürtel at de Singel in Antwerp)

Njirić+Njirić are a phenomenon in their own right; they have made it again for the umpteenth time with their exhibition in the Antwerp's de Singel. Ms. Vandermarliere, the director of the architectural program in de Singel as the most prestigious of places to show and discuss architecture in Belgium, was quite curious to find out what were the Njirićs like at the last Biennale in Venice. My reply, of course, was that her choice was more than excellent, that she should pursue her e-mail correspondence with the Njirićs, and that the exhibition was bound to be good. What did Katrin expect to get from the Njirićs? Perhaps a whiff of fresh Balkan air, an outstanding performance, something to top Steven Holl, Wiel Arets, and other figures that had been familiar to the Belgian and Dutch audience. Something new and unexpected in any case, as the audience has grown a bit tired of Koolhaas' undisputed intelligence, Neutelings's structural mathematics, Cristiaanse's pragmatism, and Stephan Bell's perfection. The Njirićs were expected to show some new songlines from the transitional chaos.

So, for the umpteenth time and with the great and imaginative support by Ivan Marušić Klif[74] and the rest of the crew, njirić+njirić rose to the occasion and asserted their status in Europe.

The thing is that the Njirićs are thoroughbred European architects: they were educated in Zagreb (Croatia), worked in Graz (Austria) for a long time, where Hrvoje also taught at the University; their major buildings are in Maribor (Slovenia); their monograph is being published in Barcelona (Spain); and their work is reviewed by Manuel Gausa, Irénee Scalbert, and Yorgos Simeoforidis. How they are treated at home is quite another matter and I am reluctant to go there for the treatment is awful, even though not surprising, considering that they are outsiders who have surpassed their own milieu. The only thing I can promise to the Njirićs and to the whole European generation of outstanding Croatian architects like them is that time will show how they have been treated by the Croatian architectural establishment. From that perspective, this establishment will look like an Afghani Taliban who tried to wipe out an entire generation. Without success, obviously, for the Njirić, Puljiz, Randić, Radonić, 3LHD, and a lot of them have managed to find their own way and space to show their work in a much broader context that spans from Japan to Antwerp. The only question is when will this generation take over Croatia as well, but this might have to coincide with the political decision to join the European Union. Until then, the interest for the Njirić and the like will be limited to Europe and the world.

After Toyo Ito's million-dollar exhibition in Aachen, Kalvariengürtel is the most interesting architectural show I have had the pleasure to attend recently.

What started as a low-budget exhibition, driven by an obsession to present themselves in the best light possible, has been sublimed in an unbelievably interesting interactive show. As an idea and the title, Kalvariengürtel may be brimming with a variety of meanings; this is the name of the street where the Njirićs used to live in Graz in the early 1990s; this is also the area in the shopping mall where the customer is required to take the cart and drive it through the exhibition as if it were a store, only to be frisked at the exit like a shoplifter,

74   Ivan Marušić Klif (Zagreb, 1969) is a prominent Croatian visual and media artist.

and finally, this is the Calvary as the context for the Njirićs' operations from their Zagreb headquarters. If you remove all this unnecessary symbolism, what remains is a super active presentation of their architectural production over the last ten-odd years. This representation of the Calvary involves several stations, each using its own level of interaction to present a subject of particular interest or a group of projects. So let us take the cart and pay a visit to the njirić+njirić store.

The first station, tagged by the authors as the decorated site, is an interactive theater with five canvass screens and five Kodak carousel projectors. When the visitor enters this round room encircled by five semi-transparent canvasses for projection, they have to press one of the eight buttons, each for one major project. Each project is represented by a logo, which is a basic drawing. By pressing the button, all projectors are set in motion and start to project on all five canvasses. All of a sudden the visitor is in the middle of McDonalds, Baumax, and other projects. When the show is over after 60 seconds, the visitor can repeat it or move on to another project by pressing a different button. This installation takes the visitor to see the Njirićs' architecture from the first drafts to the photos of the completed building. The initial draft and the corresponding logo are "verified" and explained through a series of pictures of the completed building. This is an afterthought of the Njirićs' argument with Yorgos Simeoforidis that logo represents the "basic organizational model", which should be easy to understand, useful, and which should encourage further project development.

The second station – cinemascope – shows two different contexts and two different projects: the memorial on the occasion of 900 years of the city of Zagreb and the international port terminal in Yokohama. It is hard to imagine two things more disparate than this – the umbrellas of Šestine[75]

and the Japanese fish on the interactive front of the terminal – yet the joint presentation of the two projects flows so naturally because it does not look into the context but into the concepts of characterizing a city, which is what both projects share. Both are presented as a video accompanied by "contextual" music. This video projection overlaps with slides and text, which is quite a peculiar way to present architecture in a gallery.

The third station – this is tomorrow 2.0 – is a closed, 1 by 6 by 2 meter black box for presenting the "world around us" in a series of slides and accompanying text. The inscriptions on the box such as subversion, fundamentals, wonder, love, brains, and progress call the visitor's attention and invite them to come near and take a peep through a hole. The slides offer an interesting view of the future as the Njirićs' see it. Nearly all of them show "our contemporary chaos" and the controversies of the modern world, as they alternate newspaper clips, advertisements, press releases, and statistical data. Hardly any of them shows a piece of architecture or bears a cultural reference. Instead, the visitor sees the global context and the way the Njirićs' interpret it. This black box could fit into any museum of contemporary art as a cross-section of the times we live in, but here it clearly speaks about the Njirićs' complete immersion in the global world of information and their critical attitude toward this world. The criticism becomes clear when you connect the inscription on the peep hole with the text on the slide.

The fourth station – electro-cadavre exquis – brings the most ambitious interactive setup possible. The visitor faces a box with 12 slots. Three Plexiglas disks where placed by the box for the visitor to slide into the slots. This starts a projector to show one of the architectural pieces by the Njirićs. However, to finish this game, the visitor needs to complete the picture by sliding the other two disks and consequently starting the other two projectors. This is how they get to compose the image by combining different production levels of their piece. They become part

---

[75] Šestine is a picturesque village, once adjacent to Zagreb, Croatian capital, now a part of it. Šestine's symbol is a big, red umbrella that gradually became another symbol of Zagreb.

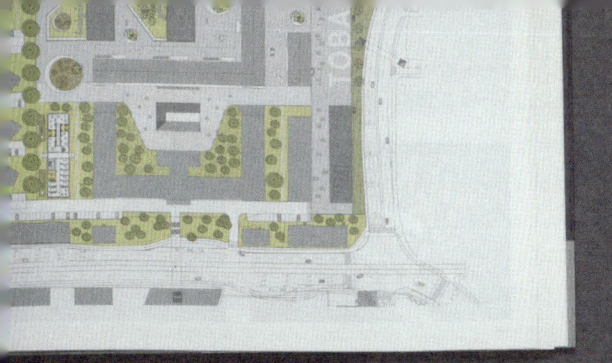

ORIS 48

Zagreb, 2007

Vedran Mimica : New Tobačna, Strictly Controlled Smoking

Janez Koželj
Markus Schaefer
Marijn Spoelstra
Dekleva and Gregorčič
Kebel and Cimolini
Sadar and Vuga
Černigoj and Grmek
Helena Njirić

Čovjek i prostor, LI/07-08

Zagreb, 2004

New authenticity and the guardians of the critical consciousness
interview with Vedran Mimica by: Ana Bakić, Alan Kostrenčić, Maroje Mrduljaš

Čovjek i prostor, 1-3

Zagreb, 2001

Vedran Mimica
Balkan Teletubbies
and Deconstruction
of Modernism

Kees Christiaanse
Bart Lootsma
Darko Fritz
Helena Paver Njirić
Hrvoje Njirić
Katrin Vandermerliere
Steven Holl
Wiel Arets
Stephan Bell
Klif Marušić
Manuel Gausa
Irenée Scalbert
Yorgos Simeoforidis
Pero Puljiz
Saša Randić
Bojan Radonić
3LHD

of a Dadaist game of producing new images from ready-made components. The first slide overlaps with the second and the third as if to deconstruct the meaning and the very display of the piece. The visitor is no longer a passive observer of the perfect image, but an active participant who gets to compose a "new" image of the Njirićs' architecture.

The fifth station – diagrams' flow – is a huge, two-faced screen showing computer animations that tell educational stories about the Njirićs' projects. I find these animations the best part of the exhibition, as they show how a project develops from the first idea to virtual reality in a very intriguing way. Hrvoje Njirić authored the "shooting script", and Lala Raščić, a visual and media artist, did the animation that combines the tradition of the Zagreb School of Animated Film, Cedric Price-like cartoon narrative from the 1960s, and the peculiar cross-sectional and axonometric drawing style of the Njirićs. The screen is set in a hall, and as visitors approach it, they trip a laser beam to start a projection. This is yet another of the small wonders from Ivan Marušić Klif's studio: your movement along the hall triggers a series of projections.

The final station is the 1:1 mock-up. In the real-life scale it shows a moving walkway (tapis roulant) in a business building with a view to two diametrically opposed environments: office and wildlife. The mock-up is set in de Singel's hall whereas the man-made and natural sceneries are shown on huge panels. As you pass this station, your Calvary is drawing to an end, but before you leave the "store" and return the cart, you will be frisked. Truth be told, the curator has not embraced this idea without reserve.
The Calvary is over now, and you feel genuinely amazed and excited about the world of the Njirićs. Firstly, because you have just seen an architectural exhibition that is not a series of historical, still images, but an interactive experience that questions whether it is really possible to represent architecture as much as it questions the character of architecture in the times when the market dominates over culture. Secondly, because there is a new wind blowing from the European southeast, witnessing that the intercultural exchange with the West is absolutely possible and necessary, as long as we speak about the Njirićs' level of production. Once again, this exhibition has confirmed that the work of njirić+njirić belongs to the top European practices at the beginning of a "new" era, and that the "Balkan aliens" can take you to the core of their work with infinitesimal budget and infinite imagination.

The correspondingly modest and imaginative exhibition catalog takes you through Kalvariengürtel with a series of texts about the Njirićs and four manifestos they issued.
All four, namely the 1997 "upgrading/updating", the 1999 "end of modernism", and the 2000 "xx vs xxi" and "9 points for students in architecture" speak in clear, almost computer terms about downloading files for future operations in the architecture of the third millennium. Their deconstruction of the modern paradigm, which in itself is quite eclectic and ornamental, has become the new, complex, collective, digital, fluid architecture of new possibilities and organizational forms.

Where does this poetic force and inspired optimism come? The Habsburg-Yugoslav-Croatian modernist background? No European "consumer" can answer this question. But what about me? Did I miss something?

CHILDREN'S ROOM

Edited version of the essay published in "473"[76], ed. Vladimir Mattioni, UPI2M Plus, Zagreb 2003

Regarding architecture and urban planning, as an element of cultural production (or attempting to prove that assumption), the phenomenon of the "Children's room" is rendered even more interesting. A group of young people has, in the beginning of their professional activity, found themselves in an environment of institutionalized yet non-hierarchical production. That rarely happens in this part of the world. The only way for young, self-educated people with aspiration towards Europe – who miraculously appear in Croatia every year – to continue their professional career is to start an individual practice, as detached from institutions as possible. The country's large number of mini-practices with only two or three employees serves as a proof. However, the "Children's room" was part of a large institution, City of Zagreb, Urban Planning Office. This institution, in the mid-90s, in collaboration with the Berlage Institute, began a series of international seminars called Frames of the Metropolis, wherein the "children" started out as technical support, only to become equal participants in later seminars.

With every phenomenon having a simple explanation – and myself being a person who has spent a large amount of time abroad, which left me illiterate in relation to the complicated and coded situations of the new Croatia – my opinion is that Vladimir Mattioni served as a primary *spiritus movens* of the "Children's room." Its existence would probably not have been possible without the special energy of Slavko Dakić, which was necessary to create a new type of institutional performance, as well as the professional and conceptual support of Borislav Doklestić, Ratko Miličević, Niko Gamulin, Ivan Čižmek and others. The basic advantage for Mattioni comes from the fact that he previously did not live in Zagreb and thus did not take part in the city planning institutions of Zagreb. Instead, his situation made it possible for him to develop, in parallel with his city-planning work, an artistic conceptual project within something called "New Yugoslav Art Practice" of the 1970s. Mattioni arrived at the office at the same time as the members of the "Children's room." He did not have a room to work in either. But, according to the nature of his artistic work, he had a project. And the nature of that project was collective, interactive and based upon the intellect and cooperation of each participant. Mattioni succeeded in putting intelligence before hierarchy, an achievement so simple yet rarely seen in Croatia. The project became more important than relations and subsequent production made the project more important than interrelations, and production became the sole reason for discussion. The "children" as such could not be better than they were, but, at the same time it is necessary to realize that children are good by default, which results in disappearance of difficulties and effort, and encourages adventure.

To explain the "Children's room" production it would be interesting to compare the *Krašland* project with the contemporary project for extension of the Maksimir soccer stadium. This comparison presents the complete difference between the "children's" world and that of the "adults." While on one side a horrifying evidence of totalitarian theory and practice was being constructed, with new architecture destroying architectural history and preventing democratic future from happening in the case of Dinamo[77] Zagreb soccer stadium; the other side, only a couple of hundred meters down the road, witnessed the development of a space of postmodern leisure and urban (even though presenting a consumerist way of life) quality which remained non built.

---

76 Book "473" resulted from the endeavour of the several authors (Hrvoje Bakran, Ivana Crnošija, Tea Horvat, Zdravko Krasić, Dražen Plevko and Vladimir Mattioni). That group of authors was famous under different names and in different formations: first as "Childrens' room" (1996-1998), then as the web-site "urbanizam.net" (1999-2001) and finally as a company "Urbane tehnike" (Urban techniques) after 2002.

77 Dinamo is Zagreb's local soccer club.

Almost all projects that came out of the "Children's room" attempted to create a setting for a way of life that has not yet been established in Croatia, and if it were, these projects and strategies would carry urban and vivacious quality, bringing this part of the world closer to the democratic standards of Western European urbanity. This conclusion leaves a feeling of unease, because the genesis of these projects comprised the analytic process of mapping and sampling of the local phenomena. The project's answers come from the research results. So it seems logical to ask "Why not?" Why is it not possible to imagine implementing such projects, because they do not belong to the playful domain of the children, but present a logical and intelligent answer by a new generation of Croatian architects to the extremely controversial surrounding of transition, post-modernism and post-history?

However, the "Children's room" adventure continues, and it would be a good thing for the children never to grow up. As for Vladimir, I know, he never will.

Hrvoje Bakran
Zdravko Krasić
Vladimir Mattioni
Saša Randić
Kenneth Frampton
Dalibor Martinis
Helena Njirić
Hrvoje Njirić
Ivan Čižmek
Goran Rako
Alejandro Zaera-Polo
Slavko Dakić
Nikola Polak
Rem Koolhaas
Zaha Hadid
Daniel Libeskind
Alessandro Mendini
Niek Verdonk
Mario Botta
Thom Mayne
Gorki Žuvela
Fumihiko Maki

Toyo Ito
Jean Nouvel
Slavoj Žižek
Norman Klein
Dražen Lalić
Goran Ivanišević
Diego Maradona
Bojan Radonić
Herman Hertzberger
Bojan Baletić
Veljko Olujić
Tonči Žarnić
Mladen Jošić
Dafne Berc
Norman Foster
Oliver Dragojević
TBF
Braco Dimitrijević
Goran Trbuljak
Biafra
Zvjezdana Fio
Vladimir Šlapeta

URBANIZAM.NET

UPI-2M PLUS, Zagreb, 2004

Free Croat in the Hague,
interview with Vedran Mimica
by Hrvoje Bakran, Zdravko
Krasnić, Vladimir Mattioni

473

UPI2M, Zagreb, 1990

Vedran Mimica
Children's Room

Joschka Fischer
Boro Doklestić
Ratko Miličević
Niko Gamulin
Ivan Čižmek
Vladimir Mattioni
Children's room: Ivana Crnošija
Tea Horvat
Zdravko Krasić
Hrvoje Bakran
Dražen Plevko

▶ razgovarali: Zdravko Krasić i Hrvoje Bakran

Next Europe

U RAZGOVORU ZA ČIP VEDRAN MIMICA IZNOSI, KAO SUDIONIK 10. ARHITEKTONSKOG KONGRESA U BEČU NA TEMU "SLIJEDEĆA EUROPA", SVOJE VIĐENJE PERSPEKTIVA RAZVOJA ZEMALJA ISTOČNE EUROPE, POSEBICE HRVATSKE S ASPEKTA ARHITEKTONSKE I KULTURNE PRODUKCIJE, TE NJIHOVA UKLJUČIVANJA U "PROŠIRENU" EUROPSKU UNIJU

Oris 89

Zagreb, 2014

Vedran Mimica
Unique Cultural Project

Čovjek i prostor 11–12

Zagreb, 2002

Vedran Mimica
Next Europe

Dietmar Steiner
Wolfgang Petritsch
Slavoj Žižek
Lluís Hortet
Deyan Sudjic
Andrej Hrauski
Walter Maria Stojan
Michael Ignatieff
Milan Kundera
Daniel Libeskind
Braco Dimitrijević
Joseph Beuys
Igor Zidić
Tonko Maroević
Vjeran Zuppa
Njirić+Njirić

Čovjek i prostor, 5-6

Zagreb, 2006

Vedran Mimica
New School of
Architecture in Split

Manfredo Tafuri
Ante Kuzmanić
Eugen Širola
Ivo Babić

NEXT EUROPE

Edited interview with Zdravko Krasić and Hrvoje Bakran about 10th Congress of Architecture in Vienna
Published in Čovjek i prostor 11-12, 2002

In the interview for ČIP, from the 10th Vienna Architecture Congress "Next Europe", Vedran Mimica brings his own views of the architectural and cultural development of Eastern European countries, Croatia in particular, and their part in the EU "enlargement."

ČIP In the early November 2002, the Architekturzentrum Wien (Vienna Architecture Center) organized the 10th Vienna Architecture Congress with an indicative title "Next Europe." Since you participated as one of the invited speakers, could you tell us what the key topics were?

Vedran Mimica Dietmar Steiner has been organizing these congresses in Vienna for ten years already, and last year he started a new series to be dedicated to the EU enlargement or the "New Europe," as he calls it. The enlargement concept behind the New Europe was endorsed at the recent accession meeting in Athens by ten new member states. Consequently, it broadens, or should I say "enlarges," the scope of our discussion. Steiner's congress seeks to encompass this scope through multidisciplinary and multicultural or multinational discussion about the emerging phenomena. Curiously enough, I was invited to speak about Croatian transitional issues, even though Croatia is still far away from joining this New Europe. I suppose Dietmar wanted to "fill in the blanks," so he needed another "Balkan expert." This is how he announced my lecture. I can hardly call myself an expert for the Balkans, but since I had worked on the Randić and Turato monograph and the Frames of the Metropolis and wrote several articles for ČIP, Oris, Arhitekturni Bilten and other regional periodicals, I found Dietmar's invitation interesting, if not entirely appropriate. Truth be told, I already had two lectures on a similar subject, one in Geneva in 2000 as part of a seminar entitled "Reconstruction and Memory" and the other in Skopje in 2002, at the First conference of the Balkan schools of architecture. The first lecture – "East-West: Blurring Territories" – was about the Balkan wars and their consequences, and the second – "The Future of Architectural Education in the Time of Globalization" – was about how to overcome these consequences through education. This third lecture in the series – "Croatia between Postdaytonian Arcadia and Transitional Darkness" – was to answer Dietmar's question how to develop architectural discourse in this next or new Europe.

ČIP   What was Dietmar Steiner's take-home message at the Vienna congress?

VM   His take-home message was that only if we, both from the Western and Eastern world, intensify our dialogue and start to show different experiences, than the European project could really develop. People from the east should not then be considered as newcomers but as peer citizens, cultural workers, architects, and historians. We should ask ourselves whether the Croatian architectural scene has been presented to Europe in this context. I find it particularly disastrous that Croatia does not participate in the Mies van der Rohe Award, which is an EU award, and that it is poorly represented at the Venice Biennale. These two are the major European events that evaluate the quality of national architectures. This year, as I became the Mies van der Rohe Award specialist, I was in a position to nominate an architectural piece for the award and I asked the award director Lluís Hortet why I could not nominate works from Croatia whereas most other Eastern European countries were eligible. He told me that Bruxelles had told him that Croatia was still not politically eligible for the award. I got the same answer from the Venice Biennale: that Croatia, Slovenia, and then Yugoslavia (now Serbia and Montenegro) could not agree about sharing the Yugoslav pavilion, so the Biennale director Deyan Sudjic reached an awkward decision that only the leftover Yugoslavia should be exhibiting in the former common pavilion. My objection, backed by my Slovene colleague Andrej Hrauski, was that this was the Yugoslav pavilion and not Serbian and Montenegrin alone. I strongly feel that the Croatian architectural establishment should have formally challenged the ownership of the Giardini pavilion and requested permanent exhibition rights at the Biennale. The same goes for the inclusion in the Mies van der Rohe Award.

ČIP   Does Europe view Croatia through its association with the Balkans?

VM   Croatian political and cultural circles find the Balkan attribute unacceptable. Many will go the length to explain that Croatia is not nearly as Balkan as it is European. Walter Maria Stojan, a Professor of Greek history at Vienna University, published an interesting essay The Balkans: A European Tragedy[78] in which he challenges the common perception of the Balkans as a 'mysterious European subcontinent, … dark and soaked in blood and almost wild,' especially over the last ten years. Instead, he claims that, despite grave historical turmoil, the Balkans have been the main land bridge between Europe and Asia Minor, that has carried all the important cultural influences over to Europe in the unlikely times when two worlds, West and East, Christianity and Islam, collided. It was the Balkans, and Bosnia in particular, where these contrasted worlds had coexisted for centuries. He recalls the fantastic image of Sarajevo with the Catholic bell tower, Orthodox bell tower, minarets, and a synagogue. Stojan argues that the Balkans will be home of the new future. Some of his arguments may seem naïve, but they are nonetheless accurate: 'nature intact, mountains leaning over the sea, different cultures in a small area, rich European history, and untapped resources for future development offer a variety of potentials.' He also admits that it will take a lot of time before we abandon the stereotypes and the stigma. There is no denying that the Balkans have a

---

[78]   Maria Stojan, W. (2001) "Balkan – evropska tragedija".
Source: www.alexandria-press.com/newprint/011_balkan_tragedija_stojan.htm, accessed August 22, 2016

stigma. Whenever I mention where I am coming from, I am perceived as a Balkanite. I personally have no problem with this, but you can sense the prevailing stereotype, you do feel kind of stigmatized. Stojan continues by saying that he wanted to impart his feeling for the Balkans to his Austrian children, and that the feeling is nice. Now, this romanticized view of the Balkans aside, the hard facts have not been working toward removing that stigma lately. They still seem to influence the European perception of Croatia.

ČIP This brings us to the Old Bridge in Mostar. How paradigmatic is that case for our discussion?

VM Michael Ignatieff, MIT professor, has recently published an article in The New York Times about the research of a French engineer Gilles Pequeux, who is now trying to rebuild the Mostar bridge. Pequeux found out that when the bridge was originally built, two stone cutting techniques were used in an incredible symbiosis, one Western, Catholic, and the other Eastern, Muslim. His replica is going to use them both. In the article, Ignatieff recalls the history of coexistence of these two worlds and speaks about the unique construction of the bridge. Many of the exemplary works in this corner of the planet have combined these two dominant cultures. This overlapping, as opposed to exclusion, is not only paradigmatic for the future of the Balkans, but for the future of the enlarged Europe.

ČIP What do you think is necessary to restore the dialogue in the Balkans?

VM The countries of the former Yugoslavia should start to speak to each other if they want to join the EU, and I mean on all levels. This is one of the key EU requirements. At the Vienna congress I argued that the communication between these countries required a higher state of mind and gave three examples. The first was how Willy Brandt dealt with the German historical guilt from WW2. For the second, literary example, I took Milan Kundera, who has best described the complex spiritual world of the so called Eastern Bloc. At the moment, one could safely claim that the discourse of these countries has surpassed the West, at least on a theoretical level. The third example comes from the world of architecture. It is the work of Daniel Libeskind, his addition to the Jewish Museum Berlin in particular. Libeskind argues that architecture can turn historical tragedies into flourishing new concepts that generate new cultural discourse, which is what his museum does.

ČIP Is there a way to objectively view the recent Balkan events from a historical perspective?

VM I think that no one can really explain or speculate about the Balkan conflicts without finding himself or herself on thin ice. The history of the Balkans, like no other, has been a slippery concept. Cases in point are the last generations spanning from grandfathers to grandchildren. For a while, my own father believed that Stalin was a charismatic leader; my generation in turn believed that Tito was a great world statesman, and the new generation of Croatians thought as much of Franjo Tuđman. Yet we have benefited recently from the open and democratic dialogue that has made us aware of the new information about the character of these leading figures. In other words, we should not be surprised if, in a future history book, another replaces an established historical fact, and by saying it I mean the close future. It does hurt me a bit, though, that this region was incredibly open in the 1970s and 1980s, that it ventured into alternative economic and political systems and developed alternative cultural projects, even if it politically did take the form of a sort of enlightened authoritarianism. Along these lines, I had an interesting conversation with Braco Dimitrijević about his workshop with Joseph Beuys in Belgrade in 1974 and about Gorgona, New Tendency, and New Painting. It will be interesting to see how things will develop at future Vienna seminars, say in 2015, when we will hopefully gain a critical perspective on the European enlargement project and on the events at the fringes of Europe.

MISSION IMPOSSIBLE? I DON'T THINK SO

Published in Oris 9, Zagreb 2001

Art has to be forgotten: Beauty must be realized.[79]

Piet Mondrian, 1938

Non-figurative art is created by establishing a dynamic rhythm of determinate mutual relations, which excludes the formation of any particular form. We note thus, that to destroy particular form is only to do more consistently what all art has done.
The dynamic rhythm, which is essential in all art, is also the essential element of a non-figurative work.[80]

Piet Mondrian, 1937

During the last few years, Vitić's[81] residential building in Zagreb has become a landmark for Croatian post-war Modernism and a canonical example for the discussion of modernist projects. When Post-modernism replaced Modernism at 1980 Portoghesi Venice Biennale titled The Presence of the Past with a main exhibition Strada Novissima, it opened a Pandora's box of the most diverse architectural scenarios for the end of the millennium. The completion of the modernist project was reviewed, from Frampton to Jencks and from Habermas to Deleuze. From critical regionalism via the critical reconstruction of Berlin to the technological and global approach of the 1990s, architecture has sought new inventions in tradition or in new technologies. The recycling of all past utopias without the creation of new paradigms and new canons has opened a domain where "anything goes" was not only a possibility, but a promising "liberty."

In resisting globalization, traditional cultures insist on the values of local milieus, as a pledge for their cultural identity, and make the effort to discover historical values. History is a dynamic category, so that it is not irrelevant which page of history is read or appears in the media space of today. The post-modernist reading of history usually reveals national cultural values which are then reinterpreted as solid and traditional. The historical reading of Modernism during the past two decades in Croatian architecture has resulted in a series of neo-modernist buildings which have explored the possibilities of completing the modernist project.

During the past decade, Vitić's building has been used, in a variety of ways and through a series of coincidences, as an argument, as an illustration, as a flag, as proof. Of what? It is the modest ambition of this text to answer the question: why have we discovered Vitić after 40 years? Perhaps because nothing has been done on Ivan Vitić, for example, a monograph,[82] a text, a film, an exhibition, a discussion, a publication, a website.
And Vladimir Turina, Kazimir Ostrogović, Drago Galić, Božidar Rašica, Neven Šegvić, Aleksandar Dragomanović, Radovan Nikšić, do they deserve a post-historical promotion or not? We simply do not have a personality like Vladimír Šlapeta[83] to

---

79   Quoted from: Holtzman, Harry & James, Martin.S. (1987) The New Art, the New Life: The Collected Writings of Piet Mondrian (Documents of Twentieth-Century Art). London: Thames & Hudson Ltd

80   Ibid.

81   Ivan Vitić (1917-1986), a famous Croatian modernist architect, whose extraordinary works are to be found across Croatia – from the Croatian capital over his home city Šibenik to the Island of Vis.

82   This injustice was rectified to the certain extent when in 2006 the Croatian Association of Architects issued a special edition of the Arhitektura, another longstanding Croatian architectural journal (established in 1947), dedicated entirely to the legacy of Ivan Vitić. Arhitektura, No. 1 (217) / Year LIV 2005 (Printed in 2006).

83   Vladimír Šlapeta is an architect, architecture historian, a professor at the Brno University of Technology, Faculty of Architecture, Head of Department of Theory.

YUGOSLAV MEMORIAL
CENTRE BOŠKO BUHA
IN GRADINA

project study
1980

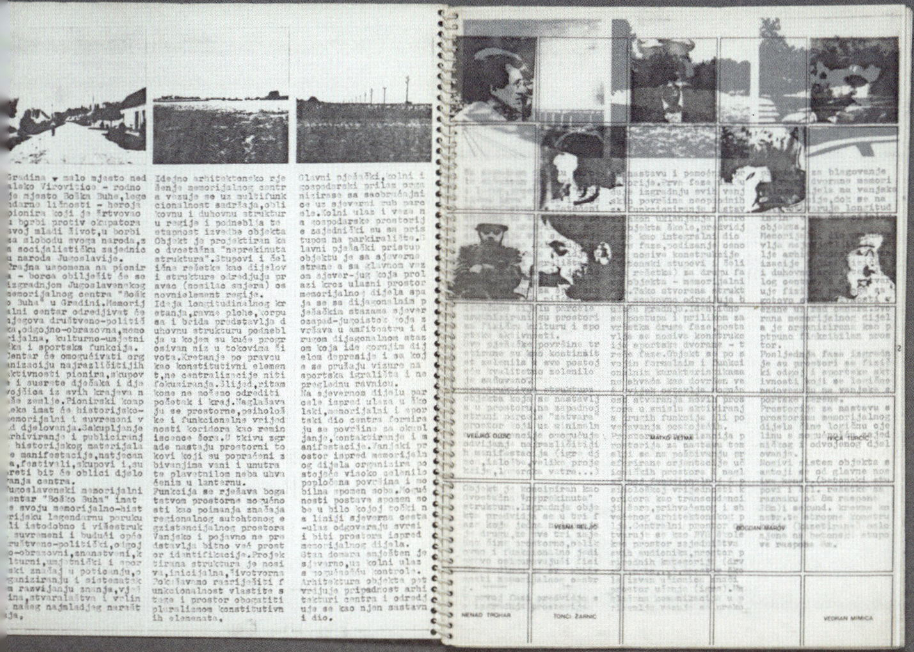

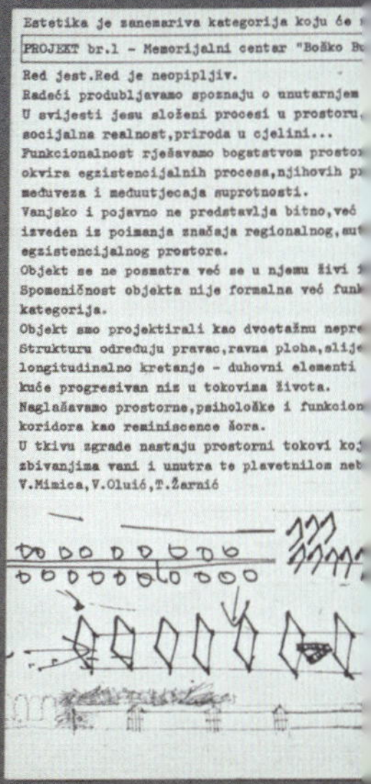

ORIS 9

2001

Vedran Mimica
Mission Impossible?
I Don't Think So

Kenneth Frampton
Charles Jencks
Jurgen Habermas
Vladimir Šlapeta
Aldo van Eyck
Yap Hong Seng
Pero Puljiz
Theo Bosch
Aleksandar Laslo
Jorgos Simeoforidis
Njirić+Njirić

present and show Croatian Modernism through a series of monographs and exhibitions. Be that as it may, during the past ten years or so, I have mapped a series of coincidences connected to Vitić and his building in Laginjina Street in Zagreb.

Coincidence 1

The Berlage Institute. Home of Aldo van Eyck. South Amsterdam. 1991. Yap Hong Seng, the first Berlage director, asks Pero Puljiz, a student of the first generation, if he perhaps knows who designed three residential towers at Olympia Plein Stadium, which was part of a project completed in the first semester. From the description given, Pero believes it is his project, but also stresses that the project arose as a strong reference to the 1958 project of architect Ivan Vitić from Zagreb. Hong Seng explains that Theo Bosch, a visiting professor, has offered his teaching fee to the student who designed the project, for the next semester scholarship.

Coincidence 2

Frames of the Metropolis, the International town planning workshop seminar. Zagreb. 1995. Saša Laslo[84] stops a minibus full of participants in front of the building in Laginjina Street. Kenneth Frampton and Jorgos Simeoforidis approach him with a perfectly understandable question: "...so who is this Vitić and why don't you have any books on this author? Do you realize that you don't exist in the world history of architecture, yet you have such an accomplished work dating from the late 1950s?"

Coincidence 3

The Faculty of Architecture in Zagreb. "Platform 9.81". The year 2000. Members of Platforma 9.81 showed me a series of slides taken on the Island of Vis. While scanning the situation on Vis, they discover Vitić's Army Headquarters building and literally clean it of layers of refuse and years of neglect on the part of the local authorities.

Coincidence 4

Singel, the centre for art and architecture in Antwerp. The opening of the exhibition of architects Njirić and Njirić from Zagreb entitled Kalvariengürtel. The year 2001.

In his introductory lecture during the opening, the positively eloquent Hrvoje Njirić presents his conceptual "background" through a series of slides. To the left, Vitić's building in Laginjina Street, dating from 1958 in back and white; to the right, the same building shot in color in 2000, with its crumbling façade.

Let us repeat the question. Why do we discover Vitić after 40 years? Why do Theo Bosch, Aldo van Eyck's partner and an architect whose houses almost all have a strong, organic, circular shape, discover Puljiz's work as the most interesting among the works of 15 students? Why does Frampton believe he has missed an important page in the history of post-war European architecture? Why do students clean Vitić's army barracks in Komiža on the Island of Vis? Why do the Njirićs, so "obscenely" successful outside Croatia, present Vitić's building in Laginjina Street as their conceptual backdrop? And why has Andrija Rusan been "pestering" me for months to write an article on Vitić for Oris?

To write about Vitić, or anyone belonging to the brilliant generation of Croatian post-war modernists, is almost "obscene" without first doing careful research into the context in which these works were created, the importance of the work in relation to the architect's opus; without a comparative analysis of the work in relation to culture; to the cultural, social, artistic and political landscape of Croatia and Europe during the said period. This is why this contribution should be viewed, on one hand, as an appeal for such endeavours, and, on the other hand, as an attempt to find an answer to the fascination with Vitić after 40 years.

84   Aleksandar Saša Laslo (1950-2014), a Croatian architect and prominent architectural historian, dedicated most of his writing to Croatian modernism.

What fascinates us?

Vitić's building in Laginjina Street speaks of the possibilities of the modernist code to intervene in the existing urban context, thus causing a "complete" change in the building rules and principles to create a startlingly adapted environment to the context. By creating a void instead of a solid corner building, Vitić's modernist code deconstructs Lenuci's block matrix extension to the east, thus creating a public space. Empty instead of full is the perfect twist that creates a public area in front of the building, thus negating the courtyard as a place of a new urban identity. There is no courtyard and there never was, as it never fulfilled the expectations of Lenuci and urban planners at the beginning of the 20th century; instead it was transformed into a rural environment. A plaza stands instead of the courtyard, a super urban void in front of the housing. It is only at first glance that the building seems to be a perfect symbiosis between Corbu and Mondrian, and these references are apparent. However, further analysis must anticipate the perfect contextuality of the project, which has, perhaps, only been achieved through Niemeyer's interventions in Rio and São Paolo.

The building is a perfect example of the effort needed to interpolate Corbusier's code into a block matrix. The main building is a clear interpretation of Corbusier's five basic rules of modern architecture, whilst the western and northern buildings create a "second generation" of the same code which, through volume and design, respects the framework of the block. However, the ingenious detail of mobile shutters (the product of Vitić's Mediterranean background) used on the main building creates a different interpretation of the Unité façade. The dynamic rhythm found in Mondrian's sentence from 1937 is used here as an almost Mediterranean reinterpretation of Le Corbusier and as a collage in which the citizens participate to create the urban image. The elevation of the central building is exactly that canonical surface on which "everything" is changeable. It is here that the bourgeois, solid, traditional, central European architecture of Zagreb's city is transformed through Vitić's code. This code is modern, yet not eclectic, although it does create a dynamic field of collages with Arp's force and rapture. All the principles of original Modernism are respected and acknowledged, but their contextual interpretation through the dynamic field even today speak in support of Habermas's statement on the open possibilities of completing the modernist project.

If nothing else than through Docomomo, the international organisation which promotes the protection and conservation of monuments of Modern Movement architecture, we need to preserve and restore, publicize and present to the world Vitić's building in Laginjina Street as an example of the ultimate achievement in Croatian architecture and, I would venture to say, as the fundamental pledge for a milieu's cultural future.

And I conclude with one more question: how can we transform our fascination with Vitić into a fascination for the future where, within the global environment, we will be able to read the true values of Croatian history? Mission impossible? I do not think so.

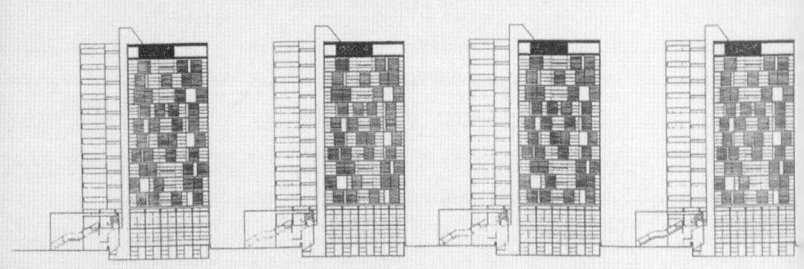

Pero Puljiz: Projekt za Stadionplein / project for Stadionplein, Amsterdam, Nizozemska / Netherlands, 1990.

diskusija, publikacija, web stranica o Ivanu Vitiću. A Turina, Ostrogović, Galić, Rašica, Šegvić, Dragomanović, Nikšić – zaslužuju li oni postpovijesnu promociju ili... Mi jednostavno nemamo našeg Vladu Slapetu da našu modernu pokaže i prikaže kroz serije monografija i izložbi,

film, an exhibition, a discussion, a publication, a website.
And Turina, Ostrogovic, Galic, Rasica, Segvic, Dragomanovic, Niksic, do they deserve post historical promotion or not? We simply do not have a Vlado Slapeta to present and show Croatian

Iz foto arhiva Toše Dabca / Photo archive of Toša Dabac

Bilo kako bilo, ja sam u zadnjih desetak godina "mapirao" niz slučajnosti vezanih uz Vitića i Laginjinu.

SLUČAJNOST 1

Berlage institut, Južni Amsterdam. Godina 1991. Yap Hong Seng, prvi direktor Berlagea, zaustavlja studenta prve generacije Peru Puljiza i pita zna li on možda tko je projektirao tri stambena tornja na Stadion Pleinu u tek završenom projektu u prvom semestru. Peri se iz opisa čini da se radi o njegovom projektu, ali napominje da je nastao kao snažna referenca na zagrebački projekt arhitekta Vitića iz 1958. Hong Seng mu pojašnjava kako se gostujući profesor Theo Bosch odrekao svog honorara u korist studenta koji je napravio taj projekt, a tim će mu se novcem platiti školarina za iduće semestre.

SLUČAJNOST 2

"Okviri metropole", međunarodni urbanistički seminar, Zagreb, godina 1995. Saša Laslo zaustavlja minibus pun sudionika seminara u Laginjinoj. Kenneth Frampton i Jorgos Simeoforidis mi prilaze sa sasvim normalnim pitanjem: "Pa tko je taj Vitić i zašto nema knjige o tom autoru? Je li vama jasno da ne postojite u svjetskoj povijesti arhitekture, a imate ovakve realizacije iz kasnih pedesetih?"

SLUČAJNOST 3

AF Zagreb. Platforma 9.81. Godina 2000. Studenti iz Platforme pokazuju mi seriju dijapozitiva s Visa i zamišljaju akciju na tom otoku tijekom ljeta 2001. i 2002. Događaj Mega EASA, međunarodni studentski seminar. Tijekom "skeniranja" situacije na Visu "otkrivaju" Vitićev Dom JNA te ga - doslovno

Modernism through a series of monographs and exhibitions. Be that as it may, during the past ten years or so, I have mapped a series of coincidences connected to Vitić and his building in Laginjina Ulica.

COINCIDENCE 1

The Berlage Institute, Home of Aldo van Eyck, South Amsterdam, 1991. Yap Hong Seng, the first Berlage director, asks Pero Puljiz, a student of the first generation, if he perhaps knows who designed the three residential towers at Plein Stadium, which was part of a project completed in the first semester. From the description given, Pero believes it is his project, but also stresses that the project arose as a strong reference to the 1958 project of architect Ivan Vitić from Zagreb. Hong Seng explains that Theo Bosch, a visiting professor, has offered his fee to the student

ORIS 9

2001

Vedran Mimica
Mission Impossible?
I Don't Think So

Ernest Weissmann,
Foundation and Clinical Hospital in
Zagreb, competition entry, 1931

EXERCISING EUROPE

Text is a result of Vedran Mimica's conversation with Alan Kostrenčić and Maroje Mrduljaš on EUROPAN, Published in Arhitektura 1 (216), Zagreb 2005

European Context

Boris Groys is probably right when he compares the new Europe with the former Soviet Union and speaks about the large community of countries not founded through a democratic process but led by the vast bureaucratic apparatus from Bruxelles, which attempts to control the large territory with countless regulations and laws. The only difference, for now, is that the European project, in comparison to the Soviet one, is progressing splendidly and has all the more supporters. Europan is, as its name suggests, one of the Paneuropean initiatives generated within the context of the union of European states. Europan is a cultural interpretation of the architectural creations of young architects/professionals (under 40) on the theme of housing and calls on architects to be involved in milieus to which they do not originally belong. The opening of local centers to the European exchange of architectural ideas and strategies is the basic feature of Europan and its success, in a particular way, is parallel to the success of the project of the united Europe.

Housing Program / Living Program

Didier Rebois, Yorgos Simeoforidis, Manuel Gausa, Dietmar Steiner and many other "believers" of Europan's premise have been promoting and advocating the ideas of new forms of housing in European cities from 1989. During the 1980s, a radical post-modernism was used as an attempt to resolve the crisis of European cities and the modernist movement whereby the reconstruction of Bruxelles, London and many other cities was under the obvious influence of the Strada Novissima (1980) and Berlin's IBA (from 1977 and on). However, already at the end of the eighties it became clear that the post-modern discourse would not be able to be significantly used on the reconstruction of European cities and that new ways would have to be created of its perception, first theoretical ones and then technical and strategic ones. A parallel conclusion was that housing was still an important program in building cities, especially for countries of the new Eastern Europe where the shortage of housing was obvious. The same applied to the former colonial forces which had a large influx of inhabitants from the former colonies in Asia and Africa. This changed the national structure and multicultural picture of European metropolises. Europan began as a laboratory for housing programs, but not those of a CIAM or monofunctional nature, but rather in the sense of housing as a part of life. That which was once a housing program became a living program linked to the themes of mobility, identity, typology, the relation between infrastructure and housing, hybrid programs.

United Europe as a project became quite obviously successful through a series of political, cultural and, most importantly, economic formats. In that sense, the success of Europan is at once the success of the European project both on an individual level of all actors tied in with Europan, as well as on an international level of cultural exchange which is fundamental for a New Europe. Local boundaries disappear, as do local authorities and the local becomes European. Many theoreticians, especially those who were close to the idea of the dying off of the national state as the underlying format for the development of culture, were close to the Europan criteria and visions. Europan was a test balloon for many countries in the sense of questioning their possibilities for participation in European processes. It was interesting for all to see how the different countries that were members of Europan adapted to these ideas.

Exercising Europe and the Exchange of Cultural Values

Europan is still, which is surprising, probably the most popular competition for young architects in

Europe. If one only counts the number of people, teams and work hours invested by young European architects in order to respond to interesting project tasks, and if one knows that this organization is led by only 5 or 6 people, then one needs to understand that this is a real architectural-cultural phenomenon. One of the fundamental reasons for Europan's popularity is that it places architects more in the position of producer of new cultural values and less as producer of project documentations. Second, Europan jury members are always carefully selected, followed by critics who formed their thoughts around specific Europan campaigns and who later quite seriously and critically documented the awarded works. Ninety percent of the frustrations of those awarded and who did not build is actually well compensated through promotions, presentations, catalog, exhibitions and through their presence within European architectural discussions. Europan's network has covered almost the entire Europe and beyond European political boundaries, which is especially important for Croatia.

A comparison could be made between Europan as an architectural workshop and Europe as a political workshop of new concepts of relations between national states. However, this comparison would be too imprecise as Simeoforidis and the others were less impressed by the political processes in Europe and more concerned about the reconstruction of European cities. Didier Rebois is perhaps a successful politician-architect, and he needed to be so for the entire process to receive resources and support. However, Simeoforidis and Gausa were almost exclusively interested in the application of some of their theoretical research with their inclusion in the competition's task on the one hand, and on the other hand they were interested in seeing what kind of relation there was between the various architectural schools and national architectures within Europe. This intense connection could not be seen through other international competitions, biennials, triennials, or larger regional exchanges of architectural exhibitions. In that sense, Europan was far ahead of all the others. Simeoforidis was, as were many others, very critical towards his own Greek milieu and he believed that the exchange between north and south Europe was inspirational in both directions. He never thought that this was a one-way process. He had great support on the part of Dietmar Steiner who claimed that the New Europe was now being redefined through eastern Europe, in a way that what was not able to be made in the west, was now being exercised in the east, where Eastern Europe with all its values, be they historical, be they quite contemporary, could have an essential influence on western Europe. In this regard, the Njirić architect team is an interesting example, as they do not seem to belong to the western-European context by the many characteristics of their work. That openness and positive naiveté is something that the Western Europe has forgotten. Simeoforidis and Steiner's argument was that those people and those cultures, or rather, their ways of thought, could contribute to the creation of a new European spirit which is essentially defined by exchanges between diverse milieus, characters, and different traditions.

Simeoforidis also posed the new questions of European cities, especially peripheries, non-places, deteriorating places or undefined spaces. In one moment architects, together with sociologists, were learning about the physical production of spaces without identities or recognizability. What became an interesting question was the potential of such places, whether or not they were inevitably negative and in which manner such places become or not become spaces for new ways of life. These themes shifted the direction of architectural discussion and education from the functional toward the real and contextual. The new lifestyle of inhabiting the city became important in relation to the conceptualization of physical frameworks from the postulates of radical modernism. It was precisely for this reason that there was a very strong resistance toward Europan tasks which were subversive in some way. Functionalist positivism no longer seemed possible as an approach, just as a postmodern Disneyland did not look real. This was encompassed even in films and video spots and in other forms of visual expression in which the new lifestyles were shown in specific spaces. However, there is an enormously empty space between the creation of an image that exists only in the imaginations of architects or film directors and that which is the result of political and economic involvement and this kind of naiveté was present quite distinctly within the Europan, positive in its own way but very ineffective. What was more acceptable and somewhat more effective was the research linked to a typology and the relations of infrastructure and building, as these were closer to mild changes in actuality. The reality of European cities could not be changed radically as in, for example, Asia. For this reason, there were enormous differences between the winning competition works which looked revolutionary and local interpretations of that work. It is incredibly difficult to build such complex hybrids which are too advanced even for Germany, the Netherlands or Scotland. There was no social structure of conferring so that such projects could be actually built.

Critical or Operative Model?

On the one hand, it is true that the relation toward invention or revolution of urban life within Europan seemed perhaps even falsely radical and that it did not achieve the results, which were fundamental in relation toward changes in the city. On the other hand, if one looks at the successful young architects in Europe today, what can be seen is that they have all, in one way or another, emerged from the Europan kitchen. The interesting question that was present throughout all the Europans was that of the possibility of the involvement of architects in milieus foreign to them and in which way were they in the position to produce values that were urban or cultural. Europan endeavored in a very concrete way to compress time and to present such discussions a lot earlier then they would normally come into play through the customary system of deliberation. It can be said that it was a more critical than operative

Hunch 6/7

Berlage Institute Report
Rotterdam, 2003

hunch 47

Masterclass with Liz Diller, Sylvia Lavin, Vedran Mimica, Greg Lynn, Kelly Shannon, Bart Lootsma, Martine de Maeseneer, and Wiel Arets.

Elia Zenghelis came to the Berlage for a jury in the spring of 1993 and has remained ever since. Zenghelis's educational experience and his amazing ability to follow different projects simultaneously made him an ideal person for the second year thesis program. According to Hertzberger (and not only Hertzberger), Zenghelis is the world's best teacher of architecture. Rem Koolhaas, Zaha Hadid, and Greg Lynn were some of his students. For years, Zenghelis has managed to maintain a love and passion for teaching; a rare gift. He never tires or refuses to sit for hours with students and to help them to deliver quality work. Elia describes our students as "pregnant" with an idea or argument or concept, and himself as a "midwife" helping young architects to deliver. He has an amazing ability to recognize the particular obsession of each and every student and to "architecturalize" it, to develop it to its final stage.

The Berlage's pursuit of final, individual theses was always a controversial issue. Some critics argue that only the very best students are able to engage in individual research. Others support individual-based theses that do not develop personal preoccupations and obsessions but contribute to a larger body of collective research. Regardless of the argument, Elia was able to lift each particular student's production to its ultimate level.

model but there was always the belief that it could be operative too. In Spain, Antonio Velless always sought locations in which local urban planners, politicians and developers would be ready to participate. Many of these Europan projects were even built.

If we look at the Croatian situation, Europan was the most successful by its presentation of one entire new generation in a European context. This new "European" generation of Croatian architects was identified as being very interesting not only by what they were doing in their offices but also for their new European perspective on architecture, only that this time they were coming from the southeast. The Njirić team would often end up on the covers of Europan books and they were frequently looked upon as those who had won the Europan. It is a completely different story of how our Europan heroes fared on their "home" court. Unfortunately, not one project has been implemented in Croatia. I was a jury member for the Vukovar location and I was all for the excellent winning project to be carried out, not only for national-emotional reasons; but precisely for the reason that this project is important for the development of the Vukovar riverfront, which is an essential precondition for the postwar reconstruction of the town. Europan made many ideas, which may have seemed avant-garde in some milieus to be almost normal and acceptable. However, the leading people of Europan never wished to influence the local Europan competitions, which were always independent units.

Expiration Dates and Iconography

Every cultural format has its expiration date and in contemporary times their expiration is all the shorter and shorter. It is all the more difficult to conceive a festival, institution or project which could carry on over a number of years and be successful. I am of the belief that there is a specific type of consciousness or self-criticism among the generation of architects under forty and that they are conscious of the fact that a specific type of Photoshop aesthetic is no longer convincing or credible and that on the basis of this no one can win an award at the Europan. The question that is opened here then is what is convincing in today's iconographic plan. The dominant global architectural discourse is obviously post-neo-deconstructivist so that there is a serious problem of presenting any other type of iconography. It is precisely marginal countries that were not under the media or finance pressure of sources of power and decision-making that now have the possibility of producing a different type of iconography be it on their own territory, be it that they suggest it for somewhere else. In that sense, Europan is perhaps not yet exhausted as a format, as it continues to call for contributions. An interesting question here is whether it could be exchanged or developed toward some other forms and this is always present. It is difficult to criticize something that is so successful; at one time students worked continuously on Europan at the Berlage Institute, and then in one moment we became critical towards Europan mannerisms. Some countries such as Belgium and the Netherlands have already done so much in the way of promoting not only their own but also foreign young architects that Europan no longer seems serious for them. Many young architects have managed to make a name for themselves even without Europan as they are supported by their milieus. I certainly agree that Europan created a specific canon, but there were always surprises as well. Perhaps the format itself is no longer congruous with the way the younger generations think and the interesting ones no longer apply to the Europan as it no longer presents a challenge. Europe has already integrated itself so much that the mobility of architecture is such that an Europan promotion is no longer necessary. In the situation of the line between the Baltic's to the Adriatic Europan values of presentation and the exchange of architects still remain important and in the future Europan will certainly be more popular and necessary in the eastern than in the western part of Europe.

BORDERS: THE OTHER SIDE OF
GLOBALIZATION

In the catalog of the 38th Zagreb Salon curated by Stefano Boeri, Zagreb 2003

Europe keeps redefining itself historically. The difference in this process now and before is that Europe does not any more go far to the East or to Africa, but it uses its own territory for redefining.

Suddenly millions, who were European for centuries, are excluded from Europe. They are The Others now. Europe is reconstructing itself using the Eastern Europe for that. A new power discourse is being set up. On the one hand we have norms that are frequently western, but eastern countries have not yet been considered ready for such norms, because they had a difficult past and need help to become ready, compatible with the norm. The established power discourse is a necessary tool for the ones controlling resources, so that they could maintain control over them. I am often a part of that construction of Otherness. I have been The Other many times and I am frequently tired of it, I do not want to be The Other.

From an interview with Joanna Regulska conducted by Igor Marković.
Zarez, Zagreb 1999

The dream of a completely fluid and passing world-space is maybe the last Utopian idea of the 20th century. It is a characteristic quality, supposedly inborn to the world of today, but if we look at that space more closely, it leaves a different impression.

One of the immediate results of global interconnecting and movement seems to be the proliferation of borders, security systems, checkpoints, physical and virtual demarcations. That phenomenon can be observed on the micro-level of our environment, as well as on the large scale of global flow. That means that borders are everywhere around us. They are at the same time conventional, geographic, abstract and real, usual and controversial. A general overview of this flow pattern (of people, commodities, ideas...) and limitations specific of particular areas, reveals the complexity of individual and collective identities, which are at the same time created and divided by the experience of crossing a border.

Stefano Boeri, Multiplicity 2003

The international Internet competition of the 38th Zagreb Salon with the topic Borders: the Other Side of Globalization is conceived as the conceptual redefining of the Republic of Croatia's border with the European Union.

Ideas and suggestions for redefining the border area are expected it the fields of architecture and city-planning, landscape architecture, graphic design, industrial design and all other disciplines rooted in the visual interpretation of reality.

Particularities and/or differences in the economical, cultural, and social and landscape context represent the basic conceptual frame for suggestions. All suggestions should anticipate the inclusion of Croatia into the European integration in the period from 2007 onwards.

The intervention space defines the border area with present and future members of the EU, Italy (border at sea), Slovenia (border at sea and on land) and Hungary (border on land).

As a world process, globalization has a major influence on everything happening in local context. Globalization processes can be visualized almost like a weather forecast, an inevitable process, and new ecology. As farmers do not ask why it is going to rain tomorrow or why it is windy, so the local authorities (politicians, investors, 'culture-people' and others) should not lose time specifying global influences, but use it to understand and manipulate them. For the architectural discourse, it is especially interesting to diagnose the influences of the global flow on local physical reality.

The investigation in this segment leads us to Saskia Sassen and her hypotheses 'that if we take digitalization seriously, then we shall soon realize that global flow influences the local physical environment creating "interstitial" or "counter" spaces.'[85] They are places where the global flow has partially, but evidently influenced the formation of a city's physical environment. Further on, Sassen states that precisely at those spots and in those spaces, alternative projects can be conceived and visualized.

Following Sassen, we can characterize alternative projects as the ones which will not blindly and literally follow the globalization processes, but form a certain opposition towards them. Such projects will accept the global, but will build the local as an alternative expression of the global. Strategies of such projects must engage a certain amount of imagination, true understanding of global processes and finally, a special visual culture. The border competition counts on such strategies in solving the task. The border itself is exactly that space "between", that "different" space where the global and the local world overlap and touch each other.

Croatia is a transitional country and transition is its first and real ecology. But in the Croatian context, transition is not any more just a phenomenon where a single political party system and a controlled market are replaced by parliamentarian democracy and a free market.

In spite of the specific Croatian experience full of crises (homeland war), controversies and stumbling over obstacles, this first transition phase is evidently reaching its end. However acceptable at the beginning of the 1990s the motto: "Time is a luxury which East European countries cannot afford in transitional process" seemed; today we speak about possibly positive characteristics of the "strategies of delay." In the case of Croatia it would be hard to believe that those "strategies of delay" are conducted with complete awareness or strategically, because here everyone, it is at least declared to be so, hurries to Europe. But if we consider Slaven Letica, a former intellectual, who vested in governor Jelačić's costume brings apples and good news to Slovenian task forces on the border between Croatia and Slovenia, more precisely on the peak of Sveta Gera,[86] one has to ask whether even that "strategy of delay" is not partially deliberate, although completely cut off any reasonable critical discourse. The question who needs this peak in embark hills and which conquering armies will watch each other from it once Croatia enters the EU is also interesting. It is, however, equally clear that for Letica and the HSP (Croatian Rights' Party), but also for the Slovenian daily paper "Dnevnik," the border represents a field for political and identification discussions. A border is an area that always generates tensions. The border contest should use this dynamic identification field to create new possible situations for border regions. It is interesting that even after abolishing the borders between European countries, border areas retain their special meanings, dynamics and contents. However, we must also note that the European region is getting more and more unified, that bureaucratic directives from Brussels have been taken seriously in the East. Those European investors tend to unify European urban programs. Europe is becoming an area with same hotels,

85   Saskia Sassen's lecture at the Berlage Institute during the masterclass "Case Study Amsterdam", February 2002.

86   Sveta Gera or Trdina Peak along the border between southeastern Slovenia and Croatia is the highest peak of the Žumberak Mountains. It is subject to a border dispute between Croatia and Slovenia.

Joanna Regulska
Igor Mirković
Stefano Boeri
Saskia Sassen
Slaven Letica

8. ZAGREBAČKI SALON :
ARHITEKTURA 2003

UHA, DAZ, Zagreb, 2003

Vedran Mimica: Borders: The
Other Side of Globalisation

same restaurants, a common infrastructure, an area abandoning its particularities. A border has always been a place of difference, a place where change is happening, and a place of some other identities...

Those identities should not vanish; moreover, the new Europe needs them desperately. The European expansion to the East has sense only in that context, as a social and cultural project. "New" European countries, which, however, have always been European, should not contribute to European culture only by their medieval monuments, but rather through relevant modern production. The role of architecture, city planning, landscape planning, graphic and industrial design and all other visual disciplines is of utmost importance for the European cultural exchange. In that context, strategies of delay can help Croatia to realize a different, less restricted level of urban environment, until it is integrated into the community. The border competition initiates a discussion about particularities of Croatian visual identity, as well as strategies for the development of urban environment in border areas. The time until the admittance into the Union should rather be comprehended as a chance for development of a specific concept than as an obstacle for achievement of European "ideals."

To end or begin the story about the Croatian territory visual redefinition contest, let us try to outline a story about children born in the 21st-century Croatia. When Croatia comes close to the EU they will have finished the primary school, and when Croatia is really integrated, they will have to be completely ready for European exchange. They will all drive through Bregana and Šentilj at 75 mph without stopping and questions from customs officers, towards European destinations instead of ending their trip on the Trieste-Graz line. The reason for the journey will not be shopping, but mostly business or relocation reasons. Passing the former borders between European countries they will ask themselves why their grand grandfathers, grandfathers and fathers have fought wars and what is so essential and important for their Croatian identity. Pictures of Dubrovnik, Kaptol[87] and Split, Kraš[88] nougat sweets, Vegeta[89] condiment, Pliva[90] aspirin and ties[91] will be insufficient and maybe unimportant for their national identities. In their minds, they will carry images of the new Croatian reality, which will be different, special, specific and interesting to Europe, like Scandinavian industrial design, Italian fashion or German cars. Croatia of their youth will be a country, which they remember not only for its preserved nature, but also a sensibly built environment, a communication that means culture and developed infrastructure. The 38th Zagreb Salon and the border competition announced as one of the Salon's activities, maybe represent the first probe towards building up strategies which one-day would make this story real. Suggestions for redefining the visual in border areas, as well as a discussion with leading Croatian politicians, theoreticians, curators, architects, planners and public interested in this topic, might constitute the initial elements for development strategies. There is not really much time for drawing up and then implementing those strategies if we like "stories for children."

87   Kaptol is a part of Croatian capital Zagreb, the seat of the Roman Catholic archbishop. It is one of the two hills that the medieval Zagreb originated from.

88   Chocolate and sweets factory "Josip Kraš" in Zagreb was one of the strongest factories during the socialist period, and one of the rare ones that successfully continued its business in the transitional period.

89   Vegeta is a sort of condiment, primarily a mixture of salt and flavor boosting compounds, spices and vegetables, invented in 1959 by a Croatian scientist Zlata Bartl. Since then, Vegeta has become a strong brand of "Podravka" factory (another industrial survivor of the transitional period) from Koprivnica town and a product sold worldwide.

90   Pliva has been the largest pharmaceutical company in Croatia and one of the leading companies in Southeast Europe since 1926. After had been juggled with in the transitional period, in 2008 it became a member of the Teva Group, one of the largest global pharmaceutical companies.

91   In the 1990s Croatia reinvented its tradition of wearing a tie, claiming to be the country where the tie was invented.

NEW SCHOOL OF ARCHITECTURE IN SPLIT

Proposal for a new school of architecture by the Berlage Institute.
Published in Čovjek i prostor 5-6, Zagreb 2006

I think that it is extremely difficult to adequately understand the values of our heritage if we have not learned how to live in the present and accepted, among the efforts for renewal and development, the ones that represent true values of the qualities of harmony and equilibrium. It is very difficult to evaluate the cultural influence of the past if our cities are not built on modern standards.

Manfredo Tafuri, 1995

The Berlage Institute Suggestion – Foundation of the European Architectural Academy in Split

At the threshold of its European integrations the Republic of Croatia is defining a strategy of cultural development for the transitional period that will last until the integration into the European Union is completed. In this process, education will be a very important field in the process of adjusting to European standards. Founding of new and the reform of the existing educational institutions are necessary for Croatia with a new European orientation. The Dalmatian and especially the cultural and urban environment of Split are a ground of high potential for those oncoming processes.

Split could be an interesting environment for a new school of architecture. Split is a phenomenon where 1.700 years of building tradition merge with the Mediterranean landscape into the final and total cityscape. The spirit of Split, its genius loci has never been frozen, but it has always been re-interpreted anew, by centuries-long activities of generations of builders and architects, all the way from Diocletian's Palace, over St. Martin's Chapel above the northern gate of the Palace, to Ante Kuzmanić's and Eugen Širola's re-interpretation of Bačvice. The architectural discourse in Split is a dialogue with the previously existing construction layer and the Mediterranean landscape. It is this new contemporary interpretation of the spirit of the place that builds the basis of Split's modernity, in this artistic and/or architectural interpretation. Diocletian's Palace and the Mediterranean landscape have the equal value and meaning.

The new architectural school in Split must find space for inspiration in historical context, in the space of "confrontation" with today's time. The main task of the new school is the education for young people – in order that they might become architects and be able to appear on the Croatian and European cultural and architectural market about 2007, precisely the time when, as we believe, Croatia will also be becoming a part of the European Union. In this context, the only criterion for a school can be the European and the world criterion for educational processes and institutions.

Academy or Faculty

Historically speaking, architectural education has always taken place between the scholarly, technical and rational spirit of poly-technical colleges and architectural faculties and a free, creative and informal spirit of architectural academies. The Croatian history of architectural education is divided into two periods: the first one, after 1918 when it followed European standards and when architectural studies were possible both at the Technical Faculty and at the Art Academy, and the second one, after 1945, when studies were possible only at the Faculty of Architecture, Civil Engineering and Geodesy, later at the Faculty of Architecture. It is almost useless to explain why a new school of architecture in Croatia should be radically different from the totally retrograde Faculty of Architecture in Zagreb. The Split Academy should be a school with European standards in all its aspects, which, in short, means the following: the appliance of international standards in the selection of lecturers; the school curriculum adjusted to the principles of the Bologna Declaration; management of the institution where the public and the private sphere complement each other in financing; dynamic publishing activities and continuous public presentation of the school's production within the cultural environment. The Architectural Academy conceptualizes two strategies: one is the education of young people for the understanding of the context in which architecture happens, i.e. in which it is being built, and the other is the development of cultural identity of an area, region and/or state through architecture and city-planning. Architects who graduate from the Academy should be publicly visible intellectuals, "managers of change," and socially and culturally active independent professionals.

Academy and the Principles

The Academy should above all be an educational environment for sound reasoning, where the cumulative intelligence of students and lecturers will overpower the hierarchical logic and bureaucratic precision; in other words a "no nonsense place." The European Architectural Academy in Split will act on the principles equal to the ones in similar, best European and world schools like the Architectural Association in London, Sci-Arc in Los Angeles or the Berlage Institute in Rotterdam.

Academy and the Curriculum

The undergraduate curriculum is the main structure for the education of architects.
The Academy's curriculum must understand the Dalmatian cultural and urban space as a reader, and by no means only as local value, but in the first place as a historical and global inspiration, because the foundations of Croatian culture are eminently urban and this urban historical infrastructure is that which connects Croatia with European cultural context. Split and Diocletian's Palace, as a paradigmatic story about the process of transforming eminently private property (emperor's palace) into eminently public property (a Croatian city), will in that case become the most important chapter in the reader. Trogir and Dubrovnik are only further pages of that reader. The re-conceptualization of the existing and the creation of the new is the basic characteristic of the Academy's curriculum. It will also have to enable the perception of innovations as new values in transitional times.

The outline of the curriculum is a division in three levels: the basic two-year level, the one-year intermediate level and the two-year graduate level. The basic level is the educational environment that must "completely" enable the student to act within the discipline of architecture and city-planning within two years. Unlike architectural faculties at technical universities, where this level is burdened by a large number of technical subjects, mostly completely unnecessary for the future architectural practice, the Architectural Academy will enable the future architects to acquire relevant knowledge from the very start of their schooling.

Architectural and urban design, understood as simultaneous and uniform discourse, will be the main interest of the basic phase. Engineering and the technical aspect of architectural production should be a parallel focus. History and the theory of architecture should be a guideline through all the years of study. In this phase, the knowledge of English language and computer program skills should reach the proficient level.

The intermediate phase will prepare the student for the final graduate phase and show his/her true abilities and advantages in relation to different fields of architectural activity. The first complex city-planning and architectural task will be solved during this phase of study.

The studies on this level will be broadened by the knowledge of new technologies and materials, of the development in the media, organizational structures, and global economic and social trends. The graduation unit will be the final, two-year design based research work and planning of a complex thesis developed by the student in concordance with the tutor. This complex and multi-disciplinary research will also include experts from tangential disciplines in relation to the task's topic.

The basic character of learning will be the work in an atelier or a workshop, which means that without regard to the subject, the syllabus will always be carried out in small groups, reaching eight students at most and the tasks will be solved through group work. No matter how complex a subject or a task is, and regardless of their character, the principal strategy of the Academy is creation. Everything that is produced is liable to critical discussion with several critics, which means that the evaluation and assessment of students' works is always public and collective. "Marks" are obtained through critical discussion of a student with the jury, consisting of guest critics and students tutor(s).

Academy and the Students

From their first year on, students should be devoted to architecture. The applicants will be chosen on the basis of their submitted portfolio and an interview with the enrollment commission. The Academy should take up thirty students a year. It would be ideal if students came from all parts of Croatia and foreign countries (Slovenia, Bosnia and Herzegovina, Croatian emigrants), but it is expected that the majority of students would be from Split and Dalmatia. The studies until graduation should last five years, so that the maximal number of students at the Academy would be 150.

Academy and the Teaching Staff

It is very important for the new school to start its activity with young teaching staff, which should have European education. There is already an entire generation of young Croatian architects who completed their post-graduate studies at European and world schools of architecture. The majority of lecturers at the Academy should be employed on part-time basis, meaning that apart from education they should also be active in architectural practice, or other practices and institutions. The academy should, of course, also have steadily employed teachers and other staff. The Barcelona example, with five teaching syllabus directors, could function as a model for the Split Academy. The function of the director is to carry out and organize lectures, the selection of faculty, financial planning, editing of publications and all other activities connected with the educational process. Other employees with "lecturer" status are: a head of the audio, video and computer studio, head of the model workshop, librarian, and a head of the office for publication of the Academy's issues.

Academy and the Building

The building program of the Academy should count with hundred and fifty students who all should have a place for work with a computer connected to the central system (a high-end solution). Other facilities are: a library, model workshop (wood and metal), an exhibition hall, lecture halls, audio and video laboratory, management offices, a store with books and other materials, canteen and a "bar".

The Academy must be permanently open, seven days a week, in the capacity of a school but also as an "open culture center" for architecture. The Academy must also be present on the social media.

Academy and Financing

By approaching the European Union, from January this year Croatian universities have the possibility of being included into the Union's programs for improvement of university schooling. The Tempus Program means are already accessible. This program advances the means for opening of new institutions. The program and the concept of the European Architectural Academy in Split would certainly be supported by similar European institutions, which would enable a successful application for the long-term financing by the Tempus Program means. Those means would enable technical equipment of this institution, as well as international exchange of teaching staff and students.

Academy and the World

The Academy will be connected to Mediterranean schools of architecture (Venice, Genoa, Barcelona, Valencia, Athens, Beirut and Alexandria) and in this way, through different forms of exchange, appear on the international scene. Three international seminars in the organization of the Berlage Institute (INDESEM, 1988; 1700+Diokletian's Palace, 1997; and Traffic Terminals in Split Harbor, 1999) showed the interest of eminent European architects and institutions for Split and the exchange with Split. The basic relation of the Academy to the outside world would be publishing. Every year the Academy would have to publish the papers by its students and teachers in English and Croatian.

The suggestion for the foundation of the European Architectural Academy in Split was put forward in 2000. It followed the request of the Split University Chancellor, Ivo Babić, concerning architectural education in the post-graduate studies. In drawing up the proposal, the author of the study, Vedran Mimica from the Berlage Institute suggested the model of European Architectural Academy in Split as the most adequate one in the context of starting architectural education in Split. The proposal has not been considered at the University in any of its aspects. New architectural studies at the Civil Engineering and Architecture Faculty in Split were started from the undergraduate level, as a copy of the program in Zagreb.

ORIS 46

Zagreb, 2007

Vedran Mimica
The Power of Architectural Thought

In order to get a final impression of the Koprivnica gymnasium, it would be necessary to engage in a critical dialogue between the architects and users about the horticultural arrangement of the school park, the graphic standard of visual communications in the school and the sports hall, and, in particular, the possibility of installation of another interactive building membrane for the purpose of visual and media communication between the hybrid and the wider environment.
In the architectural environment of the Koprivnica gymnasium, young high school graduates should have no trouble reading "Fran Supilo's Spirit", an essay by Miroslav Krleža from his collection *Ten Bloody Years*. A view from the building's interior to Croatian reality on the outside will thus be clear to them, and they will find themselves close to dreams of a different Croatia shared by both Supilo and Krleža.

GIMNAZIJA I SPORTSKA DVORANA / GYMNASIUM AND SPORTS HALL
Ulica dr. Željka Selingera, Koprivnica, Hrvatska/Croatia
autori / authors Lea Pelivan + Toma Plejić / STUDIO UP
arhitektonski ured / architectural office STUDIO UP
projektni tim / project team Lea Pelivan, Toma Plejić, Saša Relić, Marina Zajec, Katarina Lukačina, Danka Tišljar, Ana-Dana Beroš, Mojca Smode, Marina Smokvina, Ana Boljar, Maša Mujakić, modeli/models 1:50, 1:100 Željko Gorubić, Jeronim Mladinov, Dujam Ivanišević, Silvija Leković, Mateo Biluš, UPI-2M: Berislav Medić, Goran Janjuš, Andrej Marković, MAX.ING: Zvonimir Franjčisković, ENG-90: Milan Bjelko, Ernest Kevo, Siniša Radić, INSPEKTING: Milan Carević
investitor / client grad Koprivnica, Koprivničko-križevačka županija, Tehnika SPV (privatni partner) / Koprivnica Municipal Authority, Koprivnica – Križevci County, Tehnika SPV (private partner)
površina parcele / site area 2.4 ha
izgrađena površina / built-up area 11.600 m²/sqm
projekt / project 2003.-2006.
realizacija / completion 2007.
cijena / cost 10.956.904,00 €

ORIS 47

Zagreb, 2007

Vedran Mimica
Gymnasium / Quantum Leap in Miroslav Krleža Street

MINES OF CULTURE

Town of Labin & Platform 9,81, 2007

A continuation of a project Croatian Archipelago
New Lighthouses: Labin - Subterranean Town

GYMNASIUM / QUANTUM LEAP IN MIROSLAV KRLEŽA STREET

Published in Oris 47, Zagreb, 2007

It is precisely this sort of thinking about the great responsibilities borne by contemporary architecture in Croatia that prompted us to select the projects presented here, the ones capable of rising above the simple functionalist response to the problem posed by the client, and it convinced us to award the architects who have proven themselves capable of transcending stylistic preoccupations and linguistic classifications.

Stefano Boeri, 38th Zagreb Salon Catalog 2003

Joining in on the European cultural discourse with a slight delay, the Croatian architects association invited Stefano Boeri to judge the 38th Zagreb architecture salon in 2003. Boeri thus became the first internationally renowned architect invited to select the best among the 450 entered works as a "dilettante" (at least as far as "genuine" familiarity with Croatian architecture is concerned). What transpired was a "Stefano's leap", which has become a theorem on the quality and European focus of Croatian architecture only four years later.

Boeri recognized quality in the exceptionally young generation of Croatian architects, and first prize was evenly divided between Studio UP (Lea Pelivan and Toma Plejić) for their design for a secondary school (gymnasium) in Koprivnica, Petar Mišković for "Parasite", an "improved" diploma work in the class of professor Tonči Žarnić, and Hrvoje Njirić for the project "A Construction for One Thousand Hands" for the international exhibition of architecture in Nanjing.

Out of these three exceptionally high-quality (from a conceptual standpoint) projects, only the gymnasium in Koprivnica came to fruition, and thus confirmed numerous arguments from Boeri's text/theorem in the introduction to the catalog of the 38th Zagreb salon. Boeri pointed out: 'We selected those projects that are capable of realistically approaching the conditions of the real estate market and dealing with the client's demands, but always committed to the thought of producing a symbolic and functional "added value." We give priority to a few that are able to make use of the power of individual and fragmented energies for the creation of spaces that turn to local communities and call on them for interaction, exchange, competition and comparison of thought. This convinced us that even in Croatia, the future of architecture, as a discipline of general social benefit, is measured by the ability to discover new spatial qualities and new planning tools. The members of this small group share something that is altogether more important: extravagant, breakthrough generosity.'

Boeri focused on individuals and projects of new Croatian architecture with exceptional precision, and anticipated the contours of a possible positive development. However, the gymnasium and sports hall complex by Studio UP in Koprivnica was additionally surprising in that it was quickly and precisely completed, and it created a quantum leap in relation to Croatian architectural production, particularly in view of the cultural and historical landscape of Podravina. The agile mayor of Koprivnica and County prefect launched an ambitious project to build the gymnasium for 900 pupils in one shift and a sports hall that seats 2,500, as well as other complimentary city facilities, in addition to the public-private partnership in construction of the gymnasium and sports hall in Koprivnica. The idea of building two complementary urban facilities in a single building also arose, which is relatively new in Croatia. Hybrid facilities overlap with the public-private partnership concept, where the hybrid complex is leased and managed independently of the newly formed institution. Studio UP used the programmatic hybrid of the sports hall and the school and other facilities as the basis for the building composition. The spatial and visual overlapping of the facilities and the synergy of use constitute the basic operative logic underlying the building.

Abitare 480

Milan, 2008

Gymnasium / Quantum Leap
in Miroslav Krleža Street

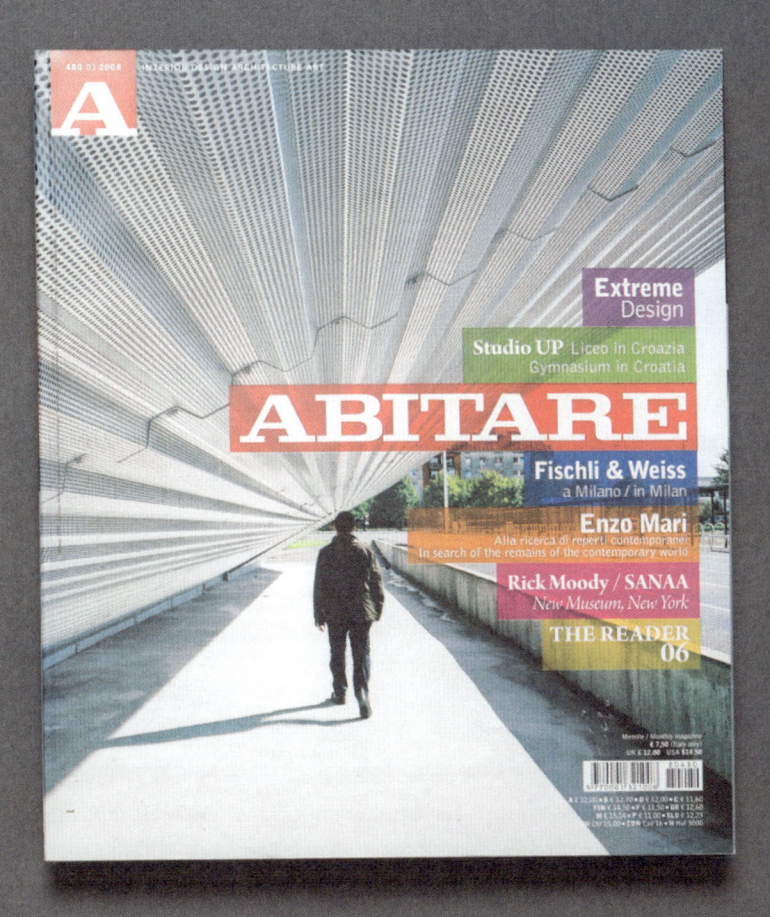

ORIS 54

Zagreb, 2008

Vedran Mimica
Exits Are Clearly Marked

In the text accompanying the competition work, Studio UP also insisted on conceptual dualities, which define the plot (tabula rasa) on Koprivnica's periphery. A specific relation is established between part of the plot oriented toward the city and part oriented toward the residential neighborhood. Studio UP employed dualities in their vocabulary: "black and green," "full and empty," "cold and warm," and "spiritual and physical." According to Studio UP, in a field of these opposing lines of force, the following will be created: "an enigmatic compressed mono-volume of the gymnasium and sports hall complex with intricate spatial relations in contrast to a vast plain landscape, placed centrally on the plot, forming a gymnasium – a common place – a contrasting rectangular whole lacking a foreground or background, without hierarchy or authority." The selection of an abstract mono-volume, with a transparent membrane and another membrane which should ideally contain visual messages and communicate with the environment, is a radical break with the modernist tradition of building schools and sports facilities as three-dimensional interpretations of bureaucratic disposition schemes. The "common place" concept examines the stability of the hybrid, and enables the most diverse interpretations both in terms of use and interpretation of significance of the building.

A multi-floor covered and zenith-lit central street is the building's hub. The unexpected, almost metropolitan density of spatial overlapping was created here. It is an exceptionally dynamic "urban landscape" full of galleries, bridges, penetrations, vistas and niches. Studio Up architecture focuses in particular on the use of material, and the colorist control of the building's interior and exterior. The main construction material is steel as load-bearing structure for the gymnasium and the sports hall. Steel is rarely used in Croatian architecture, so that a certain "low tech" aspect is present in this facility as well. However, the details used by studio Up in harmonizing the basic steel construction with aluminum glazing in the gymnasium tract, and "translucent" Lexan envelope of the sports hall create an almost high-tech impression like that of Herzog and De Meuron's work.

Control of the color palette in the building's interior, particularly of the central street, classroom spaces and the lavatories in the school building, is a true contribution to the cultural atmosphere of the educational space, and an apparent response to the vulgar Americanization and commercialization of the media reality, as experienced by Croatian youth. In order to get a final impression of Koprivnica gymnasium, it would be necessary to engage in a critical dialogue between the architects and users about the horticultural arrangement of the school park, the graphic standard of visual communications in the school and the sports hall, and, in particular, the possibility of installation of another interactive building membrane for the purpose of visual and media communication between the hybrid and the wider environment.

To what extent this kind of architecture is "ahead of its time" in the age of "simultaneity" of time, to what extent it is local and national in the age of globalization, to what extent it has transcended stylistic preoccupations and linguistic classifications in the age of defining "new" cultures, remains to be seen and studied carefully after this first critical presentation. Today, after the first visit to the school, immediately before the opening, we can point out that the first completed project by the Studio UP is a remarkably mature, intelligent and well-thought out work for such "scandalously" young architects. The "under-40" classification should obviously be changed to "under-30", at least in Croatia. In the architectural environment of the gymnasium in Koprivnica, young high school graduates should have no trouble reading Fran Supilo's spirit, an essay by Miroslav Krleža[92] from his collection Ten Bloody Years. A view from the building's interior to Croatian reality on the outside will thus be clear to them, and they will find themselves close to dreams of a different Croatia shared by both Supilo and Krleža.

---

92   Miroslav Krleža (1893-1981) was the most famous and influential Croatian writer of the 20th Ct. Fran Supilo (1870-1917) was a journalist and politician who openly stood against the Austro-Hungarian domination prior to WWI.

EXITS ARE CLEARLY MARKED

Published in Oris 54, Zagreb 2008

The highest form of moral is not to feel at home in one's own house.

Theodor Adorno

Prologue

When I come to Zagreb, and especially during the Days of Oris, my friends, who were my generation at university, usually ask me: "How's it going, Mimac, where do you say you live?" My answer is that I more or less live at Schiphol, Amsterdam airport, and I travel for about six months a year. Otherwise, I live in Rotterdam, but only a few hundred meters from Rotterdam airport. I love to travel beyond the ordinary, and I also love airports. For example, the one on the Altiplano above La Paz bordering Titicaca Lake at 4200 meters above sea level, with a four-kilometer long landing strip due to the thin air which brings aircraft to a stop with difficulty and with a luggage conveyor belt made of wooden strips. The old terminal at Kastrup in Copenhagen is the most beautifully designed airport interior – you feel here as if you are in a Jakobsen hotel. It is difficult to forget the old local airports in Rio de Janeiro or Hong Kong, where aircraft used to land almost between the houses. I also remember that half destroyed one in Sarajevo, which was devastated in the last war, with French soldiers and technicians.

Of the big ones, 'my' Schiphol is the best, most functional and most efficient, and has won awards year after year in these categories.
Foster's Hong Kong is impressive, and what Beijing is like – I cannot wait to see!
Of the small ones, I would like to mention the one in Chandigarh, where Sikh soldiers with turbans and Kalashnikovs will welcome you; the one in Ohrid, where the director has to be found 'to open it' and finally, the one on Unije Island in Kvarner Bay, where the grass landing strip touches the Adriatic and corn fields and everybody calls it the Airport.

Introduction

At the beginning of October 1994, a new generation started their studies at the Berlage Institute and the dean, Herman Hertzberger, made the programmed plan for the following semester. The highlight of the semester was supposed to be Master Class Week. Herman, influenced by the aircraft tragedy in Bijmermeer near Schiphol airport when 43 people died, proposed to dedicate the master class to the design of a memorial to the innocent victims of the tragedy. An obvious question arose: "Who could be a guest professor, the 'Master' architect for that task?" Daniel Libeskind, Zaha Hadid, Aldo van Eyck were names proposed by us and by the students. The choice fell on Zaha, and I was given the special task of going to London and talking her into cooperation. I got a ticket for the British Midlands flight from Schiphol to the new London airport, Stansted, opened in March 1991.

I found myself in Foster's high tech paradise, a perfect "social condenser," as Kenneth Frampton, a member of the first Mies van der Rohe Award jury for the most successful European realization of the year, characterized this building. Frampton perceived the power of architecture in the creation of public spaces, spaces for everyday life. Entirely in opposition to the somewhat later theories of French anthropologist Marc Augé about airport buildings as non-places. In Foster's work, Frampton sees the realization of a possible architecture of the kind heralded by the Russian Constructivists and Suprematists of the revolutionary 1920s. Stansted as a "social condenser" is exactly a place for meeting, exchange, transition from one state into another, a perfect airport where passengers who are departing and passengers who are arriving meet on the same level, and pass the route from the airport building to the terminal by riding on a monorail driverless vehicle. Welcome to the future.

At that time in 1994, Zaha's office looked like a painter's atelier with seven employed architects. Large formats of Zaha's drawings, oil paintings, collages were scattered all around the entire space. Peak, Vitra, Düsseldorf, and Berlin were some among the projects I had known, but not in that format. The neoconstructivist revolution began here; its source and inspiration were here. Zaha graduated from the AA in 1977 in the class of Koolhaas and Zenghelis with her work entitled Malevich's Tectonics and a motto: "We can only perceive space when we break free from the earth, when the point of support disappears." Elia Zenghelis, her first employer in the original OMA always emphasized that the competition for The Peak in Hong Kong in 1982 changed everything, and that it meant a paradigmatic break which other deconstructivists (only) followed.

I managed to convince Zaha that the Berlage was a school with excellent students and that the master class would receive huge publicity in Amsterdam. Zaha accepted the invitation and took Patrik Schumacher, then a young assistant, with her to the Berlage.

What has this introduction to do with the competition for Zagreb Airport Pleso? Nothing at all, or perhaps something. Namely, when I realized what had happened with my Iraqi friend and Lord Foster in the competition for Zagreb Airport, I asked the editorial board of Oris if I could write an article about this case.

How it should not be done or Bavarian hygienists at work

All packages with models were opened carefully, separately and successively and checked for any damage. An additional check of special functions e.g. light effects was performed. Some minor repairs were made.

The six-digit code on the models was either removed or masked with the four-digit code according to the related plans and forms.

General overviews were done in Munich at the office of K+P.

The new code-letter list and unopened authors' envelopes were locked in a secured place.

All models, brochures and presentation material were packed carefully and arrived in Zagreb undamaged and in good condition. The arrangement of the models and plans at the rooms of the jury meeting was executed together with representatives of Zagreb Airport and Mr Jošić of the CAA.

Final jury report prepared by: Ms Elisabeth Riha, Architect K+P Organizer and Mr Mladen Jošić, Zagreb & Munich, 18 September 2008

If we focus on the theme of the new Zagreb airport, we can say that airports today are anything but independent aviation hubs on city peripheries. More and more airports are becoming cities in themselves. The Airport, with every terminal attached to shopping malls, serviced by hotels, cinemas, saunas, swimming pools recently even casinos and art galleries, embodies all the characteristics of an urban center – dense, congested, and overlaid with rich programmatic accumulations, served by efficient intermodal transportation networks.

The company Zagreb Airport, when organizing a national, limited, single-stage, anonymous design and urban planning competition for the new passenger terminal of Zagreb Airport imagined exactly such an image, with invitations to foreign and domestic architectural offices.

The number of passengers in Pleso has shown exponential growth, up to 15% per year, and the expected long-drawn-out and desired acceptance of Croatia into the European Union will only accelerate this growth. Pleso annually processes 2 million passengers in relatively non-standard conditions for a European airport. In 2012, when

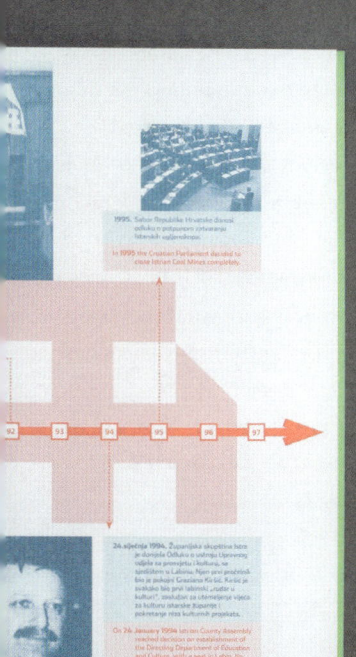

ORIS 54

Zagreb, 2008

Vedran Mimica
Exits Are Clearly Marked

MINES OF CULTURE

Town of Labin & Platform 9,81, 2007

the new airport could be completed,[93] the traffic through Pleso will be near 5 million passengers. Speaking hypothetically, with good management and state-of-the-art facilities, it could enter the race with Budapest, Belgrade, and Vienna for a slice of the cake as a south-eastern European regional hub. Even if it remains solely "the gate to Croatia and Zagreb" the new airport is more than needed. Not only as "the gateway to the nation and the window onto the world", as some competitors at the competition marked it, but also as a structural element of a new metropolitan infrastructure, the modern European Croatia. The old airport is still full of beautiful original architectural details by Bernardo Bernardi[94] and very valuable segmented interventions by the architects Ćurković and Zidarić, as well as of probably intimate memories of generations of passengers; a unique place where you can still get cheese and cream for $ 2, from a waitress in Borosana shoes (these were generally accepted comfortable working shoes in the former Yugoslavia).

The planning of a new airport, as well as the planning of many fundamental infrastructural interventions in Croatia was developed during the 1990s and at the beginning of the 21st century, usually without a uniform strategy, serious financial analysis and in an environment of typical transitional instability. If it is to be judged according to the media reporting, after the recently completed competition which was supposed to investigate the possibilities and define the scope, price and responsibility for serious work on the project of an airport city, the situation has only become more complicated. Local newspaper headlines, statements by members of the jury, and awarded and "offended" architects, condemnations related to plagiarism and the setting up of the jury, political rhetoric from the top and the bottom and the formation of a new commission for evaluation of the first five awarded works should not be perceived too seriously. This is, namely, the usual folklore in most countries in the world when important and large projects are involved. However, if we really want to use the new Pleso in 2012, then "top-class world architecture is like a tango, and it takes two to tango," in the words of the new Pritzker Prize laureate, Jean Nouvel. In Croatian reality, unfortunately, it seems that often it takes three to tango. The third party is, apart from the architect and client, politics. One too many, if we consider Croatian local politics. Therefore, it would be necessary to accumulate "intelligence" in Croatian conditions between architects, investors, and politicians in order to finally make something good. However, the way in which things have started certainly will not result in anything good.

Energetic concept: Entries with codes 1001, 1015, 1008, and 1004 must be significantly improved to meet the demands.

Final jury report prepared by: Ms Elisabeth Riha, Architect K+P Organizer and Mr Mladen Jošić, Zagreb & Munich, 18 September 2008

Namely, Zagreb Airport is the contracting authority behind the competition, and their work was consulted by Koch+Partner, architects from Munich, the CAA (Croatian Architects' Association) and the DAZ (Zagreb Architects' Association). This diverse but ambitious company made a series of fundamental errors in the organization and execution of the competition. To be more precise, the usual practice in the world is not "sticking codes in Munich" onto the works of architectural Nobel winners (Pritzker Prize laureates) and not cramming them into sealed envelopes, but inviting these people to present their work personally. As it was, Lord Foster ended up among the candidates for elimination in the first round of the Zagreb competition, if one can trust "The Final Report of the Jury", because "in work 1004, the concept of energy should be significantly improved in order to satisfy the criteria of Koch+Partners experts." In this first round, two members of the jury voted for elimination of Foster from the competition,

---

93 In 2016 it was not completed.

94 Bernardo Bernardi (1921-1985), one of the prominent Croatian architects of the second half of the 20th Ct and the most engaged in interior design.

probably under the influence of the K+P experts' report. Such a misunderstanding would certainly not have occurred if members of the jury had had the opportunity to participate in a personal presentation by the architects.

My last meeting with Lord Foster occurred at the Urban Age congress in Berlin last year, organized by Ricky Burdett, professor at the London School of Economics and director of the Venice Biennale in 2006. Foster was invited to talk about sustainable buildings for the 21st century. In an incredibly impressive presentation, he presented ecological arguments as fundamental for development of the world in the future, by displaying the phenomenon of the development of Asian cities.

He compared the development of Heathrow Airport in London and the new airport in Beijing, which was being constructed at that time on the basis of his project. These two airports are of similar size and capacity, the only difference being the fact that 86 years were needed for Heathrow and 5 for Beijing to reach their present capacity. Namely, Foster's project for Beijing's Terminal 3 was built in five years and its size is equal to the size of all five terminals at Heathrow. Such fast growth, according to Foster, primarily poses the question of the energy sustainability of buildings and cities. In the project presentation for Beijing airport, Foster least talked about impressive dimensions and architectural qualities, but stressed the incredible success of his engineers in reducing energy consumption and CO_2 emissions by more than 30% in comparison with airports built so far.

Members of the jury and interested audience could have had the same or similar lecture in Zagreb. If not, then at least they could have spent a little more time in a more serious study of work 1004 and perceived the concept of the airport city's "ecological development."

When the world's top class architects are invited, should not we ask ourselves, perhaps even conclude, that these architects would demand a similar jury?

Similar in terms of "mentality," international level of recognition, being informed and having a certain status. Except for Professor Eberle, unfortunately not one of the members of the Zagreb new airport jury (so far) has had that kind of status. As we know, Professor Eberle declined to participate in the jury. Therefore, the jury consisted of one economist and one surveyor, three architect-politicians, three international architects who run successful, but extremely commercial offices and two prestigious local architects. Most jury members have not had any international jury experience. Each member of the jury had equal voting rights, and the jury decided to choose the winner by anonymous voting in several rounds. In order to confirm the credibility of the system, the jury organized the opening of the sealed envelopes in front of local journalists who, again, could not restrain themselves from uproarious laughter after the winning work was announced. The president of the jury then explained that it was not "the best work" that won, but it was, in his opinion, the most integral work, and that the price was probably approximately 280 million euros. "Only" 40 million euros more than the anticipated financial construction.

Since all architecture, and especially architecture of huge public buildings, is a political, social, cultural and ecological fact, such architecture should be chosen accordingly. In this kind of interesting constellation, the jury chose, perhaps with surprising preciseness, award-winning and appreciated works, but was entirely wrong, in my opinion, in the ordering of the first five works.

What now?

Zaha Hadid: If we all go for a competition, we know one of us would win, unless it's unfair or it's very political and so on; it's acceptable.

From Charlie Rose television interview with Pritzker Prize laureates Zaha Hadid, Renzo Piano, Frank Gehry and Jean Nouvel.

Source: www.charlierose.com

Parametric or associative design is a new technique of designing, developed in the last ten years in leading architectural offices and postgraduate schools of architecture around the world. Hundreds of young architects have gone through paperless study at Columbia University in New York, the DRL (Design Research Laboratory) study at the AA (Architectural Association, London) and Associative Design study at the Berlage Institute and they are the main labor force today in the leading offices in the world. Patrik Schumacher, partner of Zaha Hadid, and Brett Steele, director of AA, initiated the DRL (Design Research Laboratory) at the AA in 1995 with the idea of developing topological studies of new architectural forms and computer usage in the creation of parametric families of objects.

Topological studies comprise the study of the properties of figures that are independent of size or shape and are not changed by stretching, bending, knotting, or twisting as well as the study of changes in topography that occur over time and, in particular, of how such changes taking place in a particular area affect the history of that area. In other words, design does not tend to create one unique object in a parametric world, but to create a family of objects because the final form is obtained by "input" of parameters in a computer program which generates form, usually the structural parts of the object and the object's membrane. The work of Hadid Architects office for Zagreb airport is the result of such a procedure. The jury was presented this approach to design in a very didactic manner in form of a textual explanation of the project.

Precisely Patrik Schumacher and the DRL are significantly responsible for the planetary success of Zaha Hadid and the growth of her office from 7 to 270 employees. In spite of this incredible growth, the office has lost almost nothing of Zaha's powerful designer imagination. Exactly the opposite, parametric logic has magnificently overlapped with its formal expression. The project for Zagreb airport has indeed shown the best sides of both procedures.

Parametric logic determines the design of a basic element which reconciles all the technical and technological demands of the client, and multiplication of the basic construction element creates spectacular airport spaces, a series of unique places where you have to be extremely architecturally insensitive or uneducated not to feel the signature of a brilliant woman architect and production of a highly professional office. Just look at the perspective of the access road to the airport and airport building, and you will understand that top architecture produces something that is called added value in economic theories.

Zaha is not building twenty of the most important cultural, industrial, infrastructural and business buildings all around the world at this very moment because some local managers and mayors are "in love" with her architecture. It is more than clear to this group of technocrats, from Vilnius, via Dubai to Guangzhou (Canton), that with Zaha's architecture institutions will obtain supreme business, tourist and cultural promotion. 'Take Easy Jet to Zagreb, Croatia and shop at Zaha's airport' could be an expected advertising slogan in the new Wallpaper. Such a potential value on the European market would probably be very easy to sell, make a profit (if we had to, even give in concession) of at least double the price of the construction and, for example, finally complete the University Hospital on Zagreb's river, the Sava.

Zaha certainly did not need the publicity of the competition. Even this kind of jury must have been aware that work 1006, neatly sealed, re-coded, and controlled again in Munich, came from London. However, I have to emphasize again, if "the diva had been allowed" to explain this to the jury, as well as to an audience in Zagreb, it would certainly have been an excellent cultural and educational event. Namely, it would be interesting to see "our surveyors and German hygienists" explaining to Zaha that her work was significantly worse than the works by her competition. If the members of the jury had had a chance to participate in a series of Zaha's lectures, especially in "the sad" period of the middle of the 1990s when she won the competition for the Cardiff opera house, they would have found out that her arguments were never (only) aesthetic, artistic, but much more a result of research on new geometries for creation of space of new public, democratic domain. Literally. Zaha is not a laureate of the Pritzker Prize because her drawings are nice; therefore, one can find her on the cover pages of almost all world class magazines. Zaha is simply one of the most important persons of modern architecture and certainly the most important woman architect in history.

Zaha's "excursion" to Zagreb is an almost paradigmatic case for students of sociology – to investigate what in its essence creates the mediocre relation of one society, city, environment towards remarkable individuals and their works.

However, despite of all the above said, the authors of the winning work should be sincerely congratulated. They won with a large majority in conditions where the jury worked and/or discussed the quality of individual works. The Civil Engineering Institute of Croatia (Institut građevinarstva Hrvatske, IGH) is a private company whose name did not change during the transition, and according to some commentators, whose monopolistic behavior has also not changed when all significant infrastructural jobs in Croatia are considered. The Civil Engineering Institute of Croatia employed two rather small architectural offices for this task, led by two architectural immortals (at least in Croatian conditions), Croatian academics – Velimir Neidhardt and Branko Kincl.

The work of IGH was extremely professionally performed in all aspects which the task for the competition work required from the competitors, and they obviously managed to impress the jury. The jury had an almost unanimous opinion about the remarkable values of work 1007, which you would understand if you carefully read the opinion, written in a somewhat stenographic manner, about this work.

The almost apologetic opinion of the jury should, in my opinion, be opposed by at least two important factors. One is the architectural quality of the project and its textual explication which the jury quotes in a rather uncritical manner. The other is the anticipated price of the building's construction and the price of its maintenance.

Let me first quote a sentence which the jury states at the beginning of its report as the key explanation of the airport building's architectural concept: 'The terminal building resembles an extended flagpole displaying the combination of a long linear inductive pole structure, softly wrapped in a dynamic envelope, which unwraps itself to levitate above the terminal hall generating the free dynamics of the structural net – the flying roof – an iconic expression of the landscape.'[95]

It is very difficult here not to ask oneself what the jury and competitor really want to say. Namely, what is similar in this work to the "flag carrier" or "flagpole" is probably the airport piers. But, if we engage in connotative analyses, then we should at least ask ourselves why architects think that the airport building should remind us of a horizontal carrier of flags and why the jury thinks that it is good that airport building should resemble anything. The problem also occurs further in the sentence where "inductive pole structure," "dynamic membrane," "free dynamism of structural net" and eventually "flying roof" (they probably meant floating) appear as an "iconic expression of the landscape." In order to still try to understand the architectural concept that generated this work, we would find a significant theoretical contribution in the explanation by the winning architects: "Specific architectural form is generated by the unique blend of both aesthetic phenomena and functional requirements which

[95] From the textual explication of the competition entry 1007.

Transparentnost aerodromske zgrade u pogledu sa prilazne ceste.

Transparency of the airport building, viewed from the access road.

↓ Izvor: Citat s prvog panoa natječajnog rada ureda Foster+Partners

tektonsko remek-djelo i vjerojatno najisplativiji projekt za novi terminal.

782184 ¶ Zagrebački aerodrom – novi putnički terminal ¶ '... Kad god sam pošao tom šumom, svaki put sam nešto nova vidio, nešto nova naučio; nije ona crna, gluha, mrtva kako se izdaleko na obzorju crta i prikazuje, nego u njoj diše život i svijet izvoran...' ¶ Josip Kozarac (1858.-1906.)

S Fosterovim radom upoznao sam se sredinom 70-ih kad sam svoje studentske ljetne dane provodio u Londonu. Škola za engleski jezik koju sam pohađao bila je u Tottenhamu, a nedaleko od nje bio je ured Foster Architects. Zauzimao je cijelo prizemlje stambene zgrade, a od ulice je bio odijeljen očigledno novom high-tech staklenom stijenom. Iza stijene, kao u izlogu, bile su velike makete natječajnih i prvih izvedenih radova. Prvu subotu nakon otkrića Fosterovih izloga našao sam se u vlaku za Ipswich da bih bezuspješno nagovarao domara u zgradi osiguravajućeg društva Willis Faber Dumas da me pripusti u bazen u prizemlju i na travnatu terasu zgrade uz restoran za zaposlene i klijente. Već u ovom prvom svjetski priznatom radu Foster je pokazao razumijevanje velikih majstora moderne, u ovom slučaju Miesa, te osobitu brigu za socijalni aspekt arhitekture. Sainsbury centar za umjetnost u prostoru Sveučilišta Istočne Anglije na periferiji Norwicha, iz 1977. godine, prvo je od desetak ključnih objekata svjetske arhitekture u posljednjih tridesetak godina, sagrađenih pod vodstvom Lorda Fostera. Zato danas Foster predstavlja pravi arhitektonski fenomen, ne samo kao uspješni arhitekt, već još više kao osnivač najuspješnije arhitektonske kompanije novog vremena koja zapošljava gotovo tisuću ljudi. Foster je, u stvari, promijenio prirodu arhitektonske prakse stvarajući

the most successful architectural company of mo which employs almost one thousand people. Fos fact, changed the nature of architectural practice b a highly motivated 'machine' which can produce b the highest technical quality in a global context. ¶ what has this architect offered Zagreb? In one sen created a new gateway to Zagreb and Croatia. in his own words, architecture that embodies light and openness,' an airport that represents onto the world. Architecture that creates a sense Architecture of unique identity and iconic design. impressive is that this airport looks 'as if it doesn as if it is dematerialized and overlaps with the s forests. The terminal is not perceived and experi building, a spectacular volume, a technological building is almost not there and this is the ab greatest value of this work. Iconic, and yet 'in masterpiece. This project looks almost as if it co a Semper architectural reading book; it is like a primitive hut of the 21st century or like Bruno T pyramid. And finally, Foster's reading and evalua fantastic southern Zagreb landscape (the quote fro

MINES OF CULTURE

Town of Labin & Platform 9,81, 2007

visoko motiviranu 'mašinu' koja je u stanju proizvesti objekte najviše tehničke kvalitete u globalnom kontekstu. ¶ I konačno, što nam je ovaj arhitekt ponudio za Zagreb. U jednoj rečenici – stvorio je nova vrata Zagreba i Hrvatske. Stvorio je, po njegovim riječima, arhitekturu koja utjelovljuje 'poeziju svjetla i otvorenosti', aerodrom koji predstavlja prozor u svijet. Arhitekturu koja stvara osjećaj 'mjesta'. Arhitekturu jedinstvenog identiteta te ikoničkog dizajna. Ipak, najimpresivnije je što taj aerodrom 'kao da ne postoji', kao da je dematerijaliziran i preklapa se s okolnim šumama. Terminal se ne percipira i ne doživljava kao objekt, spektakularni volumen, tehnološki 'mjehurić'. Zgrade gotovo da i nema i to je apsolutna i najveća vrijednost ovog rada. Ikoničan, a 'nevidljiv'. Remek djelo. Projekt gotovo da izlazi iz Semperove arhitektonske čitanke, kao 'karipska primitivna koliba' 21. stoljeća ili kao Bruno Tautove staklene piramide. I konačno, Fosterovo čitanje i vrednovanje fantastičnog južnozagrebačkog krajolika (Kozarčev citat) osnova je konceptualne inspiracije za dizajn, ne samo terminala već cijelog aerodromskog grada. Tako jednostavno, nepretenciozno i jasno, kao čitanka za osnovnu školu. Meni apsolutno nije jasno kako bilo koji arhitekt (da opet ne spomenem članove žirija), gledajući u perspektivu

is the basis of the conceptual inspiration for the design, not only of the terminal but of the entire airport city. So simple, unpretentious and clear, like an elementary school reading book. I absolutely do not understand how any architect (not to mention again the members of the jury), when looking at the perspective of the access road to the airport building which emphasizes its transparency, the perfect relationship with the existing natural environment and spectacular and at the same time simple roof, is not able to foresee the creation of certainly one of the most beautiful airports in the world and a building which would put Croatia on the world map of recognizable destinations. ¶ I dare say – of similar power as the walls of Dubrovnik or Diocletian's Palace. Especially if we know that Foster's renderings are never far from reality. ¶ Foster + Partners must have also used the important experience of Stansted; nevertheless, their Zagreb airport integrates landscape and architecture in a much more direct manner. Namely, Foster does not only build a terminal, but also

Socijalni prostor putnika u odlasku i dolasku, s potpunom transparentnošću prema aerodromskoj pisti i pogledima na Medvednicu.

Social space for passengers who are arriving and departing, with complete transparency to the landing strip and views of Medvednica Mountain.

Jasnoća i jednostavnost konstrukcije u presjeku kroz centralni aerodromski prostor.

Clarity and simplicity of construction: cross - section through the central airport space

combine environmental, symbolic and historical paradigms of human development with openness to both global principles and the inherent local culture. On the one hand, the creation of the architectural form relies on the strictly functional philosophy of the complex terminal structure, while on the other, the ultimate architectural form is the result of the unique urban landscape and environmental context which allows for different aesthetic attributions and denotes the symbolism of meaning using indexes, signs and symbols.'[96]

If we were able to understand this theory, we would conclude that this must be about the titanic ambition that all these, obviously entirely opposed in terms of concept, categories should be reconciled in one airport terminal and about obtaining something that is called a unique blend. It is about a method of overlapping where functionalism is not present yet, but the final form is still the result of a unique context, which allows for different types of aestheticism and symbolism. Here, we are theoretically in the 1980s, in a postmodern discourse when there were attempts to create a new language, a language of indexes, signs and symbols through contextuality.

Another huge problem of this work is the price of construction and the price of maintenance. I definitely do not consider myself an expert on the financial evaluation of individual buildings on the basis of elaborated design projects, but some facts related to the winning work are somewhat disturbing. In contrast to Foster's or Hadid's repetitive system of support construction, IGH proposes an extremely hybrid-like solution in which each individual part requires the application of a different building technique. Almost all the basic elements of the support construction are of different dimensions and of "irregular" geometry. Although there is discordance between the visualization of the winning project and its technological studies, it is clear that this is a very sophisticated "greenhouse" with a double membrane and powerful energy plant for heating and cooling, as well as air ventilation of the building. It is interesting to compare this solution with Fuksas' one for Terminal 3 of Shenzhen International Airport in southern China. The web-site worldarchitecture-news.com will explain this to us: 'The design considers ecological effects by using an innovative two-skin layer which will reduce energy consumption and allow natural light to permeate the structure'. Shenzhen is located in a somewhat different climate zone than Zagreb, but the basic principle of energy sensitivity is probably valid for both projects, in this way similar in terms of both construction and space.

The other argument which Fuksas uses in the explanation of his awarded work is: 'In construction terms, its design optimizes the performance of materials selected on the basis of local availability, functionality, application of local skills, and low-cost procurement.' Remarkably, 'it will have been designed and built in just few years,' as www.dezeen.com informs us.

To conclude, this is a high-cost procurement, and therefore the last in a number of initiatives by the Prime Minister and the Mayor of Zagreb to "have a commission arranged to investigate the construction price of the new terminal at Zagreb Airport" is probably a logical consequence of the concern about the price of the awarded work in times of global economic recession. According to www.poslovni.hr, the Prime Minister Sanader stated: 'We will appreciate the principle that an investor does not have to choose the project that won first prize because the decision by expert jury as an associate body does not have to be final for the investor. We lack the financial dimension and in this moment, we cannot, out of responsibility for our citizens and appropriations, spend another kuna.'

Interesting here is the "journalistic" formulation that the jury is an associated body to the investor and that as such, an "associate" – it does not really have to be taken into consideration. The CAA (Croatian Architects' Association) and DAZ (Zagreb

96 Ibid.

Architects' Association) will surely dislike such formulations; however, since they formed the jury with the investor it is difficult not to agree with the Prime Minister. Of course, my arguments are of a "somewhat" different pretext than the Prime Minister's, but it is a real pity that the jury was not in a condition to recognize architectural qualities, and then the financial consequences of the first five awarded works.

Therefore, I will explain in a further text why the work of the Foster + Partners is a potential urbanistic and architectural master piece for the new Zagreb airport city and probably the most cost-effective project for the new terminal.

782184

Zagreb Airport – New Passenger Terminal

"Each time I passed through the forest I discovered something new, I learned something new; it is not somber, silent or lifeless – even if it appears so on the horizon. Inside the forest breathes life and the world glistens".

Josip Kozarac (Croatian writer, 1858–1906)

Source: quote from the first board of Foster + Partners competition work

I became familiar with the work of Foster in the mid 70s when I spent some of my student summer days in London. The English language school I attended was in Tottenham, and not far from it was the Foster Architects office. It occupied the entire ground floor of a housing building and was separated from the street by an obviously new high-tech glass wall. Behind the wall, like in a shop window, there were large models of competition and first accomplished works. The first Saturday after discovering Foster's windows, I found myself on the train for Ipswich in order to unsuccessfully try to convince the janitor in the building of insurance company Willis Faber Dumas to let me see the pool on the ground floor and the building's grass terrace, next to the restaurant for employees and clients. Already in this first globally recognized work, Foster showed he understood the big masters of modernism, in this case Mies, and his special care for the social aspect of architecture. The Sainsbury Arts Centre on the University of East Anglia campus from 1977, on the outskirts of Norwich, was the first among ten key buildings of the world's architecture in the last thirty years built under the guidance of Lord Foster. Therefore, Foster represents a real architectural phenomenon today, not only as a successful architect, but even more as the founder of the most successful architectural company of modern times, which employs almost one thousand people. Foster has, in fact, changed the nature of architectural practice by creating a highly motivated "machine" which can produce buildings of the highest technical quality in a global context.

And finally, what has this architect offered Zagreb? In one sentence – he created a new gateway to Zagreb and Croatia. He created, in his own words, architecture that embodies "poetry of light and openness," an airport that represents a window onto the world. Architecture that creates a sense of "place." Architecture of unique identity and iconic design. Yet, most impressive is that this airport looks "as if it does not exist," as if it is dematerialized and overlaps with the surrounding forests. The terminal is not perceived and experienced as a building, a spectacular volume, a technological blob. The building is almost not there and this is the absolute and greatest value of this work. Iconic, and yet "invisible." A masterpiece. This project looks almost as if it comes out of a Semper architectural reading book; it is like a Caribbean primitive hut of the 21st century or like Bruno Taut's glass pyramid. And finally, Foster's reading and evaluating the fantastic southern Zagreb landscape (the quote from Kozarac) is the basis of the conceptual inspiration for the design, not only of the terminal but of the entire airport city. So simple, unpretentious and clear, like an elementary school reading book. I absolutely do not understand how any architect (not to mention again the members of the jury), when looking at the perspective of the access road to the airport building which emphasizes its transparency, the perfect relationship with the existing natural environment and spectacular and at the same time simple roof, is not able to foresee the creation of certainly one of the most beautiful airports in the world and a building which would put Croatia on the world map of recognizable destinations.

I dare say – of similar power as the walls of Dubrovnik or Diocletian's Palace. Especially if we know that Foster's office renderings are never far from reality.

Foster + Partners must have also used the important experience of Stansted; nevertheless, their Zagreb airport integrates landscape and architecture in a much more direct manner. Namely, Foster does not only build a terminal, but also proposes a very interesting "ecological development of the entire airport city."

Here, greenery represents the dominant character of the master plan and it serves as pollution control, carbon sink, microclimate control and recreation.

The terminal building is designed in a simple modular system which enables great flexibility with extensions and changes related to the Schengen/non-Schengen status of Croatia. The entire terminal is set on a concrete podium, therefore no excavation of the terrain (which has a high local water table) is anticipated which certainly reduces costs and enables a short construction time. The concrete platform represents a very simple construction (three floors in the part with garages), in a twelve by twelve meter module, from which steel pillars are erected, carrying the roof grid.

The roof is absolutely the most significant element of the composition that creates the elementary atmosphere and character of the building. It is valuable to quote what Foster people say about the design of the roof: 'The location of the new terminal in proximity to the existing forest inspired the design. As the forest spontaneously grows, so the roof is easily expandable and extremely flexible. As the forest blends together different trees in one entity, so the roof system is built by combining simple and very repetitive modules in a way that creates a unique visual identity. As a natural canopy filters the sunlight through the layers of leaves, so the layers of diffusers and reflective panels distribute the natural light efficiently in the terminal, providing a comfortable environment for the passengers.'[97]

The roof is a simple steel spatial grid, which is assembled of just two basic rhomboid modules. The height of the grid is 1.80 m and it is carried by irregularly arranged pillars with a distance ranging from 12 to 30 meters. The roof, together with the glass walls, represents the basic architectural, but also energy-related membrane of the building.

Let us repeat – Foster's key functional arguments are painfully simple, but probably have to be underlined one more time: 'Zagreb airport will be convenient, safe and technically advanced since it will allow for flexibility for future growth and flexibility in operation. It will provide first-class design standards for all passengers and optimized operational opportunities. The terminal building will be quick to build and will represent value for money and will be very sustainable.'[98]

Here, we have to pose a question which at first sight is utterly simple: "Do we, as a community, believe these arguments by one of the most successful architectural offices in the world or are we proverbially suspicious about them"? And perhaps this question: Can Zagreb (for the nth time), after Adolf Loos, Alvar Aalto, Jaap Bakema, Jean Nouvel, Thom Mayne and Daniel Libeskind, also thank Zaha Hadid and Lord Foster on their efforts to build a significant piece of architecture in Croatia?

I really seriously think it cannot. It cannot because Croatia would certainly like to become a European Union country with high European standards which include selecting the very best international practitioners in developing its future.

97 From the textual explication of the competition entry 1004.
98 Ibid.

WHERE IS (CROATIAN) ARCHITECTURE HEADED

Published in Čovjek i prostor 7-8, Zagreb 2010

The editorial staff of the journal Čovjek i prostor organized the panel discussion Freedom of Expression in Architecture in June this year and asked me to comment on the topics and questions which defined the very discussion. Enticed by the critical mass of questions posed and by many years of my own efforts to answer similar ones, I wrote this article from quite a distance, yet perhaps "close enough" to utter something about Croatian architectural topics.

To design means primarily to think. That "mantra" of my teacher, Herman Hertzberger, used to be his answer to the postmodern discourse, in relation not only to education, but also to the creation of an authentic architectural culture, a global-Dutch in his case. To make it very simple, we may say that the past twenty years have been a period when the most influential architects in the world, alongside construction, wrote books, taught in schools, researched new urban phenomena and finally accepted a Faustian deal by becoming very prominent (star system), while their social role lost some of its significance. Rem Koolhaas, the most important protagonist of the past two decades, shows such a state of present-day architecture in OMA exhibition at the Venice Biennale; questioning to a certain extent the purpose and meaning of architecture in the "post-historical" times.

Croatian architectural and social scenes found themselves amidst historic discontinuity in the early '90s, but since the year 2000 they have sort of set out to consolidate the discontinuity.

The overall economic and social crisis in the country has, hopefully only temporarily, stopped that process. The panel discussion questions reveal some of the aspects of this "consolidation" so I shall try to respond to them briefly.

If we asked whether an inhibited social discourse leads to inhibited architecture, the answer might simply or in general be: yes, it does, because architecture is always, to a certain extent, a reflection of the environment where it is produced. Perhaps, though, one should note that the term "inhibited" is probably of a lower genus than "transitional", and that "discourse inhibition" is but one aspect of transitional changes. Transition, at least in theory, enables the presenting of different ways of working or constructing different discourses, which was clearly shown by the early Njirić's in Njirić+Njirić arhitekti hints at the exhibition in Antwerp Singel 2001, or Randić and Turato in the text Načela/Principles in Arhitekst's monograph The Architecture of Transition from 2000. Both the exhibition and the book made for an excellent operational platform for the "consolidation of discontinuity," which most certainly lacked the critical mass needed for avoiding "social inhibition". However, there was no lack of energy or intelligence of "thinking" architects, for creating a new "national" architecture. Clearly, this is not just about two interesting pairs of architects, but about an entire new generation.

The criteria for encouraging excellence or, in case of Croatia, for recognizing new European values were perhaps set in the 1990s primarily by the Frames of Metropolis, international seminars organized by the Planning Office of the City of Zagreb and the Berlage Institute, and more locally and precisely by Stefano Boeri as the first foreign selector of Zagreb Salon, in 2003.

If we add to these activities the efforts made by the Oris magazine, the Croatian Architects Association, Platforma 9.81 and the Croatian government's program of affordable housing (POS), Croatian architecture appeared quite blissful compared to the regional or "ex" Yugo-East-European zone. Strangely, even without the development of a real critical discourse, defining serious criteria, developing new forms of education, and despite the minimal influence on the cultural social sphere.

The main problem in the development of criteria for encouraging excellence is the problem of critical mass or size. Within the xenophobic nature of living in Croatia, expressed best in the cultural scene of

Čovjek i prostor, 5-6

Zagreb, 2006

Vedran Mimica
New School of
Architecture in Split

8. ZAGREBAČKI SALON :
ARHITEKTURA 2003

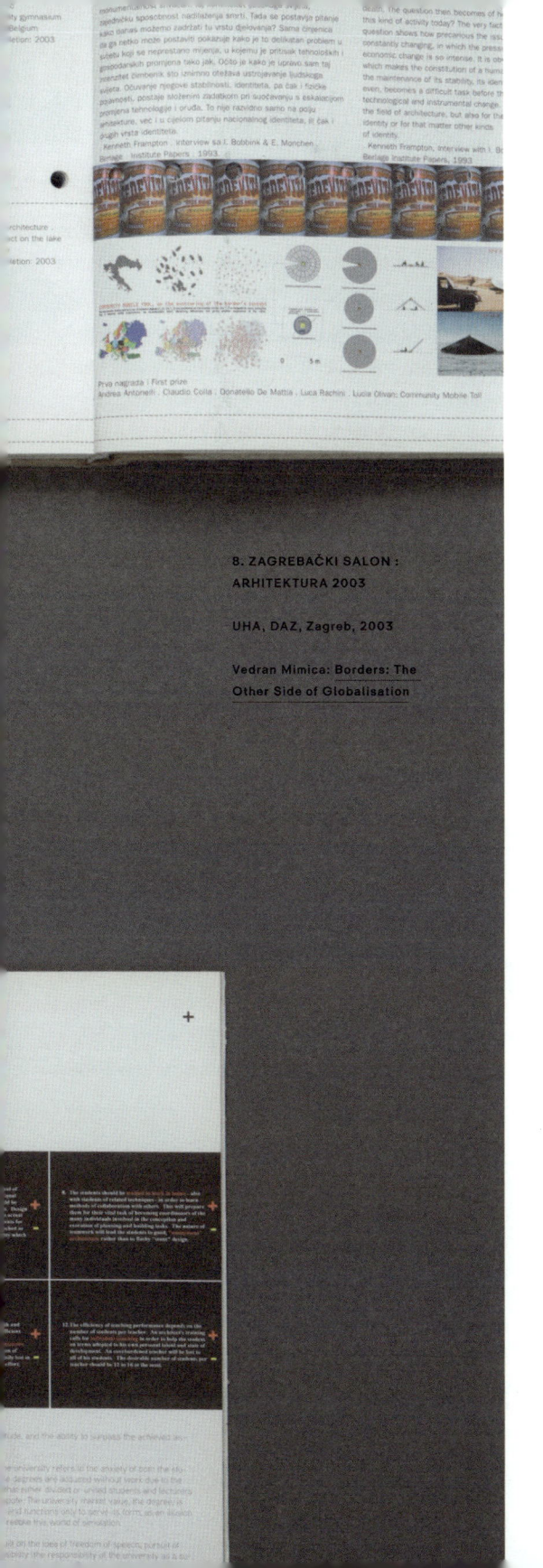

UHA, DAZ, Zagreb, 2003

Vedran Mimica: Borders: The
Other Side of Globalisation

Zagreb, everything looks big because almost nothing exists on the outside. However, should we regain consciousness and see that we are, or should be, a part of the world, or at least of European culture, we shall see that the cultural relevance of Croatia is worth approximately as much as the total shares of Croatian economic exchange in the EU, which is 0,1 %. It is thus not strange that the Njirićs were described by Belgian journalists as Balkan Teletubbies, little Martians, while Studio UP and "little" Mies have already confirmed the change of view towards Croatian architecture. One should definitely mention the "uncritical" infatuation of Manuel Gausa and especially Hans Ibelings with Croatian architecture.

In order to speak seriously about architectural culture in Croatia, one should first and foremost make a radical quantum leap. After that imagined leap, on the way to the European Union we would not face just two architectural magazines, two unreformed schools of architecture, two or three true critics and an entirely undefined governmental policy towards the question of which social production category architecture and urban planning belong to. If we add to the above-mentioned factors the professional associations of architects, architectural offices and NGOs dealing with space, we should realize that everyone must develop some criteria of excellence within their field as the basis for their social involvement. Only with a big, organized, collective effort and massive state subsidies with 100% use of European funds (not 20%), Croatian architecture can become a relevant subject in the European exchange, rather than a peripheral, if not provincial one. This has almost ceased to be a question of whether we care about that exchange and become a question of how we can take part in it.

In order to dream about such strategies in these times of a crisis, I shall briefly respond to some of the other questions of the editorial staff. Having a mono-cultural quality layer does definitely not benefit any "national" architecture. However, it does make it recognizable and makes perception and presentation somewhat simpler. In order to create a new "poly-cultural" quality layer, we shall have to wait for new generations which will not unavoidably depend on educational formats, economic inabilities and a dysfunctional market. Hereby I also implicitly speak about questioning some of the sacred dogmas of Croatian architecture, such as "aesthetic functionalism", "Zagreb School," the unquestionable status of institutional action and the impossibility of criticizing them. Questioning definitely does not mean and should not be perceived as erasing, eradicating and forgetting, but on the contrary, as transformation, transgression and redefinition.

The role of people of authority (however we define or determine them) is crucial in that very process of redefining a dogmatic perception of the world and architecture. Namely, my humble experience says that real global architectural authorities were always ready to accept and understand contemporary social changes and take a stance towards them. In the contemporary, postmodern period you cannot "teach the 1980s curriculum" because it will probably exclude you from the category of people of authority in a serious discussion. We may notice it is even more dangerous that such authorities often have groups of "admirers" and followers, and are firmly built into social decision-making networks.

The cluster of questions about education is quite "painful" because, on one hand, there is a naive, almost "student" faith in the idea that everything would be better if our university education worked, while on the other we realize that they probably represent the most unreformed segment of the social knowledge production. It is generally considered true that knowledge or "social capital", which can be recognized in the knowledge of certain social groups, is absolutely fundamentally important for the development of contemporary society. We also realize that young experts in their professional engagements between Lastovo and Edinburgh will simply never use more than 70% of the knowledge taught at unreformed universities. We probably also realize that a curriculum has to relate to real challenges of building in a certain region and be very contextual. Thus, if we assume that these totally basic premises for reform and the development of architectural education are clear, one should try to eliminate all obstacles to "common sense" in order to reform our two faculties, or else the time has perhaps really come for the creation of explicitly elite regional private schools. The School of Architecture at the POLIS University in Tirana, Albania, which I recently visited, is an extremely interesting example. Google it if you are really interested in the topic of educating architects and urban planners in a transitional environment.

And finally, the group of questions about the relationship of our profession and practice, and of censorship and auto-censorship, to freedom of creation or expression. Two concepts which might enhance the attempt at answering these somewhat difficult questions come from Frampton and Koolhaas (mentioned in the opening paragraph). Kenneth Frampton wrote in the conclusion of his essay Between Monumentally and the Immaterial in Arhitekst's[99] "little brick" book Contemporary Croatian Architecture: Testing Reality: 'How can one not wonder what is left for architects in our times, especially Croatian architects? That question is equally painful here as anywhere else and there is no satisfactory answer. One might only say that a responsible architect must equally be constantly engaged in the political discourse and the promoting of political ideas, as in the design of buildings.'

It is not so hard to extract the common inspirational theorem from these two approaches. If you want to be an architect in these times, start thinking and acting politically.

[99] Arhitekst is a Croatian publishing house.

CITIES CAN CHANGE THEIR IDENTITY

Interview by Damir Šarac. Published in Slobodna Dalmacija, daily newspaper, Split 2013

Damir Šarac We have dedicated a series of articles to mapping, a type of research that sets grounds for defining development strategies for many successful cities, regions, and countries, but which is completely new to the current Croatian practice. What use is there of mapping? In simple terms, it gives an exact insight into the current state of things. Not only is this insight necessary for planning but mapping also makes it enormously easier. What does mapping mean for a Mediterranean city like Split?

Vedran Mimica We look at mapping as a possibility to articulate particular urban features into the Mediterranean context. If mapping is a method to analyze the complex processes going on in modern cities in order to understand the social, cultural, economic and historical realities of a city such as Split, then it should be particularly sensitive to its Mediterranean context. For instance, if one maps the musical scene of Split and Dalmatia taking the hip hop band Dječaci (The Boys) and the a cappella group Cambi as input data, one gets completely contrasted images of the city and the region. Each of these images will be true, but the one based on the hip hop band will be much more useful for developing a strategy of change. As an analytical method, urban mapping relies on objectivity that is always difficult to achieve in complex environments such as city of Split. Even so, when and if one develops a high degree of sensitivity to the context one is analyzing and to the change one intends to implement, one will most likely end up taking sides that are ideologically opposed to the dominant, parochial views of what Split and Dalmatia are because parochialism excludes all but a single model of development. As a rule, this model is in conflict with the results and development strategies based on mapping. A few years ago, Tonko Gugić, the mayor of Vela Luka on the island of Korčula, asked me an interesting question as he was pointing to the dry stone walls stretching all over the local landscape. He said: "Mime, look at this beauty and tell me frankly how can we develop and stay the same?" The answer to this perfectly logical question as well as to your question about what mapping means for Split would probably be that we need to define our fundamental values and organize development models around them, so that the two do not clash but correspond with each other. I speak of correspondence in Adorno's sense of the term as the only criterion of tradition that we should follow. To use his own words, this correspondence 'sheds light on the present and receives from the present its own light. Such correspondence is not one of empathy and direct relationship, but requires distance.'[100]

Q To which areas is mapping applicable?

VM Mapping is applicable to any area of city production or the production of social reality in the Lefebvrean sense of the term.

Q What does this mean in terms of heritage and monument evaluation?

VM In the early 1980s, I took a postgraduate course in Split on the preservation and renovation of architectural heritage. There we learned about the value of our heritage and the importance to preserve it by using a method of active preservation. Even though we did learn a lot, we knew then and there that our extraordinary professors Marasović, Babić, Prijatelj, and Cambi did not care much about the true relationship between the heritage and contemporary urban life. In the west tower of Diocletian's Palace where our classrooms were situated we often could not hear our fine teachers because the neighbors would play music full blast. I think it is hard to really understand our heritage unless we learn to appreciate the present we live in. Renovation should identify

---

[100] Coulson, Shea (2007) Adorno's Aesthetics of Critique. Newcastle, UK: Cambridge Scholars Publishing

and reflect those values of our heritage that bring true quality, harmony, and balance. We can hardly evaluate the cultural influence of the past unless our cities are built on modern standards. Heritage cannot be evaluated based only on scientific interpretation of its historical layers, but also on the specifics of contemporary life of the residents who live in these layers.

Q What does this mean for cultural development and ties with the region?

VM Cultural development, whatever you mean by this term, is fundamental for the development of any city and its ties with other cities and regions in particular. I see culture as any social activity, from ballet to graffiti. Croatian culture is often referred to in its traditional forms: opera, ballet, theater, poetry, prose, painting… This means that most of the national revenue is allocated to these traditional forms, even though their influence on the real cultural production is minimal. In terms of modern city development, particularly in transitional countries, we are more interested in non-traditional, sub- or anti-cultural forms such as Split soccer fan club Torcida. If you map the movement of the fans from the local community Blatina to the northern section of the Poljud stadium and back, you get to know the real culture of an important subcultural group. If you go to see the opera Aida at Peristyle of the Diocletian's Palace, you will learn much less about culture in Split, at least about that part of (sub)culture that has some influence on the character and the life of the city. If you go to see Peristil when the head of the city tourist bureau impersonates Diocletian and delivers a speech to the tourist, you will see the city thematized or disneyfied, which is a recent trend over here.

Q What does mapping mean for tourism, especially in terms of understanding the ongoing changes? How does it reflect on planning, controlling, and implementing tourism development?

VM At the Split Summer Festival just a little while ago, Platform 9.81 organized an earnest panel discussion about tourism and culture. Perhaps the key take-home message was that the best development strategy for Split as a tourist destination is if it is developed for the benefit of its own residents. While this is perhaps an oversimplification of a very complex issue, you have to bear in mind that the tourist season at the Adriatic lasts for about 75 days, and you do not need advanced mapping to get to this conclusion. Common sense will do. Tourism is an important industry that can substantially increase the city revenue, but if we do not develop our cities so that tourists and residents can live together and that the new hybrid architecture is operational throughout the year, we will remain in that dual state of mind on and off-season. Successful tourist countries such as Austria, France, or Norway do not know what seasonal tourism means. Moreover, Austrian summer revenues top the winter ones.

Q Has the time finally come for Split, a city with more than 20,000 university students, to acknowledge and start to make use of its creative and intellectual potential?

VM When the Berlage Institute planned for the new university campuses in Zadar and Dubrovnik, we mapped annual student consumption and compared it with the consumption of hotel guests in these two cities. The comparison has shown that students spend more per year and that investment into universities – and I do not mean buildings alone, but the new programs – is more beneficial for city development than investment in strictly tourism-related businesses!

One positive strategic move to bring university students from the EU to Split is the post-graduate study program called Master in Architecture in English recently launched by the Split University, Faculty of Civil Engineering, Architecture and Geodesy. Unfortunately, I have not noticed that the city of Split makes any direct use of its creative and intellectual potential, as you call it, even though I am sure there is one. Instead, when it comes to decision making about city development, my Split university colleagues and friends seem to have been marginalized by the semi-literate political elite. A word of caution though – I do not live there or any other part of Croatia, so my views are the views of a "man [who] has been abroad for long, so you should not hold that against him," as my dear friend Gorki Žuvela once explained in my defense.

Q   What would mapping mean for Split in terms of capital investment and new ideas?

VM This is the fundamental question, as it concerns the relationship between globalization and local community. In Split it seems to have taken an unfortunate turn, considering that the city has not developed much since the opening of the first McDonald's in Marmont Street ten years ago. Globalization is inevitable, it is like the rain; you can take cover under the umbrella and make no use of it or you can collect it in cisterns and use it for irrigation. These metaphors for the four-year olds may not answer your question, but one thing is certain – development outside the globalizing world is hardly conceivable. Whether globalization is brought by businessmen from the other parts of the country or comes from South Korea will soon become irrelevant, as long as it saves the local shipyard. The condition is that everything is for sale on the neoliberal global market. The EU project, even though in a certain crisis at the moment, seems to be the only light at the end of the tunnel and a real opportunity for development. What worries me is Croatian incapability to make the best of the available EU funds and to understand what EU really means as a global project.

Q   Are you saying that the city needs a new, global identity?

VM Let me give you an illustrious example from South America. More than six years ago, a coalition of several parties won the local elections in Medellin, Colombia with a narrow margin, and the newly elected mayor sent a clear message to drug cartels who had run the city until then: "You cannot buy us!" Some found this declaration suicidal in what was then the worst, most dangerous and backward city in South America, but these politicians endured and showed the world that things can change. Thanks to the mapping of its recent progress in politics, education, and social development, this February Medellin was declared the most innovative city in the world. Recently, it has also been declared the most inviting destination for corporate business in South America. These changes came with substantial capital investment in educational, cultural, and public transport infrastructure that engaged the very best architects from the region through public competitions. In other words, cities can change their identity. Even those that feel strongly about their local spirit, genius loci. Today, for the genium locum to remain alive, it needs to be constantly reinterpreted. You cannot freeze it in time but should understand it in terms of the current needs. This dynamic understanding of a "place" is the only possible starting point for creative immersion in global surroundings. I am saying this from an experience with hundred-odd cities across forty countries of the world. It is quite interesting to see how cities compete on the global stage, both on the theoretical and quite practical level, and how they seek the balance between global influences and local resistance to them. At the Illinois Institute of Technology College of Architecture in Chicago we deal with issues such as "the meaning of metropolitan identity in the age of undifferentiated globalization." To do that, we have been working on new generation models of complex urban conditions in Chicago that could directly influence city development models all over the world at some later point. Using parametric design processes and emerging social media, we seek to create urban development models that will strike the balance between the pressures from the globalizing world and local architectural interpretations. As you probably know, broader Chicago area is the home of American jazz and the McDonald's franchise, but what is even more relevant for us, of the first skyscrapers. The question for us now is: what's next?

6IX PACK:
CONTEMPORARY SLOVENIAN ARCHITECTURE

Published in 6IX Pack: Contemporary Slovenian Architecture,

Vale-Novak Publisher, Ljubljana, second edition, 2006

The following text is a result of a series of conversations with Igor Kebel and Mika Cimolini (the Berlage students from Slovenia) that took place at the Berlage Institute in spring 2005.

We are beyond good and bad.

Rem Koolhaas at the Berlage Institute, 1993

Double Exchange

Question   Slovenia's transition has either disappeared or has become reversed, namely, this transition is no longer so much about Slovenia approaching Europe; it is more about Europe approaching Slovenia. Under what circumstances did this reversal take place?

Vedran Mimica Slovenia entered a major transition after the fall of the Berlin wall in 1989, as did all the other former socialist states in Europe. One may officially declare the transition completed in 2004, when Slovenia was admitted as a full member to the European Union. Nevertheless, if one looks into Slovenian society, culture, architecture, and the economy, then one may witness the continuation of various processes of transition. Slovenia became European by a political decree. The discussion here, however, concerns the cultural and architectural issues linked to the country's new political and economic processes. Since Slovenian culture and society are now the part of the larger EU, the promotion of any strategy must be framed within this larger European context. Obviously, Slovenia cannot forget its history, its culture, its links with the East, and the West. Being an EU member, Slovenia must contribute to the diversity of European cultures. This is a two way process – on the one hand, Slovenia comes to Europe; on the other hand, the EU coming to Slovenia also complements this process. Nevertheless, it is crucial that in the aftermath of the transition, Slovenia now engages in processes of consolidation, cooperation, and exchange. This creates a politically, even ideologically, and definitively economically and culturally, challenging state of affairs. Under what circumstances could this reversed process take place? Now there is neither extensive knowledge nor experience of such processes in Slovenia. Perhaps the architectural competition for redesign of Kolizej[101] in Ljubljana could be deemed a first test of how to organize a big competition deploying practices which are regular in western Europe, how to understand the role of the developer, find how to select international jury. The fact that such a competition process was shocking, even unacceptable, to the local inhabitants and culture, proves that Slovenia has yet to appreciate and become conscious of the European way of doing things. After signing an incredible number of EU memorandums and agreements that frame the legislative package, the more challenging, performative aspect of relations with the EU has begun. This is where Slovenia, and all other countries new to Europe, will need a decade to start understanding, shaping and influencing these processes. No doubt, the shock of the rejection of the EU constitution by the referendum in France and the Netherlands has been unsettling for the most recently accepted states to the EU. Recently, the Polish prime minister approached Tony Blair to lift the deal made for Poland entering the EU in lieu of compensation of Polish peasants. Blair replied by saying that "it is not about money it is about principles." However, the question is really what principles are we talking about? Ironically, the dynamism of EU politics is surprising to the new members, yet it is the very condition that they must understand and maneuver within. Three years ago, Dietmar Steiner invited me and a couple of other so called "eastern European experts," including Andrej Hrausky and people from Hungary, Poland, Czech Republic and Slovakia, to discuss the Next Europe. Steiner organized this discussion in the Architekturzentrum Wien in Vienna. He argued that all these nations that were being accepted into Europe had indeed always been part of Europe;

101   Kolizej (Coliseum in German, originally Amphitheatrum Flavium) is a type of a monumental multipurpose and multilevel building that emerged in Austria in the 19th Ct.

even if we go back 1000 years, they have always been a constitutive factor of European culture. The region's rich urban and architectural histories are European: the Diocletian palace in Split, Plečnik in Slovenia, and the modernism of Czech architecture. Today, these nations' architects, practitioners, and theoreticians, are new to Western Europe. Steiner claimed that the attitude of them being "new" to Europe is wrong, and insisted that we consider them as always having been European. We should concentrate on what they can teach western Europe through their tradition, architecture, culture, and recent production. This is an interesting viewpoint, and perhaps the right conceptual frame, by which to consider Eastern Europe. When one presents such an attitude in places like Prague, Zagreb or Ljubljana, then the cultural establishment starts talking about history. However, the so called New Europe is less interested in history than it is in contemporary performance. Obviously, Czech modernism was terra incognita before Šlapeta opened an exhibition at AA; Plečnik was terra incognita before the exhibition in the Pompidou center; and Croatian modernism will remain terra incognita until its legacy is either exhibited or published. By presenting these movements, one presents history. This, of course, remains important. It is, however, also necessary for all these countries to present recent work. To date, contemporary work has usually been presented through events such as the Venice Biennale, and other established occasions of the kind, as well as through a handful of magazines. This is absolutely not enough, since all of the curators of such big exhibitions and magazines are presenters of the establishment anyway. Slovenian architecture is something that could be presented as a contemporary movement, without any big manifestos, or big ideological statements. Recent Slovenian work could provide a basis for debate concerning local particularities within the larger frame of cultural transformations taking place in Europe. The quality of local performance vis-à-vis global pressures will be critical if one is to achieve a higher quality of architectural production.

Q Integration with Europe through culture and education, the merge is established between particular cultural heritages and with intrinsic heritages and with intrinsic values of local practices. As smallness is gaining attention, can we anticipate an exhaustion of bigness? Is "bigness" finally going beyond self-sufficiency or is this just a fake move? Is Europe a cultural melting pot?

VM Europe is culturally diverse and this diversity will remain. The more pressing questions are how are "little cultures" going to negotiate with "big cultures", and what is the level of EU integration with regards to education and other cultural policies? Education is now very important for the process of integration. According to the Bologna declaration, from 2007 onwards, every young graduate from any EU country will be able to study anywhere in EU and receive full recognition for these studies. This is an amazing concept – it will allow students to start their studies in Ljubljana, continue in Venice, graduate in London and receive one and the same diploma for their efforts! Interesting things will start to happen when, because of their multi-national education, these students will no longer be representatives of particular national schools. These processes are, almost by default, positive. Most east European educational institutions are, at the moment at least, not performing up to par. Because they did not reform their curriculum structures, make them more aligned with new west European practices in education. The intelligence of young people is already in striding conflict with the structures of these institutions. By creating a multinational educational environment, and encouraging mobility of students and teachers, the Bologna process will slowly change these institutions. They will be forced to change. At the same time, however, no one would ever want an educational institution in Ljubljana to be completely the same as a school in Edinburgh, for instance. Diversity and specificity should remain a competitive edge. In the future, one could study architecture in Ljubljana because of Plečnik or the Sixpackers;

precisely these differences will provide the positive context influencing the choice for studying in Slovenia. New Slovenian students will have a choice that was not possible in a society that previously had been too singularly determined. Education is an increasingly consumer oriented activity. Students or graduates from the high schools of the future will be shopping by looming into curricula, into lifestyle in a particular city; they will be choosing pleasurable or hedonistic settings. They will be critical of the life they will be living in a particular country. The boom of the schools in Barcelona is not at all surprising – the city has a pleasurable setting, while the interest in schools in London may be credited to its powers as a metropolitan magnet.

The so-called "little places" or "little schools" will not suffer in this process. On the contrary, especially the eastern EU countries are incredibly interesting for so called "westerners" as the East can offer something that does not exist in the West. In this sense, Europe's extension to the east is an extremely exciting project.

As the world of architecture becomes globalized, with many offices worming with different addresses, and branches all over the world, or with the rise of big architectural offices such as Herzog & de Meuron or Foster that employ hundreds, it must be remembered that the majority of architectural practices nonetheless remain small and local. They are performing under very particular relations between architects and politicians or developers in particular setting. There is enormous space for local expression and for local specifics. The question then is – what is the quality of these activities and how can these local expressions gain some sort of more general qualities. One has to look at the work and then place or qualify the work within their particular contextual forces. These forces are never completely local nor completely global, they are always both.

Q Sixpackers' attitudes in resolving global issues through local practice. How is Sixpack dealing with the absence of heroic radicalism? What is Sixpack breaking, if breaking is no longer a necessity?

VM Sixpack, and the new generation of architects, are the best of what could have happened to Slovenian architecture, and to a certain extent Croatian architecture, too. In the beginning of the 1990s, there was a period in which the most dedicated and ambitious young architects from Slovenia simply felt that they needed additional education and experiences; this feeling was genuine and contextual. It was obvious that the desire for gaining knowledge through further education and to be able to operate in new contexts was the result of a completely conscious decision. I personally witnessed such an attitude among the Sixpackers from the Berlage and AA; these students were all infected with a particular architectural virus. They differed from the previous generation of architects in that they did not see Ljubljana or even Slovenia as their exclusive terrain/frame of operations.In the beginning of the 1990s, the Slovenian frame was too small, too traditional, and too "difficult." The younger architects could not accept the incredibly hierarchical social structure at play in Slovenia. The fact that one would have to work as an assistant in both the university or within an architectural office for the first 25 years of one's career was simply unacceptable to them. These people did not believe in this, they had a different point of view. Their attitudes were more reflective of the European standpoint, and this was in stark contrast with the more traditional, Slovene socialist frame of reference. Importantly, these people came to Western Europe with a particular pool of knowledge and skills that cannot be considered minor in any circumstances. On the contrary, their skills were comparative and on par to those of their colleagues from the West. It was important for them to understand that they had similar knowledge and an understanding of architecture as their colleagues from Western Europe. This was a critical discovery, because it imbued them with confidence and gave them a different view of the cultural setting from which they came. The main reason to study in London or the Netherlands was not to better understand

TERRITORIES, IDENTITIES, NETS:
SLOVENE ART 1995 - 2005

eds. Igor Španjol, Igor Zabel
Moderna galerija, Ljubljana, 2005

Vedran Mimica: Three Rooms, Curatorial Politics

SIXPACK : CONTEMPORARY SLOVENIAN ARCHITECTURE

ed. Andrej Hrausky, Sixpack architects
DESSA, Ljubljana, 2005

Vedran Mimica : Sixpack : Contemporary Slovenian Architecture

Vasa Perović
Matija Bevk
Aljoša Dekleva
Tina Gregorič
Mika Cimolini
Igor Kebel
Tomaž Maechtig
Urša Vrhunc
Rok Oman
Špela Videčnik
Jurij Sadar
Boštjan Vuga
Vladimir Šlapeta
Tadej Glažar
Dado Katušić
Hrvoje Njirić

these cultural contexts, but for the Slovenians to form new insights about Slovenia. Perhaps they could never fully understand Ljubljana and Slovenia if never lived and worked anywhere else. From personal experience, I can say that studies at the beginning of the 1980s in Delft were more instructive about Zagreb, for instance, than would have been the case if I had been doing research, lecturing and teaching in Zagreb.

Self-confidence of skills and knowledge, together with the possibility to learn more, and form a critical attitude towards the cultural setting of one's origins, have been super important for the future instrumentality of Sixpackers. The Berlage and AA operate in terms of strategies and scenarios and these young architects immersed themselves in these ways of thinking that inevitably relate future performance to forces far beyond those that are merely local. In the mid-90's, Slovenian political culture proclaimed that only the EU represented the future for Slovenia, and that EU standards had to be applied to various aspects of social, economic, political and other forms of life. Although a group of very different architects, the Sixpackers nonetheless have in common the fact that they worked within these EU standards.

Q Sixpackers as driving beyond the cultural, political and territorial boundaries in their break with historical and local movements, their break with icons of Slovenia's past as well as local practices. With its Sixpack exhibition abroad, the group has made an impact on the local scene. How do you explain that? What is the potential of Sixpack? Conversely, what would a criticism of Sixpack consist of, what are the possible opportunities missed by the group?

VM In the context of Middle Europe that is one of Slovenia too, there is a great culture of debate in architecture. At the beginning of the 20th century, the Secessionist architects had an incredible conflict with the Historicist architects. Later, modernists became embroiled in a conflict with the postmodernists. There exists a culture of conflict. At the

TERRITORIES, IDENTITIES, NETS:
SLOVENE ART 1995 - 2005

eds. Igor Španjol, Igor Zabel
Moderna galerija, Ljubljana, 2005

ORIS 48

Zagreb, 2007

Vedran Mimica
New Tobačna, Strictly Controlled Smoking

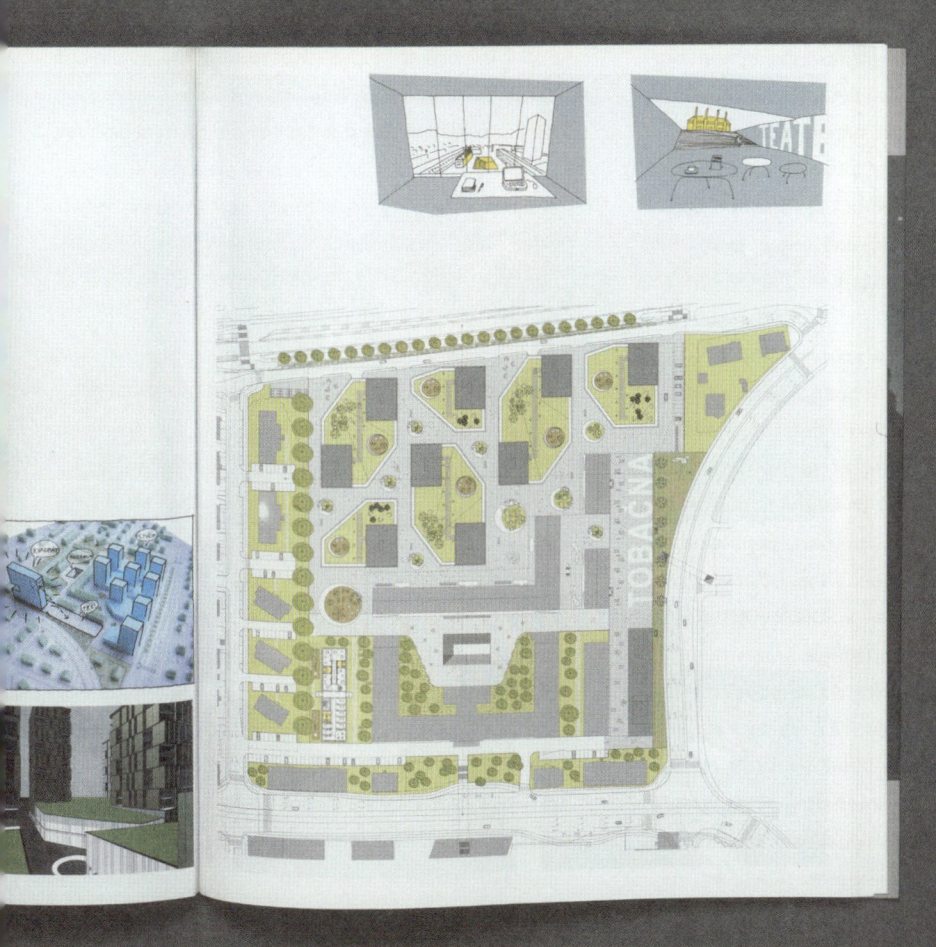

- Janez Koželj
- Markus Schaefer
- Marijn Spoelstra
- Dekleva and Gregorčič
- Kebel and Cimolini
- Sadar and Vuga
- Černigoj and Grmek
- Helena Njirić

same time, there is also a culture of a political control over certain markets. These two cultures do not easily coexist with each other, namely, the first culture involves a critical or cultural debate concerning new generations of architects, while the second includes political and economical maneuvers to control the market historically, and „the establishment" has never been sympathetic to change. The nature of the establishment is such that it can perform well only if there is no change or only if it controls and accommodates change. The question then becomes if change is inevitable or positive? One could say that it is inevitable and possible with regards to Sixpackers cultural performance and if one would like to see the development of Slovenia architecture. I share the opinion of Herman Hertzberger – namely, that places such as the Berlage were explicitly established in order to equip the people with the knowledge of how to change local conditions. Recently, I was invited by Tadej Glažar and Tina Gregorič to curate an exhibition concerning the last ten years of Slovenian architecture. After one looms at the result of this, one that objectively selected 56 buildings, one understands that the buildings of the Sixpackers are fundamental to shaping the new Slovenian architecture. If one was invited to make an exhibition covering 2005-2015, it would without doubt be influenced by the Sixpack generation. This is very fortunate for Slovenian architecture. This balancing of global influences with local interpretations is an interesting prospect for the immediate future. Sixpackers and other Slovenian architects will define the models, prototypes, strategies, and urban scenarios in order to engage with Slovenia's landscape. One would like to continue to see a difference, as introduced by the Sixpackers. The Berlage and AA somehow, innocently or incidentally, have influenced local Slovenian architecture and the international cultures of their institutions are indirectly linked to the fact that Slovenia has "allowed" foreigners such as Vasa Perović or Dado Katušić, to practice in its midst. Such openness has invariably enriched the otherwise very local culture. In this sense, it is interesting when people like Andrew Benjamin or Brett Steele, or other international professors are so fascinated when visiting such a small place as Ljubljana and discovering all the layers that it is made up of. Obviously, the last layer is one that has been fundamentally shaped by the Sixpack generation. Although it was not a strategy designed by neither Hertzberger nor Mohsen Mostafavi, one must admit that both the AA and Berlage network have been fairly efficient. On the one hand, the schools' graduates were supported and moderately promoted; on the other hand, all the work that is done by Sixpackers is hard work done by professionals. It has nothing to do with the Berlage and AA networks, but is simply due to the performance of these architects locally. But being in the network, knowing people, knowing the right information, knowing the different theories and strategies, and being linked with knowledge, is super important in contemporary global society. If you are disconnected from this network, you are in an invalid position. The position of the Sixpackers was a position in which one was able, in a rather limited amount of time, to accumulate performative knowledge. This knowledge anticipates that architecture needs more layers of mediation. Architecture has to be mediated through perhaps tangential disciplines such as literature, film, narratives in general, and journalism. It would be very difficult to establish an architectural production in a society by remaining only architectural in the strict sense of the word. Architectural production needs to adopt strategies from the media and the market in order to present itself better to the world at large. What seems to be incredibly important for the future, is the relation between the architect and the client. Architects will be more and more in a position of educators; they will be those who bring clients up to a higher level of understanding. Finally, as architecture is a material practice, it is the knowledge of technology, of new materials, and evolving lifestyles, that will be a most interesting field of operation. Slovenia's Sixpackers will have great responsibilities and opportunities in building the next European architectural culture. We are looking forward to the upcoming productions.

STRICTLY CONTROLLED SMOKING

Essay New Tobačna, Strictly Controlled Smoking. Published in Oris 48, Zagreb 2007

Ljubljana, as a "new" European city, is searching for development strategies to move toward a European milieu. Architecture and urban planning should uphold this ambition, presenting new values and methods for planning, programming, "management" and construction of a new European Ljubljana. The city government and developers engaged many local and international experts in the task of creating a vision for a new Ljubljana. This should culminate in the presentation of a new general master plan and all strategic projects for the upcoming period, when it will be possible to use EU cohesion funds to the fullest.

Recently a new city government assumed office in Ljubljana, headed by the agile Mayor Janković and Deputy Mayor Koželj, an authority on architecture and urban planning. It was Janez Koželj who in a development study for Ljubljana, produced in 2004, listed almost forty large-scale projects for city development, of which none were implemented, with the exception of a bypass, several public institutions and the BTC shopping center. The question that arose in 2005, particularly after the Kolizej case,[102] was more than obvious: why is Ljubljana not developing, why were the great expectations after Slovenia joined the European Union not fulfilled, and what were the reasons for such a state of affairs? The Berlage Institute was asked by the City of Ljubljana to prepare an independent view of the city's urban development opportunities.

A team of five students supported by Vedran Mimica, Director of the Institute, and external advisers analyzed the city, studied issues such as development in the new EU capitals, new and old urban typologies, possible development scenarios and case studies on development mechanisms, with the aim of defining a series of specific strategies and projects for the city. The two semesters' studio work in the 2005/06 academic year was led by Markus Schaefer of Hosoya Schaefer Architects (architecture) and Marijn Spoelstra of Mountainworks (financial consulting). Its main interest was defined by the collaborative and creative cross-section of these two often separated disciplines. The Berlage Institute diagnosis underlined the following symptoms of the current state of blocked development:

The constantly changing municipal political environment leads to ambiguity and a non-existent strategy and long-term vision for the development of the city.

After the first phase of transition from (liberal) socialism to (controlled) capitalism, there is still a lack of strategic planning tools, proper legislation and clear policies, a lack of knowledge and resources in the city government and incomplete organization (for example, there is no a city development department).

A lack of clarity in matters of land ownership due to the denationalization process (even the city government is currently unaware of its own status of land ownership), which makes it very difficult to implement new zoning laws, the main driving force of development).

A lack of understanding of the development mechanism and public and private responsibilities in it, together with a lack of trust between public and private parties due to blocked or failed projects, bureaucracy and lack of structure, legislation and policies,

---

102 Kolizej was the first architectural contest after the admission of Slovenia into the EU. 'The outcome and the exhibition of project proposals gave rise to a heated controversy among Slovene architects. Eventually this has led to everyday media encounters and reached a cultural-political meta-level, which is no surprise. This, in every sense high-standard competition, has inevitably rubbed salt on the wounds of the smug Ljubljana architectural scene by raising the following issues: Can the city center accommodate virile new projects? How to increase public awareness and how to challenge the idea of the city gate on the Ljubljana ring. How to stop the trend towards the displacement of urban functions, services, and entertainment to the outskirts (e.g. the BTC shopping center) and the consequent emptying of the city's parterre' (quoted from Boris Podrecca's article Kolizej Area Competition, published in Oris magazine No 30, 2004).

results in a lack of freedom and opportunities for private parties.

On the one hand, the city fears change (for example, the cultural heritage protection program is exaggerated, resulting in difficulty of renewal or redevelopment).

On the other hand, expectations for the future are high due to joining the EU. But being a part of the EU does not necessarily and automatically result in Slovenian development. The state of frozen development results in higher demand than supply for real estate. Together with high expectations from the "EU-effect" this results in relatively very high rents and prices of construction land and real estate, which can have a negative effect on the facilitation of new projects implementation.

The Berlage Institute study Light Capital: Urban Scripts for Ljubljana was presented at the Venice Biennale in 2006. After Venice, it was also presented in Ljubljana City Hall as an exhibition and public discussion. I believe that the exhibition, and in particular the subsequent public discussion, also resulted in the invitation to the author of this text to participate in a jury for the conversion of a former tobacco factory complex near the center of Ljubljana. After visiting the site of the former factory, and particularly after initial talks with IMOS[103] representatives, we were once again convinced that the analyzes of the difficulties in Ljubljana's development were very precise. Still, the idea that a private investor in agreement with the City and the Slovenian Chamber of Architecture and Physical Planning would announce a competition and initiate development of the center of Ljubljana seemed interesting. It was interesting in the sense that the Kolizej case should not be repeated, and that

cooperation between the private and public sectors would finally generate the desired results in Ljubljana. The invitation for a jury was interesting to this author also with reference to verification of the results of the Berlage Institute study in an "actual reality."[104] Namely, after the Kolizej case, which, due to the specific organization of the competition, the controversial program and the volume of construction, postponed project development for over three years, the competition for conversion of the tobacco factory, New Tobačna, was carefully and exhaustively prepared.

All aspects of a new city business, housing, cultural and commercial center were carefully analyzed and measured. A critical assessment of the existing facilities was particularly well elaborated concerning protection of the cultural heritage, traffic accessibility and general user safety. To a certain extent, such elaboration was slightly paradoxical, but also strongly contextual with reference to legislation and the character of transitional processes and cultural discussions in Ljubljana.

The first slightly paradoxical argument was the idea that all more or less preserved halls of the former 19th century factory should be preserved as a memorial and even identification landmark of Ljubljana in the 21st century. We could surely develop a very open critical discussion by asking if it is inevitable that the development of Ljubljana be subjected to a high degree of protection in the central zone, to what extent such protection protects the true value of the historical heritage, and to what extent it is an expression of bureaucratic mechanisms that persist from past times. What values of ordinary, functional 19th century industrial architecture are to be included in the creation of new memories of contemporary Ljubljana? By asking these questions, we by no means favor

---

103   IMOS is one of the leading Slovenian companies in the field of conducting complex engineering for all types of buildings. In more than four decades of successful operation, IMOS has designed countless apartment, business, school, medical, retail, tourist, and production buildings in Ljubljana, Slovenia, and abroad.

104   That particular Berlage Institute study was accompanied with the publication Light Capital: Urban Scripts for Ljubljana, Schaefer, M., ed. published by the Berlage Institute, Rotterdam in 2006.

bulldozing all historical buildings, but we do want a very critical discussion of the possibilities of creating new identities by using the historical background.

By using them, and not inevitably by protecting them, particularly when they have lost all connections to contemporary life.

The second paradox is that the competition program elaborated in detail the housing, business, cultural and commercial content, as though it implied nostalgia for the times when the system was able to build such city complexes. Namely, it is clear that IMOS as the construction organizer would have to "sell" certain parts of the New Tobačna complex to various investors who will certainly have their own ideas and demands which will probably not fully comply with the projected competition program.

The arguments for defending these two paradoxes are certainly in the domain of Ljubljana's development, where the Kolizej spirit is still present, as well as the IMOS wish to simply attract new investors by "high resolution" projects regarding the real presentation not only of urban design but also of the architectural and typological characteristics of single complexes.

Despite the "high resolution," or precisely because of it, we somehow cannot resist the impression that architects again "spent" their time relatively unfocused on certain aspects of the project which certainly will not influence implementation in the future.

The competition finally resulted in a series of very well elaborated projects, which we hope will be used for the elaboration of a detailed and hopefully flexible plan for further planning and design of a very prospective part of metropolitan Ljubljana's urban core.

If we look closer at the list of awards for the New Tobačna, we may conclude that a generation of young Slovenian architects, which presented itself through the exhibition and publication Sixpack a few years ago, "grew up" very quickly and showed that it was fully capable of solving complex urban development tasks. Dekleva and Gregorčič, Kebel and Cimolini, and Sadar and Vuga employ the knowledge which they accumulated during their postgraduate studies in London and Rotterdam, the experience from numerous competitions and clear understanding of the situation in which they work. Their work is perhaps the closest to the idea of an "up-scale" Ljubljana, a Ljubljana with an enhanced and denser scale. As we have already pointed out, their work is significantly influenced by the task at hand, but they manage to present an almost "natural" increase of a scale for the development of a new complex urban density.

The first prize that went to Dekleva and Gregorčič team is characterized by an extremely intelligent reading of the spirit of the city of Ljubljana, and of a historical matrix of the urban complex of the old Tobačna. By overlapping and analyzing these two scales, they create an operative three-dimensional diagram for the organization of new typological complexes on the site. Dekleva and Gregorčič have carefully and thoroughly designed a series of new typologies of housing, business premises, a representative hotel, cultural facilities and hybrid complexes, probably anticipating the potential process of a development of the site. We must hope that at least something of this almost encyclopedic product will be preserved and implemented in the detailed projects for the New Tobačna.

LIGHT CAPITAL :
URBAN SCRIPTS FOR LJUBLJANA

Berlage Institute research report No.07

2005 / 2006

ROME: THE CENTRE(S) ELSEWHERE

Berlage Institute Project study

SKIRA, Milano, 2010

LOS ANGELES STRANGER THAN FICTION

Berlage Institute research report No.33

2009 / 2010

TIRANA METROPOLIS

Introduction to the book Tirana Metropolis,
Published by the Berlage Institute, Rotterdam 2004

Now there is a new Tirana, colorful, happy, with a new and improved infrastructure and cultural life. I think Edi Rama is the man that has done the best for his country and for Tirana's citizens...

Tirana resident after Edi Rama's election as World Mayor 2004

Technical Utopia: Tirana after Communism

Perhaps a celebration of Tirana's mayor, Edi Rama, is an inappropriate introduction to a publication of the Berlage Institute's research studio Tirana, a Modern European Capital. Nevertheless, Rama's election as the World Mayor in 2004 is unmistakable evidence of a phenomenon that has emerged in Tirana since 2000 to the present.

This research report presents the contemporary situation in Tirana and anticipates its future developments. In an attempt to describe Albania and Tirana during the Communist regime, the interview with Edi Rama that follows can be seen as a medium to guide western readers through a complex historical situation in the Balkans, and particularly in Albania. Enver Hoxha's regime was perhaps the most severe communist experiment in the European history, with devastating consequences for the Albanian culture, life, and development. From late 1940s until the mid 1980s, Hoxha completely isolated Albania from the world, exercising utopian communist strategies that resulted in the erasure of everything outside his ideology. In the 1990s, after the fall of the Berlin Wall, Albania underwent a transition – a radical liberation movement expressed in the extreme anarchistic behavior of the majority of population.
When, in 2000, Edi Rama became mayor of Tirana, it was probably the worst possible job one could take.

Edi Rama
Boris Groys
Slavoj Žižek
Elia Zenghelis
Pier Vittorio Aureli
Hans Blankenburg

RANDIĆ & TURATO : THE ARCHITECTURE OF TRANSITION

Kenneth Frampton, Darko Glavan, Vedran Mimica
Arhitekst, Zagreb, 2010

Vedran Mimica : Architecture of Transition and the Production of Meaning

TIRANA METROPOLIS

Berlage Institute research report
2004

Vedran Mimica : Technical Utopia : Tirana After Communism

One may perhaps theorize, following Boris Groys' discourse, about the technical experience of Utopia: 'if you only know how to get to Utopia it is inoperative, but if you know how to get in and then out again, it is operational; it is technical.'[105] This going in and coming out is a post-communist experience that should be understood as a completion of the communist experience. To forget Utopia means to forget technical knowledge. It is precisely this technical Utopian knowledge – political wisdom and tactical brilliance linking the aesthetic experience to real human conditions – that allowed Edi Rama to construct a miracle in Tirana in only four years.

Slovenian philosopher Slavoj Žižek's concept of a "third way" is a projection of a new way of dealing with capitalism after communism in Russia. He argues that late capitalism is equally devastating for Russian society as was communism. Perhaps only Edi Rama, the mayor of Tirana, is creating an alternative, third way of development through his urban and social policies as real applications of technical aspect of utopian knowledge. One would hope that all these efforts would redirect and manipulate the strong currents of global capital flows into the creation of an authentic and specific architectural and civic culture, which will contribute to European cultural exchange. The invention of new realities might not be a mission impossible in Tirana.

The Berlage Institute staff and participants were deeply inspired by working with Rama and his staff to pursue radical changes in the development of the city of Tirana. We sympathize with the painful lack of understanding of the Albanian situation expressed by some European critics and aim to support them in their attempt to gain insights into the policies of Edi Rama. Elia Zenghelis initiated the Berlage Studio in Tirana with persuasive power and imagination. Dutch Ambassador Hans Blankenburg and the Ministry of Foreign affairs conceptually and financially supported the project, and Deutsche Gesellschaft für Technische Zusammenarbeit GTZ supported the Summer Academy. We are deeply grateful for their trust in the Berlage Institute's productive imagination.

Publication presents the visions of Berlage Institute participants for the new European capital at a precise moment in the history of Tirana. The approach of the studio was super-contextual – presented as an exercise in deep understanding of the Albanian context. This knowledge was superimposed with the advanced theories and methodologies from the Berlage Institute. With the intensive guidance of tutors Elia Zenghelis and Pier Vittorio Aureli, five team projects for the development of Tirana's urban structure, as well as two designs for parks, have been developed. Projects for the City of Tirana and the Great Lake Park debate the conceptual and strategic premises for the development of the regulatory plan for Tirana. The project for the Central Park might be the first realized urban intervention on the basis of the Berlage studio investigations.

---

[105] From a transcript of Groys's lecture at the Domus workshop in Zagreb, 2004.

SIX ANSWERS ON ALBANIA
BY VEDRAN MIMICA

Questions by Gudrun Hausegger and Gabriele Kaiser for www.nextroom.at, 2010

Vedran Mimica, currently director of the Berlage Institute in Rotterdam, is an outstanding connoisseur of the Balkans. As he was serving as an advisor to Edi Rama, the charismatic mayor of Tirana, he is the right person to provide glowing reference on Albania, too.

Q   Which books would you recommend to read in order to get a deeper understanding of the Balkans?

VM If it was only one for the "beginners," then I would recommend Robert D. Kaplan's Balkan Ghosts: A Journey through History. Kaplan is an American journalist who traveled through the Balkans during the "pre-large catastrophe" in the late 1980s and early 1990s. His political travelogue fully deciphers the Balkans' ancient passions and intractable hatreds for outsiders. The book is the most insightful and timely work on the relation between history and the contemporary madness found in the Balkans. For more advanced readers, I would suggest the complete oeuvre of the Croatian writer Miroslav Krleža. In his novels, dramas, essays, letters, speeches, and poems he covers the entire 19th and 20th century relations of the Austro-Hungarian Empire and the Balkan states, focusing on the two great wars. Krleža is an erudite author who covers the entire cultural production of the region in the socio-political context of the time.

Q   As a Croatian architecture critic and currently the director of the Dutch Berlage Institute, how would you describe your relationship to Albania and its capital Tirana?

VM Edi Rama, the mayor of the city, invited me to Tirana in 2004 – an invitation, based on the imagination of Elia Zenghelis, who was a member of the international jury for the city center's master plan a year earlier. Zenghelis believed that the Berlage Institute could work with the municipality of Tirana on the „vision" for the new European capital. Tirana is the young capital city of a twentieth-century state whose inhabitants rank amongst the oldest Europeans. Tirana was a small-scale city of serene beauty, grand infrastructure, and early modernism – where, after the Second World War, time stood still for nearly half a century. Since the collapse of the notorious and unique communist regime that had isolated the country from the rest of the world, the city underwent some 13 years of uncontrollable growth and thoughtlessly aggressive development, threatening its survival as both a city and sustainable environment; during this short period, its population tripled and so did its size, reflecting the tremendous energy release that had accumulated during half a century of repression. Thanks to the city's enlightened governance, this energy has turned into a drive that for architects (among others) constitutes the most ideal framework for the construction of a model, modern European state. Indeed, contrary to other Eastern European states that emerged after the collapse of communism, Albania eagerly anticipated its future with optimism and confidence. In this context of suspended animation, we were invited by the city to provide it with a vision that would rise to the level of its expectations.

Q   To what extent do former socialist structures in Albania still continue to have an impact on contemporary processes of architecture and city planning?

VM I would add the impact on social production and civic life as well. We now know that Enver Hoxha's regime was perhaps the most severe communist experiment in the European history, with devastating consequences for Albanian culture, life, and development. From the late 1940s until the mid 1980s, Hoxha completely isolated Albania from the world by exercising utopian communist strategies that resulted in the erasure of everything outside his ideology. In the 1990s, after the fall of the Berlin Wall, Albania underwent a transition – a radical liberation movement expressed in the extreme anarchistic behavior of the majority of population.

Q How would you judge the potential of "external" city planning projects in the Balkans (such as those by Winy Maas or Dominique Perrault) versus "internal" initiatives (such as those by Co-PLAN)?

VM Here we are talking about two very different approaches, if you would agree. One is perhaps top down, including big, powerful investments and creating the mega city projects. Another is the work on new forms of architectural initiatives where the work of NGO alike structures is juxtaposed with professional architectural deliveries. This approach is much more bottom up orientated, trying to involve the civic society as a constitutive part of planning and development. The first approach is perhaps risky in terms of public or social benefits, which will be possibly achieved through the large-scale operations in an environment without the democratic control. The second approach could suffer from a form of populist determinacy, usually not helpful for creation of advanced architecture.

Q As for architecture and city planning, do you have a personal vision for Tirana – do you have one for its political or socio-political future?

VM I was serving as an adviser to Edi Rama and my views are clearly very congruent with his policies and procedures. More personally or perhaps more theoretically, I would hope that Tirana and Albania would build some third way policies, following Žižek's term, in order to create a unique culture of new forms of welfare for its citizens, after the shocking histories. If, and perhaps the question is more when, Rama wins the next general election, there will be a real chance to construct a truly unique socio-political landscape in Albania. Albania should then enter the European Union, as an example of what should have been done in the rest of the Eastern European countries during the transition from socialism to capitalism. This sounds mega-utopian, but I can commit to it fully.

A VISION BEYOND PLANNING

An interview with Tirana's Mayor Edi Rama by Joachim Declerck, Bart Melort, Vedran Mimica, Marc Ryan and Martino Tattara, conducted on November 17, 2004 for the book *Tirana Metropolis*, published by the Berlage Institute, Rotterdam 2004

Question The campaign to paint Tirana's facades that began in 2000 had an incredible impact on the city. Could you explain the context in which you became the mayor, and how you came up with the idea of repainting the facades? Why do you think this program was so successful?

Edi Rama We entered the building of the municipality of Tirana in October 2000, after exactly ten years of freedom. In 1990, when the former regime collapsed, a completely new chapter opened in the life of our city and our country. It created an incredible space of freedom for everyone – without rules, institutions or infrastructure. Albania has been experiencing a huge demographic change: the population of Tirana has increased from 230,000 to around 600,000 in ten years. (The population is still growing; because there is no instrument of census, we cannot even say precisely what the number is.) In the areas surrounding the old city – in all the suburbs that were once agricultural land – there is now a mushrooming of illegal settlements. Becoming the mayor of Tirana in 2000 meant taking on the burden of running a chaotic and depressed city. It was like a train station in a lost area of the world where everybody was waiting for a train, for a plane, for a horse, for a blank marriage, or whatever miraculous vehicle that would enable them to escape the station. It was also a city where everybody was throwing the remains of their last meals everywhere without caring; Tirana at that time was full of dust and garbage. At that train station, nobody cared who the manager or who the cleaner was; they both looked the same. So there was a total lack of credibility – a lack of trust – in all institutions. In this situation, running the city was first a matter of establishing communication with the people. We had to tell the citizens that with the October elections something was changing and still needed to change,

LIGHT CAPITAL : URBAN SCRIPTS FOR LJUBLJANA

Berlage Institute research report No.07

2005 / 2006

SIXPACK : CONTEMPORARY SLOVENIAN ARCHITECTURE

ed. Andrej Hrausky, Sixpack architects

DESSA, Ljubljana, 2005

TIRANA METROPOLIS

Berlage Institute research report

2004

and to make this change happen, someone elected by them, somewhere in this city, was preparing something. I should remind you that the municipality of Tirana in the year 2000 was a very desperate place in matters of budget, organization, structures, people, motivations, and human resources. When I walked through the corridors of the City Hall for the first time, I felt trapped inside a book by Kafka – drowning in a deep gray, with a terrible smell of smoke. There was no one single computer, but many televisions in the offices and ashtrays everywhere, revealing a total abandon of public service. So we had to give a sign of life, and establish communication with the world outside this Kafkaesque building by means of a low-budget operation. That is where the idea of color came in. It was not intended as an aesthetic intervention; it was not an artistic provocation. It was a very political action because colors could have the very strong, immediate, and direct impact we were looking for, with a very low budget. Color had the power to shock – it broke the grayness like a curtain that suddenly opens somewhere and light enters. I remember the first building – it was the beginning; after spending only one hour putting some orange on top of the gray, people started to congregate around the building as if it had been the site of a car accident. Some people were completely shocked, some were irritated, and others were just laughing. The supervisor, who was French – because this was a European Union project – stopped the painting and said, "This work cannot continue! It is scandalous because these colors are impossible! It does not conform to any European standard." That was the beginning of Tirana's path towards becoming a European capital.

Q This project was obviously influenced by your background as an artist, but it was also clearly based on a specific political idea. How do you see the relationship between your educational background and your political strategy?

ER Surely my artistic background – 40 years of watching reality through colors, drawing, and through artistic perception – informed my decision. Perhaps the decision was prepared years ago, before I ever could have imagined that I would someday have the opportunity, as a mayor, to witness the deformation of these communist era buildings. It is incredible to see how communist era buildings, without any architectural expression beyond the need for extreme functionalism, have been deformed by the people inhabiting them in their search for more space. The facades were totally empty, without any kind of architectural physiognomy or individualism, and now they are being deformed in an extremely brutal way by an anonymous deconstructivism that is the result of the achieved freedom. The residents have expanded the spaces where everyone used to live before. These changes were made without any aesthetic concern. These buildings become monuments of the lack of communication between interior and exterior, between what people do inside and what they do outside. After years of intense inner renovation and outdoor deconstruction, the city became schizophrenic. Inside, families were living according to a new standard while outside; the streets were full of the garbage and debris from the renovation works. People were throwing everything that they had to replace into the streets. The extension of their inner space was their first and last concern. The exterior appearance was not on their agenda. The result of this operation was an "archaeological" architecture. At first, we faced the situation created by the urban planning of Hoxha's regime: prefab buildings made by communist architects. Afterward, we had hundreds of thousands of architects who lived with their families, pushing with their hands from the sides and deforming the surfaces of the buildings. The colors were the third intervention. The colors had the function of transforming the city from the labyrinthine nightmare it was, into a place with a certain harmony among buildings, where you could understand where you were. My background has definitely influenced my decisions as mayor. As an artist, I have always been convinced of the power that colors can have on human beings and the power that beautiful forms can have on a community.

Q In respect to other cities in the Balkan region, we are impressed by the optimism that you have breathed over the city of Tirana. It is a specific, unexpected condition that compensates for the severe problems that the city and its population are confronted with. We feel that this optimism has been generated by the communication of a vision. Also in the studio at the Berlage Institute, we have been asked to propose an urban vision for Tirana. What is the role of a clear vision in setting up urban policies for a city today? How would you define the meaning of this vision for Tirana as a capital city in the process of European integration?

ER In Albania communist ideology was expressed in the most brutal and violent manner. This made Albania a very different case from Croatia, or from the former Soviet empire. Brutalization of the individual dignity was the result of a patriarchal version of communism, but also of a history without a democratic chapter. I strongly believe that Croatia, Slovenia or Romania, – not to talk about Poland, Hungary and the Czech Republic – have a much more comprehensive way of moving towards European integration and democratic standards. This has to do with the fact that in Albania, ideology has acted like an atomic bomb whose radiation still shows its effects. The anarchism that followed the collapse of the regime is linked to the nature of the Balkan people. They can be very individualistic, but are also keen to be absorbed by ideological dictatorship like Russian Matryoshkas: dictator after dictator, from the highest political level down to the family sphere. Regarding the necessity of a vision for the urban development of Tirana, I believe that it is difficult to act academically in these circumstances; I never have the courage to talk about our work in Tirana as something that can be taken as a model. At the same time, I think that we cannot follow models of elsewhere, because our specific reality is putting us in very different circumstances. What is happening in Tirana is the effect of the huge energy on the levels of the individual, the family, and the community, spreading like a river with no predetermined direction. This energy can and should not be stopped by any academic or legal planning process. The planning process therefore has to include the energy of the citizens in the promotion of every idea. We try to work in both directions: planning and developing without really leaning towards one or the other extreme.

Q What is interesting in the United Nations High Commissioner for Refugees policies is the recognition that after oppression and bombing of Kosovo, the redevelopment in the province went faster than in any area in the world ever affected by military conflict. It seems that there is a specific capacity for self-reinvention.

ER Yes, there is a distinctive propensity in the Balkan people to tailor their attitudes so that they can be at their best in every situation, the best promoters, and the best opponents of an idea. A friend of mine once said Albanians are like Tarzan: the most agile monkeys among monkeys and the most refined gentlemen among gentlemen. If you go to Kosovo after five years of the United Nations administration, there is no sign of an established culture of planning. You find the same illegal settlements, the same energy and disorganization spreading around as it used to be in Tirana in the 1990s. This troubled me as it was not the Albanian government, but an international administration that did not respond to what was going on in the territory. In this context, urban planning needs to be visionary but should also take into consideration the energy that is present in the context. If you try to stay too glued to the academic process, your plan will be a failure, like a constitution that has no practical application but is buried in the library.

Q After the fall of the Berlin wall in 1989, two western concepts were projected onto former socialist and eastern European countries: parliamentary democracy and free markets. It seems that while parliamentary democracy was embraced, a free market was interpreted differently. Many theoreticians believe that Western Europe did not develop in a positive direction and that the delay in the development of cities like Bucharest, Sofia, and Tirana could work to their advantage. Do you believe that this delay could help Tirana to develop in a more fertile way?

ER Within this discussion, the continuous "radiation effect" of communism on the cultural level has to be taken into account for the Albanian case. Our parliamentary democracy is still very young, and as a political system, it is not even part of our history. The current political situation is a direct result of a history in which both the concepts of political opposition and cultural alternatives were not thinkable. In the 1970s, Albania was a country that put people in prison for liking the work of Vincent Van Gogh, and that abolished the English horn from the orchestra because Albania did not have any diplomatic relations with Great Britain. Twentieth-century culture was abolished. I could not read Kafka or listen to the Beatles or to Stravinsky. What would be the result if all of this brainwashing were overlooked by parliamentary democracy? A collection of political parties with different visions and programs run by the people that served the former regime because there was no other choice. I am convinced that this has nothing to do with a kind of specific sin in the culture of the Balkan people, but it has to do with the fact that our human resources have been totally contaminated. It will take a long time to create a new political class or cultural elite. Today if we switch on a TV in Tirana or Albania, we listen to the European integration propaganda as much as we used to listen to the Red Horizon. And just as we did not oppose it in the past, we are not opposing it today. So the delay you are imagining is interesting to talk about, but it is not something physical. We have to make our lives more livable through the small and seemingly unimportant details, which are the essentials of life — not the very important theories. So I would be very skeptical about every possible discussion until we have an environment that promotes discussion and debate.

Q Looking at your political agenda, we would identify a new balance between policies of deep control and laissez-faire. It seems that in certain ways the municipality is acquiring more control, while in other ways it is opening the door to private interests and initiatives. What is your policy in this respect? How is the negotiation between private interests and the public good occurring?

ER In the years of transition, the city faced two kinds of abusers: the developers and the squatters. The first immediately recognized that the demographic change could be their fortune and invested all their money and energy into the construction of housing for the newcomers. The latter were the self-made architects that colonized the public land to build their roof. All our effort has been focused on dividing these two categories very clearly. For the developers we have been an annoyance, while for the squatters we are trying to provide a chance. The annoyance results from the need to make them understand that they cannot continue to abuse and speculate on what will be the future of the city, its environment, and its physiognomy — the place where our children and grandchildren will have to live. In relation to developers, we are trying to set up a new building standard. In the year 2000, building permissions were still granted without a concept of land management and any idea of harmony between buildings. Everybody could build what they wanted on their property without accurate static calculation and without meeting any security standard. We are also telling big developers that we will no longer accept any architectural project that does not add quality to the city. These projects need to mark the urban development of Tirana, especially in city hot spots around the center. To guarantee this quality, we have adopted the strategy of holding international competitions for important buildings. The chance, for the squatters, comes with us telling them that what they built illegally is a tradition of sorts, and can be a chance for the economical development of our city. These houses are incredible products. The people who built them are from the poorest class in society, but their houses represent a huge capital that has to be managed in their own interest and with their own economic possibilities. We have now undertaken a huge action to legalize these illegal settlements and to give these people title properties, as well as to compensate the old owners who cannot have their land back anymore. We are trying to create the possibility for everybody to start a new economic life. But even if the intention is clear, to implement the law we need a huge reform of the structures of territorial control to avoid that this law can also be a push toward new illegal development. So their houses have become title property. With this title property they have to pay a debt to the city for legalizing their building, and they have to start a business in order to start life. It is incredible to see that in these two, three, four-floor villas, incredibly poor people are thinking about where to find the next brick to make the next floor.

Q   In your first address to the students in Rotterdam, you spoke about the transition from the communist regime into freedom, and how people had conceptualized freedom as the ability to attack nature or public space. In that context, you talked about the relationship between the interior and exterior city.

ER   The fact that architecture could promote democracy and new cultural life in Tirana is linked to the transition from communism towards the European integration. There is something fundamentally problematic in our society that has to do with the relationship between human beings and nature, and with the "radiation effect" that communism has had on our cultural life. Creating the highest standards for the environment has paradoxically alienated the human being from the natural environment. These standards were created to protect the sea, forests, water sources, and air, in a country with only 600 cars during communism. In this paradox, the high environmental standards were perceived by human beings as the treasure of the enemy. And just as revolutionaries entered castles and wrecked everything in bourgeois houses, the environment was also wrecked. In 1991, exactly after the folding of the regime, people perceived that they were free, that they could move and speak freely, and that they could act freely. Like in ancient times, they destroyed castles – or schools – in order to take the stones and build their houses. They broke down the walls of hospitals; they cut trees to make space to build illegal houses. The international media treated their activity as a barbaric attitude of the wildest Balkan community, but in fact the result of 50 years of frustration and fear. It was like blowing up the bridges from where the enemy retreated, and destroying everything that reminded people of communism and of the terrible presence of the state.

Q   After the Colors Program – the painting of Tirana's facades – you began a battle against illegal construction all over the city, ordering the demolition of hundreds of illegal buildings. What was the Albanian reaction to this battle? There exist a growing desire for order and control among a large part of Tirana's society. Could this perhaps indicate that the huge wave of "anarchic liberalism" that appeared during the post-regime era might be ending?

ER   We made it clear from the beginning that we would not touch any structure that a family had built for itself, but that we would demolish every other structure built for commercial use on public land. So there has been a clear distinction and we had a clear strategy. Today we are demolishing every building that has been occupying our public spaces. We had two distinct cities, the interior city (in the apartments, the living spaces and the shopping spaces) and the exterior city – a no-man's land. We are now trying to connect the exterior and interior cities, trying to convince people that they do not need just a nice house, apartment, and living room in the middle of the garbage, but also a nice exterior – a nice street, garden, lighting, sidewalks and so on. This has helped us to work in the interest of the many and not in the interest of the few. When we started demolishing the 460-some buildings and removing 120.000 tons of concrete, of course we did not have thousands of supporters in the streets behind the bulldozers but the public support was clearly in the air. We did not make the mistake of differentiating among who had friends in the municipality or the government and who did not. They had to leave without differentiation; everybody felt that this was a just action, aiming at building a new space for the city. It was clear to everybody that when the injunction of the municipality arrived, one just had to take all of his belongings and leave. So we have been able to avoid making two basic mistakes: the first being to enter into an impossible and unjust fight by attacking houses, and the second mistake being to privilege some and be arrogant to others. So in front of everybody was a bulldozer that did not have cousins.

Q We would like to discuss the future development of the city center and greater Tirana. The plan by Architecture Studio for the city center will now be implemented. You are therefore inviting talented young European architects to work in Tirana. Is this because of a fear that Tirana could become like Warsaw, Krakow, or Prague where corporations have shaped the reality of the city in a very generic way? Do you think you will be able to persuade international architectural and planning firms to be sufficiently sensitive to the particular cultures and landscapes of Tirana?

ER This is a difficult task. I would be honored to make Tirana into the city where all the frustrations that architects have about their own cities would be impossible. We are trying not to freeze the center of Tirana, but to give developers the opportunities to develop their properties. But I hope that the implementation of this plan will not recycle the images we already know. If these towers are simply copies of the stereotypical towers we see in every city, the discontent would be deep. In the competition for the towers we hope the invited architects and participants will react to the reality of Tirana. We hope to let them build towers here that they would not be able to build elsewhere, not only because technology here is not as sophisticated as it is elsewhere, but especially because

of the specific context. We have made it clear to developers that these towers are to be the will of the architects or they will not be built. We hope that they will grow out of a dialogue with us and will bear a "sense" of the city. When the architects visited Tirana, we showed them not only the center but also the illegal settlements and some old movies to let them understand our past. I do not know what the result will be, but I hope these towers will give to the French plan what it is now missing. The plan itself has a huge potential to generate new public and green spaces as the Berlage Institute project for Central Park demonstrates. We hope that these projects bring a quality to the city that stimulates people's hope for the future. I believe what architecture can do in Tirana is fundamental for democracy, for the culture, and for the future of Albania.

Q What do you think about the collaboration between the municipality of Tirana and the Berlage Institute in terms of framing, shaping, and presenting ideas for the city of Tirana?

ER For the future of Tirana's urban development, the municipality team has been very satisfied with the sensibility of the Berlage participants and the deep understanding of the context that Elia Zenghelis and Pier Vittorio Aureli have shown from their first encounter with the city. What the studio has done is exactly what we are expecting from international partners and professionals: getting down to the context and coming out with a product that is an understanding of place and combines theoretical education and background. The result merges their experiences in Tirana with what they knew before coming here.

Q For the visitor, one of the most striking aspects of Tirana is the huge peripheral city that has formed around the historical city center. What is the specific policy of the municipality for this periphery? Is it necessary to develop a new urban policy and project?

ER There has been some criticism of the municipality's so called focus on the city center. But, we have made a huge amount of investments in the periphery. Especially in the past year we implemented designs that provided specific illegal settlements with roads, lighting systems, switches, trees, and sidewalks. These plans will help the peripheral parts of the city to integrate with the infrastructure of the city. It is important to emphasize that our plans are also dramatically subjected to the amount of resources and data available. Yet it would be a mistake to focus only on the outskirts. The city center in the end is important not only for the people living there, but also for those in the periphery, in Schodra and Saranda. So the center expresses the message about what the future of this place can be. I strongly believe the action has to be combined. At the same time, I strongly believe that with the means we have we also must promote quality. Talking about peripheral areas is talking about the context of a very poor city. A lot of work has to be done – especially in the illegal settlements. Poverty has to be solved not only with the quantity of bread delivered to the people but with the quality of images that you give them. Because trying to tackle poverty by delivering the bread without the images is a disaster – just as quality images without bread can make people very angry. People should be neither hungry nor angry.

Q What are the potentials for cooperation with other territorial bodies, both on the periphery of Tirana and nationally? Are there potential relations with, for example, the National Ministry of Planning, or some other government body?

ER Elia Zenghelis introduced the studio in Rotterdam, he pointed out that there is a general awareness of the necessity to promote control, urban planning, and sustainable development. There is also a general awareness of the high risk of investments that are not the result of urban planning, but only of capital. At the moment, we desperately need human resources; planning is not a matter of having nice ideas and producing slick PowerPoint presentations, but is strongly interwoven with the mechanisms of the state. It is a matter of citizens' awareness of the structures of economical promotion, trade control and social security. In the monumental organization of international bodies and structures that take care of underdeveloped countries in transition, there is not one paper that talks about the necessity of urban planning. This is frustrating because as mayor of Tirana one understands that urban planning is about the concept of life in a community. It is very distressing that there is not one penny of European Community funds designated for urban planning.

Q You stated that true beauty could overcome certain resistances. What do you mean by this?

ER I have to tell you about these sports fields we built in the most difficult and peripheral area of Tirana. When I became mayor there was not one road in this area, even though thousands of people lived there. When we built the roads, I asked the city council to put aside some money that we could later invest in a playing field for the kids, since having football and cars in the same streets was not an option. It was the first sports field that the municipality built in Tirana. When I asked them to create something with artificial grass and lights in a place where there was no roads and lighting, everybody opposed me, saying, "They'll break the lights and steal the artificial grass!" And I said, "Okay, but we still have to try it." This new sports field was a great success. The kids and the parents are protecting it now; it gives them pride. Shortly afterward, an international foundation invested in some sports fields at a school in the center, but the sports fields were of very low quality. Theoretically speaking, the kids in the center are more educated, yet the fields were destroyed in a month. This is a case that reveals the importance of the quality of the image, and the power that quality images can have in a community.

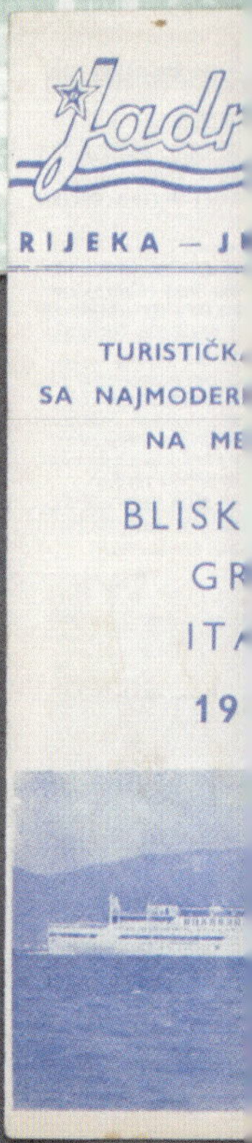

Jadrolinija, Yugoslavia

Rijeka, 1966

INDESEM 88

photograph

Split, 1988

INDESEM '88

reports
Faculty of Architecture,
Delft University of Technology

Split, 1988

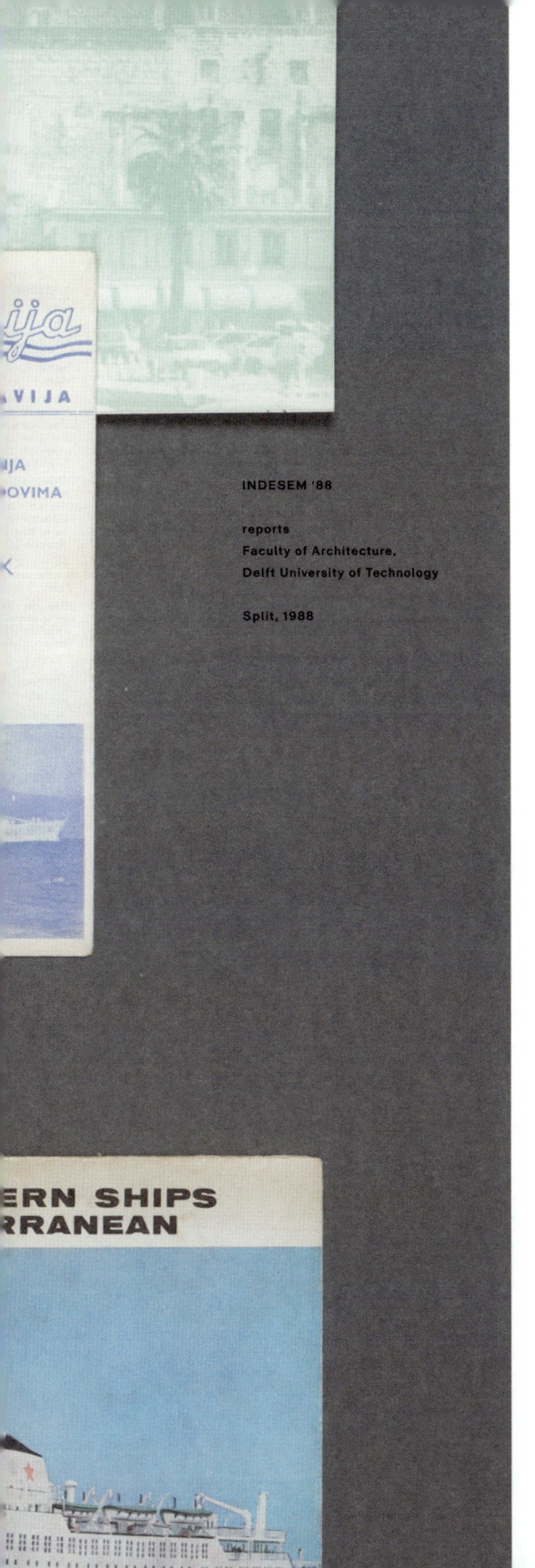

TOURISTS IN THEIR HOME TOWNS

Based on the interview by Kristina Jerkov for the on-line magazine Analitika, Kotor 2014

Professor Vedran Mimica is the Associate Dean of Research at the Illinois Institute of Technology (IIT) College of Architecture in Chicago. He has worked on a number of research studies and projects on contemporary architectural expression and heritage, most of which were done in Croatia. He also taught at this year's Architecture Prison Summer School (APSS) in Kotor, Montenegro, which is a part of the Kotor Art event. Behind the unusual title of his lecture, (Don't) Try This at Home, is a story about globalized tourist industry – a phenomenon we are all familiar with – and its effects on local communities. Especially the effects of tourist resorts that have been spawning across the Montenegrin coast over the last few years and that will spread to the north of our country, if one is to believe the announcements made by the government.

'Tourism is the leading industry of today's world, employing over 280 million people and contributing to 10% of of the world GDP. WTTC's latest annual research, in conjunction with partner Oxford Economics, shows Travel & Tourism's contribution to world GDP grew for the sixth consecutive year in 2015, rising to a total of 9.8% of world GDP (US$7.2 trillion). The sector now supports 284 million people in employment – that's 1 in 11 jobs on the planet'.[106] The feeling that we are all tourists is quite overwhelming. Statistics show that 13% of the world population are tourists and that 12% of BDP is generated by tourism. This means that tourism is a large industry that greatly affects the development of many countries. In addition, tourism is a global phenomenon. Some define tourism as the "people's binary wish to trade something commonplace for something uncommon or extraordinary". It is that wish that makes us tourists. Global, mass tourism –

[106] Source: www.wttc.org/research/economic-research/economic-impact-analysis Copyright @ WTTC 2016, accessed October 7, 2016

exercised for years by countries such as Spain and Italy — is slowly fading away and is no longer appropriate for the year 2014, because it has created a sort of mono-cultural tourism, an aspect of global tourism that has increasingly been challenged. Alternatives have taken many forms: congress tourism, environmental tourism, rural, cultural, religious, event, medical, and gay (LGBT) tourism. All these forms treat the host area in a completely different way than mass tourism.

Two countries, Costa Rica and Norway have made the greatest progress in what we could term as sustainable tourism. In fact, it has reached massive proportions in these two countries but has remained sustainable in the way tourist facilities are distributed in the host countries and the way tourists are allowed to relate to genuine local communities and values. What do we mean by sustainability? There is no single definition, as it involves a balance between three factors: economy, society, and environment. Tourism that is economically successful is likely to endanger the social and environmental parts of the equation. Eco-tourism will probably not be as successful economically. Sustainable development involves interdependency and requires a serious strategic approach. The Berlage Institute worked on one of the Matra projects by the Dutch ministry of foreign affairs that we called Croatian Archipelago New Lighthouses. The primary focus of this project was not tourism but social transformation of a country acceding the European Union. The project was the result of collaboration between the Croatian Architects' Association and the Berlage Institute and led to a simple yet interesting conclusion. If you associate local development with tourism, then you should first have in mind the people who live there. Not only because local residents often become tourists in their own towns, but because you want to create a place that encourages a productive relationship between tourists and residents. This kind of relationship is possible where the interests of the hosts and guests go hand in hand. What this exactly means is hard to tell. But it definitely does not mean that all local population should be cooking and waiting at tables and that all foreigners should be guests. It is rather a kind of cohabitation of the two. This model of tourism will probably grow in the years to come. The guests will feel less like "guests" and locals less like "hosts." Having this in mind, we should also be aware that leisurely holidays such as long summer beach vacations are growing scarce and that tourism has increasingly become work-related. This is why models such as congress, medical, event, cultural, and environmental tourism attract professionals.

The resort concept

East Adriatic development strategies should consider coastal towns as the key generators of alternative forms of tourism to tourist resorts. At the moment, nearly every coastal district in Croatia plans to build at least two resorts. Most of the towns have a population of less than 2000 people. Clearly, these plans are overambitious and we are lucky that they have not even started. As a model, the resort has had success in the third-world countries of the tropical and subtropical belt, whose climate allows for the season to last year-round. A group of the Berlage Institute researchers analyzed the economic effects of resorts in the Caribbean and concluded that only 13% of the profit remains in the country — Dominican Republic in this particular case — whereas 87% goes to international tour operators. I do not know if this is the case with Montenegro, but something tells me it could be. When I discussed this issue with one of TUI's executives — TUI being one of the world's leading tour operators — at the Rotterdam Biennale, he told me that the figures were not so much in favor of global capital and that we should understand the global reasons for building resorts around the world, considering that TUI alone has more than 140 million clients. I said that I did understand, but that he too should understand the local communities in which these resorts are built. The Berlage Institute worked with Markus Miessen and Tina di Carlo on a study that investigated how a resort can generate the economic development of the

Atlantic coast in northeastern Brazil, provided there is a parallel plan for the development of the local economy in respect to the resort. They came up with a strategy to micro-finance local population in the production sector in preference to services. The idea was for the resort to become a generator of local economy instead of feeding on global economy like a parasite. This kind of strategy requires a fine ear to tune up the interests of local population and tour operators; something that is seldom seen in the global tourist industry.

Tour operators, developers, and local communities

There are models of tourism development that have improved the relationship between local residents and guests, but these are still outside the scope of big tour operators and developers. And there is so much to learn about the tourist industry by looking at how Club Med develops resorts. Club Med is one incredibly interesting and successful company specialized in resort development. The Berlage Institute worked on a research project on year-round resort that would be less than one hour and a half flight away from Paris. We selected the town of Vrsar on the west Istrian coast. Our idea was to set up a resort that would produce energy instead of wasting it and the guests would also work there in a way. People at Club Med found the idea intriguing but added that the market was not ready for this kind of progressive thinking. Still, they liked great many of our ideas about using and saving local resources, such as the frugal use of water for golf courses or use of land in property to produce food for the resort. The problem lies in the climate on the east Adriatic coast, with only 90-odd days of warm weather. This problem is even greater as the tourist season does not even last that long. To have a year-round tourist season, the coastal towns need a program that would also involve their residents. I refer to courses for foreign students, I refer to congresses, events, seasonal employment of non-residents and medical tourism for the elderly from the European Union. For this you need a critical mass of coastal town residents who share this idea and who are willing to put a stop to hibernation of their hometowns over the winter. The case in point is Dubrovnik, with the stark contrast between summer and winter and practically a suicidal practice of selling out real estates in the old town to people who will not spend there more than a month or two over the year. The Dubrovnik old city thus counts less than 800 residents in the winter and is no more than an abandoned museum. In contrast, towns like Rijeka, Split, and Zadar, with the critical mass much higher than that of Dubrovnik, are slowly getting the hang of the idea of year-round urban tourism that is different from resort or hotel-type tourism.

The first tourist resorts date back to the late 19th century. In England, Belgium, the Netherlands, and France they were a reaction to the negative impacts of the industrial revolution. People from industrial cities resorted to the quiet of small towns. This basic idea seems to extend to the resort models of the future. However, in this part of Europe we will not be able to really talk about sustainable tourism for a long time. I do have faith in certain "recipes" for change, but, regrettably, have to admit that tourist industry is not ready to accept them. We first need to accept that students, business and retired people are also tourists. The demographic structure of Europe is disastrous. Over the next two decades Europe will have an enormous number of retired people. I am against ghettos for the retired of Northern Europe on the Adriatic. Although, we have to realize that the European demographic structure and real estate market will see fundamental changes. And even the mayors of Croatian small towns may soon be foreigners, which is something unthinkable at the moment. However, it is happening in Spain, where the mayor of Ibiza is a German, elected by the majority of its residents. This is a shift toward democratization and modernization that replaces local with European standards, but here in Croatia or Montenegro, a German national would hardly even run for, let alone be elected mayor. A little while ago, Sweden appointed a 27-year-old woman of Bosnian origin as the new minister of education. She immigrated to Sweden as a refugee in 1995, when she was five. This kind of political openness is simply out of the question in South East Europe, yet it is crucial for its future.

BERLAGE T
ZAGREB S
AND NEW LI

METROPOLITAN FRAMEWORKS
Zagreb 1996
ZAGREB, TAKE A NAP
Zagreb 1996
A CONVERSATION WITH KENNETH FRAMPTON
Zagreb 1996
URBAN RULES
Zagreb 1996
"NEW" NEW ZAGREB
Zagreb 1996
SMALL CHANGES
Zagreb 1999

DEMOCRATIZATION OF PUBLIC SPACE
Zagreb 1999
MARE NOSTRUM
Rotterdam 2005
NEW LIGHTHOUSES
Split 2005
CROATIA — THE MEDITERRANEAN AS IT COULD BE
Zagreb 2005
SPACE IS THE BASIC CROATIAN RESOURCE
Zagreb 2008
INTERVIEW AT DAZ
Zagreb 2012

TRANSFERS, SEMINARS LIGHTHOUSES

The texts in this section gives an account of the Berlage educational postgraduate program and how it was inseparable from my architectural and urban research production, curatorial practices, publication, and transfer of new knowledge and experience from both the European and global environment towards the urban developments in Croatia.

During the 1990s a group of architects from Slovenia, Croatia and Serbia enrolled in postgraduate studies at the Berlage. The Berlage idea was that, after their studies, these architects could be ideally engaged in urban developments in the cities and countries which they originated from. Therefore, I passionately engaged in a support of this generation by inventing and introducing different forms of public architectural and cultural formats linking local governmental and non-governmental institutions with our alumni.

The results of these initiatives from the Berlage Institute to engage in the transitional nature of urban developments in Croatia are presented in the following chapter.

The studies on Zagreb urbanity stem from the observation that the city has found itself in a condition of incapability to understand its urban realities through a single set of imposed values, as the city seeks definition of its post-yugoslav status in the new geopolitical, social and cultural realm.

In Zagreb Seminars[107] the city was envisioned as a new European capital as it transitioned

[107] There were altogether three Zagreb Urban Planning seminars. The first (Frames of the Metropolis, 1995) and the second (Frames of the Metropolis – Urban Rules, 1996) resulted in the book Frames of the Metropolis. Zagreb Urban Planning Seminars 1995&1996 (edited by Vladimir Mattioni, published by the City of Zagreb and the Office for Development Planning and Environmental Protection in 1996). The third seminar titled Frames of the Metropolis – Small Changes took place in 1999.

along with the series of urban fragments located between its historical center and the modernist peripheries. The aim was to investigate this urban fabric and try to imagine "new newness" as visions for the future of the city. These visions should then ideally fertilize imagination of politicians, investors, architects and citizens of Zagreb.

Croatian Archipelago New Lighthouses project deals with the fundamental issue of creating a sustainable coastal development strategy within the transitional socioeconomic environment. The project anticipates tourism as the generator of a process of social transformation, and the development of cities and landscapes along the Croatian coastline. Project focus is on decaying and neglected sites at seven coastal cities which should ideally turn into the lighthouses of social changes. Conceptually all projects should primarily improve the city infrastructures while simultaneously improving basis for tourist industry.

Within Croatia's distinct post-socialist experiences, the studies introduce the influence of civil society as a fundamental element for carrying out development plans through democratic and transparent processes. Therefore, the new planning methods presented by the New Lighthouses project include transitional changes in governing systems and civil society, helping Croatia to understand and accept concepts of social, economic and ecological sustainability in development. It is important that the urban culture continues to converse with its historical ties, in the reality of foreign investments and localized architectural production.

METROPOLITAN FRAMEWORKS

Published in Frames of the Metropolis, City of Zagreb and the Office for Development Planning and Environmental Protection, Zagreb 1996

The City of Zagreb Office for Development Planning and Environmental Protection and the Berlage Institute Amsterdam, Postgraduate School of Architecture, are inviting an international group of young, devoted architects and professional figures of prestige (as guest lecturers and critics) to the Frames of the Metropolis, Zagreb urban planning seminar, from 17 to 22 April 1995.

As the end of the century is approaching, Zagreb, as a city in a peripheral European condition (in between European community and turbulent east), is framing a strategic territory for metropolitan development. This process could be based only within a global scenario of inevitable physical and electronic links to the rest of the European common market and cultures.

The Zagreb urban tradition bridges 900 years of city development within western European context with a clearly readable set of historical urban layers. The seminar will reflect upon that Zagreb urban tradition and try to imagine a new newness.

Today, in a post-socialist condition within a heterogeneous social and cultural realm, the city of Zagreb can no longer understand its urban realities through a single conceptual construction or a single set of established values. The seminar will have to anticipate the discontinuous nature of what we call "reality". The use of these (existing) realities will not disguise the fact that the urban planning almost always involves the invention of another reality.

In the new economical and political conditions of Zagreb, a concept of public domain should be redefined. New urban planning strategies could imagine collective spaces which are neither public nor private, but both at the same time. Public spaces absorbed by private users, or private spaces used by the collective. A city railway as a public transport network is a collective space par excellence and a fundamental element of metropolitan life.

Seminar work studios will operate within a central area of a city along a railroad. The site consists of a series of urban fragments located between the historical center and the modern peripheries. The site is a sort of a "zone of disturbance", a zone of urban voids and interstitial areas. However, the area of the city north of the railway could be characterized as stable, with certain historical or symbolic weight, a sort of rootedness and permanence (as inevitable conditions for usual perception of urbanity). South of the railway are a series of atmospheres governed by instability, movement, fragility and mobility. The site of the project bridges from the Zagreb west railway terminal to the Oil Factory and is 3.5 km long and 1-2 km wide.

Today, in the highly unstable and hybrid conditions of contemporary realities, it is almost inappropriate to determine a singular assignment for the seminar. Rather, we wish to introduce a series of frames of different qualities and aims as possible issues to be tackled within the project.

Urbanism vs. Architecture Operating predominantly within the urban planning domain, the project has to liberate itself from the atavistic notions of urbanism and architecture as separate activities. The substance of the project will be the answer to such dilemmas as: urban planning or anti-urban planning, order or disorder, and continuity or discontinuity. The project has to face the contemporary chaos lucidly, perhaps without giving up the establishment of (necessarily unstated) principles of order. The project has to establish a relation between the general and particular, system and fragment, city and object. It has to introduce a capacity for simultaneous seeing the object as a city and the city as topography.

Territory Within the flexible edges of a given site, the project should anticipate critical research into territories with potential, and mark fields that could accommodate metropolitan processes. A series of sub-territories and places could be established that have their own vitality and certain quantities.

FRAMES OF THE METROPOLIS:
ZAGREB URBAN PLANNING
SEMINARS 1995 & 1996

Horetzky, Zagreb, 1996

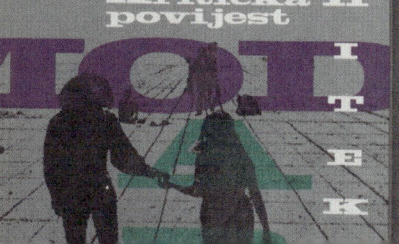

PROJECT ZAGREB : Transition as
Condition, Strategy, Practice

Eva Blau and Ivan Rupnik
Actar, Barcelona, 2007

Vedran Mimica : Tendencies

ZAREZ, I/6

Zagreb, 1999

Democratization of public space,
interview with Vedran Mimica

CASE STUDY 16
Frames of the Metropolis: Transition as Practice

Between 1995 and 1999, architects and planners in the Municipal Department for City Development Planning and Environment Protection organized a series of annual seminars under the rubric Frames of the Metropolis to create new urban strategies and make scenarios for the future city. The "frames" in the title were intended to designate both a range of vantage points and a conceptual field that would encompass both local and global perspectives, resulting in a spectrum of readings and projections. By focusing on interstitial zones—conceived spatially and temporally—the seminars sought to understand the modalities of change, growth, and decay that have characterized Zagreb's urban development. The seminars generated a series of design workshops in the late 1990s for private developments in which the Association of Croatian Architects (UHA) was, and continues to be, heavily involved. Several projects rework and expand transitional strategies of the past.
The Frames of the Metropolis workshops educated two generations of architects (the last socialist-trained and first postsocialist-trained) about the possible methods of operating in the new transitional environment. The "teacher" in these workshops was truly the city, both the real, lived city and the virtual city of unrealized plans and unsatisfied desires. The participants in the workshops in the mid-1990s are now the architects working in and on the city.

MODERN ARCHITECTURE :
A CRITICAL HISTORY

Kenneth Frampton

Globus, Zagreb, 1992

Urban typologies The project could anticipate the formation of a series of hybrid urban typologies to express sets of tensions which new realities could be articulated with and new programs accommodated.

Urban Programs The project could suggest several new urban programs such as hypermarkets, fairs, stadiums, large car parks, cinepolis, shopping malls, floating markets, new industries, gastronomic exchange, etc., as well as standard urban programs like housing, offices, shopping, and hotels. The project should provide the right conditions for interaction, and design urban territories and typologies for allocation of these programs.

Density A future of urban planning in Zagreb will basically depend on issues of quantity. The project has to research the potentials of new space and anticipate future densities in terms of m2/m2, ideas/m2, ambitions/m2, dreams/m2, $/m2...

Voids The site of the project is a configuration of urban voids or interstitial areas. The project has to articulate and structure these "negative" spaces. The void-space and cityscape may be a "controllable" form of the project with crucial importance for public or collective programs.

Public transport – metropolitan infrastructure The project has to anticipate "technical manipulation" of the city railway lines for intensification and diversification of related territories and its potentials.

Time Time as a process has to be anticipated within the project and certain material organizations or plans should embody a notion of change and some sort of topographical flexibility.

Final frame We hope that seminar work studios will operate from the perspective of Zagreb citizens and supporters yet initiate a critical process of re-establishing the need for visions for the future of the city. These visions should then fertilize the imagination of politicians, investors, architects and citizens of Zagreb.

FRAMES OF THE METROPOLIS:
ZAGREB URBAN PLANNING
SEMINARS 1995 & 1996

Horetzky, Zagreb, 1996

ACTES DU COLLOQUE:
URBICIDE - URGENCES -
DURABILITE: RECONSTRUCTION
ET MEMOIRE

Geneva: Institut d'Architecture
de l'Universite de Geneve, 2005

Vedran Mimica
East-West: Blurring Territories

ZAGREB, TAKE A NAP

Published in Frames of the Metropolis, City of Zagreb and the Office for Development Planning and Environmental Protection, Zagreb 1996

The Berlage Institute Team: Vedran Mimica, B. K. Boley, Robin Limmroth, Tamara Roy and Dimitri Waltritsch

Intro

We hope to provide a modest contribution to the seminar in the manner of a conceptual approach or device for further thinking about this growing city with an enormous empty lot right in the center of it.

We are offering a way to consider an open space in the city's geography and future history which is full of opportunities, expectations, and pitfalls.

City in Waiting

Looking around us, we saw that Zagreb is a city in waiting. There is a gap between the aspirations the city has for itself and the means available to achieve those aspirations. We recognize that when investment does happen, it should not be unrestricted and only cater to today's short term needs but instead take into account in a civic manner that future realities will inevitably change.

Zagreb Take a Nap

Our working title is Zagreb Take a Nap. But napping is not just falling asleep; it is preparing oneself for waking up. Some people want to sleep a short time, some for a long time. If you want to take a short nap, you need to make preparations before you rest.

Everything should be arranged and ready to go. If you are planning on a longer sleep then you can take your time, make your bed nicely, and dream about your future decisions while you rest undisturbed.
Some people never sleep.

When a City Takes a Nap

So, if a city prepares to take a nap, what is the first thing it needs? A pillow.

Urban Pillows

Pillows have the advantage of being able to reserve area for something else while dressing the space up a little bit. They can also make a particular spot more comfortable + appealing to occupy. And they can easily be moved, adjusted or compressed.
Within the corridor structure of Zagreb, we have laid down a field of urban pillows, which create spheres of interventions, preparations and processes. The city is a great bed where sleepers with strong dreams and ideas search the site for the right pillow. Their aspirations can be the activating elements of the area. Some dreams are grand and require global interest and support while others came from the values and desires that stir within the community.

Sites for Pillows

To determine where and where not to place the pillows, we did a subjective assessment of the site. We looked at some areas of decay and denial. Areas of misuse, under-use and over-use.

Areas of civic disproportion and contradiction. And we looked at those hungry areas waiting to be satisfied and areas already awake which did not need pillows. These are all the areas of possibility and potential.

Pillow Plan

Our pillow plan locates areas and ideas which are close to waking up as well as those reserved for longer sleep. It is an attempt to show the actors in different phases of desired readiness.

Some of the hot spots marked on the diagram are just the consequential development of conditions already present on the site. For others, a punctual injection was chosen in order to stimulate a new process of development.

Types of Pillows

Ready to Wake

The ready to wake pillows prepare an area to be more attractive and comfortable for development and investment, which means a certain level of infrastructure should be provided.

Most areas we have marked orange are already near this level of infrastructure. In other words, it would not be too expensive or difficult for the city to achieve this in the ready to wake areas shown.

Sweet Dreams

The sweet dreams pillows reserve areas of the site while covering them with a temporary role in the city. The minimum effort required to satisfy the territory is all that is necessary for preparations. In this way, territories or processes in decay or abandonment can be prepared to become places of use and worth.

These pillows are used to buffer, or direct, development by the reservation and preparation of open spaces. To insure that sweet dream areas can be managed over a longer period of time, an occupying idea or program must reserve it. This is essential in order to allow Zagreb the chance to consider processes as they unfold in the future.

Ghosts and Sleeping Beauties

These two are two types of deep sleepers:

1. Ghosts

Ghosts are temporary users of the pillows. They are programs, landscapes, etc. that will temporarily satisfy the areas, and thus reserve the open space. These ghosts are already floating around in a site. You must stir up existing ghosts.

2. Sleeping beauties

These are dream ideas strong enough to make the community want to keep its future places undisturbed. Ghosts can occupy the pillows until the sleeping beauties awake.

What is sleeping next to you?

As pillows awaken we assume that over time they may activate pillows beside them. As awake of ones will grow, they will search out connections to other active areas and enhance the networks of the city.

Final Comment

To take one's time for development by strategically achieving free zones for future use is a highly controversial act in a reality that shows accelerating optimization of use. This device offers an aggressive defense in order to gain a freedom not from something, but a freedom to do something.

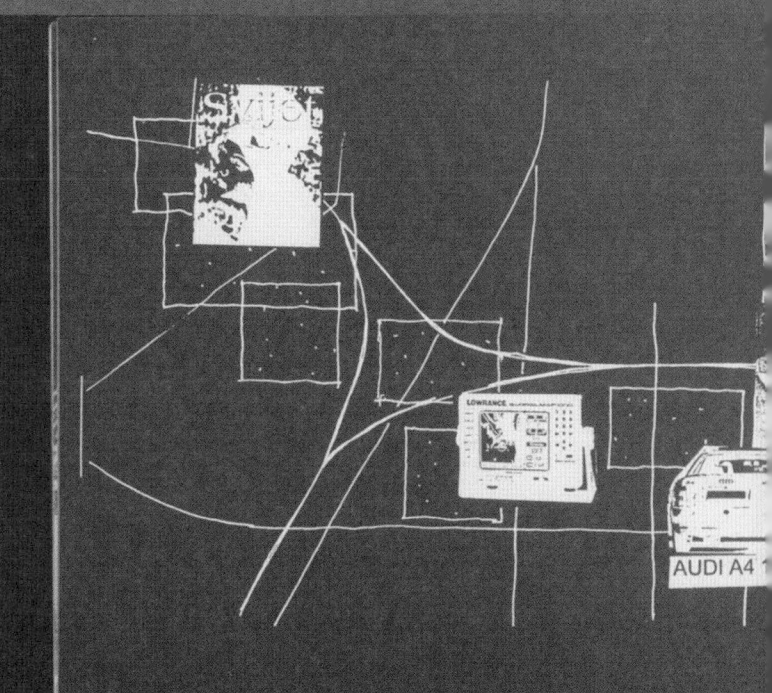

READY TO WAKE UP AREAS

train every 15 minutes • tram ever
• parking areas • $$ • global compu
investment money • tax incentives
lights • electricity • water • sewer •

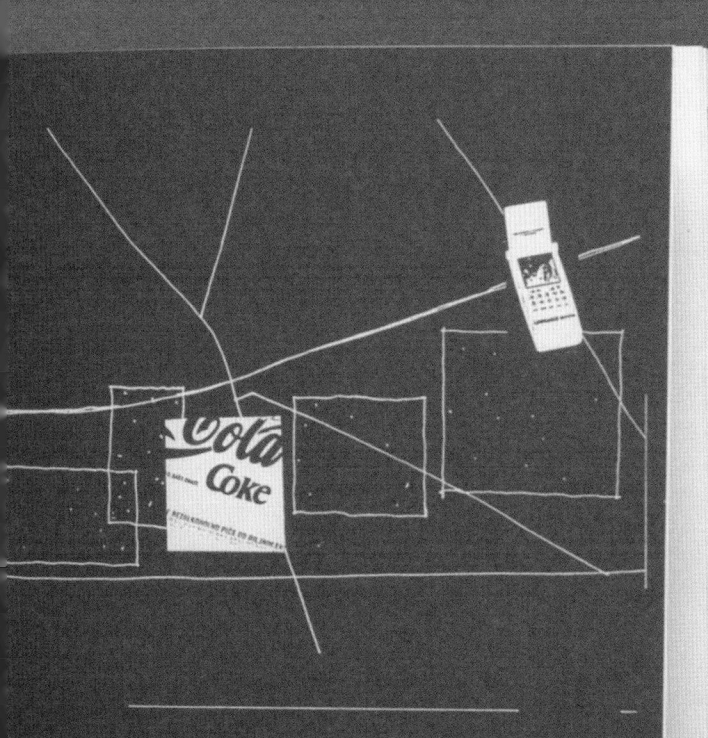

**FRAMES OF THE METROPOLIS:
ZAGREB URBAN PLANNING
SEMINARS 1995 & 1996**

Horetzky, Zagreb, 1996

Zagreb, Take a Nap Project

Vedran Mimica, B. K. Boley,
Robin Limmroth, Tamara Roy
and Dimitri Waltritsch

A CONVERSATION WITH KENNETH FRAMPTON

Published in Frames of the Metropolis, City of Zagreb and the Office for Development Planning and Environmental Protection, Zagreb 1996; based on the conversation with Nada Beroš, Miće Gamulin, Vladimir Gudac, Aleksandar Laslo, Vladimir Mattioni, Vedran Mimica and Feđa Vukić.

Question   Last week we tried to decipher what was supposed to be the new urban strategy for Zagreb as a town with metropolis potential. A great amount of energy from young architects was used, with the goal of forming a frame for the metropolis Zagreb on the location of the two modern Zagreb towns – the one from the time of the railway, and the other from the automobile time. After all those efforts, where your personal contribution was of great significance, is it possible to say something more about the identity of Zagreb?

Kenneth Frampton   For obvious reasons it is difficult for an outsider to give an adequate answer. In more general terms this split between two different modes of urbanization is an inherent conflict that it intrinsically resists any easy resolution. It is obviously difficult to integrate the relative stability of the capitalist metropolis fed by rail, with the dynamism of the multi-national capitalist megalopolis fed by automobile. It remains miraculous that cities like Helsinki, Copenhagen and Barcelona have been able to achieve some sort of symbiosis between these different forms of urbanization. While some tendency towards high-rise "Manhattanization" remains throughout the developed world it is perhaps less prevalent today than in the 1970s and 1980s due to the introduction of computers and downsizing of corporations and bureaucracies. However, the "historical delay" in places like Zagreb may provoke a certain amount of high-rise speculation that ought in my view be resisted or at least contained as the French did on Paris in La Défense or the Front de Seine where they sequestered the high rise form in two main clusters, except for the unfortunate anomaly of the Tour Montparnasse. Needless to say this response does not treat with the issue of identity that may lie behind the question.

Q   When you talk about the level of architecture, you point out some architects who iconize their architecture and the other side when constructions pretend to poeticize. If that signifies the point which can help us to value architecture, what that aspiration to poeticize means, how can we be sure that one architecture is valuable and the other is not?

KF   This question is not less difficult since it evokes the issue of taste. Since the end of the seventeenth century we have acknowledged that universal positive beauty could only mean geometry, precision of execution and richness of materials. Aside from any arbitrary beauty or "stile" buildings may be subtly inflected and enriched in terms of style, light access, mode of entry and even in terms of tradition. All these inflections may be developed as poetic articulations as opposed to works which are exclusively determined from a functional, economic or productive standpoint. However, buildings may also be reductive in an aesthetic sense in that the building is reduced to a seductive image, to a "decorated shed" in which there is nothing beyond the envelope or skin; formalism in fact. We may add to this Walter Benjamin's insight that ordinary people experience architecture as a state of distraction. I take this to mean that while the full cultural resonance of a work may not be legible to the uninitiated, they are nonetheless susceptible to its subliminal aspects at the unconscious level. Experience indicates that people sometimes feel at ease in quite abstract spaces without knowing why. I think that a truly mature architecture should have different levels of meaning inscribed within it, so that it may be appreciated by different subjects at different levels.

Q   When you talk about the optimum level, which means that one part of society has the same language of architecture that recognizes certain values, than we are talking about the elite, you call it laconic architecture. In Croatia it covers very small number of people and we should wait for about ten years before it becomes the dominant language of our production.

KF This raises the issue of the societal status of architecture in a given country, at a particular time. In the first four decades of this century there were moments, particularly among the new nations of Europe after the First World War, when modern architecture was ideologically representative of the cultural and political identity of the nation. Two different modernizing industrial states from this period come to mind, Finland and Czechoslovakia. They each produced a distinctive architecture that was expressive of their aspirations and circumstances; an articulated syntax that immediately gave the lie, so to speak, to the homogeneity of the so-called International Style. Even today, one encounters different national priorities with regard to architecture and this, by necessity, encourages the public to see architecture differently. Every public building of consequence that is opened in Barcelona is an occasion for local celebration. Thousands of people attended the vernissage of Richard Meier's Museum of Modern Art in Barcelona when it stood, as it still does now without its collection. In Finland, since its inception, the identity of the state has always been tied up with architecture and the same has long been the case in the Netherlands where the government spends an enormous amount of money on architecture and sponsors among other things a National Institute for Architecture and an annual publication featuring the best buildings of the year. In such countries the state evidently accords a value to architecture that is missing, such as England, for example, where it has taken over twenty years to build a national library. Such a national reluctance to build the institutions of the nations would be unthinkable in France, where from the time of Valéry Giscard d'Estaing onwards the French state has placed an enormous emphasis on architecture and urbanism extending from the realization of the Center Pompidou to the recent achievement of the Bibliothèque nationale. On the other hand, throughout the period 1945-1965 French architecture languished in a state of total decadence, under the aegis of the moribund École des Beaux-Arts and it was only after the student revolt of 1968 that everything changed. Throughout the regime of François Mitterrand the state organized competitions for young architects when even the second and third prize winners were given a small commission. Unfortunately, such a sponsorship of architectural culture is unthinkable in a country like the United States, which seems to be locked onto a socio-political course which is totally reactionary; witness the American position at the recent international exhibition staged in Seville, where the richest nation in the world could not bring itself to pay for more than two second hand geodesic domes! If the state accords prestige to architecture then the society as a whole will take interest in its cultivation.

Q It is very unpopular that a state stands above the architecture?

KF We like to deceive ourselves into thinking that desire is an all but natural process that emerges of its own accord. Our cupidity in this regards – nothing short of astounding, given the enormous amounts of money spent on advertising. When we evoke the idea of popular culture, it is also a matter of engineering taste. That the state has come to be discredited in the former countries of the so called Eastern Block is understandable but in this, as in most matters, it is still preferable to maintain a certain balance, as Václav Havel reminds in his recent address to the responsibility of the intellectual. The end of the Cold War would seem to favor the wholesale Americanization of the planet since America clearly emerges from this as the victorious "other." What America now has to contribute culturally aside from its omnipotent media industry is another matter and in this regard it is possible to discern an American loss of confidence. I think it is true to say that American intellectuals no longer believe in the validity of its culture particularly in the realm of architecture where the post-modern condition has favored the wholesale proliferation of pluralist kitsch. The earliest stages of capitalist formation in America saw the emergence of bourgeois patrons (the so-called Robber Barons!) who entertained a vision of an American civilization and sought an architecture in which it could be realized at a level which was capable of surpassing the European

192

predavanje/lecture:
Kenneth Frampton (New York)
SVJETSKA ARHITEKTURA I REFLEKSIVNA PRAKSA
subota, 22. travnja u 14.00 sati
WORLD ARCHITECTURE AND REFLECTIVE PRACTICE
Saturday 22nd April, 2 p.m.

193   233

FRAMES OF THE METROPOLIS:
ZAGREB URBAN PLANNING
SEMINARS 1995 & 1996

Horetzky, Zagreb, 1996

basis from which it stemmed. Hence the triumph of the Beaux Arts in the United States and the quite remarkable creation of prestigious public institutions of all kinds, the state houses, the universities, the museums, the law courts, the railroad stations, the libraries, and last but not least Washington itself. To all intents and purposes this confidence in the manifest destiny of the Pax Americana came to an end with the denouement of the Vietnam War, bringing about a fiscal crisis from which America has yet to recover. It is far from clear that the new médiatique private sector will guarantee any kind of future civic patronage and from this Europe should draw its lesson.

Q   What do you think about the new environment questions and ecology and the new moment in architecture all over the world? What is your opinion about this new ecology movement and city development, since city is artificial and not natural?

KF   Well, nothing is purely natural anyway since the species have forever been engaged in the modification of nature for its own purposes. As far as architecture and urbanism are concerned one of the key issues in all this is land settlement pattern; that is to say the question of how close people are prepared or able to live together and the related counter issues of density and speculative suburban subdivision. The distinguished Austrian architect Roland Rainer has been preoccupied with the low-rise, high-density housing throughout his life and has been able to demonstrate his thesis in built work, above all in the so called Puchenau Siedlung under continuous development on the banks of the Danube near Linz throughout the last twenty-five years. His critical, ecological attitudes is set forth in his book, Livable Environments of 1974 in which he challenges the current patterns of land settlement prevailing in Austria, Germany and elsewhere. From a global standpoint there is little doubt, as he advocates that environmental legislation should be enacted and adhered to worldwide, from increased automotive fuel efficiency to exercising care with regard to non-reliable resources, such as water, timber and open land. In all of this the negative term is maximization; a process that addresses itself solely to the commodification of everything, solely for the purpose of maximizing profit. Hence, the profligate waste of energy in the air-conditioned irrigated motopia of Los Angeles. This also accounts for the ecological countermove in Europe where architects like Renzo Piano, in collaboration with Ove Arup and Partners are trying to devise ways, such as the ventilated curtain wall, where the buildings of future will minimize the use of air conditioning. It is also possible to maximize energy conservation with the result that all other criteria become totally compromised. Thus one oscillates between the formalist building where ecological criteria are ignored and environmentally conscious structure that is bureaucratically over determined. This last, as Germany results in a provision of total brutal forms of fenestration in order to totally eliminate any form of a "cold bridge." Once again, this is maximization in the over-determined economic sense, only this time coming from bureaucracy rather than from speculators. Somewhere between these extremes lies the mediatory role of architecture conceived as a sensitive manifestation of critical culture.

Q   This question is connected to our present situation: if a monument is lost, but its designs are existent, should we reconstruct it, half-reconstruct it, make it fake or make a new building on the same spot?

KF   I think it is very difficult to give one general answer to this question because I do not have much experience in this area either, but there will have to be some kind of comparative, specific decision. There are all sorts of funny paradoxes involved; it is possible to clean the building, I am thinking about the US examples, but you can clean them in such a way that in the end they look fake. Even the Palazzo del Te, which was restored by the Italians recently, can give a very uncomfortable feeling. It has been restored in such a way that it looks plastic, so even if the thing is there and not destroyed, it is also very delicate to restore it. All these arguments about cleaning the ceiling of the Sistine Chapel, this mania for cleaning, evokes a question of cultural discretion – the maximization which can also be a maximization of profit, and the mentality under the divided labor of society, that ex, who is a cleaner of the Renaissance paintings, wants to maximize the result, like the surgeons desire to maximize his capacity to do a certain kind of surgery on somebody who is already half-dead, but since he is a technocrat he has to do it right. It is very delicate how much you restore something and exactly in what way you restore it. The question of restoration is a totally different level of decision. I think I am right. Some parts of Warsaw were rebuilt after the Second World War completely from drawings and you say it is a kind of fake, but there are fakes and "fakes" because it is a kind of cultural act as well. It may be possible to rebuild a work in such a way that if one is very sensitive one can indicate it. In any case the technology is not going the same as it was at the time when it was made, and the question of how this is expressed, I think it can be expressed. Scarpa, for example, is a master in this point of view, for restoring and making boundary between a creative work and maintenance and restoration, both articulated and paradoxical. But one also has to cultivate both architect and proprietor.

Q In our very turbulent history in most places the only continuum is architecture. People identify architecture as a symbol of a place. Some of those symbols are now destroyed. For us it is very important to have them, even fakes, just to keep this symbol.

KF Maybe the answer is also to make it back, but indicate that it has passed through this process somehow.

Q A short comment on Steven Holl's winning of competition for the Museum of Contemporary Art in Helsinki?

KF I think it is a complex business; there was also a voting in Parliament for the project to go on. But there were some Finnish architects who thought that it was not the best solution. Maybe that was chauvinist a little bit, but they thought it should be made by Finnish architects. The mixture of culture and political life are not really avoidable. I do not see it in terms of traditional betrayal, I believe in this importance of tradition, but it also involves transactions and from that point of view embodying a foreign architect in Helsinki to build this building, a very good American architect, was a sort of fertile thing to do. It could be that it is not as refined work from the point of view of its spatial distribution as maybe some designs submitted to the competition by the Finns, and on those grounds one could say that it was not the building to build.

Q Today you saw a part of modern architecture in Zagreb, what do you think about it?

KF It is a difficult question to answer. I am very surprised at the Ban Jelačić Square[108], it is extremely rich and dense and in very good condition, and lived in, even the department store is still the department store. Of course, it may seem funny that I would find this significant, but in the US there are many cities where the department store exists, but it is no longer the department store because it has been destroyed in another way, through market and development, because the center of the city no longer means anything, the suburbs have drawn all the economic force out of it and that kind of vitality vanished. Another thing that also happened in so called "developed" countries, for example Bedford Square, Bloomsbury section where up to 1939 people lived there, but after WWII it transformed into offices. This is not specifically an intrinsic architectural quality, but in terms of the culture of the city I think it is very alive and in a very good condition, also fully lived. I was also very impressed by Novakova[109] street of modern buildings for their quality, although they are in very bad condition. In the discussion about how Modern architecture was not human and how it was all a disaster, after seeing a housing like that, you realize how this is all nonsense.

108 The main square in Zagreb, Croatian capital.

109 Novakova St. is a Zagreb's version of the Weissenhof Estate in Stuttgart, a series of modernist urban villas built between two world wars.

URBAN RULES

Published in Frames of the Metropolis, City of Zagreb and the Office for Development Planning and Environmental Protection, Zagreb 1996

The urban planning seminar Frames of the Metropolis initiated in 1995 concentrated on finding the strategies for metropolitan development of the city of Zagreb, focusing on the central city area by the railway. The Frames of the Metropolis 1996 seminar has Urban Rules for its subject. It focuses on six morphologically different parts of the city and is in search of the new planning methodology instruments. The Urban Rules anticipate development of new regulation plans for metropolitan development of Zagreb. Through a workshop, lectures, presentations and exhibitions the Urban Rules Seminar set a framework for answers on questions related to conceptual and practical possibilities of architecture and urbanism in development of a city under the post-socialistic conditions. Six task groups within the Seminar workshop focus on six parts of the city as segments of new regulation plans. During two periods of time prior to the Seminar, the workshop develop Urban Rules for six morphologically different parts of the city which shall be formed into urban typologies for individual locations during the Seminar. Therefore, the task groups have a double role: as the "institutional planners" in real setting and as the "off-institutional" makers of urban and architectural design for concrete tasks. In this way the conceptualized workshop demonstrate urban rules as a stimulating contradiction of limits and possibilities.

The Frames of the Metropolis seminar on the subject of Urban Rules is a public, cultural and specialist project which opens for the second time a critical argument on potentials the urban planning has in the process of Zagreb transformation. The Seminar results could directly affect future development of the city, whereby the ideas, projects, lectures and discussions would excite imagination of politicians, investors, architects and citizens of Zagreb.

During the Urban Rules Seminar the task groups tackle the below topics and issues within the discourse of urban planning and design.

concept   At the end of the century, in highly unstable social circumstances, a number of questions have to be answered on both theoretical and ideological background for setting up the urban rules.

urban network   Presentation and/or result of each urban plan is an urban grid, urban matrix or urban texture. How can urban rules induce development of new urban grids for the future development of the city?

urban density   Development of Zagreb urban character depends on increase in urban density. What is the anticipating of urban density increase through urban rules under the recent conditions of urban restriction?

public space   Under new economic, political and first of all cultural conditions Zagreb must redefine the concept of public urban space. What is the way of setting new urban rules for public urban space?

urban amenities   The urban rules are to anticipate new and standard urban programs and possibilities of various activities overlapping on the same territory in different time intervals.

urban landscape   The urban rules are to determine an attitude toward transformation of natural and/or suburban landscape into the urban landscape.

urban typologies   The new urban rules should offer the possibility of conceiving a number of new urban typologies.

The seminar is directly oriented towards execution of the office's tasks assumed from the municipal assembly through acceptance of the program of measures for improvement of spatial conditions: the city of Zagreb municipal assembly concluded that preparations were to be commenced for generation of a new city master plan which would be a strategic document for development of physical and regulation plans and executive documentation. The results of the seminar should be used on both levels.

232 **236**

URBAN RULES

FRAMES OF THE METROPOLIS:
ZAGREB URBAN PLANNING
SEMINARS 1995 & 1996

Horetzky, Zagreb, 1996

"NEW" NEW ZAGREB

Published in Frames of the Metropolis, City of Zagreb and the Office for Development Planning and Environmental Protection, Zagreb 1996

Lada Hršak/Vedran Mimica/Zoka Skorup

The Context

Zagreb, a city with a potential of a future European regional center, at present on a periphery of European happenings, and at the end of the century in post-socialist period, needs to set the new strategies for urban development. The idea of building a city within the agreed margins (GUP[110]1992) asks for a set of quality different scenarios for development of particular parts of the city. It is not possible to understand or project the urban reality of Zagreb today as a singular conceptual construction or a unique result of predetermined values.

New Zagreb is a town-building vision of the Mayor Holjevac from the late 1950s. The new city, based on tabula rasa principle, was completely planned and built by a generation of urban planners and architects brought up on pragmatic basis. CIAM's apotheosis south of the Sava river created in the 1960s clearly shows revision efforts in the 1980s and 1990s with every new built housing settlement. In all, New Zagreb was pronounced as a "form that is following a fiasco," as a city bedroom, as a part of the town with no identity, as socialist controlled space, as a betrayal of the modern mission, as a releasing principle that captures.

Today however, in the era of transition and instability where the emphasized idea of the return to historical offers at least a scenery security, it seems almost necessary to prepare new method for disorder exploitation and understanding the logic of permanent conflicts. The return to the historical in the areas of New Zagreb means the recognition of quality of the modern, (also Holjevac) as historical categories with amnesty potential. The amnesty for New Zagreb is reading the context towards the creation of the new. New Zagreb represents a unique Zagreb's and European area where the patterns of modern way of life present the traditional value. The culture of inhabitants of New Zagreb is eminently urban with mainly affirmative relation towards the immediate environment. Presentation of urban planning of a modern European city with new typologies and programs, with developed infrastructure, as a part of metropolitan space of Zagreb, makes the most sense essentially in New Zagreb.

The Concept

The amnesty for New Zagreb is a conceptual frame for creation of the "new" New Zagreb. Affirmation of the new project, but also its unfinished state, is the inspiration for the project. The project redefines a modern city and the basic rules. Our amnesty concept means releasing from the charges and starting the new while understanding the past. The past is a tradition of a utopian idea about building the new city on CIAM's principles. After the "amnesty" we necessarily change the meaning, consciousness and view about New Zagreb. Changed destiny for the entire part of a city cannot be only a post-modern taboo, but a unique opportunity for construction of the new. The new of the new is based on a reconstruction of the existent historical, cultural and technical infrastructure. Corridor-avenues (the basic street pattern of New Zagreb) are being finished and densely planned, so as to create streams of passing pedestrians, cyclists, trams and cars, covering the entire territory of New Zagreb. The relation between corridor-avenues and New Zagreb mega-block housing spaces is redefined. Mostly empty and urbanely undefined marginal zone of mega-blocks becomes denser with new buildings and immediate connection towards the corridor-avenue.

The programmed character of the ground floor is exclusively public, and the rules for parcels enable accessibility of central mega-block zones. Thickening of the urban matrix greatly influences the ground floor part, changing the character and atmosphere of the CIAM town.

[110] General Urban Plan (GUP) is a kind of a master-plan.

New urban planning of New Zagreb opens possibilities which architecture should utilize. Paradoxically however, the borders between urban planning and architecture have to fade. Only urban planning itself, which affirms architectural design as its own inspection and constituency, enables the usage of its potentials. The design anticipates heterogeneity and public character of new programs in a way which completes the unfinished New Zagreb's housing settlements; but also constitutes programmatic layers which, applied in the new part of the city, provide an important identity and character radically different from other parts of the city, especially from the historic center.

New Zagreb needs to become an entity for itself in a metropolitan Zagreb area, but also a center of regional interest. For bringing this kind of vision into life, we present a series of URBAN RULES of different scales and qualities as graphic-textual conceptual diagrams. Diagrams question the GUP-PUP[111] (existing planning schemes) ideology and anticipate the conceptual directions of the new regulation rules as flexible and dynamic instruments of a new urban practice.

New Zagreb – Debate about the Project

Amnesty for New Zagreb is an urban vision, created in March 1996 on The Berlage Institute. The debate about the project took place during Zagreb's workshop Frames of the Metropolis, beginning of April. The panels present seven topics discussed during the debate about the project.

1 The Title
New^2 Zagreb is a title that metaphorically and more precisely determines the character of the study, than Amnesty for New Zagreb title. New^2 Zagreb expresses the anticipation of the future through affirmation of the present. New Zagreb is presented as a unique Zagreb and European area where types of modern way of life present traditional values. The very area of New Zagreb makes by far the most sense possibilities for urban projection of modern European city with new typologies, programs and developed infrastructure.

2 Ideogram + Infrastructure
The main characteristic of New Zagreb ideogram is an anticipation of development based on modern infrastructure. New Zagreb can be developed as a sole urban programmatic entity within the region of Zagreb, only if it develops the existing infrastructure and connects it with other parts of the city and the region. The basic orientation of the new infrastructure is quick city railway direction Ban Jelačić square-Main Railway station-Trnje-New Zagreb-Zagreb Airport Pleso-Velika Gorica.

3 Dynamics of Development
In present times it is not possible to conceptualize urban plan as a static image or representation. New^2 Zagreb presents an urban strategy that anticipates dynamics of development as a constituent thesis. Dynamics of development treats the area of New Zagreb as a compact one, and does not predict concentrated building in certain parts.

4 Characterization of Corridor
The basic idea of the study is thickening of the avenue infrastructure – corridors. The characteristic section shows fundamental change of character for New Zagreb avenues where we plan lines of quick city railway or tram, additional car roads, cyclist and pedestrian roads. New programs appearing by the corridor in the marginal zone of mega-blocks are connected with the corridor zone through public pedestrian areas so as to define the zone of intervention between the inside of the block and the corridor. We also plan underground pedestrian connections vertical to the corridor direction. All existing and new buildings belonging to the mega-block get a "house" number in relation to the corridor and are connected through the public area with the corridor.

[111] Provedbeni urbani plan (PUP) means the plan that is approved to be carried out.

5 Transparency

Urban building rules for marginal zone of mega-blocks anticipate the transparency of the zone towards the inside of the block as the main characteristics. Closing of the inside of the block in relation to the corridor cannot be the result of the applied rule of maximal length of street elevation of 40%. To ensure the transparency there is an additional rule which limits the length of the building in relation to the corridor to 100 m at the most.

6 Topography of Buildings

The relation between the building and the terrain in the marginal zone of mega-blocks is defined by topography of the building. The topography then establishes a dynamic spatial relationship between the public zone of the corridor, public programs in the ground floor level of the building and inner part of the block.

7 City Identities

The final debate topic about the project, again establishes the vision about New^2 Zagreb as spatially and programmatically clearly expressed entities within Zagreb metropolitan area, which likewise contains other urban entities.

Većeslav Holjevac Avenue (north-south) is a central, representative and symbolic axis that connects New Zagreb with central city area across the Bridge of Freedom (Most Slobode). Infrastructure backup of this avenue, especially the direction of the new fast city-railway, presuppose widening and reconstruction of the bridge and also the corridor in the recreational zone of Bundek lake. In this zone we do not offer programs immediately connected with Holjevac Avenue.

In the zone between Zagreb Fair and Središće settlement we predict a city train station with a series of new programs in the marginal zone by the corridor.

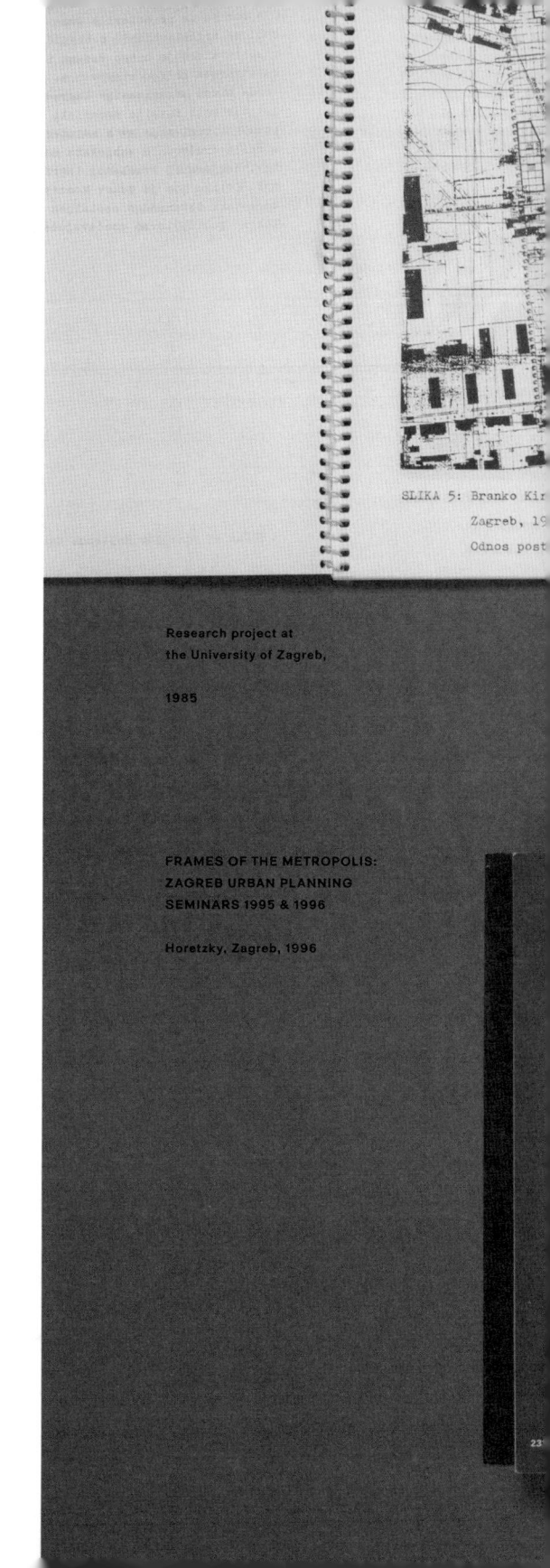

SLIKA 5: Branko Kir
Zagreb, 19
Odnos post

Research project at
the University of Zagreb,

1985

FRAMES OF THE METROPOLIS:
ZAGREB URBAN PLANNING
SEMINARS 1995 & 1996

Horetzky, Zagreb, 1996

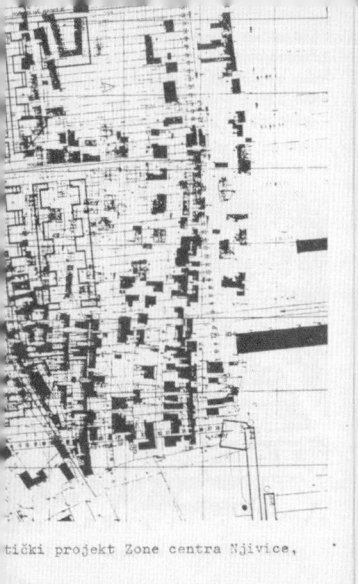

ACTES DU COLLOQUE:
URBICIDE - URGENCES -
DURABILITE: RECONSTRUCTION
ET MEMOIRE

Geneva: Institut d'Architecture
de l'Universite de Geneve, 2005

Vedran Mimica
East-West: Blurring Territories

SMALL CHANGES

Seminar Brief for the third seminar titled Frames of the Metropolis – Small Changes, Zagreb 1999

Zagreb is the capital of Croatia, a country in transition located between the European Union and the unstable East European region. In the immediate future we envisage that the city's development will follow the "third way" (between East and West). This vision must be conceptually defined as a transition process without a real time frame for the countries inclusion in the global process of European Union enlargement.

small changes must envisage "new newness" which will explore the possibilities for changing traditional institutions. Institutions in this context imply new urban development plans and documents, new local government institutions, new citizen's interest groups, which will be able to establish interactive links with the new planning documents. We imagine the establishment of non-hierarchical, contextual, adaptive and clever mechanisms capable of initiating urban development in a transitional environment. These mechanisms must accept the new market logic while maintaining a public interest of the city.

small changes recognize the "real reality" as their area of activity, thus including in their scenarios local government institutions and/or the clearly defined interests of the citizens. The new city spaces must be defined simultaneously as public and private with a very precisely defined relationship between public use of space and the public interest of its leasing.

small changes concentrate on "disturbance" zones, urban voids and gaps that generate numerous instabilities in the city atmosphere. Designs that will introduce "new novelties" have to show a high level of sensitivity when re-conceptualizing these atmospheres and when designing scenarios for changing the context of certain areas.

small changes are not interested in utopian projects. Designs must define a relationship between the general and particular, the whole and part, city and individual objects, as a relationship of one reality with another. These realities must be defined and conceptualized within given limits. The task is unique and related to one site.

small changes must envisage a new typology or urban activities that constitute new "topography." New "topography" must be defined in a way that accepts the new activities of new institutions. The new programs and activities that will be located in the new "topography" must be defined so as to reflect the real capabilities of local communities. For the real and successful implementations of new programs their pragmatic, simple and clever proposals must recognize the atmosphere of the local environment and assume the participation of community.

small changes must take exceptional care when linking new "topography" with the existing urban city infrastructure.

small changes must introduce time in its daily, weekly, monthly and seasonal rhythm on new "topography."

small changes must be implemented without delay and with minimum costs.

ZAREZ, I/6

Zagreb, 1999

Democratization of public space, interview with Vedran Mimica

SMALL CHANGES

program brochures

1999

Vedran Mimica, voditelj radionice *Male promjene*

Demokratizacija javnoga prostora

Za zemlju u tranziciji sada je vrijeme da definira što ona jest i kako djeluje u javnom gradskom prostoru

Silvia Kolbowski, konceptualna umjetnica

Paralektički pogled

Ono što mi se činilo zanimljivo u konceptu malih promjena jest da su one specifične za Zagreb. Tu nema velikih sredstava, možda čak ni jake volje za izvršavanjem promjena

DEMOCRATIZATION OF PUBLIC SPACE

Interview by Sabina Sabolović for Zarez, monthly paper for culture, year I, No 6, Zagreb 1999

Zarez What is the concept behind the series of the workshops Small Changes? It seems to rely on Koolhaas' tenets of new newness, especially in regard to new institutions.

Vedran Mimica I believe that this is what transitional countries need. I refer to the ones that have shifted from one system to another without having substantially changed their institutions. This is why I insisted that programs for these locations should be new, urban, and supported by new institutions, because the old ones are not capable of seeing any changes through. The idea of the seminar is to produce highly ambitious projects, and the take-home message is that these new institutions should be able to delineate a new cityscape. All projects should meet two basic requirements: to keep within the current economic limitations and to be independent of any subsidies. The real question is who should establish these new institutions. I believe the initiative should come from the civic society. I also believe that these projects could be financially viable, and that Zagreb treasures an immense number of clever young people who are jobless because old institutions have no interest for them. Laying down the foundations for the workshops, I had in mind a program that would be social and even political in a sense, tailored specifically for this community in any case. It is high time for a transitional country such as ours to define its identity and its actions in the public urban space. It should acknowledge the tradition no doubt, but should also build its image on the urban culture that is already there but has no space or an institution to represent it at the moment. Skaters, for example. We've talked about them at the workshops, yet they have no place of their own in this town. I'm talking about things that may not be crucial, but can easily be done, and cheaply for that matter, and would satisfy the needs of a minority subculture, such as hip-hoppers.

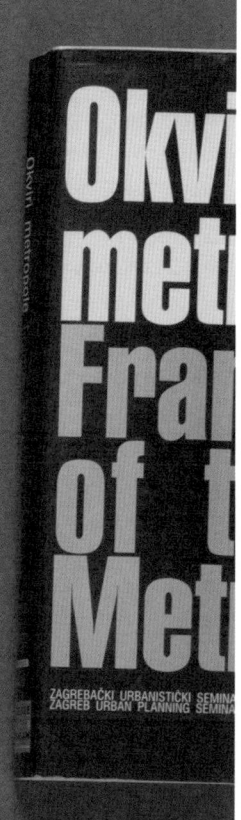

FRAMES OF THE METROPOLIS:
ZAGREB URBAN PLANNING
SEMINARS 1995 & 1996

Horetzky, Zagreb, 1996

ZAREZ, I/6

Zagreb, 1999

Democratization of public space,
interview with Vedran Mimica

Zarez — You have given one example. How about other content your workshops have come up with?

VM — Most of the projects deal with new urban content such as this and is mostly related to how the youth sees urban space. There are playgrounds for children and gardens for senior citizens, that is, group-specific content that allows them to transfer their hobbies and interest, their identity so to speak, to public urban space. After all, these projects are about new ways to democratize public space, which may include semi-private and semi-public spaces. These spaces are clearly defined by their users, their physical arrangement, and design.

Zarez — Can "small changes" really create these new spaces and new content? Judging by the workshops, it seems to me that many of the projects disregard the given frames and require big investments.

VM — You are right to an extent. Some locations are pretty demanding. The case in point is the railway "Bermuda Triangle" near the Student Center. Elevating the railway and building a viaduct have little to do with small or low-cost changes. But of the fifty-eight project locations, many require minimal construction work. There is a backyard in the neighborhood of Kustošija that would cost very little money to be repurposed. The real problem is that this requires a new way of thinking, a new practice and a consensus, so that marble and brass cafeterias stop being the only place for the youth to gather in and the only kind of public places that makes money. Look at the other metropolises all over the world; they have parks, boutique museums, community meeting rooms, and similar content that is absolutely feasible and acceptable. They are not part of the global franchises such as McDonalds, but make use of community resources to be of everyday use for their residents.

Zarez — You have mentioned that these Small Changes would really change the image of the city if they were really implemented.

VM — Imagine that all these proposals see the light of day in a short time frame, say, a year. I find this idea very intriguing. Zagreb would become an amazingly interesting place. Its overall appearance would not change the least bit, yet its use would be revolutionized. I am inclined to believe that some of these locations would become highly popular gathering places for certain subcultures, cult places of sort, as once were Teatar ITD,[112] Zvečka[113] or the Tuškanac playground. Some would become distinct focal points.

Zarez — One of the seminar organizers was the City Office for Development Planning. Do you think it might stand behind some of the proposed projects?

VM — The City Office for Development Planning stands behind this whole thing. Even so, I do not expect that a traditional institution such as this should bring these changes. This is simply out of their frame of thinking. They just organized the seminar, went public with it, will launch an exhibition, publish a monograph, and release a CD. And I do not think they will go beyond that. If they do, the City Assembly and the mayor will find themselves in a real "trouble", having to seriously consider these projects and what they would do for Zagreb. They will then have to establish a new institution, headed by young, ambitious, and intelligent people who would run operations and mediate between new investors and the City Office. This new institution would then take over seeing these projects through.

[112] Teatar ITD (Theater ETC) was a place of the enormous importance for the cultural life of Zagreb in the 1970s.

[113] Zvečka was a cafe in the center of Zagreb, a place of informal gathering of architects, artists, designers, journalists, etc. In the times without the Internet, it served as a kind of a social networking hub.

MARE NOSTRUM

Introduction to the Croatian presentation at the 2nd International Architecture Biennale Rotterdam

Mare Nostrum is an international and research-oriented exhibition for the second International Architecture Biennale Rotterdam. Architects all over the world have been asked to analyze the development of their country's coasts. In the exhibition they will present their findings and alternative proposals, for the coasts of Australia, Belgium, Brazil, the Caribbean, Croatia, France, Israel, Italy, Mexico, Scotland, Slovenia, South Africa, Spain, Taiwan, Turkey and Ukraine.

Mare Nostrum is concerned with one of the most conspicuous trends in globalization, namely the rise of mass tourism, and its relation to the presence of water. Specifically, it focuses on the coastlines of countries, in temperate and sub-tropical climates, that during the past centuries, decades or recent years have become a favorite destination for recreation and retreat. Starting off in the 19th century Britain, coastal tourism has gradually spread over the world, with diverse cultural, environmental, economic and political implications. Once considered a haven for poets and painters, a refuge for intellectuals to become lost in contemplation, and a playground for the happy few, the coastal resort has gradually become synonymous with mass tourism. During the past century the world has seen the growth of urbanized strips just a few kilometers wide and hundreds of kilometers long, with populations in the millions that have no economic link with the coast, yet generate an entirely new economy base on the proximity of water.

Whereas the roots of the phenomenon lie in the Mediterranean, the Mare Nostrum of the Roman Empire, the conquest of coastlines through tourism has by now become a worldwide phenomenon. Ever-cheaper long distance flights have made distant shores a commonplace destination for those who can afford them. Large numbers of affluent people of the third age are relocating along foreign coasts, to spend the last of their days in milder climes, all the while remaining just a few hours of flight away from their grandchildren. However, these grandchildren travel the same routes, perpetually in search of new thrills, part of a rising international beach culture, exchanging news of the best sand and surf on the internet. And the busy generation in the middle seeks rapid recovery from stress and fatigue with lightning visits to fully catered environments, or high-priced Robinson Crusoe bareness with all mod cons just round the corner.

These travelers, thrill seekers and settlers are the Romans of the 21st century colonizing coastlines all over by new means, namely those of the tourists and the industries that cater to them, and turning the global seas into their Mare Nostrum, aided, moreover, by an army of property developers, tour operators, policymakers and politicians. As one of the largest and fastest growing sectors of the global economy, tourism plays an important part in the development of many of the poorer areas of the world. At the same time this development threatens to engulf the original cultural and environmental assets of these areas, or has already done so. The question is, of course, how to retain these assets while exploiting them at the same time.

Croatian Archipelago
New Lighthouses Project

Croatian Archipelago/New Lighthouses anticipates tourism as the generator of a process of social transformation, and the development of cities and landscape along the Croatian coastline. Croatia's prosperity and economic growth are tightly linked to the development of a tourism industry that perceives the unique landscape of the Adriatic coast as a value that forms the tourism product. Croatia sells the image of virgin landscapes, summarized by the slogan "Croatia – the Mediterranean as it once was." These branding and marketing strategies present an image of Croatia as a traditional, summer-only destination for the mass market.

The proposals by seven teams of Croatian architects represent paradigmatic examples of an alternative approach, constructed on the precondition that spatial changes are the product of collective intelligence, representing (the means of) the democratization of society.

An alternative approach has the capacity to critically engage the metaphysical and political programs that operate in a given society. The exhibition at the Rotterdam Biennale is an integral part of the Matra Projects Program – a program of the Dutch Ministry of Foreign Affairs that aims to support the process of social transformation in the countries of Central and Eastern Europe. The Berlage Institute and the Croatian Association of Architects are aiming at implementing seven pilot projects along the Croatian coastline.

Powerful metaphor of the lighthouse is presenting a relation between historical heritage and a need for new visions of development. Croatia sells the image of virgin landscapes, summarized by the slogan "Croatia – the Mediterranean as it once was".

Seven concepts by seven teams of Croatian architects (three of the teams composed of Berlage Institute alumni) for seven critical sites along Croatian coast presents different strategies of interventions imagining Croatia as Mediterranean as it could be.

Strategy 1

Labin is Mine, Opening Horizons
Architectural team: Platforma 981
(Luciano Basauri, Dafne Berc, Damir Blažević, Lada Hršak, Vesna Jelušić, Jerolim Mladinov, Marko Sančanin)
NGO /research/ Endem
(Maja Skvaža, Ivan Šurina)

The project proposes to use the symbolic heritage and the infrastructural legacy of the mine industry as means for promoting and re-establishing local cultural production in order to empower Labin's identity.

Strategy 2

Plateau for half million people
Architectural team: Randić-Turato d.o.o.
(Saša Randić, Idis Turato, Iva Franolić, Gorjana Drašković)
NGO /research/ Društvo za poljepšavanje Omišlja
(Dražen Abramović, Dejana Brozić)

The strategy of re-qualification sees the void of a quarry as a generating element of the transformation where most of the territory should remain unbuilt and will be defined with open temporary programs.

Strategy 3

Re: Island 44°52′N/14°49′E, Goli otok –
reconstruction of the communist-era prison.
Architectural team: STUDIO UP
(Lea Pelivan, Toma Plejić, Marina Dilberović, Saša Relić)
NGO /research/ O tom po tom
(Sanjin Kaštelan, Slave Lukarov)

The strategy of cognitive cartography is resolving leftover issues of memory, history and politics. Past-future coding is criss-crossed as a new strategy for the society that does not worship "labor" any more but high and green technology as a mirror image of sin-absolved society.

Strategy 4

Symbiotic Game
Architectural team: de Architekten Cie, Croatia
(Branimir Medić, Pero Puljiz, Sunčana Rapaić, Ida Polzer, Zvonimir Marčić)
NGO /research/ Studentski Savez Sveučilišta u Zadru (Nikola Turčinov, Ivan Čirjak)

The working principle is a game of negotiations and strategies among three parties: the City of Zadar, University of Zadar and a developer. It is a symbiotic system, a cause effect of different relationships:

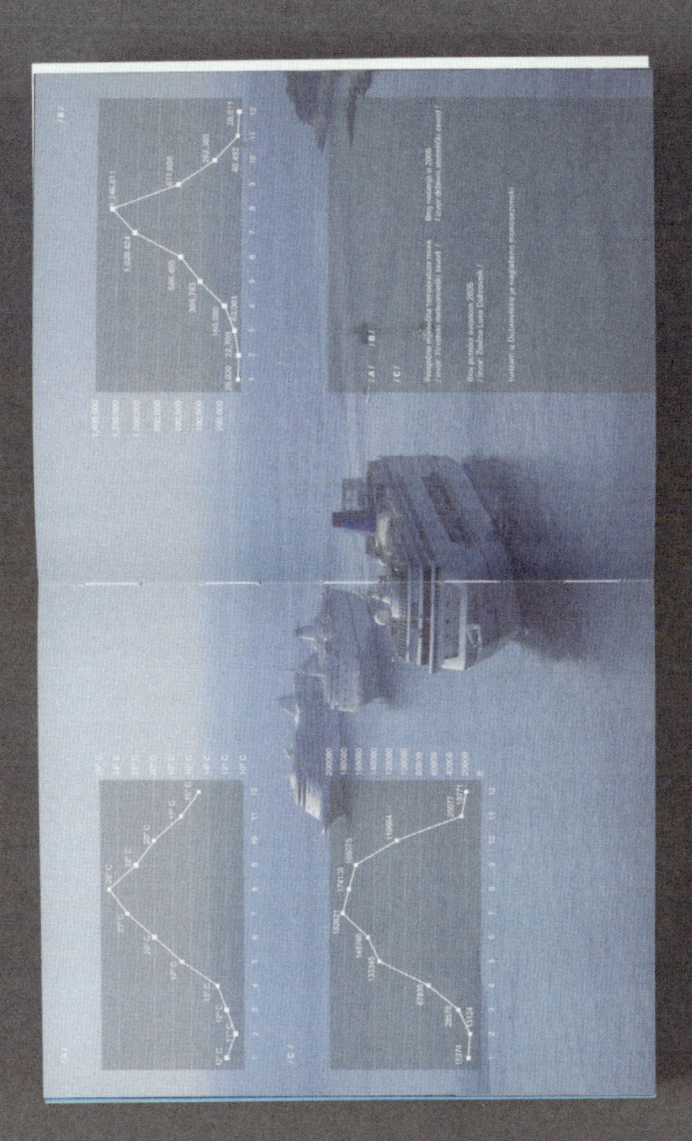

Nives Kozulić
Lionel Veehr
Saša Randić
Lea Pelivan
Toma Plejić
Rolling Stones
Pope
Davor Katušić
Dubravka Šuica
Branimir Medić
Pero Puljiz

CROATIAN ARCHIPELAGO : NEW LIGHTHOUSES

Berlage Institute, Croatian Architects/ Association,
Zagreb, 2006

Never-ending Summer,
Educational Park in Dubrovnik
Architectural team: 3LHD

CROATIAN ARCHIPELAGO : NEW LIGHTHOUSES

Interim Substantial and Content Report nr. 2
01/11/2005 - 30/04/2006

public private partnership, high densities on the site and sharing model among the capital, space-time organization and the knowledge management applied on the site.

Strategy 5

"URBOTANSCAPE"©
(urban – botanic – landscape)
Architectural team: arhitektonski biro Ante Kuzmanić d.o.o.
(Ante Kuzmanić, Samuel Martin, Dujmo Žižić, Mihaela Bašić, Andrej Čikeš, Sanja Matijević)
NGO /research/ Mladen Banović

The strategy is to accept the densification of the mainland coast in order to keep nature resources on the Dalmatian islands preserved. 1km2 CITY = 10km2 NATURE. Dugi Rat's plain shall provide the region of central Dalmatia with public urban facilities and generate a 24h – 365 days vivid urban – botanic – landscape = "URBOTANSCAPE"©.

Strategy 6

Sweet Water, the New Civic Center, Stari Grad, Island of Hvar
Architectural team: Produkcija 004
(Davor Katušić, Juri Armanda, Ranko Lipovac)
NGO /research/ Pulentoda
(Frano Radonić, Ivica Moškatelo)

The strategy brings up the subject of water by stressing the aspect of ecology/activism vs. commerce in creating a public-private hybrid of a new Civic Center.

Strategy 7

Never-ending Summer, Educational Park in Dubrovnik
Architectural team: 3LHD
(Saša Begović, Marko Dabrović, Tanja Grozdanić, Silvije Novak, Silke Fisher, Iskra Kirin, Iva Marčetić, Irena Mažer, Krunoslav Szorsen)
Model / Mario Škarijot, Jelena Grlić, Tomislav Kolarić
NGO /research/ AW Lazareti
(Ana Marinković, Srdjana Cvijetić)

The strategy is based on the reconstruction of the abandoned old hospital site by inserting new educational and public program in breathtaking natural park. The creation of a new cultural density and social structure should introduce new forms of educational tourism where citizens and visitors should study, in this Arcadian environment, throughout whole year.

The proposals by seven teams of Croatian architects represent paradigmatic examples of an alternative approach, constructed on the precondition that spatial changes are the product of collective intelligence, representing (the means of) the democratization of society.

An alternative approach has the capacity to critically engage the metaphysical and political programs that operate in a given society.

NEW LIGHTHOUSES

Interview by Nives Rogoznica,
Published in Slobodna Dalmacija, daily newspaper, Split 2005

Vedran Mimica, the associate dean of the Berlage Institute in Rotterdam is one of the leaders of the Croatian Archipelago New Lighthouses project presented at the Biennale in Rotterdam between 25 May and 25 June 2005. The project however is not about lighthouses but about seven locations along the Croatian Adriatic coast that will become the beacons of further architectural development, once they are completed. The project has been presented at the exhibition Mare Nostrum, which investigates the effects of mass tourism on the coast. Among the seventeen teams from the five continents, the Croatian team has received the jury mention for having presented "an interesting option for dealing with capital investments in the pristine coast" or as the authors like to say of the "Mediterranean as it could be." The "Lighthouses" are the first in a series of activities of this two-year collaborative project by the Berlage Institute and the Croatian Architects' Association, funded by the Dutch Ministry of Foreign Affairs as part of the Matra program. This fall, the project will also be presented in Zagreb at the respective locations. Its completion shall involve public discussions, exhibitions, and workshops, whose objective is to include civil society in decision-making about their environment. One of the seven locations is Zadar with a new campus and the working title "Symbiotic Game." The new campus is to be constructed on the premises of the former military base Stjepan Radić. It has been supported by the University of Zadar, the city of Zadar, and the County, and according to the town planner Nives Kozulić complies with the town's development plan.

Nives Rogoznica This project was in fact not a coincidence, was it?

Vedran Mimica Adriaan Geuze, the curator of the second International Architecture Biennale Rotterdam, invited me because he knew that I had not given up on Croatia, even though I have been in the Netherlands for 15 years. He proposed that we present the Croatian coast as part of the Mare Nostrum project that should present the development of 16 national coasts under the pressure of mass tourism. To get the funds that would ensure our participation at the Biennale we applied for the Matra program of the Dutch Ministry of Foreign Affairs. The aim of this program is to encourage the development of civil society in the EU candidate countries. Lionel Veehr, Dutch Ambassador in Croatia and Saša Randić, chair of the Croatian Architects' Association supported the idea, and an "innocent" presentation at the Biennale suddenly became a serious project involving seven locations along the Adriatic coast. The project will last for two years and has the ambition to help civil society get involved in design, planning, and public presentation of these locations. It has the ambition for Croatia to define design and planning methods that will reflect the needs and expectations of its transitional society. As fund raising is a long and cumbersome process due to strict application procedure, we could not afford to wait, so our teams of architects agreed to volunteer and take the risk.

Q What conceptual guidelines did the esthetics and the use of new tourist buildings follow?

VM Tourism is the leading industry employing over 200 million people and cashing in 3 trillion US dollars. It is a straightforward consequence of the process we refer to as globalization, and globalization is like weather forecast saying, "it will definitely rain." It is there, whether you want it or not. I have had the opportunity to attend to several theoretical discussions about Croatia, and they all come down to opposing globalization. As if you could oppose the rain! The only thing left to do is to get an umbrella. Globalization can be adapted to our needs by developing political, economic, social, and finally architectural and planning practices that will modify our tourism into a force that fosters the development of the local community instead of abusing the nation's fantastic natural resources.

Q You refer to the social and economic benefits of the project. What about esthetics, which seems to be in short supply in recent local architecture?

VM If you prefer to talk about esthetics, let me tell you that I have selected the most interesting emerging architects in Croatia today, and they all have worked on the Adriatic. Esthetics aspect of the work will come from their emerging practice. If we speak of the quality of architecture in Croatia in general, what happens is that many foreign investors who come to the Adriatic to buy property or a concession or to develop tourist programs bring along their own architects. The result are projects such as the Russian Solaris in Šibenik, which is a sore thumb in the context of Croatian architectural culture. Instead, we believe that foreign investors should consider local context and architecture, if they wish to add value to their investment.

Q Croatian tourism faces two big issues: buildings dating from the age of socialism and the so called apartmentalization[114] that persistently defies control of town planners. What was the reaction of the local authorities to your projects, especially the most avant-garde such as Labin underground and Goli otok?

VM We are yet to present the project in Croatia. We will open with a workshop and exhibition in Zagreb and I hope we will be able to show it at the Museum of Arts and Crafts. We have been in contact with local mayors, district heads, and NGOs, all of whom had supported the project even before we applied for funding. As for the Labin underground town or the controversial Goli otok, we are presenting our views of two locations that have no straightforward connections with tourism. The Labin underground town could accommodate lecture halls, clubs, and other interesting content, including a winery. It could give a new brand to the entire town on the surface and connect it with the touristy Rabac with its underground passages. This very communication could be a tourist attraction, accompanied by other content such as wine cellars.

Goli otok, on the other hand, is very controversial and challenging. It is the brainchild of our youngest and perhaps most intriguing architects Lea Pelivan and Toma Plejić of the Studio UP in Zagreb. So far, they have examined the topography and the mapping of the location and have been highly sensitive to its history.[115] At the moment, Goli otok is concessioned to a hunting society from Lopar on the island of Rab and is reserved for rabbit hunting. One quite serious idea is to set up an entertainment, cultural and art tourist center with workshops and lectures, but there are also ideas about a casino complex, and even about a ski center. With all these ideas on the table, what follows is to make a specific research. It will be carried out by an NGO from Rijeka, and we hope to get precise information about what sort of content should best suit Goli otok.

Q Equally interesting is the idea about the conversion of the quarry in Omišalj. Into what exactly?

VM We have not decided yet. The only thing we know for the time being is that this is a fantastic and probably the largest flat area on the Adriatic that can easily accommodate half a million people. In other words, a Rolling Stones concert or Pope's sermon in the open or any other mass attraction. Architects who have worked on this project recommend that

---

114 Apartmentalization refers to a terrific boom in construction of mostly illegal houses, usually with several apartments for rent, which are in use solely during the high season (in Croatia it means only July and August). Most of these constructions affected the coastline in an array of negative ways, however, one has to consider that for the impoverished nation where many people were forced out of work in more than often unfair and nontransparent processes of privatization, renting apartments in high season was the only way to feed the family.

115 Goli otok was a prison between 1949 and 1989, most of whose prisoners were political dissidents, treated in a horrendous way by their warders, but also forced to act brutally towards each other among themselves. Goli otok was a kind of Yugoslav Gulag. It is still a contested ground.

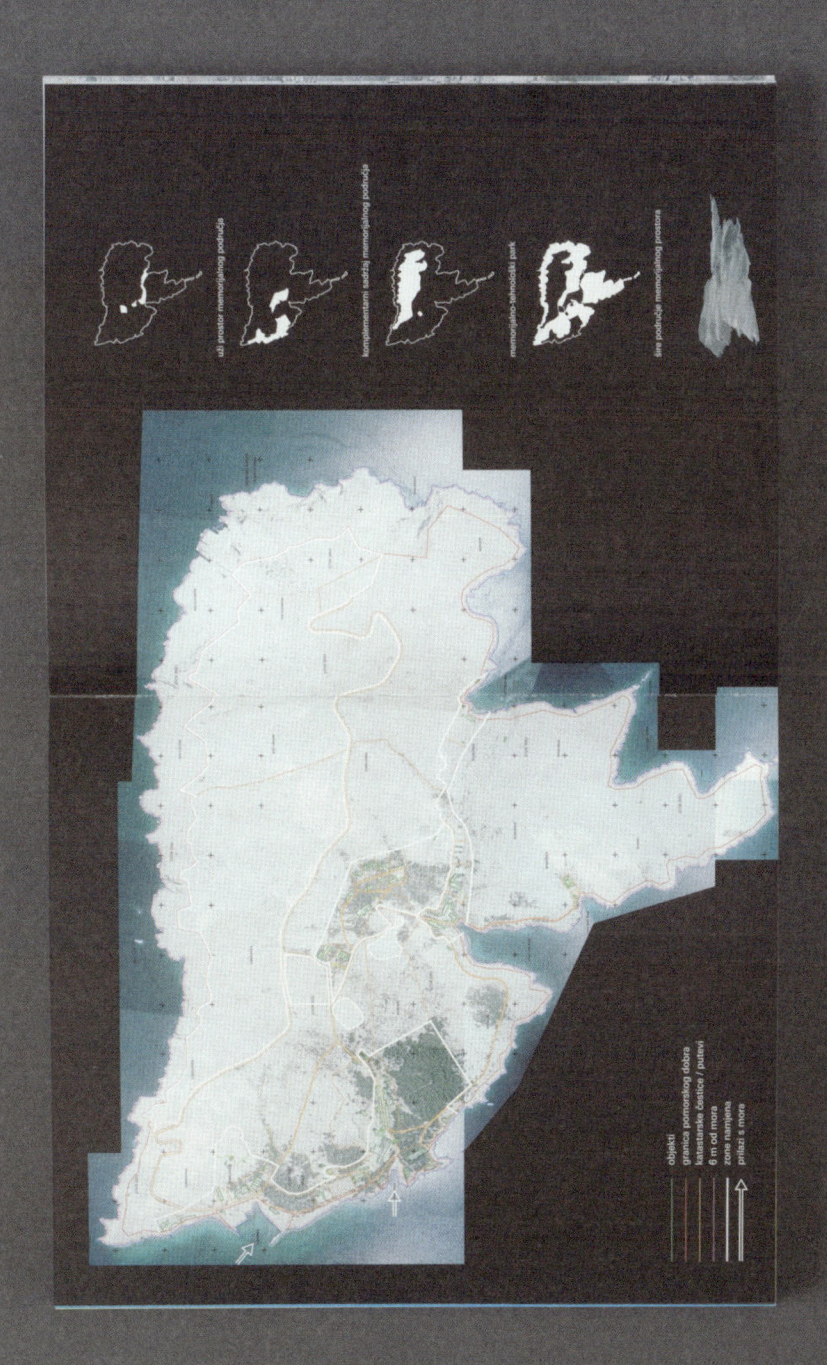

CROATIAN ARCHIPELAGO : NEW LIGHTHOUSES

Berlage Institute, Croatian Architects/ Association, Zagreb, 2006

Re: Island 44°52'N/14°49'E, Goli otok — reconstruction of the communist-era prison.
Architectural team: STUDIO UP

this area is left unbuilt, despite the vicinity of the Rijeka city airport, but to serve as a backup with only minor necessary construction work to be done. The idea is still in its early, conceptual stage and needs further development to get more realistic outlines for future construction. Omišalj will no doubt be developing for the next twenty, thirty, maybe even forty years, and we will propose a strategy and chronology.

Q Changes proposed for Dugi rat and Stari grad start from the conversion of buildings completed back in the socialist times. Considering that there are so many of them along the coast, how do you think they can be improved?

VM Dugi rat is an interesting task, especially in view of its pending privatization. One corporation is keen on buying the old ferrochrome factory and several other leftover factories from the period of coastal industrialization in the 20th century. I hope this happens by the end of September this year. We believe that some of the buildings could be salvaged, keeping in mind however that this area is highly contaminated and needs a thorough cleanup, which includes tearing some of the buildings down. As for Dugi rat, it needs a novel approach to tourism. The corporation I refer to plans to build a five-star hotel, a new marina with berths, and we have dropped a few more ideas including a local sailing club, water polo club, the firefighters, healthcare facilities, kindergartens and daycare, and residences. Dugi rat is to become a new small town. Clearly this is a huge project. On our end it is being carried out by Ante Kuzmanić, and it will be very interesting to see how will the corporation representatives respond to our proposal, which is, by the way, supported by the district head.

As for Stari grad, we have an eyesore construction site from the 1960s. It is an unfinished concrete bunker on the waterfront. Davor Katušić from Produkcija 004 sees it as a hybrid of the unfinished drama theater converted into a multimedia center and marina facilities. While this project may not be as big as the remaining six, it is very interesting, as it draws its idea from the medieval Hektorović Castle only a hundred yards away and brings the final touch to the waterfront of this small community with an incredibly open local government.

Q Zadar and Dubrovnik stand apart, as their primary objective is not tourism or entertainment, but education. What is the difference between the campus in Zadar and the educational park in Dubrovnik?

VM At first glance tourism does not seem to be their objective, but the adoption of the Bologna process will greatly increase student and teacher mobility. Not that you can call them tourists proper, as they are more of a nomadic sort, but from 2010 on, Zadar, Dubrovnik, and Zagreb will be accommodating people from 25 EU countries and extend the tourist season. Hence the title of the Dubrovnik project – "The Never Ending Summer." Ambitiously run by the Dubrovnik University Rector, the new music and art academies will extend the stay of foreign and Croatian students. The difference between Dubrovnik and Zadar is that Dubrovnik already has two schools in the park: the Inter-University Centre (IUC), founded by Ivan Supek[116] in the 1970s, and an American school for hotel management established in the mid 1990s. Dubrovnik's Mayor Dubravka Šuica has supported our idea to transform this park into one unit, not to turn it into a campus, though, but a public park proper, which is not the case right now, because there is an old hospital complex. The main building will be converted into an administrative building of the rectorate or the university and other buildings into practice or lecture rooms for the music and art academies or any other university department.

The situation in Zadar is similar; it is an old military complex whose area nearly equals the area of the

---

116 Ivan Supek (1915-2007) was a Croatian physicist, philosopher, writer, playwright, peace activist and humanist.

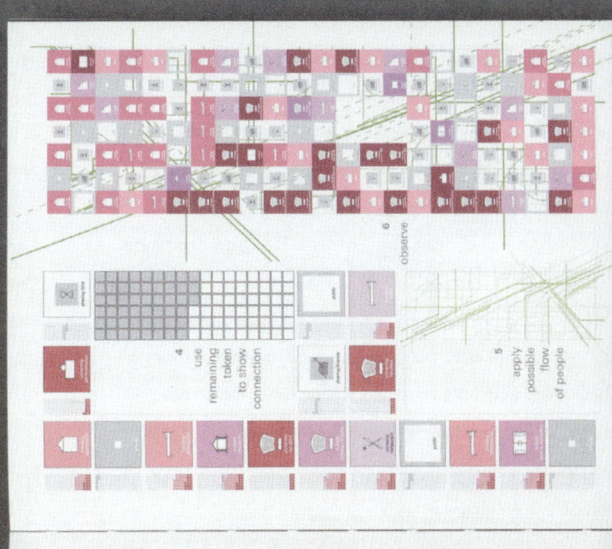

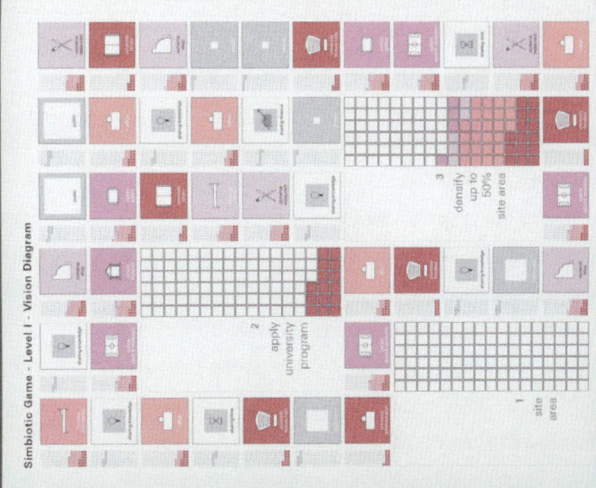

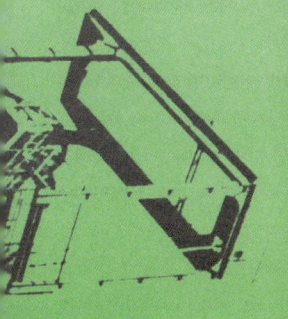

CROATIAN ARCHIPELAGO : NEW LIGHTHOUSES

Berlage Institute, Croatian Architects Association, Zagreb, 2006

Symbiotic Game
Architectural team: de Architekten Cie, Croatia

MINES OF CULTURE

Town of Labin & Platform 9,81, 2007

Zadar peninsula. Its potentials are enormous. Over the last couple of years, Zadar has been flourishing thanks to the highway connection to Zagreb and Split, and also thanks to what to me seems an enthusiastic administration. This definitely makes Zadar an interesting place for a new university campus. The project itself has been developed in collaboration with an architecture studio from Amsterdam, whose partners are former Berlage Institute students Branimir Medić and Pero Puljiz. Their ten year experience in the Netherlands has given them a good insight into how public and private partnerships work. Zadar location differs from Dubrovnik in its importance, area, and will quite likely differ in the program.

Q The first association our readers will have when they see the word campus will be the image of US campuses from the movies. What is the difference between a modern, 21st century campus and the American concept of the 20th century?

VM We should not re-create the American type campuses in Croatia. The design of many campuses, such as the one in Split, is such that they might have the same destiny as the movie campuses; they may end up isolated from the rest of the community. Considering the location in Zadar, this should not happen. Instead, it could be a new town center with residences, businesses, and culture and university buildings. In many European cities, campus and university isolation has turned out to be a bad decision. The new campus of the 21st century and the life of students in general will be more focused on the media, on the Internet, on quick information exchange than on the location. Curiously enough, students prefer living and studying in the city to an isolated campus.

Q Every day we see a new case of illegal building, with the island of Vir being just an extreme example. But we also see legal architecture that poorly fits its environment. What do other Mediterranean countries do? Do they seek to preserve their traditional architecture by adjusting it to modern technologies? How does the Netherlands preserve its traditional architecture?

VM This one is hard to answer. What we like to see as good architecture is usually presented as such in journals. All the countries in the world, even the Netherlands with perhaps the most interesting modern architecture in Europe if not the world, can boast about two to three percent of buildings that have an esthetic value. The rest is far less exciting. The Netherlands is excellent at urban planning and zoning. Urban planning is a discipline that does not go after esthetics or colors or facades or styles, but limits itself to organizing space, public and private alike. Dutch town planners project large areas, big cities, and can propose architects for individual buildings. Now that is a curiosity. Here in Croatia, we have been pretty fortunate with subsidized housing, as the project proposals mostly came from young architects, and the buildings turned out to be of high quality. In contrast, independent construction – and I do not refer to Croatia alone – was often in collision with the Croatian history of architecture and even more so with the landscape. Croatian landscape is marvelous and exciting, and the kind of architecture you have referred to when you mentioned Vir reminds me of Mexico. This phenomenon is not our specialty; you can find it in any corner of the world, including Europe. Illegal building is preposterous in the Netherlands or Austria, but you can still find ugly architecture, sore thumbs that stick out in their environment, but much less than here.

Q The county of Zadar has been working on an adaptation of the general hospital with the aim to downsize energy consumption. This brings us to the issue of self-sustainable homes. What is the situation with this kind of building in Europe?

VM At the Berlage we have been working on self-sustainable projects for a while now.
This year, we will set up a studio in Madrid that will work only on such homes. These housing programs

have been supported by all EU countries. In the Netherlands the recycling industry of construction materials is highly developed. There is no such thing in Croatia, for now. Croatian construction industry has remained rigid in its traditional ways. It uses traditional materials that involve consumption of enormous amounts of energy for heating and cooling. When Croatia becomes a serious candidate for EU accession, new funds will open, and Croatia will surely make use of the advanced know-how from Madrid or any other European country that fosters self-sustainable housing. The only problem is that these housing estates are costlier than the regular ones and that our construction industry has not yet reached the level required to meet these standards. In addition, the EU funds will not cover the entire cost of a project. Europe and the world will definitely move in that direction, especially with public buildings. There is no doubt about that. Our project, when it reaches the energy planning stage in two years' time, will surely include elements of sustainable development.

Q What I can read between the lines is that large investors might oppose the "Lighthouses," is that right?

VM Currently, the political tensions are high and the pressure from large investors is rising. The corporation investing in Dugi rat is Austrian, Croatian, and Swiss. It is very important how we present our projects and negotiate with players like this one. The prevailing feeling in Croatia is that players like these can do whatever they please, as long as they have met red tape requirements for the locations. We, in turn, believe that local communities, government administration through planning instruments, and NGOs' can have their say about what and how is to be built.

We cannot allow any private sector to come in the possession of public land or marine resources, as has happened with Solaris, quite on the contrary, we should develop mechanisms that will persuade – not coerce, mind you – investors to invest into public resources and support civil society. Provided, of course, that corruption is minimized, which is a huge issue. It will be interesting to see how it works out. I cannot wait to see how our pilot project will influence these processes.

Q The Lighthouses project speaks a lot about the role of civil society, which is still in its early stages in Croatia. You have presented the Zadar project as a game with three players: the university, the town, and the investor. Hence the name "Symbiotic Game." Everything seems to run smoothly for the moment.

VM The circumstances in Zadar are much better than elsewhere, as there are enough clever people working together; this is what we like to call "accumulation of intelligence". Intelligence seems to drain whenever either investors or politicians or architects think that their plan should prevail and negotiations come to a stall. When we speak about civil society, we do not only mean NGOs, but all citizens, who are entitled to comment on the proposed plans. The problem is that their interests often do not go further than whether their olive orchard will become land for development or remain agricultural land. But if we manage to raise their awareness of the value and the role of land for the future development of coastal towns through a series of public discussions, quite different from what they are now, we will be moving toward European standards. This project may have a Promethean ring to it, but this is exactly why we call it Lighthouses, because it has the ambition to beacon the way out of Croatian transitional darkness.

CROATIAN ARCHIPELAGO :
NEW LIGHTHOUSES

Berlage Institute, Croatian
Architects/ Association, Zagreb
2006

Labin is Mine, Opening Horizons
Architectural team: Platforma 981

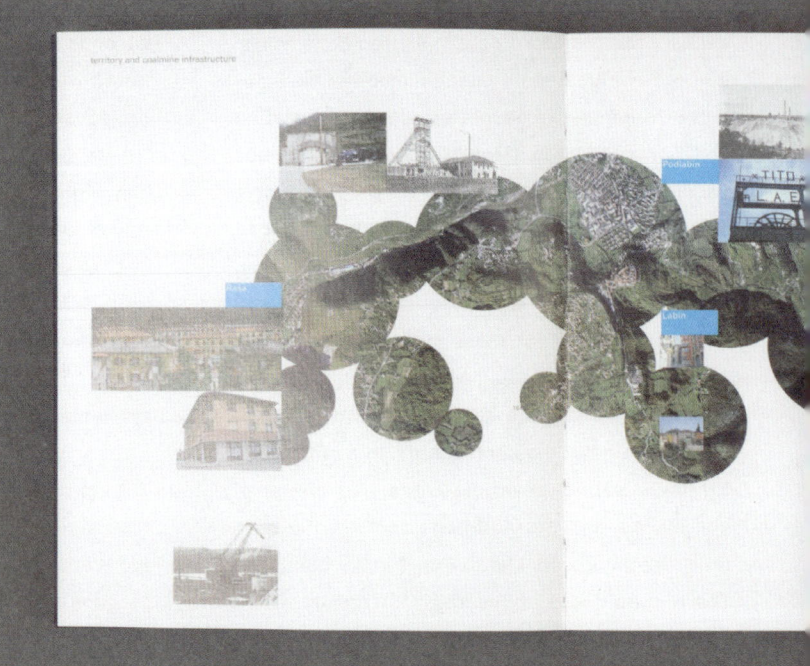

MINES OF CULTURE

Town of Labin & Platform 9,81, 2007

A continuation of a project Croatian Archipelago
New Lighthouses: Labin - Subterranean Town

VISIONARY POWER :
Producing the Contemporary City

3rd International Architecture Biennale

Rotterdam, 2007

CROATIAN ARCHIPELAGO : NEW LIGHTHOUSES

Interim Substantial and Content Report nr. 2
01/11/2005 - 30/04/2006

CROATIA – THE MEDITERRANEAN AS IT COULD BE

Introduction to the book Croatian Archipelago New Lighthouses
Published by the Croatian Architects Association & Berlage Institute, Zagreb 2005

There is an ideal, and hopefully not utopian, scenario for the future life of the book you are holding in your hands; it should become a "handbook for fixing and building" the Croatian part of the Adriatic coast. It includes analyzes, operating methods and a list of instructions for the construction of seven specific locations in the Adriatic. It is arranged and designed as a handbook where you can easily find all the aspects and participants of the process of shaping the development strategies for the locations of Labin, Omišalj, Goli Otok, Zadar, Dugi Rat, Stari Grad and Dubrovnik. In the spirit of the metaphor of New Lighthouses and with a certain level of ambitions and faith in the project's future, we present the operational character of the development strategies and their usability for other parts of the coast too.

Fortunately, most of the Adriatic coast (85 per cent) is pristine nature of exceptional beauty, which does not need "fixing." Therefore, this "handbook" will instruct how to fix the Adriatic in the parts that were devastated by prior construction and how to build the untouched territories. The development of the Croatian Adriatic is not just unavoidable, it is a necessary process. The main idea of Croatian Archipelago New Lighthouses is building "the Mediterranean as it could be" instead of "the Mediterranean as it once was."

Sustainable development, avoiding the unavoidable disaster

A look at the urban Mediterranean coast can be worrying. From Gibraltar to the Bosporus, if we consider only the European side and especially the Spanish and Italian coasts, mass tourism spells disaster for the Croatian coast too. Italy and Spain are examples of unsustainable development or a development that makes it hard for future generations to change the situation.

The project of Croatian Archipelago New Lighthouses shows how the coast can be developed in a sustainable way. "Sustainability concept" is virtually the only possible model of land development under the pressure of the global market. Mass tourism is a major aspect of the global market and will radically affect coastal development in the future.

The central issue answered by this project is: what kind of development? The sustainability of the development of a territory can be defined as the relationship between three segments: economic, social and ecological. A project will be sustainable only if the relationships between these three segments of social reality are improved and not worsened. This means that a project trying to push economic development should not endanger the environment or stop the expected social transformation; a project trying to preserve the environment should not worsen the economic status or stop social transformations; finally, a project trying to support social transformations should not stop economic development or endanger the environment. Such "sustainability" becomes almost an operating concept balancing the economic, social and ecological aspects of development. On the other hand, the concept of sustainable development is not a magical, ideologically and structurally well-defined method that should be blindly followed in order to eventually fulfill expectations. Sustainable development is primarily a multilayered process; in case of Croatia, it represents a (transitional) transformation of society towards new democratic standards. This transformation is not and cannot be supported or developed unless it is based on qualitatively different projects and processes. Fortunately or not, a system can never be copied into another social context. The copy-paste method usually does not work or does not produce sustainable results. Therefore, high quality development strategies and their specific context are the pledge of any successful future.

The second transition:
Future in the European Union

The issue of the London journal The Economist describing the countries that joined the European Union in 2005 has a very interesting table. A diagram shows when these countries which joined EU in 2004 should reach the level of the developed countries that founded the Union. Countries from Slovenia to Lithuania are expected to take between 30 and 50 years to reach that standard according to the current economic and political indicators. By joining the Union, these countries completed the "first transition," i.e. moved from one-party political system and regulated state economy to parliamentary democracy and free markets. After complying with the Union standards and becoming its members, they still face the hard task of actually reaching those standards. Of course, this is not only about the gross domestic product, but primarily about democratization and social transformation.

Social transformation, as the parallel process overlapping with the political and economic transformation, is particularly important for reaching the standards of the developed societies of Western Europe. In fact, the Matra program of the Dutch foreign ministry is one of the mechanisms of the developed western countries that should motivate such transformations and reduce differences in the new united Europe. The Croatian social landscape is still in the "first transition" phase. In many social aspects, Croatia significantly lags behind the European standards that should bring it closer to the European Union in the near future.

Space management and truly democratic, transparent decision-making about the genuinely most valuable Croatian resource is crucial for the development of the entire country. Croatian Archipelago New Lighthouses sees urban planning and architecture as the fundamental disciplines for the overall development and social transformation of Croatia to reach the standards of the European Union. The crucial issue for joining the European Union is not when Croatia will be formally accepted, but how much and in what way it will have developed by then. After centuries of instability, regime changes, wars and marginal existence between or against systems, the Croatian project for Europe is an almost incredible chance for a more stable development over a longer period of time.

Urban Planning and the Civil Society

The urban development strategy of the Croatian coastal area should primarily focus on the development of towns or villages and should control the expansion of the built territory. The urban densification and new contents of the inhabited areas have a vital importance for both inhabitants and tourists. The construction of new infrastructure and the overlapping with new city contents, respecting the existing urban qualities, should create new qualities in coastal towns and villages. This is the question answered by Croatian Archipelago New Lighthouses: how to shape those strategies and initiate the development processes? The development in the new conditions should be accompanied by new planning methods. The planning process itself should link the top-down and the bottom-up approaches. In other words, the plans of fundamental importance for specific locations should be made with the widest possible participation of all the development stakeholders. In that process, architects and urban planners will have the strategic role of coordinators and choreographers of new urban processes. They directly cooperate with the local community, NGOs and the potential users of the premises. This project considers architects as "change managers," initiators of development. The project uses new methods to explore territory — public discussions and presentations of draft plans, examination of potential interested users, public opinion surveys — and directly communicates with the local community to make agreed plans for the development of particular locations. In this way, the influence of the civil society in the widest sense may be fundamental for carrying out development plans through democratic and transparent processes. The new planning methods presented by Croatian Archipelago New Lighthouses include transitional changes in governing systems, civil society development and the understanding and acceptance of the sustainability concept. Institutional changes and growing awareness of stakeholders are long-term processes, specific for transitional areas. But the implementation of the project-generated processes and any experiences arising from project efforts may significantly accelerate the "adaptation" to new standards.

CROATIAN ARCHIPELAGO : NEW LIGHTHOUSES

Interim Substantial and Content Report nr. 2
01/11/2005 - 30/04/2006

ISKUSTVO VANJSKOG PROSTORA
OPENDOOR EXPERIENCE

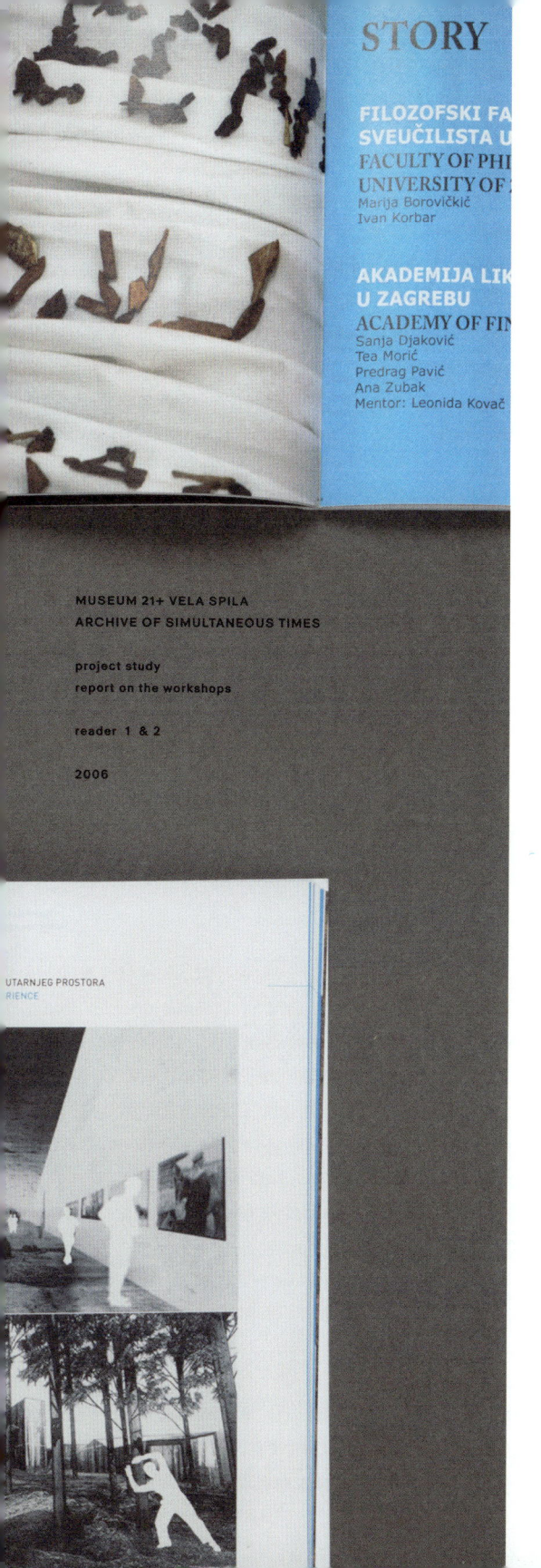

SPACE IS THE BASIC CROATIAN RESOURCE

Interview by Barbara Matejčić. Published in Vjesnik,[117] Zagreb 2008

Barbara Matejčić Thanks to the close connections with the Berlage Institute, Croatian architecture is often associated with the Dutch. What do you think they have in common?

Vedran Mimica One can hardly speak of national architectures these days; our lives and work are greatly influenced by the global exchange of information, ideas, and knowledge. The fountains of knowledge for the new generations are Google and Wikipedia. Yet we can still talk about idiosyncratic architectural discourses that reflect a specific social, economic, or political context. In that sense, Croatian architecture is determined by transition, whereas Dutch architecture is produced in a developed, neoliberal setting. Working on the monograph Randić & Turato: The Architecture of Transition in the mid 1990s, I asked Kenneth Frampton to write the foreword. In that foreword, he keenly observed that modern Croatian architecture was greatly influenced by Rem Koolhaas and his disciples, even though Koolhaas had never worked with Croatian architects. Dutch architecture of the 1990s was simply an inspiration for young Croatian architects who could not side with radical postmodernism. Instead they adopted Koolhaas and other Dutch schools as their second modernist movement, as architecture free of dogma. Another influence may have been the series of seminars The Frames of the Metropolis, organized every year, which introduced them to Dutch architecture.

Q How do you explain that the ideas and the projects resulting from The Frames of the Metropolis and the Small Changes workshop have never been integrated into the development plan of Zagreb?

[117] Vjesnik was a Croatian daily newspaper, and also a publishing house. The first issue of Vjesnik was printed in June of 1940. It played especially important role during the socialist times, when it was the most significant political newspaper in the Socialist Republic of Croatia and among the most influential in Yugoslavia. Vjesnik ceased to exist in 2012.

VM   The Berlage is a research institute, and implementing urban development strategies is not our primary task. However, our research and development strategies have been implemented in many communities whom we worked with. Zagreb was our testing ground for the hypothesis that transitional planning requires a radically different approach from the one in socialism. Unfortunately, judging by the prevailing view of the role of planners and planning, of investors, local administration, and civil society, the remnants of the times past are still very strong in Croatia.

The Frame of Meropolis workshops addressed this issue as early as the mid 1990s and proposed reasonable development strategies for the city of Zagreb. The fifty-odd projects that came out of the Small Changes workshop had the potential to substantially change the run-down, nondescript neighborhoods with minimal budget requirements. I refer to projects for public areas such as neglected backyards, tram and bus stops, and playgrounds. Even then we pointed out that these projects could not be implemented unless local administration were reformed. Our ideas may have been premature or – paradoxically – overdue for what we were trying to prove: that we needed to focus on small things instead of big, on public instead of private, on the poor members of the community instead on the rich. Even so, our Small Changes saw the light of day, but the location shifted to the Albanian capital Tirana, thanks to the support of its charismatic mayor and painter Edi Rama, who aptly combines his artistic and political experience to boost and improve one of the most neglected capitals in Europe.

Q   Are you saying that the course of changes is entirely up to one person, as long as they are high enough on the ladder, just like it has been throughout our history?

VM   Not necessarily, but to make a leap in quality that will really turn things around you need a partner who is high up in terms of intellect, ability to grasp new concepts, and politics. Or as Koolhaas would put it, you need an extraordinary cumulative intelligence of architects, politicians, and investors combined.

Q   At your recent presentation of the Berlage in Zagreb you asked "Who builds cities today?" Can you answer that question yourself?

VM   There is a consensus that city development should be sustainable, and theoretical discussions about the sustainability of cities keep bouncing between the three points of the economy-society-environment triangle. If the mayor's interest lies with economic development, city administration should be able to understand the relationships between economic and social developments as well as between economic development and environmental protection.

Like in most transitional countries, the prevailing opinion in Croatia is that the only motor of city development is the market. However, our latest research in Eastern Europe and China challenges this opinion, especially in terms of a well-defined concept of sustainability. Market reasoning simply cannot cover all the angles of a sensible city development strategy.

And to finally answer your question: cities are built by a consensus between all stakeholders in its development. This means that the voice of the civil society is essential. The negotiation between the parties largely depends on the level of the society's democratization. The higher the level, the negotiation takes longer and involves more parameters and stakeholders. If the level is low, negotiation takes less time and often has only one "winner," so to speak. The consequences are seldom sustainable and are more likely to be disastrous for the society and environment.

Q   Speaking of sustainable development, the project New Lighthouses started from this premise. Do you think that this concept is being implemented on our coast?

VM What I think is that there is a positive attitude toward its implementation, at least in theory. And it goes against the grain of foreign and domestic capital investment, whose only interest is to build. People are becoming more and more aware that a consensus is necessary, and not only on the seven locations included in the project over the last two years. We seem to have realized that space is the fundamental national asset and that it must not be squandered. But we also have to realize that it is essential for the development to be sustainable and by no means oriented exclusively to tourism. Perhaps it is a bit naïve to expect that global tourist corporations should really stick to the tenets of sustainable development on our coast, but the recent, slightly bizarre news about the engagement of Daniel Libeskind in the Orco Group projects on the island of Hvar seem to witness that shift in attitude.

One of the successful models that forces the stakeholders to negotiate about coastal development is the so called "public-private partnership." In Croatia, this model has not yet taken root. Instead, the only negotiating parties are the developer (investor), who represents private interests, and local administration, who are supposed to represent the public. So when it happens, as has happened with the Dugi Rat factory, that the site is sold – no questions asked (beyond a percentage for the bribe) – to a global financial giant, Landmark in our case, then there is no room left for negotiation and the influence of the local community and civil society is minimized. This is why the coast should be developed using the public-private partnership model as much as possible, instead of selling it and trying to influence development post festum through obsolete traditional zoning and planning instruments.

Q I find quite interesting your argument that what places Croatian culture in the European cultural setting is not literature or art but its historical towns.

VM I believe that what distinguishes and promotes Croatia, and sets the course of its future development is our architectural heritage, perhaps even more than our music or literary heritage. I may be professionally biased, but developed countries know little about what distinguishes Croatia from Slovenia or Slovakia, just as we know little about the differences between Latvia, Lithuania, and Estonia. And yet, almost everyone has heard of Dubrovnik and Diocletian's Palace in Split. Visitors to Croatia are often astonished and then enchanted by our historical towns and landscape. Ston could serve as a textbook example of urban development, a lesson for architects on how to treat space. Diocletian's Palace, on the other hand, clearly illustrates how an imperial villa was transformed into a functional town, teaching us about a dynamic approach to architectural typology.

I think it is important that we show our advanced urban culture and its historical ties with space to foreign investors and architects, but this also goes for our recent architectural production. This is what we tried to do in the book <u>Contemporary Croatian Architecture: Testing Reality</u>, which can serve as a guidebook for foreign developers in Croatia. The first thing you do when you come to a new environment is to get hold of publications on the history and current architecture of that area, but publications in English that would introduce foreigners to our architectural past and present are still in short supply.

INTERVIEW AT DAZ *

Vedran Mimica, the Berlage Institute for www.d-a-z.hr/hr/vijesti/intervju-vedran-mimica-institut-berlage,1599.html, published on August 8, 2012

The Berlage Institute as we know ceased to exist on August 1, 2012. At the same time, a new institution by the name of the Berlage Center for Advanced Studies in Architecture and Urban Design was established at the Delft University of Technology Faculty of Architecture. These two events are the familiar consequence of the economic crisis that forced Dutch administration to cut out the Berlage from the "basic infrastructure of cultural institutes."

DAZ Are you going to stay the dean of the Berlage?

Vedran Mimica My mandate ends with the old Berlage. It lasted from 2007 to 2012, during the period in which the Berlage strengthened its position as a leading international research institute of architecture and urban planning. I insisted on the social, or if you will, political and ideological aspects of sustainable building and redevelopment of metropolitan areas. What we had in mind was a new kind of "welfare" state or city and worked on a new theory that would define new realities. The global crisis from the early 2008 has once again confirmed that this kind of thinking is necessary, but it has also posed even greater challenges for our concepts. We were generating concepts and strategies for a new urban development of the world that would respond to the needs of all people and not only some of them. But to answer your question: no, I will not remain the dean, which is in line with the good tradition of the Berlage Institute. We will publicly announce the vacancy for the new head, but I will strongly advocate that preference is given to our former students who have contributed to what we call the Berlage legacy.

Q What has the future in store for the Berlage?

* DAZ, acronym for Društvo arhitekata Zagreba – Zagreb Society of Architects.

VM Uncertainty. My colleague and general director of the Berlage Institute Rob Docter suggested in an interview for ArhiNed that shutting down the Berlage due to general cuts in the public sector was a thoughtless act, and that he did not see any particular gain in its shift to Delft. Regretfully, I concur. Even though we have been given the opportunity to continue with our work and are deeply grateful to the new management of the Delft Faculty of Architecture, our future will depend on the number of students who can afford to enroll in this very expensive school. The thing is that the Faculty of Architecture has to cut more than 20% of its annual budget to survive, and there will be no money left for the development of the Berlage Center.

Q In what else will the Delft TU Berlage differ from this one?

VM Our work at Delft will be limited to the postgraduate master program and to organizing public lectures by leading architects and theoreticians on behalf of the Faculty of Architecture. The new Berlage will no longer have its own PhD program or a "contract-research program" (you probably remember the Croatian Archipelago New Lighthouses project). It will no longer publish the periodical Hunch or research reports, as all will be digital and in a way commercial.

The advantage is that the program will be accredited, and that the students will receive 90 ECTS credits and a diploma for a three-semester study.

Q Can this immersion into the academic system actually sink the Berlage?

VM The Berlage you know sank on August 1, 2012. The Delft Berlage is, to all intents and purposes, a new institution/foundation, that will keep some aspects of its predecessor. Some type of symbiosis is definitely possible. Metaphorically speaking, it will be like one of those small fish swimming around a big shark and cleaning its teeth.

Q   The Berlage provided education and experience to many young Croatian architects. How will these changes in business affect the enrollment of new Croatian generations in the Center?

VM I do not see many young architects from Croatia or Southeastern Europe turning up at the Delft Center. The greatest hindrance will probably be the 22,500 Euro tuition fee for the three-semester study. My humble opinion on the other hand is that this is one of the best investments in your career future in Europe.

Q   In late October last year you signed the so called Memorandum of Understanding between the Berlage Institute and the University of Rijeka. Will that collaboration continue?

VM This project counted on the EU IPA fund intended for the advancement of school programs in Croatia. We put our heads together with a team of fantastic people from the University of Rijeka and submitted an application for the first specialist study of architecture and urban planning in English in Croatia. The idea was to establish a regional research center for urban development in the Mediterranean. However, the evaluation we received said that this project was not relevant enough within the Croatian educational framework. The evaluating agency did not bother to explain any further, and the opportunity to establish a transparent and argument-driven dialogue with the IPA fund went out the window. As we are absolutely convinced of the relevance of this project, the University of Rijeka will start an accredited lifelong learning program next year. It will consist of a series of workshops for young architects and final-year architecture students, and we hope that it becomes a two-semester postgraduate study any time soon. Collaboration with the Berlage in Delft is yet to be negotiated.

Q   What is your view of the current situation in Croatian architecture from the position of a head of an acknowledged international institute?

VM Within its current social context, Croatian architecture has made many exceptional cultural and professional achievements. But what bothers me is this troublesome social context. I do not see any signs of social or economic improvement in Croatia that would be beneficial for architecture and urban planning in particular. It is really mind-boggling that not even current EU integration processes have generated new enthusiasm or ideas.

CLOSIN

LIFE AFTER THE DEATH IN VENICE
Zagreb 2006
CLOSING TIME!
Zagreb 2009
UTOPIAN JOURNEYS
Zagreb 2010
E LA NAVE VA
Zagreb 2014

G TIME

For over a century, the Venice Biennale (La Biennale di Venezia) has been one of the most prestigious cultural institutions in the world. Over the past thirty years, the Biennale has given growing importance to the Architecture Exhibition.

Paolo Portoghesi as the director with the committee (Vincent Scully, Christian Norberg-Schulz, Charles Jencks, among others) in 1980 organized the 1st International Architecture Exhibition titled La presenza del passato (The Presence of the Past), which was a consideration of the Postmodernist movement.

Portoghesi main exhibition was named Strada Novissima, a hypothetical postmodern "street" made up of twenty facades that sparked a historical debate about the "lost language of architecture."

Since 1980 I have been involved with the Venice Biennale in various capacities. First as a visitor from the nearby city of Zagreb where I lived in the 1980s; then as the director of Biennale student workshops in 2000 and 2002, curator of the Croatian exhibition and director of production of the Berlage Institute exhibition in 2006, and later as a speaker at openings of national pavilions and panelist in various symposia at the Venice Biennials.

The texts included within this section are meant to discuss the question of cultural and social importance of exhibiting architecture and architectural research. Each biennial discussed in this section has distinctive challenges in their respective periodic contexts. Biannually, a new appointed director is faced with the threats of wide criticism of whether the contemporary responses to the changing urban domain is presented comprehensively enough in the architectural language.

The essays include personal perspectives on the success of the biennial exhibits, with self-reflections on the acquired insights to better position the Berlage Institute postgraduate research based design discourse as well as Croatian architecture on the global stage.

Moreover, the biennials of this decade have been defining the ethical qualities of architecture as a discipline with more globalized views, recognizing the departure of the Modernist utopian pursuit as an important concept in the historic legacy of previous biennials. The Venice Biennale catalyzes significant international discourse about the accessibility of architecture in its innovative and experimental quests, at the same time it spurs an ongoing conversation about culture and identity while cultivating advanced models of urban developments and research.

LIFE AFTER THE DEATH IN VENICE

Published in Oris 42, Zagreb 2006

Now that the 10th Architecture Biennale in Venice is closed, I would like to open this critical reflection in the context of exchanging ideas about cities, architecture, and society with a brief press clipping overview of leading international journals.

Edwin Heathcote of the world's opinion maker Financial Times opens his article by placing Venice in its context and reflecting on Richard Burdett's response to the established tradition of the world's greatest architecture show:

Venice is an absurd city, a city of incomparable loveliness sinking into its own stinking canals, a city in which, as Italo Calvino points out in his Invisible Cities, we can see anything we want reflected, from decadence to decay, immorality to sublime beauty. It is the proto-heritage city, the first urban theme park, a city insistent on exhibiting itself and one that exists more in the imagination and memory than it does in reality. It is, then, the most potent place to hold architecture's biggest visionary event and even more perfect that it should host this year's particular theme of cities.
The Architecture Biennale, the world's most influential architecture festival, is usually focused on the promotion of "starchitecture", big new showstoppers from the jet-set design divas. It had, in fact, become a little dull, a blown-up version of coffee-table hagiographies. I ask Burdett how the "Cities" theme would fit into this tradition. "The Biennale," he replies, "is rediscovering its potential not just as a mirror but as a way of influencing thinking on the development of the discipline. There is a desire that Biennales should have a message. Over 100,000 people come to the shows and there are about 150 separate events in the city. It's important to realize that the architecture events are part of a bigger cultural program."

Follow Heathcote's critical deliberations on Burdett's show:

Burdett's show is more earnest. It is a supreme effort to bring architects back to the reality of the streets, to reintroduce the tough issues of poverty, transport, politics, immigration, crime and so on. But ultimately, the show offends no one. The statistics are over-familiar; the solutions are too general, too glib. The show tells us cities are diverse. They are getting bigger. Olympics will happen in some cities. Cities are full of people. Transporting people publicly is good. Corruption is bad. This much we already know.
But Burdett has made a start. He has already created a stir in the architectural world by broaching the bigger issues, his intentions are good and he is to be congratulated on a complex, big and engaging (if slightly tiring) effort.

Nicolai Ouroussoff of The New York Times openly criticizes the absence of architectural design:

What the show provides, in place of inspired architecture, is a window on a dystopian future. But the architecture is engulfed by the statistics. There are no models of actual buildings and few technical drawings. The architectural designs, in many cases presented on small video monitors, with one image following another and no opportunity to pause and study, are treated as afterthoughts, as if architects had little to contribute to the conversation. But it also reminds us of what good architects do: optimists by trade, they give concrete form to a future of their own imagining, transporting us to an elevated plane of existence. In Venice this goal was somehow lost.

> And to end the press clippings, a Hugh Pearman opinion as published in the RIBA Journal, London, and the Architect's Newspaper, New York:

Burdett has done a very risky thing. He has made this Biennale very serious indeed. Although the title is "Cities, Architecture and Society" he has largely ignored the second of those three words. We are in a world of statistics, density, population growth projections, cell phone data, general demographics, and analyses of cities which are expanding and those which are shrinking. Seldom has Google Earth and its equivalents been so much in demand for overhead views. Never have so many images of ordinary life in ordinary cities been gathered together in one place. It is all immensely worthy. It is also, with some exceptions, monumentally dull.

> Richard "Ricky" Burdett, the director of the 10th Architecture Biennale is a professor at the London School of Economics and Political Science (LSE) and consultant for urban development to London's mayor Ken Livingstone. Even Burdett's appointment to curate the Biennale had an air of the extraordinary about it, for his work had been focused on urban development through research of areas where society, economy and politics overlap, rather than on specific architectural issues. His LSE program Urban Age, taught by professors such as Saskia Sassen and Richard Sennett, proposes that the most obvious consequence of globalization is the development of cities as new megalopolises. The world has only now stepped into a new "urban age" in which more than half the Earth's population lives in the city. This piece of information may seem less awesome if we consider the population boom over the last 40 years. In 1966, the Earth's population was about three billion people, and now it is six billion. In other words, humankind has doubled over the last 40 years. Urbanization has shifted from the West to the East, to countries such as China and India, the new generators of city development or entirely new cities. According to projections based on the current GDP growth of 10% per annum, China alone will populate its cities with 400 million people by the year 2020. This is the entire Croatian population multiplied by one hundred.

In Europe urbanization seems to be taking the opposite direction. A number of European towns are shrinking. One of the reasons is the adamantly restrictive immigration policy of the EU countries, another is the economic reconstruction Europe is going through, and yet another is the negative population growth. To present these issues to a wider architectural public, Burdett made them central to the Venice Biennale. All shows before this one fostered a kind of interdisciplinary discussion, but now it has become multidisciplinary. In his mini-manifesto on the relationships between cities, architecture and society, Burdett proposes a thesis that the ultimate issue of this century is the understanding of these processes and of socially relevant urban development strategies and visions, including those of entirely new cities. Burdett also offered an operational motto that shoving reality down one's throat will not do, and neither will tons of graphs; that this reality, however spectacular in

RANDIĆ & TURATO :
THE ARCHITECTURE OF TRANSITION

Kenneth Frampton, Darko Glavan, Vedran Mimica
Arhitekst, Zagreb, 2010

Vedran Mimica
Architecture of Transition and
 the Production of Meaning

IN-BETWEEN :
A book on the Croatian coast, global
processes, and how to live with them

Saša Randić, Idis Turato

Rijeka, 2006

HUNCH, BEYOND MAPPING :
PROJECTING THE CITY

Berlage Institute Rotterdam, 2006

Engaging Reality
interview with Vedran Mimica by
Jennifer Sigler and Roemer van Toorn

Lagos, China, Las Vegas or Eastern Europe, still needs an architect's help with a scenario, a strategy, a concept of change.
This one cannot be argued in the face of the criticism Burdett had to take from the world's leading journals.

Quite another issue is how deeply architects will be involved in this new city construction business, if at all. Recently Rem Koolhaas held a lecture at the Berlage Institute in which he claimed that architects were completely excluded from construction of new cities. Koolhaas pointed to a paradox that architectural manifestos on new cities disappeared by the 1960s, the decade that saw the population boom and the development of new megalopolises such as Tokyo, Los Angeles, Lagos, Bangkok, Mumbai and Mexico City, in which architects played only a marginal role. Over the last 20 years, no city greater than 10 million people has been developing according to planned urban strategies or under an architectural influence worth mentioning. This paradox is clearly the consequence of globalization, of decentralized decision-making, of the collapse of totalitarian regimes, but a no lesser paradox is that architects are outstandingly popular as a profession which creates icons for a city, but not the city itself. Even though national pavilions, national issues and national architectures have been overrun by the global exchange of ideas, goods, services and people, interpretations of global processes are still local and very specific. This is what Burdett had in mind when he suggested that national teams, with or without pavilions in the Giardini, should address the central themes of the Biennale titled <u>Cities, Architecture and Society</u>.

Burdett put up a small competition for some fifteen countries still without the Giardini pavilion, looking for a proposal that would fit the central, Italian pavilion. The proposal entitled "In Between the Systems" of the architectural office Randić & Turato, lobbied for by Commissioner Andrija Rusan and curated by the author of these lines, got Croatia into the central

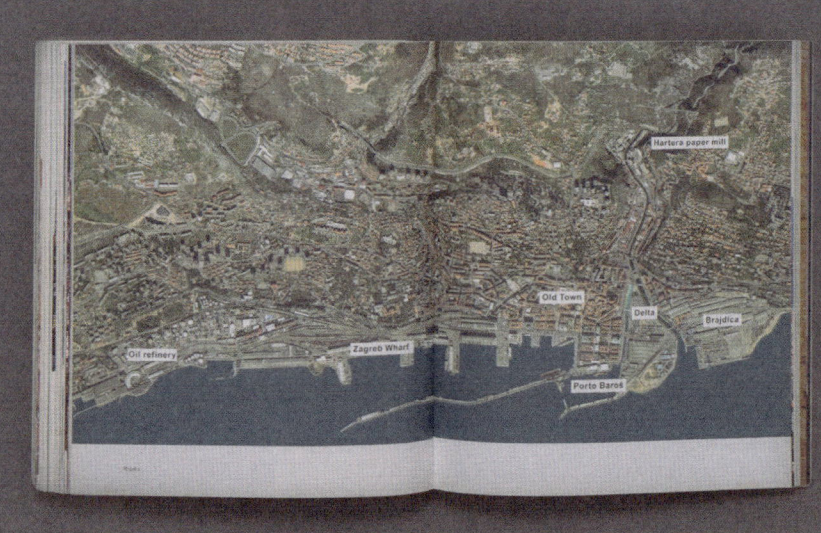

IN-BETWEEN : A book on the Croatian coast, global processes, and how to live with them

Saša Randić, Idis Turato
Rijeka, 2006

HUNCH, BEYOND MAPPING : PROJECTING THE CITY

Berlage Institute Rotterdam, 2006

pavilion in the select company of South Africa and Argentina. Curiously enough, from the competition entry to the Biennale opening, the Croatian multidisciplinary team formed by Randić and Turato and the Commissioner himself worked with extraordinary enthusiasm, and the financial support by the Croatian Ministry of Culture was absolutely forthcoming.

If we put it in the conceptual framework of the given themes, that is, cities, architecture and society, perhaps we can understand how national exhibitions work, or more specifically, how Croatia can present itself on an international exchange forum of architectural ideas.

In our postmodern age or the post critical age, as some fancy critics have recently started to call it, any kind of utopia or critical discourse is likely to be readily commodified and assimilated into the structures of the market and the media.

And while good old modernism believed in the "utopian spirit," allowing for the past to be fundamentally transcended by the future, in the developed Western world by nearly all contemporary accounts, avant-garde is dead and utopias are obsolete. Instead, the modern world is overrun by information technology, lifestyles and media; identity, brands and commodities are what society is demanding and consuming. This is why Ricky Burdett, starting from his LSE Urban Age program that has been substantially influenced by the research of Saskia Sassen and Richard Sennett, asked the Biennale participants to answer questions for which he claimed to be far more fundamental than "brands and commodities": What are the distinctions of the new urban age? How do you see the urban boom in Asia and in the world? Is public space vanishing? How do urban sprawl and concentration affect city development? What is the role of infrastructure in it? How does the labor market define new urban regions? How do cities treat the socially underprivileged? How do "governance and legal structures" keep up with city development or even initiate it? The Urban Age program has become an incubator of ideas for the central Arsenale exhibition, and national teams were "expected" to incorporate these absolutely important topics into their own presentations.

However, if we consider a country such as Croatia, whose population corresponds to an average Shanghai district and is two million short of the Mumbai slum population, it is evident that only a presentation of specific, transition-related urban issues could possibly justify Croatian participation, in fact its central position, in the Venice Biennale. With its objectionable opportunistic and technocratic development policy, the only Croatian metropolis, Zagreb, disqualified itself from the presentation; instead Burdett was counting on Italian and even global interest for the Croatian Adriatic towns as those having the greatest potential in Southeast Europe for an authentic sustained development, which is clearly evident from the recent architectural practice of offices such as Randić & Turato.

This is why our negotiations with Burdett focused on Rijeka, Split and Dubrovnik, on an area that has already become, and will shortly be fully influenced by the global market, especially its tourism segment. Tourism is now the world's largest industry; it employs 200 million people and makes 3.6 trillion USD a year. As only 15% of the Croatian Adriatic coast has been urbanized, possibilities for the development of new or alternative models of global tourism are enormous.

To quote the Croatian entry proposal: "In Between the Systems performs urban research which will focus on port transformation and the potential of local practices to contribute to the redefinition of port/city relationships". This choice of three developing ports is perhaps the most logical for a presentation within the city-architecture-society framework.

However the Croatian team set up a room with five multimedia walls staging five synchronized shows, with an interactive HG robot and presented a book In-Between, a book on the Croatian coast, global processes, and how to live with them.

Just like two years before, the Croatian architects

worked their ideas out in close collaboration with authors from "tangential disciplines" who substantially contributed to the concept, design and the structure of the exhibition. There were Ivana Franke, multimedia author of the 2004 campaign, rock musician Damir Martinović Mrle, and video clip director and cameraman Radislav Jovanov Gonzo, who participated in this Venice Biennale.

The Croatian presentation was a bundle of emotions, verging on drama. Mrle's music and Gonzo's video clip editing were practically shouting, "Here we are, Venice, standing before the whole world." But the presentation does not answer the question: "What are we here for?", and neither does any deeper investigation into the relationship between the HG robot and the synchronized video wall projections help to understand the messages their authors wanted to get across within the time compressed to TV standards. The answer should probably be looked for in the book In Between.

Its authors and editors, Saša Randić and Idis Turato, have collected their research there, and organized it in four sections: Prehistory, Transition, the New Millennium, and Fusion. This book and the exhibition start from the assumption that a context is more important and fundamentally more interesting than a concept. It is in a space in between, a space of permanent instability, of latent chaos, of ironical conceptual overlapping such as that of Croatia that the "state of affairs" is also their essence, what they really are. This is why the book unfolds like a collage non-linear puzzle, replacing critical and committed discourse with rhizomatous, post critical, and contextual discourse. This is why some of the critics and the public must have been somewhat disappointed, as they expected not only this spectacular display of the state of transitional affairs past and current, but also a proposal of how to deal with them.

An argument in favor of the Croatian presentation could be the post critical view that the market and media have consumed so-called utopias and that there is no critical discourse within the late-capitalistic mode of production. However, if we can theoretically declare the unfinished modern project to have finally been abandoned, we must ask ourselves what is there to fill the void? Perhaps we may remember that although literally grounded in reality and the present, architecture has the capacity to transcend particular contexts and moments in time and that the fundamental power of architecture in the creation of culture, through materialization of new and fundamental values, is manifested in the projections of the urban environment.

At the closing ceremony, for the second time in a row the Biennale jury awarded a national team that gave up national issues in favor of global processes. After Belgium, that was awarded for its presentation of life in Congo's capital Kinshasa in 2004, the Golden Lion Award for national pavilions was awarded to Denmark for project CO-EVOLUTION, Danish/Chinese collaboration on sustainable urban development in China. This is how the jury argued its decision:

"This pavilion shows us a country looking outward rather than inward, bringing its expertise to bear on the ecological problems faced by cities in China. The Danish pavilion does more than a catalog of these ecological challenges; the Danish planners and architects propose concrete solutions to water and energy management through visual forms of aesthetic merit. And the Danes show what they themselves learned from their Chinese colleagues. We salute the creativity, intelligence, and generosity of the Danish pavilion.

In addition to these awards, the Biennale jury would like to single out three exhibitions for outstanding merit: the Japanese Pavilion designed by Terunobu Fujimori for the integrity of its forms and for the sheer pleasure it provides to the visitors; the Iceland Pavilion for an outstanding collaboration between the artist Ólafur Elíasson and the architectural office Henning Larsen; the Pavilion of the Former Yugoslav Republic of Macedonia curated by Minas Bakalčev and Mitko Hadži Pulja for the depth and poetry of its thinking about urban form, rendered simple by chalks words and images on a black board."

The Venice Biennale is over, the awards distributed; Burdett has survived his adventure into the new age of viewing architecture through city development. This may be the right time to address the future development of Croatian architectural discourse.

After the totalitarian 1990s and life in relative isolation, save for occasional breakthroughs such as Europan, Frames of the Metropolis and the Days of Oris, Croatian architectural discourse revived communication with the public at home and abroad with the First Congress of Croatian Architects, the 38th Zagreb Salon curated by Stefano Boeri, Croatian participation at the Rotterdam Biennale, with the joint project named Croatian Archipelago New Lighthouses of the Croatian Architects Association and Berlage Institute, with the EU Tempus program for reform of high education, and finally with Croatia's full eligibility for the EU Mies van der Rohe Award for contemporary architecture. These events, rising publishing industry and strong NGO activity brought Croatian architecture closer to a European-style interactive communication with a wider social context. However, it would be absolutely wrong to conclude that Croatian architecture has now become a peer of other countries participating in international exchange. What happened is what was bound to happen anyway; figuratively speaking, we rose to our feet. As ever, we rose to our feet thanks to enthusiasts and architecture lovers and no thanks to a structured national architecture and urban development policy that should otherwise play a key role in Croatian integration into the European cultural and political environment.

A certain number of architectural enthusiasts gave Croatian architecture a chance, however theoretical and remote, to produce an authentic and consistent cultural discourse.

This year's Venice Biennale and Zagreb Salon tell us to pay more attention to the critical aspect in its development.

I believe that "critical and committed" mean that the key mission of architecture in Croatia (but not only in Croatia) is to protect and develop the public domain. Saskia Sassen's warning at the opening of the Venice Biennale that the urban public domain is under the threat of global capital's plans for contemporary cities and Rem Koolhaas' call for architects to act like public intellectuals reinforce the argument that architectural discourse must develop sensitivity toward public, shared space. Surrounded by transitional controversies, Croatian architects must commit themselves to the development of architectural practice through permanent education, theoretical research, international exchange, and publishing and specialist studies. Only through these will they be able to understand the social, economic and environmental domains of global processes. As a unique creative social force, architects first need to understand and then to shape the sensitive relationships between these domains into an authentic and sustainable projection of the Croatian city of the future.

Before a critical view can become an operational strategy, it is also absolutely necessary for government institutions to change and provide structural support to architecture and city planning as disciplines promoting critical approach in Croatian territory development. Needless to say, this process goes in many directions and works back and forth, and I would like to stress it one more time that only critical and highly professional architects can gain equal footing with global capital flows, political pragmatism and powerful media.

Finally a word of advice to those careful readers who noticed that the author of this text was also the curator of the Croatian exhibition at the Venice Biennale: this article should be read as a self-critical reflection.

BUILDING RELATIONS:
THE BERLAGE PLATFORM

Zagreb, 2008

ORIS 5

Zagreb, 2000

ORIS 55

Zagreb, 2009

Vedran Mimica: Closing Time

Bojan Radonić
Goran Rako

CLOSING TIME!

Excerpts from Interview with Aaron Betsky (Director of the 11th International Architecture Exhibition Out There: Architecture Beyond Building) conducted by Vedran Mimica and Andrej Radman in Amsterdam on November 29, 2008, published in Oris 55, Zagreb 2009

Q   How do you look in retrospect at that time from 2001 to 2007, when you worked as director of NAi (The Netherlands Architectural Institute)? You came after The SuperDutch (Bart Lootsma) had been published, when Dutch architecture was one of the most inspiring and interesting worldwide. How do you find the performance of the Dutch system of funding and promoting architecture, the structure which was basically installed by Hedy D'Ancona, the former minister of culture in the early 90s? She argued that architecture is very important for the Dutch culture, economy and international prestige and therefore the NAi, the Berlage Institute and the Netherlands Architecture Fund would be substantially funded by the country's budget for culture.

AB   Well, I do not think it started just with Hedy d'Ancona, there was a group of people. I think that when I was in the Netherlands I argued that it was a confluence of a very long tradition and basic facts of the artificial landscape which have been sketched out by a lot of people; with the appearance of a number of very bright people, let us not forget that having the presence of Rem [Koolhaas], and then Winy [Maas] and Willem-Jan Neutelings, and a whole group of people created one of those moments like in Los Angeles when Thom and Michael and Eric Moss, Frank Gehry, all happened to arrive in the same city. People come up with lots of theories why you get these nests of people. What of course is especially interesting is that that nest of people appeared just about the same time as the nest of people around Droog, with Renny Ramakers and Gijs Bakker, pulling together people like Hella Jongerius and Jurgen Bey and Marcel Wanders, people who now are world famous in their own field. And for me especially the relationship between them is very important, the relationship between them and the earlier generation of Anthon Beeke and Wim Crouwel and Total Design, and this notion that you have beautiful trains running through the whole country and beautiful stamps and money; the part of the whole state apparatus is extremely important. What is interesting is that it has been done without any good school of architecture, what is usually what causes it. It was done really without large commissions of the "showy" sort that you would have in England, France or America – it was done much more in the background. I think also I was lucky, because when I came here not only had ten years before this mechanism been set up with the NAi, Stimuleringsfonds, The Berlage – I mean, there was a whole nest of different organizations set up, originally the Design Institute as well – and my predecessor, Kristin Feireiss, had done a fantastic job using that to make the NAi into a hub in international discussion about architecture. Just as the Berlage had become with Hertzberger and Wiel [Arets] who made it a hub within this international discussion of architecture and those things together, really, were powerful. What was interesting to me was that when I arrived there what I found was chaos because, in so doing, Kristin had almost literally worked herself to death, she got carried away, it would work anyone else to death, so for the first time in my life my role was to say, "Ok, take a deep breath, let us be calm, we do not have to do everything at the same time." But I think that after I had been there for a few years I managed to actually get the place to where we could be a very powerful engine for focusing public attention on the design environment through exhibitions and debates and I did that despite all of the cutbacks in government funding. It was an interesting time to be in the Netherlands.

Q   And now, to come to the present, you are now in Cincinnati where you had to build an extension to the museum, if I understand the process correctly, and then to run it?

AB   We have a fantastic old museum with a very large collection, and when I arrived there I was told that they were ready for a major expansion renovation: they had done a masterplan; they were ready to hire an architect to get it going. When I arrived there I found out that it was not quite true. People have sort of said, "Yes, we'll do it," without really knowing what that really meant. So I had to spend the first year and a half there getting people to the point where this last summer they said, "Yes, we believe in this," "We're going to do this," and "This is how we are going to do it," and that also took reorganizing the staff and all those kinds of things. And now, of course, unfortunately right at the point where we were beginning to raise money we had to suspend that because of the economic crisis. So that is on hold. But what I have done in the meantime is to try to really understand what this art museum is about and what an encyclopedic art museum in general is about, and to understand that here the roots are really in the Arts and Crafts Movement. And that using art as a way to understand where you have come from, where you are and where you are going, can make it a very powerful tool in the community. And I have tried to redirect exhibitions and the programs to accomplish that and that of course would be an ongoing effort.

Q   And then you must have received a phone call from the Biennale….

AB Yeah, it was very strange. I was doing this extension; I was actually in the offices of Neutelings Riedijk, talking about plans. My secretary calls and says, "A fellow called, Mr. Baratta, from Italy, and wants to talk to you," and I said, "Well, give him my cell phone number" and he called me and said, "Hello, I am Paolo Baratta, I have a problem – maybe you can help." And I said, "Hello, Mr. Baratta, who are you and what is your problem?" And he said, "Well, I have just been made the president of the Biennale and I found out we do not have a curator." And I said, "Interesting that you should think about this, since I was commissioner for the Dutch pavilion three times, and visited a lot, and I have always thought you should think about this and that and wish that a biennale could contain this and that." [Betsky received a Golden Lion for the best foreign pavilion in 2002.] After a moment of silence he said, "I think you have solved my problem." And I said, "Well, not so fast because, you know, I have a job." And he said, "We must talk." Then I said, "OK, look. I am going on vacation. But I am going on vacation in Amalfi where one of my board members found this incredible hotel for us and we are going to and stay in Amalfi." He said, "I will come to see you." I said, "Well, I am not going to come to Rome." He said, "No, no, I will come to see you." So we go to Amalfi and the next day this guy shows up with his chauffeured car from Rome. He proved to be a fantastic man, very intelligent man, we had a fantastic conversation and then he said, "Look, at least go to Venice and look at it." There goes my vacation. I drove up to Venice from Amalfi, and the whole time I am driving there I am going, "I'm not going to do this, I'm not going to do this, it is crazy, it is insane, I can't do this…" And then I get there and this guy Max, Massimiliano – he is fantastic – meets me and takes us to the Arsenale. It was minus one degree. We were all bundled up, and he opens up the door and there is the whole Arsenale completely empty. And he just goes like this [outstretching his arm] and I look at Peter, my husband, and Peter looks at me and says, "Well, there goes 2008. What do we do in 2009?" Once you see that space you cannot, you cannot…

Q   You seem to be very conscious of historicity. I was hoping that you would draw a rough genealogy of the Venice Architectural Biennale for us. You have recently stated that the current Biennale has worked out the facts and figures of the previous one into a form.

AB You cannot help but think, when you work on the Biennale, of this incredible start that it had. Remember that the Architecture Biennale is a "Benjamin", the late son of the Art Biennale. It started with this incredible moment of the Strada Novissima, and with this notion that they could assemble the collective image of what architecture was thinking about them. And then Aldo Rossi's Biennales with the Teatro del Mondo, which for me was the very symbol of how you could install a new kind of architecture in the city, rather than just pointing at it. One starts, I think, with the notion that one actually makes architecture there, not postcards. Because, even more than most exhibitions, the Biennale is at such a scale that putting up postcards of buildings makes no sense. Of course, it went through much turmoil in which I saw myself responding first to Fuksas who said, "Why are we making buildings, what is the ethical quality of buildings?" Then Sudjic asked, "OK, good question, but first of all we have to make good buildings." Then Foster responded, "These two are not really opposites, we have to think about what the form and the meta-form of architecture are, they really are one," and Ricky Burdett followed, "Yes, but we have to understand that they are part of a larger social construct which is embodied in the city." I said, "OK, now that we have all of this on the table, the question is – what do we do with it?" Because, I do not think that buildings are any longer enough to answer the kind of questions that have been raised and already in Foster and all these people you begin to see that the most interesting experiments were not in the creation of autonomous buildings, but went beyond that. I think that Sudjic really got the best of the autonomous buildings and then what do you do after that? This was called "Next", but this is maybe "After".

Q But before we turn to "Architecture vs. Building", which is the topic that we would really like to discuss further, this year marks a very special anniversary. You have been asked this before but it is important to dwell on it again – 1968 – forty years on, what is its legacy in general terms, but also in relation to the issues of utopia and technology in particular?

AB Yeah, to me this is also very important – this is also my PhD at the Berlage if I can get back to it – there was a moment between 1968 and 1973 that Modernism died. And Modernism died because Modernity died, which is to say the self-perpetuating automatic production of technologically based advances in every aspect of our lives ground to a halt. The Vietnam War turned into a quagmire, the economy stagnated, the oil crisis happened, we realized the limits of growth with Club of Rome Report and the social contract that had allowed this incredible post-war boom to occur came undone. All of this happened between May 1968 and the summer of 1973, or the fall of '73. In between were the Prague revolution and all these other events. The point that I try to make for architecture is that it meant, therefore, that architects who also, by the way, at that point had no work, had to think about what they were doing and the notion that what one was producing in architecture was a promissory note to utopia – in other words, that every building one did was a building stone for utopia that might not be realized there, but this was one building stone of it – had to be abandoned, and with it the notion of systemic thinking. And what one saw instead was a notional interest in systems as incomplete and self-contradictory and the re-emergence of narrative, stories to be told whether they were histories or whether they were stories like detective stories, like Bernard Tschumi.

Q Or Voluntary Prisoners of Architecture (Koolhaas with Zenghelis)...

AB Right. And at the intersection of system and narrative what I call experimental architecture appeared, which is an architecture that still believed that one had to do more than make buildings that were functional but did not believe that there was a fixed utopia to which one was moving, but instead saw its task as experimenting. The two loci of that kind of experimentation were in London at the AA [Architectural Association] and in New York, at the Institute of Architecture and Urban Studies. Many things were happening at the same time in Italy (Superstudio) but those two were really the cores. My contention is that the people who came out of that, who now are amongst the most important and influential architects in the world, Rem, Tschumi, Zaha, and all these people have then generated by now two or three generations of students who have kept this experimental architecture practice alive. With this Biennale basically I want to say, "This is what I feel is right in architecture, what I am interested in architecture, what I think architecture should be about in this mode of experimentation."

Q   In the Italian Pavilion you juxtaposed Gehry from the 1970s and Zaha from the 1980s with the new generations.

AB I was trying to say, "Here is the tradition," here is what I want to call the "OGs", the "Original Gangsters", people who had been doing this since the 1970s, and here are the people who are working on it today, who are carrying this tradition forward. It has formal implications, it has environmental implications, it has political implications, and so I tried to show that whole messy array of what comes out of what people were doing in the 1970s and 1980s, and continue to do to this day. The one person who I left out was Peter Eisenman, mainly because he had been so featured in the last Biennales.

Q   The subtitle of the Biennale, "Out There", could be read in opposition to "in here" [points to his forehead]. It places an emphasis on the encounter. All these architects who kept experimenting could be tied in with the notion of an "enacted utopia" as Slavoj Žižek would have it, that is to say, something that one does out of pure urge rather than through conscious planning or teleological contemplation.

AB There are a lot of overtones but quite frankly the origin of the title goes back to the lecture series that I put together in Los Angeles when I founded the Los Angeles Forum for Architecture and Urban Design and we did a lecture series called "Out There Doing It" which they have resurrected since, as I understand. And it was basically on kids who left their firms, like me, and were out there doing it. Of course, it also means "out there beyond what is normal, acceptable" you might even think of it "sexually out there," everything that is out there, beyond.

Q   You often stress that architecture needs to deal with what is already there.

AB I mean it literally. I am very interested of course in taking the discoveries of Droog design into the realm of architecture with the notion that the last thing we need is new buildings. What we need is to rethink, reuse, and reconceptualize what already exists. I was surprised that architects did not get upset about this and they got upset about all other kinds of things I thought were absurd, but probably the most radical thing I thought is you should always ask yourself the question of Neutelings' "lazy architecture," "Do I really need to make a building here?", "Do I really need to make something?" This is the other reason why the Delft situation is so fantastic because after the literal failure of the brutalist technological fortress the re-inhabitation is so much more fantastic. It is such a great way also to be able to stand there with students and point to the unfinished ceiling in relationship to the windows and say, "This is how it works, this is where you start." So that to me is fantastic. [Betsky is referring to the adaptations made to the building temporarily housing the TU Delft Architectural Faculty after fire demolished the 1970 van den Broek / Bakema building in the spring of 2008.]

Q   On the issue of the ground you keep talking about framing and staging, about architecture that makes us feel at home. This is another unexpected (Heideggerian) move that is much appreciated.

AB The theory there that I worked with is based on the work of Tony Giddens, although when I asked him about it he said that I had completely misunderstood what he was talking about. [They laugh.] He talks about the fact that what we essentially do in our lives, everything we do, is an attempt to try to create a stage in which we can act in the role that we believe we are destined to act in. And we try to find fellow actors and we try to find a stage. I think that architecture as the staging of an environment that we feel is proper for us is its central task.

Q   Giddens' discourse was obviously influential in "staging a stage" for the Arsenale show. Your modus operandi was to invite leading practitioners and to construct a sort of architectural promenade. How would you describe this journey from Coop Himmelb(l)au to Nigel Coates?

AB I am not sure that there was a logical progression. I mean, it was more a question of the rhythm. We went through something like 28 different variations of placements of these things. So much had to do with pragmatic things, you know, like Zaha showed up at the last moment with something I could not get through the door. You know, when I saw what Nigel Coates was doing it seemed very much like a kind of altarpiece so it should come at the end, a moment of rest, a moment of return to the body. It seemed very much like an end piece. But there was a sense that in the Arsenale tried to install the building blocks for architecture beyond building, and the Italian pavilion was a series of tactics and strategies, you know, a sort of flailing around if you will.

Q How would you evaluate individual curatorial answers, for example the Danish pavilion which went into kind of eco-politics or the Swiss which would argue that education is perhaps beyond architecture, presenting "Explorations in Architecture", a design-research method introduced at four leading Swiss architectural schools?

AB The ones that most interested me were things like the Japanese pavilion that was very beautiful – it was absolutely gorgeous, I thought the German pavilion which took it to the kind of logical; techno-utopian extreme was quite fantastic; I loved the Belgian pavilion (Party is Over), that was really fantastic. I think it is remarkable – and president Barata said this several times – that there was much more response to my theme than there had been in the previous Biennale, so I was happy with that. The Polish pavilion, of course, which won the Golden Lion, I thought they were quite interesting. It is interesting because I did not see the Swiss one as being about education. The result, what you saw, was actually building blocks for architecture which was what I thought was interesting about it. That incredibly sexy wall, which had roots in Thomas Jefferson's walls and beyond that was fantastic because it exactly made the point that you can make architecture beyond building, you can make a series of components that do not necessarily have the elements of what one would think of as a building.

Q Biennale somehow marked the end of an era. What followed was the credit crunch, the end of deregulation, marked by states taking on a new role in planning and brokering new deals. Many critics and even pragmatic practitioners have lately been contemplating architectural engagement with politics. Did you observe such tendencies already in your Biennale?

AB The one thing that I was very clear about, which I thought was clear but apparently was not communicated well enough was that this was not going to be a Biennale that was going to present solutions. In fact several critics said, "Well, we doubt it's going to be good because it ignores the social-economic-environmental problems of the world," and my point was, "Haven't you realized that when you ask architects to solve the social-economic-environmental problems of the world they make it worse?" Do not ask architects to solve it! Ask architects to ask the right questions, to open up your eyes, to do the right thing and then let people work on that to provide the building blocks. Certainly do not expect either, as has been done in the past, not to give to architects any money, to give them immense social problems, like social housing and say, "We are giving no money, we are giving you insolvable social problems – fix them!" You will just get more prisons.

Q However, I think the Italian and Chinese national pavilions tried to deal with that issue in a very interesting way.

AB Yes, and that is fine. But, again, I was not looking for solutions or looking for people to offer solutions. Not that I do not think there are problems, I just think that there are things that we need to do as citizens, and as citizens we can offer a certain amount of expertise which comes from our discipline and we should not pretend to be the Albert Speers of the ecological war.

Čovjek i prostor, 5-6
Zagreb, 2010

ORIS 28
Zagreb, 2004
Vedran Mimica: Acanthus
Branimir Medić
Pero Puljiz

ORIS 5
Zagreb, 2000

UTOPIAN JOURNEYS

Published in Čovjek i prostor 5-6, Zagreb 2010

Why we hate the Utopian with such fervor? Because it makes too many demands? Even Google cannot help you out here... The current moment has almost no idea how to negotiate the coexistence of radical change and radical stasis that is our future.

Quotes from Rem Koolhaas/OMA/AMO, the exhibition Cronocaos at the Venice Biennale 2010.

Kazuyo Sejima, the first ever female architect, the director of the 12th International Architecture Exhibition at the Venice Biennale, presented the participants, the 54 national teams and selected architects, with a cluster of seemingly simple thematic relations under the umbrella People meet in architecture. Sejima clarified her approach with the following words: 'The idea is to help people relate to architecture, help architecture relate to people and help people relate to themselves [...] There will be independent spaces for each architect or each country, which means that the participants will be their own curators. In this way contributors will design their own space and make presentations that consider the experience of the visitor both physically and conceptually. It will be a series of spaces rather than a series of objects.'[118]

The Croatian author-group of architects, selected by Leo Modrčin, the commissioner of the Ministry of Culture of the Republic of Croatia for the Croatian participation at the 12th International Architecture Exhibition in Venice, set out on an extremely ambitious project as a possible answer to Sejima's thematic relations about how people relate to architecture, architecture to people, and people to themselves. Here is a quote by the group, from the official web-site: 'Without project and all its formats (the realized pavilion, the exhibition installation with blueprints, photographs and a film, the posters for compiling a book, the book, the web-site), we passionately wanted to affirm and illustrate the idea of a floating pavilion which takes Croatian exhibits every year across the sea to the Venice Biennale. We wish to repair the damaged pavilion, present it in Venice, and after the Biennale closes, hand it over to the Museum of Modern and Contemporary Art and exhibit it in Rijeka.'

This is/was an extraordinary effort to carry out almost all possible formats of exhibiting a national architecture within a world exhibition.

If you read the book / catalog Brod / The Ship / La Nave: A floating pavilion for Croatia at the Venice Biennale, which very precisely represents the process which the group and the commissioner underwent between the end of March and the end of August 2010, you will have to conclude that the project's conceptual premises, work-process and final realization had, along with the obvious ambition, a clearly Utopian dimension.

The very idea of building a national floating pavilion for the permanent representation of architecture and art at the Mostra in Venice is in conflict with almost all, urban, maritime, organizational, financial, and probably also political givens concerning the relationship between the Venetian Maritime Territory and foreign countries. The catalog and the book have very precisely mapped the commissioner's and architects' efforts to convince the Venetians otherwise. The last country which built a pavilion in the Giardini was Korea, although a "prefabricated" one with no foundations, following an extremely long and complicated process. And Singapore was the last country with a promotional, commercial floating pavilion anchored in the Arsenale.

The second somewhat Utopian aspect was the idea to entrust the project with a group of 15 architects and to practice the method of collective decision-making in all aspects of the presentation in Venice. The third one was probably the relation between

[118] Etherington, Rose (2010) Venice architecture biennale announced. Published on January 28, 2010. Source: www.dezeen.com/2010/01/28/venice-architecture-biennale-theme-announced, accessed September 17, 2016

ambition and resolution on one, and attainable resources on the other hand.

Furthermore, the faith in "improvisation", "disorganization", and "intuition", "lucky moments" and "still sea" testifies to a truly Utopian "drive" of this group of people who are totally dedicated to architecture and its mission.

Despite all that, or precisely because of it, the result of the group's work has a historic meaning for Croatian architecture. Hereby I primarily speak about the architecture of the built pavilion.

In order to perform a connotative analysis of the realization, I would like to refer to Boris Groys, Russian philosopher who visited Zagreb during DOMUS magazine workshop in 2004. Groys then stated, while speaking about countries which grew out of socialism, that real Utopian concepts are those in which the participants, having "journeyed" to Utopia, leave it.

According to Groys, if we knew merely how to get to Utopia, that knowledge would not be useful, but if we know how to come and go, that knowledge is useful, "technical". A Utopian project is in fact a project for an endless journey, but also a project whose most important aspect deals with the technical knowledge of Utopian activity or journey. If we paraphrase Groys again, we might say that the author-group created a thoroughly special collective design. I believe that within the process of the pavilion's realization they created a special collective aesthetic experience, but unfortunately without the consciousness about how to handle it. It is/was a collective emotional thrill, an aesthetic experience. The experience is present while you are there and then also when you leave. Groys will have finally concluded that creating contemporary public space (as well as a pavilion for international exhibitions) by artistic, architectural or political means is precisely such an experience.

If we return to recent history for just a moment, we have to conclude that, apart from the authors-architects, just the few lucky visitors to the pavilion in Rijeka, before it embarked on its tragically voyage to Venice, had the privilege of experiencing that. The transport of the barge and the pavilion to Venice perhaps required that one forgets about Groys' technical aspect of the Utopian experience and opt for the purely technical knowledge of professor Sabljak's structural engineering basic principles.

This aspect of the national participation at the biggest architectural exhibition in the world particularly deserves criticism, but the author of these lines does not feel entirely capable of it beyond the Vitruvian lesson of firmitas,[119] which inevitably points to a certain level of the authors' responsibility for the "stability to the Utopian voyage" of the pavilion, to Venice. The history of modern architecture could almost be told by the history of building national or corporate pavilions for the World Fairs (EXPO) and international architectural biennials. From the Mies pavilion in Barcelona 1929 and its resurrection in 1986 to Moshe Safdie's Habitat in Montreal 1967, from le Corbusier's l'Esprit Nouveau at the Paris EXPO of 1925 to MVRDV's Dutch pavilion for the Hannover EXPO of 2000, from Melnikov's Soviet Russia's pavilion at the Paris EXPO of 1925 to Diller&Scofidio's Blur Building at lake Neuchâtel at the Swiss EXPO of 2002, a pavilion is the theme and task in which architecture ponders its limitations and capabilities, and presents new canons in response to the thematic environments of particular events. Croatian history of exhibitions/pavilions has noted Drago Ibler's expressionist/protomodernist design for the exhibition in the theatre section of the Yugoslavian pavilion at the Paris EXPO of 1925, Vjenceslav Richter's pavilions for the Bruxelles EXPO of 1958 and the Pavilion of Self-Government and Free Time for the Milan Design Triennial of 1963, Ivan Crnković's participation at the 5th Venice Architecture Biennale of 1990, Branko Silađin's Croatian pavilion at the Lisbon EXPO of 1998, and 3LHD's at the Japan's EXPO of 2005.

The Croatian pavilion for the 12th International Architecture Exhibition in Venice is a fundamental contribution to the history of "pavilion" architecture, not

---

119 One of the three qualities of any structure that Vitruvius emphasized in his book De architectura is firmitas, which means firm, solid.

Rem Koolhaas
Kazuyo Sejima
Leo Modrčin
Boris Groys
Drago Ibler
Vjenceslav Richter
Ivan Crnković
Hannah Arendt
Kenneth Frampton
Christian Keres
Kersten Geers
David Van Severen
Marko Dabrović (3LHD)

MEDITERRANEAN CRUISE BROCHURE

Jadrolinija, Yugoslavia

Rijeka, 1966

Čovjek i prostor, 5–6

Zagreb, 2010

Vedran Mimica: Utopian Journeys

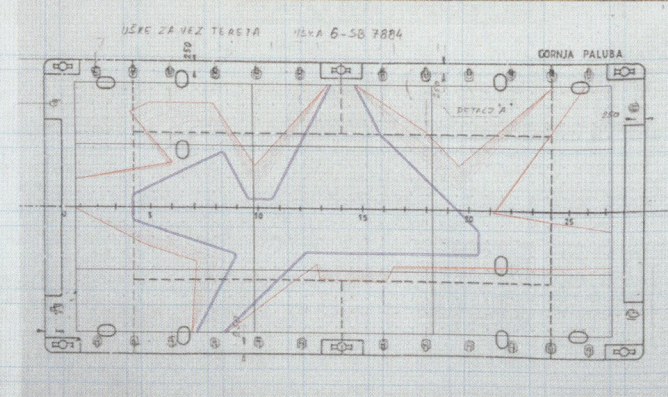

only within the Croatian context. The author-group, perhaps even somewhat unconsciously, almost rhizomatically, extremely intelligently responded to or, one should say, reinterpreted Sejima's dual relations. Even a virtual walk through the pavilion, at the moment, unfortunately, the only possible one, is enough for one to recognize clearly that an elementary architectural structure can "help" establish relations between people and architecture, architecture and people, and people with themselves. In an extremely direct way, this pavilion shows the true capability of architecture to elevate us to a higher level of spatial existence. That is probably one of the basic purposes of architecture and architectural action. Thus the very positive reaction of Kazuyo Sejima, during her conversation with Leo Modrčin and myself in Venice about the "incoming" Croatian pavilion, came as no surprise at all. Through the publication about the pavilion, I believe that Sejima recognized one of possibly inspiring interpretations of her curating efforts.

It is perhaps less important to answer whether the pavilion and its "completed" presence are the results of inspired authorship, coincidence, collective effort of individual spur-of-the-moment inspiration; one should rather try to explain the contextual-connotative aspects of the realized work. The contextual aspects primarily refer to the link the pavilion, as an artifact, establishes with the general, common atmosphere of the Biennale.

I would like to mention that the Golden Lion for the best design at the exhibition People Meet in Architecture was awarded to the design Architecture as Air: Study for Château la Coste by the architect Junya Ishigami, with the following explanation: 'The jury would like to acknowledge the unique and uncompromising vision of its author, Junya Ishigami. The work pushes the limits of materiality, visibility, tectonics, thinness, and ultimately of architecture itself.'[120]

It is a delicate spatial installation, a 1:1 model of a building, dealing with creating transparency which is not limited by massive, solid structures. The work of the young Japanese architect, Ishigami, is most certainly different from the work of the Croatian author-group, but some obvious conceptual similarities are more than present and to a certain extent they define what probably are the most interesting contributions of this year's Mostra through their radical investigations of the capabilities of architecture as a tectonic discipline. In those investigations tectonics are not primarily perceived as "load-bearing", but rather as the means of creating space of public appearance – having borrowed a phrase of Frampton's taken from Hannah Arendt's philosophical discourse. Another serious reading of Frampton can help us to conclude that perhaps the most interesting contributions to the Venetian exhibition are the works of those architects (Christian Kerez and the "little silver lions" from Belgium, Kersten Geers and David Van Severen) who "rediscovered" tectonic as an irreducible aspect of architecture, involving an oscillation between presentation and representation, between the constitution of the thing as such and its manifestation as form.

The connotative line of analysis of the Croatian pavilion has to touch upon the very concept of "space of public appearance", which brings us once more to Frampton and his argument: 'I prefer the word civic as opposed to public because of the political connotations of this word. I think that every truly public building must be conceived so that it works – to use Hannah Arendt's phrase – as "the space of public appearance." That is, as the space in which the society recognizes itself, its own identity, and therefore of course its political and cultural potential.'

If we ponder for a moment the civic spaces of our transitional reality, then the pavilion of the group of Croatian architects does not speak – rather it "screams" about the need for a radical change of code, canon, model of creating space in which an individual can feel as though a part of the society. The "Croatian"

[120] Etherington, Rose (2010) Golden Lion awards winners announced at Venice Architecture Biennale. Published on August 31, 2010. Source: www.dezeen.com/2010/08/31/golden-lion-award-winners-announced-at-venice-architecture-biennale/, accessed September 17, 2016

* Title of the last film by Federico Fellini with a story that took place in 1914

Pavilion thus represents one plausible "radical stasis" from the sentence by Koolhaas at the beginning; it is its fundamental value even if we do not accept too quickly Rem's statement that something like that is unavoidably necessary for "our" future.

Let us conclude. If we accept Alvaro Siza's aphorism 'Architects do not invent anything, they transform reality,'[121] then it simultaneously warns both the society and architects about the delicacy of architectural action, and this warning should be taken very seriously by both sides.

Recommendations

Critical and partly theoretical texts do not usually end with recommendations, but the author asks to be forgiven for his weakness and succumbing to the temptation of entering the public discussion on the "pavilion case".

Firstly, Croatian cultural and professional public should finally accept the fact that in this country there is an extraordinary generation of architects who raised Croatian architecture to an enviable and recognizable European level, as a unique national architecture in comparison with all other transition countries.

Secondly, the pavilion for the Venetian exhibition must be rebuilt and such a decision must not take 57 years to make, like with Mies in Barcelona.

Thirdly, future Croatian participation in world exhibitions require a completely different organizational-logistical system. Do I think any of these "recommendations" will be seriously considered and accepted? Of course not! So, I feel something like that morning when Marko Dabrović answered my call from the Riva dei Sette Martiri about the arrival of the pavilion to Venice with,"Mime, damn, it broke."[122]

E LA NAVE VA * (AND THE SHIP SAILS ON)

Published in Oris 91, Zagreb 2014

The manifestation of the wind of thought is not knowledge but the ability to tell right from wrong, beautiful from ugly. And I hope that thinking gives people the strength to prevent catastrophes in these rare moments when the chips are down.

Quote from a movie Hannah Arendt by Margarethe von Trotta, based on five articles on the trial of Adolf Eichmann by Hannah Arendt, published in The New Yorker in 1963.

La Biennale

The astonishing beauty of thought, as Hannah Arendt describes it when she talks about the possibilities of active life (vita activa) in different realms of activity, may apply for the period of 34 years of Rem Koolhaas' presence at the Venetian Mostra. From the Strada novissima of 1980 to Fundamentals, his brainchild exhibition, Koolhaas' "manifestation of the wind of thought" has fundamentally affected the development of the global architectural discourse. The author of these lines has had the privilege to attend all the Biennials so far, in a variety of capacities, and has had the privilege to work in the Netherlands for the last 25 years under the strong influence and shelter of Rem Koolhaas' cloak, to paraphrase Dostoyevsky's words: 'We have all come out of Gogol's cloak.'[123]

This is why "we all" had been awaiting Fundamentals with great interest – to get the fundamental, if not the definitive, definition of Rem's "cloak."

Rem Koolhaas and the Biennale president Paolo Baratta came up with an ambitious "entertain-

---

121   Bouman, Ole & Van Toorn, Roemer. Desperately seeking Siza. A Conversation with Alvaro Siza Vieira. Source: http://www.roemervantoorn.nl/interviewalvaros.html, accessed October 10, 2016

122   What Dabrović actually said was "Mime, jebi ga, puk'o je", which is difficult to translate to proper English (Note by the editor).

123   The Overcoat (Russian: Шинель, translit.Shinel; sometimes translated as The Cloak) is a short story by Ukrainian-born Russian author Nikolai Gogol, published in 1842. The story and its author have had great influence on Russian literature, as expressed in the above paraphrased quote, attributed to Fyodor Dostoyevsky: "We all come out from Gogol's 'Overcoat'." Source: E.H. Carr (2014) Dostoevsky 1821-1881, London: Routledge, 2014

ORIS 91

Zagreb, 2015

Vedran Mimica
E la nave va – And the Ship Sails On

IN-BETWEEN :
A book on the Croatian coast, global processes, and how to live with them

Saša Randić, Idis Turato

Rijeka, 2006

ment" program for the global audience in Venice for the season summer/autumn 2014. Baratta gave Koolhaas two years plus a delay until summer to make the architectural exhibition the backbone of the entire program – to be fleshed out with other exhibitions, film, dance, music, and plays.

This idea of blending a variety of art forms under the same program, in which the architectural exhibition would be the central event, is a merger of Baratta's perception of the Venice Biennale as a cultural product of a "dying" city and of Koolhaas' idea of publicly displaying architecture through research practice. Fundamentals consisted of three exhibitions that "together illuminate the past, present and future of our discipline," to use Koolhaas' words, namely: Absorbing Modernity: 1924-2014 (national pavilions), Elements of Architecture (Central Pavilion), and Monditalia (Arsenale).

> Language is grammar. So, if architecture is to be considered a language, 'elements' do not matter. So for me what is missing [from the show], purposely missing, is the grammatic. [...] Koolhaas does not believe in grammar.

Cynthia Davidson, Eiseman's life and business partner made an extra effort to complement Eisenman's criticism with 24 critical reviews of the Biennale on nearly 50 pages of the magazine Log. The most eloquent and most critical was the text by Marco de Michelis, architecture history professor from Venice. He first presented the whole history of OMA/AMO exhibitions to conclude that Monditalia is an exhibition that "lacks attention to the general direction of a project altogether incapable of producing an original critical meaning." About Elements De Michelis is no less critical:

> A little bit Wunderkammer and a little bit trade show, Elements does not succeed in putting into focus the real, essential problem: the invention of a "new" system of rules that would allow us to relate the "elemental" elements of the building.[124]

This criticism has but one basic flaw: it attributes the entire Biennale setup to a single person, as if this person were a semi-god who does not have the privilege to error – even more paradoxically – who is supposed to be saying and showing only what certain critics would like to hear or see.

Even though most of the criticism aims at Rem Koolhaas the man and the author, only a few of the critics really know that Rem's work is primarily based on collective effort to generate specific intelligence. Hence the view of the three Biennale exhibitions as Rem's own, as the children of his own research, which is far from truth.

I am convinced that, despite the criticism, Fundamentals will stand out as a milestone in the history of the Venice Biennale and architecture. Not because architecture has remained without "grammar" or because Rem declared "the end of all things," but because he has turned a new page at the opening, Baratta said to the press:

> With Rem Koolhaas our aim is to create an exceptional, research-centered Architecture Biennale. It will be significantly innovative, as Rem has conceived a project that involves the entire Biennale, which fully exploits its potential.

> I must remind everyone that la Biennale embraces various disciplines beyond Art and Architecture (Dance, Music, Theatre, and Cinema), and here too Koolhaas didn't miss the opportunity. The Monditalia section of the exhibition will also act as a container for activities pertaining

---

[124] De Michelis, Marco (2014) Fundamentals. In: LOG 32, New York City: Anyone Corporation

to these different arts ensuring that they are not happenings alongside or overlapping with the Architecture Exhibition. Dance, Music, Theatre, and Cinema will be incorporated to epitomize the articulated and living contexts in which architecture may be conceived or imagined.

And here Koolhaas goes straight to the point. With great courage and ambition, after having traced the history of modernity over the past 100 years to the present, he identifies and presents the elements that should act as references for a regenerated relationship between us and architecture (Elements of Architecture).[125]

> These words clearly show to which extent has his fascination with Koolhaas' ideas about presenting architecture influenced the Venice Biennale.
> After Baratta, Koolhaas also addressed the press with the following words:

Architecture, not architects… After several architecture Biennales dedicated to the celebration of the contemporary, Fundamentals will look at histories, try to reconstruct how architecture finds itself in its current situation, and speculate on its future.

Elements of Architecture will pay close attention to the fundamentals of our buildings, used by any architect, anywhere, anytime: the floor, the wall, the ceiling, the roof, the door, the window, the façade, the balcony, the corridor, the fireplace, the toilet, the stair, the escalator, the elevator, the ramp…

By looking at the evolution of architectural elements shared by all cultures, the exhibition will expand the architectural discourse beyond its normal parameters, and include a broad public in an exploration of the familiar, the erased, and the visionary dimensions of architecture.[126]

In one of his last lectures at the Berlage Institute Rem Koolhaas talked about exhibition projects carried out by his studio AMO. He showed a photo from the opening of the Content exhibition in the Berlin Neue Nationalgalerie Mies van der Rohe and said, "I am a public intellectual."
Koolhaas' intellectual journey started from the post-1968 Netherlands in which he wrote for newspapers and films. He then studied architecture at the Architectural Association School of Architecture in London with Elia Zengelis, Cornell University with Mathias Ungers, and at Eisenman's New York Institute of Architecture and Urban Studies, where he worked on the Delirious New York. He is now the director of OMA and AMO, Harvard professor, and one of the most influential contemporary architects in the world.

The thin red line that connects the dots along this road is his incessant questioning of every single canon of modern architecture and society. His approach to reality is above all intellectual, anarchistic and surreal, and he produces meaning by fundamentally changing the structure and the rules of behavior in architecture. Rem has always rubbed the norms, standards, generally accepted beliefs and values the wrong way. No wonder then that his Biennale has rubbed a number of critics the wrong way. The first to publicly declare the "end of Koolhaas" and his age was no other than Peter Eisenman in his interview with Valentina Ciuffi for the web magazine DeZeen. This is what Eisenman said:

---

125 Source: www.labiennale.org/en/architecture/archive/14th-exhibition/14iae/ accessed September 7, 2016

126 Ibid.

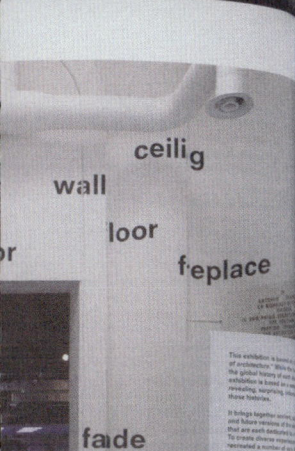

oploditi mnoge umove, uroditi različitim akademskim oblicima i stvoriti nov način razmišljanja o fasadama. Ukratko, radi se o uobičajenom obliku pisanja o arhitekturi kojemu je cilj izgradnji novu stvarnost, a ne vjerno reproducirati već postojeću. U izloženoj postavi, a osobito u svakom poglavlju knjige o fasadama, Zaera-Polo donosi povijesne izvore te suvremene primjere izgrađenih fasada na jedinstveno zanimljiv način, razmatrajući materijalne, tehnološke, semiološke, političke, socijalne, ekološke, ideološke, estetske i futurološke aspekte fasadizma. ¶ Druga knjiga u seriji od petnaest elemenata kojoj treba posvetiti pažnju je Stair (Stepenice). Ovdje se radi o Trübyjevom otkriću Friedricha Mielkea, 93-godišnjeg njemačkog arhitekta koji je sav svoj radni vijek posvetio izučavanju stepenica. Mielke je od 1957., kad je doktorirao na temu stepenica u potsdamskim građanskim kućama, napisao dvije knjige, 5 vodiča te 20 brojeva Scalalogije, serije knjiga posvećenih istraživanju stepenica. Fantastičan razgovor s Mielkeom dio je izložbe Elements, a kratki Venice Statement, koji je napisao za izložbu, završava definicijom scalalogije: 'Scalalogija' se od čisto tehničkih istraživačkih metoda koje rabi 'Stair Research' razlikuje svojim duhom. Ona stvara filozofsku superstrukturu za istraživanje svih svjetovnih dosega. ¶ Ako ste pažljivo proučili izložbu Elements, a potom jednako pažljivo pročitali 15 volumena od poda, preko zida, stropa, krova, prozora, fasade, balkona, hodnika, kamina, zahoda, stepenica, pokretnih stuba, dizala... neizbježno ćete se naći u konceptualnoj superstrukturi za istraživanje svjetovnih dosega arhitekture, kao što to predlaže Friedrich Mielke.

MONDITALIA ¶ I dok je za rad na izložbi Elements Koolhaas koristio uglavnom svoje snage, zaposlenike OMA-e i AMO-a, studente s Harvarda te ranije suradnike, izložba Monditalia nastala je kao otvoreni poziv arhitektima, kritičarima i kustosima da predlože teme u odnosu na povijest, sadašnjost i budućnost Italije. Koolhaas je na uvodnoj konferenciji za medije o Monditaliji istakao sljedeće: U trenutku ključne političke pretvorbe odlučili smo Italiju prikazati kao »fundamentalnu« zemlju, potpuno jedinstvenu, po ipak takvu koja pokazuje određena svojstva – napose nemjerljivo bogatstvo, kreativnost, stručnost i potencijal, ruku pod ruku s političkim kovitlacem – koja ju čine prototipom sadašnjeg trenutka. ¶ Monditalia je trebala napraviti povijesni i suvremeni prikaz Italije kroz 41 arhitektonsko istraživanje, 82 filma te seriju plesnih i kazališnih performansa. Sama struktura, ali i ambicija projekta, bila je ipak iznad vremenskih, tehničkih, pa i financijskih uvjeta u kojima se projekt trebao ostvariti, ali i iznad mogućnosti percepcije publike. Ako su Elementi bili prvenstveno namijenjeni arhitektonskoj subkulturi, Monditalia je računala i na opću publiku koja je zainteresirana

Rem Koolhaas presents the Biennale as la fine [the end]: The end of my career, the end of my hegemony, the end of my mythology, the end of everything, the end of architecture. Because we don't have architects [in the biennale]. We have performance, we have film, we have video; we have everything but architecture.[127]

> Any discussion about the influence of architecture on the construction of social reality.
>
> Elements
>
> Speaking about the Biennale's backbone, Elements, Rem Koolhaas stressed the following:

Under near-microscopic attention, the apparently mundane elements of architecture are revealed as unstable compounds of cultural preferences, forgotten symbolism, technological advances, mutations spawned by intensifying global exchange, climatic considerations, fluctuating thresholds of comfort, mythical desires, political calculations, regulatory requirements, neoliberal economics, new digital regimes, and, somewhere in the mix, the ideas of the architect.[128]

> Now, people who cannot see that Elements were the first to tackle a host of influences on architectural production beyond "grammar" in a way that taps into infinite possibilities of rethinking architecture, well, these people are simply myopic. This shortsighted criticism of Koolhaas, including the criticism of Eisenman and his followers, can be attributed to under-

standing architecture as an independent discipline. When Rem's 15 research teams produce Elements, and when the designer Irma Boom summarizes that effort in 15 booklets, they by no means speak about old or new, pillars, toilets, stairs, or facades, but they "trigger ideas", to use Alejandro Zaera-Polo's words in his "disclaimer" on the Facade:

This is not an academic paper, but a historical speculation, a technological fiction not suitable as an exhaustive source, but as a trigger of ideas in which we firmly believe. It is not thoroughly researched nor peer-reviewed. It is partial, opinionated, and inexact. But we hope it will fertilize many minds, spin off different forms of scholarship, and originate a new form of thinking about facades. It is, in short, a standard type of architectural writing, aimed at the construction of a new reality, rather than the faithful reproduction of a pre-existing one.[129]

> In his exhibition, and especially in every chapter of his booklet on facades, Zaera-Polo gives historical references to and contemporary examples of facades built in unique ways, and discusses the material, technological, semiological, political, social, environmental, ideological, esthetic, and futurological aspects of "facadism."
> The second of the fifteen booklets on the elements that deserves attention is the Stair. It is in fact Stefan Truby's homage to Friedrich Mielke, a 93-year-old German architect who has spent all of his working life studying stairs. Since 1957 when he defended his doctoral thesis on staircases in Potsdamer residences, he has published two books, five guidebooks, and 20 issues of Scalalogy, a series of volumes

---

127 Ciuffi, Valentina (2014) Rem Koolhaas is stating "the end" of his career, says Peter Eisenman. Published on June 9, 2014. Source: www.dezeen.com/2014/06/09/rem-koolhaas-at-the-end-of-career-says-peter-eisenman/ accessed September 9, 2016

128 Source: http://www.myvenice.org/print-675.html, accessed September 7, 2016

129 Alejandro Zaera-Polo in the statement issued in connection to his "sudden resignation from the Post of Dean of the School of Architecture at Princeton University on October 30 2014." Source: www.arquitecturaviva.com/media/Documentos/carta_zaera(1).pdf , accessed September 7, 2016

dedicated to the study of stairs. Elements include a fantastic interview with Mielke and a brief Venice Statement that ends with a definition of scalalogy:

Scalalogy differentiates itself in spirit from the purely technical surveying methods employed by Stair Research. Scalalogy creates the philosophical superstructure to cover all profane accomplishments.

If you have studied the exhibition carefully and read the 15 volumes (floor, wall, ceiling, door, roof, window, façade, balcony, corridor, fireplace, toilet, stair, escalator, elevator, and ramp) with equal attention, you will – just as Friedrich Mielke suggests – find yourself in a conceptual superstructure that investigates architecture's profane accomplishments.

This is why we can conclude that Koolhaas' team has completely met Baratta's "requirement" to '[identify and present] the elements that should act as references for a regenerated relationship between us and architecture.'[130]

Monditalia

While for Elements Koolhaas mostly relied on his own human resources, including the OMA/AMO employees, Harvard students, and earlier collaborators, Monditalia was an open invitation to all architects, critics, and curators to come up with projects related to the past, present, and the future of Italy. This is what he said about Monditalia at the press conference:

The physical presence of the Arsenale is interpreted as an ideal set. Rather than a sequence of individual episodes that typically do not connect to form a single narrative, we propose to dedicate the Arsenale to a single theme – Italy – and to mobilize other festivals of La Biennale di Venezia – film, dance, music, theatre – to collectively represent a comprehensive portrait of the host country.

In a moment of crucial political transformation, we decided to look at Italy as a "fundamental" country, completely unique but showing certain features – particularly the coexistence of immense riches, creativity, competences, and potential combined with political turbulence – that also make it a prototype of the current moment.[131]

The intention with Monditalia was to make a historical scan of Italy through 41 architectural research projects, 82 films, and a series of dance and theater performances. Its structure and ambition, however, was not only to go beyond the temporal, technical, or financial boundaries imposed on the exhibition, but also beyond the perception of the audience.

If Elements were, by and large, intended for architectural subculture, Monditalia counted on general public interested in a variety of art forms. The force that was supposed to glue these interests together comes from the concept of Italy as a "fundamental" country for the understanding of the relationship between the recent neoliberal chaos and the possibility to fully unlock a country's potential. Many of the 41 research projects were able to show their own specific values and importance, but had hard time establishing a relationship with the film projections and dance performances. Only when an audio guide for Elements and Monditalia became available one month after the exhibition opening the visitors acquired the access to the short and

130 Frearson, Amy (2014) Venice Biennale "will severe connections with contemporary architecture", says Rem Koolhaas. Published on March 11, 2014. Source: www.dezeen.com/2014/03/11/rem-koolhaas-venice-biennale-2014-more-details, accessed September 8, 2016

131 Quintal, Becky (2014) Latest Details Released on Koolhaas' Venice Biennale 2014 "Fundamentals", published on March 12, 2014. Source: www.archdaily.com/484728/latest-details-released-on-koolhaas-venice-biennale-2014-fundamentals, accessed September 7, 2016

ORIŠ 91

Zagreb, 2015

Maroje Mrduljaš i Ana Dana Beroš, snimljeni u atriju Galerije Klovićevi dvori, Zagreb, 2014., unutar postava izložbe Arhivi, preraspodjele i premjeravanja, kustosi Reinhard Braun i Sandra Križić Roban, autorica postava: Ana Dana Beroš

Maroje Mrduljaš and Ana Dana Beroš, photographed in the atrium of the Klovićevi Dvori Gallery, Zagreb, 2014, inside of the exhibition set up Archives, Re-Assemblances and Surveys, curators: Reinhard Braun and Sandra Križić Roban, author of the set up: Ana Dana Beroš

(MM)

ekologije, ali i napetka digitalnih tehnologija na državne granice koje se obično doživljavaju kao nepromjenjiva datost. Vaš rad, s kojim Monditalio započinje, problematizira pitanje imigranata na slučaju otoka Lampeduse, prvog mjesta kontakta na putu od Afrike prema Italiji, Europi i onome što nazivamo zapadnim svijetom. Vaš rad treba čitati kroz socijalnu kritiku i pitanje politike migracija koje Vi povezujete s tržištem rada, ali mislim da je u jednom naglašenije prostornom smislu Vaš rad zanimljiv i po tome što pokazuje da granica nije crta ili točka, nego dugotrajni proces, dramaturgija tegobnog i po život opasnog puta, neizvjesnog iščekivanja u imigrantskom kampu, zatim i neizvjesnosti koja slijedi nakon eventualog konačnog prolaska administrativno-birokratske granice. Dakle, nacionalne, ali i druge granice su višestruke, a njihov utjecaj na iskustvo pojedinca, naročito onih koji dolaze s druge strane, vrlo je složen. Iz moje perspektive, svi smo mi često u statusu deprivilegiranih imigranata koji dolaze s druge strane i suočavamo se s transgresijama normi i granica, prelascima iz jednog statusa u drugi, bilo da se radi o sasvim institucionalnim ili pak intimnim kontekstima. Stanje imigranta također je priča o strepnjama, neizvjesnostima, ali i o vitalnosti, naročito o jednoj gotovo naivnoj okrenutosti prema budućnosti. No, zašto ste se Vi zainteresirali za temu granica i imigranata? Hrvatska je u liminalnoj situaciji; u EU, a izvan Shengena, jedan prostor između, i ovdje i ondje ili nigdje istovremeno, s iskustvom dugog pristupa EU koje je

and recently especially due to changes in the snow an in the Alps. The Italian border therefore shows how cli change, global ecology as and the advancement of d technologies affect state frontiers, which are often perce as an unchangeable given. Monditalia starts with your in which you problematize the issue of immigrants, takin the case of the island of Lampedusa, the first place of con on the path from Africa to Italy, Europe and everything call the Western world. Your work should be read throug lens of social criticism and the question of migration po which you link to the labour market, but I believe your to be interesting also for showing that a border is not a nor a dot, but a long-lasting process, the dramaturgy arduous and life-threatening journey, including the anx wait in the detention centre, as well of the incertitude follows if a pass through the administrative bureaucrat der is eventually acquired. There are thus multiple nati and other borders, and their effect on the experience individual, especially those arriving from the other si very complex. From my perspective, all of us often find selves in the status of unprivileged immigrants arriving the other side, in which we face transgressions of norms borders, transitions from one status to the other, wh those contexts are entirely institutional or partly private immigrant's situation is a story of fears, uncertainties also a story of vitality, especially of an almost naïve d tionality toward the future. What made you intereste the theme of borders and immigrants? Croatia is curr in a liminal situation, in the EU, but outside the Sche zone, a space in-between, both here and there or now simultaneously, with the experience of a long-lastin accession process that seemed and still seems like a lon in the purgatory of a migrant camp. Therefore I believe Lampedusa experience can also relate to the current C tian identity. To what extent does Lampedusa interest as a concrete case, and to what degree as a broader rule perhaps a metaphor? Can you explain the aspect of the p human view you bring in to introduction of your resea

¶ ANA DANA BEROŠ — The issues of illegal migrations, inequality, the impossibility of belonging to a place, and consequences in urban and social reality – these I consid be key issues in Europe today, issues that we can no lo avoid in Croatia either. In the contemporary moment o imperative of mobility, which is compatible with the imper of work flexibility, the forced territorial migrations of pre ous but very often highly educated workers are parallel t wanderings and detentions of illegal migrants. Both of t

didactic explanations from the lion's (curator's) mouth about the setup.

For example, explanations of the "stops" in Monditalia clarify the relationship with the classics of Italian cinematography such as Roberto Rossellini, Michelangelo Antonioni, Federico Fellini, Pier Paolo Pasolini, Luchino Visconti, or Lina Wertmüller.

Monditalia focuses on social issues such as emigration, industrial heritage, sex, entertainment, crime, travel, housing, sanctity, radical education, ruins, and boundaries, which are intended to create a collective "selfie" of Italy accompanied by a 316 meters long geography map of Tabula Peutingeriana[132] from the 4th or 5th Ct. Ideally, a stroll down the Arsenal halls should take the visitor into a world of phenomena, films, and dance that investigates the possibilities of knowledge through the relationships between the body, image, model, and movement.

Of special interest for the Croatian architectural culture is the participation of two young researchers whose project won the competition for Monditalia, namely architect Ana Dana Beroš and art historian Luka Skansi. Ana Dana investigated illegal immigration from North Africa to the Italian Lampedusa Island in an installation she has entitled Intermundia. In it she defines illegal immigration to the European "fortress" as the State of Urgency, illustrating it with humongous books and inscrutable boxes. Intermundia is the third stop of Monditalia and it invites visitors, one at a time, to experience the box-like space and the audio-visual effects that accompany it. The sound effects are original and have been recorded at the ship graveyard of Lampedusa, a place where many of the African immigrant boats have ended their journey to Italy. After spending a short spell in the pitch dark of the boat's bowels, so to speak, the lights turn on to show a graffito on a black wall saying "We are all Africans." Just like the sounds, the graffito has been taken to Venice from its original location. Ana Dana has found an intelligent way to communicate to her audience the many layers of her investigation into migration driven by existential necessity by exposing them to an immediate, even if brief, experience and by giving them an insight into the global social problem through her well-structured installation. Luka Skansi is a Croatian-Italian art historian with a master's degree from the Venetian school of architecture (IUAV) in 2002 on the thesis Texts and projects by Rem Koolhaas, 1963-78 and with a doctoral degree on pre-revolutionary Russia, 1900-17. At the exhibition he presented his research on Italian industrial architecture from the boom period of the 1950s and 1960s entitled The Remnants of the Miracle. Over the last two years, Skansi has focused on researching and documenting the "pearls" of modern Italian industrial architecture that fell into oblivion. A generation of designers and engineers, most notably Pier Luigi Nervi, built an array of factory buildings, warehouses, and business towers that belong to an interesting heritage, but also give room for their reinterpretation in a post-Fordian sense. As Skansi's multimedia presentation follows the birth, growth, and finally the death of several economic sectors in Italy, it seems to prepare us for a new "miracle" that would restore these buildings to life.

Absorbing Modernity: 1914-2014

National pavilion exhibitions around the title Absorbing Modernity: 1914-2014 are the result of yet another of Koolhaas' attempts to attain a higher level of consistency and correlation between the Biennale exhibitions. This is how he describes it:

Participating countries will engage in a single theme – Absorbing Modernity: 1914-2014 – and will show, each in their own way, the process of the erasure of national characteristics in favor of the almost universal adoption of a single modern language and a single repertoire of typologies. But

---

[132] Tabula Peutingeriana is an illustrated itinerarium (road map) showing the cursus publicus, the road network in the Roman Empire.

the transition to what seems like a universal architectural language is a more complex process than we typically recognize, involving significant encounters between cultures, technical inventions, and hidden ways of remaining "national." In a time of ubiquitous google research and the flattening of cultural memory, it is crucial for the future of architecture to resurrect and expose these narratives.[133]

In 1914, it made sense to talk about a "Chinese" architecture, a "Swiss" architecture, an "Indian" architecture. One hundred years later, under the influence of wars, diverse political regimes, different states of development, national and international architectural movements, individual talents, friendships, random personal trajectories and technological developments, architectures that were once specific and local have become interchangeable and global. National identity has seemingly been sacrificed to modernity.[134]

Stephan Petermann, Koolhaas' associate at AMO/OMA in charge of the initial research team for the Fundamentals and of the set up for Absorbing Modernity: 1914-2014 invited me to a meeting in Rotterdam in the early summer of 2013 to discuss if I could help with research of the Mies van der Rohe Archive in Chicago. Rem joined the meeting, and after a discussion about Mies's contribution to the "elementary" development of Modernism, focused on the setup of national pavilion exhibitions. I observed that the period between 1914 and 2014 to be covered by the exhibition also included

[133] Quintal, Becky(2014) Latest Details Released on Koolhaas' Venice Biennale 2014 "Fundamentals". Published on March 12, 2014. Source: www.archdaily.com/484728/latest-details-released-on-koolhaas-venice-biennale-2014-fundamentals, accessed September 7, 2016

[134] Source: oma.eu/news/rem-koolhaas-announces-themes-for-2014-venice-architecture-biennale, accessed September 16, 2016

70 years of Yugoslavia. Koolhaas replied that he was most interested in modernization of Yugoslavia during socialism and in the export of Yugoslav architecture to the non-aligned African and Asian countries. We discussed the conundrum about the succession of the Yugoslav pavilion in Giardini that still has not been resolved and agreed that I should look into the hypothetical possibility of organizing a joint exhibition of the succeeding countries. This hypothetical possibility should not have necessarily corresponded to utopia, because we had an outstanding success with the Unfinished Modernisations, curated by Maroje Mrduljaš and Vladimir Kulić, which gave hope for continued collaboration on Absorbing Modernity. However, the selection of national curators took too long, Mrduljaš and Kulić did not enter any of the national teams of the succeeding countries, and this put an end to the hypothetical possibility to organize a historical exhibition that would receive full support by the Biennale's chair. Instead, architecture of the old and new Yugoslavia between 1918 and 1990 was "presented" through six separate national exhibitions. The Serbo-Croatian team working on the Serbian presentation picked an unfinished project by the Croatian architect Vjenceslav Richter from 1961 – the Museum of Revolution of the Yugoslav Nations and Minorities. The Macedonian exhibition focused on the influence of Japanese Metabolism on Macedonian architecture. Curators from Kosovo decided to ignore Yugoslav Modernism, treating it as an aspect of the repressive regime, and focused on the local vernacular. This is probably why they failed to show the most interesting blend of the two discourses, the National Library of Kosovo in Priština, by the master Andrija Mutnjaković. The Slovene exhibition looked into space travel, based on the ideas of Herman Potočnik Noordung, whereas the Montenegrin team analyzed the abandoned socialist buildings designed by the Slovene architect Marko Mušič, Bosnian architect Zlatko Ugljen, and Montenegrin architect Vukota Tupa Vukotić.

The Croatian contribution to Absorbing Modernity: 1914-2014 was entitled Fitting Abstraction. Its authors Karin Šerman, Igor Ekštajn, Nataša Jakšić, Zrinka Barišić Marenić, Melita Čavlović, Mojca Smode

ORIS 91

Zagreb, 2015

IN-BETWEEN :
A book on the Croatian coast, global processes, and how to live with them

Saša Randić, Idis Turato

Rijeka, 2006

Cvitanović, and Marina Smokvina concluded that 'Modernity in local Croatian architecture does not dissolve or compromise earlier national architecture, but, thanks to a series of historical events, it is the main bearer of the national cultural memory and identity.'[135] Responses to Koolhaas' invitation to look into the history of "national" architectures over the past 100 years are quite interesting. The great majority of commissioners/curators opted for a phenomenological approach, while a minority preferred a chronological and encyclopedic one. Most tried to present and explain a certain phenomenon, concept, practice or a theme taken from another culture, which influenced or overlapped with one's national architecture. The Swiss exhibition, for example, looked into the relationship between the English architect and teacher Cedric Price and the Swiss sociologist Lucius Burckhardt, whereas the Scandinavian countries focused on the export of modern Western architecture to the south, most notably African and Asian countries, and the US presented the influence of its designers on other countries, including Croatia, (Hotel President at Babin Kuk Resort in Dubrovnik, designed by Edward Durell Stone).

The Croatian team belongs to the minority who sought to provide a comprehensive, almost encyclopedic presentation of a variety of concepts and the results of absorbing modernity by diverse "national" geographies. Karin Šerman, the commissioner and curator, explained their attempt as follows: 'Abstraction is one of the central formal and conceptual characteristics of architectural modernism. Our claim is that within the local circumstances, for a number of concrete historical reasons, architectural modernism – although deeply marked by this abstraction – emerges as a legitimate bearer of local architectural identity. In this way abstraction here becomes "rhetorical" and "representative."'[136] Her deputy, Igor Ekštajn, added that Koolhaas' invitation which was as cynical and provocative as explicitly genuine, more dedicated to the archives on architecture than design genius, focused on history rather than modernity, intended for nerds rather than bloggers – provokes a variety of responses. The Croatian response to Koolhaas is genuinely "nerdish" and deserves an A+ for the effort, but also requires a serious review of the fundamental premises from which their "assignment" had sprung. The one thing this review should address is the very notion of abstraction. As we all know, abstraction is the process of isolating what is relevant in something, whereas an abstract work is the one that does not represent a being, object, situation, or event. Architectural or geometric abstractions, as it were, are concepts that have greatly contributed to the construction of Stonehenge, Egyptian pyramids, Palladio's villas, or the Rietveld Schröder House. In these, abstraction is in a way "rhetorical" and "representative." The argument that 'architectural modernism [...] emerges as a legitimate bearer of the local architectural identity'[137] may ring intriguing to incorrigible adorers of the Croatian architecture and culture, but it cannot create a serious conceptual platform for any fruitful global exchange.

The other concept that needs a review is the historical continuity or, in the Croatian case, discontinuity. The basic premise is that Croatian identity over the last 100 years belongs to the modern project despite territorial divergence influenced by three radically different European cultures – Ottoman, Venetian, and Austro-Hungarian – three catastrophic wars, and five government systems. Six, if we count the Independent State of Croatia[138], but it would be wiser to leave it out. Any serious research on the Croatian territory has to acknowledge divergent identities, completely different circumstances in the

---

135 Source: www.fittingabstraction.com, accessed September 15, 2016

136 Source: Croatian Real Estate Newsletter Vol 97 (PDF), September 2014, Interview with Karin Šerman, filipovic-advisory.com/UserFiles/File/cren/CREN_97_092014_EN.PDF, accessed September 15, 2016

137 Source: Croatian Real Estate Newsletter Vol 97 (PDF), September 2014, Interview with Karin Šerman, filipovic-advisory.com/UserFiles/File/cren/CREN_97_092014_EN.PDF, accessed September 15, 2016.

138 So called Independent State of Croatia was epitomization of the worst of WWII, and certainly not independent. It was a quisling state that applied genocide laws, while trying to exterminate Serb, Jewish and Roma population.

production of the built environment, and conceptual discontinuities of the three disparate periods of national architectural development, namely the beginnings of modernism between the two world wars, post-war (socialist) unfinished modernization, and the architecture of the transition in the last 25 years.

Ever since the Njirićs' exhibition in the Antwerp Singel, this last period has, formally and programmatically, been detached from modernism. This is perhaps the most interesting, and definitely the best documented part of the Croatian architectural history. Šerman and her team, instead, prefer Eisenman›s discourse over Koolhaas›, because their Fitting Abstraction speaks about autonomy, continuity, distinctive architectural language and grammar, all with the intention to show the accomplishment of the planned goal to 'have successfully built the desired identity and to have achieved a broader cultural ambition.'[139]

I absolutely welcome the effort of the Croatian university team to define the fundamentals of architecture in Croatia over the last 100 years. I cannot help observing, though – without the least bit of ill will – that this is what most of the team members do for a living, but we also have to admit how hard this task is, especially because the results of the Atlas of Architecture, a research project conducted by the Faculty of Architecture, are barely visible and so is the production of Academia Moderna, whereas the activity of the Museum of Architecture in research, presentation, documentation, and promotion of (modern) architecture in Croatia is marginal. This leads to a conclusion that Šerman and her team found themselves in a territory without clear landmarks, historical facts, and critical references. They put a great effort to fill this void, even though it is an insurmountable obstacle to conceptualizing national architectural culture. This void is best described by an anecdote from the defense of the doctoral thesis by Tomislav Premerl[140] at the University of Zagreb Faculty of Architecture in 1985. Professor Šegvić asked the candidate one question only: "Dear colleague Premerl, why do you call architecture, which you so diligently studied, Croatian and modern?" It would do much good to Croatian national architecture and culture – if this is what it is all about – to answer this simple question. In global terms, Koolhaas has successfully closed another chapter as he usually does, and started a new one by replying to the question how has architecture reached where it is now and what can be its future. To answer these questions in near future we will need an outstanding "manifestation of the wind of thought" that reaches beyond the Arendt's sense of the term.

When the great Venetian show lowered the curtain, 228,000 people had already seen it. According to the magazine Domus and the University of Milan, which have analyzed over 60,000 posts in English commenting on the performance of the Koolhaas' and national teams over the six months of the exhibition, the vox populi architectonici on social networks is 58.8% neutral, 35% positive, and 6.2% negative. Elements received 83.2% positive comments vs. 16.8% negative, if we exclude the neutral, and Monditalia 75.7% positive vs. 24.3% negative. Domus concludes the article as follows:

This is the social ranking of the 2014 Biennale, based on personal and sometimes idiosyncratic opinions, naturally. As a whole, however, it speaks of a successful Biennale, with a great deal of light and the odd small shadow.[141]

---

139 Source: Croatian Real Estate Newsletter Vol 97 (PDF), September 2014, Interview with Karin Šerman, filipovic-advisory.com/UserFiles/File/cren/CREN_97_092014_EN.PDF, accessed September 15, 2016

140 Tomislav Premerl (1939) is an architect and architectural historian whose book Croatian Architecture Between Two World Wars was a milestone in re-evaluation of Croatian modernism.

141 Novozhilova, Maria (2014) Venice 2014: social ranking. Published on November 25, 2014. Source: www.domusweb.it/en/architecture/2014/11/25/venice_biennial_socialmedia.html, accessed Septemper 29, 2016

EPILOG W

WIEL ARETS

U dobroj se

Interviewed in Chicago, 23 August 2013

¶ My conversations with Wiel Arets started in 1991, wh
met in the orphanage of Aldo van Eyck, at the Berlag

EL ARETS

fotografije photographs by
Jan Bitter

portreti portraits
Łukasz Kowalczyk

razgovarali u Chicagu, 23. kolovoza 2013.

Moji razgovori s Wielom Aretsom započeli su 1991. godine,
smo se sreli u nahodištu Alda van Eycka, na Berlage Insti-
u južnom Amsterdamu i nastavili su se sve do onih koje

WIEL ARETS

A Good

'Another important benchmark in 1990 was the formation of the Berlage Institute in Amsterdam. The Berlage was founded by the Dutch architect Herman Hertzberger as an educational workshop. Wiel Arets became dean in 1994 and rebranded the school as a "laboratory," emphasizing speculative design research and global urbanism. Throughout the 1990s the Berlage played a double role. On the one hand, under the entrepreneurial guidance of the Dutch architect Wiel Arets, it became an important node in the international network, a place for visiting architects and students from the USA, Asia, and Europe to meet and exchange ideas. Like the Architectural Association in earlier decades, the Berlage emerged as a preferred international destination for North American architects and teachers. It was emblematic of a growing internationalism in design education, both giving younger faculty from the US important international exposure and anticipating the global educational initiatives that were to emerge in North American schools after a beginning of the new century. The Berlage was also an active promoter of a generation of younger architects, taking advantage of this institutional support, these young practitioners were able to turn their academic visibility into professional credibility.'[142]

In his 2012 article, Stan Allen points toward aspects of my tenure as Dean of the Berlage Institute in the 1990s as a creation of a "bridge" between North American architects and institutions and Dutch architectural education and culture. When I was invited to become Dean of College of Architecture at the Illinois Institute of Technology in Chicago in 2012, in a sort of reverse process I invited Vedran Mimica to join me, since he had been the Associate Dean during my tenure at the Berlage Institute. In preparation of my being the Dean of an architecture school so connected to the 'Shadow of Mies van der Rohe', who led it from 1938-1958, I decided to prepare a publication that announced the major changes to the college that would occur, in NOWNESS I.[143] Having known from my time at the Berlage Institute that institutional publications are of the essence to their communication, Hunch was the publication I started at the Berlage Institute as a platform to disseminate the work of not only our students, but also the faculty, and visiting teachers, and the thoughts and ideas of others within the orbit of the school. Hunch was, at that time, edited by Jennifer Sigler.[144] In a process of becoming a tenured professor at IIT, Mimica submitted a lengthy portfolio that documented his vision on the academic climate, as well as his own work as an architect, educator, and writer. I had suggested that he perhaps publish a book, by critically editing submitted material—focusing on his tenure at the Berlage Institute, where he worked for 22 years – and how this ties into his work at IIT in Chicago. The result is The Berlage Affair, which in its seven chapters, tracks the many projects of Mimica and his views on today's architectural field. The influence of an academic setting has much more to do with just being a school; schools should be sites of discourse, for all involved. Even a school's young students must feel empowered to participate. During his tenure at the Berlage Institute, he established new educational programs and urban planning workshops, which

143 Wiel Arets, Sean Keller and Vedran Mimica (2013) Nowness 1: IIT Architecture Chicago 2013-2014. Chicago: IITAC

144 Jennifer Sigler (ed.), Hunch 1 (Rotterdam: The Berlage Institute, 1999); Jennifer Sigler (ed.), Hunch 2 (Rotterdam: The Berlage Institute, 2000); Jennifer Sigler (ed.), Hunch 3 (Rotterdam: The Berlage Institute, 2001); Jennifer Sigler (ed.), Hunch 4 (Rotterdam: The Berlage Institute, 2002); Jennifer Sigler (ed.), Hunch 5 (Rotterdam: The Berlage Institute, 2002); Jennifer Sigler (ed.), Hunch 6/7 (Rotterdam: The Berlage Institute, 2003).

142 Allen, Stan (2012) 'The Future That is Now: Architectural Education in North America, 1912-2012.' In: Architecture School: Three Centuries of Educating Architects, Joan Ockman, ed. Cambridge, MIT Press/ACSA, p. 209

Figure 109
"Ring Roads of the World,"
poster for Rice University School of Architecture, 2009. Graphics by Thumb Design (Jessica Young and Luke Bulman). The designers graduated from Rice's M.Arch. program and began doing posters for the school in 1999.

any other figure in this period, Koolhaas defined the model for a practice focused on competitions and a parallel body of exhibitions, publications, and speculative urban research, leading over time to major institutional commissions. The present-day fascination with large-scale interdisciplinary urban design work—inspired in part by OMA's projects of the late 1980s, and certainly jumpstarted by the publication in 1995 of his book *S M L XL*—could also be traced back to the publication in 1987 of the inaugural double issue of the journal *Zone*, entitled "The Contemporary City," edited by Michael Feher and Sanford Kwinter. Drawing from art, architecture, politics, and literary theory, the editors saw the city as the privileged site for interdisciplinary study. The *Zone* issue gave ambitious young architects a model for working on the city that was far from the pieties of the New Urbanism, but also distinct from the formal approaches of mainstream practitioners such as Meier or Stirling. The effect of these two books would be visible later in the decade with the emergence of the interdisciplinary practices of landscape urbanism and the data-driven studio work of the Harvard Project on the City, directed by Koolhaas.

There were a number of important transitions in schools of architecture around this time. Bernard Tschumi began his deanship at Columbia in 1988. Having won the Parc de la Villette competition in 1983, Tschumi had spent much of the next five years in France, overseeing that project. In the United States, he was still considered something of an outsider, known primarily for his theoretical writings and an early polemical project, "Advertisements for Architecture." Modeled loosely on the Architectural Association, where Tschumi had taught in the 1970s, Columbia became known for its early embrace of the computer in the 1990s. At Harvard's Graduate School of Design, Rafael Moneo had completed his term as chair, which had been characterized by a return to disciplinary concerns and an opening of the school to visiting faculty from Europe. His successor, the Atlanta architect Mack Scogin, would be more pluralistic in his outlook. Computer specialist William Mitchell assumed the deanship at Massachusetts Institute of Technology in 1992, building on M.I.T.'s technological legacy and the presence there of the Media Lab. Lars Lerup, who had been teaching at the University of California at Berkeley and was known for his drawings and urban speculations, became dean at Rice University in Houston in 1993. Lerup invited intellectuals such as Kwinter, a theorist who was not professionally trained in architecture, to the school, and focused the curriculum on the American city and emergent forms of urbanism. **Figure 109** Stanley Tigerman at the University of Illinois at Chicago would also cultivate a younger generation of architects and theorists, including R. E. Somol, Catherine Ingraham, and Greg Lynn. **Figure 110**

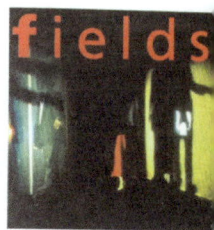

Another important benchmark in 1990 was the formation of the Berlage Institute in Amsterdam. The Berlage was founded by the Dutch architect Herman Hertzberger as an educational workshop. Wiel Arets became dean in 1994 and rebranded the school as a "laboratory," emphasizing speculative design research and global urbanism. Throughout the 1990s the Berlage played a double role. On the one hand, under the entrepreneurial guidance of Arets, it became an important node in the international network, a place for visiting architects and students from the United States, Asia, and Europe to meet and exchange ideas. Like the Architectural Association in earlier decades, the Berlage emerged as a preferred international destination for North American architects and teachers. **Figure 111** It was emblematic of a growing internationalism in design education, both giving younger faculty from the U.S. important international exposure and anticipating the global educational initiatives that were to emerge in North American schools after the beginning of the new century. The Berlage was also an active promoter of a generation of younger architects. Taking advantage of

206

ARCHITECTURE SCHOOL: THREE
CENTURIES OF EDUCATING
ARCHITECTS IN NORTH AMERICA

Ed. Joan Ockman
The Mit Press, 2012

served to initiate a wide array of stimulating debates. There is now a growing sense of urgency around questions of global urbanization; much of The Berlage Affair is dedicated to the research of the contemporary metropolis. Architecture writings are very well positioned to offer a synthetic overview of philosophical debates about the contemporary metropolis, by taking into account: the economy, ecology, sociology, art, civil engineering, history, literature, politics, religion, and ideology. In this sense, the target audience of this book is large and diverse. Simultaneously, the book is primarily written for architecture students and architects, public administrators working within urban development, cultural and social workers, activists, and those who seek to promote contemporary architecture. The Berlage Affair speaks to residents of cities and countries currently undergoing rapid economic, social, and cultural transition — while reflecting on the laboratory atmosphere the institute enabled through "Progressive Research," and freedom of thought. After 22 years at the Berlage Institute, Mimica moved to Chicago with his family, where I invited him to work with me to develop new programs at the IIT College of Architecture. Before the Berlage Institute closed in 2012, its former deans published books on educational and conceptual strategies used during their tenures. After the book Lessons for Students in Architecture, by Hertzberger,[145] Stills,[146] and The Sniper's Log by Alejandro Zaera-Polo;[147] The Berlage Affair concludes a large historical chapter on one European educational project — the Berlage Institute — while also reflecting on IIT's academic climate, the "Rethinking Metropolis" agenda, as well as Nowness: all of which were introduced to IIT, during 2012. Early in the Berlage Institute's infancy, Tadao Ando was invited to the school to give a master class, though he was adverse to the idea and proclaimed to the students that he did not believe in schools, and instead encouraged the students then at the Berlage Institute, to educate themselves. That is, to become autodidacts. Ando went on to give an incredibly memorable lecture that week at the school, and reinforced his statement that one has to constantly rehearse to understand one's own intuition. After three years of the school's existence, Hertzberger understood I was, perhaps, the best person to lead it next. After all, it was me who he had asked to bring Tadao Ando to the school, since I knew him from visiting him in Japan in the early-1980s, as well as exhibiting his work, and publishing his first works, in the European media. Hertzberger had known of my architectural work, prior experiences in education, which were then already numerous, and the resulting international network of practicing architects and educators that I had come in contact with, during my own teaching. For instance, I was connected to the networks present in London, especially at the AA, where I first taught the Diploma Unit One Master, for five years, under its then long time dean, Alvin Boyarski. I then began teaching at Columbia University, where Bernard Tschumi—who taught at the AA for many years—was the Dean, and where Kenneth Frampton was and still is, a key figure. In these early teaching experiences of mine on the East Coast of the USA, I began to come in contact with other academics and architects throughout the country, such as Bob Somol, who was then active in LA, and now Chicago, and Greg Lynn, who was active in the Midwest as well as on the West Coast. The documentation of these early, back and forth movements of so many American and European architects and scholars, is largely unwritten history; this is only partially alluded to, within Stan Allen's epigram on education, at the beginning of this essay. I was then invited to teach at the Cooper Union, by John Hejduk, who had an ongoing discourse with Peter Eisenman, whom I remember was then giving a series of lectures, to which he admitted only ten

---

145 Hertzberger, Herman (1991) Lessons for Students of Architecture. Rotterdam: 010 Publishers

146 van Toorn, Roemer ed. (2010) Stills: A Timeline of Ideas, Articles & Interviews 1983-2010. Rotterdam: 010

147 Polo, Alejandro Zaera (2012) The Sniper's Log: Architectural Chronicles of Generation-X. New York: Actar

ARCHITECTURE SCHOOL: THREE
CENTURIES OF EDUCATING
ARCHITECTS IN NORTH AMERICA

ed. Joan Ockman
The MIT Press, 2012

ARCHITECTURE SCHOOL

THREE CENTURIES OF EDUCATING ARCHITECTS IN NORTH AMERICA

JOAN OCKMAN editor
with REBECCA WILLIAMSON research editor

students. Of course it was the IAUS, and Oppositions, which Peter directed, that had a large impact on the urban discourse. It was Boyarski who invited me to go to Mexico to research and experience the work of Luis Barragán and prepare an AA publication on him – I travelled for 16 weeks in total. A bit later I traveled throughout South America; in Buenos Aires, I was long connected with its Biennale. And lastly, I have always been fond of Japan, and the country continues to be a source of fascination and inspiration to me. I actually published seven articles in the early 1980s, about Japanese architects such as Shinohara and Maki, after I had studied their work carefully in the library, by writing to them, and later talking to them, as I traveled throughout their country, right after I had graduated. I had even traveled in Russia, mostly in Moscow and St. Petersburg, to study the early-twentieth century radical work. I was, at this time, also starting to build my first projects as a young architect, and I entered many competitions, mostly to develop my skills and to learn how to tell my own story. Earlier in my career, in the late 1970s, I spent much time in the archives of the Dutch architect FPJ Peutz, who was active in my hometown of Heerlen; I went on to publish a book about him and his work, in 1981. I was then invited to teach at Princeton, by Anthony Vidler, right at the same time that I was approached by Hertzberger, who enquired about me being appointed as his successor as the Berlage Institute's next Dean. Knowing this diverse and wide-ranging international background of mine, Hertzberger soon had convinced me to be the Berlage Institute's next Dean. Luckily, hesitantly, yet happily, I accepted his offer. And so instead of teaching at Princeton, I instead became a member of Princeton University's Advisory Board. Whereas Hertzberger had had a deep understanding and an appreciation for the Montessori school system, and he had applied this system of thought to the early structuring of the Berlage Institute – I had teaching experience, around the globe, which I was able to draw influences from and apply to the institute's laboratory approach. For me "Progressive Research" was the idea that spurred the creation of a PhD at the Berlage Institute. And it was due to Mimica's capacity to balance the "exploratory" and "laboratory" modes of approach – that the institute was further strengthened. The position and the influence of an academic setting has more to do with its realm and atmosphere, than it just being considered a school; it should be the place for discourse, manifested and stimulated by master architects, though also young and less established architects, who must understand that they have to take a stance of their own, immediately. Last but not least, is the role of institutions as a place for "Progressive Research;" schools should be a "laboratory" where great thinkers, architects, and philosophers collaborate to develop new ideas, in a free climate, with fluid exchange of thought.

Just as at the Berlage Institute; when I came to the IIT College of Architecture as Dean, I was able to apply all that I had previously learned and gained to the structuring of the curriculum, but also the larger strategies, such as publications, lecture series, awards, and one-off events. At IIT Mimica worked with me as the Associated Dean of Research, Director of Master of Science program and as a curator of "Cloud Studio" design based research program. Mimica was thoroughly involved in many aspects of my tenure. We co-edited NOWNESS I with Sean Keller, which announced the changes at the College of Architecture, and defined the discourse of "Rethinking Metropolis" as central to composition of new curriculum. Mimica and his wife Sasha Zanko also worked with me on the Mies Crown Hall Americas Prize (MCHAP), as did Dirk Dennison, who is its director. NOWNESS II shows this and many other major accomplishments of the school, alongside excellent work by our students. Mimica was also involved in the creation of the "Dean's Lecture Series" and "Cloud Talks," and joined the interviews with our guest lecturers. The book Crown Hall Dean's Dialogue: 2012-2017,[148] published by ACTAR and IITAC in 2017, partially

---

148   Arets, Wiel & Siemionow, Agata (2017) Crown Hall Dean's Dialogues 2012-2017. New York/Chicago: Actar & IITAC Press

serves to record his involvement in the continuous debates with visiting figures at the college. Mimica is a unique individual, with a rather gifted sensibility to trigger faculty and students to debate and encourage the sharpening of their arguments. Being with him during my tenure at the Berlage Institute and at the college as Dean, and on our many trips throughout the globe – to, among others, Cape Town, São Paolo, Mexico City, Buenos Aires, Beijing, Tokyo, Chandigarh, Montreal, New York, Los Angeles, and the Venice Biennale – it was always a pleasure to see how he takes a position; always in favor of those who have something to say, and sometimes very critical about others. During our time as academics in Europe and the Americas, we came to understand and promote the nuances of the debate process, which is so critical to students' education, as they will design the cities of tomorrow.

As the Director of the Master of Science program and curator of "Cloud Studio" design based research program, Mimica created an intellectual climate in which it was possible to reflect upon the forces shaping the contemporary world, and their implications for architecture, landscape, and urbanism. The studio and thesis production was oriented toward the development of new strategies and future urban models with the aim of advancing the knowledge of relationships between urban thinking and materiality, technology, energy, ecology, emerging media, and socio-political and cultural concerns. Working with Vedran Mimica at the IIT College of Architecture during my tenure as its Dean allowed us to expand the "bridge" we constructed in the 1990s at the Berlage Institute, in order to create a new globally oriented and astutely distinguished educational setting, within the wonderful City of Chicago.

Professor Wiel Arets
Architect

NOWNESS

co-edited with Wiel Arets and Sean Keller
IIT Press, Chicago, 2013

MUSEUM 21+ VELA SPILA,
ARCHIVE OF SIMULTANEOUS TIMES

project study
report on the workshops, reader 1

Rotterdam, 2006

THE CITY AS A PROJECT

Berlage Institute, 2009

BUILDING RELATIONS:
THE BERLAGE PLATFORM

exhibition and seminar

Croatian Museum of Architecture,
Zagreb, 2008

WIEL ARETS : STILLS
A TIMELINE OF IDEAS,
ARTICLES AND INTERVIEWS,
1982 - 2010

010 Publishers, Rotterdam
2010

dezajn
HERMAN HERTZBERGER
PSIHOLOGIJA
ALDO VAN EYCK
ARCARCHIS
LIGHT CAPITAL
BERLAGE INSTITUTE
the flood
THE ARCHITECTURAL REVIEW
Public events spring '95
the BERLAGE institute AMSTERDAM
fields
BERLIN
PARIS
DIPLOMA
Urban Reports
The Istrian Heritage

AFTER THE SELF MANAGED CITY ?
art & sport
Okviri metropole Frames of the Metropolis
TITO
HRVATSKA MODERNA I SAVREMENA ARHITEKTURA
95'05
oris
Randić & Turato
čip
čovjek i prostor
rudnici kulture mines of culture
The Sniper's Log
ČOVJEK I PROSTOR
CENZURA, AUTOCEN-ZURA
NOWNESS
STILLS
THE CITY AS A PROJECT
Croatia
4988

WHO IS VEDRAN MIMICA? THE BERLAGE PLATFORM   LEARNING WITHOUT TEACHING   BERLAGE EXCHANGERS   WEST

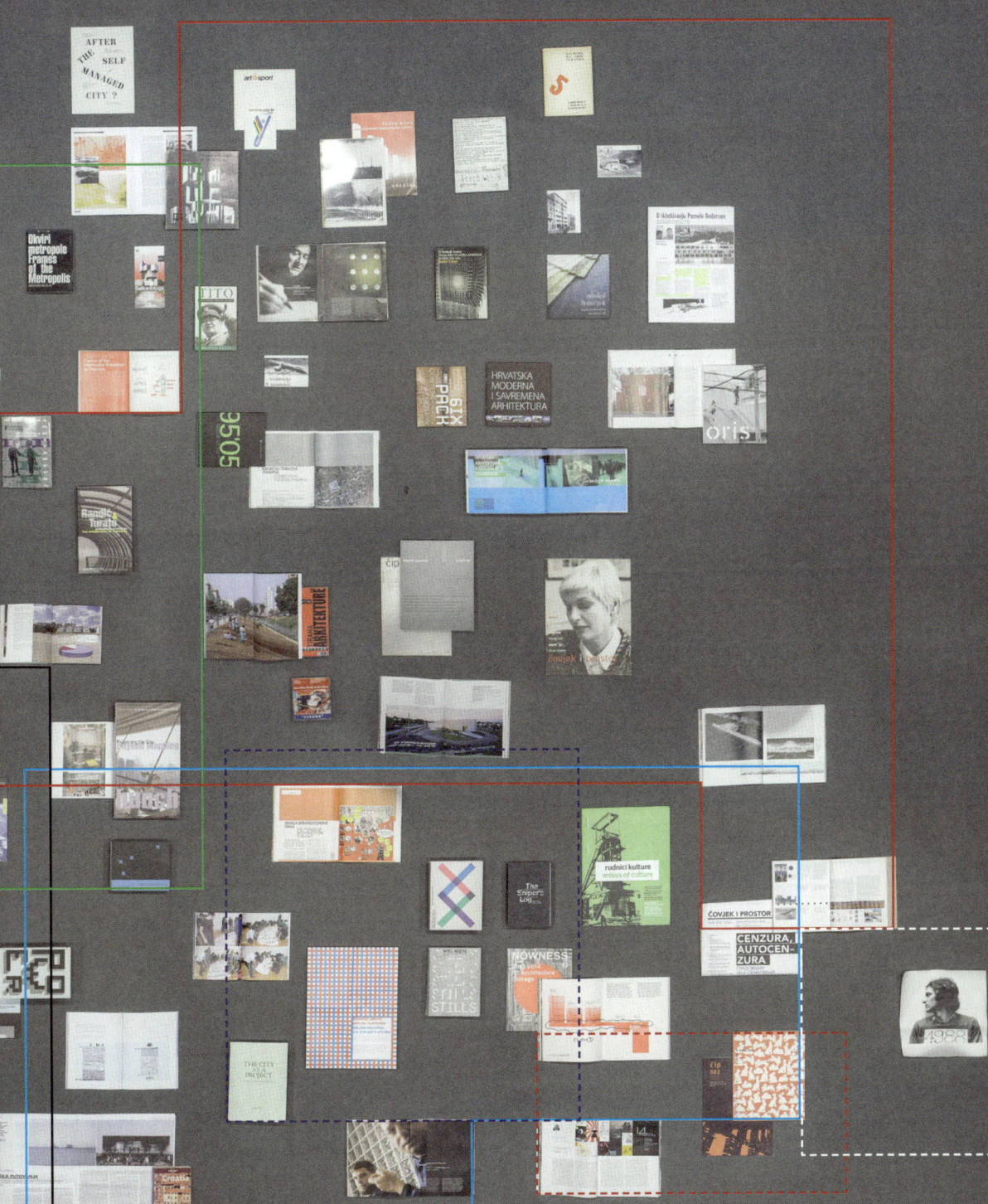

AIR AND ARCHITECTURE OF TRANSITION   BERLAGE TRANSFERS, ZAGREB SEMINARS AND NEW LIGHTHOUSES   CLOSING TIME

WHO IS VEDRAN MIMICA?

REPORT ABOUT SPECIALIZATION

ČOVJEK I PROSTOR 1996 1/2

TITO : THE STORY FROM INSIDE

Vedran Mimica: Croatia could easily home 24 million people. And quite comfortably at that.

PALACES IN A ROW, IN A POWER : Producing the Contemporary City

CROATIAN ARCHIPEL - NEW LIGHTHOUSES

CONFIRMATION of the specialization

MINES OF CULTURE

ARCHITECTURE WEEK
CHEERFUL GUIDE TO PARIS
CROATIAN ID CARD
PERSONAL PHOTO

LIFE AFTER THE DEATH IN VENICE

DIPLOMSKI RAD DIZAJN CENTAR ZAGREB ILICA

LETTER FROM REMI BAUDOUI

ARCHITECTURE STUDENTS' NEWSPAPER No 5 (LSA 5)

CLOSING TIME

CROATIAN ARCHIPELAGO : NEW LIGHTHOUSES, the book

REF SPE

LYBIAN DESIGN ACADEMY 2012 VISION FOR THE FUTURE

CROATIAN MODERN AND CONTEMPORARY ARCHITECTURE

ARCHITECTURE STUDENTS' NEWSPAPER MEDITERRANEAN CRUISE BROCHURE

THE BERLAGE CAHIERS 1 STUDIO '90

SPACE IS THE BASIC CROATIAN RESOURCE

SKJ MEMBE FEE BOOKL

TIRANA: ARCHITECTURE & COMPETITIONS 03-2005

DESIGN FOR BOŠKO BUHA MEMORIAL CENTER

ARCHITECTURAL AGENCY MPG 1992/1995 : TADEJ GLAŽAR, BRANIMIR MEDIĆ, PERO PULJIZ

LET RUS OF

CULTURAL SUMMER 96 IN OMIŠ

TIRANA METROPOLIS

ACTES DU COLLOQUE: URBICIDE - URGENCES - DURABILITE: RECONSTRUCTION

SMALL CHANGES
S. RECOMMENDATION
:tures,
.andscapes,
CONSTRUCTION

THE BERLAGE EXPERIENCE

EN UNIVERSITY TECHNOLOGIES SARAJEVO IG
PROTOTYPES

XX

GO

Oris 5

BUILDING RELATIONS: THE BERLAGE PLATFORM

Tourists in their home towns

CROATIA NOT READY FOR THE SHOCK OF THE FUTURE

REAL ET MEMOIRE THEORY: A I Theory Project (Symposium)
After the Self-Managed City?

LETTER TO HERMAN HERTZBERGER

VERSLAG 2007 : 3e Internationale Architectuur Biennale Rotterda

THE POWER OF ARCHITECTURAL THOUGHT

INVENTORY CARDS

A COMMON GROUND : NARRATIONS FOR IMAGINING RETURN

BE 201

PARIS EXCURSI

RECOMM

POSTGRADUATE SCHOOL OF ARCHITECTURE

COLLEGIUM ARTISTICUM: GREEN DESIGN

A VISION BEYOND PLANNING

LYBIAN DESIGN ACADEMY 201 VISION FOR THE FUTURE

HOMMAGE TO IVAN MEŠTROVI
THE FLOOD :
A 2nd International FICTI Architecture SUMMIT Biennale

INFORMATION FOR DUTCH PASSPORT FORM

MISSION IMPOSSIBLE? I DON'T THINK SO
-URBAN AGE BER YUGOSLAVIAN MEMORIAL CENTRE
VORKING AND BOŠKO BUHA
ON IN GRADINA -EDGE

INFORMATION FOR THE VISITORS SCHOLARSHIP

FIELDS : THE BERLAGE CACHIERS 5 : STUDIO

Vela spila svjetski muzej 21. stoljeća
Projekt nizozemskog instituta i

HUNCH, BEYOND MAPPING : PROJECTING THE CITY

BERLAGE INSTIT

NEW AUTHENTICITY AND THE GUARDIANS OF THE CRITICAL CONSCIOUSNESS

PROJECT ZAGREB
ZAHVALJUJEM ition
TI MIME
as Condition,
Strategy, Practice

ECOLOGICAL CHILD PSYCH

RANDIĆ & TURATO : THE ARCHITECTURE OF TRANSITION

INFORMATION ON POSTGRADUATE MASTERS STUDIES

EN RESEARCH PRODUCTION AND OUTPU :011

TERRITORIES, IDENTITIES, NETS: SLOVENE ART 1995 - 2005

ARCHITECTURAL-URBAN DESIGN OF KASARNE-KULTURPARK, KOŠICE
ROME: THE CENTRE(S) ELSEWHERE

PHOTOGRAPHS

BULDOŽER

GUIDANCE BOOKLET : MEXICO

1700+ : international symposium on
THE SNIPER'S LOG : ARCHITECTURAL personal photograph
OF GENERATION X
OBLIQUE STRATEGIES

473

YUGOSLAVIAN PASSPORT

FIRST ARCHI BRIGADE : THE UTMOST INCOMPLETE ARCHIVE

SIXPACK : CONTEM SLOVENIAN ARCHIT

APPLICATION FORM

BERLAGE INSTITUTE PROSPECTUS
PERSONAL PHOTO

MUSEUM 21+ VELA SPILA
PUBLIC EVEN RESEARCH FELLOWSHIP
SPRING '95 1985-1986
ZOKA, I LOVE YOU!

LI
SIMULTANEOUS TIMES

SKJ CARD

BALKAN TELETUBBIES AND DECONSTRUCTION
OPEN OF MODERNISM
OF TH 20th DAVIES/S SCHOOLS
CENTURY OF ENGLISH

M(2x)
RICTLY CONTROLLED OKING

PERSONAL DOCUMENT
ER'S LICENSE   PLAN DE PARIS   BEETHOVEN IX. SYMPHONIE   BERLIN : EXCURSION   URBAN REPORTS
- Urban strategies
DEMOCRATIZATION   MIRANDO AL   and visions
OF PUBLIC SPACE   THE BERLAGE   FUTURO RECOMMENDATION   in mid-sized
ART & SPORT   2.0   TO THE FUTURE   WIEL ARcities in a
: STILLSlocal and global
A TIMELINEcontext
OF IDEAS, ARTICLES
AND INTERVIEWS,
INDESEM '88   1982 - 2010   WITH ALL DUE
INTENT
2000 SHANGAY:
THE SPIRIT   MAKING THE
LETTER OF CONFIRMATION OF MEGA   CITY BY THE
BOSKO BUHA   SEA
MOLBA   : YUGOSLAVIAN
MEMORIAL CENTER

NEW LIGHTHOUSES LOGARITHMIC
OF THE CRO TABLES   INVOICE
ADRIATIC
PROGRAM OF
FRAMES OF THE   Povijest suvremene   THE SPECIALIZATION
METROPOLIS: Hrvatske -   NOT QUITE OBVIOUS
ZAGREB URBAN   it iz arh FELLOWSHIP   DENSITIES   PEOPLE DO STILL
PLANNING SEMINARS   ugla FPROPOSITION   LIVE IN PLACES
1995 & 1996   knjiga SuvreTIRONA
AMNESTY FOR   hrvatska arhitektura   SIX ANSWERS
NOVI ZAGREB: - testiranje   ON ALBANIA
FELLOWSHIP   ROATIAN ARC stvarnosti   BY VEDRAN MIMICA
CONTRACT   NEW LIGHTHOUSES,
NEW KNJIGA OPĆENA   LATI AMALIA, CONCERT,
AWINGS FORA- MONOGRAFIJA   LISBON   LEARNING FROM   PROJECT OF
ROJECT IN SFMIMICA   MALEŠNICA   THE MONUMENT POVENJAK 2009
škola arhitekture   ON PBALKON ZUM
u Splitu)   GORBALKAN
2009-2010 PROSPECTUS
TUTE   URBAN AGE   WAITING FOR
SPECTUS   PAMELA ANDERSON
MIMICE : NAVAL   CONTEMPORARY
CHRONICLE   CROATIAN ARCHITECTURE   VISIONARY POWER
- TESTING REALITY   : Producing
8. ZAGREBAČKI   the Contemporary
SALON : ARHITEKTURA   City
2003
SFRJ ID CARD   GYMNASIUM /
RECONSTRUCTION QUANTUM LEAP   IMAGINATIONIIS : HERMAN Brochure of
CERTIFICATION   A DELFT TRANSPORT MIROSLAV   LY BIAN DESIGNERtourist busses
OF CARD   KRLEŽA STREET   ACADEMY   JT Vin Oaxaca
BUILDING IN
THE AREA OF
NEXT EUROPE   THE OLD HOSPITAL
PERSONAL PHOTOGRAPH   URBANIZAM NET
CONFIRMATION
JADROLINIJA'S   OF THE RESEARCH
PHOTOGRAPH   TOURIST TRIPS STRUCTURE OF   FELLOWSHIP
/ Switzerland)   STAFF AT THE   THE CA1985-1986
NOTES ON CHILDREN,   BERLAGE INSTITUTE   SCHOOL OF ENGLISH
AN HERTZBERGER MENT   MARE NOSTRUM   OF IDEOLOGY
BITION HITECHURE   AFTER THE SEL WHERE IS (CROATIAN)   AND ARCHITECTURAL
CHITECTURE   CITY?   ARCHITECTURE   EDUCATION
STUDIO '92   HEADED?   CROATIAN MODERN 000
- '93 : THE   ARCHITECTURE DIPLOMA LONELY PLANET: SE
NEW PUBLIC   Electronic   CROATIA   JRE
REALM, the   airplane ticket   CONGRESS 2009
Be conference
2 "The urban   IN THE FUNCTION   BUSINESS CARD
image in post-so OF A SIGN -
- perspectives   DRAGO IBLER
from Zadar"   AND THE CROATIAN
ARCHITECTURE
S ON CHILDREN,   BETWEEN TWO
RONMENT   EWARS
ARCHITECTURE,   STUDY LANDSCAPES   NEW MOSQUE
up   OF HERMAN HERTZBERGER'ECTUS   & MUSEUM OF
NEW VOCABULARIES   '97 '98   TIRANA & RELIGIOUS
FOR THE EURMIMICE CROATIA   HARMONY DESIGN
CITY   COMPETITION

LOTUS INTERNATIONAL
19
ELGRADE   CREATION OF   LETTER TO HERMAN   PSYCHOLOGY
CAPITAL   NEW WORLDS   HERTZBERGER   EXITS ARE CLEARLY   for the 3rd
IN MINIATURE   THE MATERIAL   MARKED   grade of high
WORLD OF CHILDHOOD   school

DAMIR ŽIŽIĆ

VLADIMIR MATTIONI

DAMIR GAMULIN

VEDRAN MIMICA

CAMERA UTILITY

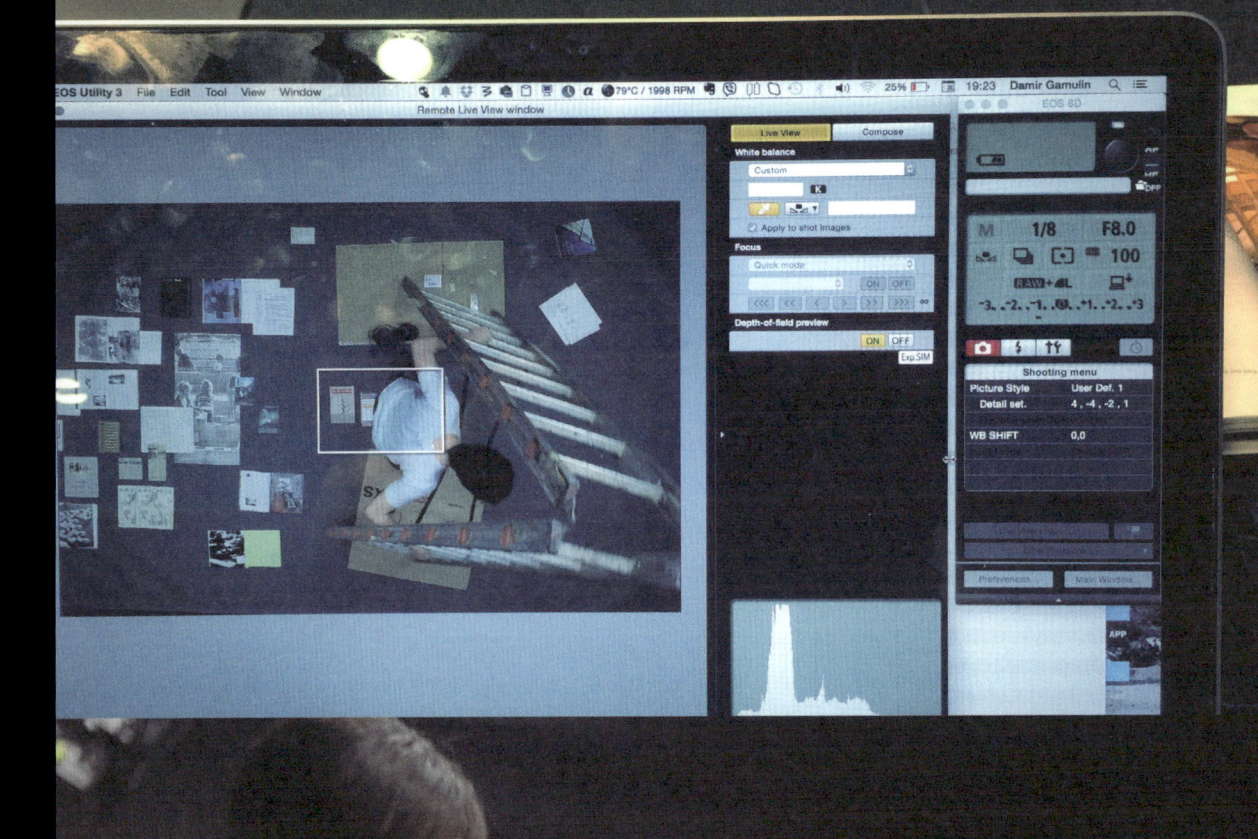

ANA ŠKEGRO

BEGIN SORT

SONJA LEBOŠ

fields

GERMAN CITIES
SUCCESS BEYOND
GROWTH?

SORT

INDEX

A

Abramović, Dražen [304]
Adorno, Theodor [227, 243]
Allen, Stan [39, 362, 364]
Ando, Tadao [11, 18, 104, 364]
Antonioni, Michelangelo [355]
Arets, Wiel [7, 9, 11, 14, 18, 26, 32, 36, 39, 40, 42, 44, 53, 104, 119, 150, 153, 159, 193, 337, 360-361, 362, 363, 367]
Arendt, Hannah [40, 346, 347, 359]
Armanda, Juri [306]
Arup, Ove [174, 290]
Augé, Marc [227]
Aureli, Pier Vittorio [8, 57, 59, 260, 268]
Azimi, Nassrine [9, 170]

B

Babić, Ivo [9, 222, 243]
Bakalčev, Minas [334]
Bakema, Jaap [182, 238, 340]
Bakker, Gijs [337]
Bakran, Hrvoje [9, 197, 201]
Balić, Emir [178]
Banac, Ivo [170]
Banham, Reyner [89]
Banović, Mladen [306]
Barragán, Luis [366]
Baratta, Paolo [338, 347, 349, 350, 353]
Barišić Marenić, Zrinka [356]
Barragán, Luis [39, 366]
Barthes, Roland [72]
Bartl, Zlata [218]
Basauri, Luciano [304]
Bašić, Mihaela [306]
Bašić, Nikola [184]
Baudouï, Rémi [164]
Baydemir, Osman [48]
Beaudouin, Eugène [80, 81, 82]
Beck, Ulrich [34]
Beeke, Anthon [337]
Bekaert, Geert [152, 153]
Bell, Stephan [193]
Benjamin, Andrew [252]

Benjamin, Walter [286]
Berc, Dafne [304]
Berlage, Hendrik Petrus [81, 183]
Bernardi, Bernardo [230]
Bernfest, Miljenko [187]
Beroš, Ana Dana [355]
Beroš, Nada [286]
Betsky, Aron [9, 15, 337, 338, 340]
Bey, Jurgen [337]
Bijvoet, Bernard [100]
Bilić, Ante Nikša [184]
Blankenburg, Hans [260]
Blažević, Damir [304]
Bobbink, Inge [40]
Boeri, Stefano [183, 185, 215, 224, 239, 335]
Bofill, Riccardo [104]
Bohigas, Oriol [11, 32, 104, 123]
Boley, B.K. [282]
Bonnema, Abe [97, 100]
Borruey, René [144]
Bos, Caroline [39]
Boševski, Zoran [184]
Bouman, Ole [347]
Boyarsky, Alvin [11, 152, 153, 366]
Bradić, Saša [174]
Branzi, Andrea [85, 120]
Brillembourg, Alfredo [60]
Brozić, Dejana [304]
Buchanan, Peter [90]
Bunschoten, Raoul [8, 39]
Burckhardt, Lucius [358]
Busquets, Joan [123]
Burdett, Richard [15, 50, 231, 328, 329, 331, 333, 334, 339]
Burton, Richard [168]
Bosch, Teo [206]
Broz Tito, Josip [164, 166, 168, 170, 171, 178, 179, 180, 203,]

C

Cache, Bernard [55]
Calatrava, Santiago [123]
Cambi, Nenad [243]
Castells, Manuel [84, 85, 120]

Cimolini, Mika [9, 246, 255]
Ciriani, Henri [11, 32, 104]
Ciuffi, Valentina [350]
Chareau, Pierre [100]
Chomsky, Noam [72]
Christiaanse, Kees [11, 32, 104, 131, 134, 191, 192]
Churchill, Winston [164]
Coates, Nigel [341]
Coenen, Jo [11, 32]
Colenbrander, Bernard [32]
Cook, Peter [105, 152]
Corsellis, Timothy [114]
Costa, Lúcio [123, 272]
Coulson, Shea [243]
Crnković, Ivan [184, 344]
Crnošija, Ivana [197]
Crouwel, Mels [11, 32]
Cvijetić, Srdjana [306]

Ć

Ćurković, Tomislav [184, 230]

Č

Čavlović, Melita [356]
Čikeš, Andrej [306]
Čirjak, Ivan [304]
Čižmek, Ivan [197]

D

Dabrović, Marko [306, 347]
Dakić, Slavko [197]
D'Ancona, Hedy [29, 337]
Davis, Mike [136]
De Cauter, Lieven [8, 60]
De Carlo, Giancarlo [11, 32, 104]
Declerck, Joachim [8, 262]
Dennison, Dirk [366]
De Geyter, Xaveer [11, 32, 163]
De Graaf, Reinier [8, 175]
Dehaene, Michiel [60]
Dekleva, Aljoša [255]
Delić, Stipe [168]
Deleuze, Gilles [204]
De Meuron, Pierre [226, 248]

De Michelis, Marco [349]
Descombes, Georges [104]
De Vries, Marina [57]
Di Carlo, Tina [272]
Dilberović, Marina [304]
Diller, Elizabeth [39, 344]
Dobrović, Nikola [105]
Dodd, Nigel [107, 114]
Docter, Rob [44, 322]
Doklestić, Borislav [197]
Doshi, V. Balkrishna [11, 30, 32]
Dostoyevsky, Fyodor Mikhailovich [347]
Dragomanović, Aleksandar [204]
Drašković, Gorjana [304]
Dudok, Marinus Willem [72]
Duiker, Johannes Jan [72, 81, 82, 90]
Durell Stone, Edward [358]

E

Easterling, Keller [59, 135]
Ekštajn, Igor [356, 358]
Elíasson, Ólafur [334]
Eisenman, Peter [30, 42, 104, 153, 340, 349, 350, 352, 359, 364,]
Ergić, Ivana [187]
Ergić, Vedrana [187]
Etherington, Rose [343, 346]

F

Fabijanić, Nenad [184]
Fellini, Federico [346, 355]
Feireiss, Kristin [337]
Fischer, Joschka [179]
Fisher, Silke [306]
Fiolić, Boris [184]
Foster, Norman [227, 228, 230, 231, 236, 238, 248, 339]
Foucault, Michel [72]
Frampton, Kenneth [6-7, 11, 14, 18, 32, 34, 40, 42, 60, 81, 90, 101, 104, 105, 115, 153, 171, 175, 184, 185, 204, 206, 227, 242, 275, 286, 319, 346]
Franke, Ivana [334]
Franco, Francisco [123]

Franolić, Iva [304]
Fritz, Darko [193]
Fuksas, Massimiliano [236, 339]
Fujimori, Terunobu [334]

G

Galić, Drago [183, 204]
Gamulin, Niko [197]
Gamulin, Miće [186, 286]
Gausa, Manuel [193, 210, 211, 241]
Geers, Kersten [346]
Gehry, Frank [132, 231, 337, 340]
Genscher, Hans-Dietrich [167]
Geuze, Adriaan [11, 32, 57, 307]
Giddens, Anthony [140, 340]
Giedion, Siegfried [90]
Gigantes, Eleni [110, 111]
Glavan, Darko [176]
Glažar, Tadej [8, 175, 252]
Gogol, Nicolai [347]
Graves, Michael [30, 104]
Gregorič, Tina [252]
Grichting. Anna [9, 164]
Grlić, Danko [70]
Grlić, Jelena [306]
Grozdanić, Tanja [306]
Groys, Boris [180, 181, 210, 260, 344]
Gudac, Vladimir [286]
Gugić, Tonko [243]
Gullichsen, Christian [11, 32]

H

Habermas, Jürgen [184, 185, 204, 207]
Hadid, Zaha [34, 132, 152, 227, 231, 232, 236, 238]
Hadži Pulja, Mitko [334]
Harvey, David [137]
Hausegger, Gudrun [9, 261]
Heathcote, Edwin [328]
Heidegger, Martin [70]
Hein, Alan [70]
Held, Richard [70]
Hertzberger, Herman [6, 8, 11, 14, 18, 20, 29,30, 32, 34, 36, 39, 42, 44, 46, 53, 57, 62, 64, 65, 71, 72, 74, 76, 78, 84, 88, 90, 93, 94, 96, 97, 98, 100, 101, 104, 105, 107, 108, 110, 171, 175, 182, 227, 239, 252, 337, 364, 366]
Herzog, Jacques [226, 248]
Hejduk, John [364]
Himmelblau, Coop [132]
Hitchcock, Henry-Russell [82]
Hitler, Adolf [89]
Ho, Kurt C.H. [129]
Holl, Steven [11, 30, 112, 114, 193, 291]
Holjevac, Većeslav [294, 296]
Holtzman, Harry [69,203]
Homer [120]
Hong Seng, Yap [8, 30, 44, 206]
Horvat, Tea [197]
Hortet, Lluís [202]
Houben, Francine [57]
Hoxhà, Enver [258]
Hrauski, Andrej [202]
Hršak, Lada [8, 294, 304]

I

Ibelings, Hans [241]
Ibler, Drago [96, 183, 344]
Ilić, Vanja [187]
Ishigami, Junya [346]
Ito, Toyo [104, 110, 112, 193]
Ivanko, Aleksej [168]
Ipšić, Sanja [175]

J

Jacobsen, Arne [83]
Jakšić, Nataša [356]
James, Martin S. [69, 203]
Janković, Zoran [253]
Jeanneret, Charles-Édouard
"Le Corbusier" [89, 100, 105, 174, 191, 207, 344]
Jefferson, Thomas [341]
Jelušić, Vesna [304]
Jencks, Charles [152, 204, 326]
Jerde, Jon [125,126]
Jerkov, Kristina [9, 271]
Johnson, Philip [82]
Jongerius, Hella [337]
Jošić, Mladen [228, 230]

Joustra, N. [114]
Jovanov, Radislav "Gonzo" [334]
Jurić, Marija "Zagorka" [120]

K

Kahn, Louis Isadore [70]
Kaiser, Gabriele [9, 261]
Kantor, Robert E. [70]
Kaplan, Robert D. [261]
Kasun, Vladimir [187]
Katušić, Dado [9, 252, 306, 310]
Karadžić, Radovan [162, 167]
Kaštelan, Sanjin [304]
Kebel, Igor [8, 9, 246, 255]
Keller, Sean [362, 366]
Kemper, Joke [8, 44]
Kerez, Christian [346]
Kezić, Neno [184]
Kincl, Branko [233]
Kirin, Iskra [306]
Klumpner, Hubert [60]
Kloos, Jan Piet [72],
Kolarić, Tomislav [306]
Koolhaas, Rem [11, 14, 15, 29, 32, 34, 40, 42, 60, 61, 104, 114, 126, 129, 135, 138, 140, 152, 178, 184, 193, 228, 239, 242, 246, 301, 319, 320, 331, 335, 337, 339, 343, 347, 349, 350, 352, 353, 355, 356, 358, 359]
Kostrenčić, Alan [9, 210]
Kovačić, Viktor [183]
Kozarac, Josip [237]
Kozulić, Nives [307]
Koželj, Janez [253]
Kraus, Karl [40]
Krasić, Zdravko [9, 197, 201]
Krleža, Miroslav [7, 8, 161, 224, 226, 261]
Kučar, Savka Dapčević [166]
Kulić, Vladimir [356]
Kundera, Milan [120, 203]
Kusturica, Emir [171]
Kuzmanić, Ante [9, 184, 219, 306, 310]

L

Labrouste, Henri [100]
Laslo, Aleksandar Saša [206, 286]

Lavin, Sylvia [39]
Larsen, Henning [163, 334]
Lathouri, Marina [8, 175]
Lau, Christoph [34]
Lenuci, Milan [121, 182, 207]
Letica, Slaven [216]
Letilović, Iva [187]
Lévi-Strauss, Claude [72]
Libeskind, Daniel [36, 203, 227, 238, 321]
Limmroth, Robin [282]
Lipovac, Ranko [306]
Lisinski, Vatroslav [120]
Livingstone, Ken [329]
Lods, Marcel [80, 81, 82]
Loher, Robert [187]
Lončarić, Davor [184]
Loos, Adolf [70, 238]
Lootsma, Bart [8, 39, 191, 192, 193, 337]
Löwy, Slavko [183]
Lukarov, Slave [304]
Lynch, Kevin [71]
Lynn, Greg [34, 39, 364]
Lyotard, Jean-François [61, 134]

M

Maas, Winy [8, 39, 46, 138, 262, 337]
Maki, Fumihiko [366]
Matejčić, Barbara [9, 319]
Marasović, Jerko [243]
Marcianò, Ada Francesca [94]
Marčetić, Iva [306]
Marčić, Zvonimir [304]
Mardešić, Ante [184]
Marguc, Petra [168]
Marinković, Ana [306]
Marković, Igor [215]
Martin, Samuel [306]
Martinović, Damir "Mrle" [334]
Marušić, Ivan "Klif" [193]
Marx, Roberto Burle [123, 125]
Matijević, Sanja [306]
Mattioni, Vladimir [9, 14, 179, 180, 186, 187, 191, 197, 276, 286]
Mažer, Irena [306]

Mayne, Thom [11, 84, 110, 111, 114, 168, 238]
McCarter, Robert [150]
Medić, Branimir [8, 175, 185, 304, 312]
Medić, Tatjana [9]
Meier, Richard [30, 287]
Melnikov, Konstantin Stepanovich [140, 344]
Melort, Bart [262]
Mielke, Friedrich [352-353]
Miessen, Markus [48, 272]
Miličević, Ratko [197]
Milošević, Slobodan [162, 166, 167, 171, 178, 179]
Milutin, Vesna [187]
Mimica, Aljoša [171]
Miralles Moya, Enric [123]
Mišković, Petar [185, 187, 224]
Mitrašinović, Miodrag [9, 104, 107]
Mladić, Ratko [167]
Mladinov, Jerolim [304]
Monchen, Ellen [40]
Modrian, Piet [69, 204]
Modrčin, Leo [185, 186, 343, 346]
Montessori, Maria [32, 34, 46, 65, 69, 72, 74, 78, 84, 88, 93, 94, 101, 366]
Morssink, Mick [8, 14, 44]
Mostafavi, Mohsen [252]
Moss, Eric [337]
Moškatelo, Ivica [306]
Mravinac, Vesna [187]
Mrduljaš, Maroje [9, 210, 356]
Murtić, Marko [187]
Mussolini, Benito Amilcare Andrea [83, 89]

Mušič, Marko [356]
Mutnjaković, Andrija [356]

N

Neidhardt, Velimir [233]
Neutelings, Willem Jan [11, 32, 39, 104, 193, 337, 338, 340]
Neutra, Richard [82, 174]
Niemeyer, Oscar [123, 174, 207]
Nijsee, Rob [157]
Nikšić, Radovan [204]

Norberg-Schulz, Christian [326]
Nouvel, Jean [11, 100, 104, 230, 231, 238]
Novak, Silvije [306]
Novozhilova, Maria [359]

NJ

Njirić, Helena [6, 9, 160, 185, 187, 190, 191, 192, 193, 194, 196, 206, 211, 239, 241, 359]
Njirić, Hrvoje [6, 9, 14, 160, 185, 187, 190, 191, 192, 193, 194, 196, 206, 211, 224, 239, 241, 359]

O

Ockels, Wubbo Johannes [39]
Ockman, Joan [362]
Opstelten, Ivo [57]
Ouroussoff, Nicolai [328]
Orwell, George [136]

P

Pallasmaa, Juhani [11, 32]
Pasolini, Pier Paolo [355]
Pavelić, Dinka [9]
Pavelić, Tom [184]
Pearman, Hugh [329]
Perrault, Dominique [262]
Perret, Auguste [81, 100]
Pestalozzi, Henri [69]
Piano, Renzo [11, 29, 104, 231, 290]
Piacentini, Marcello [89]
Pičman, Josip [183]
Piñón, Helio [123]
Pinós, Carme [123]
Pelivan, Lea [9, 224, 304, 308]
Perković, Lovro [183]
Perović, Vasa [8, 107, 252]
Petermann, Stephan [356]
Peutz, FJP [366]
Plato [69, 181]
Planić, Stjepan [183]
Plavec, Ivica [187]
Plečnik, Jože [183, 247]
Plejić, Toma [9, 224, 304]
Plevko, Dražen [197]
Podrecca, Boris [253]

Poković, Toni [174]
Polak, Nikola [184]
Polzer, Ida [304]
Popić, Nikola [184]
Portoghesi, Paolo [174, 179, 184, 204, 326]
Potočnik, Herman Noordung [356]
Premerl, Tomislav [359]
Price, Cedric [20, 174, 196]
Prijatelj, Kruno [243]
Prouvé, Jean [81]
Prpić, Lovorka [187]
Puljiz, Pero [8, 175, 185, 193, 206, 304, 312]

Q

Quintal, Becky [353, 356]

R

Radić, Stjepan [166, 307]
Radonić, Bojan [9]
Radonić, Frano [306]
Rainer, Roland [290]
Rajčić, Branimir [187]
Rako, Damir [174]
Rama, Edi [48, 53, 57, 163, 258, 260, 261, 262, 320]
Ramakers, Renny [337]
Randić, Saša [8, 9, 174, 175, 176, 193, 239, 304, 307, 319, 331, 333, 334]
Rapaić, Sunčana [304]
Rapoport, Amos [70]
Rashid, Hani [39]
Raščić, Lala [196]
Rašica, Božidar [8, 96, 183, 204]
Read, Herbert [69]
Rebois, Didier [210, 211]
Regulska, Joanna [215]
Reidy, Affonso Eduardo [123]
Reiser, Jesse [39]
Relić, Saša [304]
Richter, Vjenceslav [356]
Riha, Elisabeth [228, 230]
Risselada, Max [8, 11, 18, 34, 105]
Riley, Terence [39]
Rogoznica, Nives [9, 307]
Roosevelt, Franklin Delano [164]

Rose, Charlie [231]
Rossellini, Roberto [355]
Rossi, Aldo [83, 104, 174, 338]
Rossum, Van [157]
Roth, Alfred [69]
Rotondi, Michael [337]
Rousseau, Jean-Jacques [69]
Rowe, Colin [40]
Roy, Tamara [282]
Rudolph, Paul [83]
Rusan, Andrija [9, 61, 187, 206, 331]
Ryan, Marc [8, 262]

S

Sabolović, Sabina [9, 301]
Sadar, Jurij [255]
Safdie, Moshe [344]
Sanader, Ivo [236]
Sančanin, Marko [304]
Sartre, Jean-Paul [72]
Sassen, Saskia [11, 17, 49, 60, 135, 137, 216, 329, 333, 335]
Scalbert, Irénée [193]
Scarpa, Carlo [291]
Schaefer, Markus [57, 253]
Schneiter, Liliane [9, 171]
Schumacher, Patrik [228, 232]
Schumacher, Thomas [88]
Schüller, Nicola [131]
Scofidio, Ricardo [344]
Scott Brown, Denise [126]
Scully, Vincent [326]
Seissel, Josip [183]
Semper, Gottfried [115, 121, 237]
Sennet, Richard [136, 329, 333]
Sejima, Kazuyo [15, 343, 346]
Shannon, Kelly [8, 80, 88, 107]
Kazuo, Shinohara [366]
Sigler, Jennifer [9, 44, 50, 362]
Sikkema, Aryan [154]
Silađin, Branko [344]
Simeoforidis, Yorgos [34, 193, 194, 206, 210, 211]
Siza, Alvaro [104, 347]

Skansi, Luka [355]
Skorup, Zoka [294]
Skvaža, Maja [304]
Smithson, Alison [182]
Smithson, Peter [11, 32, 81, 182]
Smode Cvitanović, Mojca [356]
Smokvina, Marina [358]
Solà-Morales, Ignasi de [34, 115, 123]
Somol, Bob [364]
Speer, Albert [341]
Spoelstra, Marijn [57, 253]
Stalin, Joseph Vissarionovich [89, 164, 166, 180, 203]
Steele, Brett [232, 252]
Steidle, Otto [104]
Steiner, Dietmar [9, 201, 202, 210, 211, 246]
Stirling, James [105]
Stojan, Walter Maria [202]
Sudjic, Deyan [202, 339]
Supek, Ivan [310]
Supilo, Fran [226]
Szorsen, Krunoslav [306]

Š

Šarac, Damir [9, 243]
Šegvić, Neven [8, 20, 96, 183, 204, 359]
Šerman, Karin [356, 358, 359]
Širola, Eugen [219]
Škarijot, Mario [306]
Šlapeta, Vladimír [204, 247]
Šuica, Dubravka [310]
Šurina, Ivan [304]
Šuvar, Stipe [96]

T

Tadej, Mira [184]
Tattara, Martino [8, 262]
Taut, Bruno [105, 237]
Tchumi, Bernard [104]
Terragni, Giuseppe [42, 82, 83, 88, 89, 90, 94]
Tigerman, Stanley [30, 104]
Truby, Stefan [352]
Trummer, Peter [8, 55, 57]
Tuđman, Franjo [164, 203]

Tupker, Hans [8, 152]
Turato, Idis [9, 173, 174, 175, 176, 201, 239, 304, 319, 331, 333, 334]
Turčinov, Nikola [304]
Turina, Vladimir [183, 204]
Turner, Judith [152]

U

Uehara, Yushi [57]
Ugljen, Zlatko [356]
Ungers, Mathias [350]
Urry, John [60, 135]
Usseling, Mirjam [30]

V

van Berkel, Ben [11, 32, 39, 97, 152]
van den Broek, Johannes [97, 340]
van der Rohe, Mies [90, 123, 143, 159, 202, 227, 335, 350, 356, 362]
Vandermarliere, Katrien [193]
van Eyck, Aldo [11, 18, 20, 26, 29, 30, 32, 34, 72, 83, 96, 97, 104, 150, 175, 182, 206, 227]
van Herk, Arne [32, 104]
van Rijs, Jacob [39, 138]
van Rooy, Max [97]
van Severen, David [346]
van Toorn, Roemer [8, 9, 34, 42, 44, 50, 347, 364]
Venturi, Robert [40, 70, 71, 126]
Verhoeven, Jan [72]
Veehr, Lionel [307]
Viaplana, Albert [123]
Vidler, Tony [153, 366]
Visconti, Luchino [355]
Vitić, Ivan [183, 204, 206, 207]
Vlahović, Morana [187]
Vranić, Dubravka [187]
Vuga, Boštjan [255]
Vukić, Feđa [179, 180, 286]
Vukotić, Dušan [190]
Vukotić, Vukota Tupa [356]

W

Waltritsch, Dimitri [282]
Wagner, Otto [183]

Wanders, Marcel [337]
Wang, Wilfried [1, 15]
Wertmüller, Lina [355]
Wilson, Colin St.John [11]
Wilson, Peter [152]
Weeber, Carel [20]
Weissmann, Ernest [183]
Wollenberg, Petra [9, 131]
Woods, Lebeus [168]

Z

Zaera-Polo, Alejandro [8, 11, 14, 42, 44, 46, 50, 53, 136, 352, 364]
Zanko, Sasha [366]
Zemin, Jiang [129]
Zemljak, Ivan [183]
Zenghelis, Elia [8, 11, 14, 34, 39, 40, 46, 110, 111, 114, 143, 152, 228, 260, 261, 268, 269]
Zidarić, Zoran [184, 230]
Zloković, Milan [105]
Zevi, Bruno [88]
Zola, Zoka [9, 140, 186]

Ž

Žarnić, Tonči [8, 185, 224]
Žižek, Slavoj [260, 262, 340]
Žižić, Dujmo [306]
Žuvela, Gorki [9, 245]

VEDRAN MIMICA'S SELECTED BIBLIOGRAPHY

PUBLISHED BOOKS

Contemporary Croatian Architecture: Testing Reality
co-authored with Maroje Mrduljaš and Andrija Rusan, Arhitekst Publishers, Zagreb, 2007

Randic & Turato, The Architecture of Transition
monograph with the essay 'An Architecture of Transition and the Production of Meaning', Arhitekst Publishers, Zagreb, 2000

Notes on Children, Environment and Architecture
Publikatieburo Boouwkunde, Delft, 1992

BOOK CHAPTERS – CONTRIBUTIONS AND EDITORIAL WORK

Grad Split i arhitekt Ante Kuzmanić
Editor and co-author, to be published by University of Split Press, Split, 2017

Crown Hall Dean's Dialogues
Interviews with Wiel Arets and lecturers in Deans Lecture Series at Illinois Institute of Technology, IITAC and Actar, Chicago and Barcelona, 2017

Nowness Two
co-edited with Wiel Arets and Luis Ortega
To be published by IITAC Press, Chicago, 2017

Njirić+Njirić: Children of St. Peter's Street
essay in a monograph "Aftermath",
to be published by Actar

Making Architecture Politically
In 'We need it – we do it', a book accompanying the exhibition 'Reporting from the Front', representing Croatia at the 15th International Architecture Exhibition a/ La Biennale di Venezia 2016, Platforma 9.81, Split, 2016

Nowness
Illinois Institute of Technology Architecture Chicago 2013-2014
co-edited with Wiel Arets and Sean Keller,
IITAC Press, Chicago, 2013

Building Consciousness
In 'The Berlage Survey of the Culture, Education, and Practice of Architecture and Urbanism', NAi Publishers/ Berlage Institute, Rotterdam, 2011

Croatian Archipelago New Lighthouses
Croatian Architects Association/Berlage Institute, Zagreb, 2005

Technical Utopia: Tirana after Communism
In 'Tirana Metropolis', Berlage Institute, Rotterdam, 2004

Making the City by the Sea
In 'The Marseille Experiment', Actar, Barcelona, 2003

The Marseille Experiment
Interview with Elia Zenghelis. In 'Making the City by the Sea Forum & Workshop Marseille,' Berlage Institute – Fundació Mies van der Rohe / IFA – Institut Français d'Architecture, 2003

Preface to Five Minutes City
In 'Five Minutes City', Episode Publishers, Rotterdam, 2003

Utopia as Tradition: the Architectural Schools of Hertzberger and Terragni
co-authored with Kelly Shannon
In 'Kid Size: The Material World of Childhood', Vitra Design Museum, Skira Editore, Milan, 1997

Frames of the Metropolis
In 'Frames of the Metropolis', City Development Planning and Environmental Protection Office, Zagreb, 1996

The New Public Realm: Berlage Cahiers 2
co-editor; 010 Publishers, Rotterdam, 1992

BOOK CHAPTERS – CONTRIBUTIONS

Vedran Mimica talks to Petra Wollenberg about the mid-sized city
In 'Urban Reports – Urban strategies and visions in mid-sized cities in a local and global context', Nicola Schüller, Petra Wollenberg and Kees Christiaanse (eds), gta Verlag, ETH Zürich, Zürich, 2008

Tendencies
In 'Project Zagreb' by Eve Blau and Ivan Rupnik
Based on GSD Harvard Studio Research, Actar, Barcelona, 2007

Essay on six young emerging offices in Slovenia
In '6IX Pack: Contemporary Slovenian Architecture', Vale-Novak, Ljubljana, second edition 2006

Three Rooms, Curatorial Politics
In 'Territories, Identities, Nets, Slovene Art 1995-2005', Igor Španjol, Igor Zabel (eds), Moderna galerija, Ljubljana, 2005

East-West: Blurring Territories
In 'Actes du Colloque Urbicide~Urgence~Durabilité: Reconstruction et Mémoire'
(Actes of the Colloquium: Urbicide, Urgency, Durability: Reconstruction and Memory) Rémi Baudouï and Anna Grichting (eds), Institut d'Architecture de l'Université de Genève, Geneva, 2005

Free Croat in The Hague
Vedran Mimica talks to Vladimir Mattioni. In URBANIZAM.NET, UPI2M plus, Zagreb, 2004

Venice Zone, Pedestrian Infrastructural System
In 'Vivere Venezia', publication about workshop at the 8th International Architectural Exhibition Next at Venice Biennale, Marsilio Editori, Venice, 2004

Children's Room
In '473', UPI2M plus, Zagreb, 2003

Borders: the other side of globalization
In the catalog of the 38th Zagreb Salon curated by Stefano Boeri, Zagreb 2003

Utopia as Tradition: The Architectural Schools of Hertzberger and Terragni
Co-authored with Kelly Shannon. In 'Kid Size: The Material World of Childhood'
Skira Editore, Vitra Design Museum, 1997

PUBLISHED ARTICLES
Oris Magazine, Zagreb

A Shift in Perspective
Interview with Darko Fritz by Vedran Mimica and Maroje Mrduljaš, Oris 98, 2015

E la nave va
Oris 91, 2014

Unique Cultural Project
Oris 89, 2014

A good building makes you feel at home
Wiel Arets in conversation with Vedran Mimica
Oris 83, 2013

Study Landscapes of Herman Hertzberger
Oris 68, 2011

Oblique Strategies
Interview with Davor Katušić (Berlage alumni)
Oris 65, 2010

Closing Time!
Interview with Aaron Betsky
Oris 55, 2009

Exits Are Clearly Marked
Oris 54, 2008

New Tobačna, Strictly Controlled Smoking
Oris 48, 2007

Gymnasium / Quantum Leap in Miroslav Krleža Street
Oris 47, 2007

The Power of Architectural Thought
Oris 46, 2007

Life after the Death in Venice
Oris 42, 2006

Not Quite Obvious Densities
Oris 28, 2004

Zoka, I Love You!
Oris 27, 2004

Creation of New Worlds in Miniature
Oris 20, 2003

People Do Still Live in Places
Oris 14, 2002

Mission Impossible? I Don't Think So
Oris 9, 2001

PUBLISHED ARTICLES
Čovjek i prostor (ČiP) Magazine, Zagreb

Utopian Journeys
Čovjek i prostor 5/6, 2010

Where is (Croatian) architecture headed?
Čovjek i prostor 7/8, 2010

New school of architecture in the city of Split
Čovjek i prostor 5/6, 2006

New Authenticity and the Guardians of the Critical Consciousness
Vedran Mimica in conversation Ana Bakić, Alan Kostrenčić, Maroje Mrduljaš. Čovjek i prostor 7/8, 2004

Identity: Croatian Archipelago New Lighthouses
Čovjek i prostor 9/10, 2004

Next Europe
Vedran Mimica in conversation with Zdravko Krasić and Hrvoje Bakran
Čovjek i prostor 11/12, 2002

Interview with Herman Hertzberger on education in architecture
Čovjek i prostor 4/6, 2001

Balkan TeleTubies and Deconstruction of Modernism
About Njirić and Njirić exhibition at Single in Antwerpen, Čovjek i prostor 1/3, 2001

Frames of the Metropolis
With Vladimir Mattioni
Čovjek i prostor 11/12, 2000

2000 Shangay: the Spirit of Mega
Čovjek i prostor 1/2, 2000

TemA produkcija
About architectural production in Croatia
Čovjek i prostor 1/2, 2000

Expecting Pamela Anderson
Čovjek i prostor 7/8, 1998

Godišnja nagrada Viktor Kovačić 1996
About Tonči Žarnić and Hildegard Auf Franić's Nursery and Kindergarten in Zagreb
Čovjek i prostor 11/12, 1997

PUBLISHED ARTICLES
other magazines

Gymnasium / Quantum Leap in Miroslav Krleža Street
Abitare 480, Milan 2008

Exercising Europe
Vedran Mimica in conversation with Alan Kostrenčić and Maroje Mrduljaš on EUROPAN
Arhitektura 216, Zagreb 2004

Don't cry Croatia
Domus 873, Milan, September 2004

The Berlage Experience
Hunch 6/7, Rotterdam 2003

Bounded Freedom. Montessori College Oost in Amsterdam, the Netherlands
With Kelly Shannon
Architektur Aktuell 07/08, Vienna 2000

Njiric+Njiric: Inventing Landscapes
Domus 779, Milan 1996

RELEVANT INTERVIEWS WITH VEDRAN MIMICA

Tourists in Their Home Towns
Kristina Jerkov for the on-line magazine Analitika, Kotor 2014

Cities Can Change Their Identity
Damir Šarac, published in Slobodna Dalmacija, daily newspaper, Split 2013

Six Answers On Albania By Vedran Mimica
Gudrun Hausegger and Gabriele Kaiser for www.nextroom.at, 2010

Space is the Basic Croatian Resource
Barbara Matejčić, published in Vjesnik, Zagreb 2008

Engaging Reality
Jennifer Sigler and Roemer van Toorn. In 'Projecting the City, Beyond Mapping', a special issue of Hunch, The Berlage Institute, Rotterdam 2006

New Lighthouses
Nives Rogoznica, published in Slobodna Dalmacija, daily newspaper, Split 2005

Democratization of Public Space
Sabina Sabolović, published in Zarez, monthly paper for culture, year I, No 6, Zagreb 1999

The Berlage Institute
Miodrag Mitrašinović, published in the magazine Communication, January 1992, Belgrade 1992

VEDRAN MIMICA'S SELECTED CURATORIAL WORK

Third International Architectural Biennale Rotterdam. Power – Producing the Contemporary City, Rotterdam, 2007

Mare Nostrum
Croatian section of the exhibition 'The Flood' at the 2nd International Architecture Biennale Rotterdam
Rotterdam 2005

Inbetween: on the Croatian Coast, Transitional Processes, and how to live with them
Croatian exhibition in the Italian Pavilion as a part of the 10th International Architecture Exhibition Cities, Architecture and Society at Venice Biennale
Venice 2006

Venice Zone-Pedestrian Infrastructural System
(with P.V. Aurelli)
Part of Vivere Venezia Exhibition at Museo Corer as a part of the 8th International Architecture Exhibition 'Next' at Venice Biennale, Venice 2002

Six Years of BiA
(with H. Hertzberger)
Netherlands Architecture Institute
Rotterdam and Amsterdam 1997

Strategic Sites for the Hague
(with J. Kroes)
The Hague City Hall, The Hague 1996

The Architecture of Innocence
(with W. Arets)
Heerlen Town Hall, Heerlen 1992

Herman Hertzberger, Architecture
Museum of Applied Art, Zagreb, 1987